RED MIGRATIONS

Red Migrations

*Transnational Mobility
and Leftist Culture after 1917*

EDITED BY PHILIP GLEISSNER
AND BRADLEY A. GORSKI

UNIVERSITY OF TORONTO PRESS
Toronto Buffalo London

© University of Toronto Press 2024
Toronto Buffalo London
utorontopress.com
Printed in the USA

ISBN 978-1-4875-4388-4 (cloth)   ISBN 978-1-4875-4389-1 (EPUB)
                                  ISBN 978-1-4875-4390-7 (PDF)

Library and Archives Canada Cataloguing in Publication

Title: Red migrations : transnational mobility and leftist culture after 1917 / edited by Philip Gleissner and Bradley A. Gorski.
Names: Gleissner, Philip, editor. | Gorski, Bradley A., editor.
Description: Includes bibliographical references and index.
Identifiers: Canadiana (print) 20240347331 | Canadiana (ebook) 20240347390 | ISBN 9781487543884 (cloth) | ISBN 9781487543891 (EPUB) | ISBN 9781487543907 (PDF)
Subjects: LCSH: Soviet Union – History – Revolution, 1917–1921 – Influence. | LCSH: Soviet Union – Emigration and immigration – Political aspects. | LCSH: Transnationalism – History – 20th century. | LCSH: Intellectuals – History – 20th century. | LCSH: Ideology and literature – History – 20th century. | LCSH: Slavic literature – 20th century – History and criticism. | LCSH: Aesthetics, Modern – 20th century.
Classification: LCC DK265.9.I5 R43 2024 | DDC 947.084/1–dc23

Cover design: Hannah Gaskamp
Cover image: Regina Bilan/Shutterstock.com

We wish to acknowledge the land on which the University of Toronto Press operates. This land is the traditional territory of the Wendat, the Anishnaabeg, the Haudenosaunee, the Métis, and the Mississaugas of the Credit First Nation.

University of Toronto Press acknowledges the financial support of the Government of Canada, the Canada Council for the Arts, and the Ontario Arts Council, an agency of the Government of Ontario, for its publishing activities.

 Canada Council for the Arts Conseil des Arts du Canada

 ONTARIO ARTS COUNCIL
CONSEIL DES ARTS DE L'ONTARIO
an Ontario government agency
un organisme du gouvernement de l'Ontario

 Funded by the Government of Canada Financé par le gouvernement du Canada

To the memory of Helen Fehervary and Katerina Clark.

Contents

List of Images ix

Acknowledgments xi

Introduction: From Internationalism to Transnationalism 3
BRADLEY A. GORSKI AND PHILIP GLEISSNER

Part I. Forms

1 "How They Do It in America": Cosmopolitanism and Cultural Arbitrage in Soviet Russia 25
SERGUEI ALEX. OUSHAKINE

2 Transnational Theory of the Avant-garde: János Mácza, Artistic Praxis, and the Marxist Method 88
IRINA DENISCHENKO

3 Staging Revolution: Stalinist *Drambalet* in the German Democratic Republic 129
ELIZABETH H. STERN

4 *Hegelienkov*: Eval'd Ilienkov, Western Marxism, and Philosophical Politics after Stalin 160
TREVOR WILSON

Part II. Geographies

5 Guides to Berlin: Exiles, Émigrés, and the Left 185
ROMAN UTKIN

6 "Syphilis, Dirt, and the Frontiers of Revolution": Langston Hughes and Arthur Koestler at the Borders of Disgust   214
BRADLEY A. GORSKI

7 The Intellectual Migrations of the British Communist Ralph Fox during the 1920s and 1930s   239
KATERINA CLARK

Part III. Identities

8 Revolutionary Violence with Chinese Characteristics: Chinese Migrants in Early Soviet Literature   267
EDWARD TYERMAN

9 The Feeling and Fragility of Modernity: Red Mobility against the Grand Tour in Nikolai Aseev's *Unmade Beauty* (1928)   299
MICHAEL KUNICHIKA

10 Blackness in the Red Land: African Americans and Racial Identity in the "Colourless" Soviet Union   319
KIMBERLY ST. JULIAN-VARNON

Part IV. Communities

11 The "Father of Russian Futurism" in America: David Burliuk and the *Russian Voice*   345
ANNA ARUSTAMOVA, TRANSLATED FROM THE RUSSIAN BY ISAAC STACKHOUSE WHEELER

12 Exilic Experiments in Education: The Multiple Lives and Journeys of László Radványi, pseud. Johann-Lorenz Schmidt   375
HELEN FEHERVARY

13 Haunting Encounters: Reimagining Hermina Dumont Huiswoud's Trip to the Soviet Union, 1930–1933   398
TATSIANA SHCHURKO

14 Desiring the USSR: Writers from Two Germanys in the Soviet Contact Zone   429
PHILIP GLEISSNER

List of Contributors   459

Index   463

Images

1.1. Boris Zelenskii: A poster for Grigorii Aleksandrov's *Circus*   26
1.2. Douglas Fairbanks and Mary Pickford in Moscow, 10 August 1926   32
1.3. A poster for the film *Frauennot, Frauenglück*, 1929   34
1.4. Soviets in Hollywood, September 1930: Grigorii Aleksandrov and Charlie Chaplin   36
1.5. Soviets in Hollywood, September 1930: Grigorii Aleksandrov, Sergei Eisenstein, Walt Disney, and Eduard Tisse   37
1.6. Grigorii Aleksandrov at the Ford Factory in Detroit, 9 June 1930   39
1.7. The permutation of circles   45
1.8. Localizing the globe   45
1.9. Playing with the globe   47
1.10. Marion (with a local Chaplin) before, during, and after her canon number   48
1.11. The mirror staging of the West and the USSR   49
1.12. A *"fizkult reviu"* (physical culture revue)   50
1.13. Playing with water and fire   52
1.14. The circus/circles of adoptions   54
1.15. Hospitality enacted   55
1.16. Palimpsests of belonging   56
1.17. A lullaby that worked vs. a lullaby that didn't   58
1.18. Mikhail Khazanovskii, a poster for the film *Sud chesti* (*A Trial of Honour*), 1948   59
1.19. "Rereading Belinskii": a passportless tramp, *Krokodil*, 20 March 1949   67
1.20. The syllogism of the FAKC. Nikolai Kondakov, *Logika* (1954)   69

x Images

1.21. Iulii Ganf, "A vulture from the overseas: 'They use my feathers to write all these things,'" *Krokodil*, 30 March 1949 74
2.1. Alfred H. Barr Jr., dust jacket of *Cubism and Abstract Art* (1936) 89
2.2. F.T. Marinetti, manuscript diagram of Futurism 90
2.3. János Mácza, "The Social Origins of New Art and Literature" (1926) 92
2.4. János Mácza, a page from "The Black Tomcat," published in *Ma*, 15 September 1921 99
2.5. Sándor Barta, image poem from "Crystal of Time: Moscow" in *Ék* (1923) 103
2.6. János Mácza, "The Interrelationship of Schools in New Art and New Literature" (1926) 106
2.7. János Mácza, "The Division of Coercive Social Forces" (1926) 108
2.8. János Mácza, "The Social Origins of New Art and Literature" (1926) 110
2.9. János Mácza, "The Origins of Activism" (1926) 111
5.1. Cover of Andrei Bely's *One of the Mansions of the Kingdom of Shades* (1924) 199
6.1. Langston Hughes and Arthur Koestler in Soviet Turkmenistan 215
8.1. "Peace and Freedom in Sovdepia." Kharkov OSVAG (Information-Propaganda Agency of the Armed Forces of Southern Russia), 1919 268
8.2. Peter the First and Shi Huangdi. Engraving by V.N. Masiutin in Boris Pil'niak, *Povest' Peterburgskaia ili Sviatoi-kamen'-gorod* (1922) 278
8.3. Title page for "Sankt-Piter-Burkh," in Pil'niak, *Povest' Peterburgskaia* (1922) 279
11.1. The front page of the *Russian Voice* on the reactions to Lenin's funeral, 24 February 1924 349
11.2. A typical Literary Thursday with poems from Futurists Aleksei Kruchenykh, Nikolai Aseev, and David Burliuk, 15 May 1924 350
13.1. Undated photographic image of a veiled woman* 402
14.1. Intertextual geographies: "Central Asia in the Times of Kisch" 442

Acknowledgments

All books are journeys, and this has been – appropriately – an especially long, peripatetic, and collaborative one. We put together our first Red Migrations event – a round table at the annual ASEEES convention – in November 2018. The enthusiastic response there helped the idea blossom into a long-term collaborative research project. We hosted another series of panels at the AATSEEL conference in spring 2019, and just as we were putting together a workshop for the papers-in-progress that eventually coalesced into this volume, the COVID-19 crisis closed borders and stymied mobility in a way we never thought possible in the twenty-first century. Through that difficult time of isolation, however, our research on the idealistic transnationalism of the post-Revolutionary years became something of a lifeline for us. Our international travellers – the leftists, artists, and revolutionaries who fill these pages – had brought us together for years, and now they connected us even during lockdown. The Red Migrations virtual seminar series spanned the fall of 2020 and provided yet another opportunity to refine the research collected here. In this way, this book is a product of the pandemic. It was finally worked out in the months of isolation, through computer screens, and in two dimensions. And perhaps for that reason, it is everything the pandemic was not. It is expansive, idealistic, collaborative, and we hope inspiring. For that, we have many people to thank.

First, we want to thank all of our collaborators. Those whose contributions fill this volume stuck with us through many iterations, several rounds of edits, and the inevitable silences of academic publishing. Their work is the best tribute to their efforts. But many more worked with us along the way. The first round table included inspiring work by Elena Ostrovskaya and Thomas Kitson. Kaitlyn Tucker, Holly Myers, Elise Thorsen, Elena Zemskova, Katherine Reischl, and Milla Fedorova presented polished research that pushed our panel series and seminars to a higher level. Galin Tihanov launched the seminar series with an incisive keynote that added depth to the way we connected transnational movements and aesthetic theories. Greg Afinogenov, Rossen Djagalov, and Helena Goscilo volunteered their time as discussants and provided invaluable commentary that advanced the research further.

We would also like to thank the various institutions that have supported this project, including the program committees of ASEEES and especially AATSEEL, which provided Red Migrations with a stream of panels at its 2019 conference. Thanks also go to our home institutions, Georgetown University and the Ohio State University, both of which provided us the stability and support necessary to carry out such a long-term project. Georgetown University supported this research through a Summer Salary Supplement grant that facilitated the completion of the manuscript. The College of Arts and Sciences at Ohio State awarded Red Migrations a Conference Support grant and generously allowed for it to be used as a book subvention grant, after we had to cancel our in-person conference, replacing it with a number of virtual events.

We would also like to thank our tireless editor at University of Toronto Press, Stephen Shapiro, who has championed this project from its early days and has seen the manuscript through many iterations, transmogrifications, and blown deadlines. His stewardship of the project has been invaluable. The intellectual generosity of the two anonymous reviewers helped sharpen and deepen the book's arguments, and we would like to express our sincere gratitude for their willingness to carefully review this lengthy volume.

Finally, we would like to acknowledge that the long and oftentimes joyful process of creating this volume also included two moments of profound grief. On 13 April 2023, our contributor Helen Fehervary passed away unexpectedly in Albuquerque, New Mexico. Her impressive research on leftist German literature, and especially Anna Seghers, documents with great depth and genuine personal involvement the history of the transnational mode of intellectual life in the twentieth century. Less than a year later, we lost Katerina Clark on 1 February 2024. A pioneering scholar of socialist internationalism, Katy defined the field to which this book contributes. She attended our very first round table and gave characteristically generous and incisive feedback to everyone throughout the process. As her work has been at the heart of this research project from the beginning, it is only fitting (though unplanned) that her contribution finds its place at the very centre of this volume. We dedicate this volume to the memory of these two enthusiastic and inspiring scholars and colleagues, and express our heartfelt sympathy to their families, friends, and students.

RED MIGRATIONS

Introduction: From Internationalism to Transnationalism

BRADLEY A. GORSKI AND PHILIP GLEISSNER

As we enter the third year of Vladimir Putin's brutal and unprovoked war against Ukraine, it may seem an odd time to think about transnational movements sparked by the 1917 Russian Revolution. But it is precisely at such moments of isolationism, xenophobia, and rising nationalism that we need to examine alternative ways of being, to recall the hopes and possibilities that drive cross-border movements and create hybrid identities. Indeed, new transnational imaginaries often coincide with isolation, separatist tendencies, and state violence. When Russia launched its full-scale invasion on 24 February 2022, borders closed and travel (not to mention archival research) became more difficult. The invasion itself was based on a delusion of Russian exceptionalism and a paranoid fear of Ukraine's increasing openness to the West. The Ukrainian people have suffered immeasurably because of that delusion and paranoia. But Ukraine has only become more a part of the "collective West" (as Putin often characterizes his "true" enemy). Flows of refugees, monetary aid, and military support have criss-crossed the Ukrainian border. The war has forged one of the strongest international alliances in recent memory to impose sanctions on Russia and support the Ukrainian cause. Even Russia, despite its increasing isolationism, has become more transnational, not less, as a wave of conscientious objectors settled abroad in the first months of the war, and another wave fled mobilization in October 2022. Nearby capitals from Tbilisi to Tallinn have been overrun with Russian citizens, who still maintain ties – economic, informational, affective – with those within Russia proper. New transnational solidarities have been formed, often with Ukrainian artists and activists in the lead, that are rallying support from international organizations and allies from around the world. Far from stamping out personal and economic transnationalism, Russian brutality has made such ties more important than ever.

Red Migrations looks back across the century to the aftermath of the 1917 Revolution as a very different moment of intensive transnational connectivity to understand what previous movements, networks, and solidarities might have to offer us today. What emerges is a complex constellation of transnationalism that cuts against two dominant narratives of the post-revolutionary moment. The first, characteristic of traditional émigré studies, frames the revolution as a rupture, a breaking of ties between Russia and the rest of the world. That narrative, as we argue below, was long at the heart of the discipline of Slavic and East European Studies as it grew up among the binary thinking of the Cold War. An important counternarrative, which has attracted renewed scholarly attention in recent decades, centres on the Communist International and the Soviet Union's ambitions for world revolution. That counternarrative, however, tells only part of the story. At least as important as the Soviet state, we argue, were the transnational movements and networks of individuals motivated by desires, hopes, fears, and affections. For this reason, *Red Migrations* proposes a third way of thinking about spatial displacement after 1917 – through the lens of transnationalism – in order to expand the two paradigms of traditional émigré studies and Soviet internationalism. *Red Migrations* sees mobility after 1917 as infused with the hopes of world revolution and activated by protean networks of individuals, institutions, geographies, and ideas. It is a version of leftist internationalism, but informed by theories of transnationalism: an internationalism from below.

The Revolution and World Culture

The decade immediately following the revolution – the 1920s – was one of intense intercultural ferment. Although initial hopes that the 1917 Revolution would immediately spark a worldwide communist conflagration were stymied when Polish forces repelled the Red Cavalry in 1921, the Third Communist International, or Comintern, founded two years earlier, actively developed communist parties throughout the world. This political internationalism was always accompanied by cultural analogues. Maxim Gorky founded the "World Literature" publishing house immediately after the revolution. By 1920, Anatoly Lunacharsky, the People's Commissar of Enlightenment, had found himself head of a (short-lived) Kul'tintern or Cultural International. Later, at the Fourth Comintern Congress, Lunacharsky would propose an equally short-lived Literary International. In 1927, under the auspices of the Russian Association of Proletarian Writers (RAPP) and the International Bureau of Revolutionary Literature (Mezhdunarodnoe biuro revoliutsionnoi literatury, MBRL), Moscow hosted the First International Conference of Proletarian and Revolutionary Writers, with attendees from fourteen countries. Early the following year, the *Herald of Foreign Literature* (*Vestnik inostrannoi literatury*) began publication, with Lunacharsky as its chief editor. In Berlin, the International Workers' Aid Organization or Mezhrabpom was formed; it soon focused its efforts on its film studio, which would connect not only German and Soviet filmmakers but also other representatives of leftist world cinema.[1]

The 1930s are usually remembered as the decade in which Stalin's "socialism in one country" won out over the hope for world revolution. (Indeed, by the late 1930s world revolution had become associated with the Trotskyite "left opposition.") But on the cultural front, the 1930s were perhaps even more international than the 1920s. In 1931 the journal *Literature of the World Revolution* (*Literatura mirovoi revoliutsii*) launched, continuing the work of *Herald of Foreign Literature*, and changing its name to *International Literature* the following year. Associated now with the newly founded International Association of Revolutionary Writers (Mezhdunardonyoe ob"ednienie revoliutsionnykh pisatelei, MORP), the successor organization of MRBL, it maintained its commitment (for the time being) to publishing a broad array of literature in first four and then six world languages.[2]

The anti-imperialist play *Roar China*, which Sergei Tret'iakov had written after his own travels east, premiered in Moscow and then travelled the world from New York to Guangzhou.[3] In fact, as Soviet cultural policy narrowed towards the adoption of socialist realism in 1934, cultural leftism spread around the globe in sometimes planned and sometimes unexpected ways. The Communist Party of the United States founded John Reed Clubs as havens for proletarian literature, while the New York-based émigré newspaper the *Russian Voice* – and its literary editor David Burliuk – actively cultivated Russian-language leftist poetry in the US (see chapter 11 in this volume). In 1935 in Paris, the Comintern sponsored the anti-fascist First Congress for the Defence of Culture; a Second Conference would follow in 1937, at the very peak of the Stalinist terror at home. Leftist cultural institutions also moved farther afield; for example, the Marxist Workers School (MASCH), expelled from Berlin in 1933, was reimagined by its visionary director as a workers' school in Mexico City (chapter 12 below), and the Indian Progressive Writers' Association convened its inaugural conference in Lucknow in 1936.[4]

This cultural ferment of the 1930s was inextricable from the diffusion of political leftism in the same decade. As the Soviet vision of world revolution faded, different leftist political imaginaries took hold in various parts of the world. Mao Zedong's peasant-focused collectivism had found popularity in the southeastern Chinese province of Jiangxi, where he was elected chairman of a semi-autonomous "Soviet Republic" amid growing political instability in the country. The American communist Harry Haywood enthusiastically adopted what he called the "Black Belt" thesis, which argued that African Americans within the US constituted an oppressed nation. The Russian-Jewish poet Osip Mandelshtam interviewed an emerging communist leader from French Indochina, who would later take on the name Ho Chi Minh, and heard in his words "not European culture, but the culture of the future ... the approach of tomorrow, the oceanic silence of universal brotherhood."[5] In Britain, a small group of influential Trotskyists lamented the abandonment of world revolution and what they saw as Stalin's betrayal of leftist ideals. One member of the group, the Trinidadian historian C.L.R. James, wrote the first book-length study of the Comintern, *World Revolution, 1917–1936*, which appeared in 1937. For James, these decades represented Moscow's best attempt to disseminate communist politics and culture throughout the world.[6] But it is not James's story, nor any of the other stories sketched above that has dominated the study of East European cultural or political transnationalism in the 1920s and 1930s. That story has been dominated by the so-called white émigrés.

White Culture, White Politics

The First World War, the Revolution, and the Russian Civil War displaced an enormous number of Russians, anywhere between one and three million according to various estimates by international organizations conducted in the early 1920s.[7] Although many were prisoners of war who were eventually repatriated, nearly a million remained abroad permanently.[8] This "first wave" of Russian emigration, as it came to be called, shaped the interwar and even post-war Western imagination of both Russia and the Soviet Union. It was often suggested that "Russia Abroad" at this time was a more authentic version of Russia than that which had fallen to the Bolsheviks.[9] "The revolution and the civil war split Russia in two – literally and figuratively," Marc Raeff wrote in the opening of his classic study *Russia Abroad*. "One lost the very name of Russia and became first the RSFSR and then the USSR; the other, defeated by Lenin's government, rejecting and escaping the newly created RSFSR, constituted itself into a Russia beyond the borders, Russia Abroad."[10] Here, characteristically, the two Russias are presented as vying for legitimacy (Russia "split in two"), but the advantage is clear: one has transformed itself into a changing series of acronyms, while the other still constitutes "Russia," only now beyond borders.

A more recent book by Greta Slobin invokes the same binary opposition and assigns the groups their now familiar colours: "The October Revolution of 1917 and ensuing Civil War divided the citizens of the Russian Empire into the Reds and the Whites, creating a political schism."[11] In this framing, it is the whites who constituted the authentic Russia beyond borders, Russia Abroad.[12] It is true that many of those fleeing the revolution had some affiliation with the White Army (the Great Soviet Encyclopaedia was happy to claim, dubiously, that "within the white émigré community there are at least 1,000,000 participants in the White Army") and that others were monarchists – the political affiliation most directly associated with the term "whites."[13] But the emigration was much more diverse than this description allows. Burliuk, for instance, an anarchist, painter, and Futurist poet who found his way to New York, where he worked for "a firmly Soviet newspaper" in what he called "the country of predatory capitalism," would be counted among the first wave and by implication the white émigrés, as would many Social Democrats, Mensheviks, and other leftists.[14] Chapter 5 in this volume addresses this ambivalence of the first wave, which often maintained a surprising openness towards continued association with the Soviet state.

Researchers often acknowledge this political diversity, yet it is commonly downplayed in the historical narrative and all but lost in the popular imagination. Gleb Struve's encyclopaedic *Russian Literature in Exile* (*Russkaia literatura v izgnanii*, 1959) features a thorough index of émigré personalities, including many who appear in this volume: Shklovsky, Ehrenburg, Gorky, and even Burliuk. The protagonists of the narrative part of Struve's book, however, are different: the firmly anti-Soviet writers Ivan Bunin, Dmitry Merezhkovskii, Vladislav Khodasevich, Zinaida Gippius, Viacheslav Ivanov, and so on. When Bunin gave his 1924 speech "The Mission of the Russian Emigration," he noted that there were three million Russians in emigration but suggested excluding from that number any who might be secret supporters or even sympathizers of the Soviet Union and who had found their way abroad only "in order to shame us in front of foreigners and to sow discord."[15] Belonging to the true Russian emigration, in other words, was determined by political affiliations and was arbitrated by powerful cultural figures.

This exclusive community had a mission, as Bunin further elaborated: to be a "threatening sign to the world and capable fighters for the eternal, divine fundamentals of human existence that nowadays, not only in Russia, but everywhere have been shaken."[16] For Bunin, as for many of the influential figures of the first wave, the revolution was a downfall of biblical proportions, and embracing it was a sin.

Emigration, he proposed, was a matter of choice, a demonstration of rejection at the price of leaving everything that was once held dear. The fashioning of exilic reality as a moral choice among the white émigrés is nowhere as pronounced as in the slogan "We are not in exile; we are on a mission" ("My ne v izgnanii, my v poslanii," commonly ascribed to Merezhkovskii and Gippius, although it originated in a 1927 poem by Nina Berberova).[17] As the white émigrés' self-fashioning was embraced in scholarly works, that slogan became something of a truism, synthesizing ideological uniformity and political commitment that framed migration in moral terms, as a deliberate act of negating the revolution.

But if emigration was a political statement, it was often oversimplified into the "absolute rejection of the Bolshevik regime." And it was also expressed primarily through culture – specifically a high, largely literary culture, which saw itself as detached from politics.[18] "Culture, for the Russian émigrés," writes Raeff,

> was an essential aspect of their national identity, of the identity as educated, at whatever level, Russian people. It consisted of all those manifestations of … "high" culture: the literary, artistic, and scientific or scholarly creations of the nation, which are promulgated by such institutions as church, school, theater, books and journals, informal clubs, societies, and organizations. In all of these manifestations, however, there was a specifically *Russian* identity.[19]

This assertion that culture, not politics, constituted the core of Russia Abroad is at the centre of many such accounts.[20] Indeed, the priority of an authentic culture untouched by the volatile politics of the twentieth century became an essential aspect of the Russian emigration's self-fashioning. Vladimir Nabokov, perhaps the English language's most forceful spokesperson for this view, would later write that "a work of art has no importance whatever to society."[21] But of course, culture *is* important to society, and it *is* political. Indeed, the politics of the Soviet Union, where culture could not be divorced from politics, was the major (and political!) reason why the white emigration insisted on a culture that rejected politics.[22]

The vehement denial of politics was a political stance in itself. Moreover, the fixation on the "whiteness" *and* cultural purity of the first wave of the Russian emigration carried significant political baggage.[23] And that baggage has, to a large extent, defined not only émigré studies but the field of Slavic and East European Studies more broadly. In the post–Second World War period, many of the white émigrés and their descendants made their way across the Atlantic just at the time when the US was ramping up both its funding for area studies and its anti-communist messaging. The white émigré narrative of a pure culture disinterested in politics (aside from an "absolute rejection of the Bolshevik regime") found fertile ground in the burgeoning field of Slavic Studies. Many early Slavic departments employed or were founded by white émigré scholars and teachers, and the field's major publications, according to a recent meta-analysis, showed a marked tendency in the post-war decades for discussions of "high," largely pre-revolutionary, culture as detached from direct political concerns.[24]

Without denying the many invaluable contributions to Russian and world culture made by the first wave of Russian émigrés, *Red Migrations* is meant, in part, as a corrective to the mythology and mystique of the white émigré narrative. It interrogates the very roots of Slavic Studies in North America in order to reconceptualize this originary moment as something more open, diverse, and progressive. While émigré studies (and diaspora studies more broadly) posit movements as unidirectional – which, in this case, means *away from* Soviet Russia – *Red Migrations* sees multidirectional and overlapping trajectories: of emissaries sent from the young Soviet Union; of idealists, journalists, and workers attracted to the socialist project; and of émigrés and exiles who later decided to return. Where the white émigré narrative is driven by the single-minded flight from political persecution, *Red Migrations* sees both attraction and repulsion, desire and fear, hope and need as drivers of transnational movements in the years after 1917. By questioning the monolithic vision of the white emigration and introducing a broader spectrum of political allegiances, geographical movements, and international networks, *Red Migrations* brings to light the long-overlooked diversity at the very heart of the field's emergence.

Internationalism as Counternarrative

As a counterbalance to the white émigré narrative, socialist modes of global mobility have gained significant scholarly attention in recent decades. Such accounts inevitably start with the Comintern, Moscow's project for forging an international alliance of communists in the 1920s and 1930s. In these decades, Moscow became – in Katerina Clark's provocative phrase – "the fourth Rome," but not because of the Stalinist doctrine of socialism in one country, the increasingly paranoid repressions, or even the military build-up to war. In fact, it became a global centre *despite* all of these tendencies and because it encouraged cultural and aesthetic exchanges that intersected with an idealistic internationalism in a moment of increasing oppression of leftist politics by the emerging fascist regimes of Europe. The recent volume *Comintern*

Aesthetics highlights this inner contradiction of socialist organizing across national borders in the 1930s: the Comintern's "subservience to Soviet state interests and Stalinist realpolitik," on one hand, and, on the other, its "unrealized and perhaps unrealizable dream: to balance centripetal control with local struggle, internationalism, and nationalism."[25] Art and literature that were internationalist in either their organizational practices or their aesthetics, that volume argues, embodied the spirit of the Comintern, creating an alternative network of world culture that decentred traditional hubs, especially Paris. But, as the editors note, "the sheer variety of contexts ... made clear the pitfalls of simply replacing the Parisian centre with a Muscovite one."[26] The culture of the world revolution, albeit heavily shaped by the Soviet Union, was in reality polycentric.

By focusing on mobility and transnational networks and treating the Comintern as only one of many factors in cross-border pursuits, we aim to further broaden the discussion of global leftist culture. Even the Soviet Union itself often played an affective role that went beyond the institutional efforts of the Comintern. For many it was a beacon of hope. It embodied the promise that revolutionary change was possible, it supported the anti-colonial struggle, and – as large swathes of Europe descended into economic depression and fascism – it offered a model of a more just society. Publications around the world – some with direct financial or logistical support from the Soviet Union through the Comintern, others independently – celebrated the revolution and called on working people from the Americas to East Asia to think in new ways about economic and social justice. Emissaries from the Soviet Union travelled throughout the world, some of them agitating for revolution, others cultivating cultural ties, many doing both. These travellers populate the following chapters – Roman Utkin, for instance, introduces the reader to Ilya Ehrenburg, Andrei Bely, and Viktor Shklovsky as they contemplate, not without ideological ambivalence, returning from Berlin to the Soviet Union (chapter 5); Serguei Oushakine follows Sergei Eisenstein, Grigorii Aleksandrov, and Eduard Tisse as they meet Walt Disney and Charlie Chaplin in Hollywood (chapter 1); and Michael Kunichika traces Nikolai Aseev's trip through Europe, where he meets, among others, Maxim Gorky, whose villa in Sorrento serves as a hub of the red migrants (chapter 9).

What unites the chapters of this volume is that they put mobility itself at the centre, demonstrating how the temporary and long-term movements of artists, culture workers, and cultural theorists and the concrete mechanisms of cultural exchange around them shaped their ideologies, social theories, and artistic practices. For many of those drawn towards the Soviet centre, the institutions of internationalism provided a justification and an infrastructure to pursue a wide variety of projects. In the 1920s and especially the 1930s – the period at the core of the phenomenon Clark describes as Moscow's role as the "fourth Rome" – the country hosted travellers and migrants from the world over. Prominent Marxists like Georg Lukács and Antonio Gramsci came to study at the Marx-Engels Institute, but the institute also attracted lesser-known figures whose trajectories and contributions are explored in this volume for the first time, such as the British Communist Ralph Fox (chapter 7) and the Hungarian Dadaist and Marxist theoretician János Mácza (chapter 2). Others were interested in the Soviet Union as a land supposedly free of prejudice, where Black American workers like Margaret Glasgoe and Robert Robinson could form an identity not entirely determined by race (chapter 10) and where communists and fellow travellers like Arthur Koestler and Langston Hughes could negotiate the relative values of social boundaries (chapter 6).

Chapters in this volume that are less engaged with physical relocation trace the parallel and concurrent circulation of ideas, cultural forms, and even language, as in Trevor Wilson's chapter on the cross-border exchanges and publication of late socialist works on Marxist philosophy (chapter 4), Elizabeth Stern's chapter on the import of socialist realist ballet to the GDR (chapter 3), and Edward Tyerman's discussion of Chinese migrant workers as a literary trope (chapter 8). What unites all these contributions is that they reveal how neither the paradigm of (white) émigré studies nor the focus on Comintern internationalism in isolation allows for an exhaustive treatment of mobilities to, from, and around the Soviet Union in the twentieth century.

Internationalism, Cosmopolitanism, Transnationalism

Using the tension between émigré studies and research on socialist internationalism as its point of departure, *Red Migrations* straddles two ongoing and vibrant scholarly conversations in distinct fields. The first, in Slavic Studies, re-examines the role of the Soviet Union on the world stage, especially in the interwar period and, to some extent, also after the Second World War. The second, in Migration Studies, addresses the urgent need to understand transnational movements and how they interact with interpersonal networks, economic drivers, political exigencies, and desires. Each of these debates has helped focus the research in this volume, not least by generating a scholarly vocabulary that can be loosely grouped around three key concepts that are essential for understanding movements across borders in this time period: internationalism, cosmopolitanism, and transnationalism.

Internationalism figured prominently in communist thought long before the Bolshevik Revolution, and in the post-1917 era it became the favoured label for the vision of a world revolution – sponsored by the Comintern – that would spread from Moscow to Europe and soon around the world. The Comintern's internationalism, as noted earlier, was a constant negotiation between an aspiration to "horizontal affinities across the lines of nation, race and culture" and a desire for central control.[27] Some, like Tyerman, see this negotiation as a productive tension "between the theoretical power of a Soviet-centric perspective on global history and the need for forms of translation and localized interpretation."[28] Others, like Brigitte Studer, see the Comintern's efforts at solidarity as flawed, at best "hierarchical but polycentric."[29] In its "turn to Stalinist centralization" in the late 1920s, the organization became increasingly unforgiving towards local variation in political positions.[30] Indeed, "internationalism," in Clark's estimation, was used at times as little more than "a euphemism for the cause of Soviet ideological hegemony throughout the world" and the violence that entailed.[31] Amelia Glaser and Steven Lee argue that in order to resist "the overall trend towards centralization" within the internationalist framework, scholars should "emphasize local agency against notions of the Comintern as monolith."[32]

Red Migrations takes up that challenge by focusing attention on the hyperlocal, on the movements and networks of individuals and small groups of cultural and political actors. Additionally, this volume probes another assumption undergirding internationalism, namely its tendency to view its actors within the boundaries of their respective nation-states. Expressed in the term inter-*national* – between nations – this foundational assumption continues to inform world governance today in organizations like the United Nations, NATO, and even the European Union, each of which has at its core the undisputed belief in the autonomous nation-state as the constitutive element of international organizations. This too was the challenge of the Comintern, which started as the *Third* International, a renegotiation between the values of communist solidarity across borders and those of national commitments, a conflict of interests that had fractured the *Second* International on the eve of the First World War.

Ilya Ehrenburg offers a powerful exposé of nationalism within the Second International in his 1921 picaresque novel *The Extraordinary Adventures of Julio Jurenito and His Disciples*. The narrator elaborates that while he had seen many things in life, from the urinals of Paris to Tatlin's project for the Monument to the Third International, nothing compared to this scene of internationalist discontent. At a fictive hotel in (neutral) Geneva where socialist representatives from both factions of the war were meeting, "the two delegations stayed in two separate buildings: in order to avoid compromising themselves, they not only refused to meet, they even refused to correspond with each other, since they all were good, honest patriots. But, being socialists and members of the International, they all aspired to the renewal of comradely relations just as soon as the war had ended."[33]

Ehrenburg the polyglot reveals here in a comical key the flawed nature of the Second International on the eve of the First World War. National interest and identity become the inherent limitations of the project of internationalism, and the different parties communicate only through posters and slogans displayed in their respective hotel windows. Internationalism, Ehrenburg suggests, inevitably runs up against the nation; the logic of its constituent elements becomes its biggest obstacle.

Cosmopolitanism, on the other hand, has always sought to transcend the idea of the nation. The term can be traced back to the fourth century BCE, when Diogenes the Cynic called himself a citizen of the cosmos, rather than of the political state of Athens. In the Soviet context, cosmopolitanism was not much used by the Comintern and thus did not become a cover for Soviet hegemony. Indeed, its Soviet legacy is something of the opposite: it evolved into a strongly pejorative term, especially during Stalin's increasingly paranoid post-war purges, which chiefly targeted Soviet Jews (see chapter 1 in this volume). At this moment, even Ehrenburg himself, who had so shrewdly observed the lack of leftist solidarity across national borders, now found himself in an impossible position: between opposition to this amalgamation of antisemitism and nationalist insecurity on the one hand, and cooperation with the Soviet state on the other.[34] In today's Russia, the term cosmopolitanism has been revived to add a conspiratorial valence to charges against so-called "foreign agents" and others with international ties. In this way, cosmopolitanism has the dual advantage of moving beyond the nation-state and also being opposed to the distinct history of Stalinist hegemonic aspirations and their connections to state violence.

Like internationalism, cosmopolitanism also articulates a tension between two aspirations, but it is not between the horizontal and the vertical. Cosmopolitanism does not conjure images of central control; even the "kinless cosmopolites" of Stalin's paranoid imaginings are dangerous not because they are active agents of another power, but because they are so dissociated from their own country that they are susceptible to outside forces. The tension in the term cosmopolitanism, then, is not between solidarity and central control, but between universality and cultural particularity. Indeed, in today's critical vocabulary, the term has been used to signify an aspiration to both universality and particularity at once. Cosmopolitanism is (in Martha Nussbaum's words) the "allegiance to the worldwide community of human beings," but at the same time (in Paul Rabinow's) it is "an ethos of macro-interdependencies, with an acute consciousness ... of the inescapabilities and particularities of places, characters, historical trajectories and fates."[35] Recognizing this tension between the universal and the culturally specific, Kwame Anthony Appiah writes that "there is a sense in which cosmopolitanism is the name not of the solution, but of the challenge."[36]

The challenge, for Bruno Latour, is understanding that the "cosmos" in "cosmopolitan" might mean very different things to different actors. Drawing on Isabelle Stengers's work *Cosmopolitique* (1997), Latour proposes a "constructivist cosmopolitics" that would interrogate and value the construction of what it means to be universal, instead of assuming that the "allegiance to the worldwide community of human beings" means the same thing to all those humans.[37] Indeed, the years after the 1917 Revolution provide a particularly clear example of competing cosmoses. If the white emigration imagined a worldwide community based on ideals of individual liberty, aesthetic genius, and dissociation from political concerns, then the Soviet Union imagined something quite different: a universal brotherhood of working people and oppressed nations, and an anti-colonialism that would reject the exploitation of capitalism and ultimately work towards the world revolution. The Soviet vision, perhaps surprisingly, was the one more anchored in the nation-state. Indeed, in Stalin's programmatic text "Marxism and the National Question" (1913), the path to universalism was mapped out in positively Wilsonian terms. Socialism would protect "the right of nations to self-determination"; at the same time, it would agitate "against harmful customs and institutions of that nation in order to enable the toiling strata of the nation to emancipate themselves from them."[38] The insistence on national self-determination continued throughout the interwar era, both within the Soviet Union and internationally through the Comintern, becoming something of a banner of the anti-colonial struggle. It was, in fact, the white émigrés – largely displaced persons and stateless actors – who abandoned the nation-state as a necessary aspect of political identity. In many ways, the white émigrés might be seen as cosmopolitans. Between the internationalism of the Comintern, then, and the cosmopolitanism of the white emigration, those who populate the following pages would need a third term.

The term transnationalism, which provides the conceptual backbone for this volume, describes a different mode of organization across borders. As a framework in the social sciences, transnationalism has enjoyed great popularity over the past twenty years for its potential to reveal activity that disrupts clear-cut notions of the nation and its boundaries. It describes social practices created through global mobility that conceive of migration not as individualized incidents of relocation but rather as events embedded in a constant back-and-forth, a continuous negotiation of fluctuating identities and values in multiple places. Since the mid-twentieth century at least, the mobility of migrants has been enhanced by affordable air travel, the financial networks of global capitalism, greater tolerance toward dual citizenship, global systems of communication, and the circulation of political involvement and cultural forms these things facilitate. Increases in labour migration and population flows in the post-colonial and post-socialist era have come to rely on these infrastructures.[39]

Although these kinds of mobility may seem unique to late capitalism, multidirectional movements have long been part of global migration regimes. Many scholars now agree that transnationalism indexes "a novel perspective, if not a novel phenomenon."[40] Even in the earlier history of immigration to the United States, return migration and complex patterns of mobility between Europe and America were more common than often assumed. For instance, in 1921 roughly 800,000 new immigrants arrived in the US, but around 250,000 *left*, either disillusioned by the New World's unkept promises or having fulfilled their financial goals.[41] Although these kinds of mobility were not conceptualized as transnationalism at the time, recent developments in transnationalism studies have heightened awareness of return and circular migration patterns and systems of remittances as consistent elements of global mobility throughout human history. In migration studies, these observations have led to the questioning of the modern immigrant narrative as a story of singular relocation followed by a process of assimilation and negotiations around multiculturalism.[42] Indeed, it is reasonable to assume that if migrants continue to be mobile, concomitant social changes may not be so linear as the one-way narrative of assimilation suggests. Transnational identities remain in flux.

Early applications of this concept in migration studies have used the term transmigrants to refer to those "immigrants who develop and maintain multiple relationships – familial, economic, social, organizational, religious, and political – that span borders," leading to a "multiplicity of involvements" in both countries of origin and countries of settlement.[43] Studying global mobility from this angle means eschewing a narrow focus on statistics of relocation and inventories of motivations and challenges. Indeed, defining who is a migrant as such has become somewhat of a moot point, a shift reflected in the current definition suggested by the United Nations: a migrant is any "person who moves away from his or her place of usual residence, whether within a country or across an international border, temporarily or permanently, and for a variety of reasons."[44] This volume reflects such diversity of displacements. While some chapters focus on diaspora communities either as cultural agents or as a theme, others focus on lengthy travel or on temporary relocation, and yet others focus on more static subjects surrounded by agile networks of circulating cultural forms and influences. These kinds of mobilities are often interconnected: long-term relocation is entangled with the circulation of aesthetics, travel is embedded in networks of cultural exchange, and so forth. "All displacements are not the same," as Caren Kaplan reminds us, yet they often adhere to the same laws of attraction that set them in motion, shaping similar spaces for cultural exchange and social encounters.[45] More importantly, all kinds of mobility addressed in this volume lead to a similar multiplicity of involvements characteristic of the transnational.

The transnational lens of our volume reflects a diversity of displacements, each treated distinctly in its individual chapter. What these chapters have in common is a conscious shift away from state-sponsored institutions as the main source of agency, which is not to say that institutions do not matter. Quite the contrary. But the chapters in this volume show how institutions functioned as frameworks and facilitators, rather than exclusively as authorities and control mechanisms. Various actors inhabited institutional frameworks in different ways. Ralph Fox, for instance, parlayed his position within the Communist Party of Great Britain to become a leading adviser to the Soviets on South Asia (chapter 7), and German writers in the 1960s used the Writers' Union as a boutique travel agency, even as they withdrew their commitment to post-war socialist literature (chapter 14). In such instances, institutions do not control the movements of subjects. Instead, active subjects make use of institutions as they build transnational networks, motivated by their own hopes, desires, and solidarities.

Committed to the conceptual framework of transnational mobility with its multidirectional and parallel entanglements, this volume resists the urge to organize its chapters in terms of dominant directionalities (outreach versus influx), perceived quality of the relocation (short- versus long-term, voluntary versus forced), or even varieties of political commitment. None of these categories hold up to close scrutiny, which is, after all, one of the central arguments of this volume: mobilities are multidirectional; the duration of relocation is not indicative of its impact; subjective formulations of the desire to move and coerced migration are hard to separate; and ideological orientations are flexible, subject to pragmatic and at times even cynical transformations. For this reason, we instead organize this book around four key terms, which emerged in the series of workshops preceding this volume: *Forms, Geographies, Identities,* and *Communities*.

The first section, *Forms*, collects four chapters that trace the movement of aesthetic forms across borders to develop theories of Marxist mobility that are deeply informed by the experience of transnational movements as well as by leftist aesthetics. Serguei Oushakine's chapter locates the cosmopolitan origins of Stalinist cinema in Hollywood and provides a genealogy for the downfall of the late-Stalinist anti-cosmopolitan campaign. By following a particularly influential filmmaker, Grigorii Aleksandrov, to Hollywood and back in the 1930s, Oushakine shows how cultural arbitrage – the process of transporting a cultural product across a border in order to increase its value – is key to understanding both the development of Stalinist cinema and the post-war anti-cosmopolitan hysteria. Irina Denischenko traces a different vision of cultural transfer: she follows the Dadaist playwright and Marxist theorist János Mácza from the short-lived Hungarian Commune to Moscow, where he used his diverse experience of contemporary art to create the first transnational theory of the avant-garde – a theory previously all but unknown in English-language scholarship. Mácza's theory – complete with striking visuals – posits a concrete historical, rather than simply a formal, commonality among the artistic movements known as the historical avant-garde. Contributions by Elizabeth Stern and Trevor Wilson turn to the post–Second World War era to unearth how ideas travelled between the Soviet Union and its neighbours. Stern demonstrates how East German dance under Soviet rule relied on the belated circulation of Stalinist approaches to depicting the revolution on stage. Importing the Stalinist form of *drambalet*, she shows, proved essential in East Germany's development of a postwar socialist aesthetic that would simultaneously incorporate and deny the classical traditions of music and dance, traditions that had been tainted by Nazi involvement. Wilson reveals how the philosopher Eval'd Ilienkov developed his reconceptualization of dialectical materialism in correspondence with Bulgarian philosophers and the Italian Communist Party. Ilienkov was part of an active trans-European network and was first appreciated in Italy; his work demonstrates that the separation between Western and Soviet Marxism "was defined much more generationally than geographically."

The second section, *Geographies*, argues that red migrations, although traceable on a map, created their own geographies, attaching specific meanings to places, making some of them more relevant and thus bringing them into closer mental proximity than a map might lead one to believe. In Roman Utkin's chapter, that place is Berlin, which emerges through the performative practices of the literary environment as a politically and aesthetically multivalent space with fluctuating loyalties to the Soviet state. Berlin becomes at once a place of exile, an empty space, and finally a place from which to return, as many of Utkin's émigrés leave Berlin for the East, back to the Soviet Union. With its unusual focus on émigrés commonly associated with the Russian diaspora rather than the Soviet state, the chapter reveals that red migrations are often phenomena of great ideological ambiguity, in which political alliances are as fluid as the actors are globally mobile. In Bradley Gorski's and Katerina Clark's contributions, Central Asia serves as the locus of productive engagement with the project of the revolution. In Gorski's chapter, Langston Hughes and Arthur Koestler experience Soviet modernity as it overcomes boundaries and breaches barriers between ethnicities, genders, and life practices. In their later memoirs, both Hughes and Koestler express these frontiers in terms of disgust – one urging stricter boundaries, and the other celebrating their breach. For Clark, Central Asia becomes a space of political ambitions on a Eurasianist scale, where the British communist Ralph Fox migrates towards Soviet communism through his imaginations of the Eurasian space. Simultaneously, the Central Asian steppe opens onto vistas of historical possibilities, where the legacies of Tamerlane and Genghis Khan can work as foils for current debates on despotic leaders, empirical expanses, and transnational nomadism.

The geography of the Soviet Union, straddling Europe and Asia, makes it particularly fertile soil for the negotiation of national, ethnic, and racial identity in the context of socialist modernity, as the third section, *Identities*, demonstrates. Edward Tyerman traces the trope of the Chinese migrant worker in Russian modernist and early Soviet writing, in which East Asian identities are exploited in order to express ideological positions during the Russian Civil War. He shows how the literary trope of the Chinese migrant focalized at once the desire for solidarity, the anxieties of national stability, and the "limit of community." Michael Kunichika follows the Futurist poet Nikolai Aseev on an "unsentimental journey" to Italy, where Roman ruins become a litmus test for Aseev's commitment to the aesthetic program of modernity. Aseev, Kunichika argues, ultimately travels to reaffirm his identity at home. By contrast, the red migrants who populate Kimberly St. Julian-Varnon's chapter are able to explore their identities away from the strictures placed on them at home. Following several African American migrants to the Soviet Union, St. Julian-Varnon shows how Soviet anti-racist rhetoric and practice opened up a space for (re)formulating racial identities across classes in the 1920s and 1930s.

The new socialist context inspired new identities while also bringing together new configurations of creative, educational, and political actors, as the fourth section, *Communities*, demonstrates. Anna Arustamova shows how one of the key figures of the pre-revolutionary leftist elite in Soviet literature, the Futurist David Burliuk, organized an unexpected community of socialist cultural production in the United States. Burliuk's attempt to create a "proletarian" literature in America, she argues, undermines many common tropes of émigré culture and reconfigures what we know about both the politics and the aesthetics of interwar Russia Abroad. Helen Fehervary's study of the nomadic intellectual and Hungarian-German socialist László Radványi reveals his involvement in numerous endeavours in workers' education from Weimar Germany to Mexico City. Fehervary shows how education – a particularly important but underappreciated cultural undertaking – creates networks that are essential to émigré and transnational communities. Tatsiana Shchurko's meditation on an image from the Hermina Huiswoud archive demonstrates how, even when the realities of travel inhibited engagement between visitors and Soviet citizens, solidarities could be imagined based on shared experiences of racially determined oppression. Her chapter envisions a potential network of radical feminist solidarity that would connect Black Americans, Soviet Central Asians, and even researchers and activists today. Philip Gleissner's chapter traces how German writers in the 1960s took advantage of Soviet initiatives for cultural exchange to build networks of friendship and kinship across borders that bypassed official ideological commitments. He argues that desire – romantic, geographic, cultural – should be centred in studies of the formation of transnational networks that worked both within and beyond institutional frameworks.

Each of these sections unites multiple historical periods, from the early Soviet years to high Stalinism and the post-war era. It is our hope that this chronological diversity will give rise to new ideas about socialist culture's transnational mode of being and will highlight the agency of individual writers, artists, and activists. Introducing a fuller spectrum of political allegiances, geographical movements, and international networks, and their motivations, *Red Migrations* seeks long-neglected diversity in order to question the monolithic vision of émigré studies that is a central point of origin for the Slavic field and that has shaped our perceptions of mobility and global entanglements of Russian culture and politics to this day.

Notes

1. For a detailed timeline of cultural organization around the Comintern, see Amelia Glaser and Steven S. Lee, eds., *Comintern Aesthetics* (Toronto: University of Toronto Press, 2019), xiii–xxi.
2. In 1935, MORP was dissolved and *International Literature* was made an organ of the Soviet Union of Writers. In 1943, the journal was discontinued. For a history of the journal, see Elena Ostrovskaya and Elena Zemskova, "Between the Battlefield and the Marketplace: *International Literature* Magazine in Britain," *Russian Journal of Communication* 8, no. 3 (2016): 217–29; Elena Ostrovskaya and Elena Zemskova, "From *International Literature* to World Literature: English Translators in 1930s Moscow," *Translation and Interpreting Studies* 14, no. 3 (2019): 351–71.
3. See Edward Tyerman, "Resignifying 'The Red Poppy': Internationalism and Symbolic Power in the Sino-Soviet Encounter," *Slavic and East European Journal* 61, no. 3 (2017): 445–66.
4. Katerina Clark, *Eurasia without Borders: The Dream of a Leftist Literary Commons, 1919–1943* (Cambridge, MA: Harvard University Press, 2021), 283–4.
5. Osip Mandelstam, "An Interview with Ho Chi Minh – 1923," trans. Clarence Brown, *Commentary*, August 1967. https://www.commentary.org/articles/osip-mandelstam/an-interview-with-ho-chi-minh-1923. The original ran in *Ogonek*, 23 December 1923.
6. Christian Høgsberg, "Introduction," in C.L.R. James, *World Revolution, 1917–1936: The Rise and Fall of the Communist International* [1937] (Durham: Duke University Press, 2017).
7. Boris Raymond and David R. Jones, *The Russian Diaspora, 1917–1941* (Lanham: Scarecrow Press, 2000), 8–9; John Glad, *Russia Abroad: Writers, History, Politics* (Washington: Birchbark Press, 1999), 105–8.
8. Marc Raeff, *Russia Abroad: A Cultural History of the Russian Emigration 1919–1939* (Oxford: Oxford University Press, 1990), 24.
9. WorldCat lists at least four books with the title *Russia Abroad*, along with several more with Russian titles such as "Rossiia za rubezhom" and "Zarubezhnaia Rossiia," alongside canonical studies that continue to shape Western perceptions of Russian émigré culture, such as Glad, *Russia Abroad*; and Raeff, *Russia Abroad*.
10. Raeff, *Russia Abroad*, 3.
11. Greta N. Slobin, *Russians Abroad: Literary and Cultural Politics of Diaspora (1919–1939)*, ed. Katerina Clark, Nancy Condee, Dan Slobin, and Mark Slobin (Boston: Academic Studies Press, 2013), 14.
12. It is worth noting that in this regard, the exodus of the 1920s and current departures from the Russian Federation do not align. Whereas Russia Abroad claimed cultural purity and continuity in opposition to the Soviet

state, the conservative or even nationalist position is today taken by the Russian state itself.
13 Encyclopedia qtd. in Glad, *Russia Abroad*, 107.
14 Burliuk, letter to Erich Gollerbakh, 1929, qtd. in Arustamova, this volume.
15 Ivan Bunin, "Missiia russkoi emigratsii: Rech', proiznesennaia v Parizhe 16 fevralia," *Rul'*, 3 April 1924: 5.
16 Bunin, "Missiia russkoi emigratsii."
17 Liliia Podicheva, "'Ia ne v izgnanii, ia v poslanii' Niny Berberovoi: Kanonizatsiia frazy," in *Tekstologiia i istoriko-literaturnyi protsess: Sbornik statei VII Mezhdunarodnoi konferentsii molodykh issledovatelei* (Moscow: Buki vedi, 2018), 143–57.
18 Raeff, *Russia Abroad*, 8.
19 Raeff, *Russia Abroad*, 9–10.
20 Greta Slobin likewise sees "an impressive story of remarkable literary, linguistic, and cultural continuity." Slobin, *Russians Abroad*, 14.
21 Vladimir Nabokov, *Strong Opinions* (New York: Vintage, 1989), 33.
22 Evgeny Dobrenko's research has revealed this continuity between politics and culture in great detail with regard to socialist realism. He demonstrates how from the 1930s on the aesthetic doctrine of Soviet art was not merely the purely artistic method that it claimed to be but rather functioned as a political institution. Its "basic function," he argues, was "to create socialism – Soviet reality and not an artifact." Evgeny Dobrenko, *Political Economy of Socialist Realism* (New Haven: Yale University Press, 2007), xii.
23 Whiteness here is meant predominantly in the sense of Civil War–era political commitment but ultimately also in terms of Slavic and Christian identity. For late-Soviet consequences of a similar position, see Rossen Djagalov, "Racism, the Highest Stage of Anti-Communism," *Slavic Review* 80, no. 2 (2021): 290–8.
24 Marijeta Bozovic, et al. "Knight Moves: Russifying Quantitative Literary Studies," *Russian Literature*, Special Issue on "Digital Humanities and Russian and East European Studies" (2021): 113–38, esp. 128.
25 Glaser and Lee, *Comintern Aesthetics*, 5.
26 Glaser and Lee, *Comintern Aesthetics*, 529.
27 Edward Tyerman, *Internationalist Aesthetics: China and Early Soviet Culture* (New York: Columbia University Press, 2021), 7.
28 Tyerman, *Internationalist Aesthetics*, 8.
29 Brigitte Studer, *The Transnational World of the Cominternians* (Basingstoke: Palgrave Macmillan, 2015), 24.
30 Glaser and Lee, *Comintern Aesthetics*, 10.
31 Katerina Clark, *Moscow the Fourth Rome: Stalinism, Cosmopolitanism, and the Evolution of Soviet Culture, 1931–1941* (Cambridge, MA: Harvard University Press, 2011), 4.

32 Glaser and Lee, *Comintern Aesthetics*, 11.
33 Il'ia Erenburg, *Sobranie sochinenii v deviati tomakh*, vol. 1: *Khulio Khurenito. Trest. D.E. Trinadtsat' trubok* (Moskva: Gosudarstvennoe izdatel'stvo khudozhestvennoi literatury, 1962), 137–8.
34 Joshua Rubenstein, *Tangled Loyalties: The Life and Times of Ilya Ehrenburg* (New York: Basic Books, 1996), 258, 262.
35 Paul Rabinow, "Respresentations Are Social Facts," in *Writing Culture*, ed. James Clifford (1986), qtd. in Bruce Robbins, "Introduction Part I: Actually Existing Cosmopolitanism," in *Cosmopolitics: Thinking and Feeling beyond Nation*, ed. By Pheng Cheah and Bruce Robbins (Minneapolis: University of Minnesota Press, 1998), 1.
36 Kwame Anthony Appiah, *Cosmopolitanism: Ethics in a World of Strangers* (New York: W.W. Norton, 2006), xv.
37 Bruno Latour, "Whose Cosmos, Which Cosmopolitics? Comments on the Peace Terms of Ulrich Beck," *Common Knowledge* 10, no. 3 (2004): 450–63.
38 Joseph Stalin, "Marxism and the National Question," *Prosveshchenie*, nos. 3–5, March–May 1913, https://www.marxists.org/reference/archive/stalin/works/1913/03.htm.
39 Thomas Faist and Başak Bilecen, "Transnationalism," in *Routledge International Handbook of Migration Studies*, 2nd ed. (Routledge, 2019), 499.
40 Lewis H. Siegelbaum and Leslie Page Moch, "Transnationalism in One Country? Seeing and Not Seeing Cross-Border Migration within the Soviet Union," *Slavic Review* 75, no. 4 (2016): 973.
41 Roger Daniels, *Coming to America: A History of Immigration and Ethnicity in American Life*, 2nd ed. (New York: Harper Perennial, 2002), 287–8.
42 Faist and Bilecen, "Transnationalism," 505.
43 Nina Glick Schiller, Cristina Szanton Blanc, and Linda G. Basch, *Nations Unbound: Transnational Projects, Postcolonial Predicaments, and Deterritorialized Nation-States* (Langhorne: Gordon and Breach, 1994), 7.
44 *Glossary on Migration*, International Migration Law 34 (Geneva: International Organization for Migration, 2019), https://publications.iom.int/system/files/pdf/iml_34_glossary.pdf, 132.
45 Caren Kaplan, *Questions of Travel: Postmodern Discourses of Displacement* (Durham: Duke University Press, 1996), 4.

PART I

Forms

1 "How They Do It in America": Cosmopolitanism and Cultural Arbitrage in Soviet Russia

SERGUEI ALEX. OUSHAKINE

The tendency in Soviet Russia today towards western standards is merely a reflection of the general tendency of the Russian bureaucracy away from revolutionary Marxism.
— David Schrire, 1936[1]

Figaro quì, Figaro là. Machines here, machines there.
— Sergei Eisenstein, 1927[2]

Béla Balázs did not mince words in his review of a new musical from Grigorii Aleksandrov, released in 1936. Published in the main Soviet cinema journal, *Iskusstvo kino* (*The Art of Cinema*), Balázs's review began bluntly: "At first glance, the film *Circus* is overwhelmingly dubious (*somnintel'nyi*), just as Aleksandrov's overall style is." Immediately after this confession there was an unexpected turn: "But we like it. We are laughing, and we are touched." Then – another one:

> Still, many of us are tormented by doubt: how can we applaud this kind of bourgeois art now if we used to despise and scorn it only recently? Hasn't the genre of melodrama been compromised forever? This mélange of jazz and melancholic tango; the sensations, the acrobatics, and the glitter of the revue; the circus humor and the hit number of the star – we have been calling all that "kitsch" in the West. How could such a film possibly succeed here? How could we possibly like it?[3] (figure 1.1)

Balázs's answer to this socio-aesthetic conundrum was both simple and complicated; it was structural and historical. First, he reminded his readers of old "folk wisdom," claiming that even when two different people do the same thing, the things they produce in the end are rarely

Figure 1.1. Boris Zelenskii: A poster for Grigorii Aleksandrov's *Circus*. Moscow: Kinofotoizdat, 1936. Courtesy of the State Central Museum of Cinema (Gosudarstvennyi Tsentral'nyi muzei kino). Goskatalog No: GTsMK KP – 3000.

the same. Then he reframed his idea with the help of Karl Marx's "scientific definition": the difference between the-same-things-that-are-not-the-same is rooted in "the change of function." As Balázs clarified, "in different historical and social conditions the same fact receives very different importance and has very different impact."[4] Hence, revues and melodramas in the West are not the same as revues and melodramas in the East: their obvious (formal) similarities mask their fundamental (functional) differences. The glamour of the "bourgeois revue" – "with hundreds of women, torches, spinning wheels, and glittering lights" – was escapist and misleading; its goal was "to tone down the gloom of poverty." In the Soviet context, the role and function of glittering revues were dramatically transformed: "There is no need to blind the Soviet viewer with glamour. Yet, he should have some aesthetic enjoyment in his life." Drawing a sharp bottom line, Balázs concluded his essay with a programmatic statement: "We have no reason for promoting ascetic tastes. We are not going to let bourgeois art monopolize glitter and beauty."[5]

In this essay, I follow Balázs's intriguing point about linking (formal) repetition and (functional) difference. I am interested in exploring further the mechanics whereby genres and art forms change their function in the process of transcultural and transnational migration. Certainly, by now, Balázs's main idea – function does not follow form – is rather familiar. Throughout the last century, various scholars and artists showed how spatial or temporal recontextualization of a cultural form implies its repurposing. Marcel Duchamp's exhibits of ready-mades, Yuri Tynianov's works on parody, Roman Jakobson's study of aphasia and shifters, Jacques Derrida's investigation of the affordances and effects of citationality, and Christian Boltanski's *objet trouvé* art installations have demonstrated convincingly that there is nothing mechanical about the reproduction of form.[6] Iteration is always already a re-formation that can (and often does) radically dispense with intentions, meanings, and goals that were originally associated with the form.

My main concern, however, is not with the structural affordances that enable the form to constantly reinvent its function. Rather, I want to understand specific historical settings, artistic devices, and discursive frameworks that served to domesticate or estrange a particular cultural form. Simply put, how does a Hollywood revue become a quintessential Stalinist artefact? Or, alternatively, what does it take to transform a home-grown cultural product into the ultimate sign of an alien or foreign culture?

While following Balázs's overall move towards destabilizing the link between form and function – *the same things done by different people in different places are never quite the same* – I will slightly complicate its functionalist orientation with two additional components, which I borrow from studies of cosmopolitanism and ongoing debates about the sociology of finance. Balázs's insightful observation about changing functions of the "same" thing carefully avoids any discussion of the procedural/processual aspects of this change. The functional change simply and literally *takes place*, emerging as an outcome of the revue's geographic movement from West to East. Yet the very process of *taking* place is rarely automatic or mechanical; it implies a particular set of chosen actions. Taking place by way of invasion is different from taking place, say, through adaptation, mimicry, parody, or grafting. In other words, art forms are culturally embedded and historically specific, so their functional change and the geographic movement depend on agents and vehicles – *function-changers* – capable of transforming bourgeois kitsch into Stalinist classics. I will use the term *cultural arbitrage* to describe this functional transformation of art forms through geographic transposition.

The basic definition of arbitrage could be as simple as this: "Arbitrage is trading that exploits price discrepancies."[7] What makes arbitrage in general and cultural arbitrage in particular so interesting is that this "exploitation" demands the simultaneous deployment of "connectivity, knowledge, and computing."[8] Or, slightly differently, it relies on three main operations implicitly suggested but not spelled out by Balázs in his review. First, cultural arbitrage requires simultaneous access of its agents to two (or more) cultural environments (e.g., the West and the East); second, it is based on disparities in the evaluation of the same thing that these different environments generate (e.g., melodrama as an object of scorn or applause); and, finally, it is achieved by "moving" undervalued commodities from one environment to another ("no monopoly on glitter and beauty").

With its focus on the movement and circulation of people, objects, technologies, and ideas, cultural arbitrage is somewhat similar to "cultural transfer." Localization happens in both cases – but on different levels and with different consequences. Adapting Coca-Cola to the tastes of consumers in Papua New Guinea during the Second World War (a case of cultural transfer) is radically different from the introduction of sugar in Great Britain at the end of the seventeenth century, which brought about dramatic changes there.[9] Like any arbitrage (and unlike the process of cultural transfer), *cultural* arbitrage concerns itself only to a point with the intricate relations that the move from the "culture of origin" to the "destination culture" engenders.[10]

At the same time, there is a significant difference between the logic of cultural arbitrage that I explore below, and the orientation of economic arbitrage proper. While access to non-overlapping fields of commodity circulation (i.e., "markets" or "cultural spheres") is crucial in both cases, *cultural* arbitrage allows me to focus less on the dual "citizenship" of the form, and to highlight instead the change of function that takes place after the form crosses the border. In this respect, the decidedly non-market nature of Soviet society helpfully reveals the fact that arbitrage is hardly reducible to economic reasoning only: ideology and aesthetics, as Balázs suggested, could be just as effective for changing the value (and function) of the (cultural) form. The change here is an outcome of the ongoing comparative re-evaluation. Far from being an act of mimicry or reproduction, cultural arbitrage performs a transformative transposition of a cultural form by situating it in a new environment and by connecting it with already existing networks and institutions, in order to generate a new value for the arbitrageur (and the consumer).

The crucial role of placing and the constitutive importance of spatial difference determine the global scope of cultural arbitrage, which capitalizes on specificities of local contexts while partaking in worldwide flows of ideas, forms, and resources: "arbitrage [i]s at once particular and universal."[11] Studies of cosmopolitanism add an important dimension to this interplay between the particular and the universal. In his comments on the ongoing efforts to make the concept and practices of cosmopolitanism relevant for contemporary social theory, David Harvey passionately insisted some time ago that both post-Kantian attempts to view cosmopolitanism as a form of ethical imperative, and post-structuralist attempts to document "vernacular" or "really existing" cosmopolitanisms, are rooted, so to speak, in the same form of geographical blindness. The supporters of universalism invite us to transcend differences produced by geography; meanwhile, the defenders of localized versions of cosmopolitanism turn politics into a "fetishistic" enterprise by freezing "existing geographical structures of places and norms forever."[12]

Instead of equating cosmopolitanism with the normative or the ethnographic, Harvey suggests that we pay attention to the forms of *geographic* knowledge that every type of cosmopolitanism presumes. As Harvey frames it, "cosmopolitanism bereft of geographical specificity remains abstracted and alienated reason, liable, when it comes to earth, to produce all manner of unintended and sometimes explosively evil consequences. Geography uninspired by any cosmopolitan vision is either mere heterotopic description or a passive tool of power for dominating the weak."[13]

The examples of cultural arbitrage that I discuss in this chapter acknowledge and display the geographic within the cosmopolitan (and vice versa). To demonstrate the logic of cultural arbitrage, I will focus on Aleksandrov's *Circus*, which appropriated Hollywood forms, plots, and devices, transformed them, and inscribed them on a Soviet narrative without fully domesticating them. Even while being modified, these forms retained their "foreign" flavour, texture, and accent. The visual nature of Aleksandrov's medium allows me to avoid the somewhat misleading language of translation in dealing with foreign art forms. In his *Circus*, forms were not simply reconstituted in a different language. Rather, they were *re*situated in new local settings; they were *re*attached to local actors, and they were *re*inscribed onto locally relevant (visual) narratives. I finish the chapter with a reverse example of the tendency mapped out by Aleksandrov. By looking at the 1948–9 "fight" unleashed by the Soviet party-state against the "anti-patriotic group of theatre critics," I explore the geographic externalization and political alienation of domestic cultural forms. In this case, cultural arbitrage was performed discursively and retrospectively by officials, but it similarly relied on the operational deployment of "connectivity, knowledge, and computing." By changing the function of the theatre critics' activity, the authorities reframed their publications (or a lack thereof) as a coordinated campaign for establishing and maintaining a particular regime of aesthetic judgment that continuously "underpriced" and "devalued" domestic art forms, while "hyperinflating" the worth and significance of the foreign. Having determined the operative logic of arbitraging, the party-state quickly translated it into a language of belonging to two incompatible (ideological, aesthetic, and geographical) spheres. Local cultural critique was effectively estranged by being branded not only as unpatriotic but also as bourgeois and quasi-imperialist. The result was a "complex story of variegated forms of exchangeable social capital traded across geography," as Kevin Platt phrased it in a different context.[14]

When read together, these examples outline different ways of dealing with cosmopolitan aspirations, while usefully pointing to the unremitting fascination of Soviet cultural producers with the global context of their local activities. Stalinist culture might not look like the best candidate for analysing the complexities of universalist aspirations, yet, it would be conceptually misleading and historically erroneous to perceive it as "an ever more hermetic place of cultural autarchy."[15] I show below that this culture provides plenty of examples that demonstrate a palpable concern with models and practices of extraterritorial belonging that would imply neither radical self-isolation, nor colonial submission, nor imperial domination. In this context, cosmopolitanism – be it practised or merely imagined – was manifested as a historically available form of cultural arbitrage, as the ability to negotiate imbalances and irregularities of cultural flows by transposing cultural forms from one geographic field/market to another.[16] Cosmopolitanism emerges here as the outcome of an implicit international transaction or an explicit dialogue between the particular and the universal, the concrete and the abstract, the domestic and the foreign, the local and the global.

The Arbitrageur in Training

Proof will no longer be needed of the rumor that Soviet audiences will accept only American films or home-made copies of them. How much truth is there in this gloomy legend?

– Cedric Belfrage, 1936[17]

On 7 August 1928, *Sovetskii ekran* (*The Soviet Screen*), a trade magazine for Soviet filmmakers, published a statement (*zaiavka*) signed by three important Soviet directors – Sergei Eisenstein (1898–1948), Vsevolod Pudovkin (1893–1953), and Grigorii Aleksandrov (1903–1983), who was Eisenstein's assistant director on *Battleship Potemkin* (1925) and a co-director of *October* (1927).[18] The troika insisted in their letter that the time of the silent cinema was over and that Soviet filmmakers should learn the art of the sound film first-hand.[19]

"First-hand" in this case meant going to Hollywood. The editorial lead-in for the *zaiavka* symptomatically warned the audience that some statements in the article "could not avoid being controversial and not quite clear for the unprepared reader." More crucially, though, the editorial fully agreed with the filmmakers' main point: given the lack of any possibility to test in practice the theory of sound cinema, "we have to start on this path by familiarizing ourselves with theory and by observing someone else's practical experience."[20] In 1928, the desire to "observe" American movie making in person was not entirely new. It had emerged in the summer of 1926, when Hollywood experts – including two major stars, Douglas Fairbanks and Mary Pickford – visited the Soviet Union.[21] Reporting on their visit, *Pravda* noted that the stars were "very pleased with their stay in Moscow," and quoted them as saying (after a screening of *Potemkin*) that "Eisenstein's mastery of film-drama could be compared only to Chaplin's mastery of film-comedies" (figure 1.2).[22]

Eisenstein would later recount that during his tour of the Kremlin, Fairbanks himself had invited Eisenstein and his team to visit Hollywood.[23] Aleksandrov would recall in his memoirs yet another crucial aspect of the visit: along with the film stars, Joseph Schenk had come to Moscow. Born in the Russian Empire, the president of United Artists and the future co-founder of 20th Century Fox was Eisenstein's distant relative, and, as Aleksandrov indicated, it was Schenk who had invited Eisenstein and his colleagues to familiarize themselves with the filmmaking process in the US. Both Fairbanks and Schenk would be instrumental in obtaining visas for the Soviets; yet from the very beginning the invitation was rather informal. No dates or details were ever discussed; no plans or contracts were drafted. Indeed, as Aleksandrov's archival papers and published memoirs suggest, the Soviet filmmakers were the main engine behind the trip. In 1928, Eisenstein and Aleksandrov even discussed the possibility of their US visit with Joseph Stalin, who, while supporting the trip, suggested making an extensive tour around the Soviet Union first – in order "to observe everything, to think through everything, and to make your own conclusions about everything" (the two artists obediently complied).[24]

Figure 1.2. Photo from *Sovetskii ekran*'s coverage of Douglas Fairbanks and Mary Pickford in Moscow (10 August 1926). The original caption informed the reader: "Mary Pickford and Douglas Fairbanks are in Moscow – with GTK [the State College of Cinematography] pins on their lapels."

Many years later, in his not always reliable memoirs published in the 1970s, Aleksandrov would explain this urge to see America: "It would be quite hard to create the Soviet film industry without visiting the technically advanced and industrially powerful Hollywood studios, just as it would have been impossible to rebuild AMO [the Moscow Automotive Society, later known as ZIL – SO] and to build the Gorky Auto Plant without studying the organization of the conveyer production at the Ford plant in Detroit."[25] This interest in industrial power – more precisely, in technological advancement – was not a retrospective political justification; it is plainly evident in Aleksandrov's diaries and letters written during the trip. His striving for professional knowledge, his desire to connect and to learn, is often overlooked or simply neglected; yet I think that to a large extent it determined the future success of Aleksandrov's own artistic production in the Soviet Union.

In March 1929, Anatoly Lunacharsky, the Commissar of Enlightenment, finally signed off on the governmental approval of the trip abroad (*komandirovka*). On 19 August 1929, Aleksandrov and Eisenstein, together with the cameraman Eduard Tisse, left for Europe.[26] They had not yet secured US visas, so they decided to travel around while waiting for an official invitation (in the end, it was extended by Paramount Studios in mid-April 1930).[27] In 1929, while hanging out in Berlin, the three men had their first exposure to a sound film: *The Singing Fool* with Al Jolson (dir. Lloyd Bacon, 1928). The sound in the film excited the group so much that they could not sleep that night at all, instead lying awake fantasizing about future film projects. As Aleksandrov put it: "This trip turned out to be even more meaningful than we had imagined: we became totally overwhelmed by a desire to figure out the mystery of sound film and started exploring various possibilities of participating in sound film production."[28]

To forge contacts and to pay for the trip, the group searched for new projects. The possibilities were not multiple, but they were important. In September 1929, Aleksandrov wrote to his wife Olga (who had stayed in Moscow) from Zurich: "I am writing this from a hospital where they do abortions ... To earn some money for our stay here ... we are filming a scientific picture about abortion."[29] This silent film – *Frauennot, Frauenglück* – was a combination of documentary and acted sequences.[30] The idea to create "the first national Swiss film" was initiated by the Swiss film distributor Lazar Wechsler, who was familiar with Russian cinema and had presented *Potemkin* in Switzerland.[31] Interested in "creating Swiss cinematography," Wechsler commissioned a film that called for the legalization of abortion. The result quickly generated a lot of attention and (angry) responses from Catholic communities (figure 1.3).[32]

A month later, Aleksandrov wrote from Berlin about yet another opportunity – this time, to shoot commercials for Nestlé: "The offer is very interesting – because they pay a lot, but mostly because ... it involves a trip around the world to film the company's branches everywhere. This means America, India, and Africa ..."[33]

Many of these projects did not pan out; even so, the discussions exposed the group to different ways of organizing filmmaking. Perhaps, more significantly, these conversations helped introduce the troika to various professional, political, and artistic networks. Aleksandrov would later recite ever-growing lists of Western celebrities "who became our friends: Rabindranath Tagore, Luigi Pirandello, Sigmund Freud, Filippo Marinetti, John Goldsworthy, Pablo Picasso, Albert Einstein, Thomas Edison, Theodore Dreiser, Erskine Caldwell, ... Charlie Chaplin, John Ford, Marlene Dietrich, and others."[34] Still, as articulated

Figure 1.3. A poster for the film *Frauennot, Frauenglück* by Eduard Tisse, Sergei Eisenstein, and Grigorii Aleksandrov, 1929. Source: https://www.filmo.ch

in the 1928 *zaiavka*, the group's main interest was in mastering sound. In 1929, while in Berlin, they met with the Austrian American director Josef von Sternberg, who was filming the first German sound film, *The Blue Angel*, starring Marlene Dietrich and Emil Jannings. Apart from declaring ecstatically in his memoirs that "we totally forgot ourselves when helping Sternberg" (*pomogali s upoeniem*), Aleksandrov wrote down little about the relationship the group established with Sternberg.[35] His available letters are also conspicuously silent about this part of the trip. He does say, however, that "three leading cinema powers – the USA, the USSR, and Germany – were tending the cradle of *The Blue Angel*."[36] Some scholars of Soviet cinema view this encounter as a key event that dramatically transformed Aleksandrov's own views about film production: upon his return to the USSR, he would radically replace the practice of filming mostly non-actors (honed in his cooperation with Eisenstein) with a deliberately star-driven approach, with Marlene Dietrich as the paradigm.[37]

Aleksandrov was absolutely clear about the significance of the group's experience abroad. Only three months after the troika left Soviet Russia, he noted on 20 November 1929: "Very, very many impressions; I have no energy to describe them all, but they will be … highly useful for my life and my work."[38] A year later, by then in the US, he would continue the same theme: "During this year I learned as much as I'd learned during my previous twenty-six years."[39]

To understand the political significance of this cooperation one needs to keep in mind several trends of the time. In 1928, the first widely publicized trial against wreckers and saboteurs (the Shakhty Affair) was held in the Soviet Union. Fifty-three "bourgeois specialists" (i.e., people who had been trained before the Bolshevik Revolution) were accused of counter-revolutionary activity and cooperation with foreign countries hostile to the Soviet Union. Eleven people were sentenced to death, and the rest were imprisoned.[40] One year before that, in 1927, the "left opposition" led by Leon Trotsky had been destroyed; Trotsky himself was expelled from the Soviet Union in 1929.

This internal Soviet context, with its politicization of technical expertise and elimination of political opposition, would not entirely determine the trajectory of the cultural arbitraging that so interested Aleksandrov, but it did sometimes make itself felt. When the group finally arrived in Los Angeles, it spent a lot of time and effort pitching (unsuccessfully) film projects to various producers. At one point the troika was invited to dine with Carl Laemmle, the founder of Universal Pictures. Aleksandrov wrote in his memoirs that in the middle of the evening, a telephone was brought in and Laemmle announced that Trotsky was on the line. Apparently, he had just finished a script titled *The Kremlin's Mysteries*, and he was eager for the crew that had created *Potemkin* and *October* to work with him on the film. Panic-stricken, Eisenstein cut off the conversation, and the group walked out.[41]

As is well known, the trip to America was not what the Eisenstein collective had envisioned: no Hollywood projects emerged, and no collaboration was established.[42] But the lack of success in securing contracts

Figure 1.4. Soviets in Hollywood, September 1930: Grigorii Aleksandrov and Charlie Chaplin. Photo by Sergei Eisenstein. *Vecherniaia Moskva* explained that Aleksandrov and Chaplin are singing *"Volga, Volga, mat' rodnaia"* (Iz-za ostrova na strezhen'). *Vecherniaia Moskva*, 1 July 1937, p. 3.

was somewhat balanced by other things – the group established lasting relationships with Hollywood stars and filmmakers. During their visit, Charlie Chaplin was filming *City Lights*, and Aleksandrov managed to spend some time on that set, noting in his diary later with some surprise that Chaplin's approach to filmmaking was rather amateurish (*kustarno*): he paid little attention to camera work, stage setting, or lighting: "Being an actor, Chaplin is interested in acting and nothing else ... plus, the technical possibilities of his little studio are rather limited" (figures 1.4–1.5).[43]

New friends and new settings meant a new lifestyle for the visitors. In a letter to his wife, Aleksandrov detailed their daily social routine:

> Our life goes on, following the standard Hollywood schedule. We get up at 6 am and go to the ocean for a swim; there are various lessons from 9 to 11. Right now, I take 10 hours of classes every week. From 11 onwards, we work on our screenplay. At 5 pm, we meet some of our friends for golf or some other game. Then – again, some work on the screenplay or film screening. In bed by 10:30 pm. That's our life these days.[44]

Figure 1.5. Soviets in Hollywood, September 1930: Grigorii Aleksandrov, Sergei Eisenstein, Walt Disney, and Eduard Tisse. Courtesy of the State Central Museum of Cinema (Gosudarstvennyi Tsentral'nyi muzei kino). Goskatalog No: GTsMK KP –13606/60.

His "various lessons" included learning English, practising the piano, and, of course, studying sound production. He absorbed everything he could, voraciously watching films and frequenting theatres and cabarets. After seeing Lew Leslie's musical *Blackbirds of 1930* at the Royal Theatre in New York, he noted in his diary: "This is the best thing I have seen here. Black music and singing are unmatched [*nepodrazhaemy*]."[45]

During this trip, Aleksandrov encountered the problem of racism. He recorded his first surprise in November 1929, while he was still in

London. In *The Flame of Love* (dir. Richard Eichberg and Walter Summers, 1930) there was meant to be a scene in which the Chinese American actress Anna May Wong kisses an Englishman; censors considered this an instance of miscegenation, and forbade it. Muddling his race typology, Aleksandrov commented in his diary: "A black woman cannot kiss an Englishman; so, she was allowed to kiss only his hand."[46]

Another memorable exposure happened in Detroit in the summer of the following year, when he visited the famous Ford conveyer belt operation (figure 1.6). What Aleksandrov saw there was less than inspiring. On 9 June 1930, he wrote in his diary:

> 9 am. We are at the Ford plant. Assembling takes place at the conveyer belt … Like hungry dogs attacking food, people attack parts that move along the conveyer belt and quickly do their work. The pace [*temp*] of their work does not depend on them. The pace is determined by the conveyer …
>
> At a carousel in the molding division. It's a nightmare!!! Dust, coal, speed, congestion – only black men work here; big ones; still, there are 12–15 cases of fainting daily. This is not what tourists see. Men who have fainted – with foam at their mouth – are taken outside. There is some emergency help. And then – they are back to work. Black men – giants, big guys [*zdoroviaki*] – go mad … After all I have seen here, it feels that every machine must cost millions and millions; otherwise, the labor of humans is too cruel and hard; way too much so.[47]

Yet American efficiency, compartmentalization, focus, and determination clearly had a major impact on Aleksandrov. Like many of his contemporariness – Boris Arvatov, Alexei Gastev, and Lev Kuleshov, to name just a few – he was enthralled by *Amerikanizm* as a model for the Soviet future.[48] Having partaken in various activities, he distilled his American experience into a transportable method, a reproducible technique, a universal device. In the following extract from his diary, he summarized his music lessons, but he could just as easily have been talking about assembly lines in Detroit or a filming location in Hollywood: "American methods of teaching are astonishing. Their main quality is their quick pace. Also, the system is created so that there is nothing to study but the condensate, the quintessence, the substance of the subject. Moreover, it is structured in a way that helps you understand things quickly and learn them well."[49]

Aleksandrov learned another important lesson in the US. In 1930, while in New York, he worked on a compilation film for the Soviet–American film distribution company Amkino. The film was intended to popularize the first Five-Year Plan for the American audience. Lacking

Figure 1.6. Grigorii Aleksandrov at the Ford factory in Detroit, 9 June 1930. Private archive.

his own material, the director had to use recent Soviet documentaries available in New York as his visual stock. After watching a large number of films, he concluded, somewhat unexpectedly: "October 22, 1930. The USSR is a country of incredible opportunities; but there is no humour; it is a sad country. It needs humour."[50] A few weeks later, he returned to the same idea in his diary: "It is necessary to convince everybody that films today are overstuffed with ideas; we need to unpack them a bit, without simplifying."[51] He arrived at the final stage of this train of thought two weeks later. While in Hollywood, he bumped into Luis Buñuel, the Surrealist film director from Spain who had shot the "crazy film" *Un chien andalou* (1929). Summarizing his exchange with the fellow director, Aleksandrov noted, "Buñuel told me that he won't make any transrational [*zaumnye*] pictures anymore. Only propagandistic films, realist and accessible [*naturalisticheskie i poniatnye*]."[52]

Like a good arbitrageur, Aleksandrov constantly connected with people and things, compared his experiences, and computed his chances. What was missing in this story was a real opportunity to perform an actual transaction from which he could benefit. For this to happen, he had to return to the Soviet Union. It did not take long. For months, Soviet officials had been insisting that the group return immediately, decrying Eisenstein and his colleagues as "defectors" (*dezertiry*) who "broke all ties with their country," as Stalin put it in his letter to Upton Sinclair (who had helped with funding for the troika's Mexican journey).[53] In July 1930, in a letter, Boris Shumiatskii, the head of the Directorate of Cinema at the time, firmly spelled out the message for Eisenstein: "There is a huge field of work here, waiting for its masters. This is why we are so impatient: your continuous disengagement [*otryv*] from Soviet cinematography cannot be accepted from any point of view."[54] Responding to an increasingly aggressive stream of telegrams and official letters from various Soviet institutions, the troika returned to the Soviet Union in May 1932.

Circles of Cosmopolitan Hospitality

We decided to employ achievements of American film technology at the Moscow film factory. Moreover, by saying the magic phrase – "This is how they do it in America" – we could introduce the latest things, which even Hollywood did not have.

– Grigorii Aleksandrov, 1976[55]

However unsuccessful career-wise, the trip to Europe, the US, and Mexico provided the group with a new expressive language, new ideas about the organization of film production, and new approaches to cinema itself. The trip produced a stock of imagery and plot configurations that Aleksandrov would use in his future work. The question, of course, was how to transpose this newly acquired sensibility and vision onto the Soviet context. The formative suggestion came from above. In 1932, after his return from the US, Aleksandrov visited Maxim Gorky. At Gorky's dacha he again met Stalin, who complained about the backwardness of contemporary Soviet art. In Aleksandrov's transcription, Stalin apparently said:

> Our people, our Bolshevik party have every reason to be optimistic about our future. Somehow, our art has not kept pace with our industrial construction. Our art is stuck in the past. It is well known that our people love art that is lively and life-affirming [*bodroe i zhineradostnoe*], but you do not take this attitude seriously ... Can you help us stir up the masters of laughter in our art?[56]

The masters of laughter were, indeed, stirred up. For the rest of his career, Aleksandrov would be known first of all as a director of comedies.[57] Transplanting the genre of the Hollywood musical onto Soviet soil, he premiered his first musical comedy *Happy Guys* (*Veselye rebiata*) on 25 December 1934.[58] Boris Shumiatskii reviewed the film before its release in the newspaper *Kino*, declaring that Aleksandrov had "managed to conquer the hardest of all genres": his *Happy Guys* marked the successful "creation of Soviet comic cinema."[59]

The film presented a haphazard sequence of slapstick scenes and musical numbers. It was mildly subversive, too. The music that framed the film was jazz, the same music that Gorky described in his article in *Pravda* in 1928 as "an insulting chaos of wild sounds ... played by an orchestra of madmen."[60] The combination of music, romance, and slapstick in *Happy Guys* met with an enthusiastic response from the audience. As a sign of the incredible success of the comedy, Aleksandrov cites the fact that 5,737 copies of *Happy Guys* (a rather improbable number) were distributed around the country, all of which deteriorated very quickly as a result of intensive use.[61] In turn, Rimgaila Salys in her detailed study of the film, notes that fan letters in the archive of Leonid Utesov, the lead actor-singer of the film, indicated that some viewers saw the film "repeatedly – 4, 5, 6, even 25 times."[62]

From its inception, fellow directors attacked the film as lacking a proper social agenda and, more crucially, as not sufficiently Soviet. *Kino* reported from the public discussion of the film script at the House of Scientists (Dom uchenykh) in March 1933: "If you used English names [instead of Russian] in the film, it would be a real American comedy, – [the filmmaker Esther] Shub said. The thing is totally foreign [*tselikom ne nasha*]. It's just a display of skills. It is done well; it is entertaining. But this is not ours. This is from America, from their revue."[63] Concluding, the report cast the verdict: "This comedy is not connected organically with the Soviet soil. It is a comedy as such. Splendid, joyful, witty, and creative. But no more than that."[64] Before the comedy even had a chance to hit the big screen, critics insisted that it was "a failed experiment" and an "unhealthy hybrid" that could hardly justify its reliance on the "American model [*standart*]" of doing cinema.[65] After the wide release of *Happy Guys* in January 1935, the lack of organic connection with Soviet soil was emphasized in yet another, much more public and poignant way.

To celebrate the fifteenth anniversary of Soviet cinema in February 1935, the Soviet Union hosted its first International Film Festival in Moscow.[66] The event lasted two weeks and was closely followed by the media. The festival's importance was emphasized at a meeting in the Kremlin on 28 February, where key Soviet filmmakers – from Grigorii Aleksandrov and Dziga Vertov to Aleksandr Dovzhenko and Leonid Trauberg – received major awards from Stalin and Mikhail Kalinin.[67]

Unlike René Clair's *The Last Billionaire* and Walt Disney's cartoons, the 1934 American film *Viva Villa!* (dir. Jack Conway, Howard Hawks, and William Wellman) did not compete for the festival prizes, yet in its final statement the jury celebrated *Viva Villa!* for its "exceptional artistic quality."[68] The Russian formalist Viktor Shklovsky even published an uncharacteristically glowing review of the film in *Literaturnaia gazeta*.[69] The same issue, however, printed a short but very sarcastic note from the poet Aleksandr Bezymenskii, who pointed out a dangerously striking similarity between a march from *Happy Guys* written by Isaak Dunaevskii and a revolutionary song performed in *Viva Villa!*[70] A week later, Semen Kirsanov, a Soviet poet, added more fuel to the fire. Recalling his (failed) cooperation with Aleksandrov on the lyrics for the film's songs, the poet insisted that Aleksandrov – in addition to plagiarizing some of his poetry in *Happy Guys* – demanded that Kirsanov's texts be "completely apolitical" (a requirement that the poet found impossible to meet).[71] These publications started a major media scandal, followed by a professional investigation. In their letters to the editor of *Kino*, Aleksandrov and Dunaevskii vehemently denied any accusations of "pilfering," pointing out that even though the songs in the two films were influenced by the same Mexican folk song, "Adelita, Adelita," there could be no questions of plagiarism: *Happy Guys* was filmed at least a year before *Viva Villa!*[72]

The scandal would fade away, and Shumiatskii's public and unwavering belief in the "deeply positive role" of Aleksandrov's comedic experiments would be important in this process.[73] After the controversy had passed, Aleksandrov himself would arrive at a basic conclusion: a simple cultural adaptation, a dissolution of the foreign in the local, was not enough. To succeed, arbitrage must be particular and universal *at the same time*. In his next film, he would finally realize the promise he made in 1933 (but could not quite keep then): "My main task as a film director is to link the film with Soviet soil, 'to ground' it in the Soviet style [*sovetski "zazemlit'" ego*]."[74] This linking and grounding would be evident in his *Circus* (1936).

A Soviet blockbuster, *Circus* brought together an unusual number of key Soviet talents. Its script was based on the play *Pod kupolom tsirka* (*Under the Big Top*) written by popular satirical writers Ilya Il'f and Evgenii Petrov originally for the Moscow Music-Hall (where it was shown in late 1934); it was eventually amended by such leading Soviet *literati* as Valentin Kataev and Isaak Babel. The film's inventive camerawork was a result of cooperation between Vladimir Nil'sen, the chief cinematographer of the film, the artist Georgii Grivtsov, and the stage designer Sergei Luchishkin, who meticulously sketched ahead of time crucial details of each scene of *Circus* in his *kadrofilm*. Isaak Dunaevskii, a composer who significantly shaped the genre of the so-called Soviet mass song, created the soundtrack, which included one of the most popular Soviet tunes ever – "The Song about the Motherland," with the lyrics by Vasilii Lebedev-Kumach. Kasian Goleizovskii from the Bolshoi choreographed dances for the star.[75] The costumes were designed by the renowned Nadezhda Lamanova.[76] The circus animals came from the venerable company of the Durov dynasty.

Paradoxically, the film established Aleksandrov as a key figure in "Soviet Hollywood" *and* as an icon of Soviet ideological cinema.[77] It also marked the beginning of a peculiar Soviet phenomenon: although deeply westernized in its aesthetics, the film was seen as a perfect example of Soviet propaganda.[78] Despite its clearly adopted stylistics and forms, the film was a favourite both of Stalin and of Soviet viewers.

Before I show how this example of cultural arbitrage managed to succeed in the midst of growing political and cultural conservatism in the Soviet Union, I want to make a brief conceptual detour. In *Perpetual Peace*, Immanuel Kant famously equated universal hospitality with the Law of World Citizenship. As he put it, "hospitality ... means the right of a stranger not to be treated in a hostile manner by another upon his arrival on the other's territory.... It is not the right to be a permanent visitor that one may demand ... It is only a right of temporary sojourn, a right to associate, which all men have."[79] Julia Kristeva, commenting on this passage in *Strangers to Ourselves*, wondered about the origin of this right and found the answer in Kant himself: hospitality is "naturally ... inevitable" because the earth, "as a globe," is round.[80] Limited by their commonly possessed surface of the earth, Kant suggested, people "cannot infinitely disperse and hence must finally tolerate the presence of each other." Martha Nussbaum similarly perceives cosmopolitanism as a circumferential phenomenon. Following the Stoics, she suggests that "we think of ourselves not as devoid of local affiliations, but as surrounded by a series of concentric circles ... Outside all these circles is the largest one, that of humanity as a whole. Our task as citizens of the world will be to 'draw the circles somehow toward the centre.'"[81]

I find this spherical vision of cosmopolitanism – one that envelops if not encloses the individual/collective subject – quite fascinating (even if somewhat alarming). Aleksandrov's *Circus* also offered a circular understanding of cosmopolitanism. However, the crucial task in this case was not to draw the circles "towards the centre." Instead, it was the permutation of circles – an ability to flip them, so to speak – that helped sustain both hospitality and multiple affiliations. In a sense, what we have here is the arbitrage dynamic described by Mikhail Bakhtin as a process of shaping the external or foreign (*chuzhoe*) as one's *own foreignness* (*svoe-chuzhoe*).[82]

Visually, Aleksandrov's *Circus* begins by highlighting two points of his cinematic departure. The first prologue offers an autobiographical moment by showing an old poster for *Happy Guys* being scraped of the wall to be replaced by a new – much more glamorous and refined – poster for *Circus* designed by Boris Zelenskii (see figure 1.1.). Separated by the film credits, the second prologue builds an international connection: the opening scene shows the front page of a fictitious newspaper called the *Sunnyville Courier* with a photo of a circus performer accompanied by the headline "Marion Dixon, 'Human Bombshell,' Is Center of Sensational Scandal." The next sequence of cinematic devices could easily be read as a thinly disguised intertextual reference to the finale of Chaplin's *Circus* of 1928. There, the Tramp – abandoned by everyone – gazes for a moment at a large star drawn on a piece of paper and then disappears over the horizon, being slowly swallowed by an iris shot. In the second prologue, Aleksandrov uses the same technique of the iris shot to dynamize the static image of Marion in the newspaper: her photo is literally disrupted with a circled depiction of an angry male mobster, behind whom is a barely readable sign, "Circus." Taking over the whole screen, the mobster appears to orchestrate a rowdy scene somewhere in Kansas – the "sensational scandal" mentioned by the newspaper. The exact nature of the scandal remains opaque, though; the viewer sees only an agitated lynch mob chasing a desperate woman, who manages to escape an imminent tragedy by catching a moving train at the last moment (figure 1.7).

Suddenly the camera changes its zoom and pace, cutting from the woman in distress to the emblem on a train carriage of the Southern Railroad Company: a globe marked with the acronym *U.S.A.* The globe starts spinning but eventually slows down to expose another group of letters – *C.C.C.P.* This radical geopolitical reversibility quickly becomes grounded: the USSR/USA globe turns into a ball that lands right in the middle of a circus ring in Moscow (figure 1.8).

There, in the circus, it proliferates into a multitude of globes, which are played with by all kinds of agents – from a sea lion to a juggler to, naturally, a bear. Highlighting the global nature of the entertainment business, the scene humorously but pointedly presents the planet as a play toy for different actors (figure 1.9).[83]

With these global metaphors, the second prologue sketches the film's ideological trajectory – from one circus to another. Or, to be more precise, from the world of lynch mobs (in the US) to the world of circus spectacles (in the Soviet Union); from the arena of anger and despair

Figure 1.7. The permutation of circles. a–b Chaplin's Tramp from *Circus*, 1928. c–d An angry mobster from Kansas, and a circus performer in distress, from Aleksandrov's *Circus*, 1936. Screengrabs.

Figure 1.8. a–c Localizing the globe: screengrabs from the prologue of Aleksandrov's *Circus*, 1936.

to the arena of glitter and extravagance. This prologue also exposes the film's structuralist assumption: a form acquires its meaning/function as it constantly *circulates*. What is crucial, then, is the very possibility of switching the arenas in which the movement of forms takes place: if the form is perceived as devoid of any *internal* and *stable* meaning and the switching of contexts is the only mechanism through which evaluation can be achieved, then this type of cultural production can succeed only by preserving and replicating different and distinctive (i.e., foreign to one another) *fields* of circulation. Without these distinctive fields, cultural arbitrage is impossible: it needs the foreign and one's own – *chuzhoe* and *svoe* – at the same time.

What follows the prologues, then, is a chain of endless iterations of forms as well as the switching of fields of their activity. *Circus*'s storyline is full of parallel plots and situational errors that derive from doubles, mistaken identities, and misread, misconceived, or misdelivered letters. Forms and functions do not quite follow one another here: duplication fails to produce analogues, or it simply fails to deliver the intended effects. This overall Balázsian theme of adoption as functional change is important, but I want to highlight the ideological message the film's narrative articulates. Unlike the abandoned Tramp in Chaplin's *Circus*, the American circus star finds a permanent home in Aleksandrov's *Circus*: hospitality fulfils its promise here.[84]

The story the film presents, of an American circus star in the Soviet Union, is both a digest of early Soviet–American cooperation and a useful representation of *Amerikanizm*. The initial Soviet exposure to American technological miracles *in situ* is meant to be the first step in a long process of creative adoption, which will eventually render the American experts and their technology redundant. Marion Dixon (played by Liubov Orlova), the American circus performer featured in the prologue, arrives in the Soviet Union with her abusive German manager Franz von Kneishitz (played by Pavel Mossalskii).[85] In a Moscow circus, the couple performs an act called The Flight to the Moon, in which Marion is shot out of a cannon through a paper moon and then sings a glamorous song under the big top (figure 1.10).

As the film progresses, Marion falls in love with a former Soviet pilot, Martynov (played by Sergei Stoliarov), who has been invited to create a circus number called The Flight to the Stratosphere to replace the foreign number (which is too expensive to keep for a long time). In the Soviet version, the stratosphere is to be conquered by a man and a woman together; hence Martynov and his female assistant spend a lot of time closely watching the foreigners. Much of the film is an extended portrayal of the mirror stage dynamics: the Soviets learn how to inhabit

Figure 1.9. a–c Playing with the globe: a. Promotion photograph for the film. Courtesy of the State Central Museum of Cinema (Gosudarstvennyi Tsentral'nyi muzei kino). Goskatalog No: GTsMK KP- 19568/11. b & c. Screengrabs from the prologue of *Circus*, 1936.

the frames invented by the foreigners; at the same time, the foreigners learn the basics of the Soviet symbolic order (figure 1.11).

The narrative reaches its first climax on the night of the premiere, when Martynov's female partner, who was supposed to accompany him in The Flight to the Stratosphere, goes missing (because of a

Figure 1.10. Marion (with a local Chaplin) before, during, and after her canon number. Screengrabs from *Circus*, 1936.

parallel romantic plot line). The complete domestication of the Western number cannot quite be accomplished, and Marion volunteers to fly to the stratosphere with Martynov. After the couple conquers space, Marion launches into a long solo dance that ends with a song of joy and happiness on top of a huge wedding cake-like structure, animated by multiple chorus lines of female dancers (figure 1.12).

Over the course of this extravaganza, we see another – in this case formal, not ideological – transposition. Scholars of Aleksandrov have

"How They Do It in America" 49

Figure 1.11. The mirror staging of the West and the USSR. a. Von Kneishitz vs. Martynov (in a window), screengrab from *Circus*, 1936. b. Marion with Martynov (in the piano's cover), promotional photograph for the film. Courtesy of the State Central Museum of Cinema (Gosudarstvennyi Tsentral'nyi muzei kino). Goskatalog No: GTsMK KP-19568/1.

Figure 1.12. A *"fizkult reviu"* (physical culture revue) choreographed by Kasian Goleizovskii. a. Descending Marion. b. Martynov, flying in the stratosphere (screengrabs from *Circus*, 1936). c. The song of happiness performed by Marion. Promotional photograph for the film. Courtesy of the State Central Museum of Cinema (Gosudarstvennyi Tsentral'nyi muzei kino). Goskatalog No: GTsMK KP-19568/7

observed that his musical numbers were deeply indebted to American choreographers and dancers. Fred Astaire and Ginger Rogers in *Born to Dance* (1936, dir. Roy Del Ruth), and especially Busby Berkeley, with his musical numbers in *Footlight Parade* (dirs. Lloyd Bacon and Busby Berkeley, 1933) and *Gold Diggers of 1933* (dirs. Mervyn LeRoy and Busby Berkeley, 1933), significantly influenced Aleksandrov's visual language.[86] Marion's dance is an updated and somewhat improved version of Berkeley's production number "By a Waterfall" from *Footlight Parade*.[87] In the Soviet case, the transposition of the form is also its transmutation. There is nothing fluid and liquid in *Circus*: Berkeley's static water extravaganza is replaced with a dynamic pyrotechnic show, and the wedding cake itself is firmly grounded (*zazemlen*) (figure 1.13). The details of these cultural borrowings are fascinating. Yet the question posed by Balázs remains: How did the scenes of what in ten years would be labelled as a clear example of "bourgeois decadence and perversion" become culturally justified and politically possible?

It is, of course, not by chance that Marion Dixon cannot quite finish her solo atop the wedding cake in *Circus*. The song of happiness is cut off by von Kneishitz, who appears on stage to publicly reveal the secret that ties him and Marion together. Visually resembling Hitler, von Kneishitz announces to the audience that Marion has a black baby: "This is a racial crime. She has no place in civilized society. No place among white people."

It is precisely this dramatic interruption of the spectacle of joy used for introducing racial difference into the narrative of the film that enables Aleksandrov's trafficking in cosmopolitan cultural forms to succeed. The adoption of the foreign form does not mean the erasure of its foreignness through seamless integration. The foreign is not obliterated: distinct spheres and circles of circulation maintain their presence. Yet the foreign, to recall Bakhtin, is transformed into "one's own foreignness" (*svoe chuzhoe*) as the fields of its flow are changed and previous hierarchies are abolished.

In the film, Aleksandrov visualizes this transposition literally. During von Kneishitz's outraged speech, Marion's biracial son runs away from him. The Soviet audience picks him up, and the half-sleeping child begins his own circulation around the arena: from one tier to another, from one pair of loving hands to another. The interruption of the glamorous spectacle, then, is in the end a way of bringing "life" into art – by letting the circus audience perform the role of the safe heaven. Linked together by the child, individual spectators emerge as a spontaneous collective, fulfilling their duty of hospitality.

Figure 1.13. Playing with water and fire. Top – "By a Waterfall" (dir. Busby Berkeley for *Footlight Parade*, 1933). Bottom – a scene with torches from *Circus*, 1936. Screengrabs.

To emphasize this point, Aleksandrov envelops the child in yet another narrative, this time a sonic one. As he is handed from one person to the next, the child is accompanied by a lullaby sung by audience members in different languages: Russian, indeed, but also Ukrainian, Tatar, Georgian, Yiddish, even a strongly accented Russian sung by a Black American. Through these visual and sonic devices race changes its function: it is being replayed as a part of a larger story about ethnic particularities and universal connections. Internationalism is simultaneously emphasized in manifestations of formal (linguistic) diversity and neutralized by the shared script of the performed song. Deterritorialized through its polyphony, the community is, nonetheless, enclosed – narratively, sonically, and spatially.

This heavy ideological story of adoption is somewhat softened by the comic summary presented by the circus's ringmaster, who declares that in the big Soviet family, racial and ethnic differences are irrelevant: "Have as many children as you want – black ones, white ones, red ones. If you like – even blue ones, or pink with stripes, or dappled greys!" Difference is resolutely stripped of any ontological and epistemological significance, reduced entirely to its structural effect of formal variance. Or, slightly differently: racialization is both acknowledged and disavowed in *Circus*. It is shown to be the kernel of the melodramatic arc; it operates as the constitutive narrative engine of the film. Yet when taken by itself, it is dismissed as meaningless and functionless (figure 1.14).

Having adopted the form, Aleksandrov uncouples it from its original function. In this way, race and ethnicity are presented as conditions for hospitality, not as signs of inequality. Through the process of transposition, the original racializing exclusion ("She has no place … among white people") is transformed into a set of spheric rows of acceptance. The change of function, in other words, changes the value – from the ontological to the performative, and from the essential to the formal.

The child's embrace by the (allegedly) colour-blind society is doubled in the film by the adoption of the mother as well. While the circus audience serenades the child, Martynov finds Marion hiding with shame at the back of the circus and carries her in his arms into the arena. The lullaby scene gradually morphs into the second – real! – climax of the film, in which Marion performs a song about her newly found Motherland, a country where "everybody breathes freely" and "where happiness abounds."

The cosmopolitan acquires here a clear geographic anchor; the foreign is encircled by a collective of comrades and friends. Pointedly devoid of any socio-sartorial distinction, the members of the new collective are all dressed in white, turning themselves into a perfect screen for projecting any colour or colour combination – be it red, blue, or even pink with stripes (figure 1.15).

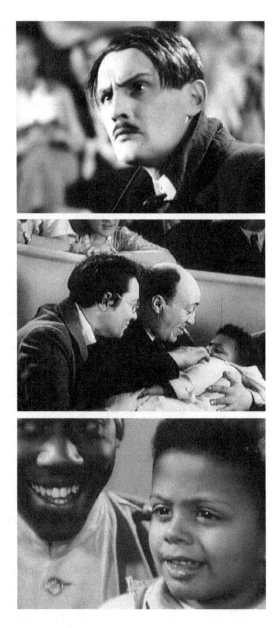

Figure 1.14. The circus/circles of adoptions. a. Von Kneishitz revealing the "dirty secret." The lullaby of acceptance, with Solomon Mikhoels singing in Yiddish (b) and Wayland Rudd singing in Russian (c). Screengrabs from *Circus*, 1936.

Figure 1.15. Hospitality enacted. a. Martynov carrying Marion. b. A circle of new friends. c. "A place among white people." Screengrabs from *Circus*, 1936.

Figure 1.16. Palimpsests of belonging. Screengrabs from *Circus*, 1936.

And not only colour. The film's final sequence visually emphasizes one more time the potential of the screen-like affordance of the new Soviet people. In this coda, Aleksandrov radically dynamizes the screen by superimposing several visual tracks. The confident walk of Martynov, Marion, and their friends on Red Square is interwoven with documentary footage of various parades and collective athletic performances. Diverse nationalities, professions, and classes come together in this whirlpool of documentary and fiction, in a sort of spectral yet multidimensional unity. And exactly at this moment we again see a quick re-emergence of the globe (an iris shot of sorts), which was so playfully displayed by Aleksandrov at the beginning of the film. Hovering above all the walking and marching people, the sphere now stays still: the meaning of the globe (and the global) is stabilized. The globe acts here as the background for the Soviet state emblem: hammer and sickle cover the planet, which itself is layered with the face of Marion and a pyramid of happy Soviet athletes, projecting themselves forward into the future (figure 1.16).

The cosmopolitan forms, skilfully deployed by Aleksandrov, did not just add some sheen of globalized glamour to Soviet propaganda. What we have here is also a palimpsest that makes the separation of circles of affiliation virtually impossible. Through the constant rotation of circles, globes, and people a potentially parochial story about finding a new Motherland is supplemented with multiple layers of meaning and even a certain "world significance," however imaginary this significance might be.

Unlike Aleksandrov's other films, *Circus* was never released in the US. When the film premiered in 1936, *The Hollywood Reporter* called it "outstanding," while bluntly noting that it had no chance of being shown abroad "as it deals with miscegenation."[88] Ignored for several decades, *Circus* was rediscovered in the 1990s by scholars who mostly downplayed the racial theme, preferring to explain its popularity as a function of its ideological narrative and iconography.[89] It is interesting, though, that films that applied a similar visual and narrative structure to promote strictly ideological issues enjoyed little success. Dziga Vertov's *Lullaby* (1937) is a good case in point. The film was conceived as a combination of episodes in which images of mothers and babies in cradles were interspersed with images of parades, musical performances, and footage of Stalin. The documentary came out one year after Aleksandrov's *Circus* and was explicitly modelled after it.

Vertov in *Lullaby* emphasized "the local," replacing the Art Deco style of *Circus* with less distant ethnographic footage of Central Asia and the Caucasus. Hoping to achieve the same popularity, the filmmaker even commissioned the film's signature song from Dunaevskii, the same composer who did the soundtrack for *Circus*.[90] Despite all his efforts, this visual display of performative patriotism – "a mighty poem of happiness," as Vertov himself described it – failed: it would be Vertov's last feature film.[91] It was shown for only five days, apparently to the clear displeasure of Stalin, and came close to vanishing.[92] Without any cosmopolitan aspirations, the national-geographic facts of Vertov's poem emerged as an incoherent montage of disconnected objects: "a passive tool of power for dominating the weak" (figure 1.17).[93]

In the final section, I will show how this logic of adoption of the cosmopolitan, the logic of cultural arbitrage perfected by Aleksandrov, was reversed. Local forms and actors were deliberately estranged by revealing their extraterritorial origin or belonging: a part of the self, to use Bakhtin again, was turned into "an alien I" (*chuzhoe ia*).[94] This type of cultural arbitrage was structured less by the transposition of forms from one culture to another (as it was in *Circus*). Rather, the flow was organized *interdiscursively* – from the field of aesthetics to the field of politics; however, the connection between two separate spheres – the Soviet and the American – was just as crucial.

58 Serguei Alex. Oushakine

Figure 1.17. A lullaby that worked vs. a lullaby that didn't. a. Marion with her baby, from Grigorii Aleksandrov's *Circus*, 1936. b. Central Asian mothers with babies in front of the portrait of Stalin with Gelia Markizova, from Dziga Vertov's *Lullaby*, 1937. Fragments of screengrabs.

Against Adoption

We were taught that "cosmopolitanism" was good; we just knew this term in Latin – as "internationalism." All they've done is to translate it back to Greek.
– Solomon Lozovskii, 1948[95]

My last set of examples is drawn from fierce public debates that took place in the Soviet Union in 1948–9. Officially, they were cast as a campaign against an anti-patriotic group of theatre critics. More commonly, though, the debates are remembered as "the fight against kinless cosmopolites" – a post-war reprise of the late 1930s purges. The by now familiar script for the show trials was restaged all over the country, in which indignant collectives applied "the law of honour" to those individuals who – allegedly – had prioritized global interests over the Motherland's concerns and needs.

These "trials of honour" were introduced by a party-state decision in March 1947. The idea was then set in motion and popularized by the

Figure 1.18. Mikhail Khazanovskii, a poster for the film *Sud chesti* (*A Trial of Honour*, dir. Abram Room), 1948. Courtesy of the State Central Museum of Cinema (Gosudarstvennyi Tsentral'nyi muzei kino). Goskatalog No: GTsMK KP-2027/323

Moscow writer Aleksandr Shtein in his play about a "corrupt" Soviet scientist who clandestinely shares important results of his scientific discovery with Americans and who is later subjected to an improvised tribunal by his colleagues.[96] An example of para-documentary literature, the play was based on an actual "trial of honour" that was staged in several institutions of the Soviet Ministry of Health on 5–7 June 1947, during which two professors – Nina Kliueva and Grigorii Roskin – were accused of providing the results of their research on a cancer vaccine to "the Americans" without official permission.[97] Written in 1948, Shtein's play *Zakon chesti* (The Law of Honour) was performed in leading Moscow theatres and quickly turned into a film by the director Abram Room (figure 1.18).

The play and the film effectively reversed the original (positive) orientation and valence of *Amerikanizm*. Commenting on the film on the eve of its premiere in Moscow (on 25 January 1949), Room declared that its main task was to portray "the fight against the servility and knee-bending adulation [*rabopelie i nizkopoklonstvo*] towards the reactionary science in the West."[98] Strongly endorsed by the media, *Sud chesti* (*A Trial of Honour*, 1948) offered a key visual representation of the fight against "kinless cosmopolites" (hereafter, I will refer to the campaign as the FAKC).[99]

Usually, the FAKC is discussed within a broader theme of the state-sponsored antisemitism in the Soviet Union. Indeed, this heavily choreographed sequence of attacks on theatre critics, which mostly targeted Jewish intelligentsia, was an important step in a chain of sinister events that transpired between 1945 and 1953. The FAKC was immediately preceded by the assassination of Solomon Mikhoels in January 1948 while he was visiting Minsk. The killing of this prominent Jewish activist – he was the artistic head of the Moscow State Jewish Theatre – led to rapid shutdowns of several Jewish publishing houses, newspapers, and theatres, and the dissolution of the Jewish Antifascist Committee (the JAC), an important Soviet organization that had been headed by Mikhoels since its inception in 1942. Mikhoels's murder had a chilling connection with Aleksandrov's *Circus* – the segment in which he sang part of the lullaby in Yiddish was excised from the film (and would not be spliced back in until 1966).[100] The dissolution of the JAC was soon followed by the arrest of Solomon Lozovskii, a prominent Soviet politician and the head of the Soviet Information Bureau (*Sovinformbiuro*), which was the JAC's host organization and sponsor. By April 1949, the FAKC attacks had fizzled out (without major casualties); however, the larger antisemitic crusade continued to unfold in an extended series of purges and public show trials, which reached their climax in the so-called "Doctors' Plot" of 1953.[101]

This historical context is essential for understanding how the assault on the theatre critics was carried out in 1948–9. Yet I think it is just as essential to pay attention to the specific arguments that were articulated and disseminated during these debates. Aleksandr Borshchagovskii, a theatre critic who became a primary target of the FAKC, usefully reminded us in his memoirs published in the early 1990s that "without clearly defined documentary ... borders and substance, the history of the fight against 'kinless cosmopolites' gets fuzzy, losing its specific 'colors' [*rasplylas' i 'vytsvetaet'*]. The chronicling of this fight was especially damaged by the wide-spread conviction that it was just a basic manifestation of antisemitism, with nothing else to discuss."[102]

Like Borshchagovskii, I contend that the campaign generated an extensive archive that allows us to see how various actors within the Soviet cultural industry envisioned relations between national culture and global influences, or between tradition and modernity, or between historical contexts and art forms. Below, I attempt to delineate some epistemological boundaries of this campaign by reconstructing its cultural rationale without reducing it to antisemitism. As I unpack the coverage of this campaign in Moscow publications, I will foreground the interplay between the geographic and the cosmopolitan, as well as between the Soviet and the American, which I have been tracing in this chapter.

I suggest that notwithstanding some sharp distinctions, this campaign exhibited the now familiar logic of cultural arbitrage: aesthetic and ideological effects of art forms were measured through the incessant comparison of their values vis-à-vis two competitive cultural fields – the domestic and the global. There was a major difference, of course. For Aleksandrov, cultural arbitrage was a way to benefit from the playful recycling of global cultural templates and models within the borders of the Soviet symbolic order. The FAKC offers us an ominous version of cultural arbitrage. The FAKC activists attacked theatre critics for their supposed advocacy of foreign cultural art forms, seeing in this sort of cultural trafficking a far-reaching process of "mergers and acquisitions," over the course of which the dominant global culture was to gradually push domestic cultural products off the market. If Aleksandrov's cultural arbitrage embedded cosmopolitan cultural forms in the synchronic amalgam of layers, superimposing different approaches, ideas, and styles, then the FAKC's participants relied on a retrospective and diachronic discovery of irreconcilable ontological and epistemological differences in the critics' works. Unlike the show trials of the 1930s, during which compromising links with the West were usually imagined, the FAKC magnified external traces and twisted connections with the foreign that were indeed present in the publications of the theatre critics. What was imagined and implied, then, was the dual logic of cultural arbitrage. Party-state functionaries performed a close reading of the already existing body of critical texts in order to change their function by peeling off all the semantic layers that supposedly obfuscated the "poisonous" core of their work.

The ontological essentialism so forcefully rejected by Aleksandrov in his films came back with a vengeance during this campaign. Ironically, in their vitriolic attacks, antisemitic combatants also attempted to root cosmopolitan cultural forms in local landscapes. However, they dramatically altered the primary goal of Aleksandrov's *zazemlenie* (grounding): the localizing adoption of *global* art forms was no longer perceived as an attempt to evolve the foreign (*chuzhoe*) into one's own foreignness (*svoe-chuzhoe*). The creative transformative abilities of cultural arbitrage celebrated by Aleksandrov's strategic *Amerikanizm* were curtailed: cultural transposition emerged as a form of unequal competition. Signs of appropriation and adoption were perceived as evidence of a major existential conflict between invasive, vagabond – *rootless* – art forms and locally grown – endemic – artistic and intellectual traditions. Within this framework, the foreign never ceased to be alien; hence, the theatre critics' interest in comparative analysis, global art forms, and other instances of "travelling" plots and "circulating" approaches was seen as indistinguishable from cultural imperialism, while the FAKC itself was framed by its proponents as a right-wing prequel to decolonization.

The fervour and the seriousness with which the Soviet political establishment launched its offensive against theatre critics generates two preliminary questions: Why theatre? And, especially, why theatre *critics*? Most likely, we will never know the exact answers to these questions; yet the statements of political leaders and the cultural politics of the time provide some important clues.[103]

After the Second World War, Soviet cinema went through a period of hibernation. The party-state's official policy of the time was "cinematic austerity" (*politika malokartin'ia*). In 1948 the Soviet film industry produced only sixteen films, in 1949 – ten, in 1950 – twelve (cf. in 1928 – 124, in 1939 – 51).[104] In her exhaustive study of the Soviet film industry, Maria Belodubrovskaya suggests that this "film famine" was mostly caused by a misconceived orientation of the party-state towards producing only cinematic masterpieces (fewer films but more prints), on the one hand, and the ever-increasing political control and self-censorship, on the other.[105] In the absence of television, professional and amateur drama became a principal form of public entertainment. Theatre and concert performances filmed for Soviet cinemas (as well as radio plays) emerged as new genres precisely in this period.

There were also ideological and pedagogical considerations. Cinema and theatre were the only media that could demonstrate in tangible and embodied ways new forms of life, providing audiences with graspable, relatable, and repeatable scenarios of social behaviour and relations. In the early 1920s, Boris Arvatov perceptively remarked that "for each given class of each given epoch theatre has produced models of human beings (embodied by actors) and patterns of *byt*-organization (envisioned by spectacles) ... Indeed, theatre, even the bourgeois kind, has been a supplement to reality, as any mimetic art would be, just as it has been a laboratory of this reality."[106] It seems that Stalin similarly understood the importance of drama and theatre, and he encouraged Soviet writers not to write long novels since "workers will never make it through them. These days, plays are the form of art that we need first and foremost. The worker can easily see a play. Through a play, we can easily popularize our ideas. Plays are the most accessible [*massovyi*] form of art in literature. This is why you should be writing plays."[107]

If the importance of dramatic theatre was defined largely by the specific cultural conditions of the time, then, the oversized significance of theatre critics was rooted in a particular theoretical assumption. Andrei Zhdanov, the key ideologue in the post-war Soviet Union, explained the vital social implications of Soviet criticism in his speech at a conference on philosophy in 1947:

> In our Soviet society, where antagonistic classes have been liquidated, the struggle between the old and the new, and consequently the development from the lower to the higher, proceeds not in the form of struggle between antagonistic classes and of cataclysms, as is the case under capitalism, but in the form of criticism and self-criticism, which is the real motive force of our development, a powerful instrument in the hands of the Communist Party. This is incontestably a new aspect of movement, a new type of development, a new dialectical law.[108]

This shift from the foundational role of the struggle between antagonistic classes to the productive dialogue between criticism and self-criticism is central, and I will come back to it later. Here, I only want to highlight the primary significance that was attached to the ability of critical evaluation to perform the function of the constitutive conflict, whose resolution – ideally speaking – should have generated new paths and forms of social development. The problem with this shift was devastatingly simple. Despite all its significance, Zhdanov's dialectical *law* failed to demonstrate its motivational force in practice. To be precise, it failed to determine the expected development – especially in the field of cultural production.

From 1946 on, various party-state institutions grew increasingly frustrated and publicly annoyed with the state of theatre production, the state of dramaturgy, and especially the state of theatre criticism. By January 1949, the level of dissatisfaction seemingly reached a breaking point, and the Department of Agitation and Propaganda of the Central Committee of the Communist Party composed a memo in which the state of Soviet dramaturgy was characterized as "highly unfortunate" (*kraine neblagopoluchnoe*) and the existing repertoire of Soviet theatres as "unsatisfactory." It also listed three main clusters of "weaknesses" in the activity of the communists working in drama theatres.

Two key weaknesses were linked with cultural shortages. The evident dearth of plays dealing with contemporary topics logically resulted in the absence of theatrical productions about contemporary issues.

Soviet theatre was not alone in this situation, though. A similar problem afflicted Soviet cinema as well. Most films of the time were either historical biopics or adaptations of literary classics. A secret report compiled for Zhdanov by the Commissar of State Security in 1946 included a telling quote from Ivan Pyr'ev, a Soviet director, famous for his peasant-style comedies. Complaining about the pressure of censorship, Pyr'ev concluded: "Our cinema knows no contemporary topics. Everyone is afraid of tackling them ... I want to film Dostoevsky. It is both interesting and safe [*ne opasno*]. Given the current state of censorship ... we can survive only by relying on history or the classics."[109]

The second shortage pointed to a lack of professional attention and interest in staging what the memo considered the "best" plays, both Soviet and classical: very few were being performed. For instance, throughout August 1948, Konstantin Simonov's *The Russian Question*, a patriotic play heavily promoted by the Soviet state, was performed in only two theatres in Russia and Ukraine, and Chekhov's *Three Sisters* in only three.

The last set of complaints in the memo was about the practice of substitution. As the party functionaries discovered, the vacuum created by the shortage of plays and theatrical performances had been filled by "ideologically and artistically deficient [*nepolnotsennye v ideino-khudozhestvennom otnoshenii*] plays." The hit of the 1948 season was not a patriotic play but *Taimyr Is Calling*, a light-hearted musical comedy of errors by Aleksandr Galich and Konstantin Isaev, which was eagerly embraced by sixty-four theatres in Russia and Ukraine.[110]

Despite all the statistics and conclusions presented in the memo, the decisive cause of the "highly unfortunate" condition of Soviet theatre was found not in the process of cultural *production* but in "the superstructure," which was deemed inadequate and misleading. Briefly noting that major Soviet playwrights had "distanced themselves from the creative production of new plays about today's life," the memo closely followed Zhdanov's logic and presented the dire situation in theatres as a failure of the critic-communists: "The absence of the principled Bolshevist theatrical criticism is a serious cause of the backwardness of our dramaturgy. Regarding several major questions, the newspaper *Sovetskoe iskusstvo* and the journal *Teatr* have assumed wrong, aesthetic and, at times, bluntly formalist positions, thereby disorienting playwrights and Soviet society."[111]

In the subsequent campaign, these "wrong, aesthetic and bluntly formalist" approaches of the critics were exposed, detailed, and substantiated. What I find somewhat unusual here is that this production of the enemy did not stop with identifying key individuals and institutions. Unlike early Soviet show trials, the FAKC not only exposed "grave mistakes and errors" but also greatly expanded its hermeneutic of suspicion in order to trace and reveal foundational frameworks – the epistemic "cornerstones" (*istoki*) – that sustained the critics' "erroneous" attitude in the first place.¹¹² Following the logic of cultural arbitrage, the attackers quickly identified the primary duality of the "cosmopolite critics," calling them *dvurushniki*, double-dealers. Ideological brokers of sorts, they were able to benefit from belonging to two opposing sides at once. For instance, the newspaper *Kul'tura i zhizn'* (*Culture and Life*) firmly linked the aesthetic and the anti-patriotic, explaining that by its very nature

> aestheticism is anti-populous, anti-patriotic, and anti-national [*antinarodno, antipatriotichno, antinatsional'no*] ... As facts show, the favorite tactical device of this group of critics is *dvurushnichestvo* (double-dealing). Recognizing that no open popularization of their anti-patriotic views is possible, they hide their views under the mask of the guardian of the high artistic standards of Soviet art ... smuggling in old, reactionary theories of "pure art" and art for art's sake.¹¹³

The core arguments of the FAKC emerged gradually, following two incompatible paths, which, nonetheless, eventually converged. One of these paths explored, so to speak, the social poetics of the "cosmopolites." As the argument had it, the critics' formalist-aesthetic (*formalistsko-estetskie*) views, approaches, and positions could not help but generate their overwhelming "apolitical" orientation, oblivious to theatrical plays and productions that dealt with contemporary issues of socialist construction. In this context, the aesthetic interest in formal aspects of art and literature was read as a lack of interest in realism, reality, and, consequently, real Soviet life. The absence of "principled Bolshevist theatrical criticism," in other words, was not an individual choice or a subjectivist mistake; it was an outcome overdetermined by the critics' methodological predilections. This line of critique was hardly new, of course. Somewhat ironically, the FAKC activists reproduced – almost verbatim – the logic and rhetoric of the anti-formalist campaign unleashed by Leon Trotsky in his *Literature and Revolution* in 1924. In the alleged "aestheticism" of the theatre critics they detected a return of the same threat of "social indifference" that Trotsky alarmingly "discovered" in Viktor Shklovsky and his colleagues, who were so eager to profess that "art was always free of life, and its colour never reflected the colour of the flag which waved over the fortress of the City."¹¹⁴

The second trajectory of attacks was a relatively novel development that grew out of different and intrinsically politicized debates about patriotism in arts and literature. The initial position was most vividly outlined by Aleksandr Fadeev, a writer and the Secretary General of the Union of Soviet Writers, in his report at the eleventh plenum of the ruling committee of the union. In his speech in June 1947, Fadeev bemoaned "the worshiping of everything that takes place abroad, the respect for and knee-bending adulation [*nizkopoklonstvo*] of everything foreign," which were still common for "some representatives of our intelligentsia."[115]

Using as his main negative example the 1941 monograph *Pushkin and World Literature* by Isaak Nusinov, a Moscow literary scholar (and a member of the JAC),[116] Fadeev scorned the author for his attempts to interpret Pushkin's "greatness" and "genius" not as "a manifestation of the specificities of historical development of the Russian nation" but as a reflection of Pushkin's desire "to extend and advance Western culture."[117] Palpably appalled by this discovery of the derivative universality of Pushkin's work, Fadeev resolutely condemned any attempts to seek the origin of Russian national traditions and canons in the West. In support of his position, he quoted from a letter written by the literary critic Vissarion Belinskii to the historian Konstantin Kavelin in November 1847: "We should stop being struck by everything European simply because it is not Asian ... We have our own national life; we are destined to share our own word with the world, to share our own thought ... I must confess, for me all those discreet sceptics, abstract human beings, and passportless tramps of humanity [*bespassportnye brodiagi v chelovechestve*] are pitiful and unpleasant."[118]

The term "passportless tramps" promulgated by Fadeev would become a default pejorative of the FAKC (figure 1.19). Another term – "kinless cosmopolites" (*bezrodnye kosmopolity*) – would be articulated a few months later by Zhdanov. During a meeting of Soviet musicians in February 1948, he continued and expanded Fadeev's train of thought, firmly presenting cosmopolitan orientations not only as anti-national but also as anti-international. Deep in dialectics, Zhdanov explained: "Internationalism in arts does not emerge from diminishing and devaluing national art. Quite the opposite: internationalism is born from the flourishing of national arts. To forget this truth [*istina*] means to lose the party's leading line; it means to lose your own face; it means to turn yourself into kinless cosmopolites."[119]

References to Belinskii's negative views on cosmopolitanism would become especially widespread in the spring of 1948, during the memorial events dedicated to the centennial of the critic's death. It was during those events that the terms "passportless tramps" and "kinless cosmopolites" would unite for the first time in the same context. In June 1948, in *Literaturnaia gazeta*, Iakov El'sberg, a literary scholar from Moscow, quoted the two pejoratives together in his essay "Belinskii and Cosmopolites."[120] A few months later, Zinovii Papernyi, a literary critic, dramatically upped the ante. Up to this point, both terms were usually evoked as abstract, albeit negative, descriptions, unattached to any concrete individual.

Figure 1.19. "Rereading Belinskii": a passportless tramp by Konstantin Eliseev, *Krokodil*, 20 March 1949. Source: https://croco.uno/year/1949.

Papernyi made an important rhetorical move by linking what had been an abstract insult to actual individuals. In "Rereading Belinskii," he ferociously attacked the outspoken literary critic and functionary Lev Subotskii for his "sinful abstracto-cosmopolitan" views on contemporary Russian literature. Reproducing Zhdanov's lines about faceless and kinless cosmopolites, Papernyi substantiated them with his own example: "L. Subotskii is precisely such a kinless cosmopolite who has lost his face."[121] Literary types had found their concrete embodiments.

These early art forms and publications prepared – linguistically, conceptually, and ideologically – the landscape for the FAKC. They also provided a large Soviet audience with legitimized pejoratives, patterns for using them, and argumentation templates. Turning "cosmopolitanism" into a negative category, they severed any plausible connections with "internationalism" and/or "world culture."

The FAKC campaign "officially" opened on 28 January 1949, when *Pravda* published an editorial with a title that clearly emphasized the singularity of the phenomenon: "About One Anti-Patriotic Group of

Theatre Critics." Apparently, the text was written by Aleksandr Fadeev and David Zaslavskii, a Moscow journalist; Stalin himself suggested three variations of cosmopolitanism: uber-cosmopolitanism, unbridled cosmopolitanism, and, finally, kinless cosmopolitanism (*ura-kosmopolitizm; ogoltelyi kosmopolitizm*, and *bezrodnyi kosmopolitizm*).[122]

The editorial brought together the two strands of criticism, which I discussed earlier. Linking formalist aesthetics directly to anti-patriotism, it "revealed" their common foundation: the unacceptable epistemology was "rooted" in an equally unacceptable ontology. Providing a list of "epigones of bourgeois aestheticism" (*poslednyshi burzhuaznogo estetstva*) who had become detached from the "life and struggle of the Soviet people,"[123] the editorial specified the main fault of these critics from *Sovetskoe isskustvo* and *Teatr*: "The sting of their aesthetic-formalist criticism is not directed against truly detrimental or deficient works of art; it is directed against the progressive and the best ones, against those who represent exemplary Soviet patriots. And this is the best evidence of the fact that aestheticizing formalism [*estetsvuishchii formalizm*] is only a cover for anti-patriotic essence."[124]

Over the next few years, this link between criticism and anti-patriotism would become a political cliché as well as a diagnostic formula that turned the figure of the critic into a social – or, rather, antisocial – type. In his textbook on logic for schoolteachers, Nikolai Kondakov presented a striking example of this. Using the terminology popularized by the FAKC, he infused the formal rules of syllogism construction with some real-life content. In demonstrating that the two negative premises of a syllogism could lead to no conclusion and, therefore, at least one premise must be positive, Kondakov offered the following example:

No cosmopolite can be a patriot.
The Critic X. is a cosmopolite.

Proceeding from these two premises, Kondakov built his *logical* conclusion by establishing a series of concentric semantic circles, which progressed from the smallest to the largest (critic → cosmopolite → patriot). The result demonstrated another basic rule of syllogism construction at work: if one of the premises is negative, the conclusion will be negative as well. Hence, the complete syllogism took the following shape (figure 1.20):

No cosmopolite can be a patriot.
The Critic X. is a cosmopolite.
Therefore: The Critic X. cannot be a patriot.[125]

Ни один космополит не может быть патриотом.
Критик X.— космополит.
―――――――――――――――――――――――
Критик X. не может быть патриотом.

Figure 1.20. The syllogism of the FAKC. Nikolai Kondakov, *Logika*. Moscow: Uchpediz, 1954, p. 227.

Of course, this juxtaposition of patriotism and cosmopolitanism is neither new nor especially interesting. What is noteworthy here is the striving to interpret mere attention to the form (as opposed to the content) as *cosmopolitan* in its essence. The question remains: Why would such attention to the form necessarily be detrimental? And perhaps even more important: Can aestheticizing formalism be patriotic? Or, to approach it negatively: What are those internal pitfalls that make cosmopolitanism utterly incompatible with the Soviet way of life?

Having launched the campaign, the initial *Pravda* article did not really address these issues. It was the follow-up discussion among artists, writers, and humanities scholars that loaded cosmopolitanism with specific meanings. Over the next three months, every major newspaper published on a regular basis reports, articles, or, at least, feuilletons that exposed yet more cosmopolites. These debates and publications reframed cosmopolitanism in a somewhat unusual way: very quickly, the word lost its connection to "universal belonging" or even "abstract humanity." Foregrounded instead was the *insufficiency* of cosmopolitan universalism; it was the *localized* origin of supposedly cosmopolitan values that was perceived as culturally denigrating and politically detrimental. Global claims of universal belonging were approached as rhetorical masks called upon to disguise a competition between two geographically distinct ideological/cultural spheres/markets. In the end, supposedly unattached forms had their own local *propiska* (residency certificate).

The day after the *Pravda* article, another Soviet newspaper, *Literaturnaia gazeta*, printed its own editorial, this one titled "The Anti-Patriotic Group of Theatre Critics Must Be Fully Exposed." This editorial drew attention to the principal method of aestheticizing formalism and explained that the very idea of *comparative* analysis of artistic forms was ideologically faulty because it was oblivious to the local contexts in which those forms emerged and developed. As the editorial framed it,

> with a grin of malicious joy [*zloradno khikhikaia*], the cosmopolite is trying as much as he can to "discover" this or that "parallel," this or that similarity

between phenomena of Russian culture and those of the West. In their vile attempts to prove that culture of the Russian people is "adopted" from the West, these pseudo-experts on culture, these people without kin or family, demonstrate all their shallowness, whose only content ... is a love "for everything foreign."[126]

The very act of formal comparison, in other words, was perceived as a process for establishing a cultural hierarchy. The "same" things were not the same at all. Cultural distinctions lost their performative power and were turned into indices of cultural superiority or deficiency. Cultural adoption, which had been so prominent only a decade earlier, was perceived now not as a mutually beneficial process of dialogue, cross-pollination, or profit but as a symptom of the insufficient cultural authenticity and cultural creativity of the locals. The very desire to highlight plausible resemblances or real similarities between cultural forms was interpreted as a gesture of "ignoring the independence, originality, and greatness of Russian culture," as one Agitprop memo put it.[127] Adoption re-emerged as a substitute for a lack of (cultural) sovereignty. I will give one example that reveals this logic in a more concrete context.

Since the beginning of the FAKC, the newspaper *Sovetskoe iskusstvo* had been running its own "trials of honour" – a series of weekly essays, each of which vitriolically exposed a particular theatre critic. Iosif Iuzovskii, a theatre scholar at the Institute of World Literature, was mentioned in the initial editorial by *Pravda*. *Sovetskoe iskusstvo* continued his exposure. What is remarkable about the Iuzovskii case is that both newspapers straightforwardly acknowledged that Iuzovskii "had been avoiding" Soviet theatre, focusing instead on world classics and Shakespeare as his main research subjects.[128] Yet this did not stop them from imputing to Iuzovskii's work the logic of cultural arbitrage, which must be global and local *at the same time*. Citing Stalin, *Pravda* claimed: "One might say that silencing is not the same as critiquing. This is wrong. As a particular way of ignoring, the method of silencing is also a form of criticism."[129] Hence, both newspapers read a *lack* of direct evidence as a *positive* clue – that is, as a sign of demonstrative distancing from urgent social problems at home. The vivid presence of the "global" Shakespeare in Iuzovskii's work was retroactively perceived as the key reason for the equally ostensible absence of "the domestic": the "native" cultural product was (allegedly) crowded out by the famous foreign playwright.

Iuzovskii's references to the universality of art went through the reassignment of function, too:

For Iuzovskii, life can change but the material of art stays. This material is invariable for all countries and periods, regardless of their historically specific economic and socio-political development, or national cultural distinctions. Therefore, for him "*Hamlet* is a mirror that every epoch looked at in order to find its own reflection. And this reflection, in turn, explained the epoch."[130] Iuzovskii thinks that our epoch ought to find its own reflection and explanation in *Hamlet*, too.[131]

It mattered little to the FAKC activists that throughout his book Iuzovskii actually argued for the need to approach Shakespeare without falling for either "ahistorical abstraction" (*vneistoricheskaia abstraktsiia*) or "historical shortsightedness" (*istorichskaia ogranichennost'*).[132] In approaching his publications as works of cultural arbitrage, they were performing a Stalinist version of the archaeology of knowledge by *connecting* Iuzovskii to different cultural spheres, by *comparing* his statements to his silences, and by *computing* the symbolic profit he might accrue in this imaginary world of transcultural exchanges. The (imputed) desire to separate art from life, and the (misperceived) invitation to look for one's own reflection in the mirrors of the world's cultures, were enough to complete the basic syllogism: "This is not a casual mistake. This is an anti-patriotic, non-Marxist system of views of the kinless cosmopolite critic."[133]

For the activists of the FAKC, critics' aestheticism had another problematic dimension. Formal resemblances could indicate a stylistic kinship that people would prefer not to notice. For instance, Aleksandr Gerasimov, the President of the Soviet Academy of Fine Arts at the time, in an article in *Pravda* criticized the Moscow art historian Abram Efros for attempting to point out a continuity between pre-revolutionary and post-revolutionary art in Russia. Dismissing Efros's conclusion that European Impressionism had strongly impacted Soviet visual art, Gerasimov implemented the Balázsian approach instead, insisting on the *political* incompatibility of the two artistic styles: "[Efros's claim] is an evil slander [*gnusnaia kleveta*] because Soviet art has strengthened and matured precisely during its uncompromising struggle against bourgeois modernism."[134] Again, not all similar things are similar in the same way: different genealogies foreground different functions, erasing the basis for any meaningful comparison. Or, as Iosif Grinberg, a film and literary critic, angrily put it in a similar context, "there wasn't, there isn't, there couldn't be … a universal art."[135]

Soviet historians were especially active in demonstrating various flaws in the metatheory that enabled such unwelcome comparisons between different periods and cultures. *Voprosy istorii* (Issues of History), the main professional journal of Soviet historians, published in

1949 its own editorial titled "On the Tasks of the Soviet Historians in the Fight against Manifestations of the Bourgeois Ideology." Among multiple examples of the "cosmopolitan" approach to history, the editorial singled out a book on Russian historiography by the Moscow historian Nikolai Rubenshtein. The book's main flaw was its approach – "the cosmopolitan perspective of 'a common stream' of development of history as a world discipline," which presented

> Russian historiography only as a repetition and a variation of schools of thought and intellectual movements that originated initially in the West and eventually travelled to Russia. In Rubenshtein's depiction, the development of historical knowledge in Russia is nothing but a filiation of ideas, detached from the historical process in Russia, from its classes and their struggle ... [Rubenshtein] fully subscribed to the anti-Marxist, anti-scientific, idealistic theory of [cultural] adoption as the foundation for the creation and development of Russian national culture. In essence, he dismisses any questions about the internal conditions, about the national and class roots of the development of Russian culture.[136]

The purposeful ignoring of the local specificity of the form, however, was only one problematic aspect of the formal comparison. The same principle of geographically bound cultural specificity was used to confront the thesis about the "common stream of development." The "*common* stream" turned out to be very particular. The source and direction of its flow were detected, and its "commonality" was recoded as a product of external imposition. As a result, the "kinless cosmopolites" and "passportless tramps" were increasingly presented as a strongly grounded phenomenon – certainly, "bourgeois" and therefore "reactionary." For example, in his article "To Defeat Bourgeois Cosmopolitanism in Cinematic Art," published in *Pravda*, Ivan Bol'shakov, the Minister of Cinematography (1939–54), criticized Leonid Trauberg, a film director from Leningrad, for attempting to highlight various links between Soviet and foreign cinema. As Bol'shakov put it,

> in his public presentations and lectures, Trauberg has praised bourgeois cinema, proving that our Soviet cinematic art is an offspring [*porozhdenie*] of American cinema; that the development of our cinema was under the influence of American, French, German directors, cameramen, and actors ... Trauberg implied that ... traces of German films could be found in Soviet cinematography, that German cameramen and actors influenced ... many

Soviet film directors. This is how Trauberg slanders the art of Soviet cinema, the most advanced cinema in the world that was developed under the leadership of the Communist Party and under the banner of socialist realism.[137]

In the wake of the Second World War, looking for German traces in Soviet art was indeed a fraught endeavour. But it was not only plausible links with fascism that the authorities objected to. Similar rebukes were aimed at those critics who insisted on learning the craft of playwriting from American and British writers.[138] Geography was important for different reasons. By "revealing" the *concrete* geographical context of what initially was seen as *abstract* aestheticizing formalism, the participants in the FAKC left no ground for *universalizing* claims. The "discovery" that cultural forms were geographically embedded gave them a reason to insist that any "talks about the form" were only "a cover,"[139] one that masked those "agents of bourgeois ideology" who had succeeded in infiltrating Soviet culture.[140] Abstract forms, in other words, had very specific sites of origin, concealed through endless exchanges "not only across multiple cultural contexts, but through multiple distinct, yet interrelated forms of social capital."[141]

Konstantin Simonov, the editor-in-chief of *Novyi mir*, in 1949 reached the logical finale by transforming early Soviet *Amerikanizm* into Cold War *anti-Amerikanizm*. Discussing at length the pitfalls of the desire to trace the origin of Soviet cinema back to D.W. Griffith and, at times, Chaplin, he passionately proclaimed:[142]

> Critic-cosmopolites keep pushing Soviet cinema to embrace American cinema and one of its creators, the director Griffith, as its progenitor … Yet, American cinema has become the most adamant, the most brutal, the most reactionary missionary of the imperialist ideas generated by the American instigators of war. It became the cinematography of anti-Soviet films, the cinematography of *The Iron Curtain*.[143] If we look in this light at the cosmopolites' theory, then it is easy to conclude that there are two different cinematographies that sprouted from the same Griffith: the modern American cinema, the cinema of imperialism, and our own Soviet cinema, the cinema of the communist society.
>
> No, my dear Cosmopolites! We do not want to adopt American cinema as our parents, or as our grandparents, or even as a twice removed grandmother. If you want to adopt as your progenitor this cinema, which began as decadence and ended as the Ku Klux Klan, then be my guest. But before you do this – get out of Soviet cinema. Get out of Soviet art. And then adopt any parents you want – but beyond our borders.[144] (figure 1.21)

Figure 1.21. Iulii Ganf, "A vulture from the overseas: 'They use my feathers to write all these things.'" The garbage box contains pages of "critical essays" signed by Aleksandr Borshchagovskii, Lev Subotskii, Iosif Iuzovskii, and Leonid Maliugin. *Krokodil*, 30 March 1949. Source: https://croco.uno/year/1949.

In a sense, Simonov was presenting in this article an absolute rejection of any possibility for the positive deployment of cultural arbitrage understood as a sustained practice of re-evaluation and transformation of global/foreign cultural forms. During the FAKC campaign, the functionalist fascination with technology, which constituted the core of the early Soviet interest in *Amerikanizm*, was completely overshadowed by the ideology of rootedness, origin, and historical belonging. (figure 1.21) Embeddedness was read teleologically. Spheres of circulations were delimited, and the borders were carefully policed. In an article published a few days later, Simonov went even further. Revisiting debates about the lack of basic conflicts in Soviet dramaturgy, he eschewed Zhdanov's plan to replace antagonistic conflicts with criticism and self-criticism. Reverting to the old and proven geopolitical and geo-ideological disposition, Simonov divided the world into "successful us" and "reactionary them," destined (doomed?) to fight each other until a complete victory:

> If we measure each of our achievements – from the very little to the gigantic – as yet another victory in our fight against the world's reactionaries; if we approach each completed construction in our country as a contribution to this fight, and if we view each act of resistance to our efforts – be this resistance purposeful or accidental – as a collaboration with our enemies, then how could we possibly think that there are no conflicts in our life?[145]

This dichotomous view, these clear-cut distinctions, left little room for adoption, cultural or otherwise. Instead it highlighted the irreconcilable difference, which was susceptible to no amalgamation or convergence. Participants in multiple meetings of artistic unions and sessions of academic institutions held in early 1949 would follow the path paved by Simonov: "bourgeois ideology" would be firmly situated in the United States. A statement produced at a Moscow conference of medieval historians on 23 March 1949 effectively summarized the new understanding of "how they do things in America":

> The promulgation [*propoved'*] of universal cosmopolitanism in Europe clears the road for the 100% presence of bourgeois "Americanism" in all spheres of culture. In the USA, linguists are already working on simplifying the English language so that it can become the single language of international communication. There is also an insistent cosmopolitan propaganda of the "cultural" unification of Western Europe under the domination of the USA … "I am for the world nation," says the Nazi of the Anglo-Saxon type, "but it is my nation that is the worldly one"; the rest should be dissolved in it, abandoning their national traditions.[146]

Somewhat unexpectedly, this political "rediscovery" of *America* as the principal source of *Soviet* cosmopolitanism effectively put an end to the attack on the anti-patriotic group of theatre critics. The FAKC stopped as abruptly as it started, less than three months after its initial onslaught. A clear geographic anchor seemed to have produced some sense of political and epistemological certainty, which was amplified further by the sharp polarization of the world at that time. On 4 April 1949, ten European states, Canada, and the US signed the North Atlantic Treaty, creating an organization (NATO) that would significantly shape global affairs in the decades to come. Anticipating all this, a Memorandum of the Soviet Government dated 1 April 1949 emphasized that the Soviet Union's exclusion from the collective system of defence could be interpreted in only one way: the newly formed alliance was to act as a clear threat to "the states unwilling to submit themselves to the diktat of the Anglo-American group of countries, interested in establishing their hegemony in the world."[147]

A week later, *Pravda* published an article by Georgii Frantzev, the head of the press office in the Soviet Ministry of Foreign Affairs, which officially ended the FAKC. Titled "Cosmopolitanism Is an Ideological Weapon of the American Reactionaries," it offered a final diagnosis, describing cosmopolitanism as "the flip side of bourgeois nationalism," deployed as an "ideological shell" by "Wall Street and its agents" in their striving for "the world domination."[148] Meanwhile, the Department of Agitation and Propaganda of the Central Committee of the Party prepared a comprehensive list of measures to increase anti-American propaganda by "unveiling the aggressive plans of American imperialism" and by demonstrating "the false nature of bourgeois democracy, and the marasmus of bourgeois culture and mores in contemporary America" (among other things).[149] The Cold War only increased tensions, leaving no chance for *Amerikanizm* to survive.

***

Moving from Aleksandrov's *Circus* of 1936 to the FAKC of 1949, I have tried to trace the evolution of the global promises of early Soviet *Amerikanizm* towards post-war grievances, anger, and anxieties surrounding *anti-Amerikanizm*. Cosmopolitanism played an important role in this evolution by suggesting frames of comparison, spheres of circulation, and flows of objects, ideas, and people. But the same cosmopolitanism was essential for channelling feelings of cultural inferiority and social backwardness.

No doubt, Béla Balázs was right: as time went on, the same things acquired very different importance and generated very different effects. For Aleksandrov, the meaning and the consequences of "how they do it in America" were strikingly incompatible with the meaning and the consequences that Fadeev, Zhdanov, Shtein, Simonov, and Room associated with it. Still, they all needed that "America" in order to justify internal goals by referring to external circumstances, or to explain the local by evoking the global. Embracing the distant other – irreconcilable yet unavoidable – they constantly compared their dispositions, computed their chances, and accounted for their successes and failures. These concentric circles of affiliation and belonging could overlap closely or diverge dramatically but they could not be escaped. Ironically, their practices of cultural arbitrage seemed to embody – again and again – Kant's basic idea: the common "possession of the surface of the earth" turns it into a vicious circle of global neighbourhood where the only solution is to learn how to "tolerate the presence of each other."[150]

Acknowledgments

This chapter has an unusually long history. In 2009, Gyan Prakash invited me to present the first version at a colloquium on "Cosmopolitanism in the Landscape of Modernity" at Princeton University; a year later, I tested my ideas in Moscow, at the annual conference organized by the journal *Novoe literaturnoe obozrenie*. Since then, the chapter has gone through multiple iterations and developments, and I am grateful to the colleagues and friends who provided their comments and suggestions on earlier versions. My special thanks to Oksana Bulgakowa, Maria Belodubrovskaya, Caroline Humphrey, Kevin Platt, Oksana Sarkisova, members of the Princeton *kruzhok*, and the Red Migration collective for their suggestions. Anna Katsnelson and Rimgaila Salys shared with me their knowledge and enthusiasm for Aleksandrov's cinema; without their expertise, this chapter would not be the same. Finally, if not for Bradley Gorski and Philip Gleissner, it would have stayed dormant for another decade. I am indebted to their energy, interest, and intellectual curiosity, which brought this project back to life in 2019.

Notes

1 David Schrire, "A Reply to 'USSR Goes Hollywood,'" *World Film News*, August 1936, 25.
2 Sergei Eisenstein, "Letter to the Editor of *Kinotechnik*, 26 February 1927"; Yuri Tsivian, ed. *Lines of Resistance: Dziga Vertov and the Twenties* (Gemona: Le Giornate del Cinema Muto, 2004), 145.
3 Béla Balázs, "Novoe reshenie temy," *Iskusstvo kino* 7 (July 1936), 42.
4 Balázs, "Novoe reshenie temy."
5 Balázs, "Novoe reshenie temy."
6 See, for example, Yuri Tynianov, *Permanent Evolution: Selected Essays on Literature, Theory, and Film*, trans. and ed. by Ainsley Morse and Philip Redko (Boston: Academic Studies Press, 2019); Roman Jakobson, "Two Aspects of Language and Two Types of Aphasic Disturbances," in Roman Jakobson and Morris Halle, *Fundamentals of Language* (The Hague: Mouton, 1956), 69–96; Roman Jakobson, "Shifters, Verbal Categories, and the Russian Verb," in Roman *Jakobson, Selected Writings*, vol. 2 (The Hague: Mouton, 1971), 130–147; Jacques Derrida, *Limited Inc.* (Evanston:

Northwestern University Press, 1988); and *Christian Boltanski* (Paris: Flammarion, 2009). For more recent studies of this dynamic, see Alexei Yurchak's exploration of "performative shift" in his *Everything Was Forever, Until It Was No More: The Last Soviet Generation* (Princeton: Princeton University Press, 2005); and my own analysis of post-Soviet aphasia and nostalgia in "'We Are Nostalgic but We Are Not Crazy': Retrofitting the Past in Russia," *Russian Review* 66 (Summer 2007), 451–82; and "Second-Hand Nostalgia: On Charms and Spells of the Soviet *Trukhliashechka*," in Otto Boele, Boris Noordenbos, and Ksenia Robbe, eds. *Post-Soviet Nostalgia: Confronting the Empire's Legacies* (London: Routledge, 2019), 38–69.
7 Donald MacKenzie, "Long-Term Capital Management and the Sociology of Arbitrage," *Economy and Society* 32 (August 2003), 350.
8 Daniel Beunza and David Stark, "Tools of the Trade: The Socio-Technology of Arbitrage in a Wall Street Trading Room," *Industrial and Corporate Change* 13 (April 2004), 370.
9 For an instructive analysis, see, correspondingly, Robert Foster, *Coca-Globalization: Following Soft Drinks from New York to New Guinea* (New York: Palgrave Macmillan, 2008); and Sidney W. Mintz, *Sweetness and Power: The Place of Sugar in Modern History* (New York: Viking Penguin, 1985).
10 For a useful representation of this approach, see Ann Thomson, Simon Burrows and Edmond Dziembowski, with Sophie Audidière, eds. *Cultural Transfers: France and Britain in the Long Eighteenth Century* (Oxford: Voltaire Foundation, 2010).
11 Hirokazu Miyazaki, "Between Arbitrage and Speculation: An Economy of Belief and Doubt," *Economy and Society* 36 (August 2007), 406.
12 David Harvey, "Cosmopolitanism and the Banality of Geographical Evils," *Public Culture* 12 (2000), 542.
13 Harvey, "Cosmopolitanism," 558.
14 Kevin M.F. Platt, "American Writing, Soviet Literary Capital, Berlin Exchange Rates: Howard Fast and Cultural Arbitrage," in Susanne Frank, Zaal Andronikashvili, and Eugene Ostashevsky, eds. *The Soviet Cosmopolis: A Project of World Literature and its Global Impact* (Berlin: De Gruyter, forthcoming).
15 Katerina Clark, *Moscow, the Fourth Rome: Stalinism, Cosmopolitanism, and the Evolution of Soviet Culture, 1931–1941* (Cambridge: Harvard University Press, 2011), 145.
16 Platt, "American Writing."
17 "Cedric Belfrage Reports on Russia's Golliwod," *World Film News* (September 1936), 16.
18 "Budushchee zvukovoi fil'my," *Sovetskii ekran* 32 (7 August, 1928), 5.
19 For details, see Lilya Kaganovsky, *The Voice of Technology: Soviet Cinema's Transition to Sound, 1928–1935* (Bloomington: Indiana University Press, 2018).
20 "Budushchee zvukovoi fil'my," 5.

21 The desire to learn from Hollywood might have been influenced by the 1925 decision of the Politburo that introduced a program of attracting foreign experts and training Soviet "students, engineers, and technicians" abroad. For details, see "Postanovlenie Politbiuro Tsk RKP (b) 'O privlechenii inostrannykh tehknikov i obuchenii nashikh tekhnikov zagranitsei'" (11 June 1925), in *Indistrializatsiia Sovetskogo Soiuza*. ed. Semen Khromov, pt. 2 (Moscow: Institut rossiiskoi istorii RAN, 1999), 203; and "Tezisy po voprosy o privlechenii inostrannykh spetsialistov v soiuznuiu promyshlennost' i o zagranichnykh kommandirovkakh sovetskikh studentov, inzhenerov i tekhnikov" (11 June 1925), in Konstantin Chernenko and Mikhail Smirtiukov, eds. *Resheniia partii i pravitel'stva po khoziastvennym voprosam*, vol. 1: *1917–1929* (Moscow: Politzdat, 1967), 490–3.

22 A.F., "Meri Pikford i Duglas Ferbenks v Moskve (Iz besedy s nimi)," *Pravda*, 25 July 1926, 7. *Sovetskii ekran* was less impressed with this visit of the Hollywood stars, though, noting that "we have not yet seen Chaplin and Stroheim … yet we are being relentlessly fed the American cuisine that consists of fairy-tale sauces prepared by Mary [Pickford]." Vlad. Korolevich, "Dovol'no Meri Pikford!" *Sovetskii ekran* 32 (10 August 1926), 13.

23 See Eisenstein's letter to Fairbanks's brother from 10 November 1926, in *Vnukovskii arkhiv. Pis'ma, dnevniki, fotografii i dokumenty zvezd sovetskogo kino iz sobraniia Aleksandra Dobrovinskogo*, vol. 2: Evropeiskii dnevnik (Moscow, 2018), 23. Hereafter, I refer to this source as VA, indicating the volume and pages.

24 As cited in *VA*, vol. 1: *Put' naverkh* (Moscow, 2017), 185; see also Grigorii Aleksandrov, *Epokha i kino* (Moscow, 1976), 106–7. For more details on the meeting, see: Boris Shumiatskii, "Stalin i kino" (January 1935), in *Kremlevskii kinoteatr. 1928–1953. Dokumenty* (Moscow: ROSSPEN, 2005), 82–3.

25 Aleksandrov, *Epokha i kino*, 122.

26 See *VA*, vol. 2, 24.

27 *VA*, vol. 2, 232.

28 Aleksandrov, *Epokha i kino*, 118.

29 *VA*, vol. 2, 34.

30 The film is available here: https://www.filmo.ch/Edition/katalog/staffel-8/frauennot---frauenglueck.html

31 Aleksandrov, *Epokha i kino*, 118.

32 *VA*, vol. 2, 34.

33 *VA*, vol. 2, 59.

34 Ivan Frolov, *Grigorii Aleksandrov* (Moscow: Iskusstvo, 1976), 16–17.

35 Aleksandrov, *Epokha i kino*, 119.

36 Aleksandrov, *Epokha i kino*, 119.

37 See, for example, Beth Holmgren, "*The Blue Angel* and Blackface: Redeeming Entertainment in Aleksandrov's *Circus*," *Russian Review* 66 (June 2007), 5–22.

38 *VA*, vol. 2, 101.
39 *VA*, vol. 3: Amerikanskii dnevnik (Moscow, 2018), 173.
40 For more detail, see Kendall E. Bailes, "The Shakhty Affair," in Kendall E. Bailes, *Technology and Society under Lenin and Stalin* (Princeton: Princeton University Press, 2015), 69–94.
41 Aleksandrov, *Epokha i kino*, 136. Recently published diaries, however, offer a much less sinister version of the event. As Aleksandrov recorded on 21 June 1930, during a breakfast with "the old Laemmle ... he asked: 'What do you think, would Leon Trotsky agree to write a film script if I commission it to him?' We responded – 'We think, he would!' *VA*, vol. 3, 72.
42 For more detail, see Ivor Montagu, *With Eisenstein in Hollywood* (Berlin: Seven Seas Books, 1969); Harry M. Geduld and Ronald Gottesman, eds., *Sergei Eisenstein and Upton Sinclair: The Making and Unmaking of "¡Que Viva Mexico!"* (Bloomington: Indiana University Press, 1970); and Ronald Bergan, *Sergei Eisenstein: A Life in Conflict* (Woodstock: Overlook Press / Peter Mayer, 1999).
43 *VA*, vol. 3, 76.
44 *VA*, vol. 3, 114.
45 *VA*, vol. 3, 173.
46 *VA*, vol. 2, 82.
47 *VA*, vol. 3, 36–7.
48 For useful discussions of this overall trend, see Jean-Louis Cohen, *Building a New World: Amerikanizm in Russian Architecture* (New Haven: Yale University Press, 2020); and Thomas Keenan, "Amerikanizm: The Brave New New World of Soviet Civilization," in Marina Balina and Serguei Alex. Oushakine, eds. *The Pedagogy of Images: Depicting Communism for Children* (Toronto: University of Toronto Press, 2021), 489–524. For "Americanist" texts by Arvatov, Gastev, and Kuleshov, see *Formal'nyi metod: Antologiia russkogo modernizma,*. vol. 4: *Funktsiia*, ed. Serguei Alex. Oushakine (Ekaterinburg–Moscow: Kabinetnyi uchenyi, 2023).
49 *VA*, vol. 3, 97.
50 *VA*, vol. 3, 172.
51 *VA*, vol. 3, 205.
52 *VA*, vol. 3, 216.
53 Pis'mo I. Stalina E. Sinkleru, 21 November 1931, in *Kremlevskii kinoteatr*, 149.
54 Pismo B. Shumiatskogo S. Eisensteinu, 24 July 1930, in *Kremlevskii kinoteatr*, 139.
55 Aleksandrov, *Epokha i kino*, 176.
56 Aleksandrov, *Epokha i kino*, 159.
57 For more detail, see the chapter "Striving for Comedy" (*Kurs na komediiu*) in Frolov's *Grigorii Aleksandrov*, 20–58; and Il'ia Kalinin, "Smekh kak trud i

smekh kak tovar (stakhanovskoe dvizhenie i kapitalisticheskii konveier)," *Novoe literaturnoe obozrenie* 121 (2013): 115–23.

58 "Veselye rebiata," *Izvestia*, 24 December 1934. For more discussion about the complicated history of the film's release, see Rimgaila Salys, *The Musical Comedy Films of Grigorii Aleksandrov: Laughing Matters* (Bristol: Intellect, 2009), 65–8.

59 Boris Shumiatskii, "Trudneishii zhanr osvoen," *Kino*, 16 December 1934, 2; see also his defence of the film in Boris Shumiatskii, *Put' masterstva* (Moscow: Kinofotoizdat, 1935), 24–5.

60 Maxim Gorkii, "O muzyke tolstykh," *Pravda*, 18 April 1928.

61 Aleksandrov, *Epokha i kino*, 186.

62 Salys, The Musical Comedy Films, 68–9.

63 "'Dzhaz-komediia': chitka i obsuzhdenie novogo komediinogo stsenariia." *Kino*, 16 April 1933, 3.

64 "'Dzhaz-komediia,'" 3.

65 B. Koval, "Neudavshiisia eksperiment," *Sovetskoe isskustvo*, 29 November 1934.

66 At the final event of the festival on 2 March, Sergei Eisenstein announced the winners. Three Soviet films shared the first prize – *Chapaev* (dir. the brothers Vasiliev), *Maksim's Youth* (dir. Grigorii Kozintsev and Leonid Trauberg), and *The Peasants* (dir. Fridrikh Ermler). The second prize was awarded to Réné Clair's *The Last Billionaire*; Walt Disney's animated films received the third prize. See coverage of the festival in *Kino*, 5 March 1935.

67 *Kino*, 1 March 1935, 1.

68 "Postanovlenie zhiuri Pervogo sovetskogo kinofestivalia," *Kino*, 5 March 1935, 1.

69 Viktor Shklovsky, "Da zdravstvuet Villa!," *Literaturnaia gazeta*, 28 February 1935.

70 Aleksandr Bezymenskii, "Karaul! Grabiat!," *Literaturnaia gazeta*, 28 February 1935. See also a special page on *Happy Guys* in *Literaturnaia gazeta*, 6 March 1935, 6. For more detail on these debates, see Salys, *The Musical Comedy Films*, 69–72.

71 Semen Kirsanov, "O pol'ze chteniia entsiklopedii, dazhe maloi," *Literaturnaia gazeta*, 6 March 1935, 6.

72 See "Pis'ma v redaktsiiu," *Kino*, 5 March 1935.

73 For more discussion, see Boris Shumiatskii, *Kinematografiia millionov* (Moscow: Gudok, 1935), 246–56. See also an important editorial in *Pravda* that defended Aleksandrov and Dunaevskii, dismissing the interventions of Kirsanov and Bezymenskii as "wrong and harmful jabbering" (*boltovnia*): "Ob itogakh kinofestivalia i besprintsipnoi pelemike." *Pravda*, 12 March 1935, 1.

74 "'Dzhaz-komediia': chitka i obsuzhdenie."

75 Guzel Agisheva, "V TsDKh otkryta vystavka 'Khudozhniki teatra K.Ia. Goleizovskogo. 1918–1932,'" *Trud*, 5 December 2012.

76 Tatiana Strizhenova, *Iz istorii sovetskogo kostiuma* (Moscow: Sovetskii khudozhnik, 1972), 34. See also Catherine Walworth, *Soviet Salvage: Imperial Debris, Revolutionary Reuse, and Russian Constructivism* (University Park: Pennsylvania State University Press, 2017), 169–70.
77 After visiting Hollywood, Boris Shumiatskii, the head of the Directorate of Cinema, would start in 1935 a massive campaign to create the "Soviet Hollywood" in Alushta, a resort on the Black Sea. The project was not realized – initially because of financial issues. Then in 1938 Shumiatskii was executed as an enemy of the people. For more detail, see *Kino*, "What the Soviet Cinema-Town Should Look Like" and especially the article by Vladimir Nil'sen "American and Soviet Hollywood" (11 January 1936, 3). For a general discussion, see Fedor Razzakov, *Gibel' sovetskogo kino: Intrigi i spory, 1918–1972* (Moscow, 2008), 82–3; Maria Belodubrovskaia, "Soviet Hollywood: The Culture Industry That Wasn't," *Cinema Journal* 53, no. 3 (Spring 2014), 100–22.
78 See, for example, Richard Taylor, "The Illusion of Happiness and the Happiness of Illusion: Grigorii Aleksandrov's *The Circus*," *Slavonic and East European Review* 74 (October 1996), 601–20; and M. Ratchford, "*Circus* of 1936: Ideology and Entertainment under the Big Top," in Andrew Horton, ed. *Inside Soviet Film Satire. Laughter with a Lash* (Cambridge: Cambridge University Press, 1993), 83–93.
79 Immanuel Kant, "Perpetual Peace: A Philosophical Sketch," in Immanuel Kant, *On History*, trans. Lewis White Beck, Robert E. Anchor, and Emil L. Fackenheim (New York: Bobbs Merrill, 1963), 103.
80 See Julia Kristeva, *Strangers to Ourselves* (New York: Columbia University Press, 1991), 172.
81 Martha Nussbaum, "Patriotism and Cosmopolitanism," in Nussbaum, *For Love of Country* (Boston, 1996).
82 See, for example, Mikhail Bakhtin, *Sobranie sochinenii*, vol. 6 (Moscow: Nauka, 2002), 433.
83 For an extensive discussion of these (and other) formal devices in *Circus*, see Anna Katsnelson, "Framed? Circus, Space, and Form in Stalinist Comedy" (unpublished manuscript).
84 For less glamourous historical accounts of Soviet hospitality at the time, see, for example, Julia L. Mickenberg, *American Girls in Red Russia: Chasing the Soviet Dream* (Chicago: University of Chicago Press, 2017); and Joy Gleason Carew, *Blacks, Reds, and Russians: Sojourners in Search of the Soviet Promise* (New Brunswick: Rutgers University Press, 2007).
85 The name of the performer might have been a coded reference to Marlene Dietrich; in 1937, some film reviews even mixed up the two names, calling the main character Marion Dietrich (see Aleksandr Khort, *Liubov' Orlova* [Moscow: Molodaia gvardiia, 2007], 108). See also Karina Dobrotvorskaia,

"Tsirk G. V. Aleksandrova," *Iskusstvo kino* 11 (November 1992); and Thomas Lahusen, "From Laughter 'Out of Sync' to Post-Synchronized Comedy: How the Stalinist Film Musical Caught up with Hollywood and Overtook it," in Dubravka Juraga and M. Keith Booker, eds., *Socialist Cultures East and West: A Post-Cold War Reassessment* (London: Praeger, 2002), 38.
86 See, for example, Lahusen, *From Laughter "Out of Sync,"* 31–42.
87 For more discussion of stylistic and narrative links of Aleksandrov's *Circus* and Hollywood, see Salys, *The Musical Comedy Films*; and Holmgren, "*The Blue Angel* and Blackface."
88 "Alexandrov Theme Taboo; Songs Tops," *Hollywood Reporter*, 10 July 1936, 6.
89 For classical examples of this approach in English, see Ratchford, "Circus of 1936"; and Taylor, "The Illusion of Happiness." For the Russian version, see Neia Zorkaia, "Bestseller Tsirk: razvlekatel'naia propaganda," in Zorkaia, *Kino. Teatr. Literatura. Opyt sistemnogo analiza* (Moscow: AGRAF, 2010): 174–85.
90 For a detailed discussion, see Jeremy Hicks, *Dziga Vertov: Defining Documentary Film* (New York: I.B. Tauris, 2007), 115–16; and Aleksei Deriabin, "Kolybel'naia Dzigi Vertova: zamysel – voploshchenie – ekrannaia sud'ba," *Kinovedcheskie zapiski* 51 (2001): 30–65.
91 Dziga Vertov, *Iz naslediia: stat'i i vystupleniia*, vol. 2 (Moscow: Eizenshtein-Tsentr, 2008), 367.
92 *Kino-eye: The Writings of Dziga Vertov*, ed. Annette Michelson (Berkeley: University of California Press, 1984), 213–14. For a discussion, see Konstantin A. Bogdanov, "Pravo na son i uslovnye refleksy: kolybel'nye pesni v sovetskoi massovoi kul'ture (1930–1950-t gody)," *Novoe literaturnoe obozrenie* 86 (2007).
93 Harvey, "Cosmopolitanism," 558.
94 Mikhail Bakhtin, *Dostoevskii* [1961], in Bakhtin, *Sobranie sochinenii*, vol. 5 (Moscow: Nauka, 1996), 366.
95 As cited in Omri Ronen, "Iz goroda Enn, 'Kosmopolit,'" *Zvezda* 1 (January 2004), 231.
96 See the decision of the Politburo of the Central Committee of the Party from 28 March 1947: "Ob organizatsii 'sudov chesti,'" *Stalin i kosmopolitizm. Dokumenty* (Moscow: Materik, 2005), 108–9. See also "Sudy chesti," *Izvestiia TsK KPSS* 11 (November 1990): 135–8.
97 For a discussion of the Kliueva–Roskin affair, see Nikolai Krementsov, "The 'KR Affair': Soviet Science on the Threshold of the Cold War," *History and Philosophy of the Life Sciences* 17, no. 3 (1995): 419–46; Vladimir Esakov and Elena Levina, *Delo KR: sudy chesti v ideologii i praktike poslevoennogo stalinizma* (Moscow: In-t rossiiskoi istorii RAN, 2001).

98 "Fil'm 'Sud chesti' na ekranakh kinoteatrov," *Vecherniaia Moskva*, 25 January 1949. See also a review of the film by Al. Abramov in *Vecherniaia Moskva*, 29 January 1949, 3. Together with several leading actors of the film, Room, Shtein, and the cameraman Aleksandr Gal'perin were awarded in 1949 the highest state award – the Stalin Prize of the first degree. For more on the official reception of the film, see German Kremlev, *Sud chesti (O fil'me i ego sozdateliakh)* (Moscow: Goskino, 1949); D. Pisarevskii, "Chest' sovetskogo patriota," *Kul'tura i zhizn'*, 30 January 1949; Vadim Kozhevnikov, "Sud chesti," *Pravda*, 25 January 1949; N. Belen'kii, "Za patrioticheskuiu chest' sovetskikh uchenykh," *Literaturnaia gazeta*, 29 January 1949.

99 In English, this "fight" is usually rendered as a campaign against "rootless cosmopolites." However, the term "rootless" does not quite do justice to the Russian original: *bezrodnyi* literally means "kinless," i.e., without any network of belonging and mutual responsibility. To maintain the negative link between cosmopolitanism and the ties of kinship, which was so paramount for the Soviets, I will use "kinless" throughout this chapter.

100 Avgusta Saraeva-Bondar' recollected in her memoirs that Aleksandrov found an uncensored copy of the film with the "compromising scene" in Czechoslovakia. See her *Siluety vremeni* (St. Petersburg, 1993), 204; see also, Salys, *The Musical Comedy Films*, 199.

101 For an extensive discussion, see Aleksandr Borshchagovskii, *Zapiski balovnia sud'by* (Moscow: Sovetskii pisatel', 1992); Gennadii Batygin and Inna Deviatko, "Evreiskii vopros: khronika sorokovykh godov." *Vestnik Rossiiskoi Akademii nauk*, vol. 63 (1993), No. 1: 61–72; No. 2: 143–15; Iu. A. Poliakov, "Vesna 1949," *Voprosy istorii* 8 (1996): 66–76; Gennadii Kostyrchenko, *Tainaia politika Stalina: Vlast' i antisemitizm* (Moscow: Mezhdunarodnye otnosheniia, 2001); Arkadii Vaksberg, *Iz ada v rai i obratno* (Moscow: Olimp, 2003); Jonathan Brent and Vladimir P. Naumov, *Stalin's Last Crime: The Plot against the Jewish Doctors, 1948–1953* (New York: Harper Perennial, 2004); and Gennadii Kostyrchenko, *Stalin protiv "kosmopolitov". Vlast' i evreiskaia intelligentsiia v SSSR* (Moscow: ROSSPEN, 2010).

102 Borshchagovskii, *Zapiski balovnia sud'by*, 76.

103 For more cultural context, see Natal'ia Gromova, *Raspad: Sud'ba sovetskogo kritika: 40–50-e gody* (Moscow: Ellis Lak, 2009), 179–296.

104 Valerii Fomin, *Istoriia rossiiskoi kinematografii (1941–1968)* (Moscow: Kanon, 2018), 586.

105 Maria Belodubrovskaya, *Not According to Plan: Filmmaking under Stalin* (Ithaca: Cornell University Press, 2017), 46–50. See also Mikhail Zhabskii, "Vesternizatsiia kinematografa: opyt i uroki istorii," *Sotsiologicheskie issledovaniia* 2 (February 1996): 27–8.

"How They Do It in America" 85

106 Boris Arvatov, "Theater and *Byt*" [1923], trans. E.V. Pavlov and S.A. Oushakine, *Russian Review* 82 (Winter 2023), 28.
107 As quoted in Kostyrchenko, *Tainaia politika Stalina*, 319.
108 Andrei Zhdanov, *Essays on Literature, Philosophy, and Music* (New York: International, 1950), 71–2.
109 "Dokladnaia zapiska narodnogo komissara Gosudarstvennoi bezopasnosti SSSR V. N. Merkulova A. A. Zhdanovu o nedostatkakh v rabote khudozhestvennoi kinematografii. 4 March 1946," in *Kremlevskii kinoteatr*, 722. For more discussion of this condition, see Maria Belodubrovskaya, "The Jockey and the Horse: Joseph Stalin and the Biopic Genre in Soviet Cinema," *Studies in Russian and Soviet Cinema* 5 (Winter 2013): 29–53.
110 "Dokladnaia zapiska Agitpropa TsK M.A. Suslovu o nedostatkakh v rabote kommunistov sektora iskusstv. January 8/10, 1949," in *Stalin i kosmopolitizm*, 215–16.
111 "Dokladnaia zapiska Agitpropa," 216, 215.
112 For a vivid example of this inquisitive search for the primary epistemological foundations (*istoki*) of cosmopolitanism (in architecture), see the monograph by Mikhail Tsapenko, a Kyiv architecture historian, *O realisticheskikh osnovakh sovetskoi architektury* (Moscow: Gosizdat, 1952), 78, 129. For a useful discussion of Tsapenko's analytics, see Vadim Bass, "Moisei Ginzburg: arkhitektor konstruktivistskoi ideologii," in *Formal'nyi metod*, vol. 4, bk. 2, 529–72.
113 "Na chuzhdykh pozitsiiakh. O proiskakh antipatrioticheskoi gruppy teatral'nykh kritikov," *Kultura i zhizn'*, 30 January 1949.
114 Leon Trotsky, "The Formalist School of Poetry and Marxism," in David Craig, ed. *Marxists on Literature: An Anthology* (New York: Penguin Books, 1975), 365.
115 Aleksandr Fadeev, "Sovetskaia literatura na pod"eme," *Pravda*, 30 June 1947.
116 Isaak Nusinov, *Pushkin i mirovaia literatura* (Moscow: Sovetskii pisatel', 1941).
117 Fadeev, "Sovetskaia literatura na pod"eme."
118 Fadeev, "Sovetskaia literatura na pod"eme." See also Vissarion Belinskii, "K.D. Kaveliny," in Belinskii, *Polnoe sobranie sochinenii v 12 tomakh*, vol. 12 (Moscow: Akademiia Nauk SSSR, 1956), 433.
119 *Soveshchanie deiatelei sovetskoi muzyki v TsK VKP(b)* (Moscow: Pravda, 1948), 139–40.
120 Iakov El'sberg, "Belinskii v bor'be s kosmopolitizmom," *Literaturnaia gazeta*, 17 April 1948.
121 Zinovii Papernyi, "Perechityvaia Belinskogo," *Literaturnaia gazeta*, 5 June 1948. For more detail about Papernyi's publication, see Kostyrchenko, *Tainaia politika Stalina*, 321–2.

122 "Ob odnoi antipatrioticheskoi gruppe teatral'nykh kritikov," *Pravda*, 28 January 1949. For more details, see commentaries in *Stalin i kosmopolitizm*; Borshchagovskii, *Zapiski balovnia sud'by*, 87.
123 Stalin added the three variations of cosmopolitanism to the final draft of the editorial the night before its publication. See *Stalin i kosmopolitizm*, 234.
124 "Ob odnoi antipatrioticheskoi gruppe."
125 Nikolai Kondakov, *Logika: posobie dlia uchitelei* (Moscow: Uchpediz, 1954), 227.
126 "Do kontsa razoblachit' antipatrioticheskuiu gruppu teatral'nykh kritikov," *Literaturnaia gazeta*, 29 January 1949.
127 "Dokladnaia zapiska Agitpropa TsK G.M. Malenkovu o sobranii sotrudnikov Instituta filosofii AN SSSR," in *Stalin i kosmopolitizm*, 318.
128 B. Kremnev, "Politicheskoe litso kritika Iuzovskogo," *Sovetskoe iskusstvo*, 29 January 1949.
129 "Ob odnoi antipatrioticheskoi gruppe."
130 See Iosif Iuzovskii, *Obraz i epokha* (Moscow: Sovetskii pisatel', 1947), 20.
131 Kremnev, "Politicheskoe litso kritika Iuzovskogo."
132 See, for example, Iuzovskii, *Obraz i epokha*, 14.
133 Kremnev, "Politicheskoe litso kritika Iuzovskogo."
134 Aleksandr Gerasimov, "Za sovetskii patriotism v iskusstve," *Pravda*, 10 February 1949.
135 Iosif Grinberg, "Propovedniki mertvykh skhem," *Iskusstvo kino* 2 (February 1949), 28.
136 "O zadachakh sovetskikh istorikov v bor'be s proiavleniiami burzhuaznoi ideologii," *Voprosy istorii* 2 (February 1949), 6–7.
137 Ivan Bolshakov, "Razgromit' burzhuaznyi kosmopolitizm v kinoiskusstve," *Pravda*, 3 March 1949.
138 See, for example, "Dokladnaia zapiska Agitpropa TsK G.M. Malenkovu o zakrytom sobranii partiinoi organizatsii Soiuza sovetskikh pisatelei 14 February 1949," *Stalin i kosmopolitizm*, 286.
139 Nikolai Gribachev, "Protiv kosmopolitizma i formalizma v poezii," *Pravda*, 16 February 1949.
140 "Stenogramma soveshchaniia redaktorov tsentral'nykh gazet i zhurnalov 29 marta 1949 goda v Agitprope TsK," *Stalin i kosmopolitizm*, 345.
141 Platt, "American Writing."
142 Singling out Griffith and Chaplin had solid historical reasons. In his classic *Iskusstvo kino* (Moscow: Tea-Kino-Pechat', 1929), Lev Kuleshov, the key figure in early Soviet cinema, stated directly: "Two world masters laid the foundations of the school of cinematography – David Griffith and Charlie Chaplin" (103; for an English version, see *Kuleshov on Film: Writing by Lev Kuleshov*, trans. Ronald Levaco [Berkeley: University of California Press, 1974], 144). Following this dogma, in 1944–45, Sergei

Eisenstein and Sergei Iutkevich opened the series of *Materials on the History of the World Cinema* with two (and only two) volumes – on Griffith and Chaplin respectively. (*D.U. Griffit* (Moscow: Goskinoizdat, 1944); and *Charlz Spenser Chaplin* (Moscow: Goskinoizdat, 1945).

143 Simonov refers here to *The Iron Curtain*, a 1948 film directed by William A. Wellman (of *Viva Villa!* fame), which was based on a series of articles "I Was Inside Stalin's Spy Ring," published in the spring of 1947 by the Soviet defector Igor Gouzenko in the international edition of Hearst's *Cosmopolitan*. For a Soviet response to the film, see Il'ia Erenburg, "Kinoprovokatory," *Kultura i zhizn*, 21 February 1948.

144 Konstantin Simonov, "Teorii i praktika kosmopolitov v kinokritike," *Sovetskoe iskusstvo*, 5 March 1949.

145 Konstantin Simonov, "Zadachi sovetskoi dramarurgii i teatral'naia kritika," *Literaturnaia gazeta*, 9 March 1949.

146 See "Stenogramma ob"edinennogo zasedaniia sektora srednikh vekov Instituta Istorii AN SSSR i kafedry srednikh vekov MGU," *Odissei: chelovek v istorii* (2007), vol. 1, 255–6.

147 "Memorandum Pravitel'stva SSSR o Severo-Atlanticheskom dogovore," *Pravda*, 1 April 1949.

148 Georgii Frantsev, "Kosmopolitizm – ideologicheskoe oruzhie amerikanskoi reaktsii," *Pravda*, 7 April 1949.

149 "Plan meropriiatii po usileniiu antiamerikanskoi propagandy na blizhaishee vremia. Dokument Agitpropa TsK," in *Stalin i kosmopolitizm*, 321.

150 Kant, "Perpetual Peace," 103.

2 Transnational Theory of the Avant-garde: János Mácza, Artistic Praxis, and the Marxist Method

IRINA DENISCHENKO

The proliferation of different -isms at the beginning of the twentieth century and their complex interactions have long attracted the diagrammatic imagination of scholars and art historians. MoMA's first curator, Alfred H. Barr Jr., created a foundational work in the genre for the 1936 exhibition *Cubism and Abstract Art* (figure 2.1).[1] Barr had taken his cue from the avant-garde, which was fond of examining, constructing, and mapping its own genealogies and networks. Diagrams such as F.T. Marinetti's tree of Futurism (figure 2.2) and Francis Picabia's mechanomorphic charts of the Dada movement were driven as much by the desire to systematize modern art movements and artists as by self-promotion, which placed one's own -ism at the root of new art and presented others as offshoots.[2]

Certain differences notwithstanding, such attempts to map out the relations among different -isms are informed by the same conception of unity that is based on notions of artistic influence and evolution. Placed in a chronological sequence, each artist or movement is presented as a source of inspiration for the next. Although undoubtedly more complex, even contemporary efforts to reconceptualize and map the avant-garde as a kind of network are partly based on these notions. For example, the interactive digital graphic that accompanied MoMA's 2013 exhibition *Inventing Abstraction* challenges the notion of a linear evolution that led to the invention of abstract art and recasts the worn-out idea of influence as multidirectional exchange among different artists who act as nodes in a "network."[3] On such a model, the development of new forms – in this case, the invention of abstraction – is not a straightforward process whereby artists operating in Western artistic capitals bequeath new artistic forms to the rest of the world. As the curators clarify, "abstraction was not the inspiration of a solitary genius but the product of network thinking – of ideas moving through a nexus of artists and intellectuals

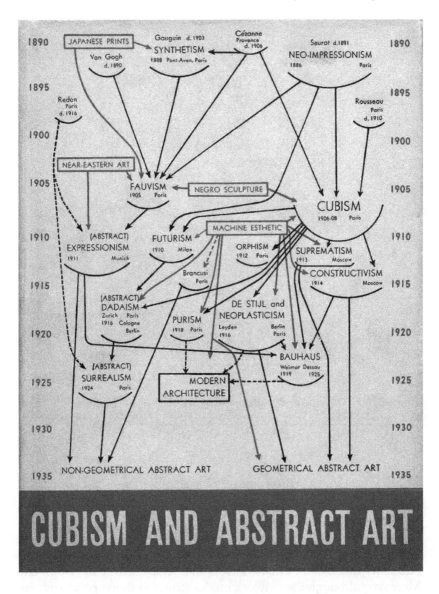

Figure 2.1. Alfred H. Barr Jr., dust jacket of *Cubism and Abstract Art* (1936). Private archive.

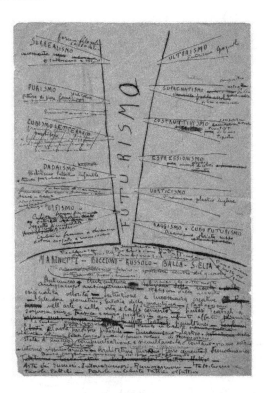

Figure 2.2. F.T. Marinetti, manuscript diagram of Futurism. Filippo Tommaso Marinetti Papers. General Collection, Beinecke Rare Book and Manuscript Library. © 2023 Artists Rights Society (ARS), New York.

working in different mediums and in far-flung places." The graphic thus aims to show that the birth of abstraction was the result of complex connections and exchanges among artists in the network. But while the concept of multidirectional exchange de-emphasizes the primacy of individual invention, this paradigm, by focusing only on artists, leaves out many other, extra-artistic factors that shape artistic development. Moreover, although the network model strives to decentre artistic canons and the hegemony of Western culture, in the end, it often reproduces that hegemony in more subtle ways.[4]

Such limitations of the network model, which continues to be influential in avant-garde studies, add urgency to the search for alternatives.⁵ One paradigm worth revisiting in formulating a new vision for a comparative studies that is not bogged down in the cultural hegemony of existing canons is Marxist sociology. This strand of theoretical inquiry emerged in Soviet Russia in the 1920s and was, at that time, simply referred to as "the Marxist method." Thanks to this new methodology, alternative conceptions of the unity of -isms were sketched out in compelling visual graphic form even before Barr captured the artistic influence–based approach in his famous diagram. Rather than mapping connections between different artists or -isms, the diagram below (figure 2.3) illustrates how each movement is shaped by the dialectical interaction of material-economic and social-psychic factors.

The organizational principle in this diagram of "the social origins of new art and literature" is not artistic influence, but extra-artistic forces that shape the development of various -isms. The diagram appeared in a 1926 book *The Art of Contemporary Europe* (*Iskusstvo sovremennoi Evropy*), by János Mácza (Ivan Matsa, 1893–1974), a member of the Hungarian avant-garde who immigrated to the Soviet Union in 1923 and soon became a leading Marxist cultural theoretician.⁶ The diagram and the book it accompanied shifted the emphasis of comparative cultural studies away from questions of artistic influence and evolution towards considerations of the economic and social factors that shape artistic production. This shift, in turn, brought certain methodological consequences that are of considerable relevance to comparative studies even today.

Together with the notion of artistic influence, the book discarded the evolution of forms as a principle for conceptualizing similarities and differences between various artistic movements. That is, long before Peter Bürger's challenge to Renato Poggioli's form-based "theory of the avant-garde" in the 1970s, Mácza's work showed that form is a misleading and unreliable factor when analysing continuity or the lack thereof between movements.⁷ The result of such a two-pronged rejection – of both influence and form – was that previously invisible movements and locations, such as the lesser-known avant-gardes of Central and Southeastern Europe, became visible and entered the annals of Mácza's art history, since primacy in the invention of new forms was no longer a requirement for inclusion. In addition to allowing Mácza to present a more inclusive survey of "the art of contemporary Europe," which included Hungary, Czechoslovakia, and Yugoslavia alongside Germany, Italy, and France, "the Marxist method" employed in the book

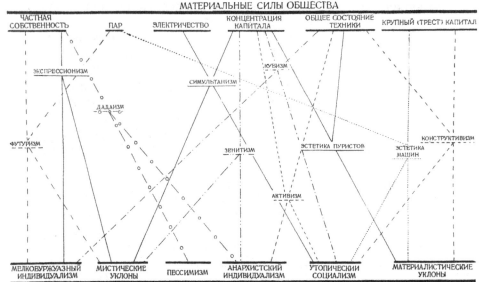

Figure 2.3. János Mácza, "The Social Origins of New Art and Literature." Diagram from *The Art of Contemporary Europe* (1926). Private collection. Across the top the diagram reads: "Material Forces of Society," including, from left to right, "Private Property," "Steam," "Electricity," "The Concentration of Capital," "The General State of Technology," and "Large 'Trust' Capital." Across the bottom the diagram reads: "Psychic Forces of Society," including, from left to right, "Petit-bourgeois Individualism," "Mystical Inclinations (or Deviations)," "Pessimism," "Anarchistic Individualism," "Utopian Socialism," and "Materialist Inclinations (or Deviations)." The artistic movements are arranged across the centre, from left to right "Futurism," "Expressionism," "Dadaism," "Simultanism," "Zenitism," "Activism," "Cubism," "Purist Aesthetics," "Machine Aesthetics," and "Constructivism." See facsimile translation of fig. 2.3 in fig. 2.8.

enabled the author to broaden its disciplinary scope. By contrast with Barr's diagram, which is concerned with visual art, Mácza's encompasses developments in literature, visual art, theatre, and music, since all art forms were shaped by the same socio-economic factors in the first decades of the twentieth century in Europe.

In this chapter, I argue that Mácza's innovative study and novel methodological insights were shaped by his transnational movements and the resulting hybrid forms of knowledge, which fused his first-hand experience of the Central European avant-garde with the Soviet search for a Marxist cultural theory in the 1920s. Together, they yielded not only the first theory of the avant-garde but also a methodology that provides valuable insights for comparative and interdisciplinary fields even today. Below, I first address the shaping of Mácza's transnational subjectivity by tracing his geographical migrations and participation in the avant-garde. Next, I show how *The Art of Contemporary Europe* systematizes Mácza's first-hand knowledge of the avant-garde, with the help of "the Marxist method." Finally, I briefly consider how leftist migration in the early twentieth century shaped theoretical knowledge production in the field of cultural studies and suggest possibilities for thinking beyond the exilic paradigm, which has defined scholarly understanding of theory and its origins.

The Shaping of a Transnational Nomadic Subjectivity

Like many participants in the Hungarian avant-garde, János Mácza was born on the periphery of the Austro-Hungarian Empire. He grew up in a small village in today's Slovakia and attended gymnasium in what is now western Ukraine. Mácza's first works appeared in Hungarian in Uzhgorod (Ungvár), where he published several articles and the slim volume on *Modern Hungarian Drama* (*A modern magyar dráma*, 1916). The significance of the multilingual borderlands in which Mácza moved in his early years cannot be overstated. Such a setting contributed to the formation of a "nomadic subjectivity," capable of adjusting to constantly shifting circumstances and sceptical of stable identities offered by nationalism.[8] Moreover, it exposed Mácza to Slavic languages, which would later ease his transition into Russian following his immigration, and set him apart from many of his fellow Hungarian émigrés, whose communication was often limited to German- and Hungarian-speaking circles in Moscow.[9]

After relocating to Budapest in 1915, Mácza joined the poet Lajos Kassák's recently launched journal *A Tett* (*The Action*, 1915–16), a revolutionary publication that is often viewed as the founding document of the Hungarian avant-garde.[10] The periodical's subtitle, "Journal of Literature, Visual Arts, and Society," pointed to its comprehensive scope, in that recent artistic developments were reviewed alongside articles on society and politics.[11] The journal's broad cultural scope and its approach to art through a sociopolitical lens also defined Kassák's next enterprise, the journal *Ma* (*Today*, 1916–25), which became an even more formative influence on Mácza's intellectual development. Founded in 1916 after the closure of *A Tett* by wartime censorship, *Ma* and its panoramic coverage of artistic life acquainted Mácza with the latest developments in European art.[12] Moreover, after the news of the Bolshevik Revolution in Russia had reached Hungary, *Ma* displayed an increasingly leftist ideological orientation, viewing art as a tool for agitation and social change.[13] By writing drama reviews for this revolutionary monthly on a regular basis, Mácza became a close associate of the *Ma* circle, a group of avant-garde artists and intellectuals that formed around the journal.[14]

In 1917 Mácza became head of *Ma*'s newly founded experimental theatre studio, which provided free education to actors; by 1919 the studio had become a leading theoretical voice of avant-garde theatre in Hungary. During the brief life of the Hungarian Soviet Republic from 21 March to 1 August 1919, Mácza became absorbed in theatre praxis and was appointed assistant director of the Hungarian National Theatre.[15] It was probably through his theatre work that he met György (Georg) Lukács, the (Deputy) People's Commissar for Culture and Education, who would become Mácza's distant interlocutor in the years to come. At this time, Lukács issued directives to the *Ma* circle, or the "Activists" as they had begun to call themselves, to organize "propaganda performances."[16] This attempt to penetrate proletarian audiences with agitational content and avant-garde forms was not always successful, however. In his autobiography from the 1920s, Kassák recounts the comical response to Mácza's play *The Individual: The Tragedy of Impotence in One Act* (*Individuum: a tehetetlenség tragédiája egy felvonásban*), staged in a theatre in the working-class neighbourhood of Újpest. Instead of the intended tragic catharsis, the melodramatic Expressionist piece elicited laughter from the audience. This experience made Mácza acutely aware of the gap between bourgeois and proletarian audiences and of the need to develop a different language for agitating among the latter.[17]

Although they initially cooperated with the Commissariat for Culture and Education and carried out its orders, the Activists soon collided with the government. Their attempt to become "the leading, definitive trend in the cultural life of the proletarian dictatorship" met with sharp opposition in the press.[18] The journalist Pál Kéri attacked what he perceived as favouritism on the part of the cultural commissariat (Lukács and Béla Balázs, in particular), initiating a press scandal. Targeting Kassák and

Mácza specifically, the press accused the Activists of being "talentless and ignorant" and depicted them as "futurists, simultanists, activists and individual anarchists," incapable of providing the official cultural program for the Soviet Republic. Central to this critique was the perceived incomprehensibility of "these Máczas" for worker audiences.[19] Lukács responded to these accusations by distancing himself from the Activists and maintaining that the new government did not promote the aesthetic program of any one group.[20] Although the commissar did not publicly denounce the group, relations between *Ma* and the government began to cool. These disagreements, fuelled by the competition for the power to define new socialist and communist art, came to a head when Béla Kun, the leader of the Hungarian Soviet Republic, publicly chastised *Ma*, labelling its literature a "product of bourgeois decadence."[21] Kassák responded to this charge in his "Letter to Béla Kun in the Name of Art," in which he suggested that the *Ma* group, which had impeccable revolutionary credentials insofar as it had opposed the "imperialist world war," organized for the "proletarian revolution," and "agitat[ed] for Communism" while Kun was still a prisoner of war in Russia, was more competent to make decisions in the sphere of art than "Comrade Kun." Although the Republic ceased to exist before the scandal could be resolved, these events and, specifically, the reinvigorated debate on the relationship of art and politics would cause irreparable internal fissures among the Activists in the years to come.[22]

The collapse of the Hungarian Commune and the repressions that followed launched a wave of leftist immigrants across Europe. Nearby Vienna and Berlin became natural first hubs, for at least some Hungarians, many of whom spoke German. The artists who were involved in the administration of the Soviet Republic generally had an easier time relocating than the political leaders, who were actively sought for retribution by the new conservative government in Hungary. While Kun, who was in danger of extradition and assassination, travelled on from Austria to Soviet Russia, many of the Activists and, with difficulty, Lukács as well, were able to settle temporarily in Vienna.[23] Although cultural histories tend to spotlight major metropolitan centres as destinations for Hungarian political refugees, the ethnically Hungarian peripheries are no less important for understanding the socialist activities of Hungarian émigrés. Out of the public eye, areas like the northern and eastern parts of the Hungarian territories within the former Austro-Hungarian Empire became hotbeds of revolutionary activity and attracted exiles like Mácza for both practical and political reasons.

After fleeing Budapest in 1919, Mácza first returned to his hometown, which by then had become part of the newly formed Czechoslovakia.

There he acquired a Czechoslovak passport, which enabled him to travel on to Vienna and reunite briefly with the Activists. While there he joined the Hungarian Communist Party (KMP) and was instructed to return to his native region, specifically to the town of Kassa or Košice, where the embers of the short-lived Slovak Soviet Republic (16 June–7 July 1919) were still glowing. According to Mácza's autobiography, he was to take part in agitational work and the building of the Czechoslovak Communist Party on Lukács's orders.[24] Arriving on assignment, he joined the editorial board of the daily Hungarian newspaper *Kassai Munkás* (*The Košice Worker*, 1907–37).[25] As editor of the paper's culture and literature section and later its editor-in-chief, Mácza published Hungarian as well as Russian, Czech, Slovak, and German avant-garde texts (among others), which he often translated himself. In 1921 the newspaper became an official organ of the newly created Communist Party of Czechoslovakia (KSČ).[26] In his capacity as editor and translator, Mácza acted as the mediator between cultures and continued to collect valuable materials that later went into the making of his book on the avant-garde.

While working in Košice, Mácza also directed mass performances and May Day demonstrations, inspired, in part, by the Soviet examples on which he reported in *Kassai Munkás*.[27] While the texts performed at these celebrations differed with respect to their style, the emphasis on worker participation remained a constant. For example, Mácza's *May Chorus* (*Májusi kórus*) employed a carefully coordinated chorus of individual and collective voices in a revolutionary musical drama acted out by "around 200 workers" for the 1 May 1922 celebrations in Košice.[28] At this time, Mácza had especially high hopes that such choruses might raise proletarian consciousness and transform workers' lives. As he reflected in his diary, this experience "in the real worker's movement, among the real proletarians," helped him understand the interrelation between "theory and praxis": "how the two complete each other so inseparably I only see now ... Only someone who has taken part in the practice of the movement, who ... personally knows the proletariat ..., can create proletarian culture."[29] Written in 1923, Mácza's diary entry echoes Lukács's contemporaneous defence of the consciousness-raising project in *History and Class Consciousness* (1923), in which the organizational work of the party, including its efforts to bridge the gap between imputed and actual proletarian consciousness, is presented as the revolution's condition of possibility.[30] Although Mácza may have been familiar with Lukács's theoretical assessment when he reflected on the importance of his own experience among the Košice workers, the former commissar's intellectual influence here should not be overestimated. Mácza seems to have arrived at similar conclusions through hands-on agitational work.³¹ The Košice chapter of his life represents the development of his Proletkult ideas regarding the role of the artist as mediator between the party and the proletariat, and, perhaps most importantly, between proletarian content and new artistic forms.³² Through his Proletkult organizational work, Mácza finally came to understand what he had failed to appreciate in Budapest: that different audiences required different forms of agitation and that in order for agitation to succeed among worker audiences, radical new avant-garde forms had to be tempered.

Alongside his editorial and agitational work in Košice, Mácza continued to contribute to *Ma*, which was relaunched in Vienna. In its second phase (1920–5), the journal became even more international and inclusive of different contemporary artistic trends, reflecting Kassák's position on the freedom of art to pursue a variety of different agendas, distinct from those of politics. The very first Vienna issue printed Kassák's bilingual (German/Hungarian) manifesto "To the Artists of All Nations!," which spoke of artists' common tasks beyond any national borders.³³ Soon after, the journal's previous, largely Expressionist idiom was supplemented by Dada and Constructivist forms and content, producing a somewhat surprising hybrid, considering the divergence of artistic strategies and worldviews between these movements.³⁴ Moreover, at this time, *Ma* was seeking to create a synthesis of the arts on its pages – to itself become a "multimedia composition."³⁵ These changes in the journal enabled its readers to keep up with the latest developments on the international art scene, to observe parallels and common trends, and to acquire a synthetic grasp of contemporary culture.

Mácza, who was the journal's Czechoslovak distributor, surely benefited from such comprehensive coverage of cultural trends and the panoramic view of artistic, political, and social life in Europe. Although far from the only source for Mácza, who was connected to the KMP in Vienna and received primary materials directly from the Party, the journal nevertheless played an important role in broadening his knowledge of contemporary art. Mácza went on to partly relay the information he absorbed from *Ma* on the pages of *Kassai Munkás*, as well as in another journal on the Hungarian-speaking periphery, *Napkelet* (*The Orient*), based in Cluj (Kolozsvár). There, no longer confined to the role of theatre critic or theoretician as he was in *Ma*, Mácza published a series of articles between June and September 1921, about an Expressionist exhibition in Košice, the Yugoslav Zenitist movement, and the contemporary artistic situation in Russia, among others. His article on Zenitism, for example, appeared in *Napkelet* just a few months after Boško Tokin's report on the movement in *Ma*. Although it is clear that Mácza used several different sources in his presentation of Zenitism, Kassák's journal remained an important guide for Mácza to contemporary cultural trends.[36] The attempt to reprocess cultural information received from publications such as *Ma* shows how the "little magazines" of the 1910s and the 1920s enabled social mobility within the avant-garde by serving as spaces of informal education and creating cultural commentators out of readers.

During this time Mácza's role in *Ma* underwent a subtle change: the theatre critic began to be featured as a playwright as well. Mácza's dramas were characterized by irreverent Dadaist humour and provocation, in line with *Ma*'s interest in Dadaism. For example, *"The Black Tomcat"* (*A fekete kandur*, 1921) begins with a typical Dadaist insult to the audience:

Ladies, gentlemen
comrades, brothers
I am stone glass steel
The spotlight's beam of light
I: sound and word canvas
Even the stage manager
And: YOU.
Go ahead and laugh!
Idiots, sponge-heads!
parrots and crowbirds
sages artists and those with V.D.
I'll draw the curtains from your eyes
Let me put the nickel in the nickelodeon
Brrr – nyek – poof
Start laughing![37]

The play goes on to parody post-war Europe through a cacophonous chorus of voices, graphically represented by different letters of the alphabet (figure 2.4).

"A," for example, is cast as a Nietzschean madman who stumbles upon the stage with a lantern, looking for God. Although the madman in Mácza's text is demoted from a mythical prophet to a fixer of advertising signs, he nevertheless plays a revolutionary role: he nudges the labourer ("G") with his stick, prompting him into action and tacitly suggesting that he is the new God now. Towards the end of the scene, however, the madman impales the worker, in a less than subtle suggestion of the danger of cooperating with such "prophets." The chaotic image of Europe presented in the play includes syphilitics, as well as antisemites who care only about women and sex. In a parody of the peace negotiations at

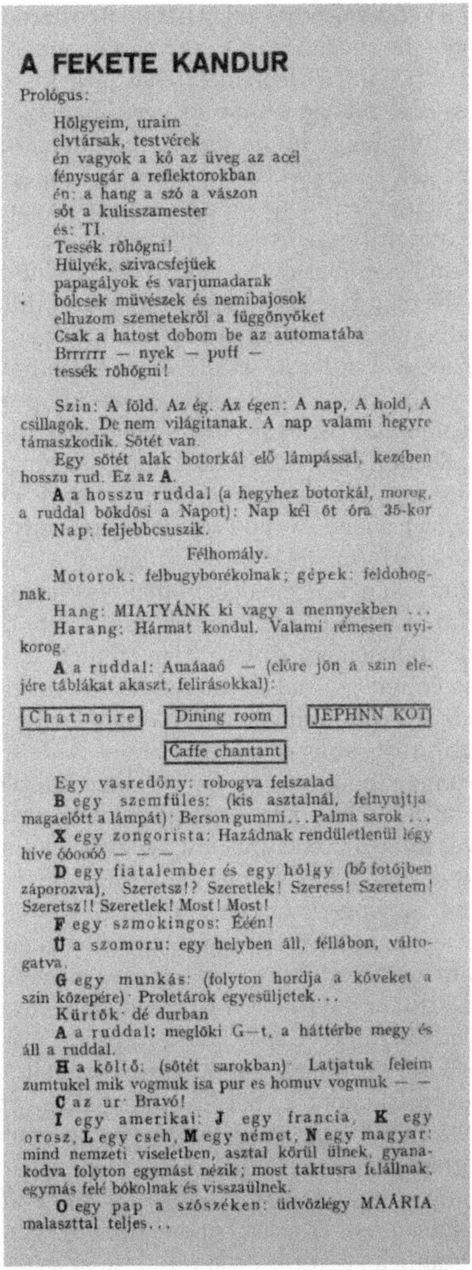

A FEKETE KANDUR

Prológus:

Hölgyeim, uraim
elvtársak, testvérek
én vagyok a kő az üveg az acél
fénysugár a reflektorokban
én: a hang a szó a vászon
sőt a kulisszamester
és: TI
Tessék röhögni!
Hülyék, szivacsfejűek
papagályok és varjumadarak
bölcsek művészek és nemibajosok
elhuzom szemetekről a függönyöket
Csak a hatost dobom be az automatába
Brrrrrr — nyek — puff —
tessék röhögni!

Szin: A föld. Az ég. Az égen: A nap, A hold, A csillagok. De nem világitanak. A nap valami hegyre támaszkodik. Sötét van.
Egy sötét alak botorkál elő lámpással, kezében hosszu rud. Ez az **A**.
A a hosszu ruddal (a hegyhez botorkál, morog, a ruddal bökdösi a Napot): Nap kél öt óra 35-kor
Nap: feljebbcsuszik.

Félhomály.
Motorok: felbugyborékolnak; gépek: feldohognak.
Hang: MIATYÁNK ki vagy a mennyekben...
Harang: Hármat kondul. Valami rémesen nyikorog.
A a ruddal: Auaáaaó — (elöre jön a szin elejére táblákat akaszt, felirásokkal):

| Chatnoire | Dining room | JEPHNN KOT |
| Caffe chantant |

Egy vasredöny: robogva felszalad
B egy szemfüles: (kis asztalnál, felnyujtja magaelött a lámpát) Berson gummi... Palma sarok...
X egy zongorista: Hazádnak rendületlenül légy hive óóoóó — — —
D egy fiatalember és egy hölgy (bő fotójben záporozva), Szeretsz!? Szeretlek! Szeress! Szeretem! Szeretsz!! Szeretlek! Most! Most!
F egy szmokingos: Één!
Ü a szomoru: egy helyben áll, féllábon, váltogatva.
G egy munkás: (folyton hordja a köveket a szin közepére) Proletárok egyesüljetek...
Kürtök: dé durban
A a ruddal: meglöki G—t, a háttérbe megy és áll a ruddal.
H a költő: (sötét sarokban) Latjatuk feleim zumtukel mik vogmuk isa pur es homuv vogmuk — —
C az ur: Bravó!
I egy amerikai: **J** egy francia, **K** egy orosz, **L** egy cseh, **M** egy német, **N** egy magyar: mind nemzeti viseletben, asztal körül ülnek, gyanakodva folyton egymást nézik; most taktusra felállnak, egymás felé bókolnak és visszaülnek.
O egy pap a szószéken: üdvözlégy MAÁRIA malaszttal teljes...

Figure 2.4. János Mácza, a page from "*The Black Tomcat*," published in the magazine *Ma*, 15 September 1921. Private collection.

Versailles, several gentlemen dressed in national costumes pretend to discuss the concept of the sovereign state and end up grabbing at the naked body of a dancer who jumps up on their table. As befits a Dadaist drama, the senselessness of events penetrates its very language, echoing Zurich Dada's critique of language in the service of nationalism and war.[38] In Mácza's play, the gentlemen who hold the fate of Europe in their hands are only capable of uttering clichés in their respective national languages, without any meaningful engagement with one another. The nonsensicality of language and communication is also reflected in the typographic arrangement of the play. The letters that represent the different characters are bolded, creating their own visual poetry on the page. Moreover, the absence of alphabetical order or of any other meaningful organization visually re-creates the senselessness of post-war European politics.

Mácza's appeal to Dadaist forms in his plays may seem incongruous with his Proletkult efforts in Košice and his membership in the KMP, since the Dadaist platform was associated with irreverence, even in regard to leftist politics, which many of the Dadaists personally subscribed to.[39] The place of Dadaist forms in Mácza's agitational strategies should be understood in the context of the debate that was taking place in Hungarian avant-garde circles. In *Ma*, Dadaist forms were initially part of a declaration of the independence of art from politics,[40] but meanwhile, in other Hungarian émigré journals, a different, more politically sharpened position on Dadaism was taking shape. Not unlike the Berlin Dadaists, some Hungarian artists sought to appropriate Dadaist techniques for leftist agitation among bourgeois audiences. For example, Sándor Barta, a poet and editor of the journal *Akasztott Ember* (*Hanged Man*, 1922–3), argued that it was futile to create constructive artworks under capitalism. In his view, rather than cooperating with "this stupid and murderous circus capitalism" or, worse, helping to build it, Western artists should aim to destroy it through satirical Dadaist forms that mercilessly attacked bourgeois culture and institutions and exposed class conflict. The only other legitimate path for the Western artist would be to create agitational art for the proletariat.[41] The Constructivist agenda was simply not an option, since, as Barta's colleague Sándor Bornyik put it, "constructive art can only be an expression of the collectivity that already exists in today's society. This collectivity is the collectivity of large capital ... Constructive art is the corresponding reflection of the organization, economy, and apparent harmony of large capital."[42] Although Barta did not articulate the political significance of Dadaist critique until the fall of 1922, his earlier Dadaist texts anticipate these positions, insofar as they contain bitter attacks on capitalism and bourgeois lifestyle.[43] The presence of Dadaist language and forms in Mácza's dramas from this period suggests that the dramatist, at least for a brief time, partly shared Barta's views.

Mácza's engagement with Dadaist techniques was also bound up with a search for new forms that could express proletarian content. He was adamant that Proletkult work could not unfold in old forms, which for him included naturalistic and psychological theatre, as well as the novel. In "The New Artists and Proletkult," Mácza staked out two positions: first, that artists must engage in Proletkult work alongside artistic projects, and, second, that old bourgeois forms were inadequate for that work. Instead of "repainting" old forms in a "'beautiful' red," new forms would have to be created, he argued.[44] The negotiation of new forms with Proletkult work is evident in his *Composition 2 (for the stage)* (*Kompozició 2 (szinpadra)*), which combines Dadaist chaos with features from worker choruses. In this play, the grotesque, spasmatic movements of the characters (who are designated by numbers rather than letters as before) are combined with instrumental accompaniment, choral speaking, and nonsensical dialogue – which is strung together from advertising slogans, platitudes, and political cries – to create a portrait of bourgeois decadence and workers' naivety. Whereas *"The Black Tomcat"* was a parody of the Versailles peace negotiations and the hypocrisy of its political players, *Composition 2* attacked the capitalist market and its fluctuations, which beckon with false promises.[45] As the play's hybrid form suggests, Mácza did not necessarily see Proletkult and artistic work as mutually exclusive; here they join forces to raise proletarian consciousness and combat the bourgeois way of life, which distracts from the revolution with its material comforts and its false promises that change is just around the corner.

Shortly before the publication of *Composition 2*, Mácza ceased to be *Ma*'s Czechoslovak distributor – a subtle indication of his departure from Košice and, more importantly, of his growing ideological differences with Kassák, whose domineering and preacherly tone had by then alienated many former Activists.[46] By the fall of 1922, the *Ma* circle was rife with conflict. In a diary entry dated October 1922, Mácza criticized Kassák and the *Ma* group for their "swing to the right" and their refusal to come off of "art's high mountain." He emphasized their indifference to agitational work, linking it to their desire to "tear themselves away from the transitional period" and their "ostrich politics." Such a position, he maintained, was "anti-Marxist."[47]

The Activists' polemics with one another unfolded not only in private diaries but also on the pages of their periodicals, such as the aforementioned *Akasztott Ember*, which was launched in November 1922.[48] After a failed attempt to found the journal *Kritika* (*Critique*) with Sándor Bortnyik in 1922 – a journal that would have participated in the creation of a "revolutionary culture movement" and "broaden[ed]" existing "Proletkult plans" – Mácza settled for a collaboration with Barta and the artist Béla Uitz on the journal Ék. *Az egyetemes kultúra orgánuma* (*Wedge: Forum of Universal Culture*, 1923–4), which featured "revolutionary" and "proletarian" content.[49] Mácza conceived of this editorial work within the framework of the Proletkult movement, which for him referred less to the development of proletarian culture by the proletariat and more to the role of the artist-intellectual (who could be of proletarian origins) in helping the development of proletarian culture within the boundaries defined by the Communist Party.[50] Thus, "critique" – broadly understood to include "theory" as well as "poetry and pictures" – played a major role in his Proletkult plans.[51] *Ék*, which partially realized Mácza's hopes for *Kritika*, would be his last project as part of the Hungarian avant-garde. In a diary entry from January 1923, Mácza noted his frustration with his co-editor Barta, whose journal *Akasztott Ember* Mácza now dismissed as "naïve and largely apolitical." While at this stage he still hoped to make *Ék* into "a good revolutionary and a good proletarian journal," by May 1923 his patience would run out.[52] His next diary entry was titled "To Russia."

With his political hopes frustrated, and increasingly exhausted by economic difficulties, the persecution of the left, and his inability to participate in the building of a socialist state, Mácza began looking to Soviet Russia as a possible solution to the challenges he faced. His dreams of a new home were further inspired by Hungarian avant-garde periodicals that published attractive reviews of the political and artistic situation there. Enthusiastic accounts of a polymorphic utopia, such as the one written by Béla Uitz following his attendance of the Third Comintern Congress in 1921, no doubt acted as a powerful catalyst for the migration of the Hungarian left to the East:

> Moscow opens up for the whole world. There is an unstoppable flood of people ... They came and came – all the peoples of Europe, Asia, Africa, America, Australia. The just came and the scoundrels, believers and those without Christ, idealists and materialists, humanists, syndicalists, anarchists, and communists. Every school of thought on earth, represented by "its very best"! Small-mindedness was not a viable option here. A spiritual storm was heading this way, such as the world has hardly ever seen before.[53]

Along with accounts of "new Russian art," its radical experiments and elevated function in society, these enchanting images of multicultural and pluralistic Moscow attracted even those artists and intellectuals who had initially fled Hungary for Vienna and Berlin.[54] The appeal

Transnational Theory of the Avant-garde 103

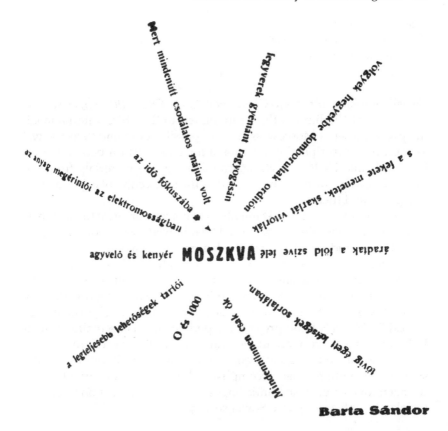

Figure 2.5. Sándor Barta, image poem from "Crystal of Time: Moscow," in *Ék* (1923). Private collection.

held by Moscow is perhaps best represented by Barta's image poem from "Crystal of Time: Moscow," published in *Ék* in May 1923 (figure 2.5):

'Cause it was wonderful May far and wide
Weapons' diamond-like brilliance
Valleys swelled up to the mountains roaringly
And black processions, scarlet sails
rose toward the heart of the earth
[all] doubts burned to the root in a row.
From all sides only they
0 and 1000
holders of the fullest possibilities

brain and bread
the touch of matter in electricity
into the focus of time
→ MOSCOW

Visually evoking Tommaso Campanella's *The City of the Sun*, as well as the spirals of Vladimir Tatlin's Monument to the Third International, the poem presents Moscow as full of "possibilities" and "electricity," as exerting a centripetal gravitational force not just on people but on historical time itself.[55] In Hungarian avant-garde materials from the mid-1920s, Moscow is often depicted as the new centre of experimental living, art, and theory.

Mácza was among the first members of his former circle to move permanently to Soviet Russia; he would be followed by Sándor Barta, Erzsébet Újvári, and Béla Uitz. Shortly before his departure, he described his decision as follows: "My decision to go to Russia has two impulses, besides economic reasons: the first is that 'I long for a home' and I think I can find this 'home' in Soviet Russia ... The second is that my book on Russian literature will not be good enough ... if I write it from abroad."[56] Mácza's book project was perhaps his last remaining intellectual tie to Kassák, who, in his evaluation of the successful October Revolution, attributed great significance to Russian literature and the spiritual revolution it had accomplished before the proletariat became the agent of change.[57] Romantic hopes aside, Mácza went on to outline his plan for integrating into Soviet society:

> For half a year minimum ... I will work in something chemical, in a pharmaceutical plant. During this time 1) I will improve my language skills to such an extent that I will be able to write simpler things; 2) get to know the Russian worker, the Russian people; 3) get to know the conditions; and 4) begin the search for literary connections. Only then and only with such preparation will I begin to be plugged in to ideological life. In the meantime, of course, I will constantly study Marxism and read helpful materials for literary history.[58]

His next diary entry, dated 10 June 1923, offered his first impressions of Moscow.[59] After working in a pharmacy for half a year, Mácza soon found himself propelled into Soviet cultural life.[60] After a few artistic attempts at experimental prose and even a propaganda film script, as well as an effort to become a reporter on Russian life for the West, Mácza turned to writing about what he knew intimately as a first-hand witness and participant: the European avant-garde.[61]

Artistic Praxis and the Marxist Method in Mácza's Theory of the Avant-Garde

The Art of Contemporary Europe (1926) was Mácza's first book published in Russian after he relocated to the Soviet Union in 1923.[62] Although this slim anthology of 150 pages uses the term "avant-garde" only once, it nevertheless focuses on movements that today are associated with the historical avant-garde, from Futurism to Dadaism and Constructivism (figure 2.6). Mácza's preferred umbrella term is "revolutionary" or "new" art and literature, which he uses in reference to the "last twenty years" of art "in the West," that is, roughly from 1906 to 1926 and spanning Western, Central, and Southeastern Europe.[63] As I argue in this section, the book is a unique intellectual product of the confluence of two diverse bodies of knowledge: avant-garde praxis and the developing Marxist theory of culture, both set in motion by Mácza's red migrations.

The Art of Contemporary Europe is informed by Mácza's first-hand experience with the avant-garde, specifically, his involvement in Hungarian periodical culture. The book, however, is not merely a descriptive-encyclopedic survey of the avant-garde, nor is it an attempt to reconstruct the genetic lineage of avant-garde movements. First and foremost, it presents a *theory* that unites these movements into a coherent whole. What distinguishes theory from avant-garde diagrams and anthologies is the attempt to conceptualize a unity behind the surface heterogeneity of artistic forms and movements. Moreover, as I show below, Mácza's understanding of the underlying unity of the avant-garde is based on neither positive nor negative influences, that is, neither on straightforward borrowing nor on the rejection of the predecessors' values. Rather, his proposed unity of "new art" in the "West" hinges on Europe's transition towards the "last stage of large capital" around the time of the First World War.[64] In Mácza's view, it is this transition, with all of its accompanying social-psychic developments, that produced the remarkable variety of -isms in the first decades of the twentieth century and unites them as a single phenomenon.[65] This theory, I argue, derives from Mácza's attempt to work out the "Marxist method" of cultural analysis on the basis of avant-garde art, a project that materialized as a result of Mácza's migration and interaction with the intellectual atmosphere of Soviet Russia in the 1920s.

Among the book's precursors and possible sources are the avant-garde anthologies *The Book of New Artists* (*Buch neuer Künstler*, 1922) and *Artisms* (*Kunstismen*, 1925), each of which, in its own way, attempted to catalogue and systematize the new artistic movements.[66] Like Barr's and Marinetti's more explicit diagrams, these early avant-garde anthologies

Figure 2.6. János Mácza, "The Interrelationship of Schools in New Art and New Literature." Diagram from *The Art of Contemporary Europe* (1926). Private collection. The movements across the top, from left to right, are "Cubism 1908," "Simultanism 1914," "Expressionism 1912," and "Futurism 1907." Below Cubism, from top to bottom, are "Glass Architecture 1916," "Picture Architecture," "Purist Aesthetics 1921," "Machine Aesthetics 1921," and "Constructivism 1921." Below from Expressionism are "Neo-Primitivism 1913," "Activism 1915," "Zenitism 1919," "Dadaism 1921," and "Haptism 1922," which joins with "Tactilism 1921" below Futurism.

reflected a genealogical conception of the unity of different -isms.[67] By contrast, Mácza's book theorizes the unity of European avant-garde art across geographic and media borders on the basis of a shared historical moment. As shown in figure 2.8, this moment was marked by the development of large capital, which led to rapid evolution in the means of production, the centralization of capital, and the heightening of class contradictions. The multiplicity of avant-garde -isms is explained by the variety of reactions of the petit-bourgeois psyche to these developments. Describing the artistic developments of the 1910s in general terms, Mácza argues that the development of capitalist production, with its dehumanizing effects, created the *dissatisfied* bourgeois individual. It is this development that found expression in new art and literature as the "struggle for the human being" and later for the "universal" human being who "combines in himself, besides the idealistic metaphysics of bourgeois 'renaissance,' the centralist tendency of developing trust capital and the technicism of capitalist production."[68] All "new art and literature" is characterized by this tendency, which distinguishes it from its predecessors, Impressionism, Decadence, and Symbolism, as expressions of a "*satisfied* bourgeois individuum."[69]

Italian Futurism, dated to 1907 in figure 2.6, is presented as a point of departure for "new art," not because it was the first to discover new forms or present a new worldview, but because it is the expression of an "active, dissatisfied bourgeois psyche."[70] Futurism viewed old forms as incapable of capturing the new "dynamic" life and sought to "destroy the narrowness of old form" in direct response to the "multiplication and acceleration of movement" in capitalist production.[71] In Mácza's view, Futurism provided a critique of the past and its forms but was unable to break with its most important legacy – idealism and metaphysics – and simply exchanged "beauty" for the equally abstract "ideal" of "physical movement."[72] He concludes that "the Futurist movement is put forth by the contemporary social force of capitalist production on the basis of a petit-bourgeois metaphysical worldview."[73]

Simultanism developed in a similar way to Futurism, but instead of responding to changes in "industrial production," it reacted to the technological developments driven by the global expansion of trade and the resulting "narrowing of space and time."[74] Expressionism, in contrast to Futurism and Simultanism, did not view these technological developments as positive, instead rejecting the "material forces of capitalist society," most radically, in its offshoot, Neo-Primitivism.[75] Although the Expressionist form, ideology, and worldview differed radically from those of Futurism and Simultanism, all three movements were in fact defined by the same material-economic developments and therefore belong together.

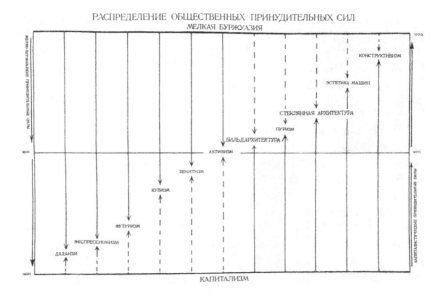

Figure 2.7. János Mácza, "The Distribution of Coercive Social Forces." Diagram from *The Art of Contemporary Europe* (1926). Private collection. The top x-axis is marked "Petit-bourgeois" and the bottom "Capitalism." The left y-axis, with arrows pointing downward, is marked "Petit-bourgeois coercive forces," and the right y-axis, with arrows pointing up, reads "Capitalist coercive forces." Arrayed across the centre from bottom left are "Dadaism," "Expressionism," "Futurism," "Cubism," "Zenitism," "Activism," "Picture Architecture," "Purism," "Glass Architecture," "Machine Aesthetics," and "Constructivism."

In Mácza's theory of the avant-garde, the First World War acted as a kind of watershed, for it made the incompatibility of the interests of the petite bourgeoisie and the capitalists impossible to ignore, laying bare class contradictions.[76] The "Imperialist war" pushed art either in the direction of "petit-bourgeois restoration," which Mácza sees in Italian Futurism's and Dada's turn to fascism, or in the direction of joining "large imperialist capital," which he observes in (International) Constructivism and its willingness to participate in the industrial production of capitalist society.[77] As his graphic indicates (figure 2.7), these directions are not absolutes, but rather occupy a sliding scale.

In this diagram, the petit-bourgeois forces act most strongly on Dadaism and most weakly on Constructivism, which embraces large capital under the pressures of the last stage of capitalism. Despite the apparent differences in reactions and ideologies, these -isms constitute a unity because they are products of the same socio-economic developments.

After presenting overviews of the different movements in his first two chapters, Mácza tries to relate each of them to the dialectical interaction between the material-economic base and social-psychic forces that characterize this stage of capitalism. However, the underlying unity of these movements is conveyed more powerfully in Mácza's diagrams than in his text.[78]

As figure 2.8 illustrates, each contemporary -ism can be linked to the "material forces of society," such as private property, steam, electricity, and so on, along the top axis, as well as to "psychic forces of society" along the bottom axis. The two-dimensionality of the graphic form allows Mácza to convey a simultaneity of movements that communicates a sense of their unity on both visual and semantic levels. Moreover, the diagram carries the promise of dialectical interaction between the top and bottom axes. As viewers study the diagram, it is as if the dotted lines transform into live animation, connecting the different movements to different forces and bringing the multiplicity of the avant-garde into play. Similar tensions and dialectics define Mácza's graphic representation of "The Origins of Activism" (figure 2.9), in which the various material and ideological forces informing the emergence of Activism and Zenitism must be animated by the viewer in a continuous circuit-like flow. In this sense, Mácza's diagrams capture his proposed theory of the avant-garde even better than his text.

In his introduction to Mácza's book, the Marxist literary and art historian Vladimir Friche, whose development of Marxist cultural sociology influenced Mácza's methodology, points out that it is thanks to the "impeccable application" of the "Marxist method" that the coherence behind the different -isms comes to the fore in the study. Although Friche exaggerates the stability of the Marxist method at the time (he himself vied to define that method in the 1920s), it is hard to disagree with his claim that "in light of this method, the initially chaotic picture of contemporary artistic condition and development in the West gains orderliness [*stroinost*], internal logic."[79] The variegated forms, politics, and worldviews of the different -isms do not get in the way of conceptualizing their unity, and the superficial parallels between them are not theorized as the source of the unity. Mácza's theory thus circumvents the obvious problem with the formalist approaches that continued to define avant-garde studies long after his book: that continuity of form is an abstract criterion, not a historical one, and, for this reason, is not a reliable factor in theorizing unity.[80] Mácza's conceptualization of the unity also avoids the traps of genealogical models, which, bound up as they are with the question of primacy, often end up excluding developments that arose later and dismissing them as secondary, imitative, and

Figure 2.8. János Mácza, "The Social Origins of New Art and Literature." Diagram from *The Art of Contemporary Europe* (1926). Private labels translated.

irrelevant. Needless to say, such models have been the primary means of reinforcing Western cultural hegemony in studies of modernism and beyond. Finally, Mácza's theory also bypasses the pitfalls of networks, which, although they decentralize influence by positing a multidirectional process of exchange, nevertheless preserve the importance of individual artist-creators (or artworks, or publications) as nodes in the network and thereby implicitly treat art as a development somewhat independent of the socio-economic sphere. In other words, they tend to distort the importance of individual agency of people and things by isolating them from other processes. Beyond avoiding such methodological traps, Mácza's depersonalized approach in *The Art of Contemporary Europe* offers specific comparative advantages.[81]

The book's scope is remarkable in its internationality and interdisciplinarity. Unlike what is often cited as the first comparative study of the avant-garde, Guillermo de Torre's *European Literatures of the Vanguard* (*Literaturas europeas de vanguardia*, 1925), *The Art of Contemporary Europe* does not privilege Romance languages and Western culture (as it is understood today), and it accords significant space to artists from Central and Southeastern Europe.[82] Mácza outlines artistic developments not only in France, Italy, and Germany but also in Hungary,

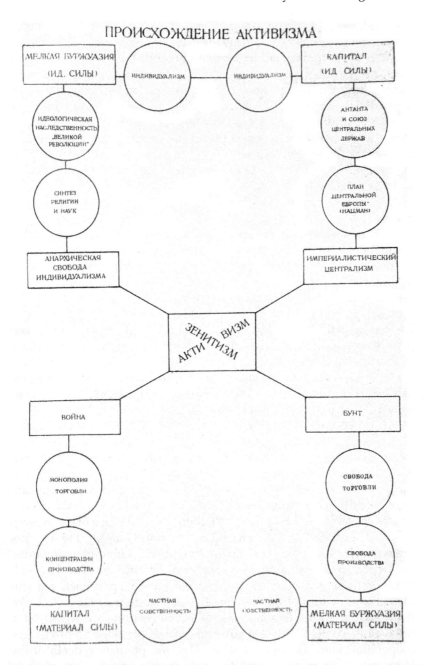

Figure 2.9. János Mácza, "The Origins of Activism." Diagram from *The Art of Contemporary Europe* (1926). Private collection.

Czechoslovakia, and Yugoslavia. The inclusion of these avant-gardes in Mácza's theory is noteworthy, for even contemporary art historical and literary narratives fail to take into account the artistic cultures of Europe's "peripheries" or "close other."[83] The avant-gardes of Central and Southeastern Europe are discussed in detail in the book; moreover, their artistic production is not treated as an epiphenomenon – that is, as a confused and imperfect imitation of artistic centres like Paris. Rather, they appear as progressive and promising examples of revolutionary art that strives to use culture as a tool for building proletarian consciousness, necessary for a successful and – in light of the several failed socialist uprisings in the region – *lasting* political revolution.

Furthermore, rather than fetishizing the uniqueness of Central and Southeastern Europe as a special site of cultural exchanges, Mácza treats it simply as part of "contemporary Europe," made one by the economic conditions of capitalism.[84] When movements are implicitly assigned greater historical significance, it is not because they were first to discover an art form or an idea, but because of the complexity of their development in relation to socio-economic and historical factors. A case in point is Mácza's evaluation of Activism, which appears at the very centre of the diagram in figure 2.7, as if perfectly balanced between petit-bourgeois and capitalist forces, which reached the height of their contradictions during the First World War.

Mácza explains that although the origins of Activism lie in Germany, its German incarnation is a less interesting example than the Hungarian variant, in part because the former's "politicization of art" ultimately failed "the test of the revolution."[85] Despite the relative "insignificance" of "Hungary and the Hungarian language," the Hungarian case provides "the best example of Activism" because it has "survived two revolutions," a "counterrevolution," and "white terror" – in short, it underwent "all possible stages of development."[86] According to Mácza's account, prior to 1918, pacifist and anarchist positions characterized the group, which rejected old forms and saw "literature as the engine of social progress."[87] After the Chrysanthemum Revolution in Hungary, the Activists came to accept that the "proletarian revolution," rather than literature, "is the most direct route to liberation of humanity." In 1919 they welcomed the Hungarian Soviet Republic and earned a prominent place in the cultural politics of the new regime. Mácza goes so far as to claim that had the Soviet Republic lasted, Activism probably would have resolved its conflicts with the government and developed a productive cooperation with the socialist state. Alas, the premature death of the Hungarian Commune stunted the movement's growth. According to his assessment, the emigration of the Activists marked the beginning of the "fall" of the movement.⁸⁸ Echoing his 1922 diary entry, Mácza claims that Activism swung "to the right" and, as a result, began to fracture.⁸⁹ Out of this fracture emerged the strand of Hungarian Activism that Mácza finds the most productive: "the left, communist wing," represented by the journal *Ék*, and the agitational art of Béla Uitz, Sándor Barta, and Aldár Komját.⁹⁰ Not surprisingly, this strand coincides with Mácza's own position before his departure for Russia. As the example of Hungarian Activism shows, the importance of a movement in his Marxist cultural theory of the avant-garde is judged not by the novelty of form or the ideological message, but rather by the complexity of its development and its reactions to the social and political conditions of its time.

Mácza's book is also distinguished by its broad interdisciplinary scope. Unlike Torre's study, it covers developments not only in literature and the visual arts but also in architecture, theatre, and music.⁹¹ Mácza's "synthetic" approach to culture is more clearly accomplished in the first two chapters, where developments in the visual arts and literature are pursued in a directly comparative perspective and treated as an inseparable whole.⁹² Although at first sight the broad interdisciplinary scope of the book may appear to be an inheritance from nineteenth-century aesthetics, Mácza's study represents a conscious reintegration of different artistic fields after their initial separation into more specialized disciplines.⁹³ Mácza eschews "aesthetic judgment," "creative activity," "artistic cognition," and the like – concepts that characterized many turn-of-the-century aesthetics and motivated their interdisciplinarity; instead, his synthetic approach to the arts is founded on a Marxist understanding of the historical stages of economic development, mainly the "transitional epoch" or the last stage of large capital, which unites the cultural field into a single whole.⁹⁴

Finally, Mácza's theory is noteworthy because of the conclusions it draws about the relative usefulness of avant-garde methods and forms in building a new socialist society, as well as its covert defence of the avant-garde experiment. Its significance is perhaps best appreciated through reference to the "Expressionist debates" that unfolded in Moscow almost ten years after the publication of *The Art of Contemporary Europe*. The central figure in these debates was none other than Lukács, who returned to cultural criticism after years of political theoretical work. By contrast with Lukács, who rejected the avant-garde under the banner of Expressionism for its supposed links with fascism and who initiated one of the great twentieth-century intellectual debates about the legacy of modernism, Mácza staked out a more nuanced position.⁹⁵ First, linked as it was to the historical situation of the 1920s, *The Art of Contemporary Europe* maintained that only certain avant-garde movements were connected to fascism, mainly, Italian Futurism and Dadaism. More importantly, whereas Lukács attacked avant-garde "methods" at the time of the intellectual witch-hunts of the 1930s on the basis of their apparent inadequacy in capturing the totality of the fragmented capitalist existence, Mácza argued that the significance of avant-garde "forms and methods" must be evaluated "dialectically" and "understood and mastered" (*okhvatit' i osvoit'*) by the proletariat, much like any other cultural forms of the past.[96] Mácza contended that since avant-garde methods "were put forth by production forms closest to us" and, for this reason, "correspond to the dynamic character of the epoch," which "demands new forms of expression," it was all the more urgent for the proletariat to appropriate them for their own purposes.[97] Mácza's defence of the avant-garde in his book was not without reservations; however, his insistence that these methods must be "tested on our own practice" in order to understand the "dialectical significance" of their results, was noteworthy amidst mounting attacks on experimental art. He concludes the book by insisting: "... only practice can show us the relationship of the accomplishments of new art and literature to our reality. And our reality, the reality of Western proletariat is class struggle, the preparation of wide proletarian masses for the coming revolution, a way to the dictatorship of the proletariat."[98] By pointing to the possible revolutionary significance of these forms, Mácza seems to at least partly invoke his earlier position on the significance of Activist agitational methods.

Red Nomadism and Knowledge Production

From Mácza's diary, as well as his initial attempts to involve himself in cultural production as an artist upon his arrival, it seems that he did not set out for Soviet Russia with the intention of becoming involved in the development of the Marxist method for studying culture. Yet, as a cultural practitioner and political agitator from the West, moreover, one who was able to function in Russian, unlike so many other revolutionary migrants, he was pulled precisely into this sphere of activity with his *The Art of Contemporary Europe*. The book was instrumental in launching his academic career and propelling him into the ranks of intellectuals who would develop the new Marxist method of *iskusstvoznanie* (art studies) within the walls of the Communist Academy, and eventually of experts in architecture and Marxist-Leninist aesthetics.[99] Perhaps the credibility he established over the course of the 1920s, coupled with his dissociation from the Hungarian émigré community and willingness to admit his "mistakes," helped him survive the Stalinist purges of the 1930s as well as attacks on Jewish cosmopolitanism after the war, while so many of his compatriots and former colleagues perished in the Stalinist camps.[100]

As I have tried to show in this chapter, the theory of the avant-garde advanced in *The Art of Contemporary Europe* is a product of the interaction between artistic developments in Central and Eastern Europe and emerging methodologies of Marxist cultural analysis from Soviet Russia. Put otherwise, Mácza's innovative transnational and interdisciplinary theory of the avant-garde is the result of a cultural exchange made possible by red migrations. While Mácza could have produced a survey, an anthology, even a genealogy of the European avant-garde prior to his emigration, a *theory* of the avant-garde, guided by a particular conception of its unity, would not have been possible without the Marxist method. Moreover, although Mácza was interested in Marxist approaches to culture before he departed for Russia, the methodology that defines his book was developed collectively with leading Soviet theoreticians in Moscow, the city of the sun and of electrifying possibilities, to return to Sándor Barta's poetic imagery.

The conditions of exile and displacement continue to overwhelmingly define scholarship that addresses the movement of agents in the first decades of the twentieth century in Central and Eastern Europe, including Russia. Yet these categories do not fully capture the experience of migration in the region, homogenizing them and casting them in a traumatic light. The experience of dislocation and exile has long defined the intellectual history of literary and critical theory in particular, linked as it is to the interwar period. In his essay "Travelling Theory," for example, Edward Said connected Lukács's influential theory of reification to his experience of dislocation after the failed experiment of the Hungarian Commune.[101] The philosopher's forced retainment in the Soviet Union in the 1930s is another moment in his biography that is often highlighted to explain the twists and turns in his theoretical output – specifically, the marginalization of his contribution to Marxist political praxis and his displacement into the sphere of cultural critique. Lukács's experience can be supplemented by countless displacements related to the Second World War that led to theoretical breakthroughs in the study of culture: Erich Auerbach writing his footnote-less *Mimesis* in Istanbul, and René Wellek founding the discipline of comparative literature in the US, among many others.

While the exilic conditions and coerced relocation hold true in relation to Mácza's departure from Hungary in 1919, the complex choreography of his movements can hardly be accounted for through the lens of exile alone. The complexity of the attending psychic state is well captured by Mácza's former colleague Béla Balázs:

> The question is this: have I been exiled when I ran abroad, or have I arrived home? … The "aura of the far-away," the feeling of foreignness gnawed at me already in my childhood like some kind of reversed home-sickness … From the Hungarian foreignness where I was not understood and was scorned as a stranger I have, by all means, come home to be among people who understand and recognize me instantly. Still, what hurts?[102]

But while Balázs frames his emigration as a kind of homelessness, Mácza's complex movements and hybrid entanglements gesture towards a deliberate embrace of nomadic existence. Throughout his life, Mácza migrated between countries, cultures, languages, and disciplines, embodying Rosi Braidotti's "nomadic subjectivity" – the non-commitment to a static individual identity, whatever shape or form it may take; the abandonment of the "desire for fixity." Rather than a "disembedded marginalized exile," Mácza, a "polyglot nomadic intellectual," occupied "an identity made of transitions," the position of "active nomadism."[103] In this sense, although the former Hungarian Activist distanced himself from his radical experimental past, he remained loyal to the idea of a permanent revolution of the mind, anticipating the next step in the march of history at each stage in his life, as is fitting for the original meaning of the *avant garde*.

Acknowledgments

The author would like to thank Erzsébet Jancsikity, who provided invaluable guidance to the Mácza archive in Budapest; the editors of this volume, the participants of the "Red Migrations" seminar, and Oliver Botar for their feedback at different stages of the article's composition; and the avant-garde research group at the Kassák Museum for cultivating my appreciation of the Hungarian avant-garde.

Notes

1 Alfred H. Barr Jr., *Cubism and Abstract Art* (New York: Museum of Modern Art, 1936).
2 Francis Picabia, "Dada Movement," *Dada*, nos. 4–5 (May 1919), and "Construction Molèculaire," *391*, no. 8 (February 1919). By contrast with Barr's and Marinetti's, Picabia's diagrams rely more on specific artists' names;

however, the different degrees of abstraction in each do not make them conceptually different. For earlier drafts of Barr's diagram, which contained more artists' names, see Manuel Fontán del Junco, "The Diagrammatic Eye and the Curatorial Imagination," in *The Genealogies of Art or the History of Art as Visual Art* (Madrid: Fundación Juan March, 2019), 20–3.

3 MoMA, "Inventing Abstraction, 1910–1925," Moma.org, 2013, https://www.moma.org/interactives/exhibitions/2012/inventingabstraction/?page=connections.

4 For example, without intending to reference specific locations, MoMA's network graphic ends up reproducing geographies that place Western Europe at the centre of artistic creation. Although specific geographical references are absent in the graphic, the artists are nevertheless distributed in accordance with the geographic locations they occupied when they began experimenting with abstraction. For example, Natalia Goncharova and Mikhail Larionov are placed on the far right, suggesting that they are in Russia; Vasily Kandinsky appears in the centre, as if in Germany; and the American artists are grouped together on the very left. The graphic also highlights the artists with the most connections in red. Almost all of them are in the centre, in the implicit place of Western Europe. Thus, although a Western bias is ostensibly absent in this graphic, which aims to reveal multidirectional exchanges, it nevertheless reasserts itself and reaffirms existing artistic canons.

5 Popularized in avant-garde studies by Hubert van den Berg, the network continues to inform secondary scholarship on the subject, including exhibition concepts. Hubert Van den Berg, "Mapping Old Traces of the New: Towards a Historical Topography of Early Twentieth-Century Avant-Garde(s) in the European Cultural Field(s)," *Arcadia* 41, no. 2 (2006): 331–49. The recent exhibition *Surrealism beyond Borders* (Metropolitan Museum of Art, New York, 2021–2), for instance, makes use of the notion of an international artistic network.

6 Ivan Matsa, *Iskusstvo sovremennoi Evropy* (Moscow: Gosudarstvennoe izdatel'stvo, 1926). Aside from citations, throughout the article I use the original Hungarian spelling of Mácza's name rather than the transliteration from the Russian. Unless otherwise noted, the translations from Hungarian and Russian in this article are my own.

7 Peter Bürger, *Theory of the Avant-Garde* (1974), trans. Michael Shaw (Minneapolis: University of Minnesota Press, 1984); Renato Poggioli, *The Theory of the Avant-Garde* (1962), trans. Gerald Fitzgerald (Cambridge: Harvard University Press, 1968).

8 In framing Mácza's subjectivity as nomadic, I am invoking Rosi Braidotti's shifting articulations of the "nomadic subject," especially in *Nomadic Subjects: Embodiment and Sexual Difference in Contemporary Feminist Theory* [1994] (New York: Columbia University Press, 2011), 21–66. "Nomadic" here does not refer to physical movement (although it does not exclude it), but

rather to changeability and fluidity of the self: "nomadism ... refers to the kind of critical consciousness that resists settling into socially coded modes of thought and behavior ... Consciousness-raising and the subversion of set conventions define the nomadic state, not the literal act of travelling" (26). For Braidotti, the formation of a nomadic subject is intimately linked with polyglotism, to not having "a mother tongue, only a succession of translations, of displacements, of adaptations to changing conditions" (21). Following Braidotti, I argue that Mácza's existence and "transit between the languages" is linked to his "skepticism about steady identities" and the resulting mobility of his thought (39). See also Braidotti, *Transpositions: On Nomadic Ethics* (Cambridge: Polity Press, 2006), 4, and "Writing as a Nomadic Subject," *Comparative Critical Studies* 11, no. 2–3 (2014), 163–84, esp. 167–9. While the transnational aspect of Mácza's subjectivity shares features with both the projected supranationality of communism and the avant-garde's *Übernationalität*, I am interested in subject mobility with respect to a number of other identity categories; hence, my preference for the term "nomadic subjectivity."

9 Galin Tihanov, "Cosmopolitans without a Polis: Towards a Hermeneutics of the East-East Exilic Experience (1929–1945)," in *The Exile and Return of Writers from East-Central Europe*, ed. John Neubauer and Borbála Zsuzsanna Török (Berlin: Walter de Gruyter, 2009), 128–9.

10 Lajos Kassák's "Programm," published in *A Tett*, no. 10 (March 1916), is often considered to be the founding manifesto of the Hungarian avant-garde. Translated in *Between Worlds: A Sourcebook of Central European Avant-Gardes, 1910–1930*, ed. Timothy O. Benson and Éva Forgács (Cambridge: MIT Press, 2002), 160–1. Depending on one's definition of the avant-garde and its relationship to modernism, *A Nyolcak (The Eight)*, who preceded Kassák's statement, can be considered the first avant-garde group in Hungary. On the latter group, see Krisztina Passuth, *A Nyolcak festézete* (Budapest: Cornivina, 1967); "The International Connections of the Eight and the Activists" in *The Hungarian Avant-Garde: The Eight and the Activists* (London: Hayward Gallery, 1980), 19–27; S.A. Mansbach, *Modern Art in Eastern Europe: From the Baltic to the Balkans, ca. 1890–1939* (Cambridge: Cambridge University Press, 1999), 272–6; and Timothy Benson, ed., *Central European Avant-Gardes: Exchange and Transformation, 1910–1930* (Los Angeles: Los Angeles County Museum of Art, 2002), 145, 149.

11 The subtitle was added in the journal's second year of existence. As Éva Forgács and Tyrus Miller note, Kassák's journal was modelled on Franz Pfemfert's *Die Aktion* (1911–32) and drew much of its information on current artistic trends from the German publication. Éva Forgács and Tyrus Miller, "The Avant-Garde in Budapest and in Exile in Vienna: *A Tett* (1915–16), *Ma* (Budapest 1916–19; Vienna 1920–6), *Egység* (1922–4), *Akasztott Ember* (1922), *2x2* (1922), *Ék* (1923–4), *Is* (1924), *365* (1925), *Dokumentum* (1926–7), and *Munka* (1928–39)," in *The Oxford Critical and Cultural History of Modernist*

Magazines, Vol. 3: *Europe, 1880–1940* (Oxford: Oxford University Press, 2013), 1128–9. See also Éva Forgács, "In the Vacuum of Exile: The Hungarian Activists in Vienna 1919–1926," in *The Exile and Return*, 113–14.

12 *A Tett* was closed in 1916 due to its pacifist and internationalist stance. Specifically, the journal was banned after the release of an international issue, which included translations of French, Russian, and other authors from Allied countries. See Forgács and Miller, "The Avant-Garde in Budapest," 1131.

13 For instance, see the "international" issue of *Ma* 3, no. 12 (December 1918). In this issue, the journal's title is printed in red and illustrated by Sándor Bortnyik's Expressionist linocut "Red Flag" on the cover. The subtitle of the linocut reads: "The state is enslaved to labor. When work is free, the state will wither away." The contents of the journal also point left: Kassák prints an article on Bolshevism by Georgii Chicherin, as well as his own programmatic essay "Onward on Our Way," which calls for the creation of "communist art alongside the communist economic system." See translation of the latter text in *Between Worlds*, 171–3. Despite the presence of Marxist rhetoric, however, the journal's overall position was probably closer to anarcho-communism.

14 Mácza published drama reviews in every *Ma* issue in 1917 and in most issues from 1918.

15 Mácza, "Életrajzom" (Biography), in *Legendák és tények* (Legends and Facts) (Budapest: Corvina kiadó, 1972), 6.

16 For example, see Lukács's directive to Kassák to organize propaganda performances and the poet's response, appointing Mácza to the task. Both reprinted in Ferenc Csaplár, *Magam törvénye szerint* (According to My Own Law) (Budapest: Petőfi Irodalmi Múzeum, 1987), 152. On renaming of the group, see Oliver Botar, "From the Avant-Garde to 'Proletarian Art'. The Émigré Hungarian Journals *Egység* and *Akasztott Ember*, 1922–23," *Art Journal* 52, no. 1 (Spring 1993): 44, 36. See also Kassák on the Activist platform, "Aktivizmus," *Ma* 4, no. 4 (April 1919), 46–51; translated in Esther Levinger, *The Structurist* 25 (1985–6), 85–6.

17 Lajos Kassák, *Egy ember élete II* (A Man's Life) (Budapest: Magvető, 1983 [1928–32]), 513. For more on this particular performance, as well as on the attempts of the Hungarian avant-garde to reach working-class audiences, see Sára Bagdi and Judit Galácz, "Green Donkey Theatre. A Case Study on Theatrical Innovations in the Name of Dadaism," in *Cannibalizing the Canon: Dada Techniques in East-Central Europe*, ed. Oliver A.I. Botar, Irina Denischenko, Gábor Dobó, and Merse Pál Szeredi (Leiden: Brill, 2024).

18 Csaplár, *Magam törvénye szerint*, 150. The willingness of *Ma* artists to cooperate with the new government is well demonstrated in "The Working Plan of the Ma Artistic Group" from March 1919, in which the artists request "tools" and "opportunities" to continue their agitational work (see 150–2).

19 Together with other documents from the press scandal, these articles are reprinted in Miklós Béládi and Béla Pomogáts, eds., *Jelzés a világba. A magyar irodalmi avantgard válogatott dokumentumai* (Signal to the World. Selected Documents of the Hungarian Literary Avantgarde) (Budapest: Magvető, 1988), 185–99 at 185, 189.

20 György Lukács, "Fölvilágosításul" (By Way of Information), *Vörös Újság*, 18 April 1919, 4. Despite this announcement of neutrality, the *Ma* circle continued to enjoy special benefits, such as biweekly (rather than monthly) publications of their journal after 15 May 1919, longer print runs, and higher-quality paper despite countrywide shortages (Csaplár, *Magam törvénye szerint*, 150). For Lukács's later take on this scandal, see *Record of a Life: An Autobiographical Sketch*, ed. István Eörsi (London: Verso, 1983), 62.

21 Published in *Vörös Újság* (June 1919), Kun's indictment is reprinted in *Jelzés a világba*, 203.

22 Kassák, "Levél Kun Bélához a művészet nevében," *Ma* 4, no. 7 (June 1919), 146–8; translated in *Between Worlds*, 230–3. For a more detailed account of the scandal, see Lee Congdon, *Exile and Social Thought: Hungarian Intellectuals in Germany and Austria, 1919–1933* (Princeton: Princeton University Press, 1991), 38–41; and Bob Dent, *Painting the Town Red: Politics and the Arts during the 1919 Hungarian Soviet Republic* (London: Pluto Press, 2018), 74–80. On Kassák's shifting positions with respect to art and politics – from his initial insistence on the artist's political autonomy, to his participation in the Hungarian Commune and attempt to exercise cultural dictatorship during this time, to his rejection of the party's dictates over culture, see Oliver Botar, "Lajos Kassák, Hungarian 'Activism,' and Political Power," *Canadian–American Slavic Studies* 36, nos. 1–2 (2002), 391–404. Kassák's shifting attitude towards the relationship of art and politics had caused fissures in the *Ma* circle even earlier, when József Révai, along with some other members, left the group in 1917.

23 On Kun and Lukács in Vienna, see Congdon, *Exile and Social Thought*, 49, 45–6. On the Activists, see Forgács, "In the Vacuum of Exile."

24 Mácza, "Életrajzom," 6. Together with Jenő Landler, Lukács became the strategic leader of the Hungarian Communist Party in Vienna. By contrast with the Moscow-based fraction of Hungarian Communists under Kun's leadership, Landler and Lukács emphasized the importance of agitational work and cooperation with the still legal Social Democratic Party for regaining power in Hungary. On the Landler–Lukács position, see Paul Le Blanc, "Spider and Fly: The Leninist Philosophy of Georg Lukács," in *Historical Materialism: Research in Critical Marxist Theory* 21, no. 2 (2013), 47–75.

25 Mácza, "Életrajzom," 6.

26 Ferenc Botka, "Sovetskaia literatura na stranitsakh 'Kashshai munkash'," in *Vengersko-russkie literaturnye sviazi* (Moscow: Nauka, 1964), 258–9. Botka also calls Mácza the "soul" of the translation project (259). See also Botka, "A 'Kassai Munkás' mint a szovjet irodalom első magyar közvetítője (1920–1930)," in *Tanulmányok a magyar-orosz irodalmi kapcsolatok köréből*, vol. 3, ed. Gábor Kemény (Budapest: Akadémiai Kiadó, 1961), 57–93; and *Kassai Munkás. 1907–1937* (Budapest: Akadémiai Kiadó, 1969).

27 János Mácza, "Forradalmi színpadok Oroszországban" (Revolutionary Stages in Russia), *Kassai Munkás*, 10 June 1921; reprinted in *Legendák és tények*, 68–70. Another possible source was the 1919 May Day celebration in Budapest. On the latter, see Dent, *Painting the Town Red*, 19–41.

28 János Mácza, typescript of "Májusi kórus," Inv. no. V. 3525/36, 1, János Mácza Papers, Archive of Petőfi Irodalmi Múzeum, Budapest, Hungary (hereafter, the archive is cited as PIM). The piece was later published in German as *Arbeiter Chor* (Dresden: Verlagsanstalt für proletarische Freidenker, 1924). For more on workers' choruses, see Dávid Szolláth, *A Kommunista aszketizmus esztétikája* (*The Aesthetics of Communist Asceticism*) (Budapest: Balassi, 2011), 191–249.

29 János Mácza, typescript and manuscript "Munkaprogramm és jegyzetek" (Work Program and Notes) and "Napló" (Diary), Inv. no. V. 3525/18, pages 5–6 in the typed pagination, pages 4–5 in handwritten, PIM.

30 Georg Lukács, *History and Class Consciousness: Studies in Marxist Dialectics* (London: Merlin Press, 1974). Although published in 1923, Lukács's study included versions of articles that had been read publicly and published earlier and that may have been known to Mácza. On the prehistory of the book, see Michael Löwy, *Georg Lukács: From Romanticism to Bolshevism*, trans. Patrick Camiller (London: NLB, 1979), 173–4.

31 Mácza's diary hints at his independence from the theoretical positions of the Lukács–Landler faction. He notes that unlike other Hungarian émigrés, he was not met by either the "Kunists" or the "Landlerists" upon his arrival in Moscow in 1923, suggesting that he acted as a politically and intellectually independent agent. Mácza, Inv. no. V. 3525/18, page 18 in the typed pagination, page 20 in handwritten, PIM.

32 As Oliver Botar notes, the Hungarian Proletkult efforts differed from their cognates in Soviet Russia. See "From Avant-Garde to 'Proletkult' in Hungarian Émigré Politico-Cultural Journals, 1922–1924," in Virginia Marquardt and Carol Hagelstein, eds., *Art and Journals on the Political Front, 1910–1940* (Gainesville: University Press of Florida, 1997), 102.

33 Kassák, "An die Künstler aller Länder," *Ma* 5, no. 1 (May 1, 1920), 2–4.

34 Marian Mazzone, "Dadaist Text / Constructivist Image: Kassák's *Képarchitektúra*," *Hungarian Studies Review* 31, nos. 1–2 (2004); Éva Forgács, "Between Cultures: Hungarian Concepts of Constructivism,"

in *Central European Avant-Gardes*, 159–61. Even after Kassák indicated his preference for Constructivist forms, he continued to publish Dadaist works in the journal.
35 Forgács and Miller, "The Avant-Garde in Budapest," 1140.
36 Mácza, "A zenitizmus?," *Napkelet*, no. 17 (1921). Mácza's reference to the printing of Aleksandr Blok's "Scythians" in the original Russian suggests that he was also in possession of primary sources, such as the third issue of the movement's journal *Zenit*, which printed the original poem in its first pages. See no. 3 (April 1921), 1–2. Cf. Boško Tokin, "Zenit, Zenitizmus," *Ma* 6, no. 7 (Jun 1921), 100. The same issue of *Ma* also printed Mácza's "A színpad" ("The stage," 87–8).
37 János Mácza, "The Black Tomcat," translated in *Between Worlds*, 320; translation modified. Original in *Ma* 6, no. 9 (September 1921), 122–5.
38 Cf. Tristan Tzara's "Dada Manifesto" (1918) in *Manifesto: A Century of Isms*, ed. Mary Caws (Lincoln: University of Nebraska Press, 2001), 297–304; and Hugo Ball's "Dada Manifesto" in Hugo Ball, *Flight Out of Time* (Berkeley: University of California Press, 1974), 219–21.
39 See, for example, Richard Huelsenbeck, "What Is Dadaism and What Does It Want in Germany?" (1919), in *The Dada Painters and Poets: An Anthology*, ed. Robert Motherwell (New York: Wittenborn, Schultz, 1951), 41–2; the original appeared in *Der Dada*, no. 1, 1919.
40 Mazzone, "Dadaist Text"; Éva Forgács, "Constructive Faith in Deconstruction: Dada in Hungarian Art," in *The Eastern Dada Orbit: Russia, Georgia, Ukraine, Central Europe, and Japan*, ed. Stephen C. Foster (Boston: G.K. Hall, 1998), 63–91.
41 Sándor Barta, "Manifesztumnak" (As a Manifesto) and "Az ige 'halálára'" (The "Death" of the Word), *Akasztott Ember*, no. 1 (November 1922). Implicit in Barta's position was the idea that different forms are suited to different audiences. The same journal issue contained Mácza's article on new Russian literature. For a more detailed discussion of Barta's position and that of other Hungarian émigré journals, see Botar, "From Avant-Garde to 'Proletkult'."
42 Sándor Bortnyik, "Művészet és proletárforradalom" (Art and Proletarian Revolution), *Akasztott Ember*, no. 5 (Feb 1923), 6–7.
43 See, for example, Barta's poem or, as he calls it, a "cadaver's manifesto," "The Greenheaded Man," published in the front pages of *Ma*'s first Dadaist issue ("A zöldfejű ember," *Ma* 6, no. 3 [Jan 1921], 22–3; translated in *Between Worlds*, 324–8, and *Tisztelt Hulláház* (Dear Morgue) (Vienna: Ma, 1921). My reading of Barta's engagement with Dadaism differs from that of Forgács, who maintains that the poet's use of Dada was less strategic than Kassák's (Forgács, "Constructive Faith," 78).
44 Mácza, "Az uj müvészek és a Prolétkult," *Ma* 7, no. 8 (Aug 1922), 60–1.

45 For example, at the midpoint in the play, after some characters dance around the corpse of a worker who could not afford to pay for his own coffin even though he always paid his union dues, the character designated as "XXIII" or "the one who is everywhere" states: "The legal circulation is increasingly disrupted to regulate the legal flow of circulation" (Mácza, "Kompozició 2 (színpadra)," *Ma* 7, no. 7 [July 1922], 42). Toward the end of the play, the character designated as "VI" or "the one who lives," who is described as "fat and swollen," states: "excuse me – the currency circulations are in order / the rise is normal go ahead feel the pulse" (43; punctuation and line breaks reproduced as in original).
46 The issue of *Ma* where *Composition 2* appeared no longer listed Mácza as its Slovak representative (*Ma* 7, no. 7 [July 1922]).
47 Mácza, "Munkaprogramm," pages 3–4 in typed and handwritten pagination. See also entries from December 1922, page 5 in typed and page 4 in handwritten pagination. His play "Én!" ("I!", September–October 1922) presents a similar critique in dramatic form. The "tragicomedy" parodies the artist-"creator," who believes himself to be above social conditions. "I am the peak and the whole world is reflected in me," the creator says to the "humble one" early in the play. By the end of the play, the creator realizes his mistake and descends from his "peak." Mácza, typescript of "Én!", Inv. no. V. 3525/30, p. 7, PIM. On the "transitional" period, see also Béla Uitz's "Az orosz művészet helyzete (1921-ben)" ("The Situation in Russian Art (in 1921)"), *Egység*, no. 2 (30 June 1922), 4.
48 *Ma*'s first émigré rival journal, *Egység* (Unity), was founded by Béla Uitz and Aldár Komját in May 1922. The second issue of *Egység* published a critique of *Ma*: Andor Rosinger, "A 'Ma' 'forradalmi' ideológiája" ("*Ma*'s 'Revolutionary' Ideology"), *Egység*, no. 2 (1922), 14–16. On Uitz's polemic with *Ma*, see Botar, "From the Avant-Garde to 'Proletkult'"; and Krisztina Passuth, "Contacts between the Hungarian and the Russian Avant-Garde in the 1920s," in *The First Russian Show* (London: Annely Juda Fine Art, 1983), 57–9.
49 Mácza, "Munkaprogramm," page 6 in typed, page 5 in handwritten pagination. On *Kritika*, see Mácza and Sándor Bortnyik, typescript of the program for the journal *Kritika*, Inv. no. V. 3525/13, 1, PIM.
50 Mácza and Bortnyik, typescript of the program for *Kritika*, 3. In this sense, Mácza's conception of the artist echoes the organizational role of the Party in Lukács's writing from this period.
51 Mácza and Bortnyik, typescript of the program for *Kritika*, 3. "Therefore, critique creates, builds: it builds the roads and possibilities toward the worldview of the collective person," which is viewed as the ultimate aim (4). Mácza wanted *Critique* to be "a journal of the groups who complete proletarian mass culture-work" (4).

52 Mácza, "Munkaprogramm," page 6 in typed, page 5 in handwritten pagination.
53 Béla Uitz, "A moszkvai nagy ünnep" (The Great Festival in Moscow), *Egység*, no. 1 (10 May 1922), translated in *Between Worlds*, 432–5.
54 Such news began to reach Central and Western Europe in the early 1920s, in part thanks to the *Ma* circle (Passuth, "Contacts," 53–9).
55 Mácza, "Munkaprogramm," page 7 in typed, page 5 in handwritten pagination.
56 Sándor Barta, "Idő kristálya: Moszkva," *Ék. Az egyetemes szocialista kultúra orgánuma*, no. 7 (1924), 4–7. On the image of Moscow as the new centre of the world, see Katerina Clark, *Moscow, the Fourth Rome: Stalinism, Cosmopolitanism, and the Evolution of Soviet Culture, 1931–1941* (Cambridge, MA: Harvard University Press, 2011). See also Michael David-Fox, *Showcasing the Great Experiment: Cultural Diplomacy and Western Visitors to the Soviet Union, 1921–1941* (Oxford: Oxford University Press, 2012).
57 Kassák, "Aktivizmus," *Ma* 4, no. 4 (April 1919), 50; translated in Levinger, *The Structurist*, 86.
58 Mácza, "Munkaprogramm," page 7 in typed, page 5 in handwritten pagination.
59 Mácza, "Munkaprogramm," page 8 in typed, page 6 in handwritten pagination. In his diary as well as brief biography, he notes that he came to Russia with the help of MOPR ("Életrajzom," 6).
60 Mácza, "Életrajzom," 6.
61 In July–August 1923, Mácza wrote his only film script, "A proletárok legendája" ("The Proletarian Legend"), and in August–September 1923, a theatrical prose piece (initially intended to be a novel) "Feltámadt város" ("The Resurrected City") in Hungarian, published in German as *Moskau: Das Evangelium der auferstandenen Stadt* (Frankfurt am Main: Der Taifun-Verlag, 1924). Besides publishing his *"Májusi kórus"* in German in 1924, Mácza also tried to publish "Literatur und Kunst in Sowjetrussland." In his biography, Mácza also notes that he planned to publish his book on Russian literature with the same publisher, but Taifun-Verlag ceased to exist ("Életrajzom" 6–7; Mácza, "Munkaprogramm," page 20 in typed, page 22 in handwritten pagination). The book manuscript remains unpublished to this day and is kept in Mácza's archive in Budapest. He also continued to publish in *Ék*.
62 The Mácza archive in Budapest contains some evidence that he began working on a survey of the avant-garde before his departure for Russia. A miscellaneous folder of writing from different years contains an eight-page text with a handwritten note that suggests this text is "a theoretical introduction" to his "book on new artistic schools," "written in Vienna in 1922" and "used in his writing of *Iskusstvo sovremennoi Evropy*." The note appears to have been added later, possibly when Mácza was compiling his archive for transfer from Russia to Budapest. See Mácza, "Mácza János

cikkei tanulmányai 1919–1973" ("János Mácza's Articles and Studies 1919–1973"), Inv. no. V. 3525/2, PIM. Based on the stylistic differences between this eight-page text and his other writing from 1922, as well as on the absence of other evidence that he was working on such a book in 1922, it seems more likely that he began composing the book after his arrival in Moscow. His diary entry from 1924 contains the first mention of an "article" on "new schools," which is likely the starting point for the book ("Munkaprogramm," pages 14–15 in the typed pagination, pages 8–9 in handwritten). Mácza's evaluation of the different movements in the eight-page archival text differs slightly from his assessment in *Iskusstvo* and is possibly an early draft of the first chapter. Mácza's introduction to the published book, dated to 1924, as well as some footnotes (Matsa, *Iskusstvo*, 93) also locate the writing of the book in 1924. The first mention of a related project – an article on Activism for *LEF* – is dated to June 1923. It is likely that this article, as well as a commissioned article on new Czech literature, dated in the diary to January 1924, contributed to his plans and vision for the book ("Munkaprogramm," pages 11–13 in the typed pagination, pages 7–8 in handwritten).

63 The single occurrence of the word "avant-garde" in the book applies to politics: "Here, before the new artists arises the question of their relationship to the avant-garde of the revolution, to the Communist Party" (Matsa, *Iskusstvo*, 122). Mácza's preference for the term "new art" is not at all surprising, since "avant-garde" was rarely used in reference to art in the 1910s and the 1920s, especially outside of Romance languages. See Matei Calinescu, *Five Faces of Modernity: Modernism, Avant-Garde, Decadence, Kitsch, Postmodernism* (Durham: Duke University Press, 1987), 95–111. Soviet reviews, which criticized Mácza's book for its narrow focus, corroborate that Mácza's primary concern was with the avant-garde (Anatoly Lunacharsky, *Novyi Mir*, nos. 8–9 [1926]: 262–6). Mácza responded to such critiques by broadening the focus of his next book, *Literature and the Proletariat in the West* (Ivan Matsa, *Literatura i proletariat na zapade* [Moscow: Izd. Kommunisticheskoi akademii, 1927], 3).

64 Matsa, *Iskusstvo*, 34.

65 Throughout the chapter, I use the term "social psychic" in place of Mácza's "psychic forces of society," as I believe this formulation more clearly indicates the collective, non-individual and socially formed quality of the "psychic" Mácza has in mind. In his introduction to the book, Vladimir Friche calls these forces "social-psychological" (*sotsial'no-psikhologicheskie*) and "psycho-ideology" (*psikho-idealogiia*), which point to the non-individual understanding of the "psychic" as well as to the absence of canonized terminology for the phenomena the term seeks to describe (Friche, Introduction, 6).

66 László Moholy-Nagy and Lajos Kassák, *Buch neuer Künstler* (Wien: MA, 1922); El Lissitzky and Hans Arp, *Die Kunstismen* (Zurich: Eugen Rentsch Verlag, 1925). Given how involved Mácza was with *Ma* at the time the

Buch was published, it seems impossible for him not to have known of at least this publication. Moreover, these anthologies are quite possibly the source of the clichés used in *Iskusstvo sovremennoi Evropy*, since many reproductions appear in all three books. Another important precedent for Mácza may have been Iván Hevesy's *A futurizmus, expresszionizmus és kubizmus művészete* (The Art of Futurism, Expressionism and Cubism) (Gyoma: Kner, 1922).

67 For example, *Kunstismen* links Constructivism to the counter-reliefs of Vladimir Tatlin, anachronistically dating the movement to 1917.
68 Matsa, *Iskusstvo*, 12–13.
69 Matsa, *Iskusstvo*, 11; my emphasis.
70 Matsa, *Iskusstvo*, 14. The extraneousness of chronology to Mácza's theory is marked by the relative absence of dates from his chapters, as well as by the fact that the sections in each chapter do not proceed in chronological sequence, as suggested by figure 2.6. For example, Cubism, which is dated to 1908 in the diagram, is treated last in chapter 1, after Futurism (1907), Simultanism (1914), Expressionism (1912), and Neo-Primitivism (1915; all dates provided in the diagram). The diagram in figure 2.6 does indeed mean to show the connections between the different schools, but it is not meant to explain the unity of the avant-garde or the continuity of its forms.
71 Matsa, *Iskusstvo*, 13.
72 Matsa, *Iskusstvo*, 14.
73 Matsa, *Iskusstvo*, 14.
74 Matsa, *Iskusstvo*, 18.
75 Matsa, *Iskusstvo*, 20.
76 Matsa, *Iskusstvo*, 34.
77 Matsa, *Iskusstvo*, 73, 86.
78 Mácza's focus on the origins of each movement in his text is generally skewed towards addressing the question of social-psychic forces. This shortcoming of the text is somewhat rectified by the more complete coverage of the diagrams.
79 Vladimir Friche, Introduction to *Iskusstvo*, 6. The 1920s reveal a wide variety of competing approaches that claimed the term "Marxist," and Mácza's book should be viewed as one attempt to develop the Marxist method. For an overview of Marxist approaches to culture in the 1920s, see Natalia Koronenko, "Literary Criticism and Cultural Policy during the New Economic Policy," and Caryl Emerson on the "sociological school" in "Literary Theory in the 1920s: Four Options and a Practicum," in *A History of Russian Literary Theory and Criticism: The Soviet Age and Beyond*, ed. Evgeny Dobrenko and Galin Tihanov (Pittsburg: University of Pittsburg Press, 2011), 17–42, 76–9.
80 See Poggioli and Bürger's critique of his formal approach.

81 Although Friche implies that Mácza's approach is entirely nameless, the book nevertheless contains many artists' names and even uses expressions like "Marinetti's Futurism." Mácza does, however, take critical distance from the treatment of artists as "inventor[s]" of forms and ideas (*Iskusstvo*, 16). In the 1920s, Soviet theoreticians adopted the idea of an "art history without names" from Heinrich Wölfflin's history of styles, needless to say, with significant revisions.

82 Torre primarily treats "vanguard" artistic developments in Spain, France, and Italy, though he does briefly mention the German Expressionists, the English Imagists, as well as the new poetry of the "Slavs," including "Poles, Hungarians, Czechoslovaks, and Yugoslavs," who receive seven of the book's 400 pages. Guillermo de Torre, *Literaturas europeas de vangardia* (Madrid: R. Caro Raggio, 1925).

83 See Piotr Piotrowski's influential critique of this gap in "Toward a Horizontal History of the European Avant-Garde," in *European Avant-Garde and Modernism Studies*, ed. Sascha Bru and Peter Nicholls (Berlin: De Gruyter, 2009), 49–58.

84 Socialists like Mácza may have avoided discourses that single out Central Europe as a special region not only because of the colonialist implications of terms like *Mitteleuropa*, but also because of the regional nationalism underpinning such views. Despite not treating Central Europe as somehow different from the West, Mácza recognizes that the different European nations found themselves at different stages of capitalist development at the turn of the twentieth century. For example, Mácza identifies Czechoslovakia as the most industrially advanced of its Slavic neighbours and therefore the most culturally literate, even before it becomes an independent nation (*Iskusstvo*, 63–4).

85 Matsa, *Iskusstvo*, 41, 45.

86 Matsa, *Iskusstvo*, 45–6.

87 Matsa, *Iskusstvo*, 48.

88 Matsa, *Iskusstvo*, 49–50.

89 Matsa, *Iskusstvo*, 50–1.

90 Matsa, *Iskusstvo*, 52.

91 Although Torre does touch on the visual arts, including a brief discussion of cinema in connection with literature, the focus of the book is nevertheless primarily on literature.

92 The last two chapters on theatre and music, although they invoke the discussions in the previous chapters, are not discussed in parallel. The peculiarity of such organization – where visual art and literature are analysed as single development, while theatre and music stand separately – possibly reflects the compositional history of the book, with the latter two chapters being added afterwards, perhaps in response to early criticism or request for more information in these particular artistic spheres.

93 For example, Mácza's manuscript on Russian literature, which he began writing in 1922, follows the Formalist method of separating out literature as an independent field of study.
94 Matsa, *Iskusstvo*, 89.
95 György Lukács, "Expressionism: Its Significance and Decline" [1934], in *Essays on Realism*, ed. Rodney Livingstone, trans. David Fernbach (Cambridge, MA: MIT Press, 1981), 76–113. Although Lukács limits his discussion of the avant-garde to the case of German Expressionism, his position has been understood as a critique of the avant-garde and modernism more broadly. For the later essays in the debate, see Theodor Adorno et al., *Aesthetics and Politics* (London: Verso, 1980). While Mary Gluck has argued that Lukács's position can be traced back to the debates that unfolded in the Hungarian émigré press in Vienna in the 1920s, there is no direct textual evidence that Lukács formulated his infamous views of the avant-garde prior to the 1930s. Gluck, "Toward a Historical Definition of Modernism: Georg Lukács and the Avant-Garde," *Journal of Modern History* 58, no. 4 (1986): 845–82.
96 Matsa, *Iskusstvo*, 126. Cf. Ernst Bloch's defence of Expressionism in *Aesthetics and Politics*, 16–27.
97 Matsa, *Iskusstvo*, 127.
98 Matsa, *Iskusstvo*, 130.
99 Mácza, "Életrajzom," 7–8. On Marxist *iskusstvoznanie*, see Irina Denischenko, "Toward a Marxist-Leninist *Kunstwissenschaft*" (ASEEES, New Orleans, November 2021).
100 On Mácza's interactions with and eventual break from the Hungarian émigré community in Moscow, see "Munkaprogramm," pages 18–9 in typed pagination, pages 20–1 in handwritten. On attacks on Mácza in the 1930s and the 1940s, see "O napadeniiakh na menia" (1974) in Mácza's archive (Inv. no. V. 4128/6/a/6, PIM), where he mentions that he was mistaken for a Jew because of his last name.
101 Edward Said, "Traveling Theory Reconsidered," in *Critical Reconstructions: The Relationship of Fiction and Life*, ed. Robert M. Polhemus and Roger B. Henkle (Stanford: Stanford University Press, 1994), 251–88. Recent attempts to complicate the exilic origins of theory include Galin Tihanov's work, "Why Did Modern Literary Theory Originate in Central and Eastern Europe?," *Common Knowledge* 10, no. 1 (2004): 61–81, and *The Birth and Death of Literary Theory: Regimes of Relevance in Russia and Beyond* (Stanford: Stanford University Press, 2019).
102 Balázs's diary, cited in Forgács, "In the Vacuum," 111.
103 Braidotti, *Nomadic Subjects*, 55, 57.

3 Staging Revolution: Stalinist *Drambalet* in the German Democratic Republic

ELIZABETH H. STERN

"In 1945, we walked through rubble; now, we are strolling along Stalinallee," wrote the East German choreographer Lilo Gruber in early 1953.[1] Gruber's enthusiastic declaration was premature, however, in its conjuring of a reality that did not yet exist. When she wrote these words, Stalin was just weeks away from dying, and Stalinallee still looked like a giant foundation pit of socialism. Newly renamed in honour of the Soviet leader, this Berlin boulevard was a tangible symbol of the German Democratic Republic's reconstruction efforts following the Second World War and of its new alliance with the Soviet Union. East German workers repurposed the rubble of their city to remake a thoroughfare in the former capital of the Third Reich in the image of Stalin's Moscow. Stalinallee was an aesthetic import and the physical embodiment of the accelerated construction of socialism in the GDR. It is thus fitting that Lilo Gruber concluded an essay on her ideas for the future development of East German dance with this hopeful yet misguided line about "strolling along Stalinallee."

Indeed, the GDR looked to the Soviet Union for guidance not only on how to rebuild its boulevards but also on how to establish a new national culture and the institutions that could foster it. This reliance provoked anxiety and animosity in some GDR artists. For others, the models offered by Soviet culture represented the only viable means by which to create a new, progressive East Germany. Dance, along with the other arts, was enlisted in the effort to forge this new culture and fashion a coherent national narrative – one that was distinct from the cultures of the Third Reich and of West Germany.

In the early 1950s, East German dance did not appear poised to aid in this cultural and ideological undertaking. As the GDR pedagogue Marianne Vogelsang put it in 1954, "the new political and cultural endeavours of the GDR unsparingly exposed the dire predicament in which dance found itself, but in this harsh exposure, there also appeared the prospects of new avenues for the art of dance."² This "dire predicament" had to do with the fact that the development of classical ballet had been curtailed under Nazi rule, and Germany's traditions of *Ausdruckstanz* (modern or expressionist dance) were seen to be ideologically suspect and too heterogeneous to constitute a national tradition.³ More stable technical and ideological foundations for dance had to be established in order for it to contribute to the formation of East German society. For a number of GDR ideologues and dance practitioners, Lilo Gruber among them, the Soviet Union seemed to provide the only possible solution for salvaging and reforming East German dance culture. This could be achieved through the cultivation of dance according to the aesthetic doctrine of socialist realism. The transplantation of Soviet repertoire (Stalinist *drambalet*) and pedagogy (Vaganova technique), however, sparked impassioned debate and required complex negotiations between artists and cultural institutions in the GDR.⁴ The intransigence of the choreographic legacy of *Ausdruckstanz* – a competing, indigenous form in the GDR – further complicated the assimilation of Soviet ballet.

This chapter examines the export viability of *drambalet* (*dramaticheskii balet*), ballet's accommodation to socialist realism and the only genre of Soviet ballet officially sanctioned until the Thaw.⁵ I have chosen to focus on *drambalet* specifically in the GDR in part because the country occupied a unique position on the front lines of the Cold War. Unlike Soviet artists, who were largely isolated behind the Iron Curtain, GDR artists, for a time, were more familiar with artistic developments in the western half of the country and with work done by former classmates and colleagues because of the still porous border between the two Germanys. GDR artists were compelled to distinguish their work from and compete with their West German counterparts while simultaneously confronting their pre-war artistic traditions and reconceiving them in line with Soviet socialist realism and the dictum "national in form, socialist in content." GDR artists and ideologues also worked in relation to two centres of power that tried to dictate dance's development: the SED (Socialist Unity Party) in Berlin and the Soviet leadership in Moscow, the former of which orbited and took its cues from the latter. Recently split from West Germany and located on the westernmost periphery of the Soviet empire, the GDR represented a border guard in the emerging Cold War. Given this set of conditions, the situation of dance in the early years of the GDR – years when it was most influenced by Soviet artistic models – offers a compelling testing ground for Soviet cultural policies. It is also an ideal arena in which to witness the emergence of hybrid cultural forms, the result of conflicts and compromises between "local" (German) artistic traditions and those of an "alien" (and dominant) political power, Soviet Russia, as the latter sought to expand and solidify its influence in the early Cold War era.

This chapter opens a window onto the early years of East German ballet, first by analysing ideological debates around dance in the GDR and then by discussing the ballet *The Flames of Paris*, the first full-fledged *drambalet* to be staged in the GDR (by Lilo Gruber for the Leipziger Ballett in 1953). Premiering during a moment of flux in cultural policy, this ballet served as a transitional work and model for future socialist realist dance productions in the GDR.[6] More importantly, the ballet served a distinct ideological function in the larger context of Cold War politics, in part by promoting a pan-Soviet idea of revolutionary culture. This chapter does not aim to provide a detailed production history of Gruber's *The Flames of Paris*; rather, it treats it as a vehicle of political consciousness – as part of the Soviet Union's broader strategy of building unity within the Eastern Bloc.[7]

Guiding this chapter is the following question: How successful was the transplantation of Stalinist *drambalet* into a different historical and national context and, in turn, how did this new set of conditions challenge Soviet models of dance? This chapter focuses on the migration of cultural forms and ideology more than on that of people, although the exchange of artists and intellectuals certainly facilitated the GDR's cultural and ideological development.[8] I limit my scope to a narrow period of time, from Stalin's death in 1953 until roughly 1957, when dance in the GDR began to evolve in a different direction, incorporating more elements of modern dance and what became known as *Tanztheater*. This period in GDR dance history is poorly understood. Only a handful of researchers have worked on dance in the early years of the GDR; even fewer have studied the evolution of East German ballet aesthetics.[9] This chapter fills this gap in knowledge by relying on little-studied archival documents, particularly from the Akademie der Künste (the Academy of Arts, or AdK) and the Staatliche Kommission für Kunstangelegenheiten (the State Commission for Artistic Matters, or Stakuko), later the Ministerium für Kultur, in order to demonstrate the challenges of tailoring "ready-made" Soviet models to the cultural landscape of East Germany following the Second World War. Taken together, these documents afford direct insight into the key questions facing dance in the early years of the GDR and sketch out why and how successfully *drambalet* was introduced.

Reshaping National Culture

Just as Soviet Russia, following the Revolution, the Civil War, and War Communism, had to replenish a class of artists and intellectuals, so too did Germany after the devastation of Nazi rule and the Second World

War. This was no easy task for the GDR. The early generation of SED members were dyed-in-the wool anti-fascists who had to contend with a generation of dance artists with ties to Nazism.[10] According to Marion Kant, this resulted in a "devious game" in the GDR: because the government desperately needed dance specialists and feared their immigration to the West, it was largely willing to overlook the questionable ideological backgrounds of dancers and choreographers.[11] Complicit figures were eager to "red-wash" their pasts, whether that involved acquiring documentation exonerating them of involvement in the Nazi regime, eliding prior political affiliations, or embellishing their communist pedigrees.[12]

The more prominent "red migrants" on the East German cultural scene were of various types. Some were hardline communists who had left Germany upon the rise of the Nazis and were now eager to help build a new, progressive society. Others had been complicit, to varying degrees, in the culture or policies of the Third Reich or were still devoted to aesthetic movements that were viewed as out of step with the times. Those working to build consensus on a way forward for GDR dance were thus a motley group of ex-fascists, lukewarm socialists, newly returned committed communists, and apolitical artists. To borrow terminology from Schiller, Blanc, and Basch's theory of transnationalism, these were people simultaneously "at home" in Germany and living in a "host society" (i.e., one occupied by Soviet forces).[13] In terms of dance, their more "native" traditions (such as *Ausdruckstanz*) were deemed ideologically unpalatable, and artists were compelled to adopt Soviet choreographic forms "alien" to them (*drambalet*). The fraught negotiations between artists and ideologues at this juncture point to the at times tortured efforts of artists to "link together their societies of origin and settlement," which, in the case of the GDR, were peculiarly in the same geographic location.[14]

The GDR borrowed artistic forms and institutional models from the Soviet Union, especially in the early post-war years. Soviet Russia exerted overt influence – for instance, it transformed the SED into a Soviet-style political party and installed leaders who pushed to "Sovietize" East German society perhaps more aggressively than Stalin himself wanted. The SED forced a merger of the Social Democratic Party (SPD) and the German Communist Party (KPD), two parties that had divided the German worker's movement during the interwar years. Wanting to avoid relitigating the bitter fighting between factions on the German left, the SED in the early 1950s essentially imported Soviet ideology and cultural policies wholesale. The Soviet Union had already laid down the path to "full communism," and the SED saw no reason to return to interwar debates. Instead, it forged ahead.[15]

The bellicose resolutions of the SED's 1951 Party Congress set the tone and agenda for early GDR *Kulturpolitik*.[16] The resolutions denounced formalism, cosmopolitanism, and kitsch as the ideological weapons of their enemies, particularly of the "imperialist warmongers" (the Americans).[17] This was not mere rhetoric. In the early post-war years, there was genuine fear of remilitarization and the outbreak of a third world war. The GDR represented a "bulwark against capitalist encroachment," and those responsible for managing national culture regarded formalist "experimentation" as "a national security risk."[18] Socialist realism was a vital "weapon" in this emerging "war" – the artistic "method" prescribed to revitalize and revolutionize the arts and to re-educate the working masses "in the spirit of socialism."[19] Curiously, however, at precisely the time when GDR cultural officials and artists were energetically advancing socialist realism, in Soviet Russia, the doctrine was already (to some extent) viewed as tired dogma that had led to creative stagnation.

In the GDR, socialist realism was now being promoted not only as the aesthetic doctrine for supporting and accelerating the construction of socialism but also as a "tool" to "legitimize East German claims for a place among the people's democracies of the Eastern Bloc."[20] The resolutions and policies laid out by the SED also called for a return to German classical heritage (*Klassizismus*, i.e., the neoclassicism of the mid-eighteenth to late nineteenth centuries) through a process called heritage appropriation (*Erbeaneignung*).[21] This was in part to lay claim to and reinterpret a tradition in a manner akin to the Great Appropriation in Soviet culture, but it was also a significant part of the cultural Cold War between East and West Germany, as both the GDR and the FRG "aimed to be the heir to the likes of Goethe, Schiller, and Bach."[22] The SED sought to bolster its cultural policies by selectively appropriating and refashioning (pre-war) German artistic traditions to fit within the framework of socialist realism. In their attempts to establish continuities with the classical heritage, officials "emphasized the development of a German national identity in East Germany" that positioned it as the "real successor to German prewar society" and the "main inheritor of German history."[23]

In the case of classical ballet, however, dance specialists did not see much in the way of a German ballet tradition with which to work. The 1951 resolutions promoted classical ballet even while explicitly noting the poor standards and "lack of ballet traditions" in German dance.[24] Germany in the 1920s had many ballet companies, but "ballet might just as well have not existed at all," according to Karl Toepfer, "so powerful was the hold of *Ausdruckstanz* on the imagination of the time."[25]

Moreover, ballet had declined during the Third Reich, after the Nazis labelled it "archaic *Tanzkunst*" and "un-German"; proponents of *Ausdruckstanz* were encouraged to reject ballet and "advance Nazi ideology through new choreographic styles."[26] As one participant at the 1953 Tanzkonferenz put it, "we do not have classical ballet in Germany ... We have no tradition at all."[27] Thus, the effort to transplant the Soviet *drambalet* genre into East Germany involved much more than a rejection of Nazi aesthetics; it also entailed the creation of a tradition almost *ex nihilo*, a new form of German ballet that would become "central to the solidification of the GDR's aesthetic agenda" in the early 1950s.[28]

Expediting Progress: The Tanzkonferenz of 1953

To address the problems facing East German dance, Stakuko, which was directly modelled on the Soviet Committee on Artistic Affairs and was closely allied with the SED, organized a conference on dance theory in Berlin. This conference was meant to be a place where dancers, choreographers, and pedagogues would discuss the development of East German dance culture and, more specifically, how to implement socialist realism. The conference aimed to root out the "formalist" and "cosmopolitan" inclinations of dance and to establish clear recommendations for improving repertoire, pedagogy, and criticism. On the knife edge separating the Stalinist and post-Stalinist eras, the Tanzkonferenz convened on 23 and 24 March 1953 – the month of Stalin's death and roughly six months before the premiere of *The Flames of Paris*.

To kick off the conference and discussion, the journal *Weltbühne* solicited commentary on what was known as "the Realism dispute." Two voices dominated the debates on dance at this time: Martin Sporck, the head of the SED's art division and editor-in-chief of the newspaper *Sonntag*; and Eberhard Rebling, a musicologist, critic, and editor of the journal *Musik und Gesellschaft*. Neither man was a dance practitioner. Both took hardline positions that deviated little from the SED's 1951 resolutions, which condemned *Ausdruckstanz* as "formalist," bemoaned the lack of progress in GDR dance, recommended learning from Soviet models, and promoted classical ballet and folk dance as "tools of socialist realist representation."[29] Rebling's article, which he read at the Tanzkonferenz, quoted liberally from Marx, Lenin, Stalin, and Zhdanov, and the buzzwords of socialist realism appeared throughout both his text and Sporck's – for example, *Parteilichkeit* (*partiinost'*, or "Party-mindedness"), *Volkstümlichkeit* (*narodnost'*, or "folk sentiment or character"), *Ideengehalt* (*soderzhatel'nost'/ideinost'*, or "richness of content/idea"), and *das Typische* (*tipichnost'*, or "typicality"). While many of these terms seem to have been repurposed from Germany's own debates in the 1920s and early 1930s, they were not reinterrogated in terms of these prior debates. Rather, these loaded terms were processed via Stalinist socialist realism, giving them a different ideological valence, and then imported to the GDR.[30] East German cultural officials, with the exception of some members of AdK (such as Brecht), largely parroted Soviet formulations instead of re-examining them in light of prior German debates or in reference to foundational German communist works. Essentially, GDR officials tended to read communist ideas through the Soviet reading of German communist texts, for example, by deferring to Zhdanov's interpretation of the communist canon rather than returning more directly to German exemplars of communist thought.[31] This partly explains why Rebling's first paragraph sounds as if it could have been ripped from a Soviet protocol on dance: "Questions of Party-mindedness [*Parteilichkeit*], of typicality, and of class conflict need to be more distinctly, sharply, and deeply worked out. The German workers, the German people demand from the art of dance an artistic representation of the life, thoughts, feelings, and sensibilities of the people of our time."[32]

While it was the task of Sporck and Rebling (and other ideologues) at the Tanzkonferenz to lead the discussion about implementing socialist realism, they largely failed to enlighten dance practitioners about the doctrine's practical applications to dance. What the dance practitioners wanted was a coherent exposition of aesthetic principles, which socialist realism did not in fact readily provide, despite it being described as a method.[33] It is thus unsurprising that, in their responses to the dance practitioners, GDR ideologues either regurgitated socialist realist axioms or held up models of successful socialist realist works, such as *The Flames of Paris*.

A typical exchange occurred on the first day of the conference, provoked by the dancer and choreographer Jean Weidt (who at this time was ballet master at the Staatstheater Schwerin). Weidt explained that he and his dancers still did not understand what socialist realism meant for dance. Despite the presence of "progressive literature" and "monthly debates about ballet and realism" at his theatre, he felt as if he had "hit a brick wall."[34] Weidt's confusion is telling – known as the "red dancer," he had a strong communist pedigree, had worked in the 1920s and 1930s to create "revolutionary" workers' dance cooperatives, and had even studied dance in Moscow in the 1930s. In his view, the primary struggle was to win over dancers who had so far "rejected" realistic dance and to aid in the ideological transformation of consciousness that would result in dancers who could "think realistically."[35] Weidt feared that they would have to "wait another four to five years" to produce a new generation of dancers, and asked, "What is to be done in order to end this bad state of affairs?"[36] Most of the other dancers and choreographers at the conference echoed Weidt's confusion and frustration. As another participant put it, "I would be very grateful for a clear and exact definition of the term 'socialist realism'!"[37] In an attempt to placate the increasingly exasperated participants, Rebling and Sporck leaned time and again on Soviet definitions of socialist realism, particularly Zhdanov's definition from the 1934 Congress of Soviet Writers. When this did not help, they simply stonewalled.

Many East German artists felt a sense of bewilderment as they attempted to learn what strategic moves were available to them in this still murky ideological terrain. For some, this was not their first experience with a new ideological parlance, nor was it their first time adjusting to new dogmatic constraints, although the style of dance rejected by the last regime was now being promoted by the current regime.[38] What becomes clear in the transcripts is that the dance practitioners had not yet mastered the choreography of this particular discursive dance – that is, what Petre Petrov calls "the ideology of socialist realism as an institutionalized practice."[39] The Tanzkonferenz can thus be read as an infelicitous staging of a ritualized performance of ideology that went off-script at times. Most participants, even avowed communists like Weidt and those supposedly learned in the tenets of Marxism-Leninism, did not yet understand the rules of this particular game.

At the Tanzkonferenz, the participants focused particularly on the slogan "national in form, socialist in content." The ideologues emphasized the second part: in their view, suitable content would produce suitable dance forms. Still unclear to dance practitioners, however, was what was meant by "national in form" – in terms of what dance forms or styles were available to them, did "national" mean "Soviet" (aka "Russian") or distinctively "German"? At this time, according to Jérôme Bazin, GDR officials were *supposed* to understand the slogan to mean that "nationalism and allegiance to the USSR could be combined."[40] Efforts to interrogate this slogan were fraught and paradoxical, however, given that the "national" element was largely understood as "Soviet." But the entire ideological apparatus of Marxism-Leninism was meant to rise above – to transcend – the national, and given that GDR officials and practitioners had to be careful to negotiate an understanding of the "national" that was distinct from the virulent nationalism of National Socialism, which had exploited specific dance styles for ideological purposes.

In the discussions, advocates of modern dance, for example, stressed the first part of the slogan to try to argue for its continuation, owing to modern dance's supposedly German origins and connections to folk dance and despite its more recent association with National Socialism. One participant, a dancer named Max Burghardt from the Erich-Weinert Ensemble, made a particularly trenchant argument for the continuation of modern dance as part of the German national heritage. His impassioned argument seems to have been based on his nationalist sentiments (with echoes of National Socialist discourse) as a "German man and a German worker," as someone who spoke German and who thus had the "thoughts and feelings of a German," as opposed to a Soviet citizen.[41] He directly challenged the transplantation of Soviet ballet to the GDR. Referring to the slogan, he explained, "Art should have national form. German dance, for which we are fighting, must be German and must be in a German [dance] language."[42] The demand that Soviet dance forms and socialist realist ideology be transposed onto GDR dance was one at which he bristled. Burghardt's comments seem to tap into what was not an uncommon fear at the time: that the Soviets simply wanted to "extract their reparations and then abandon, for all constructive political purposes, the shell of Eastern Germany."[43] It is understandable, then, that Burghardt and others mistrusted Soviet intentions and tried to resist Soviet occupation of the cultural field, including by trying to turn a slogan like "national in form" to their advantage. In invoking "national in form," Burghardt was advocating the creation of a "truly German" dance tradition based on modern dance, as opposed to the forced assimilation of non-native Soviet dance traditions and repertoire. He, along with other supporters of modern dance, wanted to continue with the style of dance that he considered indigenous and one in which they were already proficient.

The debate about modern dance largely boiled down to whether *Ausdruckstanz* was to be viewed as part of an authentic German national heritage or as a modernist deviation that had nothing to do with German *narodnost'*. Ideologues such as Rebling and, to a lesser degree, Sporck denied that *Ausdruckstanz* had any roots in German national culture and dismissed all disciplines of *Ausdruckstanz* as dangerously compromised. The official view of *Ausdruckstanz* at this time can be (somewhat reductively) summarized as follows: *Ausdruckstanz* rejects the national, therefore it is cosmopolitan, therefore it is formalist; it concerns itself with mysticism, abstraction, and the subjective feelings and experiences of the individual to the neglect of the collective; it rejects content in favour of pure form; it is unmusical and unsystematic. If classical ballet was considered a highly developed, rich, and universal language, then *Ausdruckstanz* was still split into a variety of rough local dialects with no widely agreed upon vocabulary or functional syntax. For these reasons, as well as the complicity of German figures such as Mary Wigman and Rudolf Laban in the Nazi regime, *Ausdruckstanz* was deemed largely unavailable for socialist purposes.

The internal debates at the Tanzkonferenz were wide-ranging and occasionally heated, but in the end, the adopted resolutions maintained the official Party line regarding the development of East German dance. The course of action decided upon was to follow "the model and experience of Soviet balletic art" in order to "cultivate the progressive traditions of balletic art and to limn the socialist vision of man in art."[44] The resolutions generally rejected *Ausdruckstanz* but did make a minor provision for it: thesis 3 concluded that there were some potentially salutary features of *Ausdruckstanz* – rebranded as "new artistic dance" – that could be developed under close oversight.[45] Setting aside the narrowly defined allowance for German modern dance, the published conclusions of the Tanzkonferenz were overwhelmingly oriented towards Soviet ballet. For the time being, Soviet *drambalety* were recommended to expedite the progress of GDR dance.

The aggressive promotion of *drambalet* in the GDR at this time appears somewhat ironic, however, given that many dance practitioners and critics in Soviet Russia already viewed the genre as a "dogmatic restraint on choreographic development" – emblematic of the artistic "stagnation" and "paralysis" of the late Stalinist period.[46] Rebling, Sporck, and other GDR ideologues nevertheless toed the official line when it came to recommendations for repertoire and dance education. As thesis 10 stated, "Studying the struggle for socialist realism in Soviet ballet is necessary for us to achieve socialist realism in German dance. The Soviet Union shows the only correct path for the further development of the art of dance."[47] Following the Tanzkonferenz, East German dance progressed primarily via its relationship to Soviet dance. The first real test run of Soviet *drambalet* on the East German stage was Lilo Gruber's *The Flames of Paris* in 1953.

Bringing *Drambalet* to the GDR

In the months after the Tanzkonferenz, the political situation remained unstable and the cultural climate was restrictive and perilous. Such an environment did not encourage daring artistic experimentation, and thus the choice to stage a *drambalet* like *The Flames of Paris* was a sensible one. With *The Flames of Paris*, the GDR was handed down a well-vetted ballet. It was considered a full-fledged *drambalet*; reportedly, it was Stalin's favourite ballet; it had won the Stalin Prize; it had been performed more than a thousand times; and it had already been exported to other socialist states. Some artists and ideologues encouraged choreographers to boldly reflect their new reality; Gruber, however, aware of the pitfalls of early Soviet ballet about contemporary subjects, was wary of staging a ballet about contemporary East German life or recent German history. Even the State Academic Theatre of Opera and Ballet (or GATOB, the former Mariinsky in Leningrad) and the creators of the original *Flames* backtracked after the "errors" of topical Soviet ballets, retreating to the "safer" (and more traditional) territory of history, literature, and myth. *Flames* was designed to access the ideological truths of Soviet reality but through a side door – the French Revolution, historically and geographically distant yet ideologically related material.

When it was first performed in the early 1930s, *Flames* provided the blueprint for future *drambalety*, introducing key features of the genre: the use of mass, character, and folk dance; the fusion of classical ballet, vernacular dance languages, and dramatic gesture; the heroization and dramatization typical of classical ballet; the inclusion of "ethnographic" and historical detail; the elimination of conventional ballet pantomime; dance that is motivated by the plot; high production values; and the masses positioned as the hero. According to the Russian dance historian Vadim Gaevskii, *the* defining feature of *drambalet* is its approximation of literature and dramatic theatre as means of making dance more dramaturgically comprehensible.[48] He characterizes much of the dramaturgy of *drambalety* as the staging of "confrontations between historical forces" – something embodied by *The Flames of Paris*.[49]

The basic plot of the ballet is as follows: In 1792, the Marseille battalion, led by the soldier Philippe, marches towards Paris. En route, they encounter a peasant family, including the peasant girl Zhanna, and come to the family's aid after the father is arrested by the local Marquis and his huntsmen following an altercation. The father is freed from the Marquis's estate, and the villagers and the peasant family become infected with revolutionary enthusiasm, joining the march on Paris. The second act of the ballet takes place at the royal palace, where a celebration is under way that includes a ballet within a ballet. The Marquis and his son arrive and alert the royals to the coming revolutionary forces. Two court performers see a letter that proves that the French King has betrayed the people. When they try to steal the letter, a violent altercation ensues. One court performer, Mireille, escapes and joins the revolutionary cause. In Act Three, delegates from various French provinces gather on a square in Paris. Mireille tells them that the court has betrayed the people. They join forces and storm the Tuileries. Act Four consists of revolutionary mass festivals to celebrate the people's victory.

In terms of both the ballet's content and the development of its choreographic forms, *Flames* arguably contributed to the generation of "official myths" by providing an object lesson in what Katerina Clark calls the "spontaneity/consciousness dialectic."[50] This dialectic can be seen in the ballet's depiction of the revolutionary masses and positive heroes, who, to varying degrees, transition from a state of relative "spontaneity" to a higher degree of ideological "consciousness" over the course of the ballet. This is most evident in the choreography for the court performer Mireille: she first appears as part of aristocratic rituals, playing the victim of Cupid's arrow in a court ballet; at the end of *Flames*, she performs as part of revolutionary rituals, embodying the goddess of victory in the mass festivals. Her dancing transforms in stages: from the exceptionally refined mannerisms of a court ballerina, to a more "natural" movement language when she reaches a state of revolutionary "enlightenment," and finally to a self-realized, stately revolutionary symbol.[51] The development of her movement language tracks with the awakening of her ideological consciousness.

Flames provided a solution to problems particular to early Soviet dance by demonstrating that the language of classical ballet could be used to express "realistic" revolutionary content. The production repurposed elements of nineteenth-century ballet, returning under a new guise some traditional features of full-length story ballets to the Soviet stage. In 1932, some viewed this as an aesthetic and ideological compromise liable to doom the production and further set back Soviet dance.[52] In the 1930s, however, with the "Great Appropriation" – or what Christina Ezrahi terms "artistic repossession" – the recycling of classical ballet conventions became largely unobjectionable.[53] In fact, a rapacious repurposing of the artistic material of the past (what some called "ready-made material") in *The Flames of Paris* – whether in terms of subject matter or in terms of artistic form (the conventions of nineteenth-century classical ballet) – became a major feature of *drambalet*. The "halfway policy" pursued by *The Flames of Paris* – the aesthetic and ideological "compromises" made in order to be at once appealing to the masses, ideologically inoffensive, and worthy of the former Mariinsky – became the norm.[54] In this way, *Flames* provided a "safe plan," if not a precise formula, for ballet's response to socialist realism.[55] Roughly speaking, this plan involved the following: the choice of relatively "safe" subject matter, combined with a dose of "exotica" and, ideally, "intimations of revolution"; the inclusion of an uplifting ending (even in a tragic ballet, characters should show the heroic nature of social or political struggle); the approximation of drama and literature; and the reappropriation of popular features from the classical ballet heritage.[56]

All of this was put to the service of expressing the ideological content of the era in forms that were sufficiently simple, heroic, and monumental.

While not free from controversy when it first premiered in 1932, by 1953, *The Flames of Paris*, already some twenty years old and considered part of the canon, was a decidedly safe choice, allowing those working on the production to avoid much of the blame should it be a critical or popular failure. The hope was that this production would do for GDR dance what it had done for early Soviet ballet – get dance on the "right track" both technically and ideologically. As in Soviet Russia, *The Flames of Paris* in the GDR functioned as a transitional work and offered a model of socialist realist ballet.[57]

Gruber worked quickly to stage her version of *Flames* for the Leipziger Ballett. It premiered on 4 October 1953. Gruber was an ideal, Party-minded candidate to execute this potentially loaded exercise in cultural translation, in bringing Stalinist *drambalet* to the East German stage. Like any genre, *drambalet* carried its own ideology, whose "imagined social world" could shift in meaning with recontextualization.[58] *The Flames of Paris* presented itself as a peculiar case of historical displacements: a ballet about the French Revolution, created in Stalinist Russia to celebrate the fifteenth anniversary of the Bolshevik Revolution, and imported into East Germany as an example of progressive Soviet dance. How could this ballet be recontextualized to speak to East German audiences in 1953?

Soviet officials were themselves aware that *The Flames of Paris* might not felicitously translate. Despite its success, this ballet was essentially understood as a domestic product to be circulated only within the Soviet sphere. This was recognized already in December 1932, in internal discussions about the ballet. Nikolai Shuvalov, the director of GATOB's repertoire, for example, concluded that it would be an "inappropriate ploy" (*neumestnaia vykhodka*) to stage the production in Paris, or in any other bourgeois European centre, because of its overt political nature.[59] In his and the administration's view, *Flames* was a "reflection of a particular revolutionary situation, a particular intensification of class struggle, and a particular societal catastrophe."[60] For Soviet citizens, the French Revolution, as depicted in *The Flames of Paris*, served as a metaphor for the Bolshevik Revolution and suggested a historical continuity between the two. For Parisians, however, the ballet depicted their actual history, and the Soviet ideological appropriation might come across as gauche. Even in the early 1950s, the Central Committee of the Communist Party feared that performing a Soviet interpretation of the French Revolution to the French might appear ridiculous or amount to a political blunder.[61] This ballet (a propaganda piece) might not translate well to non-Soviet audiences.

Within the Eastern Bloc, however, *Flames* was seen as an ideal cultural export because the production operated at several levels. At the level of plot/content, the ballet literally staged revolution (the French Revolution); at the level of form and genre, it "revolutionized" dance (a model *drambalet* in the grand Stalinist style); as a Soviet cultural product, the ballet was intended not only to help spur a cultural revolution in dance within individual socialist states but also to help form a coherent, transnational field of revolutionary artistic culture. The ballet was intended to make revolution tangible and visible in the Soviet Union and across socialist Eastern Europe. However paradoxical it might seem to use a Soviet ballet about the French Revolution as the model upon which to base East German dance, the transplantation of *The Flames of Paris* to the GDR, a young socialist state on the front lines of the Cold War, was in fact politically expedient.

Staging and Reception of Gruber's *The Flames of Paris*

Lilo Gruber did not seem to have any doubts that a Soviet ballet about the French Revolution would speak to an East German audience. She did, however, face serious obstacles in staging this ambitious, multi-act, and technically challenging ballet. *The Flames of Paris* was not only Gruber's first serious work for Leipzig but also her first major choreographic undertaking. There were misgivings about whether any GDR choreographer, let alone a relatively inexperienced one, could pull off the staging of a major Soviet ballet. Gruber hoped she could replicate the success *Flames* had enjoyed in Soviet Russia, and, more importantly, she hoped that, through staging the ballet, she could learn the inner workings of the *drambalet* genre to use as a springboard for the future development of East German dance. As she said in a 1952 interview, "Our ballet productions in Germany are not yet very popular – unlike in the Soviet Union. We do not yet entirely understand how to give artistic form [*gestalten*] to our new life. Classical ballet should be the foundation ... but we must build upon this foundation in order to create our own national style."[62] Gruber's goal was to bring GDR ballet up to speed, to make up for its "poor development" and traditions ruptured by the Third Reich. The staging of *Flames* was a significant and calculated step toward that goal.

It is unclear when exactly it was decided to stage *The Flames of Paris* in Leipzig, and little has been saved from the planning or staging of Gruber's 1953 version. From available sources, we know that the ballet was planned to run for three hours and included thirty-five dancers and students from the Leipzig Theatre and its ballet school, in addition to a large number of extras for the mass scenes.⁶³ It is possible that Gruber had seen excerpts from *Flames* (some scenes were later included in the 1954 Soviet release *Mastera russkogo baleta*) and that she received advice from Soviet dance artists who travelled to the GDR at this time, such as Raisa Struchkova, but it is unlikely that she had access to dance notations or a full recording. If Gruber could not fully replicate Vasilii Vainonen's original choreography, she at least attempted to reproduce key features of the ballet (the use of mass dances, folk and character dance, etc.) and the general impression that the ballet had created.

In this respect, Gruber largely succeeded. The initial response from the East German press was overwhelmingly positive, although it is likely that the critical response was to some extent scripted and predetermined by cultural officials (as it had been in Soviet Russia in 1932). In their reviews, GDR critics attempted to guide the ballet's reception and to bring it in line with their understanding of socialist realism. Sporck, for example, hailed the ballet's premiere as a moment of national significance and as the "first practical realization of what had been discussed in theory" at the Tanzkonferenz.⁶⁴ He called Gruber's *Flames* "the first successful depiction of a revolutionary subject on the German stage that was created in accordance with the methods of socialist realism."⁶⁵ Ideologues and critics proudly contrasted Gruber's ballet with the kinds of productions that were being pursued in West Germany. Pointedly, Sporck mentioned Tatjana Gsovsky, a choreographer who had left the GDR for West Germany in 1950 and whose work he called "decadent, eccentric, and full of psychopathic characters and incidents ... dance that alienates itself from the people and is heading down a dead end, from which there is only one exit – the path toward Realism."⁶⁶ In his and other critics' view, Gruber's *Flames* brightly illuminated that very path, and it quashed any lingering doubts about the viability of staging Soviet ballets in the GDR. Considered edifying and entertaining, *Flames* was both a critical and popular success. Opinion of the production in the press was in fact so unanimous that publications such as *Weltbühne* even began to reject reviews, because, as the editors put it self-consciously, "our West German readers might gain the impression that there is only this one artistic event in the GDR."⁶⁷

Intermixed with general plaudits was some mild criticism and advice to choreographers. The modern dancer and choreographer Gret Palucca (a powerful figure in GDR dance), for example, pointed to an inconsistent use of dance technique, writing that *The Flames of Paris* did not quite create a unified whole.⁶⁸ In particular, the pointe work by the character Mireille when she carries the flag of freedom to represent the victory of the *Volk* over the French monarchy was "inappropriate."⁶⁹ The primary concern, however, had to do with the technical level of Gruber's dancers. Weaknesses were most evident in the aristocratic scenes at the French court, which required expert fluency in classical ballet technique to convey the choreography's intended irony.[70]

Whatever deficiencies the production might have exhibited, *The Flames of Paris* was seen as clear evidence that East German dance theatres were indeed capable of staging Soviet *drambalety* and that this was the direction in which they should continue to work. As one critic wrote,

> Current productions in the Soviet Union show us how to overcome all the faded fairytale magic and all the old artistic gimmicks of ballet in order to bring to the ballet stage progressive dramatic content ... With its first performance of *The Flames of Paris*, the Leipzig Theater provides an impressive example of the type of combative passion [*kämpferische Leidenschaft*] by which Soviet dance artists have turned activist ballet art into a vehicle of political consciousness.[71]

As a "vehicle of political consciousness," the production had another important function: to incorporate the GDR into the pan-Soviet narrative of revolution. Exported to East Germany, *The Flames of Paris* can be viewed as effecting a double displacement of the French Revolution, in the sense that the "revolution" in the GDR (aka Soviet occupation) was built on the Bolshevik Revolution of 1917, which, through the ballet, was seen as building on the French Revolution of the late eighteenth century (and even, to some extent, the Decembrist movement, as suggested by the ballet's title).[72] The ballet thus serves as a mechanism for collapsing or folding these linked, mutually legitimizing "revolutionary" movements onto one another, eliding historical or potential ideological differences to create a unifying and structuring myth of revolution. The fact that at least one of these revolutions arose "organically" from below, while others, as in the GDR, were imposed and managed from above, was irrelevant to the revolutionary master narrative Soviet officials were advancing. And so too, in some respects, was the historical specificity of the French Revolution as depicted in *Flames* irrelevant in light of broader political ambitions. The historical and cultural specificity of the ballet's content had to be transcended (or partly obscured) in order to express a grander, more timeless revolutionary pathos and mythology: the Leninist dream of a world proletariat rising up, of revolutionary enthusiasm that would spread globally and eventually dissolve national distinctions into a single tapestry of monolithic Soviet culture. Understood in this way, it becomes obvious why Soviet cultural officials thought that *The Flames of Paris* was not suitable fare for a twentieth-century French audience, since the ballet was not really about French history as such. As a Soviet cultural product to be circulated internally, the ballet had a clear function: to help produce, or at least manufacture the illusion of, an international, unified communist culture. By the 1950s, circulation of the ballet – an aesthetically performed revolution – could fulfil this role at least in the context of socialist Eastern Europe.

The ideological provenance, content, and function of *The Flames of Paris* as a Soviet cultural product were clear to East German cultural officials and critics. Indeed, scenes from the ballet were performed a month after the Leipzig premiere at the Friedrichstadt-Palast Berlin to celebrate the thirty-sixth anniversary of the October Revolution. The program also included the Soviet anthem, the "International," Russian folk songs such as "Kamarinskaia," and a tune called "Danke Euch, Ihr Sowjetsoldaten!" ("Thank you, Soviet soldiers!").[73] Besides introducing the conventions of *drambalet*, *The Flames of Paris* served a larger political purpose for the GDR, made all the more apparent in the context of such a celebration: to blend Soviet revolutionary traditions into German culture in order to reinforce the ideological brotherhood between the GDR and the Soviet Union. The performance of the ballet, whether in its entirety or excerpted for specific festivals and events, functioned as a revolutionary ritual in Soviet Russia and across the Eastern Bloc, helping to reaffirm the idea of a transnational socialist culture.

Behind the scenes, however, more serious doubts were raised about the production and what it revealed about East German dance. Members of the Division for Performing Arts at AdK, while conceding that *The Flames of Paris* was a step forward, believed that the ballet manifested a number of "shortcomings."[74] Max Burghardt, a strong advocate and colleague of Gruber's, for example, thought that the dancers lacked the technical expertise to express the content of the production or to tackle other "big, realistic Soviet ballets."[75] Incorporating more elements of folk dance, acting techniques, and even elements of "new artistic dance" (*Ausdruckstanz* under a different name), in his opinion, would help dancers and choreographers engage more deeply with the content and give it sincere and realistic expression. In her own report sent to AdK, Gruber agreed, writing that "socialist realism places before the dancer new tasks," which she thought could not be achieved with classical ballet alone.[76] Notably, she argued that new artistic dance, in addition to folk dance, could complement classical ballet and increase its expressive power.[77] Thus, even the choreographer responsible for staging the first large-scale Soviet *drambalet* in the GDR concluded (if at first only behind the scenes) that a fusion of styles – a cultural hybrid of "local" dance traditions and "alien" ones imported from the Soviet Union – would be the most logical path forward (despite the initially stubborn conviction of officials that Soviet dance had to supplant more "native" choreographic forms).

Gruber's version of *The Flames of Paris* came increasingly to be seen as a kind of litmus test for the capabilities of GDR dance. The results of this test continued to be scrutinized in the years following its premiere. Such re-evaluation was typical of the "critical reflex" of socialist realist discursive practices: initial praise; a tempering of that praise; self-critique; and then recommendations for improvements. This critical turn also dovetailed with and was influenced by major cultural and historical shifts. Although a direct response to the demand for socialist realist ballet, *Flames* was staged during a moment of flux in the cultural policy of the GDR: Stalin had recently died, and Stakuko was dissolved by the end of 1953 – events that led to a relaxing of the campaign against formalism and a diminishment of Soviet oversight. With the loosening of restrictions, officials and dance practitioners began to look at *Flames* more critically. Despite having been hailed at the time of its premiere as incontrovertible proof that the *drambalet* model was the best way to develop GDR dance, Gruber's *Flames* was increasingly discussed less as an example to be emulated than as a warning to GDR choreographers about the challenges, technical and artistic, of assimilating *drambalet*.

Re-examining *Drambalet* after Stalin

The evolution in opinion about Gruber's *The Flames of Paris* was in all likelihood a slightly delayed response to political changes. The often rapid oscillations between periods of restriction and relative lenience in East German cultural policy created difficult working conditions for artists. In East German dance, it could take time for the reverberations of a political shift to be felt – or, more specifically, for the shock waves of a cataclysmic event such as the death of Stalin and the subsequent relaxing of restrictions to reach choreographers and ballet masters. The Tanzkonferenz of 1954 evidences early rumblings of a shift in dance practitioners' thinking – a shift that would, little by little, move away from Stalinist *drambalet*. At the conference, Gruber's *Flames* was held up for re-examination. As a staple of the Soviet repertoire and as the first successfully staged *drambalet* in the GDR, the production metonymically stood in for the entire debate about the adoption of Soviet socialist realist dance genres and methods.

The 1954 Tanzkonferenz had a distinctly different tenor and roster of participants than the 1953 Tanzkonferenz. For one, it was hosted by AdK and the Ministry of Culture, which at this time were pursuing the policy of German cultural unity. That policy included "seiz[ing] all opportunities for pan-German cooperation to cultivate and nurture a humanistic German culture."[78] The Tanzkonferenz of 1954 was conducted in this spirit, with more than twenty West German dancers and choreographers invited. But it is clear from internal documents that a joint conference was still politically delicate. "Special arrangements with the press" were made to ensure that the public naming of West Germans would not result in any political "difficulties," and West German participants were not named even in the transcripts from the conference.[79]

The 1954 Tanzkonferenz also differentiated itself in terms of its focus on "practice" (dance technique and pedagogy) as opposed to "theory" (the implementation of socialist realism). Both in the planning protocols and in the transcripts from the conference, one notes an evolution in the East German interpretation of socialist realism, allowing for greater artistic agency. This was part of a strategy to make the conference more inclusive and appealing to West German dance practitioners. Indeed, at the conference, one finds far less ideological jargon and less discussion of socialist realism as such. GDR participants and officials even tended to drop the "socialist" in front of "realism," speaking instead only of *Realismus* and *realistisches* or *dramatisches Ballett*. This, as well as the focus on technique, was part of GDR dance practitioners' effort to find common ground with their West German counterparts and to open up opportunities for collaboration and artistic exchanges.

East German participants were self-critical at times throughout the conference. The main report, delivered on the first day (2 December 1954), called the GDR's accomplishments mostly "unsatisfactory," noting only a handful of "successful results," including Gruber's *The Flames of Paris*.[80] The report credited Gruber with staging in Germany the "first and most successful revolutionary ballet," which brought the GDR "direct knowledge" of Soviet ballet.[81] Yet it also drew lessons from the production's flaws. Gruber's *Flames* was considered too preoccupied with content and plot development, for instance, to the detriment of form and actual dancing.[82] Citing the Leipzig troupe's meagre size and relative lack of technical skill, the report used the production to sow doubts about whether large-scale classical ballets and *drambalety* ought to undergird the GDR's still shaky dance scene.

To highlight the still obvious artistic gap between East German and Soviet dancers and choreographers, the chairman of the conference referred to a dance performance staged by the choreographer Anni Stoll-Peterka that the Soviet prima ballerina Galina Ulanova had seen when she and other Bolshoi dancers came to the GDR after their Paris tour was aborted.[83] Ulanova was the ballerina most identified with the *drambalet* genre and indeed had originated the role of Mireille in *Flames*; thus, her opinion of GDR dance was especially meaningful. The speaker read Ulanova's rather withering assessment aloud:

> Of course, Anni Peterka and her ensemble do not work in accordance with classical technique as we understand it. Put simply, for us, dance is classical ballet. For her [Peterka], however, any rhythmic movement accompanied by music is dance. Well, that is a perfectly legitimate point of view. We came away with the conviction that this could also be some kind of ballet. It is based on sophisticated acting, and that is, of course, a hundred times better than a bad classical ballet.[84]

Ulanova's description of GDR dance can be characterized as a distinctly qualified compliment wrapped in explicit critique. Whatever it was that East German choreographers were creating diverged from what she, and her Soviet colleagues, strictly considered dance, although it was still preferable to badly executed classical ballet.

From these words, the GDR choreographers might have hoped that they would be allowed a freer understanding of socialist dance, and even that they should not attempt to stage Soviet classical ballets. The chairman of the conference acknowledged that East German ballet had been negatively judged but added that the flaws of any given production should not make one conclude that the problem was classical ballet itself; rather, it was the poor command of classical ballet technique that resulted in the diminishment of the expressive powers of dance.[85] The speaker thought they needed to continue to "grapple" with classical ballet technique but stated that "any style of dance [should be] acceptable," so long as it contributed to and resulted in a "truthful, realistic representation of clear themes and content."[86] To boot, he noted how Soviet dance also resorted to means of expression that could not be described as strictly classical ballet technique but that extended and amplified classical ballet.[87] The speaker was thus suggesting that GDR choreographers could begin to explore a wider range of dance techniques in their own productions, including indigenous forms of modern dance. Like other critics from this time, the speaker still measured GDR dance against the high standards set by Soviet ballet, although he was able to recognize that GDR choreographers could not simply import the Soviet *drambalet* repertoire and expect to reproduce its success – a fact that *The Flames of Paris* exposed.

Transcripts from the 1954 Tanzkonferenz reflect dance practitioners' dawning realization that East German dance could and perhaps ought to broaden the definition of "realistic dance" beyond Stalinist *drambalet*. It does not appear that this stance was taken merely for show in front of West German colleagues at the conference. The conference's official resolutions conveyed this more open attitude towards what constituted "socialist" and "realist" dance, as well as a more favourable view of West German dance (which had been disparaged as "degenerate" just the year before). Those resolutions stated that "all forms of dance – classical, modern, and folk dance – should be considered," particularly when attempting to express complex and multifaceted topics or themes. The chosen dance forms, nevertheless, needed to serve the "singular goal of achieving realistic dance," and the foundation remained classical ballet.[88]

Following the 1954 Tanzkonferenz and upon the advent of the Thaw, dance in the GDR, as in the Soviet Union, began to evolve away from *drambalet* to allow for greater choreographic experimentation. Gruber, a savvy cultural operator, was able to respond to the vacillations in cultural policy, exploiting phases of ideological lenience to expand the creative possibilities of East German dance. Indeed, her creative evolution tracks closely with the general evolution of East German dance in the 1950s: an initial reliance on Soviet models and/or productions with historical precedent, followed, in the latter half of the 1950s, by greater experimentation with dance forms and attempts to create original productions on German themes. Her ballet *New Odyssey* (*Neue Odyssee*) from 1957, which dealt with the German experience of the Second World War, is a powerful example of this development.

Filtered through the timeless myth of Homer's *Odyssey*, *New Odyssey* follows a German man's journey home after the war to an imagined undivided Berlin. The ballet was meant to be political without being aggressively partisan in order to speak to *both* East and West Germans and their shared trauma.[89] While still based on elements of *drambalet*, Gruber's *New Odyssey* strove to express national content and contemporary issues in more national forms (e.g., the inclusion of modern, folk, and popular dance). The GDR critic Werner Hoersch viewed the production as a successful and uniquely German elaboration of *Handlungsballett* (aka *drambalet*), a genre that could continue to open up "rich possibilities" if choreographers used it to tell their own stories.[90]

Conclusion

Some of Gruber's work, as well as that of other GDR choreographers (e.g., Tom Schilling) particularly in the 1960s and 1970s, suggested a possible rapprochement between *drambalet* and more native theatrical traditions. After the relaxing of restrictions in the mid-1950s, artists in both the GDR and Soviet Union began to "exploit the wider political environment of de-Stalinization for their own artistic goals."[91] The demand for productions in the style of Stalinist *drambalet* receded across the Eastern Bloc, and even a ballet like *The Flames of Paris* lost its foothold in the Soviet repertoire. The production had, in Konstantin Sergeev's words, already "played its role" and become "antiquated."[92]

Yet in both the Soviet Union and the GDR, the debate about the role of art in society and about what constituted realism continued with "varying intensity and pitch."[93] Shifting interpretations led to censorship, denunciations, and a paranoid working atmosphere. Even so, GDR dance practitioners were sometimes able to take advantage of lingering ambiguity about socialist realism in dance to explore a wider array of techniques and forms, such as modern dance. This mixed messaging (perennial "revisions and clarifications") about what dance forms were allowed under the auspices of socialist realism created, in Jens Giersdorf's words, a "conundrum that would haunt East German dance to the end."[94]

But to return to a question posed at the beginning of this chapter: How successful was the transplantation of Stalinist *drambalet* into a different national tradition and historical moment? *Drambalet* largely passed this initial "stress test"; it did, however, undergo alterations, and its terms were renegotiated, when challenged by the specific cultural conditions of early Cold War East Germany. As this chapter has shown, dance practitioners and policy-makers used *drambalet*, and *The Flames of Paris* in particular, to jump-start East Germany's fledgling ballet scene in the early post-war years. This was despite the fact that the GDR dance scene could be characterized as inhospitable terrain for large-scale Soviet ballet. Yet GDR choreographers, such as Gruber and Schilling, assimilated, disrupted, or resisted some of *drambalet*'s conventions, merging them with their own dance traditions, in order to create an East German variation of socialist realist dance. In this context, *drambalet*, a portmanteau and a generic hybrid (part drama, part ballet), proved more flexible than many have assumed, given how strongly associated it was and is with dogmatic restriction and formal rigidity. The story of how East Germans grappled with *drambalet* is not only a compelling iteration of long-standing debates about the nature of dance, its form and content, but also an example of how aesthetic forms are renegotiated, enriched, and redefined as they migrate across borders and ideological regimes.

Despite the general abandonment of the genre as an artistic dead end by the mid-1960s, *drambalet* has been granted a surprising afterlife in the twenty-first century. *The Flames of Paris* has been "reconstructed" twice, by Alexei Ratmansky for the Bolshoi (2008) and by Mikhail Messerer for the Mikhailovsky Theatre (2013). Once considered a Soviet domestic product of circumscribed use, this ballet is now performed and broadcast internationally – to great (if somewhat perplexing) acclaim. Ratmansky's version, unlike Messerer's, fundamentally changes the ballet's message, from a revolutionary to a counter-revolutionary one, particularly by altering its ending to highlight the tragic personal costs of violent revolution.[95] Ratmansky largely preserved the genre's facade of grand Stalinist style while destabilizing its very foundations, its ideological content.[96] Reanimated and modified, this *drambalet* staple has become, yet again, a site for symbolic struggle and manipulation, particularly in Putin's Russia – as well as ripe fodder for debates about the art of socialist realism and how to relate to the Soviet heritage.[97] One might ask: Does the return and recirculation of a ballet like *The Flames of Paris* amount to a disembodied spectre of once vibrant revolutionary ideas – a revival of a Stalinist ritual that has lost its meaning? Or can the ballet take on a new meaning that speaks to a post-Soviet audience beyond fulfilling an appetite for "Soviet kitsch" or indulging nostalgia? The same question that had vexed both Soviet and East German dance specialists thus re-emerges: Can old forms – in this case, ones that served as propaganda for a repressive regime – accommodate new content? The answer, at least when it comes to *The Flames of Paris*, seems to be a perhaps unsettling yes.

Notes

1 Lilo Gruber, "Lilo Gruber, Leiterin der Ballettschule der Städtischen Theater, Leipzig," in *Zur Diskussion: Realismus in der Tanzkunst* (Dresden: Verlag. der Kunst, 1953), 38. Gruber's article first appeared in *Weltbühne*, no. 7 (18 February 1953). Unless otherwise indicated, all translations are my own.

2 Marianne Vogelsang, "Zur Situation des Neuen künstlerischen Tanzes," *Weltbühne*, no. 48 (1 December 1954): 1513.

3 The term *Ausdruckstanz* was coined around the turn of the last century and was associated with such prominent modernist figures as Mary Wigman, Rudolf Laban, Kurt Jooss, Dore Hoyer, Harald Kreutzberg, and Gret Palucca. Under Nazism, *Ausdruckstanz* was often called simply *deutscher Tanz*, and in the GDR it was renamed *neuer künstlerischer Tanz*.

4 The term *drambalet* refers to the body of officially sanctioned choreographic works from the 1930s and 1940s in the USSR. These ballets were typically plot-heavy and rife with ideologically sanctioned content. It should be mentioned, however, that the term *drambalet* was not consistently used in the 1930s to describe the Soviet ballets of this era. In the 1920s and 1930s,

a variety of terms were used to describe the not yet fully defined genre of *drambalet* – for example, socialist ballet, realist ballet, Soviet ballet, danced drama, choreographic drama, revolutionary ballet, socialist-revolutionary ballet, proletarian ballet, and, of course, dramatic ballet. In this article, I use the term *drambalet* to refer to the genre and the body of Soviet repertoire GDR dance was compelled to adopt.

5 In the early 1950s in the GDR, *drambalet* was typically referred to in German as *dramatisches Ballett* or *realistisches Ballett* and even, more simply, as *sowjetisches Ballett*. By the latter half of the 1950s, the term *Handlungsballett* was in regular use.

6 As clumsy as the formulation "socialist realist dance" or "socialist realist ballet" may sound, I use such terms to refer to dance or ballet that responded to socialist realism but that cannot be strictly described as *drambalet*. Indeed, *drambalet* was a response to socialist realism but was not synonymous with it.

7 My 2019 dissertation, "Politics in Pointe Shoes: The Genesis and Afterlives of Stalinist *Drambalet*," provides a thorough production history of *The Flames of Paris* in several iterations: the original 1932 production, the GDR 1953 production, and two post-Soviet "reconstructions," by Alexei Ratmansky (2008) and Mikhail Messerer (2013).

8 Soviet dancers performed in the GDR with some regularity, and clips of their dancing were provided by the USSR for public broadcast in the GDR (e.g., on the weekly program *Der Augenzeuge*). In the late 1940s and early 1950s, GDR audiences were able to see Soviet stars such as Konstantin Sergeev, Maya Plisetskaya, Natalia Dudinskaya, and Raisa Struchkova, among others.

9 Among the most prolific scholars of early East German dance are Marion Kant, Jens Giersdorf, and Ralf Stabel. The "Körperpolitik in der DDR" project connected to the University of Leipzig has also done important work on dance in the GDR.

10 The "alliance" between dancers and National Socialism has been much debated within the dance history community. See *New German Dance Studies*, ed. Susan Manning and Lucia Ruprecht (Champaign: University of Illinois Press, 2012), and especially Lilian Karina and Marion Kant, *Hitler's Dancers: German Modern Dance and the Third Reich* (New York: Berghahn Books, 2003).

11 Marion Kant, "Was bleibt? The Politics of East German Dance," in Manning and Ruprecht, *New German Dance Studies*, 143.

12 Mary Wigman and Gret Palucca, for example, were given such documentation exonerating them of complicity in the Nazi regime. Very few GDR dance practitioners were questioned during the period of denazification. Fritz Böhme was one of them; he taught race theory and dance aesthetics at the central Nazi dance institution, Meisterwerkstätten,

between 1936 and 1945, yet he was still allowed to teach dance history in the GDR and was a prominent supporter of Palucca.
13 Nina Glick Schiller, Cristina Szanton Blanc, and Linda G. Basch, *Nations Unbound: Transnational Projects, Postcolonial Predicaments, and Deterritorialized Nation-States* (Langhorne: Gordon and Breach, 1994), 7.
14 Schiller et al., *Nations Unbound*, 7.
15 The KPD's ideological platform was heavily indebted to the Soviets, since they were viewed as having already accomplished revolution.
16 Reprinted in "Der Kampf gegen den Formalismus in Kunst und Literatur für eine fortschrittliche deutsche Kultur," *Musik und Gesellschaft* (Sonderdruck zu "Musik und Gesellschaft"), no. 3 (May 1951): 1–23.
17 "Der Kampf gegen den Formalismus," 3. The descriptor "imperialistic" is taken from *Zhdanovshchina* (developed, in 1946, by Andrei Zhdanov and a repressive cultural policy that persisted until 1953), which designated the United States as "imperialist" and the Soviet Union as "democratic." These aesthetic/ideological campaigns against cosmopolitanism and formalism (less so kitsch) were largely imported from the USSR, but they were then used to fight the GDR's internal ideological battles, which to some extent differed from the Soviet ones with respect to tactics and targets. The anti-cosmopolitanism campaign in the GDR is a large topic and the subject of numerous books and articles. For anti-Semitism in the GDR's anti-cosmopolitanism campaign, see, for example, Mary Fulbrook, *German National Identity after the Holocaust* (Cambridge: Polity Press, 1999); Jeffrey Herf, *Divided Memory: The Nazi Past in the Two Germanys* (Cambridge, MA: Harvard University Press, 1997), particularly his chapter "Purging 'Cosmopolitanism': The Jewish Question in East Germany, 1949–1956," 106–61; Jan Herman Brinks, "Political Anti-Fascism in the German Democratic Republic," *Journal of Contemporary History* 32, no. 2 (2 April 1997): 207–17; and Peter Grieder, *The German Democratic Republic*, esp. 30–4.
18 Loren Kruger, "'Stories from the Production Line': Modernism and Modernization in the GDR Production Play," *Theatre Journal* 46, no. 4 (December 1994): 494–5.
19 See also Walter Ulbricht's lecture delivered to the 2nd SED Party conference and printed in the journal *Theater der Zeit*: Ulbricht, "Kampf um ein realistisches Kunstschaffen," *Theater der Zeit*, no. 16 (1952): 1–2.
20 Stephen Parker, "Brecht and Sinn und Form: The Creation of Cold War Legends," *German Life and Letters* 60, no. 4 (October 2007): 523.
21 See the collection *Classical Music in the German Democratic Republic: Production and Reception*, ed. Kyle Frackman and Larson Powell (Rochester: Camden House, 2015); and Jens Giersdorf, *The Body of the People: East German Dance Since 1945* (Madison: University of Wisconsin Press, 2013), 61–3.

22 Frackman and Powell, Introduction to *Classical Music in the German Democratic Republic*, 3; Elizabeth Janik, *Recomposing German Music: Politics and Musical Tradition in Cold War Berlin* (Boston: Brill Academic, 2005). On the Great Appropriation, see Katerina Clark, *Moscow, the Fourth Rome: Stalinism, Cosmopolitanism, and the Evolution of Soviet Culture, 1931–1941* (Cambridge, MA: Harvard University Press, 2011).
23 Giersdorf, *The Body of the People*, 62.
24 "Der Kampf gegen den Formalismus," 6.
25 Karl Toepfer, *Empire of Ecstasy: Nudity and Movement in German Body Culture, 1910–1935* (Berkeley: University of California Press, 1997), 285.
26 Jessica Payette, "The Embodiment of Collective Memory in *Neue Odyssee*," in *Classical Music in the German Democratic Republic: Production and Reception*, ed. Kyle Frackman and Larson Powell (Rochester, NY: Camden House, 2015), 98. There is some debate among dance historians about the extent to which the Nazis rejected classical ballet. Karl Toepfer contends that the Nazis did not dismiss ballet outright but hoped to establish a "German idea" of ballet (Toepfer, *Empire*, 296). By contrast, Marion Kant, like Payette, highlights the deep-seated antagonisms between *Ausdruckstanz* and ballet both before and during Nazi rule. See Marion Kant, "German Gymnastics, Modern German Dance, and Nazi Aesthetics," *Dance Research Journal* 48, no. 2 (May 2016): 4–25. See also Karina and Kant, *Hitler's Dancers*.
27 Protokolle der Tanzkonferenz 1953. Bundesarchiv Berlin. Signatur DR 1 / 6025. Ministerium für Kultur.-Staatliche Kommission für Kunstangelegenheiten. 7.3.3 Konferenzen, Kongresse, Festwochen. Bl. 25 (hereafter BA. DR 1 / 6025).
28 Payette, "The Embodiment of Collective Memory," 99.
29 Giersdorf, *The Body of the People*, 18. See also Ralf Stabel, *IM Tänzer: Der Tanz und die Staatssicherheit* (Mainz: Schott Music, 2008).
30 The term *narodnost'/Volkstümlichkeit* required particular attention by GDR officials, given the exploitation of the concept (*Volkstumideologie*) to advance murderously racist policies during the Third Reich. The term had to be ideologically laundered through the doctrine of socialist realism. In theory, National Socialist and socialist realist *narodnost'*, as it was promoted in the GDR, were different; the *narodnost'* of socialist realism was intended to erase the virulent nationalism of Nazism and replace it with the supposedly "true" nationalism that fascism had hijacked. In reality, however, the results of socialist realist and National Socialist *narodnost'* look problematically similar: the nationalism of the Third Reich was replaced by a simulacrum, however conveniently repackaged.
31 For more on the debate over socialist realism in the GDR, and in particular Brecht's contribution, see Giersdorf, *The Body of the People*, 59–62. See also Franz Anton Cramer, "Warfare over Realism: Tanztheater in East Germany 1966–1989," in Manning and Ruprecht, *New German Dance Studies*, 147–64.

32 Rebling, "Der Kampf um die Durchsetzung des sozialistischen Realismus in der Tanzkunst," in *Zur Diskussion: Realismus in der Tanzkunst* (Dresden: Verlag der Kunst, 1953), 64.
33 Socialist realism was primarily exemplar-driven via a process of retroactive canonization. See Petre Petrov, *Automatic for the Masses: The Death of the Author and the Birth of Socialist Realism* (Toronto: University of Toronto Press, 2015), 23.
34 BA. DR 1 / 6025. Bl. 17.
35 BA. DR 1 / 6025. Bl. 17.
36 BA. DR 1 / 6025. Bl. 17.
37 BA. DR 1 / 6025. Bl. 17, Bl. 10.
38 See Karina and Kant, *Hitler's Dancers*. For a study of discursive practices employed by the Nazis, see Victor Klemperer, *The Language of the Third Reich: LTI-Lingua Tertii Imperii: A Philologist's Notebook*, trans. Martin Brady (New York: Continuum, 2006); and H.M. Militz, "Victor Klemperer between LTI (Lingua-Tertii-Imperii) and LQI (Lingua-Quarti-Imperii) (Language of the Third Reich and Language of the Soviet Zone of Occupation)," *Muttersprache* 11, no. 4 (2001): 353–60.
39 Petrov, *Automatic for the Masses*, 193.
40 Jérôme Bazin, "Le réalisme socialiste et ses modèles internationaux," *Vingtième Siècle. Revue d'histoire*, vol. 109, no. 1 (2011): 3; Marina Frolova-Walker, "'National in Form, Socialist in Content': Musical Nation-Building in the Soviet Republics," *Journal of the American Musicological Society* 51, no. 2 (June 1998): 331–71.
41 BA. DR 1 / 6025. Bl. 24.
42 BA. DR 1 / 6025. Bl. 24.
43 Grieder, *The German Democratic Republic*, 21.
44 Ralf Stabel, "Und so wird daraus nichts," in *Neuer Künstlicher Tanz. Eine Dokumentation*, ed. Eva Winkler and Peter Jarchow (Dresden, 1996), 109. Quoted in Patrick Primavesi et al., "Körperpolitik in der DDR," *Denkströme. Journal der Sächsischen Akademie der Wissenschaften*, no. 14 (2015): 19.
45 "Tanzkonferenz am 23./24. März 1953, Der sozialistische Realismus in der Tanzkunst: Thesen," in *Zur Diskussion*, 75.
46 Christina Ezrahi, *Swans of the Kremlin: Ballet and Power in Soviet Russia* (Pittsburgh: University of Pittsburgh Press, 2012), 103.
47 "Tanzkonferenz am 23./24. März 1953," in *Zur Diskussion*, 75.
48 V.M. Gaevskii, *Divertisment: Sud'by klassicheskogo baleta* (Moscow: Iskusstvo, 1981), 184.
49 Gaevskii, *Divertisment*.
50 For her analysis of the spontaneity/consciousness dialectic, see Katerina Clark, *The Soviet Novel: History as Ritual* (Bloomington: Indiana University Press, 2000), 15–24. I analyse this ballet in terms of Clark's socialist realist

"master tropes" in chapter 2 of my dissertation, "Politics in Pointe Shoes." Carolyn Pouncy assesses a number of early Soviet ballets, including *Flames*, in terms of Clark's master plot; see Pouncy, "Stumbling toward Socialist Realism," *Russian History/Histoire Russe* 32, no. 2 (Summer 2005): esp. 181–2.
51 K.N. Armashevskaia with N.V. Vainonen, *Baletmeister Vainonen* (Moscow: Iskusstvo, 1971), 105.
52 See Stenogramma ob"edinennogo plenuma sektsii teatrovedeniia i muzykovedeniia GAIS sovmestno s Leningradskim Soiuzom kompozitorov (diskussiia) o postanovke baleta 'Plamia Parizha'. Protokoly zasedaniia brigady po 'Istorii sovetskogo teatra' i Sektsii teatrovedeniia. Len. otd. Gos. akademii iskusstvoznaniia [LOGAIS]. [15 December 1932–7 April 1933] TsGALI, f. 82, op. 3, d. 63. See, in particular, l. 5ob–6.
53 Ezrahi coins this term in her book *Swans of the Kremlin*; see esp. 7–9.
54 "Halfway policy" is Ivan Sollertinskii's term from a 1932 discussion of the ballet. See Stenogramma ob"edinennogo plenuma sektsii teatrovedeniia i muzykovedeniia GAIS sovmestno s Leningradskim Soiuzom kompozitorov (diskussiia) o postanovke baleta 'Plamia Parizha'. TsGALI f. 82, op. 3, d. 63, l. 56.
55 Simon Morrison, *Bolshoi Confidential: Secrets of the Russian Ballet from the Rule of the Tsars to Today* (London: 4th Estate, 2016), 290.
56 Morrison, *Bolshoi Confidential*, 291.
57 Stenogramma ob"edinennogo plenuma. TsGALI f. 82, op. 3, d. 63, l. 63.
58 Gabriele Klein, "Toward a Theory of Cultural Translation in Dance," in Manning and Ruprecht, *New German Dance Studies*, 255.
59 Stenograficheskii otchet. Ob"edinennyi plenum sektsii teatrovediia i muzikovedeniia akademii sovmestno s Leningradskim Soiuzom sovetskikh kompozitorov. [15 December 1932]. TsGALI f. 82, op. 3, d. 63, l. 63.
60 Stenograficheskii otchet. TsGALI f. 82, op. 3, d. 63, l. 63.
61 Officials decided not to bring *The Flames of Paris* to France because they worried it would not be well received there – it was of "lesser artistic interest." One can read into the obliquely worded decision that perhaps officials were still wary of bringing this piece to French audiences. See Proekty postanovlenii TsK KPSS i Soveta Ministerov SSSR. [31 April 1954]. RGANI f. 5, op. 17, d. 494, l. 103.
62 "Leipziger Bühnenkünstler stellen sich vor." [circa 1952]. Document held at Akademie der Künste (Ost) (hereafter AdK-O). Signatur Gruber 899.
63 *Die Flamme von Paris* / Boris Assafjew. Ballett-Libretto. AdK-O. Signatur Gruber 461.
64 Martin Sporck, "Ballett auf richtigem Wege (Zur leipziger Erstaffführung der Flamme von Paris)," *Weltbühne*, no. 43 (28 October 1953): 1365.

65 Sporck, "Ballett auf richtigem Wege," 1362.
66 Sporck, "Ballett auf richtigem Wege," 1363. Sporck seems to be talking about Gsovsky's twenty-minute ballet *Signale*, which did not in fact premiere until 1955. It seems his knowledge of this ballet largely came from reports he had read in the West German press.
67 Redaktion "Die Weltbühne"/Leipziger Volkszeitung an Karl Wehner. AdK-O. Signatur 451.
68 Gret Palucca, "Zur Leipziger Erstaufführung des Balletts von Assafjew: Die Flamme von Paris," *Weltbühne*, no. 47 (14 October 1953): 1295–6.
69 Palucca, "Zur Leipziger Erstaufführung," 1295.
70 "Flamme von Paris/Zur Erstaufführung des Balletts von Assafjew," *Sächsisches Tageblatt*, no. 162 (10 October 1953): 4. Held at AdK-O. Signatur 466.
71 "Flamme von Paris," *Sächsisches Tageblatt*, 4.
72 The title of the ballet was inspired by a line from a prominent member of the Decembrist movement, A.I. Odoevskii: "one spark will start a flame" (*iz iskry vozgoritsia plamia*). This line became a slogan of the revolutionary movement in Russia, with *Iskra* even chosen as the name for a Lenin-founded newspaper. Such a title (*Plamia Parizha*) helped emphasize the line of revolutionary continuity the creators of the ballet hoped to suggest between the French Revolution, the Decembrist Uprising, and the October Revolution.
73 Programm der Festveranstaltung zu Ehren des XXXVI Jahrestages der Großen Sozialistischen Oktoberrevolution. AdK-O. Signatur 464.
74 Sitzungen der Sektion Darstellende Kunst [16 December 1953]. AdK-O. Signatur 126. Bl. 216–17.
75 Max Burghardt, "Was verlangt das Theater von der künstlerischen Ausbildung seiner Theater?" AdK-O. Signatur 126. Bl. 215.
76 Lilo Gruber. [Undated report, circa December 1953]. AdK-O. Signatur 126. Bl. 221.
77 Gruber. [Undated report, circa December 1953]. AdK-O. Signatur 126. Bl. 221.
78 "Programmerklärung des Ministeriums für Kultur der Deutschen Demokratischen Republik. Zur Verteidigung der Einheit der deutschen Kultur," *Sinn und Form*, no. 2 (1954): 279.
79 This planning meeting consisted of representatives from eight editorial offices, members of the Ministry of Culture, and a number of dance specialists. See Protokoll. Pressebesprechung vom 30.11.1954 zur Tanzkonferenz. BA. DR 1 / 6025.
80 A copy of this talk, "Die gegenwärtige Situation der Tanzkunst in Deutschland und ihre nächsten Aufgaben," can be found under Losung für die I. deutsche Tanzkonferenz. BA. DR 1 / 6025. The quotes here are from Bl. 3–4. The conference was held 2–5 December 1954.

158   Elizabeth H. Stern

81 Losung für die I. deutsche Tanzkonferenz. BA. DR 1 / 6025. Bl. 15.
82 Losung für die I. deutsche Tanzkonferenz. BA. DR 1 / 6025. Bl. 17.
83 The two works Ulanova seems to have in mind were created by Anni Stoll-Peterka for the Metropol Theater: *Kleider machen Leute*, based on the comedic novella by Gottfried Keller and which had been made into an opera by Alexander von Zemlinsky (1910), and a film by Helmut Käutner (1940), as well as a piece called *Vogelscheuche*, set to Dvořák's Slavic Dances.
84 Losung für die I. deutsche Tanzkonferenz. BA. DR 1 / 6025. Bl. 24.
85 Losung für die I. deutsche Tanzkonferenz. BA. DR 1 / 6025. Bl. 25.
86 Losung für die I. deutsche Tanzkonferenz. BA. DR 1 / 6025.
87 Losung für die I. deutsche Tanzkonferenz. BA. DR 1 / 6025, Bl. 27.
88 Losung für die I. deutsche Tanzkonferenz. BA. DR 1 / 6025, Bl. 26.
89 See Payette, "The Embodiment of Collective Memory," 97–118.
90 Werner Hoerisch, "Neue Odyssee: Ballett-Uraufführung Der Berliner Staatsoper," *Neues Deutschland*, 26 November 1957. Held at Tanzarchiv Leipzig. Signatur DDR II / 72–118.
91 Ezrahi, *Swans of the Kremlin*, 103.
92 Quoted in Ezrahi, *Swans of the Kremlin*, 90. Original source: TsGALI f. 337, op. 1, d. 781, l. 77. By the early 1960s, for example, only a handful of *drambalety* remained in the Kirov's repertoire (*The Bronze Horseman*, *The Fountain of Bakhchisarai*, *Romeo and Juliet*, and *Laurencia*).
93 Cramer, "Warfare over Realism," 149.
94 Giersdorf, *The Body of the People*, 66.
95 See, for example, Alexei Ratmansky, "Aleksei Ratmanskii sdelal antirevoliutsionnyi spektakl'," interview by Ol'ga Gerdt, *TimeOut Moskva*, 30 June 2008, http://www.timeout.ru/journal/feature/2752. See also the new libretto for Ratmansky's version for the Bolshoi here: https://www.bolshoi.ru/en/performances/235/libretto.
96 Tat'iana Kuznetsova, "Kontrrevolutsiia bol'shogo stilia," *Kommersant*, 30 June 2008, http://kommersant.ru/doc/906905.
97 The ballet has taken on additional resonances following Russia's full-scale invasion of Ukraine on 24 February 2022. Ratmansky, an outspoken supporter of Ukraine, requested that the Bolshoi and Mariinsky remove his ballets from their repertoires, but they continue to perform (and profit from) his ballets, including *Flames*. In the fall of 2022, the Bolshoi and Mariinsky stripped Ratmansky's name from his own ballets. Ratmansky, in a Facebook post, commented on the added irony of the Bolshoi performing his uncredited version of *Flames*: "Did the dancers notice what happened [his name removed from the works]? Not a word from anyone. I wonder what they feel when at the end of the ballet they march towards the audience fully armed stepping over the broken hero, Jerome? Does it feel relevant to them? Do they sense an irony I intended when portraying

court dancers who in Act II perform for the revolutionaries with the same zeal they performed for the King in Act I." Alexei Ratmansky, "Yesterday Большой Театр России/Bolshoi Theatre of Russia performed my production of Flames of Paris again," Facebook, 14 November 2022, https://www.facebook.com/photo/?fbid=10222119346877498&set=a.1133754148868.

4 *Hegelienkov*: Eval'd Ilienkov, Western Marxism, and Philosophical Politics after Stalin

TREVOR WILSON

In 1956, as Nikita Khrushchev called for a return to Leninist principles of democracy and true socialism in the wake of Stalin's death, a much more subtle event took place within philosophy that sought to fulfil that same promise: Politizdat, the official publishing house of the Communist Party of the Soviet Union (CPSU), published Marx's *Economic and Philosophic Manuscripts of 1844* in a full Russian translation for the first time.[1] The publication of the manuscripts, written at the peak of Marx's engagement with German idealism, renewed Soviet interest in his philosophical development, in particular his debt to Hegel, the study of whom had since Stalin spurred accusations of "Menshevizing idealism."[2] As a thaw spread through political and cultural institutions across the socialist bloc, the call for de-Stalinization became, within philosophy, a proxy for a return to an early, "philosophical" Marx.

By far the most prominent post-Stalinist philosopher to return to the roots of Marxist thought was Eval'd Ilienkov, whose work re-examined the role of the abstract (and, in his own words, the ideal) in dialectical materialism. His magnum opus, *The Dialectic of the Abstract and the Concrete in Marx's* Capital (1960), challenged the primacy of empiricism and positivism within Soviet interpretations of Marx's dialectic that had been canonized by his predecessors under Stalin.[3] Ilienkov's philosophy was so sympathetic to the analysis of abstraction in Marx, exemplified in Marx's theory of the commodity and value-form, that his work invited accusations of ideological revisionism, eventually leading to Ilienkov's formal censure by the Communist Party. His work, however, became so popular among a younger generation of scholars that it helped dictate trends in Soviet philosophy for decades to come – in the words of his former student Vladislav Lektorskii, "[Ilienkov's] ideas and programs signalled a new boundary, a new starting point in the development of our philosophy entirely. Just as we divide German philosophy as pre- and post-Kantian, and Russian literature as pre- and post-Pushkin and Gogol, so can we divide Soviet philosophy of the postwar period into pre- and post-Ilienkov."[4]

Ilienkov's engagement with Hegel was characteristic of a generational turn towards "anthropological communism," in which Soviet philosophy pursued a more humanistic line of inquiry within the Marxist tradition, in contrast to the (to its detractors, crude) economism of its forebears.[5] The shift returned to relevance Hegelian concepts such as estrangement and alienation, reinterrogated notions of universality and the unified nature of personhood, and identified the role that socio-economic systems play in both distorting and reaffirming innate human essence. Even a decade prior, such studies would have been accused of bourgeois obscurantism, yet they rightfully invoked as their genealogical origin debates within Marxist philosophy of the early twentieth century. These debates, which had sought to canonize the philosophical origin of Marx's method, were conducted within a transnational community of scholars, political parties, and institutions. Incidentally, one such institution, the Marx-Engels Institute in Moscow, first published the *1844 Manuscripts*, in its original German, in 1932 as a collaborative effort between communists in the West and in the Soviet Union.[6]

The shift in philosophy signalled by Ilienkov was likewise global in nature. Echoing earlier collaborations that had once defined Marxism in its nascent development, Ilienkov found receptive audiences for his philosophy both within and outside of Soviet Russia: in Bulgaria, Czechoslovakia, and ultimately Italy, where Feltrinelli, the publishing house that had just controversially printed Boris Pasternak's *Doctor Zhivago* (1957), sought to publish a translation of Ilienkov's work. Re-engagement with Marx and Hegel became a unifying topic for Marxist philosophers working across Europe and the Eastern Bloc after Stalin, and it was often considered a defining feature of so-called "Western Marxism," a return of Marxism to its philosophical roots. The case of Ilienkov illustrates, however, that the phenomenon was defined much more generationally than geographically. As Louis Althusser wrote in 1961, "exegesis of the Young Marx might have once been thought the privilege and the cross of Western Marxists [but] they are no longer alone in the perils and rewards of this task."[7]

The formal criticism of Ilienkov by the CPSU, which led to his dismissal from Moscow State University, consequently came not merely from his approach to Marxist philosophy. He was also viewed as a political risk to the international philosophical community that had been tethered to Moscow: it was feared he might influence Western scholars, both those abroad and those who had been studying philosophy in the

Soviet Union, thus undermining the centralized role played by Soviet institutions in defining orthodox Marxist thought more globally. As de-Stalinization moved across the socialist bloc, the members of that bloc had begun to advocate for various degrees of political reform, all while simultaneously refuting dominant cultural models imposed by the Soviet Union.[8] A similar pluralism was under way within philosophy, conducted through informal channels such as academic exchanges and the discrete passing of manuscripts. Despite his troubles with the authorities, however, Ilienkov remained throughout his life a devoted member of the CPSU. The accusations levelled against him by the Party for his work, and the networks of his reception in the West, thus highlight the precarity of a heteroclite Marxist philosopher in the late Soviet period and the informal channels formed by communist internationalism within the philosophical community.

Early Trouble: "Theses on the Subject of Philosophy" and Georg Lukács

In 1954, Ilienkov and his colleague Valentin Korovikov, both of whom had just defended their dissertations and were teaching in the Faculty of Philosophy at Moscow State University, caused an uproar when they wrote their "Theses on the Subject of Philosophy" for discussion within Soviet philosophical circles.[9] In the theses, Ilienkov and Korovikov sought to identify the specificity of philosophy: if Marxist philosophy understands itself as the science of the general laws governing both nature and society, then what does philosophy do that science cannot? In other words, how does Marxism understand the difference between philosophical thought and scientific thought? The relationship between the two had concerned Marxists since at least the early intervention of Friedrich Engels, who in works such as *Anti-Dühring* (1878) and *Dialectics of Nature* (1883, published in 1925) sought to reconcile the Hegelian dialectical thinking that had informed Marx's political economic writings with new discoveries in the natural sciences. Engels claimed that transformative processes within the natural world (evolution, the conservation of energy, the germination of barley) could be understood dialectically. His belief that "dialectics is nothing more than the science of the general laws of motion and development of Nature, human society, and thought" later became canon for Soviet philosophical descriptions of dialectical materialism (or diamat) through the influence of Georgii Plekhanov, the "father of Russian Marxism," who relied on these scientific works by Engels when he coined the phrase dialectical materialism in 1883.[10]

With several exceptions, most Soviet accounts of diamat therefore claimed that Marxist philosophy was the study of the general rules for dialectical processes already under way in the natural world. Lenin, himself greatly influenced by Plekhanov and Engels, wrote that "the abstraction of *matter*, of the *laws* of nature, the abstraction of *value* and so on, in other words *all* scientific ... abstractions reflect nature more deeply, or rather *more fully*. From living contemplation to abstract thought *and from it to praxis* – such is the dialectical path of the knowledge of *truth*, the knowledge of objective reality."[11] Knowledge, and philosophical thinking, in other words, moved from the observation of concrete reality and into abstract conceptual thinking. In 1935, Stalin published *The Short Course of the History of the All-Union Communist Party*, which formalized this version of Soviet diamat, outlined its basic features for philosophical study, and packaged it for international export across the socialist bloc and beyond. Thus, just prior to Ilienkov, the practice of Marxist philosophy had been dominated by the "crude" or "vulgar" materialism of diamat. As Evgeny Pavlov describes it, Stalinist diamat "dispenses with 'idealist' errors: matter is primary, mind is derivative, but mind can and does know matter ('world')."[12]

In defiance of this received doctrine of diamat, that philosophy is the study of the dialectical laws of empirical reality, Ilienkov and Korovikov's theses had instead claimed that philosophy is concerned *only* with thought and the process of cognition:

> In their purity and abstractness, the laws of dialectics can be studied and isolated only by philosophy as logical categories, as the laws of dialectical thought. Only by making one's subject theoretical thought, the process of cognition, can philosophy include in its observations the most general characteristics of being – and not vice versa, as is often described. Philosophy is therefore the science of scientific thought, of its laws and forms.[13]

Philosophy does not explain the entire (natural) world, they argued, but instead studies how meaning, and conceptual categories, are made, and the role this process of meaning-making then plays in the activity of human beings.[14]

Discussions of the theses filled lecture halls and fuelled debates within the Faculty of Philosophy for years. They also quickly attracted condemnation from the academic council, which summoned Ilienkov and Korovikov to explain themselves. In particular, the connection made by the young philosophers between thought and being was denounced as a gnoseological interpretation of Marxism at odds with doctrinaire materialism. Uproar over the theses quickly spread to the district Party committee before making its way to the Central Committee of the CPSU. University members expressed concerns about the effect the teachings of Ilienkov and Korovikov might have on their students, by estranging them from the long-standing principles of diamat. At a closed meeting of the Faculty of Philosophy, one Party member in particular worried that the two men's philosophical deviations might affect relationships with communist parties in other countries, given that many young international communists came to Moscow to study Marxist philosophy: "Fraternal communist and worker's parties from foreign countries have entrusted their best sons to us. And what do we do? We allow two professors under the guise of 'creative Marxism' to cause confusion in the minds of our students, in particular in the minds of the foreign comrades entrusted to us!"[15] After a series of interrogations, Ilienkov and Korovikov were accused of violating the principles of Bolshevik Party loyalty (*partiinost'*), of attempting to prove that diamat was not an acceptable worldview, and of denying the "character of Marxist-Leninist dialectics as the science of the general rules of development in nature, society, and thought, and attempting to lead Marxist-Leninist dialectics toward a science of thought."[16] Both were subsequently removed from their positions. Korovikov abandoned philosophy entirely; Ilienkov would continue to develop the original ideas of the theses – and to attract controversy.

The concerns expressed over the theses' international implications were not unwarranted, given the growing rifts related to philosophical orthodoxy within communist parties across Europe. To garner support for their case, Ilienkov and Korovikov had written a letter to two respected foreign Marxist philosophers whose views they hoped would be sympathetic: Todor Pavlov, president of the Bulgarian Academy of Sciences, who was known for his philosophy of reflection, and Palmiro Togliatti, founder and leader of the Italian Communist Party (PCI).

In an attempt to link their own philosophical views to Togliatti's, the pair expressed admiration for the Italian politician's recent article in the leading Soviet philosophical journal *Questions of Philosophy* (*Voprosy filosofii*), "From Hegel to Marxism" (1955, originally published in Italian in 1954), in which Togliatti, too, examined early Marx within the framework of his debt to Hegel's logic.[17] Togliatti was leader of the largest non-ruling communist party; that he was also interested in the philosophical origins of Marx legitimized Ilienkov's and Korovikov's work, but it also brought to light the political dimensions of their philosophical research. After Stalin's death, Togliatti would take advantage of the power vacuum to propose "polycentrism" within communist internationalism. In defiance of Moscow, Togliatti sought to prioritize bilateral relations between autonomous parties in light of "multiple transnational trends toward socialism, variously emanating from the Communist, social-democratic, and progressive Third World movements."[18] According to a legend retold by Ilienkov's daughter Elena Illesh, during this period Togliatti even asked to meet Ilienkov to discuss the subject while on a visit to Moscow with party leaders.[19]

Philosophical positions thus paralleled geopolitical ones; the nascent claims for a more open interrogation of what exactly constituted Marxist philosophy were linked to a slowly emerging, decentralized communist transnationalism. Following his dismissal from Moscow State University, Ilienkov faced an almost immediate second trial at the Institute of Philosophy at the Academy of Sciences, where he was still employed as an instructor. After the Twentieth Party Congress, the Institute of Philosophy had enjoyed a reputation for open and invigorating philosophical thinking; censorship was less tightly enforced there, and Soviet philosophers were encouraged to collaborate with visitors from other countries in the socialist bloc.[20] Nevertheless, Party members meeting at the Institute were enraged that Ilienkov would "drive a wedge between our Soviet philosophers and foreign Marxists," thus undermining Soviet philosophical doctrine.[21] Over the course of the investigation, it was soon revealed that Bulgarian students from Moscow State University had somehow received copies of the theses and brought them to Pavlov, who was apparently sympathetic to their argument and had written a letter of support for Ilienkov to the Institute of Philosophy. In denouncing Ilienkov's work, the institute would therefore also have to denounce and insult respected foreign philosophers who shared Ilienkov's views. Ilienkov tried to use this to his advantage, requesting that the sealed letter be read at his interrogation. Party members denied this request, claiming that "T. Pavlov has many serious faults, but that does not give us communists of the Soviet Union the right to tear down Pavlov, our fraternal Bulgarian Republic's Academy president, at our meeting. It is necessary however to do so with Ilienkov."[22]

Notwithstanding the Soviet philosophers' professed respect for Pavlov and his work, the Bulgarian philosopher had also been accused of an overly gracious interpretation of idealism and subjectivity in Hegel, which supposedly undermined diamat. Pavlov's magnum opus *Theory of Reflection* (1936) returned to Lenin's writings on Hegel and logic in his philosophical notebooks in order to analyse the role of aesthetics in the mimetic reflection of reality. In the notebooks, while studying the *Science of Logic*, Lenin had sought to overcome an oversimplification of "materialism versus idealism" that was pervasive in Russian Marxist philosophy. Rejecting a "vulgar materialism," Lenin had argued that the human mind plays some role in transforming the world, through culture (laws, art, ethics, etc.) and of course labour: "man not only reflects the world, but creates it."[23] Lenin's idea of interplay between conceptual thinking and the material world centred on an analysis of the Hegelian theory of the notion [*Begriff*], in which universal (abstract), particular, and individual (concrete) categories are dialectically mediated. As Lucio Colletti helpfully describes the process, "in order to relate to themselves, finite things have to ... send themselves away *into thought* ... It is only in its Notion that it is in its *truth*, whereas in the immediacy in which it is given it is only *appearance* and a contingency."[24]

In *Theory of Reflection*, Pavlov made a similar claim for the role the mind plays in structuring and transforming the world:

> The whole matter consists in that logical judgments, the logical concepts (categories, laws) ... are a natural result, generalization, crystallization, deduction from the development of man's thought over the centuries. They are a generalization of the millennia-long human experience; and although the logical concepts as such have an abstract character, they are profoundly historical in essence. Once they are arrived at, however, they are a powerful and invaluable weapon for proper scientific knowledge and for the practical transformation of the world, as long as we do not consider them as static, dead, frozen, antithetical, but, on the contrary, as mobile, viable and interpenetrative, at that, always checked against the criterion of practice.[25]

Pavlov's theory of reflection has similarly been compared to that of Georg Lukács, who in his *Theory of the Novel* offered a preliminary definition for the modern novel as a melancholy, alienated reflection of the world by the novelist.[26] Lukács argued that in contrast to the epic, which maintained a unity of self and world in its reflection of reality, the novel form "cannot completely rid itself of its subjectivity and so appear as the immanent meaning of the object world," producing instead a tension and duplication in the narration.[27]

Lukács claimed that this process of reflection practised in literature was essential to human life in its (re)production of historical-social forms: human beings posit themselves, produce themselves, and then reproduce themselves according to their given relationship with material (economic) reality.[28] The rift in this process posited by the modern novel was a reflection of self-estrangement under capitalism. In *History and Class Consciousness* (1923), Lukács posited the overcoming of this alienation, the disjunction between a being's material and posited self, as the task of the revolution and Marxist thought. The work was considered controversial precisely because Lukács opposed his own views to those of a vulgar materialism (a proxy for Soviet diamat) that viewed the mind as merely contemplating objective reality, thereby giving birth to fatalism and a belief in the immutability of the world and undermining Marx's call for philosophy to change it.[29]

Paradoxically, then, Ilienkov, Pavlov, and Lukács were all accused of philosophical revisionism despite credibly claiming a lineage with Lenin's own philosophical views. While many Soviet philosophers embraced Lenin's adage "from living contemplation to abstract thought and from it to praxis" as their philosophical standard, they regularly neglected its final moment (from thought to praxis) in their accounts of diamat. These nuances in the practice of Marxist philosophy played out in dramatic variations across the Eastern Bloc and spilled over into Western Marxist theoretical studies, and all the while, the transformations of the post-Stalinist period threatened any sense of ideological unity across national traditions.

Ilienkov could, successfully or not, align himself with Pavlov and Togliatti in the defence of his philosophical views, but any affiliation with Lukács proved a bridge too far. In May of 1956, *Questions of Philosophy* published a positive review of Lukács's *Young Hegel* written by Ilienkov and two other philosophers.[30] Ilienkov had also been organizing a reading group of Hegel and even translating Lukács's work, consulting with philosopher Mikhail Lifshitz on Hegelian terms in the original German.[31] In the fall of the same year, the Hungarian Uprising would once more render Lukács persona non grata in Soviet intellectual circles. He briefly joined Imre Nagy's anti-Soviet government as its Minister of Culture, effectively ending (briefly) any possibility of discussion of his philosophy in the Soviet press.[32]

Ilienkov would be denounced for the review two years later, when the issue was raised at another Party meeting at the Institute of Philosophy.[33] Once again, Party members worried about the international implications of the piece: "All international communist movements study with our party ... We should not advise comrade Ilienkov to justify his mistaken article on Lukács in *Questions of Philosophy*, but instead to honestly and directly say that an error was made and that it must be corrected by a pointed declaration against Lukács and his revisionist acolytes."[34]

The renewed attack against Ilienkov and his work could not have come at a worse time. Ilienkov had just finished writing his first major work, *The Dialectic of the Abstract and the Concrete in Marx's Capital*, in 1957, but its publication had been delayed. While Ilienkov sorted out the fate of this manuscript, previous fears that he might influence foreign Marxists reached a fever pitch as Giangiacomo Feltrinelli, an Italian publisher with a soon to be troubled relationship with the Soviet authorities, expressed interest in the unpublished work.

The Feltrinelli Affair and *The Dialectic of the Abstract and the Concrete*

With the publication of *The Dialectic of the Abstract and the Concrete*, Ilienkov firmly established himself as a leading figure within the philosophical world of the Thaw. The controversies surrounding its publication, however, further intensified fears that these new approaches to Marxist philosophy might undermine the hegemonic role played by the Soviet Union in defining cultural, political, and philosophical norms across the socialist bloc. Such fears stemmed from a growing interest in Ilienkov among international communists, especially in Italy. In 1955, *Questions of Philosophy* had forwarded to Ilienkov two letters that had been sent to the journal from the Italian Society for Cultural Relations with the Soviet Union. According to Ilienkov, the society had offered to put him in contact with Italian Marxist philosophers and asked whether he had any material that might be available for translation.[35] Ilienkov had thus far published only one article in *Questions of Philosophy*; however, he told the Italians he was currently working on a book project on the same topic. To this, they replied with a request to see the manuscript and plan for its translation.[36]

A year later, in the spring of 1956, Ilienkov was again asked about the manuscript, this time by Sergio D'Angelo. D'Angelo was working in Moscow for the Italian-language division of a radio broadcaster. According to his memoirs, he had moved to the Soviet Union from Rome just a few months earlier at the suggestion of the PCI. The radio broadcaster consisted of thirty foreign-language offices located just off of Tverskaia Street (then Gorky Street), housed in two buildings near Pushkin Square. Although D'Angelo describes himself as "by no means a dogmatic communist," his work translating news from the Eastern Bloc reflected the influential role played by the PCI in Italy.[37] The Italian division had around twenty-five employees, most of them Russian, as well as several older "Soviet Italians" who had immigrated to the Soviet Union during the Stalin era, and who helped D'Angelo translate and edit materials for transmission to listeners back in Italy.

While he was leaving for Moscow, D'Angelo had been contacted by Feltrinelli, a young publisher from Milan who belonged to one of the richest families in Italy and was an active member of the PCI. Feltrinelli asked D'Angelo to keep him abreast of literary developments in the

Soviet Union and to help him contact new authors so that he could publish their works abroad. As luck would have it, one of D'Angelo's first assignments in Moscow was a culture piece on Boris Pasternak's *Doctor Zhivago*. The radio broadcast announced – prematurely, as it turned out – that Pasternak's new novel would soon be published in the Soviet Union. As part of his report, D'Angelo had travelled to meet Pasternak in Peredelkino, where the author expressed doubt that the authorities would permit him to publish the novel. Remembering his agreement with Feltrinelli, D'Angelo convinced Pasternak at their meeting to give him a copy of *Doctor Zhivago*, promising that Feltrinelli would later forward the work to other major publishers in France and England.

D'Angelo thus played a crucial role in the initial Italian publication of *Doctor Zhivago*, an event that would scandalize Soviet literary politics during the Thaw. In all likelihood, Ilienkov did not yet know about the illicit publication of *Doctor Zhivago* when D'Angelo approached him about the Italian publication of his work. Illesh, for good reason, assumes that, given the secrecy surrounding the publication of *Doctor Zhivago* abroad, D'Angelo had not informed Ilienkov about the plans despite their frequent contact.[38] Although Ilienkov had already established an international reputation as an unorthodox Soviet philosopher, D'Angelo had in fact first met him socially through a fellow journalist. D'Angelo's family soon began spending Sundays in Peredelkino at the dacha of Vasilii Ilienkov, Eval'd's father, who was himself a respected author. Given their proximity, D'Angelo could often arrange to visit both Pasternak and the Ilienkovs in the same trip. D'Angelo recounts first bonding with Eval'd over classical music and Richard Wagner – because the Ilienkovs were unable to listen to Wagner in the Soviet Union due to the composer's association with Nazi Germany, D'Angelo secretly smuggled recordings from Rome as gifts for the family.[39]

Thus, when Ilienkov was formally asked to publish his philosophical work through Feltrinelli, the request was made through a personal connection. Ilienkov could furthermore assume, perhaps naively, that it would be ideologically orthodox to work with D'Angelo and Feltrinelli, since both were members of the PCI and Feltrinelli was seeking to promote communist literature in Italy. In 1957, when Ilienkov's manuscript was finally approved for publication by the Soviet Academy of Sciences, he relayed this information to D'Angelo, who in turn requested an advance copy of the work for eventual translation (as a general rule, authorized translations of works were to be done only after the originals were published in the Soviet Union). D'Angelo chose Vittorio Strada as the translator. A respected Italian Slavist, Strada had studied philosophy at the University of Milan with Antonio Banfi, written his thesis on Soviet dialectical materialism, and was coming to Moscow to study philosophy that year.[40] D'Angelo personally introduced Strada to Ilienkov on a trip to Peredelkino, where, incidentally, the two would make a second stop to see Pasternak.[41]

The timing, however, could not have been worse for Ilienkov. As his manuscript was approved for publication in the Soviet Union, and the Italians were preparing to translate it for dissemination abroad, the philosopher fell ill with complications from tuberculosis, which he had contracted during the war. The illness required him to convalesce in a sanatorium, and while there, he left his affairs to his wife and friends. In November of 1957, while he lay recovering away from Moscow, Feltrinelli published *Doctor Zhivago*. Ilienkov would recount in his statement to the authorities that while at the sanatorium he had begun to doubt whether he had done the right thing in giving D'Angelo an early copy of his work. Still under suspicion for his earlier work, and for his positive review of Lukács, Ilienkov suddenly found himself in the unfortunate position of having his manuscript in the hands of a press that had published material banned in the Soviet Union. Thus, Ilienkov's sympathy towards unorthodox Marxist philosophy and his affiliation with foreign agents converged, once again drawing the ire of Party members while highlighting the precarity and dangers of such transnational philosophical exchanges.

In March of 1958, Vasilii, Eval'd's father, wrote his son a letter warning him that the CPSU was already aware of his interactions with Feltrinelli and that he should avoid conducting business with the publisher after it had "debased itself with a well-known novel."[42] Later that year, in November, Ilienkov was again summoned before the Party Bureau of the Institute of Philosophy to explain himself. Party members questioned Ilienkov as to why he would give his manuscript to a "foreign correspondent." The philosopher explained that D'Angelo was a communist, to which the committee replied: "Firstly, you didn't know that he was a communist. Secondly, a communist press also published Pasternak. This press also published Gustav Wetter and his anti-Soviet book. They are publishing both Togliatti and works against Togliatti. You are a grown man, you should know these things."[43]

The committee then proceeded to interrogate Ilienkov's philosophical character and question why foreign presses would be interested in his work in particular. The philosopher Petr Fedoseev argued before the committee that the Italians were drawn to Ilienkov's work for its claim that "praxis is not the criterion for truth, but pure thought is."[44] Another member complained that "several of our young philosophers are trying to oppose the older cadres, making the case that the older cadres are dogmatics offering nothing new, whereas the younger ones intend to move philosophy forward."[45] Ilienkov's past sins were yet again brought forth for condemnation: the appearance of his "Theses" in Bulgaria (and the support garnered from Pavlov), and his review of Lukács. In a consecutive, closed meeting, it was then announced that a copy of Ilienkov's dissertation had been discovered in Czechoslovakia, where Ilienkov had been declared "by a revisionist" to be one of only two Soviet philosophers writing authentic philosophical work.[46]

Ilienkov was forced to walk a very fine line: his philosophy was subjected to accusations of ideological deviance and geopolitical disloyalty, yet he had attracted international interest in the first place through the very transnational communist networks he was now accused of undermining. A series of meetings, both open and closed, followed, with the committee ultimately concluding that Ilienkov had displayed behaviour antithetical to the Party in transferring his manuscript to a foreign publisher. While Ilienkov's behaviour, they claimed, warranted expulsion from the CPSU, the committee accepted his "sincere recognition of guilt" and let him off with a formal reprimand and a demand that he heavily edit his forthcoming manuscript.[47] Notably, two years later Ilienkov would successfully request that his formal Party reprimand be repealed. That same year, *The Dialectic of the Abstract and the Concrete in Marx's Capital* would be published in the Soviet Union. (The Italian version would be published a year later, with no further scandal.)

The ease with which Ilienkov had his reprimand repealed and finally had his work published in 1960 is a reflection of two transformative shifts within Soviet society during the Thaw. First, after a series of earlier failures to apply dogmatic ideological methods to a variety of scientific fields – most notably, biology through Lysenkoism, but also other disciplines such as systems analysis, natural history, and even mathematics – party authorities in the post-war period had come to recognize the value of non-interference, in order to allow for the maximal development of scientific and technological progress within the Soviet Union and thereby enhance its global competitiveness. Oddly enough, the field of philosophy benefited just as much from this shift, as more relaxed censorship of philosophy would both further international interest in Soviet philosophy and encourage the emergence of a younger generation of philosophers devoted to new, innovative approaches to social problems.[48]

Second, and related, a series of international political crises at the beginning of the Thaw exacerbated threats to the continued predominance of the Soviet Union as the leader of the socialist world and heightened the need for a more relaxed approach to cultural matters, which had long been dictated by Moscow and the CPSU. Clearly, Ilienkov courted controversy when he engaged directly with the work of Lukács at the height of the Hungarian Revolution, but he was also protected from further reprimand through his alignment with Togliatti. As leader of the Italian Communist Party, Togliatti directly challenged Moscow on "the existence of different roads to socialism ... the need to move beyond the cold war, ... and the necessity of greater autonomy in culture and the arts" after the Soviets' disastrous response to the Hungarian Uprising and to protests in Poznań, Poland, in 1956.[49] Such clashes between communist parties and states were as cultural as they were political, and the CPSU seemingly realized that at least for a time, it would need to loosen its ideological grip on cultural production across the bloc, including within the practice of philosophy.

Ilienkov was thus able to emerge relatively unscathed from the controversies that had plagued his earlier years. Despite these initial troubles it quickly became clear that a new school had formed within Marxist thought during the Thaw. Within the Soviet Union, this school centred on Ilienkov and his numerous students, many of whom would go on to play prominent roles in late and post-Soviet philosophy. As a result of the work of Ilienkov's peers abroad, however, it was just as much a global tendency, one that developed organically, on the periphery of dominant philosophical institutions, and that was accompanied by broader political demands for decentralization across the socialist bloc.

Taking as one of its starting points the nexus of Hegel and Marx, this emergent tendency was notably much more sympathetic to questions of abstraction and ideology in its interpretation of philosophical Marxism. When Fedoseev claimed that Ilienkov's manuscript appealed to Italian Marxists because it elevated "pure thought" as the criterion for truth, he was essentially repeating the same attack as had been aimed earlier at Ilienkov and Korovikov's "Theses," where philosophy was understood as meaning-making through the formation of conceptual categories. *The Dialectic of the Abstract and the Concrete* developed this original argument further, through a concentrated analysis of the Marxian theory of value as a form of philosophical abstraction. For Ilienkov, the abstract in Marx played just as much of a practical role in daily life as anything material or concrete: "For Marx [the abstract] is by no means merely 'the purely thinkable,' merely the product of mental activity or subjective, psychological phenomenon taking place only in the individual human skull. Marx nearly always uses this term as a characteristic of real phenomena and relations existing beyond consciousness and independent of whether they are reflected in consciousness or not."[50]

Ilienkov centred his analysis of Marx's abstract on the theory of the value-form. In the first volume of *Capital*, Marx had defined a commodity as comprised of two values. The first value, use-value, comes from the object's ability to serve a particular material need – it is "conditioned by the physical properties of the commodity, and has no existence apart from the latter."[51] The second value, exchange-value, is the worth of an object as determined by its proportional relationship to other objects: a certain amount of wheat, for example, can be exchanged for a certain amount of boot polish or gold, for example, and the proportions of their exchange are determined by "congealed labor-time," that is, the time taken to produce them. For these objects to be exchangeable, they must share something between them, yet "this common element cannot be a geometrical, physical, chemical, or other natural property" of the commodities themselves.[52] In other words, exchange-value is premised not on an intrinsic physical property of a commodity; rather, it is a value formed through a network of social relations:

> Not an atom of matter enters into the objectivity of the commodities as values; in this it is the direct opposite of the coarsely sensuous objectivity of commodities as physical objects. We may twist and turn a single commodity as we wish; it remains impossible to grasp it as a thing possessing value. However, let us remember that commodities possess an objective character as values only in so far as they are all expressions of an identical social substance, human labour, that their objective character as values is therefore purely social.[53]

Ilienkov identified this *abstract*, objective, and "purely social" nature of value as Marx's unique development of preceding theories of value that had been elaborated by philosophers such as David Ricardo and Adam Smith. The social relations that determine exchange value, Marx argued, cannot be found within any one individual human mind, nor can they simply be extrapolated from the physical materiality of the object. Nevertheless, one could hardly deny that exchange-value and commodities played an active role in political economy.

While the social role played by abstract thought is particularly clear through this analysis by Marx of the value-form under capitalism, Ilienkov stressed that philosophical or abstract thinking was a universal human activity practised across socio-economic and political regimes, since collectively derived forms of meaning-making determine given cultural and societal forms: "outside and independent of the consciousness and will of an *individual* is not only the material world but also a most complicated, historically established sphere of *humankind* or society's material and spiritual culture."⁵⁴ This positive assessment of the abstract within scientific or philosophical thought undermined the predominantly empiricist theories of reflection in Soviet diamat. As Ilienkov argues, "this means that all truly scientific, and not nonsensical or empty, abstract definitions emerge in the human mind not as the result of a thoughtless, purely lucky reduction of abstract thought from concrete reflection, but rather from the systematic progression of cognition in accordance with the general, regular development of science and in the process of concretizing knowledge through its own critical transformation."⁵⁵

Ilienkov and Italian (Western) Marxism

Fedoseev was correct to identify a natural affiliation between Ilienkov's philosophy of abstraction and Italian variations on Marxist philosophy. Italian philosophers shared with their Russian colleagues a long-standing interest in Hegelianism – as Perry Anderson has illustrated, Marx's early warm reception in his own time by figures such as Antonio Labriola ensured the development of a rigorous philosophical Marxism in Italy that survived through later generations of philosophers such as Benedetto Croce, Antonio Gramsci, and Togliatti.⁵⁶ These shared intellectual heritages between Russian/Soviet and Italian Marxism, in conjunction with the outsized influence of the PCI, had created an organic community of transnational philosophical exchange between Italy and the Soviet Union, one that could be relied upon to promote Ilienkov's philosophical ideas during the Thaw.

The immediate reception of Ilienkov in Italy was through a circle of Italian Marxists dominated by the figure of Galvano Della Volpe. Curiously enough, a defining characteristic of the Della Volpe circle was its own opposition to Hegelianism within Marxist philosophy – nevertheless, Ilienkov's careful articulation of the differences between Marx's dialectical logic and Hegel's found an unlikely ally in the circle, due to the circle's persistent argument for Marxist philosophy as a rigorous, scientific method in its own right. Among Della Volpe's best-known students was Lucio Colletti, who wrote the preface to the Italian translation of Ilienkov's book. In that preface, Colletti characterizes Ilienkov, in avoiding the "old man's paraphernalia of Diamat," as the harbinger of a new school within Soviet Marxism, one devoted to a "'philosophical reconstruction' of Marxism" through an analysis of "concrete or historical abstraction" in the logic of *Capital*.⁵⁷

As Anderson notes, the interpretation of Marx as a philosopher, and not merely a political economist, had become a defining characteristic of the Western Marxist tradition, in which the study of Marx moved "from economics and politics towards philosophy, and its formal site from party assemblies to academic departments."[58] He claims further that

> Western Marxism as a whole thus paradoxically inverted the trajectory of Marx's own development itself. Where the founder of historical materialism moved progressively from philosophy to politics and then economics, as the central terrain of his thought, the successors of the tradition that emerged after 1920 increasingly turned back from economics and politics to philosophy – abandoning direct engagement with what had been the great concerns of the mature Marx, nearly as completely as he had abandoned direct pursuit of the discursive issues of his youth. The wheel, in this sense, appeared to have turned full circle.[59]

Ilienkov and the Della Volpe circle may have approached Marx differently, but they shared an interest in extrapolating from Marx's writings a rigorous, scientific logic suitable for philosophical thinking. While Anderson notes this "return to philosophy," particularly among Western Marxists, after 1956, the phenomenon of a "philosophical" Marx re-emerged in the Soviet Union as well through the work of figures like Ilienkov.

Colletti claims, moreover, that Italian Marxists were specifically drawn to Ilienkov's theory of the "concrete or historical abstraction" in Marx, which they viewed as the key to constructing a unique method for Marxist philosophy. In Ilienkov, this concrete abstraction was Marx's commodity form, interpreted as a "reproduction of the concrete in thought."[60] While the commodity, Ilienkov argued, is abstract in the sense that it bears no immediate relation to its material form, it is nevertheless concrete due to its ability to express "the given concrete historical system as a whole."[61] In other words, the commodity, which possesses both a use-value and an exchange-value, is a concrete (or historical) abstraction because, despite its "immaterial" form, it is capable of revealing the complex and competing economic forces that led to its development: "a concrete understanding of the phenomenon of the commodity-money sphere coincides with an account of all these influences exerted upon it by the developed and increasingly complicated forms of economic relations within capitalism."[62]

This identification by Ilienkov of a concretized abstraction in Marx appealed to the Della Volpe circle, because it enabled an overcoming of the reliance on Hegelian logic within Marxist philosophy that had persisted since its inception. In his magnum opus *Logic as a Positive Science*

(1950), Della Volpe sought to reverse the Hegelian logic of moving from the "abstract to concrete to abstract" with his claim for a scientific Marxian methodology of the "concrete to abstract to concrete." Paralleling Ilienkov, Della Volpe argued that "although the 'concrete' is indeed the point of departure for observation and conception, it nevertheless appears in our thought as a 'process of concentration,' as a 'result' and 'not as a point of departure.'"[63] While Marx may have largely been concerned with political economy, Della Volpe, in his argument for a scientific logic in Marxian method that could widen the scope of Marxist thought to social or cultural analysis, claimed that "we may then begin to see the shape of the relation between the *historical* economic categories and *modern* bourgeois society and its categories" due to the concreteness of the former and its articulation through the abstraction of the latter.[64] Later, in his *Critique of Taste* (also published by Feltrinelli, 1960), Della Volpe posited that the task of Marxist hermeneutics was to examine the "historical humus" of a work of art: "the story of living sediment, the historical humus whose organic presence in the work of art has properly to be demonstrated by the materialist, is to be traced back to its concrete-rational core."[65] Only in this way, Della Volpe argued, can the allegedly "immaterial" abstraction of poetry, for example, be resolved with the material, historical circumstances of its emergence.

The tradition of "Western Marxists," including philosophers such as Della Volpe, Lukács, and Althusser, in the pursuit of a philosophically rigorous method in Marx, could therefore transition from questions of strictly political economy to those of culture, ideology, and superstructure. While Ilienkov himself did not (generally) write on aesthetics, from the 1960s onward he nevertheless included culture as one of several abstract processes formed through social relations that were "inherent to human life-activity" and that he termed the "ideal": "the process by which the material life-activity of a social being begins to produce not merely a material product, but an ideal one, and so begins to produce the act of idealizing reality (the transformation of the 'material' into the 'ideal'), through which, having thus arisen, the 'ideal' becomes a critical component in the material life-activity of the social being."[66] This analysis of culture and its effect on material socio-economic relations as an ideal or immaterial product would nearly parallel arguments made by Althusser and other Western Marxists in the 1970s regarding the formational role played by ideology in the construction of social relations.[67]

What curiously arose, then, in the post-Stalinist 1950s was a transnational network of philosophers who, while no less self-avowed Marxists, nevertheless challenged dogmatic CPSU views in their return to the philosophical roots of Marx himself. Through this return to the early

Marx and his philosophical engagement with Hegel, these philosophers upended "crude economism" within Marxist philosophy and gradually incorporated questions of culture and abstraction in their work. In so doing, they challenged older *diamatchiki*, who, ironically following Engels, argued for dialectical processes already under way in nature, with the younger generation claiming instead that orthodox Marxism, in Lukács's words, was a uniquely dialectical *method* that largely concerned the connection between mind and world.[68] These philosophical challenges resonated, moreover, with the geopolitical landscape of the Thaw, during which efforts to decentre the role played by the Soviet Union in the politics of the bloc found their echo in a decentralized approach to the practice and discussion of Marxist philosophy.

It must therefore be stressed that a commonly assumed difference between "Western" and "Soviet" Marxisms was in actuality more generational than geographical, with Ilienkov and Della Volpe sharing thematic points of departure that opposed them to their respective predecessors – Della Volpe, too, would face a cold reception from Italy's PCI for his philosophical views.[69] This generational split moreover necessitated an exchange between the younger philosophers through informal channels: (often illicit) dissemination of manuscripts through cultural exchanges, informal reading groups, and the exposition of positions at odds with formal party doctrine. Paradoxically, then, while Ilienkov was first "discovered" in the West by Italian Marxists, and celebrated due both to his innovative philosophy and to the legitimacy he might bring to Italian Marxism as a Soviet philosopher, his work in fact revealed an unacknowledged continuity within various national Marxist traditions then stifled by philosophical orthodoxy.

Notes

1 Karl Marks and Fridrikh Engels, *Iz rannikh proizvedenii* (Moscow: Gosudarstvennoe izdatel'stvo politicheskoi literatury, 1956).

2 The denunciation "Menshevizing idealism" dates to the Deborinism/Mechanism debates surrounding Hegel and positivism in the 1920s and 1930s. See David Bakhurst, *Consciousness and Revolution in Soviet Philosophy: From the Bolsheviks to Evald Ilyenkov* (Cambridge: Cambridge University Press, 1991): 25–57.

3 Eval'd Il'enkov, "Dialektika abstraktnogo i konkretnogo v «Kapitale» Marksa," *Sobranie sochinenii*, vol. 2 [1960] (Moscow: Kanon+, 2019).

4 Vladislav Lektorskii is quoted in Lev Mitrohkin, *Moi filosofskie sobesedniki* (St. Petersburg: Izdatel'stvo Russkoi Khristianskoi gumanitarnoi akademii, 2005): 339.

5 Mikhail Epstein, *The Phoenix of Philosophy: Russian Thought of the Late Soviet Period (1953–1991)* (New York: Bloomsbury, 2019), 24.
6 The Institute's director, David Riazanov, had received direct support from the Soviet government to negotiate the acquisition of the manuscripts, as well as other historic socialist texts, across Europe. An account of this history can be found in Jonathan Beecher and Valerii N. Fomichev, "French Socialism in Lenin's and Stalin's Moscow: David Riazanov and the French Archive of the Marx-Engels Institute," *Journal of Modern History* 78, no. 1 (2006): 119–43.
7 Louis Althusser, *Pour Marx* [1965] (Paris: La Découverte, 2005), 47. Althusser claims further in a footnote that interest among young Soviet researchers in the young (philosophical) Marx was "an important sign of the current cultural development in the U.S.S.R."
8 Evgeny Dobrenko describes this process with regard to socialist realism in "When Comintern and Cominform Aesthetics Meet: Socialist Realism in Eastern Europe, 1956 and Beyond," in *Comintern Aesthetics*, ed. Amelia M. Glaser and Steven S. Lee (Toronto: University of Toronto Press, 2020), 424.
9 Eval'd Il'enkov and Valentin Korovikov, *Strasti po tezisam o predmete filosofii (1954–1955)*, ed. Elena Illesh (Moscow: Kanon+, 2016). For years, the original theses were lost, and their general format and argument had been reconstructed through documentation from the consequent investigation by the faculty's academic council. In recent years, however, a copy was discovered in Ilienkov's papers, and a complete, translated version can be found in David Bakhurst, "Punks versus Zombies: Evald Ilyenkov and the Battle for Soviet Philosophy," *Philosophical Thought in Russia in the Second Half of the Twentieth Century*, ed. Vladislav A. Lektorsky and Marina F. Bykova (London: Bloomsbury, 2019), 68–75.
10 K. Marx and F. Engels, *Collected Works*, vol. 25 (London: Lawrence and Wishart, 1987): 166. James D. White describes the influence of Engels on Russian Marxism, and in particular on Plekhanov, in *Marx and Russia: The Fate of a Doctrine* (London: Bloomsbury, 2019): 47–61.
11 V.I. Lenin, *Polnoe sobranie sochinenii*, vol. 29 (Moscow: Politizdat, 1969): 152–3. Emphasis in original.
12 Evgeny V. Pavlov. "Comrade Hegel: Absolute Spirit Goes East," *Crisis and Critique* 3, no. 1 (2016): 184.
13 Il'enkov and Korovikov, *Strasti po tezisam*, 146.
14 As Lektorskii describes it, "the most general aspects of reality (both natural and social) 'in their pure form' are differentiated in the categorical structure of thought. In studying this structure and the method of thought associated with it, we can attain general definitions for being itself." See Lektorskii, "Klassik otechestvennoi filosofii," in Il'enkov, *Sobranie sochinenii*, vol. 1 (Moscow: Kanon+, 2019): 9.

15 Il'enkov, *Sobranie sochinenii*, vol. 1, 77.
16 Il'enkov and Korovikov, *Strasti po tezisam*, 29–30.
17 Pal'miro Tol'iatti, "Ot Gegelia k marksizmu," *Voprosy filosofii* 4 (1955): 54–65.
18 Joan Barth Urban, *Moscow and the Italian Communist Party: From Togliatti to Berlinguer* (Ithaca: Cornell University Press, 1986), 232. Lucio Magri provides a succinct explanation of Togliatti and Italy's relationship to de-Stalinization in *The Tailor of Ulm: A History of Communism*, trans. Patrick Camiller (London: Verso, 2018), 120–37.
19 Il'enkov and Korovikov, *Strasti po tezisam*, 97.
20 Described in the recollections of philosopher Vasilii Sokolov in *Filosofskaia ottepel' i padenie dogmaticheskogo marksizma v Rossii: filosofskii fakul'tet MGU im. M.V. Lomonosova v vospominaniiakh ego vypusknikov*, ed. V.P. Shestakov (St. Petersburg: Nestor-Istoriia), 92.
21 Sokolov, *Filosofskaia*, 108.
22 Sokolov, *Filosofskaia*, 104.
23 Lenin, *Polnoe sobranie sochinenii*, vol. 29, 194.
24 Lucio Colletti, *Marxism and Hegel*, trans. Lawrence Garner (London: Verso, 1979), 16. Once a prominent Marxist philosopher in Italy, before disavowing Marx completely, Colletti wrote the foreword to Ilienkov's first publication in Italian. See n. 57.
25 Todor Pavlov, *The Philosophy of Todor Pavlov* (Sofia: Sofia Press, 1962), 54.
26 Kamelia Spassova provides an excellent comparison of the two in "Subverting the Theory of Reflection: Modernism against 'Modern Realism,'" *History of the Humanities* 4, no. 2 (2019): 357–64.
27 Georg Lukács, *The Theory of the Novel*, trans. Anna Bostock (London: Merlin Press, 1988), 84.
28 Georg Lukács, *History and Class Consciousness*, trans. Rodney Livingstone (Cambridge, MA: MIT Press, 1994), 15.
29 Lukács, *History and Class Consciousness*, 4. Abram Deborin, in his review of the work for the Soviet philosophical journal *Under the Banner of Marxism*, criticized Lukács as an orthodox Hegelian preaching the "purest idealism." See A. Deborin, "G. Lukach i ego kritika marksizma," *Pod znamenem marksizma*, 6–7 (1924): 60.
30 G. Zeidel', E.V. Il'enkov, L.K. Naumenko, "Molodoi Gegel'," *Voprosy filosofii* 5 (1956): 181–4.
31 According to Lifshitz, Ilienkov first personally wrote to Lukács in Budapest. Lukács responded with surprise that he had even been asked, when Lifshitz was already in Moscow and could answer any of his questions. Lifshitz and Lukács were close colleagues, having first met at the Marx–Engels Institute. See Mikhail Lifshitz, *Dialog s Eval'dom Il'enkovym* (Moscow: Progress-Traditsiia, 2003), 13–14.

32 Sergei Mareev, *Iz istorii sovetskoi filosofii: Lukach–Vygotskii–Il'enkov* (Moscow: Kul'turnaia revoliutsiia, 2008), 49–50.
33 Illesh attributes the delay to the slow speed with which Soviet society learned about the events in Hungary. See Il'enkov and Korovikov, *Strasti po tezisam o predmete filosofii (1954–1955)*, 39.
34 Il'enkov and Korovikov, *Strasti po tezisam o predmete filosofii (1954–1955)*, 44.
35 Eval'd Il'enkov, *Ot abstraktnogo k konkretnomy. Krutoi marshrut. 1950–1960*, ed. Elena Illesh (Moscow: Kanon+, 2017), 47.
36 Eval'd Il'enkov, "O dialektike abstraktnogo i konkretnogo v nauchno-teoreticheskom poznanii," *Voprosy filosofii* 1 (1955): 42–56.
37 Serdzho D'Andzhelo, *Delo Pasternaka: Vospominaniia ochevidtsa* (Moscow: Novoe literaturnoe obozrenie, 2007), 12.
38 Il'enkov, *Ot abstraktnogo do konkretnogo*, 47.
39 Il'enkov, *Ot abstraktnogo do konkretnogo*, 30.
40 In his memoirs, Strada described himself as uniquely capable of translating Ilienkov's work, given the dense subject matter and Strada's ability to consult directly with Ilienkov in Moscow. Strada claims that he first received a typed copy of the work in Italy and brought it with him to the USSR. See Vittorio Strada, *Rossiia kak sud'ba* (Moscow: Tri kvadrata, 2013), 491.
41 D'Andzhelo, *Delo Pasternaka*, 65.
42 Il'enkov, *Ot abstraktnogo do konkretnogo*, 48–9.
43 Il'enkov, *Ot abstraktnogo do konkretnogo*, 51.
44 Il'enkov, *Ot abstraktnogo do konkretnogo*, 58.
45 Il'enkov, *Ot abstraktnogo do konkretnogo*, 52.
46 Il'enkov, *Ot abstraktnogo do konkretnogo*, 70, 72.
47 Il'enkov, *Ot abstraktnogo do konkretnogo*, 72–3.
48 Vladislav Lektorsky, "The Russian Philosophy of the Second Half of the Twentieth Century as a Sociocultural Phenomenon," *Philosophical Thought in Russia in the Second Half of the Twentieth Century*, ed. Lektorsky and Bykova, 23.
49 Magri, *The Tailor of Ulm*, 122.
50 Eval'd Il'enkov, "Dialektika abstraktnogo i konkretnogo," 18.
51 Karl Marx, *Capital: A Critique of Political Economy*, vol. 1, trans. Ben Fowkes (London: Penguin, 1990), 126.
52 Marx, *Capital*, 127.
53 Marx, *Capital*, 138–9.
54 Il'enkov, "Dialektika abstraktnogo i konkretnogo," 25.
55 Il'enkov, "Dialektika abstraktnogo i konkretnogo," 117.
56 Perry Anderson, *Considerations on Western Marxism* (London: Verso, 1979), 40–1. Anderson notes in particular Italy and Eastern Europe's shared status

as underdeveloped economic regions, contrasting the quick appropriation of Marx by philosophers in these "peripheral" zones of Europe to his slower reception in England and France, where capital economies were more advanced and developed.
57 Lucio Colletti, preface to *La dialettica dell'astratto e del concreto nel Capitale*, Evald Vasilevic Ilenkov, trans. Vittorio Strada (Milan: Feltrinelli, 1975 [1961]), 56–7.
58 Anderson, *Considerations*, 50.
59 Anderson, *Considerations*, 52.
60 Il'enkov, "Dialektika abstraktnogo i konkretnogo," 77.
61 Il'enkov, "Dialektika abstraktnogo i konkretnogo," 80.
62 Il'enkov, "Dialektika abstraktnogo i konkretnogo," 80.
63 Galvano Della Volpe, *Logic as a Positive Science*, trans. Jon Rothschild (London: NLB, 1980) 186.
64 Della Volpe, *Logic as a Positive Science* 190.
65 Galvano Della Volpe, *Critique of Taste* [1960], trans. Michael Caesar (London: Verso, 1991),
66 Eval'd Il'enkov, "Dialektika ideal'nogo" [1974], *Logos* 1 (2009): 18.
67 See, for example, Louis Althusser, "Idéologie et appareils idéologiques d'État," in *Positions (1964–1975)* [1970] (Paris: Les Éditions sociales, 1976), 67–125.
68 Lukács controversially claimed that "[Marxist] orthodoxy refers exclusively to *method*" in *History and Class Consciousness*, 1.
69 Anderson, *Considerations*, 41.

PART II

Geographies

5 Guides to Berlin: Exiles, Émigrés, and the Left

ROMAN UTKIN

On 28 March 1922, Vladimir D. Nabokov, a prominent Russian statesman, was shot and killed during a public émigré event at Berlin's Philharmonic Hall. The attack echoed terrorist tactics used by many Russian revolutionaries in their struggle against the tsarist autocracy since the nineteenth century. In Berlin, the tables had turned: the perpetrators were the monarchists and their victim was a prominent member of the Constitutional Democrats (Kadets).[1] Nabokov's assassination was a tragic reminder that while the Bolsheviks had ultimately seized power in October 1917, they were but one group within the multifaceted Russian revolutionary movement. The Kadets were the most conservative of the progressive parties. To the monarchists, though, they were as bad as the Bolsheviks for supporting the 1905 Revolution and welcoming the abdication of the tsar in 1917.

As the Civil War drew to a close in 1921, all non-Bolshevik political parties were increasingly unwelcome in Soviet Russia. Berlin sheltered the losers of the Revolution, including monarchists and liberals, as well as the Mensheviks and Socialist Revolutionaries.[2] Among the centres of the Russian post-revolutionary emigration, Berlin of the early 1920s was the most heterogeneous. Marc Chagall, a disillusioned Soviet Commissar for Art who stopped briefly in Berlin after leaving his homeland for good, described the city in 1922 as a place where aristocrats, miracle-working rabbis, and constructivist artists crossed paths.[3] So varied was this displaced community that the poet Vladislav Khodasevich famously nicknamed Berlin "the stepmother of all Russian cities."[4] Scholars typically acknowledge the cultural and political diversity of this "Russian" Berlin, but many of its residents' leftist commitments remain insufficiently explored. The existing accounts of Russian post-revolutionary émigré culture privilege its anti-Bolshevik ethos, its sense of uprootedness, and its cultural conservatism.[5] Yet the exiled liberal intelligentsia and non-communist leftists were engaged in permanent soul-searching as Russia was being reimagined without them and on terms that were not theirs. Once the goal of the Revolution was no longer propelling leftist ideas and aesthetics, what sort of diasporic identities and sensibilities did these exiles shape?

Interwar Berlin is especially important for answering this question because of its role as "Europe's Eastern train station," as Karl Schlögel has put it. Schlögel's description emphasizes the heightened international mobility the city enabled thanks to its geographical proximity to Russia, railway infrastructure, and diplomatic agreements.[6] Although Berlin was a hub for exiles, the city also maintained consistent Soviet ties that culminated in the 1922 Treaty of Rapallo, which enabled trade and travel between Russia and Germany. As a result, Berlin grew more diverse, flooded with a new wave of Russian visitors and émigrés whose support or condemnation of the Soviet project was tentative.[7] The majority of Russian Berliners arguably favoured the Revolution as a necessary step towards establishing a democratically governed Russia, but they continually differed over the acceptability of Bolshevik policies and methods. Yesterday's political exiles from the Soviet Union were today's enthusiastic supporters of the Bolshevik state, and vice versa.[8] These conditions shaped a diasporic community that shared not only the experience of displacement but also the exposure to multiple ideologically irreconcilable political organizations, as well as the ability to cross borders. Far from being an insular and apolitical émigré enclave, Russian Berlin, or Charlottengrad – as its heart, the Berlin neighbourhood of Charlottenburg, came to be known – was a site of transnational encounters that prompted cultural producers to interrogate their positions as well as the purpose of their art in the wake of the Bolshevik takeover in Russia.[9]

Guides to Berlin: Migration and Travel Writing

Writing about Berlin, usually in autobiographically inflected genres, became an outlet for ordering the inherently disorienting experience of life abroad. That some émigrés could return to Russia – that the permanence of their exile was not definitive – meant that city writing also functioned as a rhetorical staging ground for conceptualizing this historical moment, finding new means of artistic expression, and exercising political agency despite being in exile.[10]

Consider Viktor Shklovsky's epistolary novel *Zoo, or Letters Not about Love* (1923), which catalogues the romantically rejected narrator's disappointments with diasporic politics in Berlin and ends with an official application requesting permission to return to Russia.[11] Andrei Bely's pamphlet travelogue *One of the Mansions of the Kingdom of Shades* (1924) chronicles the author's decision to leave Germany and return to Russia as he dances frenetically through Berlin's cafés and cabarets.[12] Ilya Ehrenburg's travel sketches, gathered under the title *Letters from Cafés: Germany in 1922* (1923), conjure up Berlin's inferiority, as methodically described by an author unwilling to relocate to Moscow.[13] These authors belonged to different political and aesthetic camps, but their narratives about Berlin and its Russian contingent reflect a universal sense of conflicted indeterminacy about the future. This indeterminacy also reveals how non-Bolshevik and – to use a contemporary term – politically progressive Russian writers in Berlin negotiated their stance vis-à-vis Soviet Russia and emigration by writing about Berlin.

Some avowedly anti-Bolshevik writers turned to Berlin for similar purposes. In 1925, Vladimir Nabokov, whose father had been assassinated three years earlier, published his seemingly austere short story "A Guide to Berlin," an exile's tour of a foreign city interspersed with shrewd observations on the nature of art, history, and memory.[14] Although Nabokov's text precludes a leftist reading – the narrator has nothing but contempt for communism – the story offers an original approach, in that it structures a day in the life of an émigré as a city guide. Utilitarian at its core, the city guide genre is a form of tourist propaganda that promises to unlock foreign spaces and that models ways of discovering culturally significant sites ranging from museums to restaurants. Nabokov inverts city guide logic by focusing on the mundane aspects of city life: navigating streets under construction, riding on public transit, visiting a zoo, and getting a drink at an unremarkable pub. Nabokov's protagonist cannot overcome the foreignness of the city, where he lives as a permanent stranger. Unfamiliarity with foreign surroundings might excite a tourist, but it only reaffirms the exile's alienation. That alienation is nevertheless valuable as a bulwark against assimilation. Therefore, the frame of a city guide stabilizes the uncertainty of exile while offering an outlet for maintaining difference.

At the opposite end of the ideological spectrum are discursive guides to Berlin written by Soviet visitors. For example, Larisa Reisner's essays from Berlin, published under the title *Berlin in October of 1923*, have an emphatically communist tone.[15] In Berlin as a special correspondent for the Soviet newspapers *Izvestiia* and *Krasnaia zvezda*, Reisner dispenses a sharp critique of German socialists and provides heartbreaking descriptions of the urban poor. Whereas Nabokov deliberately avoids any sort of social commentary, Reisner visits the Reichstag and Berlin's working-class neighbourhoods to describe the politicians' cowardice and the workers' poverty. She compares the Reichstag to a zoo, a casino, and a museum – anything but a functional legislative body. Her style is agitational, sharp, and accusatory. In her eyes, in Berlin "everyone is ready to do anything to avoid a social revolution" (79). This statement targets both the deputies from Germany's Social Democratic Party, who are consumed with "sausage, coffee, and anxiety" in the Reichstag's cafeteria, and the petty bourgeois, who dream of margarine at night. She sees no possibility for a revolution in Berlin, a city that in her view represents a failed promise. At the same time, she draws attention to the plight of women, many of whom are pregnant, malnourished, or socially trapped: "Very often the man does not withstand the famished devastation – the crying of the unfed children, of hunger, and of dirt. Thousands of women workers are abandoned by their husbands and lovers after a few months of unemployment" (82). Although her impressions of Berlin are thoroughly bleak, Reisner retains some hope for a better future by implying that it can be achieved through gender equality. She imagines strong future women, mothers struggling against "hunger and degeneration" with "all the strength of youth and love, all the stamina and culture of the world's singular working class," unencumbered by "not only unenlightened men but also … unenlightened women" (83).

Given how partisan Reisner's Berlin writing is, her text, while thematically fascinating, leaves little room for interpreting the possibilities of émigré identities. Unsurprisingly, her brief description of "Russian émigrés" is condescending, albeit playfully so. She describes seeing some Russian émigrés at the zoo giving a baboon "empty match boxes, pieces of old paper, and cigarette butts." The "old and smart" baboon quickly loses interest and signals his disdain by turning his "crimson-blue" behind to them (84). In Reisner's account, the émigrés are no more worthy of attention than the discarded items they offer the baboon. In contrast to Reisner, Ehrenburg, Shklovsky, and Bely consider the identities of Russians abroad a subject worth exploring. Like Reisner (and Nabokov), they elaborate their difference abroad by writing about the city. But compared to the politically uncompromising Reisner and Nabokov, Ehrenburg, Shklovsky, and Bely represent Berlin as a zone of negotiation of Russianness and political engagement in the post-revolutionary moment.

When read as city guides, Ehrenburg's, Shklovsky's, and Bely's Berlin texts lend themselves to tracking the shifts in aesthetics and politics at a moment of extraordinary geopolitical flux. The three authors position themselves neither as nostalgic exiles nor as agents of newly defunct empires.[16] In a world where newly redrawn national borders trigger transnational mobility and sharpen national identities, these writers describe the foreign city as a way of mapping what it means to be a Russian writer abroad. Reading these texts as guides opens a fresh critical perspective on a time when Russian literature was splintering into divergent Soviet and émigré modalities. In this way, these texts function as guides *out* of Berlin as much as guides *to* Berlin. These texts also complicate traditional approaches to émigré studies and provide an unexpected entry point for reassessing the problem of red migrations.

Shklovsky, Bely, and Ehrenburg arrived in Berlin in the early 1920s out of necessity. The literary critic Shklovsky fled Bolshevik persecution as a Socialist Revolutionary in 1922. Bely, the renowned Symbolist poet and anthroposophist, was allowed to leave Russia in 1921 to improve his health and settle marital affairs with his estranged wife. Ehrenburg, a former Bolshevik and committed socialist, settled in Berlin after being expelled from Paris in 1921. Unlike Nabokov and those who spent the rest of their life in exile, Shklovsky, Bely, and Ehrenburg returned to Moscow in 1923. Ehrenburg went back to Western Europe almost immediately and continued to live and work there as a foreign correspondent for the Soviet press until 1940. Shklovsky became an inimitably controversial Soviet author, while Bely died in 1934 after a series of failed attempts at ideological conformism.

Shklovsky's *Zoo*, Ehrenburg's *Letters from Cafés*, and Bely's *Kingdom of Shades* are not labelled as guides to (Russian) Berlin, and they are not meant to provide practical advice to tourists. Instead, by mixing literary and non-literary prose – as well as overtly ideological statements with intimately personal ruminations – Shklovsky, Ehrenburg, and Bely use city writing as an occasion to reflect on their own presence in Berlin at a pivotal historical moment. Approaching these texts as city guides allows us a look into what the Formalist critic Boris Eikhenbaum called "the literary everyday" (*literaturnyi byt*), understood as the dialectics of an author's embeddedness in the literary marketplace.[17] Consequently, the spatial perception registered in Shklovsky's, Ehrenburg's, and Bely's texts and these texts' publication histories reflect the development of the concepts of "Soviet" and "émigré" authorship in relation to Berlin's cityscape.

The Literary Everyday: In Search of a Genre

Russian prose genres experienced a revival in the early 1920s. The literary historian D.S. Mirsky observed, while still in emigration himself, that the "most important event in Russian literary life of the last three years is the decline of poetry and the rise of prose," which followed "the bookless years of the Civil War."[18] In Russia proper, however, Boris Eikhenbaum was far less optimistic in his assessment of contemporary prose. In his programmatic essay "The Literary Everyday" (1927), Eikhenbaum argues that in the society reshaped by the Revolution, the question of "how to write" has been superseded, "or at least complicated," by the problem of "how to be a writer."[19] As Serguei Oushakine has pointed out, Eikhenbaum's argument is less about extra-literary materialist concerns, such as the importance of information about book contracts and the make-up of the reading public, and more to do with "directing the readers' attention to the forms of authorial self-reflection regarding the writer's positionality within the system of literary production."[20] Inspired by the rapid expansion of the periodical press in the Soviet Union, Eikhenbaum put this theory into practice in his 1929 hybrid text *My Periodical*, where, in Alyson Tapp's analysis, his approach to writing "dissolves the boundaries between scholarship, autobiography and literary prose ... allowing critic, author and perhaps even literary character to mingle and move between these three modes of writing."[21] Eikhenbaum's disregard for strict genre boundaries became for him an advantage afforded by the form of a periodical publication, the newspaper or journal, which connected the disparate elements of a writer's biography and writerly activity.[22] This experimentation with genres and media, conceptualized as the theory of the literary everyday, was meant to underscore the unprecedented historical and social environment, which required new forms of representation.[23]

Although Eikhenbaum's critical concept of the literary everyday is rooted in Soviet realities, extending his theory to Russian Berlin helps us recognize how writers who lived outside Russia sought out representational forms adequate for the times. The problem of authorial agency, "how to be a writer," only sharpened in a context of diasporic displacement, especially as the likely duration of that displacement remained unclear in the early 1920s. Whereas Eikhenbaum chose the format of an idiosyncratic periodical publication for ordering heterogeneous literary material, the writers in Berlin opted for city writing as a way of cultural mapping. In Berlin, the motif of wandering extended beyond metaphor – wandering across genres – and into daily practice, reflecting the literary everyday of migrant writers.

The Migrant Literary Everyday of Russian Berlin

Russian publishing flourished in Berlin from 1920 until 1924, as the city's presses – as many as seventy-two Russian publishing houses in a city of four million – supplied books to the global diaspora and, briefly, to the Soviet market.²⁴ The major publishers had a variety of distinct profiles and rosters of authors. Ivan Ladyzhnikov Press was nominally Marxist. Zinovy Grzhebin Press, Gelikon, Petropolis, Epokha, and Otto Kirchner & Co. were established in Russia but permanently moved their operations to Berlin and served the diaspora and, for a time, the Soviet Union; most of Grzhebin's books bore a "Berlin–Petersburg–Moscow" imprint. Slovo was established by the Kadets and partly owned by the German Ullstein Verlag; it published nineteenth-century classics, early Nabokov, and the monumental *Archive of the Russian Revolution* series. Obelisk specialized in Russian religious philosophy. Mednyi Vsadnik was a monarchist press. Olga D'iakova & Co., a rare example of a publishing house run by a woman, supplied the diaspora with house manuals, family calendars, and reprints of middlebrow bestsellers.²⁵

This robust publishing environment reflected the complexity of Berlin's post-revolutionary Russian community. It also meant that authors could align themselves with particular presses serving specific segments of the reading public. That is, authors had a general sense of their audience. It is not that the presses pigeonholed their authors, but an affiliation with a given publishing house indicated a given author's political disposition. Someone like the anti-Bolshevik Nabokov, for example, never published with pro-Soviet Grzhebin or Gelikon. And Shklovsky and Ehrenburg never published with Slovo, but both Nabokov and Ehrenburg published with Petropolis.²⁶ Eikhenbaum might have called this publishing reality "literature's social mode of being," and to grasp its dynamics, it is imperative to consider how the authors conceived of their roles as writers in the polarizing Russophone community.

Ehrenburg, Shklovsky, and Bely were remarkably prolific in Berlin. From 1921 to 1923, Ehrenburg wrote and edited nearly twenty books; Shklovsky published a volume of memoirs, a novel, and a collection of essays; and Bely published sixteen books.²⁷ The city's thriving publishing market facilitated much of this activity, though most of what these authors published then was written earlier, as was the case with Ehrenburg's *The Extraordinary Adventures of Julio Jurenito* (Gelikon, 1922), the revised edition of Bely's *Petersburg* (Epokha, 1922), and Shklovsky's *A Sentimental Journey* (Gelikon, 1923).²⁸ The time these writers spent in Berlin, however, yielded a number of texts about Berlin itself. In his preface to *Zoo, or Letters Not about Love*, Shklovsky writes that his novel originated as "a series of essays on Russian Berlin" but evolved into a "book on a dispute between people of two cultures" (3–4, 267). Similarly, Bely and Ehrenburg in their respective narratives focused on migrant encounters in Berlin. And much as Shklovsky's *Zoo* turned out to be a book about more than Russian émigré life, Bely's *Kingdom of Shades* and

Ehrenburg's *Letters from Cafés* employ the theme of exile in Berlin as a means to express broader concerns about post-war, post-revolutionary European modernity.

Ehrenburg and the End of "Spatial Patriotism"

The links between the political and the poetic undergird all three of these Berlin texts. This entanglement is especially evident in Ehrenburg's work. For most of his life, Ehrenburg acted as a bridge between the Soviet Union and the West.[29] Even before becoming an indispensable figure of Soviet cultural diplomacy under Stalin, Ehrenburg tirelessly promoted abroad the literature, art, architecture, and theatre produced in Soviet Russia. While in Berlin in 1921–3, he not only published his own poetry and fiction, edited with El Lissitzky the international journal *Veshch'/Gegenstand/Object*, and wrote countless book reviews, but also secured Russian publishers in Berlin for the poetry of Boris Pasternak, Marina Tsvetaeva, and Sergei Esenin. Although Ehrenburg took advantage of the opportunities to publish in Germany, he publicly declared that "Russian culture is being created there, in Russia, and not outside it."[30]

Ehrenburg's own national status as a writer in Berlin was somewhat ambiguous. As a reviewer for *Izvestiia* put it, "the Whites consider Ehrenburg to be Red, and the Reds think he is White."[31] Ehrenburg broke with the Bolsheviks long before the Revolution, in 1909, and was not enthusiastic about the October 1917 coup. After a brush with the secret police, he left Russia in 1921, but he never self-identified as an émigré and he maintained his Soviet citizenship. In Soviet Russia of the 1920s, however, he was considered a friendly but deeply mistaken fellow traveller.[32] Some of these contradictions are captured indirectly on the cover of Ehrenburg's collection *Six Stories about Easy Endings*, published in Berlin in 1922: illustrated by El Lissitzky, the text is typeset in the pre-revolutionary orthography, bringing together the avant-garde abstraction linked with revolutionary change and the archaic letters (such as *yat*) associated with the imperial past. Many émigré writers, including Nabokov, signalled their commitment to pre-revolutionary Russia by never accepting the new orthography.

Ehrenburg was consistently critical of conservative émigrés. But he also shared a certain sensibility with them. As Ehrenburg's biographer Joshua Rubenstein has observed, "underlying his work for most of the 1920s is a brooding sadness over the fate of his country."[33] However, Ehrenburg's pessimism was of a different sort than that of the exiles bemoaning the loss of old Russia. He was attached to the idea of a pan-European unity and was concerned about Soviet Russia's isolation from the wider world. He later commented on this period by writing that "spatial [*prostranstvennyi*] patriotism" died in the trenches of the Great War: "the notion of 'motherland' [*rodina*] was swiftly replaced with 'modernity' [*sovremennost'*]."[34] For Ehrenburg, Russia's isolation meant temporal incongruity with the rest of Europe.

Strikingly, in *Letters from Cafés* Ehrenburg placed the centre of modernity in Berlin, not Moscow. He wrote that "there is only one contemporary city in Europe – Berlin" (123).[35] With backhanded praise, he called Berlin "the only imaginable capital of Europe. Among other big cities, it is Karl Schmidt, Paul Durand, Ivan Ivanovich Ivanov" (123), or, one might add, "John Smith." He found Berlin remarkably average, and saw the city as an "enormous nodal train station" at the intersection of nationalism and internationalism, socialism and capitalism, republicanism and monarchy. In the space of rival political systems, Ehrenburg's sympathies lay with the working-class districts of eastern and northern Berlin, with the singers of "The Internationale." Ehrenburg writes from the perspective of a cosmopolitan Russian traveller whose presence in Germany remains unexplained. He is neither a regular tourist nor an émigré, and his letters are written in a spontaneous and informal style. Moreover, he creates a sense of immediacy and interconnectedness by assuming that his unnamed interlocutor – any reader of his text – agrees with him. His speculation that perhaps the people who "fiercely reject the notion of motherland are the genuine patriots" exposed his own beliefs: he lived abroad to advance the cause of a class struggle unbound by national borders.[36]

Addressed to an imaginary "dear friend," his postcard-like *Letters from Cafés* combine journalistic reportage with personal ruminations and art criticism. They describe Berlin, the mountain of Brocken, the cities of Hildesheim and Magdeburg, and Weimar. Taken together, Ehrenburg's letters resemble a portrait of post-war Germany in transition.[37] The picturesque medieval towns are miniature representations of the uncertainty Ehrenburg observes in the industrially advanced but ideologically conflicted Berlin. Magdeburg is in the throes of what Ehrenburg terms "expressionist" urban redevelopment headed by the modernist architect Bruno Taut. Weimar is divided between "respectable burghers" and "blockheads" studying at the Bauhaus, the progressive art school that was headquartered in Weimar from 1919 until 1925. Ehrenburg qualifies the Bauhaus as Germany's "sole live art school" and compares it unfavourably to its Moscow counterpart Vkhutemas.[38] That is not to say that Ehrenburg necessarily finds Soviet art superior. As he visits Berlin's famed modern art gallery Der Sturm and witnesses the life of art in the provinces, his letters reflect a growing disappointment with the general popularity of leftist art. He mocks the avant-garde's resolute utilitarianism by claiming that "not a single constructivist would agree to sit on a 'constructivist' chair for more than five minutes," and he goes as far as to suggest that geometric abstraction can be violent: "the leftists have beaten feeling [*izdubasili chuvstvo*] with a ruler" (148). It is striking that Ehrenburg, who championed contemporary European art in 1922 in a book of essays, *And Yet It Spins!* (*I vse-taki ona vertitsia!*), and in his own Constructivist journal *Veshch'/Gegenstand/Object*, disparages the avant-garde once he sees it against the background of the pastoral German countryside in 1923.[39]

Ehrenburg is quick to reassure the reader of his letters that he has not switched his loyalties to the political right, but he insists on criticizing the left. Travelling through politically torn Germany makes him realize that the commitment of leftist art to "produc[ing] manifestos, excommunicat[ing] heretics, and cover[ing] walls and hearts with diagrams, equations, and charts" leads to nothing more than unusable "pseudo-constructivist" furniture (148–9). In criticizing the superficiality of such artistic practice, Ehrenburg implies that bad art translates into bad politics. And even though he is ostensibly writing about Germany, there is nothing that stops the reader from extending Ehrenburg's analysis to Russia, especially considering the international ethos of leftist art. These letters might have been written in German cafés, but they concern a commonly shared modernity.

In the impoverished Berlin of 1922, Ehrenburg saw a city on the brink of all-out class conflict. Berlin appeared to him as a "messenger [*gonets*] into the most delightful uncertainty" (133). The future would prove in the end to be far from delightful; even so, the messenger metaphor was fortuitous. Ehrenburg's idealism would be tempered with time, and he would leave Germany once France issued him a visa. But it was in post–Great War Berlin that he came to realize his own role as a messenger from and for Moscow.

Shklovsky and Diasporic Celebrity

Shklovsky was also a leftist, but he was not a Bolshevik. He participated in the Revolution and the Civil War on behalf of the Socialist Revolutionaries.[40] His support of the Provisional Government and his opposition to the Bolsheviks eventually forced him into exile in Berlin, where he nevertheless kept his distance from the anti-Soviet émigrés. Shklovsky socialized instead with Maxim Gorky, himself an exile of sorts, and published primarily with the Soviet-friendly press Gelikon.

Despite Shklovsky's ambivalence about the Soviet government – his wife was arrested and refused an exit visa, and his brother was repeatedly arrested on political grounds – he chose to return. He lived in Berlin from March 1922 until September 1923. His celebrated novel *Zoo*, published by Gelikon, secured his return to Moscow, as its last chapter was stylized as an official application for repatriation.[41]

However, before the narrator's arrival at that last chapter of *Zoo*, he ceaselessly writes letters in and about Berlin that are indicative of an earnest attempt to outline a Russian public sphere across borders. That is, as Shklovsky cycles through a diverse range of topics in his letters, the letters themselves formally act as rhetorical bridges connecting people and ideas across space and time. This public sphere is conjured by letter writing in linguistic and cultural terms, not in a geographical space. By the middle of *Zoo*, Letter Seventeen of Twenty-Nine, the narrator declares that he feels stuck in Berlin and has downgraded Russian Berliners to the status of squatters (*sidel'tsy*): "We are refugees. No, not refugees but fugitives – and now squatters" (63). Presumably, genuine refugees, exiles, and émigrés would have been galvanized by a common sense of righteous indignation and a resolve to fight for shared ideals.[42] But in Shklovsky's estimation, "Russian Berlin is going nowhere. It has no destiny. No propulsion" (63). This lack of propulsion stalls all mobility.[43] Towards the end of the novel, Shklovsky supplements the propulsion metaphor with that of a dying battery: "Our batteries were charged in Russia; here we keep going around in circles and soon we will grind to a halt" (95). The futility of "going around in circles" coupled with the lack of propulsion means that Shklovsky's letters cannot circulate properly, rendering him powerless and isolated.

Only the novel's final letter, Shklovsky's "Declaration to the All-Russian Central Executive Committee" that he cannot live in Berlin and wants to go back to Russia, achieves the intended result: the author is allowed to repatriate. In switching his addressee from the person to the state, Shklovsky styles his last letter as a declaration of defeat: "I raise my arm and surrender" (104). His surrender to the authorities reflects a deep crisis. While he experiences Russian Berlin in such a way as to conclude that "poor Russian emigration" "has no heartbeat" (95), he also concedes that "the revolution has lost its propulsion" (63). This admission of the Revolution's exhaustion, which was cut from all subsequent Soviet editions of *Zoo*, betrays Shklovsky's recognition that the utopian aspirations of the Revolution are over, together with his illusions about the possibility of life abroad.[44] Thus an attempt at starting a transnational Russian public sphere crashes against the fragmentation and inertia of Russian Berlin and the *Realpolitik* of Soviet Russia.

The original 1923 edition of *Zoo* defies easy categorization as a piece of either émigré or Soviet literature; the subsequent editions of the novel in 1924, 1929, and 1964 were made distinctly Soviet with numerous additions and strategic cuts, as Shklovsky after his return was eager to point out the deficiencies of émigré life and the foreignness of Germany.[45] In 1924, for instance, he added to his Berlin corpus such lines as "We [the émigrés] were plucked from Russia like a sieve from the water. Dark and incomprehensible is the smoke of northern, working-class Berlin."[46] Working-class northern Berlin arguably remained incomprehensible to Shklovsky even after his exile, for he never showed genuine interest in German proletarian culture. But when he lived in Berlin's wealthy and heavily Russian western part, he was fully aware of the diasporic dynamics and pursued publishing opportunities that promised to reach a wide readership.

Several chapters from *Zoo* first appeared in the journal *Beseda* (*Conversation*), an uncensored international journal aimed at informing readers in Russia of the latest developments in the arts and sciences abroad. *Beseda* was a phenomenon typical of Russian Berlin, in that it brought together as editors seemingly ideologically incompatible writers such as Gorky, Khodasevich, and Bely.[47] In 1923 they all had enough in common to work together on a journal intended for distribution in Soviet Russia. (Notably, the journal's working title had been *Putnik*, or "the wayfarer," suggesting the editors' consideration of a travel guide as metaphor.)[48] To secure access to Moscow and to attract émigré contributors and readers, the editors of *Beseda* strove to maintain political neutrality. Initially, Shklovsky was on the editorial board as well, but his colleagues excluded him after he jeopardized the journal's apolitical stance by causing a scandal during a public lecture on Russian Futurism.[49] Following this incident, Shklovsky wrote to Gorky to apologize and added, "I think that this whole affair won't compromise the journal, more so because on the Berlin market I am a relatively insignificant and easily erasable entity."[50] The last line of *Zoo*, "it is not right that I should be living in Berlin," seemed to prove his point. With this declaration, he effectively erased himself from the city and the émigré community.

Bely and the Limits of Ideological Ecumenicalism

The Soviet authorities delayed allowing – and ultimately never allowed – *Beseda* to be imported into the Soviet Union. The newly instituted censorship directorate Glavlit suspected the journal of carrying out subversive anti-communist propaganda. Among its many concerns, Glavlit took note of Andrei Bely's consistent defence of anthroposophy on the pages of the journal. Formally, Bely was a supporter of the Soviet project, living in Berlin as a Soviet citizen. He was one of the few authors with reputations firmly established before 1917 who accepted the October Revolution. But as an ardent anthroposophist, Bely viewed revolutionary change in Russia as spiritual rejuvenation. The Marxist understanding of reality in terms of competing economic forces was alien to him.[51] Although he had little in common with the Bolsheviks ideologically, he nevertheless welcomed the transformation of Russia and had gone abroad to improve his health, not necessarily to emigrate.[52]

Arriving in Berlin in November 1921, Bely discovered in the city a "swarm of Russians – a chaos."[53] It appears from Bely's Berlin diary that however chaotic the social scene, he easily grasped the distinctions among the anti-Soviet émigrés and Soviet-sympathetic intelligentsia.[54] He stayed away from the monarchists but had numerous contacts with liberals and non-Bolshevik leftists. Bely's literary everyday in Berlin reveals a writer positioning himself above the political differences on the left, if not outright disregarding them. As soon as he arrived in Berlin, he accepted the invitation of the Kadet Gessen to deliver two public lectures, one on Alexander Blok and the other on the "contemporary crisis," in support of Russian student associations abroad.[55] He was a board member of the short-lived House of the Arts, which positioned itself as an apolitical organization that functioned as an informal trade union of Russian writers, artists, musicians, and actors outside Russia.[56] In addition to serving as an editor of the politically neutral *Beseda*, he had his own monthly literary journal, *Epopeia* (*Epic*). He also contributed book reviews to the Socialist-Revolutionary daily *Dni* (*Days*). His publishers during the Berlin years 1921–3 included the Kadet press Slovo; the Menshevik Epokha; Soviet-friendly Grzhebin Press and Gelikon; and the Soviet Gosizdat. Although he harboured little sympathy for either the Soviets or the émigrés, Bely worked with both.[57]

Bely's ideological ecumenicalism ended abruptly with his decision to return to Moscow in October 1923. He was emotionally unstable while in Berlin, and his sudden departure from Germany has occasioned various speculative explanations.[58] In 1922 he believed that the possibility of going back to Russia was forever foreclosed for him, but a year later he was in Moscow, praising the spectacular achievements of the Soviet state.[59] His impressions of life in Berlin were gathered into an eccentric pamphlet, *One of the Mansions of the Kingdom of Shades*, published by Gosizdat after his return in 1924. In this book, Bely depicts Berlin as the heart of the émigré community embedded in the "kingdom of shades." The narrator locates this community's topographical centre at the spire of Berlin's Gedächtniskirche: "The spire of the remarkable church is a crossing of times and spaces: the antediluvian past is crossed here with the approaching future … The spire of that church is a point from which run [*razbegaiutsia*] the radii of Russian resettlements in Berlin within the circumference of the Charlottenburg reality." (31)

In *Kingdom of Shades*, Bely envisions Berlin in transnational terms as a mythopoetic space of intercultural encounter embodied in geometric shapes, similar to the way he described Petersburg in his eponymous novel of 1914. He sees the Berlin of 1923 in the agony of cultural exhaustion, the same way he saw the Petersburg of 1905. The despair that imbues Petersburg – a city unable to contain the forces of entropy – has come to haunt him in Berlin. For him, these two cities are inhabited by shades (*teni*), but in Berlin the accent is on the degenerate copies of real humans losing themselves in the "rhythms of foxtrot" and cocaine (60). Echoing the pessimism of *Petersburg*, Bely's narrator finds Berlin, and the European civilization for which it stands, to be but a thin veneer coating the "savage chaos of real decay and death" (69).

In a marked difference from *Petersburg*, however, *Kingdom of Shades* ends on an improbably cheerful note. The narrator moves back to Moscow, which he describes as "the source of life" and "a creative laboratory of future, perhaps never-before-seen, forms" (69, 73). The book's cover cartoonishly emphasizes the difference between black Berlin (bourgeois men and a lady in fancy hats promenading in front of a "Berliner Kafe") and red Moscow (gender-ambiguous workers in front of a massive construction site) (figure 5.1).[60] Finished in Moscow and published in Leningrad, Bely's narrative carries a pro-Soviet bias so hyperbolic that Monika Spivak has even characterized it as a "servile Soviet collection of essays."[61] Indeed, the text strives to affirm Soviet state-building at the expense of Berlin while mapping Bely's journey from Moscow to Berlin and then back to Moscow. In this way, Bely presents himself not only as a returnee but also as a refugee from the soon-to-collapse West. Having made the choice to return, Bely was diligently performing the role of a class-conscious writer, in contrast to his ideologically flexible stance in Berlin.

In the book's opening paragraph, Bely declares that Berlin had a decisive impact on him: "it's very difficult for me to share my impressions of being in Germany," he writes, because his entire life he considered himself a Westernizer and repeatedly wrote about the intellectual "poverty of Slavophilism" (5). Post-war Berlin, "this little slice of Europe," convinces Bely of the inaccuracy of his previously held beliefs. That Bely announces the challenge of narrating his life abroad by referencing the central socio-philosophical debate of the nineteenth century between the proponents of the Western model of development (Westernizers)

Figure 5.1. Unknown artist, cover design for *One of the Mansions of the Kingdom of Shades* by Andrei Bely. The cover is dated 1925, but the book was published in 1924.

and the adherents of the idea of Russia's exceptionalism (Slavophiles) is surprising. The relevance of this debate is questionable in 1924, and invoking it to announce the primacy of the nationalist Slavophiles runs counter to the Soviet ambition of a global revolution, thus undermining Bely's own aim of aligning himself with the Soviet authorities.[62] This rhetorical incongruity points to the naive superficiality of Bely's political awareness. But Bely needs the Russia versus the West binary to justify his return from Berlin and to stage his ideological transformation.

As Alexander Dolinin has observed, the theme of Europe's demise is an important presence in Bely's oeuvre from the early 1900s onward.[63] David Bethea has analysed the apocalyptic tendencies of Bely's fiction, particularly in *Petersburg*, and underscored that "his view of history as spiralling toward an end" can be detected in the structure and language of his prose.[64] Prior to moving to Berlin in 1921, Bely lamented the prospect of a European apocalypse, but it was in Berlin that he embraced the idea that Europe was in inescapable decline. Monika Spivak attributes Bely's sudden Europhobia to a string of personal misfortunes, primarily the break-up with his wife and with his mentor, the founder of anthroposophy, Rudolf Steiner.[65] Yet for all its flaws, *Kingdom of Shades* avoids the topic of personal troubles and reflects instead Bely's thorough familiarity with contemporary German art and culture. In fact, Bely's narrative aligns squarely with the gloomy millennial worldview of Oswald Spengler's widely popular treatise *The Decline of the West* (1918). Bely dismisses German philosophers, poets, musicians, politicians, and artists as derivative, concluding, "and then one begins to understand the core mood of such books as Spengler's *Decline of the West*" (43).[66] Although Bely did not accept Spengler's ideas wholesale, in the *Kingdom of Shades* he follows Spengler's model of historical evolution and identifies Berlin as the locus of Western civilizational decay.[67] For example, he claims that the popularity of such past civilizations as Egypt, India, and China among German Dadaists and Expressionists is a telltale sign of a dying society (44). By the same logic, Russian Berlin serves as an illustration of multicultural contamination and Western degeneration (26–38). Bely renounces his past attachment to Europe by way of concurring with Spengler and discursively enacting his escape from Berlin.

Paradoxically, it was Bely, who was much more ambivalent about politics than Shklovsky and Ehrenburg, who wrote the most explicitly propagandistic text against Russians in Berlin. Yet Bely's text, narrated by "Someone," is so maniacally agitational and so structurally peculiar in its condemnation of Berlin as a "bourgeois Sodom" that it borders on parody. It is likewise difficult to take at face value Ehrenburg's *Letters from Cafés* and Shklovsky's *Zoo* because these texts struggle to keep separate the fictional and documentary narrative elements. In various proportions, all three texts blend autobiographical observations, historical commentary, and political insight. They are produced by authors navigating a precarious political landscape: unwilling to become émigrés, they are reluctant to embrace the Bolsheviks, and meanwhile Russian culture is becoming increasingly divided.[68] Although these authors ultimately sided with the Soviets, the record of their publishing and public activities in Berlin shows how circuitous their paths to Moscow were. Their texts' generic inconsistency, moreover, reflects a search for means to synthesize and represent the period's contradictory cultural dynamics. To guide the reader through (Russian) Berlin in a reassuring way, Ehrenburg, Shklovsky, and Bely chart the city's topography and inscribe themselves on it. But their experiments with city writing tend to follow the same pattern: their aesthetic and spatial considerations of Berlin map ways out of it.

A Guide to the City: The Map

Ever since the advance of industrialization and urban growth, cities have served as the main locus for writing about the present.[69] In the Russian literary tradition, Petersburg exerted an outsized influence on paradigms of city writing. Bely certainly turned to some of the same tropes he used in his novel *Petersburg* when writing about Berlin in *Kingdom of Shades*. He even deliberately confused the two cityscapes: "there the street extends to the spire of the Admiralty – no, pardon me, to the spire of Gedächtniskirche" (30). Admittedly, the Saint Petersburg of the nineteenth-century classics was represented uniformly as an un-Russian and unreal place, but it was also a crucial site of personal crisis rooted in religious ethics of rebirth.[70] Berlin, a major diasporic centre, was a genuinely foreign city where existential crises were of a more immediate nature.[71] Russians flocked to Berlin not out of admiration for Prussian urban planning and lifestyle, but because the city was affordable and accessible, and because it allowed for the possibility of returning to Russia. Many Russian Berliners faced a choice between living outside Russia indefinitely or surrendering to the Bolshevik state. As we have seen, Ehrenburg repeatedly wrote about Berlin as a buzzing train station and Bely commented on its confusing mix of multiple temporalities. Shklovsky memorably compared Berlin's residential architecture to a heap of luggage: "The houses are as alike as suitcases" (304, 66). Such literary mappings of Berlin were dependent on topographical mapping, and the combination of the two was perhaps the most universally employed and productive way of narrating the circumstances surrounding the pivotal moments of the writers' lives abroad.

Schlögel has observed that Russian writers in Berlin alluded to many of the same landmarks and phenomena of the "urban interior" as they navigated the city.[72] To be sure, the Berlin Zoo, the Gedächtniskirche, streetcars, and underground trains, as well as pubs and cafés, appear frequently across various texts. What distinguished the spatial experiences of those Russian Berliners who eventually left for Moscow, however, is that they were highly aware of the social discrepancies of the neighbourhoods around specific landmarks. Most immediately, the Berlin Zoo and the Russian enclave adjacent to it were located in Berlin's wealthy western district, primarily in the borough of Charlottenburg. Whereas in "Guide to Berlin," Nabokov ignores the socioeconomic aspect of his exiled narrator's milieu, Ehrenburg, Shklovsky, and Bely emphasize that Berlin is divided into the working-class north and the bourgeois west and that most Russians live in the west. In Bely's description of his arrival in Berlin, he writes that from the train station he reached "that part of Berlin that the Russians call 'Petersburg' while the Germans call it 'Charlottengrad'" (26). He later adds, "for several months I lived in the most bourgeois quarter of Berlin" (63). Shklovsky reports laconically that "in Berlin, as everyone knows, the Russians live around the zoo. The notoriety of this fact is no cause for joy" (66, 303). Ehrenburg alludes to staying in the city's western part by sharing that he lived on the Kaiserallee, near Hohenzollernplatz (127). This topographic connection between Berlin's upscale neighbourhood and its Russian pocket established a deliberate metonymical relation between the German bourgeoisie and the Russian expatriate community.

All three writers pushed their class-informed observations further as they built their narratives on top of Berlin's existing social hierarchies as embodied in urban space. As Ehrenburg wryly put it, "as in any other city, in Berlin there are 'nationalists' and 'internationalists.' They live in different parts of the city." He explained that the "nationalists," otherwise known as "respectable people," lived in the west. The "internationalists" were factory workers living on the city's northern and eastern outskirts (126–7). This fraught geography provided a paradoxically stabilizing coordinate system in a city where everything else seemed to be in flux. In mapping the movements of their narrators within this space, Ehrenburg, Shklovsky, and Bely outlined how their respective aesthetic, social, and political considerations were simultaneously shaped by and reflected in Berlin's urban environment.[73]

For example, Ehrenburg was aware of the irony of living on a street honouring the kaiser, but he also pointed out that the symbolism of the toponyms in the post-war city was being renegotiated: "at one point the leftists proposed renaming questionably named streets. The rightists declined the proposal by citing the greatness of history and the interests of cabbies" (125). Ehrenburg's observation suggests that the insufficiency of history's greatness to justify the street's royal name – indeed, the need to pair the kaiser and the cab driver – indicates the disintegration of the link between the signifier and signified, street name and kaiser. As he witnessed, the very idea of German patriotism, "which was previously so solid it was used as granite for the monuments to Bismarck," was undergoing a fundamental transformation, "becoming an unclear, changing form," in the wake of the Great War (127–8).

Furthermore, Ehrenburg questioned the validity of any rigid political platform. He ridiculed the disintegrating monarchy and called the forces of fascism and communism competing for dominance on Berlin's streets the "redeeming agendas" (*spasitel'nye raspisaniia*) heralded by the swastika and the red star. Although he sympathized with the workers' movement, he also warned that "all those who declare their calculations and dreams to be genuine itineraries [*raspisaniia*] lie – some lie sincerely, others not" (132). Recognizing a universal desire for change on the left and on the right, Ehrenburg presents Berlin as a city where all meaning is contingent, where "everything is ersatz," a substitute for something else: the street names invoke nonexistent royalty, tobacco is made of cabbage, the political parties are interchangeable, coffee is brewed from kidney beans, churches function as commercial concert venues, and pastries taste of potatoes (130–1). This contingency thrilled Ehrenburg because it mediated the uncertainty of the historical moment – and rendered the present negotiable.

Bely was far less charitable in his view of Berlin's intersecting spatial and social planes. In his eyes, the Wittenbergplatz in the city's western part was dominated by black marketeers and rich foreigners. A rare communist demonstration disrupting the feast of consumerism appears to Bely as a mirage: "Red flags get raised and flow into the open abyss of neighbourhoods" (29). He strengthens this hallucinatory gaze by writing in a macaronic language peppered with German toponyms and idioms both in German and in transliterated Russian. Easily distracted from his thoughts on class struggle by "the rhythms of foxtrot," Bely takes the reader on a tour of various "Diele" (cafés) and "Nachtlokals" (nightclubs) where "Annuschkas" and "Nataschas" sing songs about "Wolga" and visitors enjoy "Kuljebjakas" (26–9). This lifestyle is summarized in the couplet, "Nacht! Tauenzien! Kokain! / Das ist Berlin!" (29) and reinforced in the oft-repeated slogan "Bum-Bum," the soundtrack to the imploding city.[74]

The grotesque imagery of Berlin is counterbalanced by Bely's portrayal of a sober countryside. In a passage that reads like a proletarian pastoral, Bely finds reprieve in the suburban town of Zossen. There he discovers a working-class Germany full of contempt for the bourgeois capital. Living alongside German workers, Bely reports learning from his hosts about economic ties that bind together all capitalists – what he calls "the black international of Europe" (63).[75] He is told that regardless of their nationality, bankers and factory owners have more in common with one another than with the proletariat. In his travels outside Berlin, Bely encounters two different ways that post-war Germany is coping with the burden of reparations imposed by the Treaty of Versailles: while Berlin is losing itself in dancing and drinking, Zossen undergoes a political education. Hence despite finding in Berlin a "voluptuous anticipation of a revanche, which makes one pay hopeful attention to *Sowjetrussland*" (60), Bely declares that the city is capable only of a "masquerade under the revolutionary banner" (42). Yet the memoirs of Bely's contemporaries reveal that he despised Zossen.[76] In his own diaries he called the town "a village of undertakers," and he lived there for only two months.[77] It is clear that Bely's favourable comparison of Zossen to Berlin, as well as his presentation of the city as a den of sensual excess, was a strategic move necessary to create a structural pattern showing Berlin's spatial inferiority and suggesting that it was incapable of fostering meaningful social life.

Ehrenburg and Bely inscribe social relations onto urban topography; so does Shklovsky. It is noteworthy that these writers envision themselves as outsiders without identifying a clear centre of the city, its locus of power. Instead, they conceptualize their marginality by describing their difference in the middle of a foreign space. As Shklovsky writes, "we huddle among the Germans like a lake between its shores" (67, 303). Searching for an anchoring centre throughout *Zoo*, Shklovsky's narrator travels restlessly across Berlin's western neighbourhoods from Wittenbergplatz to Nollendorfplatz, to arrive at Gleisdreieck, the engineering marvel of a train station and the novel's lyrical crescendo:

> All around, along the roofs of the long yellow buildings, run tracks; tracks run along the ground and along high iron platforms, where they intersect other iron platforms as they rise to platforms still higher.
>
> Thousands of fires, lanterns, spires, iron balls on three legs and semaphores – semaphores everywhere.
>
> Despair, émigré love and streetcar no. 164 have brought me here; I have walked a long time on the bridges over the tracks that intersect here, just as the threads of a shawl drawn through a ring intersect. That ring is Berlin. (68, 305)

The criss-crossing bridges and train tracks serve as a personal and historical crossroads where the narrator finds himself. Instead of providing a sober analysis of the historical situation, he expresses a deep conflict about love and politics. And Berlin, conceived of as a ring through which biographical threads intersect, sharpens the sense of indeterminacy about national belonging. Yet describing Berlin as a ring and tracing the narrator's circular trajectory within it allow him to break through that circle.

As Gary Saul Morson has suggested, *Zoo* exemplifies Shklovsky's theory of literature and constitutes a "menagerie of literary species."[78] Throughout the novel, the narrator inserts vignettes of literary analysis in unexpected contexts. In one of the chapters following the Gleisdreieck passage, there is a discussion of Voltaire's *Candide*. Shklovsky writes that the novel "has a nice circular plot [*kol'tsevoi siuzhet*]: while people look for Cunégonde, she is sleeping with everybody and aging. The hero winds up with an old woman, who reminisces about the tender skin of her Bulgarian captain" (92, 319). Given that the premise of *Zoo* is the narrator's own futile quest for the affection of Alya, his indifferent love interest, the reference to Cunégonde implies that Alya is similarly preoccupied with other men. Furthermore, this literary example extends to geography: while Shklovsky struggles to find a place for himself in hollow Russian Berlin, life in Russia goes on. The pattern of his walks around Berlin suggests that *Zoo*, the novel he is writing, is in danger of having a circular plot, too.[79]

However, as the novel's author and protagonist, he guides the reader to recognize the narrative's underlying structure and also shows that he is in a position to manipulate it. The critical reference to *Candide* occurs in the same chapter as Shklovsky's discovery of proletarian Berlin: "It's nice to follow the canals to the workers' districts ... There, at the Hallesches Tor, out beyond the place where you live, stands the round tower of the gasworks, just like those at home on the Obvodny Canal. When I was eighteen, I used to walk my beloved to those towers every day" (90, 318). The adjective *obvodnyi* (which denotes the quality of bypassing something) reiterates the notion of circularity but also introduces the idea of circumvention. More importantly, this passage provides a space to insert a message of solidarity with the German workers and to remind the narrator of his youthful romantic exploits in Petersburg. The invocation of workers reads almost like an afterthought here, but it is consistent with Shklovsky's sustained effort to weave together the personal and political to find a way out of the exilic impasse. The emphasized affinity with workers, even if strained, conjures up memories of personal fulfilment. By linking industrial labour and the labour of love, Shklovsky reshapes the circularity of the plot into a linear progression towards his decision to leave Germany.

The invocation of class-based solidarities in *Zoo*, *Letters from Cafés*, and *Kingdom of Shades* does not mean that Shklovsky, Ehrenburg, and Bely were Marxist thinkers. Rather, their "migrant literary everyday" reflects a performance of class-consciousness. In *Literature and Revolution*, Trotsky dismissed Bely as a representative of pre-revolutionary bourgeois culture, calling him "a corpse [who] will not be resurrected in any spirit."[80] As a formalist, Shklovsky was hostile to Marxism until he had little choice but to adopt it in the late 1920s.[81] Even Ehrenburg, who had credentials as a revolutionary exile before 1917, was criticized by his communist peers for paying insufficient attention to the "economic conditions determining the morals, customs, political system, philosophy, and culture" of the European countries he visited.[82] It is reasonable to assume that by the time the Soviet Union was established in 1922, indicating some awareness of class-based solidarity was necessary for authors living abroad wishing to receive Soviet book contracts or to repatriate. The fact that each of the three authors acknowledged in their Berlin texts local forms of class conflict indicates that they foresaw readers interested in labour issues and strained to accommodate that interest. This pseudo-Marxist impulse complicates the exilic aspects of these texts but does not negate them. For instance, the uniform focus on urban exteriors and the lack of domestic interior spaces showcases the authors' "outsideness." And while Ehrenburg, Bely, and Shklovsky reach the same conclusion that they must leave Berlin, their individual approaches to mapping the city produce three distinct conceptions of social agency that Berlin conditions. Ehrenburg finds that the present is negotiable as he hops from one café to another. For Bely, Berlin is a city best not visited because it is the realm of the undead. And romantically rejected Shklovsky shows how reading the city opens up ways of navigating it.

Exploring Ehrenburg's, Shklovsky's, and Bely's writerly activities in Berlin indicates that city writing offered them versatile plotting strategies for capturing the complexities of the social worlds they inhabited. Like Nabokov's "Guide to Berlin," the narratives of Ehrenburg, Shklovsky, and Bely are not meant to entice visitors or facilitate seamless experiences of consumerism. Instead, the internal logic of the guide provides a way of organizing the literary everyday in exile and, to an extent, exposing the precarious infrastructure of modern life. Berlin's landmarks, streets, and neighbourhoods turn into discursive tools for producing an urban space that assembles disjointed urban impressions into a coherent whole. For Ehrenburg, Shklovsky, and Bely, Berlin becomes an embodiment of dashed hopes, broken hearts, and other misfortunes – a negative city and a place "not about love." To use another of Shklovsky's locutions, they find that in Berlin "'we' is a funny word ... 'We' is I and somebody else. In Russia, 'we' is stronger" (54, 296). United by a desire for collectivity, these authors imagine it differently: as an international collectivity in *Letters from Cafés*, a a union with the beloved in *Zoo*, and a rapturous arrival home in *Kingdom of Shades*. As such, these texts also evade an easy classification into Soviet and émigré modalities. They show instead how intertwined those modalities were in the early 1920s.

Acknowledgments

This chapter is a modified version of chapter 2 in my book, *Charlottengrad: Russian Culture in Weimar Berlin* (Madison: University of Wisconsin Press, 2023).

Notes

1. The terrorists aimed at the leader of the Kadets, Pavel Miliukov, who was shielded by Nabokov. See Grigorii Arosev, *Vladimir Nabokov, otets Vladimira Nabokova* (Moscow: Al'pina Non-Fikshn, 2021), 249–55.
2. For an account of radical revolutionary émigrés in Europe before 1917 and their diversity before the Bolshevik hegemony, see Faith Hillis, *Utopia's Discontents: Russian Émigrés and the Quest for Freedom, 1830s–1930s* (Oxford: Oxford University Press, 2021).
3. Edouard Roditi, "Entretien avec Marc Chagall," *Preuves: cahiers mensuels du Congrès pour la liberté de la culture* 84 (1958): 27.
4. Vladislav Khodasevich, "Vse kamennoe, v kamennyi prolet ..." [1923] in *Sobranie sochinenii v 4 tomakh, Tom 1. Stikhotvoreniia. Literaturnaia kritika 1906–1922* (Moscow: Soglasie, 1996), 266.
5. Maria Rubins, "Conceptual Territories of 'Diaspora': Introduction. The Unbearable Lightness of Being a Diasporian: Modes of Writing and Reading Narratives of Displacement," in *Redefining Russian Literary Diaspora, 1920–2020*, ed. Maria Rubins (London: UCL Press, 2021), 15. See also Marc Raeff, *Russia Abroad: A Cultural History of the Russian Emigration, 1919–1939* (Oxford: Oxford University Press, 1990); and Robert C. Williams, *Culture in Exile: Russian Émigrés in Germany, 1881–1941* (Ithaca: Cornell University Press, 1972).
6. Karl Schlögel, *Berlin, Ostbahnhof Europas: Russen und Deutsche in ihrem Jahrhundert* (Berlin: Siedler Verlag, 1998). The most recent, expanded edition of Schlögel's book appeared with a new title, *Das russische Berlin* (2019).
7. See Karl Schlögel, *Das russische Berlin: Eine Hauptstadt im Jahrhundert der Extreme. Aktualisierte, erweiterte Neuausgabe* (Berlin: Suhrkamp, 2019), 110–13; and Lazar Fleishman, "Vysylka intelligentsii i Russkii Berlin v 1922 g.," in *Russkii Berlin, 1920–1945: mezhdunarodnaia konferentsiia, 16–18 dekabria 2002 g.*, ed. Lazar Fleishman (Moscow: Russkii put', 2006), 94–106.
8. See Robert C. Williams, "'Changing Landmarks' in Russian Berlin, 1922–1924," *Slavic Review* 27, no. 4 (1968): 581–93; and Lazar Fleishman, Robert Hughes, and Olga Raevsky-Hughes, eds., *Russkii Berlin, 1921–1923* (Paris: YMCA Press, 1983), 9–69.
9. For an in-depth study of this time period, see my *Charlottengrad*.
10. The title of Konstantin Fedin's enthusiastically received novel *Cities and Years* (*Goroda i gody*, 1924) indicates a productive formula of anchoring the historical moment as it unfolded in modern cities.
11. Victor Shklovsky, *Zoo, or Letters Not about Love*, trans. Richard Sheldon (Ithaca: Cornell University Press, 1971), 66; Viktor Shklovskii, *Sobranie sochinenii, vol. 2: Biografiia*, ed. Il'ia Kalinin (Moscow: Novoe literaturnoe obozrenie, 2019), 303.

All quotations from *Zoo* refer to these editions and will be cited parenthetically in the text; Sheldon's English translation is occasionally modified for clarity. Unless noted otherwise, all translations are mine.

12 Andrei Belyi, *Odna iz obitelei tsarstva tenei* (Leningrad: Gosudarstvennoe izdatel'stvo, 1924).

13 Il'ia Erenburg, *Belyi ugol' ili slezy Vertera* (Leningrad: Priboi, 1928), 119–49. "Letters from Cafés" were first published in 1923 in the literary journal *Rossiia*.

14 Vladimir Nabokov, "Putevoditel' po Berlinu," was originally published in the Berlin émigré daily *Rul'* on 24 December 1925. The English translation is quoted from Nabokov's *Details of a Sunset and Other Stories*, trans. Vladimir and Dmitri Nabokov (New York: McGraw-Hill, 1976), 90–8.

15 Larisa Reisner, "Berlin v oktiabre 1923g.," in her *Gamburg na barrikadakh* (Moscow: Novaia Moskva, 1924), 71–94. Her other Berlin texts from this period were published in Larisa Reisner, *V strane Gindenburga: Ocherki sovremennoi Germanii* (Moscow: Pravda, 1926). A similarly partisan account of Berlin can be found in Nikolai Nikitin, *Seichas na Zapade: Berlin, Rur, London* (Leningrad and Moscow: Petrograd, 1924).

16 Cf. Mary Louise Pratt, *Imperial Eyes: Travel Writing and Transculturation*, 2nd ed. (New York: Routledge, 2008).

17 Originally published under the title "Literatura i literaturnyi byt" in *Na literaturnom postu* no. 9 (1927): 47–52. Carol Any translates this term as "the literary milieu" in her *Boris Eikhenbaum: Voices of a Russian Formalist* (Stanford: Stanford University Press, 1994). Victor Erlich translates it as the "literary mores" in his *Russian Formalism: History–Doctrine* (The Hague: Mouton, 1969), 125. I.R. Titunik opts for the "literary environment"; see his translation of Eikhenbaum's essay in *Readings in Russian Poetics: Formalist and Structuralist Views*, ed. Ladislav Matejka and Krystyna Pomorska (Cambridge, MA: MIT Press, 1971), 56–65. In her study of Soviet Constructivism, Kristin Romberg has identified "the aesthetic of embeddedness" as a major innovation of the Russian avant-garde. See her *Gan's Constructivism: Aesthetic Theory for an Embedded Modernism* (Berkeley: University of California Press, 2018), 5–12.

18 D. Mirskii, "Molodye prozaiki," in *O literature i iskusstve: stat'i i retsenzii, 1922–1937*, ed. O.A. Korostelev and M.V. Efimov (Moscow: Novoe literaturnoe obozrenie, 2014), 103. See also his "Vozrozhdenie russkoi prozy," 50–3.

19 Boris M. Eikhenbaum, "Literaturnyi byt," in his *O literature* (Moscow: Sovetskii pisatel', 1987), 428–36. See also Any, *Boris Eikhenbaum*, 105–6; and Erlich, *Russian Formalism*, 125–9.

20 Sergei Ushakin, "Odnorazovaia periodika Borisa Eikhenbauma," in Boris Eikhenbaum, *Moi vremennik: Slovesnost', nauka, kritika, smes'* (Ekaterinburg: Kabinetnyi uchenyi, 2020), 14.

21 Alyson Tapp, "Boris Eikhenbaum's Response to the Crisis of the Novel in the 1920s," *Slavonica* 15, no. 1 (2009): 33.
22 Ushakin, "Odnorazovaia periodika," 13.
23 Ushakin, "Odnorazovaia periodika," 19; Tapp, "Boris Eikhenbaum's Response," 45.
24 Iosif Gessen, *Gody izgnaniia: zhiznennyi otchet* (Paris: YMCA-Press, 1979), 106.
25 N.A. Egorova, ed., *Zolotoi vek rossiiskogo knigoizdaniia v Germanii* (Moscow: Dom russkogo zarubezh'ia, 2013), 7–20. See also Efim Dinershtein, *Siniaia ptitsa Zinoviia Grzhebina* (Moscow: Novoe literaturnoe obozrenie, 2014), 293–376; and Raeff, *Russia Abroad*, 73–94.
26 For a brief history of Petropolis and its founder Abram Kagan's relationships with writers coming to Berlin from Soviet Russia, see *In Exile from St Petersburg: The Life and Times of Abram Saulovich Kagan, Book Publisher, as Told by His Son Anatol Kagan*, ed. Michael Atherton (Blackheath: Brandl and Schlesinger, 2017).
27 Boris Frezinskii, *Ob Il'e Erenburge: knigi, liudi, strany* (Moscow: Novoe literaturnoe obozrenie, 2013), 524–75; Vladimir Berezin, *Viktor Shklovskii* (Moscow: Molodaia gvardiia, 2014), 165–200; Mina Polianskaia, *Foxtrot belogo rytsaria: Andrei Belyi v Berline* (St. Petersburg: Demetra, 2009), 19. Publishing Russian titles in Berlin also meant that the authors established their copyright under the Berne Convention, which Russia joined only in 1995. See *In Exile from St Petersburg*, 135–6, 270.
28 Shklovsky's letter to Maksim Gorky of 16 March 1922 shows that Shklovsky brought to Berlin the print galleys for *Revolution and the Front* (published in Petrograd in 1921 and ultimately constituting the first part of *A Sentimental Journey*), its "continuation, 1918–1922" (which became the second part of *A Sentimental Journey*), and the manuscripts for *The Knight's Move* (Gelikon, 1923). Stressing his financial hardship, he asked Gorky to see if Grzhebin would be interested in publishing him. Shklovskii, *Sobranie sochinenii*, vol. 1, 184.
29 Joshua Rubenstein, *Tangled Loyalties: The Life and Times of Ilya Ehrenburg* (Tuscaloosa: University of Alabama Press, 1999), 102–3.
30 *Novaia russkaia kniga* 1 (1922): 21.
31 *Izvestiia*, 1 October 1923. Cited in Frezinksii, *Ob Il'e Erenburge*, 103.
32 Gaik Adonts, "Predislovie," in Erenburg, *Bely ugol'*, 5.
33 Rubenstein, *Tangled Loyalties*, 88.
34 Erenburg, "Vmesto predisloviia," in his *Belyi ugol'*, 10.
35 In a 1927 essay on Berlin, "Dlinnee zhizni," Ehrenburg would clarify that "during the first revolutionary years in Russia we lived in the twenty-first century." Presumably, since Soviet Russia jumped a century ahead, it found itself out of joint with the rest of Europe. See *Belyi ugol'*, 154.
36 Katerina Clark has suggested that in the 1930s Ehrenburg's international activity can be described in terms of "cosmopolitan

patriotism." See her *Moscow, the Fourth Rome: Stalinism, Cosmopolitanism, and Evolution of Soviet Culture, 1931–1941* (Cambridge, MA: Harvard University Press, 2011), 30–41.
37 Erenburg updated his German impressions five years later in a 1927 collection of essays "Piat' let spustia." See his *Bely ugol'*, 151–91.
38 Vkhutemas stands for Vysshie khudozhestvenno-tekhnicheskie masterskie, or the Higher Art and Technical Studios, which operated in Moscow from 1920 until 1926.
39 Il'ia Erenburg, *A vse-taki ona vertitsia* (Berlin: Gelikon, 1922).
40 As Aleksandr Galushkin, Il'ia Kalinin, and Vladimir Nekhotin point out, some of Shklovskii's contemporaries believed him to be a Menshevik. See Shklovskii, *Sobranie sochinenii*, vol. 1, 960.
41 Omry Ronen has argued that Nabokov's "A Guide to Berlin" and especially its English translation were written against Shklovskii's defeatism and conformism in *Zoo*. See his "Viktor Shklovsky's Tracks in 'A Guide to Berlin,'" Susanne Fusso, in *The Joy of Recognition: Selected Essays of Omry Ronen*, ed. Barry P. Sherr and Michael Wachtel (Ann Arbor: Michigan Slavic Publications, 2015), 202–31.
42 See Ivan Bunin's famous speech "Missiia russkoi emigratsii: Rech', proiznesionnaia v Parizhe 16 fevralia," *Rul'*, 3 April 1924, 5–6.
43 See Anne Dwyer, "Standstill as Extinction: Viktor Shklovsky's Poetics and Politics of Movement in the 1920s and 1930s," *PMLA* 131, no. 2 (2016): 269–88; and Britta Korkowsky, *Selbstverortung ohne Ort: Russisch-jüdische Exilliteratur aus dem Berlin der Zwanziger Jahre* (Göttingen: Wallstein Verlag, 2013), 161–7.
44 See Rad Borislavov, "'I Know What Motivation Is': The Politics of Emotion and Viktor Shklovskii's Sentimental Rhetoric," *Slavic Review* 74, no. 4 (2015): 787–807.
45 For example, the First Preface to the novel's fourth edition (1964) included the following lines: "I wanted to live and make decisions honestly: I did not want to shun what was difficult, but I lost my way. At fault and off course, I found myself an émigré in Berlin." Shklovsky, *Zoo*, 111.
46 From a Postscript to *A Sentimental Journey* added in 1924. See Shklovsky, *Zoo*, 135, 161.
47 See I. Vainberg, "Zhizn' i gibel' berlinskogo zhurnala Gor'kogo "Beseda: po neizvestnym arkhivnym materialam i neizdannoi perepiske," *Novoe literaturnoe obozrenie* 21 (1996): 361–76; and Barry P. Sherr, "A Curtailed Colloquy: Gorky, Khodasevich, and *Beseda*," in *Russian Literature and the West: A Tribute for David M. Bethea, Part II*, ed. Alexander Dolinin, et al. (Stanford: Department of Slavic Languages and Literatures, Stanford University, 2008), 129–46.
48 Sherr, "A Curtailed Colloquy," 134, 145.

49 See "Pis'ma Maksima Gor'kogo k V.F. Khodasevichu," *Novyi zhurnal* 29 (1952): 207; and Richard Sheldon's introduction to his translation of *Zoo, or Letters Not about Love*, xxii.
50 Shklovskii, *Sobranie sochinenii*, vol. 1, 197.
51 J.D. Elsworth, *Andrey Bely* (Letchworth: Bradda Books, 1972), 94.
52 Elsworth, *Andrey Bely*, 99. See also Thomas R. Beyer, "Andrej Belyj: The Berlin Years, 1921–1923," *Zeitschrift für Slavische Philologie* 50, no. 1 (1990): 90–142.
53 Andrei Belyi, "Rakurs k dnevniku," in *Andrei Belyi: Avtobiograficheskie svody*. Literaturnoe nasledstvo, ed. Aleksandr Lavrov, John Malmstad, and Monika Spivak (Moscow: Nauka, 2016), 470.
54 For example, he was curious to learn about the White émigrés' perspective on the Revolution and did so by reading the memoirs of the White Guard generals. See his "Rakurs k dnevniku," 471.
55 The news was reported in "Khronika," *Rul'*, 24 November 1921. Bely also spoke at a public meeting in support of Russian famine relief. See *Andrei Belyi: Avtobiograficheskie svody*, 613. Roman Gul' wrote in his memoir that in those days in Berlin Bely gave several well-attended public talks, but whenever "Bely touched upon political questions, unimaginable cacophony commenced. He was ready to curse the Bolsheviks, as well as to praise them." See Gul, *Ia unes Rossiiu: Apologiia emigratsii. Tom 1: Rossiia v Germanii* (New York: Most, 1984), 81.
56 *Biulliuteni Doma iskusstv Berlin* 1–2 (17 February 1922): 22. See also "Dom iskusstva," *Rul'*, 2 December 1922, 5.
57 The Soviet writer Vladimir Lidin wrote in his memoir that in Berlin "Bely was an émigré one day, and the poet of the world revolution the next." See Lidin, *Liudi i vstrechi* (Moscow: Sovetskii pisatel', 1959), 144. In 1922 and 1923 Bely also published in the Paris-based émigré journal *Sovremennye zapiski*. See E.A. Takho-Godi and M. Shruba, "Ob Andree Belom, Fedore Stepune, Dmitrii Chizhevskom i odnoi nesostoiavsheisia publikatsii v 'Sovremennykh zapiskakh'," in *Literatura russkogo zarubezh'ia (1920–1940-e gody): Vzgliad iz XXI veka*, ed. L.E. Iezuitova and S.D. Titarenko (St. Petersburg: St. Petersburg State University, 2008), 110–22.
58 Polianskaia, *Foxtrot belogo rytsaria*, 172–80; Lazar Fleishman, "Bely's Memoirs," in *Andrey Bely: Spirit of Symbolism*, ed. John Malmstad (Ithaca: Cornell University Press), 219.
59 He wrote in a letter to Nadezhda Shchupak, "маму хватил удар, а вернуться к ней в Россию нельзя: *путь отрезан*." See Boris Sapir, "An Unknown Correspondent of Andrey Bely (Andrey Bely in Berlin, 1921–1923)," *Slavonic and East European Review* 49, no. 116 (1971): 451. Moreover, as Lazar Fleishman, Robert Hughes, and Olga Raevsky-Hughes have observed, Bely was averse to the "Changing Landmarks" movement, which encouraged the émigrés to make peace with the Bolsheviks and return. See Fleishman et al., eds., *Russkii Berlin*, 221.

60 The black and red colour binary also implied an ideological distinction, since black stood for fascists and red for communists.
61 Monika Spivak, *Andrei Belyi: Mistik i sovetskii pisatel'* (Moscow: Rossiiskii gosudarstvennyi gumanitarnyi universitet, 2006), 354. Compare *Kingdom of Shades* with Bely's much more balanced essay "O 'Rossii' v Rossii i o 'Rossii' v Berline," published in *Beseda* 1 (1923): 211–36.
62 Further complications include the fact that Slavophile thought was closely connected to German idealist philosophy, as opposed to the French philosophes championed by the Westernizers. Moreover, the Eurasianist movement, which originated in émigré circles in the early 1920s, took on the mantle of Slavophilism; but Bely considered Eurasianism an "unusually bright and talentedly conceived madness and evil." See Spivak, *Andrei Belyi*, 107.
63 Aleksandr Dolinin, *"Gibel' Zapada" i drugie memy: Iz istorii raskhozhikh idei i slovesnykh formul* (Moscow: Novoe izdatel'stvo, 2020), 40–1.
64 David Bethea, *The Shape of Apocalypse in Modern Russian Fiction* (Princeton: Princeton University Press, 1989), 126–7.
65 Spivak, *Andrei Belyi*, 111, 255.
66 Bely refers to the book as *Zakat Zapada* and not *Zakat Evropy*, as it was translated into Russian. According to his diaries, he read it in the original German in 1921. Later that year he participated in a public debate devoted to the book in Petrograd. See Belyi, *Avtobiograficheskie svody*, 464, 468.
67 See Andrei Belyi, "Osnovy moego mirovozzreniia" with preface by Larisa Sugai, "Andrei Belyi protiv Osval'da Shpenglera," *Literaturnoe obozrenie* 4–5 (1995): 10–37.
68 See Lesley Chamberlain, *The Philosophy Steamer: Lenin and the Exile of the Intelligentsia* (London: Atlantic Books, 2006).
69 See Pavel Lyssakov and Stephen Norris, "The City in Russian Culture: Space, Culture, and the Russian City," in *The City in Russian Culture*, ed. Pavel Lyssakov and Stephen Norris (London: Routledge, 2018), 1–12. See also Robert Alter, *Imagined Cities: Urban Experience and the Language of the Novel* (New Haven: Yale University Press, 2005).
70 Nikolai Antsiferov's book *Dusha Peterburga* (Petersburg: Brokgauz i Efron, 1922) pioneered the study of Petersburg's representation in the Russian literary imagination. See also V.N. Toporov, *Peterburgskii tekst russkoi literatury: Izbrannye trudy* (St. Petersburg: Iskusstvo-SPB, 2003).
71 Cf. Evgenii Ponomarev, "'Berlinskii ocherk' 1920-kh godov kak variant peterburgskogo teksta," *Voprosy literatury* 3 (2013): 42–67. See also Galina Time, *Puteshestvie Moskva Berlin Moskva: Russkii vzgliad Drugogo* (Moscow: ROSSPEN, 2011).
72 Schlögel, *Das russische Berlin*, 295.
73 To use the term introduced by Michel de Certeau, walking through the city defines "spaces of enunciation" resulting in "pedestrian rhetoric." See his

The Practice of Everyday Life, trans. Steven F. Randall (Berkeley: University of California Press, 1984), 97–8.
74 "Night! Tauentzien [Street]! Cocaine! / That's Berlin"; "Boom-Boom." Notably, Bely's poem "Malen'kii balagan na malen'koi planete 'Zemlia,'" included in the book of poems *Posle razluki: Berlinskii pesennik* (Berlin: Epokha, 1922), begins with the lines "One shrieks into the open window: Boom-Boom! It began!"
75 The use of the word "black" suggests both fascism and race. Bely extended the modernist fascination with African cultures to the urban bourgeoise. For instance, he maintained that the bowler hat and formal suit of an average Berliner concealed primal "African" instincts, which manifested themselves during nighttime dancing of the foxtrot and the shimmy. Bely's problematic invocation of race deserves to be explored in depth, but such an undertaking is beyond the scope of this study.
76 See Marina Tsvetaeva, "Plennyi dukh," in her *Proza* (New York: Izd-vo im. Chekhova, 1953), 314–52. See also Monika Spivak, "Koshmar v pissuare: K voprosu o genezise odnogo emigrantskogo vpechatleniia Andreiia Belogo," *Europa Orientalis* 22, no. 2 (2003): 51–70.
77 *Andrei Belyi: Avtobiograficheskie svody*, 474.
78 Gary Saul Morson, *The Boundaries of Genre: Dostoevsky's* Diary of a Writer *and the Traditions of Literary Utopia* (Austin: University of Texas Press, 1981), 53. See also Kauffman, *Special Delivery*, 3–51; and Asiya Bulatova, "Displaced Modernism: Shklovsky's *Zoo, or Letters Not about Love* and the Borders of Literature," *Poetics Today* 37, no. 1 (2016): 29–53.
79 Cf. Carol Avins, *Border Crossings: The West and Russian Identity in Soviet Literature, 1917–1934* (Berkeley: University of California Press, 1983), 98.
80 Leon Trotsky, *Literature and Revolution* (Chicago: Haymarket Books, 2005).
81 See Shklovskii, "Pamiatnik nauchnoi oshibke," in *Sobranie sochinenii*, vol. 1, 871–8.
82 Fedor Raskol'nikov in the Foreword to the 1933 edition of Erenburg's *Viza vremeni*. See Evgenii Ponomarev, "Putevoditel' po Evrope," *Neva* 11 (2008), https://magazines.gorky.media/neva/2008/11/putevoditel-po-evrope-glavy-iz-knigi-ili-erenburga-viza-vremeni-1931.html, 24 December 2022.

6 "Syphilis, Dirt, and the Frontiers of Revolution": Langston Hughes and Arthur Koestler at the Borders of Disgust

BRADLEY A. GORSKI

Langston Hughes and Arthur Koestler met on the outskirts of the Soviet revolutionary project, in Tashkent in 1932, where they soon struck up a friendship. Together they drank tea with locals, picked cotton, attended a show trial, and travelled to the farthest southern frontier of Soviet territory. Each came to Central Asia for his own reasons: Koestler to report on agricultural developments, and Hughes to see the Soviet region that he thought most resembled the American South. Both were also interested in probing the outer limits of the Revolution, "the backward regions of Central Asia" (in Koestler's words) at "the dark frontiers of progress" (in Hughes's). Those outer frontiers repelled Koestler, but to Hughes, they suggested expansive, transgressive opportunities. In both authors' memoirs – Hughes's *I Wonder as I Wander* (1956) and Koestler's *The Invisible Writing* (1954) – these boundaries, along with the desire and danger inherent in transgressing them, are expressed in terms of disgust.[1] In their retrospective accounts, each written more than two decades after their travels, both authors deploy disgust as an aesthetic means of drawing boundaries, of reconfiguring the geography of the Revolution not only for themselves but also for the Cold War–era reader. In this way, disgust traces a transnational geography of the Revolution, one that, contributing to the larger discussions in this volume, is defined primarily not by economic need and political persecution, but rather by the affective and aesthetic impulses of desire and repulsion, community and difference.

For both Hughes and Koestler, disgust conjures the affective desire for boundaries, suggesting the need to separate inside from outside, one's own from foreign. In this way, disgust stimulates in the reader a *counter-revolutionary impulse*: it induces the rejection of internationalism and instead pushes the reader to desire stricter borders. At the same time, the very feeling of disgust suggests that those borders remain permeable. In order for disgust to be activated, after all, the object of disgust must

Figure 6.1. Langston Hughes and Arthur Koestler in Soviet Turkmenistan. Photographer unknown. Source: Langston Hughes Papers. James Weldon Johnson Collection in the Yale Collection of American Literature, Beinecke Rare Book and Manuscript Library.

threaten to transgress boundaries, which in turn provokes the desire for borders to be more fully drawn. In this way, disgust imagery allows both memoirists to suggest the contours of their own revolutionary geography without drawing the borders in a firm hand. Instead, they encourage readers to trace those lines themselves. In other words, aesthetically mobilized disgust allows boundaries to remain emergent, always almost drawn. But while Koestler induces his readers to trust their disgust, to firmly draw the boundaries it suggests, Hughes deploys disgust to sketch a revolutionary geography that invites transgression, indeed requires it.

Disgust and Revolution

Involuntary but difficult to ignore, disgust has the power to reconfigure experience both in the moment and in retrospect, and for both Hughes and Koestler, the potent affect begins to blur and redraw boundaries – of ideological, revolutionary, and interpersonal natures – within and among the timelines of their travelogues.² It is perhaps unsurprising that this extraordinarily intercultural and interracial encounter – involving an African American poet, a German-speaking Hungarian Jewish journalist, ethnically Russian Soviets, and local Turkmens (and all of their respective customs, practices, and hygienic rituals) – might produce, among some of its participants, "the fundamental schema of disgust," or "the experience of a nearness that is not wanted," to quote from Winfried Menninghaus's theory of disgust.³ Indeed, the particular conditions of Hughes and Koestler's travel brought them into close and unavoidable contact with Turkmen culture, which was itself undergoing enforced integration with the new norms of Soviet modernity. Hughes and Koestler ate, drank, and slept in close quarters with each other and with their hosts. Koestler makes multiple references to "grimy" and overcrowded conditions, to "squalor and decay" (136), and to the ironic juxtaposition of ubiquitous Soviet hygiene propaganda and manifestly unhygienic practices. Hughes mentions food prepared by cooks with dirty hands, "runny eyes and scabby faces"; he writes of melons cut with "dirty knives" and describes drinking tea from "grimy bowls" passed from hand to hand, lips to lips (148). Each traveller also describes sexual escapades alongside fears of sexually transmitted diseases, figuring sex and its inherent dangers as a powerful locus simultaneously of attraction and of disgust.

The pervasiveness of such images of disgust suggests that their place in these accounts is more than incidental. If, according to Mary Douglas's classic study, *Purity and Danger*, "where there is dirt, there is a system," then perhaps where there is this much disgust, we might say that there is not so much one system as a clash of systems – systems in various stages of transition, conflict, or negotiation.⁴ Disgust can be a powerful means of making sense of such uncertainty. Disgust draws boundaries. It demarcates the world, separating the acceptable from the unacceptable or, in Douglas's terms, purity from danger.

For Julia Kristeva, in her theory of the abject, *Powers of Horror*, the social world and the very notion of the self are defined by boundaries drawn in lines of disgust. The abject, the source of all disgust, is that which is at once unnameable and unapproachable. It forms the frontiers of the verbal self, "the border of my condition as a living being."⁵ Taboos, prohibitions, behavioural expectations are founded on and reinforced by disgust impulses, by the need to separate the abject from the self. The threat of defilement, of pollution, of the outside, provides stability to the inside, erecting and reinforcing the walls of the known world. Disgust is at once social and primordial. It is both reproducible and involuntary, part of both mimesis and reality, of both the symbolic and the real. It is simultaneously a deeply aesthetic (or perhaps anti-aesthetic) sensation, and one that transcends aesthetics to infiltrate the physical world. A successful representation of the disgusting, in other words, quickly moves beyond the bounds of its medium and makes audiences wince, recoil, experience nausea in the physical spaces of their own bodies and surroundings.

According to Daniel Kelly's survey of empirical psychological research, the sensation of disgust – whether invoked by physical stimuli or by aesthetic representations – triggers a powerful "affect program" that immediately sets off physiological and behavioural responses. The heart rate drops, salivation increases, and the subject experiences "an immediate aversion or withdrawal response" as well as a "motivation to get rid of the offending entity in [any] way."[6] Another set of more cognitive-based responses follows: a "sense of offensiveness, and contamination sensitivity," which in turn lead to "downstream effects," including moral judgments and social behaviour.[7] Poised "between conscious patterns of conduct and unconscious impulses," to quote Menninghaus again, the disgust response can bring "eminent affective powers" to bear on establishing social taboos, boundaries, and other sorting mechanisms.[8] The involuntary physical disgust response, in this way, is directly connected to ethical and moral judgments about the offending object and its sources, such that aesthetically induced disgust can be intimately connected (often unbeknownst to audiences) to normative rejection. Travelling lightly and powerfully across aesthetics, emotion, physicality, and ethics, disgust is perhaps the ultimate affect. It allows aesthetics to trace lines through the contours of the real world and encodes those boundaries in the realm of the symbolic order.

But disgust also invites the breaching of those boundaries. It is not simply a turning away (as the Russian word *otvrashchenie* would suggest); it can also be a source of attraction. It is "a vortex of summons and repulsion," in Kristeva's words.[9] William Ian Miller's *Anatomy of Disgust* further suggests that the pleasure of sex comes, at least in part, through "the mutual transgression of disgust-defended barriers."[10] The taboos around sex, often limned in terms of disgust, are "not just there to prevent pleasure, but [are] needed to heighten it."[11] Not incidentally, for both Hughes and Koestler, the pleasures and perils of sex play alongside images of disgust, suggesting simultaneously an invitation to and an interdiction against breaching the boundaries of disgust.

Although disgust might feel natural, instinctual, unlearned, the boundaries of disgust are historically and socially conditioned. They are imprinted on the symbolic order through ritual, culture, and tradition, which suppress sources of disgust from everyday experience – to flip the causal vector, as Kristeva suggests, that which culture suppresses *becomes* the source of disgust. When the symbolic order breaks down, those boundaries are breached. No longer contained, dirt is released, previous pollutants infiltrate the previously pure, and, in this absence of culturally enforced boundaries, the importance of disgust itself, disgust as an affect, is heightened. "It is thus not lack of cleanliness or health that causes abjection," writes Kristeva, "but what disturbs identity, system, order. What does not respect borders, positions, rules. The in-between, the ambiguous, the composite."[12]

In this way, disgust can play an outsized role in times of upheaval, tracing the bounds of social acceptability, the subject's place in society, and the self. The period immediately following the Russian Revolution was one such time. The turmoil, violence, and confusion of the revolutionary years activated precisely the symbolic uncertainty Kristeva highlights, intentionally disturbing "identity, system, order." Early Bolsheviks recognized such disturbances and turned to disgust in their attempts to stabilize the symbolic order. In a 1921, for instance, Lenin mobilized disgust to stamp out heterodoxy within the party. On the front page of *Pravda* under the title "On Party Purges," Lenin appealed to the "working masses," whose "fine intuition is able to comprehend the difference between honest and devoted Communists and those who arouse disgust."[13] The healthy, proletarian disgust Lenin ascribes to the working masses is meant not only to justify but also to *produce the desire for* the purges he sought. Disgust, however, has no inherent political or ideological valence, and it also proved useful for the opposite political ends. In a pamphlet that appeared the same year as Lenin's *Pravda* editorial, for instance, Bolshevik leader Aleksandra Kollontai framed disgust as a counter-revolutionary affect, accusing the petty bourgeoisie of unjustified "revulsion at and fear of revolutionary acts." For Kollontai, disgust was not a healthy attribute of the working class, but a bourgeois relic, evoking a desire for boundaries that should be overcome.[14] That disgust could be mobilized in such opposing directions (and by members of the same party in the very same year) shows just how unstable the symbolic order had become and how attractive the affective power of disgust was as a rhetorical tool for imposing some sense of stability.[15]

Beyond the symbolic order, physical disgust stimuli also proliferated in the post-revolutionary years. As early Soviet efforts at urbanization, mobilization, and communal living breached previous boundaries, more bodies crowded into smaller spaces. The destruction of the First World War, the Revolution, and the Civil War – along with Soviet ambitions for the total reorganization of society – had brought many

"Syphilis, Dirt, and the Frontiers of Revolution" 219

public services to a standstill, at least temporarily. Many urban spaces recovered only in the late 1920s and early 1930s. Meanwhile, rural areas underwent collectivization, which drove even more citizens to the cities. Dirt, grime, and filth were prominent features of the revolutionary years by nearly all accounts. The grime, general overcrowding, and faulty public services combined to raise the spectre of infection and disease. To stem contagion and concomitant public health problems, Soviet authorities launched aggressive propaganda campaigns aimed at getting citizens to observe basic personal hygiene, at times invoking disgust imagery.[16]

Travellers to the early Soviet Union often commented on the grime that seemed to coat everything. Even sympathetic travellers, like Anna Louise Strong, could not ignore the filth. An American reporter who travelled to Russia as part of a delegation of the American Friends Service Committee, Strong volunteered in a Samara orphanage, where she worked with "starving children by thousands, sick with cholera, typhus, dysentery; they had no soap nor change of underwear or clothing; they littered the floor with filth."[17] For others, like Theodore Dreiser, the dirt became central to their travels. "The huddled masses gave me a sense of nausea," he wrote in his diary on 4 January 1928. "Russia is permanently spoiled for me by the cold and dirt."[18] Strong saw the grime as evidence of poor conditions to be overcome, the mark of a society in transition, striving for something better. For Dreiser, dirt became so essential to the Soviet experience itself that, when asked to speak to VOKS (the All-Union Society for Cultural Relations with Foreign Countries; *Vsesoiuznoe obshchestvo kul'turnoi sviazi s zagranitsei*), he devoted much of his time to lecturing the young state on hygienic practices.[19]

Unlike in these accounts, however, the disgust explored in Hughes's and Koestler's travelogues is not used primarily to express something about the internal workings of the Soviet Union. Rather, it works to probe the travellers' own relationship to the frontiers of the revolutionary society they encounter. They experience grime, risk infection, and face disgust at the outer limits of the Revolution, where the reach of the Soviet project is more tenuous. Equally important, both travelogues are retrospective accounts and, in more than simple chronology, Cold War documents. Koestler's hard right turn away from his youthful Marxist ideals had culminated in the publication of *Darkness at Noon* in 1940 and his participation in *The God That Failed*, a 1949 collection of essays by prominent intellectuals renouncing their earlier interest in communism.[20] Hughes, while maintaining his commitment to progressive poetics and politics, had his own difficulties negotiating Cold War life. He had been persecuted and threatened for his "social" poetry already in the 1930s and 1940s and was called in front of the House Unamerican Activities Committee (HUAC) in March 1953, at a time when his memoir, which spends some two hundred pages in the Soviet Union, was already in the works.[21] At the same time, Hughes was involved in the developing Civil Rights movement, a dramatic shift in US race politics that found reflection in Hughes's poetics. This historical context suggests something of the stakes of these two pieces of writing. If Koestler and Hughes travelling in 1932 are probing the frontiers of revolution with their own experiences (of disgust, among other emotions), then the writers of the 1950s sketch a different – and still shifting – revolutionary geography, as leftist politics, social justice, and internationalism resonate differently with their post-war Anglo-American readerships. For this reason, it is essential to understand that disgust in these memoirs is not only – indeed not primarily – experienced. It is also deployed. Disgust becomes a literary technique that both authors use to inscribe themselves and their own ideological journeys on the contours of the revolution, to draw and redraw the boundaries of twentieth-century politics in lines of grime, syphilis, and nausea.

Hughes on the Borders of Disgust

Hughes travelled to the Soviet Union in 1932 as part of a group of twenty-two African American artists, writers, and performers invited by Mezhrabpom Film Studio and organized by Louise Thompson Patterson in order to make a film about race relations in the American South called *Black and White*. After the group arrived in Moscow, it became clear that the film would not be made, either because the material was unworkable or because of US government pressure – likely a combination of the two.[22] With the film shoot cancelled, the group dispersed. Some headed for Europe, others opted to stay in Moscow long term, and about half the group accepted an offer to tour whatever region of the Soviet Union they chose. Hughes was among the latter group. "It did not take us long," Hughes recalls in *I Wonder as I Wander*, "to decide among ourselves that the portions of the Soviet Union we would most like to see were those regions where the majority of the coloured citizens lived, namely Turkmenistan in Soviet Central Asia" (123). Beyond race relations, Hughes was also interested in the emergent revolutionary society that the peripheries of the Soviet project promised. Central Asia, he writes, "was said to be a land still in flux, where Soviet patterns were as yet none too firmly fixed" (123). His travels through Turkmen and Uzbek territories – his meetings with these Soviets of colour whose position in society would illuminate Soviet race relations – would simultaneously be encounters between those cultures and the outer edges of Soviet modernity.

Hughes's trip has been analysed before, notably in several studies in recent decades that consider encounters between African Americans and the Soviet experiment. The account in Kate A. Baldwin's 2002 book *Beyond the Color Line and the Iron Curtain*, for instance, concentrates on Hughes's fascination with the Soviet program of compulsory unveiling of Central Asian women. Drawing a connection to Hughes's long-term interest in W.E.B. Du Bois's metaphor of the veil as representative of the "double consciousness" of Black Americans, Baldwin argues that "unveiling became the representative means of establishing the extent to which the new Soviet freedom contrasted with the inequities of the color line back in the United States."[23] Central Asian unveiling became not only equivalent of breaching the colour line but also a means for Hughes to push beyond the heteronormative assumptions underlying Du Bois's original metaphor. For Du Bois, the metaphor of the veil and the understanding of double consciousness appear when he is rejected by a white girl among his schoolmates.[24] Rending the veil, then, would provide access to whiteness, not least on heteronormative sexual terms. But Hughes sees the veil differently. He identifies with the unveiling women he sees in Soviet Central Asia and not only with the male gaze he occupies. For him unveiling becomes less about sexual access and more about revelation of self. Citing a 1934 essay by Hughes in which unveiled women reveal a spectrum of skin tones, Baldwin argues that the unveilings do not primarily work to provide access to the unveiled women, nor do they allow (or compel) Central Asian women to join a normatively homogeneous Soviet world. Instead, they invite the revelation of difference.

In this light, Hughes's Central Asian trip becomes even more revolutionary, not only opening the way for racial inclusivity but also implicitly arguing for a broader spectra of differences, including, as Jennifer Wilson suggested in a later essay, "Queer Harlem, Queer Tashkent," the place of Black queer identities within the larger revolutionary project.[25] Such accounts infuse Hughes's Soviet travels with both expansive liberatory hopes – that the Soviet Union would be able to abolish race-based restrictions while simultaneously celebrating difference – and an intimate connection to domestic US race relations. As Steven Lee has argued, Hughes's travels inspired his hopes for the Revolution as a global project that could transcend the Soviet south and might even breach the American colour line.[26]

It is perhaps no surprise that after Hughes returned from the Soviet Union – and in the same years he published the essays about his trip that figure prominently in both Wilson's and Baldwin's analyses – his poetry took on more explicitly pro-communist and pro-Soviet valences. In poems like "Song of the Revolution," "Ballads of Lenin," and "Let America Be America Again," Hughes connected his Soviet sympathies directly to the fight against Jim Crow in the US. Perhaps more straightforwardly than any other, his 1934 poem "One More 'S' in the U.S.A." makes the connection explicit:

> Put one more "S" in the U.S.A.
> To make it Soviet.
> One more "S" in the U.S.A.
> Oh, we'll live to see it yet.
> When the land belongs to the farmers
> And the factories to the working men
> The U.S.A. when we take control
> Will be the U.S.S.A. then.
> [...]
> But we can't join hands together
> So long as whites are lynching black,
> So black and white in one union fight
> And get on the right track.
> By Texas, or Georgia, or Alabama led
> Come together, fellow workers
> Black and white can all be red.[27]

The liberatory hope emphasized here characterizes the expansive geography of the Revolution that Hughes developed during his time in Soviet Central Asia and that he brought back to 1930s America. This is the revolutionary geography at the centre of Hughes's contemporaneous accounts: a utopian vision of a truly world revolution – inspired by and distilled in the image of Central Asian unveiling, a metaphor of boundaries breached – that could prove capable of erasing the colour line in the US, not only for the respectable Black culture imagined by Du Bois but even for gender-fluid and queer Black identities that were so important to Hughes's experience.

When Hughes returned to his Soviet travels for his 1950s memoirs, however, something had changed. His fascination with unveiling, although not entirely absent, had significantly diminished. Instead, disgust came to the fore, and – in a related shift – a large part of Hughes's narrative was focused on Arthur Koestler. Koestler had been absent from earlier accounts, but he had gained international stature since the two had met in the 1930s, and Koestler's 1954 memoir had mentioned

Hughes, so by the time *I Wonder as I Wander* appeared in 1956, it would have been difficult for Hughes *not* to include him. Hughes casts Koestler as a foil for himself: as the two travel together, they experience a similar world, including plenty of disgust stimuli, but react entirely differently. Images of dirt and grime, nearly absent in Hughes's earlier accounts of his trip, play a central role in his 1956 narrative.[28] If tearing away the veil defined Hughes's contemporaneous experience, then by 1956, "a nearness that is not wanted" – Menninghaus's "fundamental schema of disgust" – most forcefully characterizes Hughes's remembered Soviet Central Asia.

"Turkoman hospitality," Hughes writes, "is based on sharing," which meant sharing everything, from space to spoons to bowls of tea and large vats of soup. Invited to a home-cooked meal in Ashkhabad, Hughes describes how "the food kettles had cooled enough for our hosts to reach in with bare fingers and pick up chunks of meat and tear them into smaller bits which they dropped back into the soup" before the international guests were invited to "put our hands into the warm liquid and fish around until we found a nice piece of mutton, pulled it out and ate it" (144). The evident pleasure with which this scene is described suggests that the potentially disgusting also carries an attractive charge. Similarly, both revulsion and a homoerotic undercurrent infuse the sharing of tea, which was drunk "from bowls that went from mouth to mouth, around and around in the customary ritual," and that, Hughes does not fail to mention, "dozens of strange moustaches had touched" (142).

Conditions only get grimier as the travellers make their way from Ashkhabad towards the southern border to a small village called Permetyab, a "fantastic desert community, inhabited by evil-appearing sore-covered, dirty people" (147). Invited to tea again, Hughes notes:

> There were three or four bowls, which about twenty men shared. The water had been scooped up from a filthy irrigation canal, and there was mud in the bottom of each bowl after the tea was drunk.
>
> "Koestler," I said, "we are all going to die of cholera germs."
>
> "I wouldn't be surprised," said Koestler, although he had scarcely touched his lips to any of the bowls. (147)

Their destination in this outpost of the revolution happens to be a health clinic, where they meet with a nurse just after lunch, who tells them of her troubles introducing hygienic practices, especially during childbirth: "Some of the women bite off the umbilical cord themselves, as their mothers and grandmothers did before them. Since water is scarce in this desert land, it's an old custom to wash a newborn child in sand. I have trouble with babies' eyes festering. Sometimes children lose their sight" (148). After the meeting, Hughes recalls that

> the food we had eaten had been handled by Baluchis whose hands were none too clean and some of whom had runny eyes and scabby faces. They had cut our melons with the same dirty knives with which they cut tobacco. We had drunk from their grimy bowls [and] the nurse at the clinic told us that all of the health problems there were aggravated by the fact that ninety per cent of the population of Permetyab had syphilis. (148)

If one were tracking the intensity and concentration of disgust stimuli in Hughes's account, this moment would mark its peak. Understandably, "Koestler almost keeled over," but Hughes's own response is remarkable for being so muted: "I was a bit upset myself" (148).

In fact, throughout the account, Koestler is portrayed as reacting more strongly than Hughes to the ample disgust stimuli. "Koestler was particularly perturbed at the unsanitary tea-drinking customs of Central Asia," writes Hughes, and quotes Koestler: "'Slobbering in each other's bowls,' said Koestler, 'a bloody disgusting filthy habit!'" Hughes, on the other hand, "simply went ahead and drank and re-drank with the others, and forgot about it" (134). Koestler "had a German sense of sanitation ... And every time he came back to our hotel he would wash. I had not known him long before I heard him say what I was often to hear him repeat, 'If the Revolution had only occurred in Germany, at least it would have been a clean one'" (134). Fulfilling the implicit promise, Hughes has Koestler repeat the line – which, it bears acknowledging, takes on a newly sinister hue in the post-Holocaust era when Hughes writes it – at least twice more.[29] Hughes himself – his 1932 self, the traveller, not the memoirist – seems to experience very little disgust even as he (writing in 1956) packs his prose with descriptions and images that seem designed to evoke disgust. In fact, the calm reaction to the syphilis statistic ("I was a bit upset myself") is one of the only times Hughes allows his past self to experience anything approaching a normal disgust reaction.

The incongruence between description and reaction suggests that Hughes is using disgust deliberately, so that revulsion becomes a literary technique: affect as device (to paraphrase Viktor Shklovsky). As the descriptions work on the reader, they evoke the involuntary disgust "affect program" outlined above, while Hughes himself remains impervious. If we understand disgust to be a potent means of proscribing taboos, encouraging the demarcation of boundaries, and inducing the desire for limits, then Hughes's prose suggests those borders only to show Hughes the character breaking through them. Indeed, Hughes's descriptions often suggest an attraction to the disgust stimuli, an acknowledgment that, to quote Miller, "the disgusting itself has the power to allure."[30] For Hughes, disgust not only evokes a desire for boundaries but also suggests the pleasure of breaching them.

Hughes's revolutionary geography becomes one of limits surpassed, visceral reactions overcome, and boundaries crossed. This is what he calls seeing the revolution with *"Negro* eyes" – Hughes's native optic and one that he specifically tries, in vain, to get Koestler to understand (135). "To Koestler, Turkmenistan was simply a *primitive* land moving into twentieth-century civilization. To me it was a *colored* land moving into orbits hitherto reserved for whites" (135). Just as he wants to make Koestler see the revolution this way, his poetics in *I Wonder as I Wander* are intended to make the Cold War reader see the Revolution through the hopeful eyes of a Black American coming from the Jim Crow South. The tramcars in Tashkent, Hughes notes, used to have a "Jim Crow section for Asiatics ... The old partitions were still there now, but segregation itself had gone since the Uzbeks [now] control[led] the affairs of their autonomous republic" (160). For Hughes's image of the Revolution, it is important *both* that the partitions are still visible *and* that they have become obsolete. His Cold War readers too should feel boundaries being drawn, indeed they should feel the visceral desire for those boundaries – evoked through images of disgust – and then they should see those boundaries immediately overcome.

Koestler, on the other hand, cannot overcome his disgust. Hughes titles the visit to Permetyab "Koestler Washes His Hands," and some of the last words exchanged between the two are (at least in Hughes's account): "'Dirty and ugly and dusty,' he said, head down over our meal. 'This disgusting part of the world! In Germany at least we'd have a *clean* revolution'" (158). Hughes concludes, "Were I a socio-literary historian, I might hazard a guess that here in 1932 were Koestler's crossroads ... – his turning point from left to right that was to culminate a few years later in his bitter attacks on communism" (159).

But if the key difference between Hughes and Koestler (in Hughes's account) is in their disgust responses, then the difference is one of degree rather than kind. Hughes's conspicuously calm reaction to potential infection ("I was a bit upset myself") comes right before the enigmatic line used for the title of this chapter, and it is a line uttered by Hughes in his own voice: "Syphilis, dirt, Permetyab, and the frontiers of revolution, ugh!" (148). Although he elaborates no further, directly after this exclamation, Hughes turns back from the southern border and joins

Koestler in their hotel room. Perhaps for post-HUAC reasons, perhaps as honest truth, the Cold War memoirist Hughes seems to locate the frontiers of his own revolutionary geography in the only exclamation of disgust he will allow himself, this solitary "ugh!"

Koestler's Bellyaches

Koestler's memoir, *The Invisible Writing* (1954), largely corroborates Hughes's account, but it spends less time on the relationship between the two travellers. Unlike Hughes, Koestler was more than a "fellow traveller" of the revolution. He had joined the Communist Party before his visit to the Soviet Union and had even worked briefly as an intelligence officer for the Comintern. As much an activist as a writer, Koestler spent the summer of 1932 canvassing, pamphleting, and agitating for the Communists before petitioning the Party to sponsor a writing visit to the Soviet Union. "The idea for the book" – his first book on the Soviet Union, *Of White Nights and Red Days*, published in 1934, which he recalls here in his 1954 memoir – "was to describe a journey across the Soviet Empire from its most northerly to its most southerly point" (78). The proposed book was to end with "the development of the backward regions of Central Asia." Like Hughes, Koestler was explicitly interested in the geography of the Revolution, in drawing an imagined map of development – social and technological – over the vast territory, unknown to his imagined readers, of what he calls the "Soviet Empire."[31]

When he revisits that journey in 1954, his memoir is shot through not only with hindsight but also with the wholesale renunciation of his previous communist convictions. Thus, in the memoir analysed here, a right-wing Koestler describes the experiences of his travelling leftist younger self. The narrating Koestler recalls meeting Hughes on the southern frontier of that empire, picking cotton together, and travelling with him and a writers' brigade through the Turkmen SSR. But the memoir does not openly use Hughes as a foil for the young Koestler's experiences. Nor does it emphasize Koestler's own disgust quite so elaborately as Hughes does. Disgust stimuli, however, are rife, both in descriptions of the physical world and in the choice of metaphors. The book opens with the lines (the first half borrowed from Picasso): "I went into Communism as one goes to a spring of fresh water, and I left Communism as one clambers out of a poisoned river strewn with the wreckage of flooded cities and the corpses of the drowned" (20). The Communist Party cell that Koestler joins in Berlin is described as nothing so much as a vector of infection. "The term 'cell' is not purely metaphorical; for these are living, pulsating units within a huge, sprawling organism, co-ordinated in their function, governed by a hierarchy of nervous centres, and susceptible to various diseases – to the Titoist virus, to bourgeois infection or Trotskyist cancer" (26). When Koestler gets to the Soviet Union, and especially Central Asia, the potential sources of disgust proliferate: the customs house at the Soviet border is twice described as "grimy," Central Asia is characterized by "squalor and decay," and dust and dirt are everywhere. But even as Koestler describes the dirt of the Revolution, he does not allow his younger self to express disgust explicitly at these moments. Amidst the disgust stimuli that frame his account, Koestler's narrator is apparently much more tolerant of dirt than, say, Theodore Dreiser, although he notes its existence nearly as often.

Instead, when Koestler uses words like "repellent," "revolting," and "disgust," they are in reference to something else – an internal feeling, a nausea portrayed as an ethical response rather than as a reaction to external stimuli. "Every communist," he writes, meaning his past self as much as others, experiences "disgust with Russia or the Party, when the fraudulent character of Utopia becomes temporarily apparent" (88). These moments of doubt, he writes, can be overcome only by "some repellent aspect of capitalist society" (88). In this way, the dialectic of the Revolution, for Koestler, is one of disgust, in which counter-disgust overcomes revulsion at Soviet crimes: "The show trials of 1936–38 disgusted many European Communists, but the Fascist menace, symbolized by the Spanish Civil War, disgusted them even more" (88).[32] "Party jargon," Koestler writes, "calls attacks of doubt 'bellyaches'" that must be overcome by good communists (89). Although these "bellyaches" are not explicitly connected to the dirt and grime Koestler constantly describes, more than coincidence motivates their adjacency. By describing his ethical doubts in terms of nausea and disgust alongside representations of dirt and metaphors of infection, Koestler subtly mobilizes readers' revulsion. In other words, the low-level disgust readers might well feel at Koestler's descriptions seems implicitly connected to a moral revulsion that readers are meant to sense in themselves and that they are in turn asked to associate with the revolutionary project itself.

In case the proximity of physical dirt and political nausea fails to make the point clearly, Koestler mobilizes another chain of connections that link his leftist doubts to another realm often intimately connected with disgust: sex. Sex, which shares almost all of its characteristics with disgust stimuli – closeness, boundary breaching, fluid exchange, potential for infection – is central to theories of disgust.[33] "What else, after all," writes Miller in *Anatomy of Disgust*, "makes sex so difficult, so frequently the basis for anxiety, neurosis, and psychosis?" Sexuality, in this way, might be seen as the obverse of disgust, a transgression of boundaries that evokes attraction more than repulsion. For Hughes, as noted earlier, the breeching of boundaries, whether in unveiling or the evocation of disgust, often carries an erotic charge.[34] But in Koestler's account, sex and disgust are connected not through boundary-breaking but rather through political uncertainty, and his bellyaches diminish rather than enhance his libido.

In an early chapter, Koestler assures the reader that before his political doubts creep in "the one 'diversion from the class struggle' that did not make me feel guilty was love … With most men, at least in the Anglo-Saxon countries, sex is the main source of guilt and anxiety. In my case it was the only pursuit exempt from guilt – perhaps because my attitude to women remained basically naïve and romantic" (41). However, he quickly relates two "episodes concerning women with whom I was not personally involved" that show anything but a "naïve and romantic" relationship towards sex even before his trip to the Soviet Union. In Berlin, a colleague "whose name has slipped my memory" meets a woman with "a large swastika brooch on her breast" (42). He goes home with her and finds her (agreeably) sexually aggressive. But "at the climactic moment," he writes, this "ideal *Hitler-Mädchen*" "raised herself on one elbow, stretched out the other arm in the Roman salute, and breathed in a dying voice a fervent 'Heil Hitler.'" Koestler's colleague "nearly had a stroke" (43). In the same Berlin Communist cell, a certain "Comrade Hilda" of Koestler's own Party cell feared for her safety. The reason once again connects politics and sex: "a man from the [Communist Party] District Committee … had wanted to sleep with her; … she had refused; [and] subsequently he had been accusing her of some unnamed crime against the Party" (44). "The hysterical Valkyrie and Comrade Hilda," Koestler concludes, "do not represent German womanhood; but they do represent, as extreme cases, the 'politically awakened' part of it, anno domini 1932" (44). In these two anecdotes Koestler reveals a deep anxiety about how radical politics might disturb his previously "naïve and romantic" relationship to love and sex.

But it is not until he arrives in Soviet Georgia that Koestler's own relationship to sex – previously "exempt from guilt" – wilts under the influence of political doubt. Among the peaks of the Caucasus, Koestler reports a dream in which he "was climbing up a bare rockface, when I suddenly felt a slackening of the rope to which I was attached … I woke up trembling, still waiting for the headlong fall to begin" (76). Helpfully, he interprets the dream: "The sudden slackening of the rope with … its terrifying implications, stand for the unconscious fear of losing faith in

Russia and the Communist ideal. At that date, this would indeed have meant for me a headlong fall into the physical and spiritual void" (76). He returns to the image a few pages later, when describing the book he wrote immediately after his trip, *Of White Nights and Red Days*, and his retrospective dismay at its complete omission of references to Stalin: "obviously the political libido is also subject to inhibitions and repressions, which come from the same source as the dream of the slackening of the alpinist's cord" (83). The use of "libido" might seem odd here, but it comes into focus in the next scene. On a train from Tbilisi to Yerevan, Koestler invites a young peasant woman to share his first-class train compartment:

> The girl took it for granted that she was expected to pay in the approved manner for the favour bestowed upon her. She was a peasant girl whose grandparents had probably been serfs; I was a member of the new privileged class which had replaced feudal landlords. The only difference between then and now was that in Czarist days these privileges were exercised a little less crudely, or, at least, with a certain seigneurial style.
>
> She was pretty, tipsy, and desirable. Her surprise at the wonders of a sleeping compartment was pathetic and embarrassing. When I tried to explain that I had been merely acting in a "comradely" way and that she ought not to feel under any obligation, she obviously regarded me as an even greater fool than before. To end the absurd situation, I tried to overcome the inhibiting feeling of guilt, which by now had become physical, and made an even greater fool of myself. Such incidents are merely grotesque in retrospect, but very disturbing to a vain and complex-ridden young man. The girl's undisguised derision was an echo of the healthy proletarian's contempt for the bourgeois intellectual, under which I had suffered in my early Party days. At the same time my humiliation was also a symbolic punishment, the revenge of the starving peasants on the hated bureaucracy with which I had become identified. I thought that I had become permanently impotent, and the dream of falling off the mountain assumed yet another sinister meaning. (85)

As the last line makes clear, the loss of Koestler's political convictions – a loss still inchoate, subconscious, and several years from explicit acknowledgment – already causes the loss of his erection. The experience is "very disturbing" to Koestler as a young man, not just because it impugns his masculinity but because it does so in a way that is deeply connected to his own political insecurities. In his companion's "undisguised derision" he discerns not a suspicion of his softening communist principles but rather "contempt for the bourgeois intellectual." It seems that the encounter stokes not so much his political doubt (although he frames it as such in retrospect) as his fear that he might not fit in to the vision of masculinity of a newly revolutionary society. Put differently, Koestler's fear seems to be that radical politics – the Revolution itself – might disturb his social position, his sense of self, in such a way as to interrupt his otherwise agreeable relationship to sex.

Koestler does not, however, analyse his impotence as a response to his own social and sexual uncertainty. Nor does he ever connect it to the dirt and grime he constantly describes in close proximity to his ethical queasiness at communism's crimes. Instead, he represents political doubt as something at once subconscious, essential, and deeply moral, whereas the physiological manifestations – both his impotence and his "bellyaches" – are epiphenomena, emerging from ethical concerns rather than from physical stimuli or social insecurity. Just as in Hughes's account, the encounter with the Revolution is figured in physiological and affective terms, according to which new experiences generated by the Revolution produce physiological impulses of disgust and (here, although not in Hughes) impotence. Physiology once again produces counter-revolutionary affect, and good Party members, in Koestler's telling, are supposed to ignore or overcome their discomfort.

But for Koestler, the boundaries drawn by impotence and disgust are more essential than is their overcoming. In fact, the Revolution's push to overcome boundaries is often figured as false. In an echo of Hughes's interest in unveiling, for instance, Koestler writes: "The women of Turkestan have shed their black veils, but only physically. One feels that, when looked at by a stranger, they still feel naked without the veil that used to hide a woman's most intimate features" (122). Setting aside the fact that Koestler here imaginatively appropriates the subject position of these voiceless women (a masculinist prerogative Hughes also assumes), we can nevertheless see Koestler's clear distinction that unveiling is "only physical," while something internal and, by implication, more essential persists. Koestler portrays his own disgust similarly – as essential, as something that might be overcome, but only superficially, never entirely. In this context, it is important that Koestler's disgust, while figured physiologically (as "bellyaches," nausea, etc.) comes not from external stimuli – not from the grime, squalor, or social reconfigurations he observes – but from an internal source much more closely aligned with ethical or moral centres. For Koestler, at least Koestler the memoirist of 1954, the frontier of the Revolution is a line drawn in nausea, not grime, and it should not be crossed.

Boundaries and Breaches

These two memoirs map the frontiers of the Revolution for the Cold War–era reader, each tracing boundaries in lines of disgust. Recalling the earlier discussion of disgust as affect, it is perhaps no surprise that in this era of rising tensions, Red Scares, and Iron Curtains, disgust imagery might be effective in sketching the contours of the communist world for readers in an inherently inimical capitalist West. But what is perhaps more surprising is that the same (or very similar) devices work for two writers with very different agendas, one – Koestler – insisting on boundaries, the other – Hughes – celebrating crossings. Especially among audiences who might be hostile to the Revolution, disgust proves effective *and* flexible at sketching revolutionary geographies for at least two reasons. First, disgust is emergent. It does not draw boundaries, it suggests them. It is never a line on the map, but the desire for one, the idea of a boundary always almost drawn. It can thus be mobilized to reinforce that desire or to overcome it. Second, as mentioned earlier, disgust moves quickly and powerfully among (representations of) stimuli, physical reactions, and moral judgments, without set directionality. Physical stimuli can lead to moral revulsion; but as Koestler tries to show, ethical doubts can also lead to physiological feelings of nausea. While Hughes questions some of the links along this chain of connections, Koestler insists that disgust, the boundaries it suggests, and their ethical valences should not be ignored.

But should they? Koestler builds a strong case against transgressing lines of disgust. Just before his first mention of his own nausea, he is travelling through Soviet Armenia, where he hears much about the Armenian genocide. He is shown a directive from Talaat Pasha, the Vizier of the Ottoman Empire who oversaw the massacres. The directive, which he quotes in full, ends as follows: "However regrettable it may be to resort to the means of extermination, it is nevertheless necessary to put an end to their existence without regard for women, children or sick people, without listening to the voice of conscience."[35] In the post-Nuremberg years when Koestler is writing, this directive takes on even more resonance – indeed, the Armenian genocide was cited at Nuremberg as among Hitler's favoured precedents.[36] By mentioning his own communist "bellyache" on the very same page, Koestler implicitly aligns his own nausea with the Turkish exterminators' "voice of conscience." If that is disgust, then – of course we can agree unequivocally – disgust should never be ignored. But Koestler's disgust is more slippery than that. Although he mentions in passing some of the atrocities perpetrated in the Soviet Union (the show trials occupy half a sentence, for instance), the images more likely to activate the reader's sense of disgust are his descriptions of the grimy world, its squalor and decay. Koestler's account seems to conflate three things: a low-level disgust at the environment he encounters (mostly directed at the reader), his developing nausea at communist ideology (aligned with his impotence), and that "voice of conscience" experienced and disregarded by genocidal war criminals. This conflation seems slightly disingenuous. Not all disgust is created equal. Moreover, not all disgust reflects something internal and essential. For all its physiological potency and affective immediacy, disgust, we know, is also a learned reaction. Anyone whose tastes in food have changed since childhood knows that the previously repulsive can become acceptable and even enticing. Overcoming disgust can often open up new horizons, while always heeding disgust might limit development or progress and protect the status quo. In this way, disgust is a conservative affect; to borrow from Menninghaus again, it "consists in a spontaneous and especially energetic act of saying 'no.'"[37] And while that "no" might at times be the correct response, it should not be accepted uncritically. Koestler's affective poetics suggest that the spontaneous "no," which spreads uncritically from Central Asian grime to Ottoman war crimes, is more than likely correct, whatever its source.

Hughes's account, by contrast, encourages his readers to experience disgust (even more strongly than Koestler's), to see his and Koestler's responses, and to think critically about how they might align their own reactions. This is not to say that Hughes never associated disgust and moral repulsion. Quite the contrary: in the decades following his return from the Soviet Union, and as civil rights battles heated up, he experimented with images of both moral and physical revulsion in his poetry. His poem "The Bitter River," for instance, which he wrote in response to the October 1942 lynching of two fourteen-year-old boys in Mississippi, uses the title image as a metaphor for racism and also as a way of evoking physical and moral disgust simultaneously:

> There is a bitter river
> Flowing through the South.
> Too long has the taste of its water
> Been in my mouth.
> There is a bitter river
> Dark with filth and mud.
> Too long has its evil poison
> Poisoned my blood.

> I've drunk of the bitter river
> And its gall coats the red of my tongue,
> Mixed with the blood of the lynched boys
> From its iron bridge hung,
> [...]
> Oh, water of the bitter river
> With your taste of blood and clay,
> You reflect no stars by night,
> No sun by day.[38]

The physicality of the description, which concentrates on the taste and the feeling of the river's water in the mouth and over the tongue, seems calculated to evoke the physiological disgust reaction, meant here to reinforce the moral thrust of the poem. In its use of physical disgust and moral revulsion, Hughes's river of racism is an apt (if entirely unintended) echo of the "poisoned river [of communism] strewn with the wreckage of flooded cities and the corpses of the drowned," which Koestler evokes at the beginning of his memoir. In both cases, aesthetically mobilized disgust buttresses moral repugnance.

But in contrast to Koestler, Hughes represents the filth of the river as something that he has to ingest, that becomes a part of him as a Black American faced with unrelenting racism. Similar motifs of dirt as the defining African American experience arise throughout Hughes's antiracist poetry. "The angels wings is white as snow," he writes in "Angels Wings," "But I drug ma wings / In the dirty mire."[39] More directly, in "White Man," he draws the distinction between Black and White – the colour line itself – in terms of dirt:

> Sure I know you!
> You're a White Man.
> I'm a Negro.
> You take all the best jobs
> And leave us the garbage cans to empty
> and
> The halls to clean.
> You have a good time in a big house at
> Palm Beach
> And rent us the back alleys
> And the dirty slums.[40]

Within the confines of the poem, the dirty slums and the garbage cans define the Black experience. If these images evoke disgust for the reader, they ask the reader to understand the source of the dirt as inequity, to overcome any disgust reaction, and to see the denizen of the dirt not as disgusting, but as human.

This anti-racist poetics of dirt, it seems to me, has much in common with the vision Hughes wants to induce in the reader of *I Wonder as I Wander*. For the Cold War and Civil Rights–era Hughes, lines drawn in dirt are artificial boundaries, constructed out of social inequality. They are frontiers to be questioned, borders to be crossed. In a line quoted above, Hughes writes that he wanted to get Koestler to see the Revolution through "*Negro* eyes." Explicitly, Hughes connects this vision with the newfound freedoms accorded the "colored" people of Soviet Central Asia (tramcar integration and others). Seeing the Revolution in this way means paying attention to both borders and breaches. But it also requires reframing dirt and disgust. In Hughes's poetics of dirt, social upheaval exposes dirt, releases grime, and evokes disgust. But that disgust should not be taken as a signal to forcefully put the dirt back in place, to turn away from the abject exposed. Instead, it should be an invitation to examine the source of the dirt, to question the justice of previous boundaries, and to expand the limits of the self and society. Although Hughes does not seem to succeed in getting Koestler to see the Revolution from his perspective, his memoir, through the careful deployment of disgust, gives readers the chance to try on this optic in sketching their own geographies of the Revolution and to think critically about how borders are drawn and which should be – and which should not be – transgressed.

Notes

1 The relevant memoirs are Langston Hughes, *I Wonder as I Wander: An Autobiographical Journey* [1956], in *The Collected Works of Langston Hughes*, vol. 14, ed. Joseph McLaren (Columbia: University of Missouri Press, 2002); and Arthur Koestler, *The Invisible Writing: An Autobiography* (Boston: Beacon Press, 1954). The quotes above come from Hughes 147 and Koestler 78. Subsequent references to both memoirs will be in parenthetical notes in the text.

2 I define disgust primarily as an affect. Although disgust can be evoked through images (representations) and can cause more complex feelings, emotions, and ethical and moral responses, it is at its base a physiological response. On the difference between affect, feeling, and emotion, see Silvan Tomkins, "What Is Affect?" in *Shame and its Sisters: A Silvan Tomkins Reader*, ed. Eve Kosofsky Sedgwick and Adam Frank (Durham: Duke University Press, 1995), 33–74.

3 Winfried Menninghaus, *Disgust: Theory and History of a Strong Sensation*, trans. Howard Eiland and Joel Golb (Albany: SUNY Press, 2003), 1.
4 Mary Douglas, *Purity and Danger: An Analysis of Concepts of Pollution and Taboo* (New York: Routledge, 1966), 44.
5 Julia Kristeva, *Powers of Horror: An Essay on Abjection*, trans. Leon S. Roudiez (New York: Columbia University Press, 1982), 3.
6 Daniel Kelly, *Yuck!: The Nature and Moral Significance of Disgust* (Cambridge, MA: MIT Press, 2011), 16. For a full discussion of the disgust response, both physiological and emotional, see chapter 1, "Toward a Functional Theory of Disgust."
7 Kelly, *Yuck!*, 17.
8 Menninghaus, *Disgust*, 4.
9 Kristeva, *Powers of Horror*, 1.
10 William Ian Miller, *The Anatomy of Disgust* (Cambridge, MA: Harvard University Press, 1997), 137.
11 Miller, *The Anatomy of Disgust*, 113.
12 Kristeva, *Powers of Horror*, 4.
13 Vladimir Lenin, "O chistke partii," *Pravda*, 21 September 1921, 1.
14 Aleksandra Kollontai, *Rabochaia oppozitsiia* (Moscow: 1921), 11, qtd. in Eric Naiman, "When a Communist Writes Gothic: Aleksandra Kollontai and the Politics of Disgust," *Signs* 22, No. 1 (Autumn 1996): 13. As Naiman shows, Kollontai does not always figure disgust as a counter-revolutionary affect. Indeed, in the same pamphlet, the worker's opposition is called a "swamp of opportunism," suggesting that a good party member – and not only the petite bourgeoisie – should at times experience politically induced disgust.
15 Such quotes hardly scratch the surface of revolutionary disgust, which would require a dedicated study of its own. A third type of disgust – disgust at poverty and suffering under capitalism – was widespread among revolutionary activists, artists, and thinkers. Perhaps most exemplary of this type of disgust is Maksim Gorky's tribute to Lenin, in which he ascribes this feeling to his subject: "I have never met, do not know a person, who with such depth and strength as Lenin, would feel hatred, disgust and contempt at the misery, woe, suffering of people." *Pis'ma, vospominaniia, dokumenty. V.I. Lenin i M. Gorkii* (Moscow: Nauka, 1969), 311.
16 See, for instance, Vladimir Mayakovsky's 1919 Okna ROSTA illustrations warning of the danger of typhus, which features enlarged ticks visibly infecting unhygienic citizens. Mayakovsky et al., "Hey Citizen, do you understand / That typhus is coming back stronger?," *Okna ROSTA*, 1919.
17 Anna Louise Strong, *I Change Worlds: The Remaking of an American* (New York: Henry Holt, 1935), 111–12; qtd. in Julia L. Mickenberg, *American Girls in Red Russia: Chasing the Soviet Dream* (Chicago: University of Chicago Press, 2017), 95.

18 Theodore Dreiser and Ruth Eppersend Kennell, *Dreiser's Russian Diary*, ed. Thomas P. Riggio and James L.W. West III (Philadelphia: University of Pennsylvania Press, 1996), 264.
19 Michael David-Fox, *Showcasing the Great Experiment: Cultural Diplomacy and Western Visitors to the Soviet Union, 1921–1941* (Oxford: Oxford University Press, 2012), 127–41.
20 Arthur Koestler et al., *The God That Failed: A Confession* (New York: Harper and Brothers, 1949). The collection, edited by Richard Grossman, included contributions from Louis Fischer, André Gide, Arthur Koestler, Ignazio Silone, Stephen Spender, and Richard Wright.
21 See Hughes, "My Adventures as a Social Poet" and "Concerning 'Goodbye Christ,'" in *The Collected Works of Langston Hughes*, vol. 9: *Essays on Art, Race, Politics, and World Affairs*, ed. Christopher C. De Santis (Columbia: University of Missouri Press, 2002), 207–9 and 269–77.
22 Accounts differ on this point. For Hughes's own (retrospective) take, see Hughes, *I Wonder as I Wander*, 113–14; for corroboration of unworkable material, see Baldwin, *Beyond the Color Line*, 99; for an alternate explanation that focuses on US pressure, see Steven S. Lee, "Langston Hughes's 'Moscow Movie': Reclaiming a Lost Minority Avant-Garde," *Comparative Literature* 67, no. 2 (June 2015): 185–206.
23 Kate Baldwin, *Beyond the Color Line and the Iron Curtain: Reading Encounters between Black and Red, 1922–1963* (Durham: Duke University Press, 2002), 89.
24 He writes that when the girl rejected an exchange with him, "it dawned upon me with a certain suddenness that I was different from the others, shut out from their world by a vast veil." W.E.B. Du Bois, *The Souls of Black Folk* [1903] (Penguin: New York, 1995), 8.
25 Jennifer Wilson, "Queer Harlem, Queer Tashkent: Langston Hughes's 'Boy Dancers of Uzbekistan,'" *Slavic Review* 76, no. 3 (Fall 2017): 637–46. See also Dzhennifer Uilson, "Opisyvaia 'sovetskii Iug': otzvuki postrabovladel'cheskoi Ameriki v etnograficheskikh zametkakh Lengstona Kh'iuza o Srednei Azii" [Jennifer Wilson, "Writing the 'Soviet South': Inflections of Post-slavery America in Langston Hughes's Ethnography of Central Asia"], trans. Mariia Kozlova, *Novoe literaturnoe obozrenie*, no. 141 (5/2016): n.p., https://www.nlobooks.ru/magazines/novoe_literaturnoe_obozrenie/141_nlo_5_2016/article/12188.
26 Steven Lee, *The Ethnic Avant-Garde: Minority Cultures and World Revolution* (New York: Columbia Univeristy Press, 2015), esp. 119–48.
27 Langston Hughes, *The Collected Poems*, ed. Arnold Rampersad (New York: Alfred A. Knopf, 1994), 176–7.
28 Understandably, disgust is absent from Hughes's account commissioned by the Soviet Union, *A Negro Looks at Soviet Central Asia*. But disgust and dirt (and Koestler) are also entirely absent from more candid accounts,

including essays published in the US in the 1930s and even in letters back home. See, for instance, Hughes's letter to Noël Sullivan dated 31 January 1933, in which he describes his Central Asian trip in detail, mentions unveilings, and even notes a sickness he attributes to "eating camel meat." No images of dirt, no disgust, and no Koestler are to be found (*The Selected Letters of Langston Hughes*, ed. Arnold Rampersad and David Roessel [New York: Alfred A. Knopf, 2015], 138–44).

29 Depending on how you count. "'This filthy hole!,' said Koestler. 'It will take more than a revolution to clean up this dive. I can't wash in this stinking water'" (138); "'In Germany,' Koestler said, 'strangers would be told what they'd be getting into before commencing anything like this. What a hell of a part of the world to have a revolution!'" (145); "'What a hell of a place to have a revolution,' said Koestler, or words to that effect" (149); "I asked Koestler how he found Tashkent. 'Dirty and ugly and dusty,' he said, head down over our meal. 'This disgusting part of the world! In Germany at least we'd have a *clean* revolution'" (158).

30 Miller, *The Anatomy of Disgust*, 111.

31 The resulting book, *Of White Nights and Red Days*, was published in German by a Soviet press in Kharkiv. Arthur Koestler, *Von weißen Nächten und roten Tagen. 12 Reportagen aus den Sowjet-Peripherien*. (Kharkiv: Ukrainischer Staatsverlag für die nationalen Minderheiten in der USSR, 1934).

32 Although this is the only mention of show trials in Koestler's memoir, Hughes includes a description of the trial of Atta Kurdov in Ashkhabad, which he attended with Koestler. According to Hughes, it was the first show trial Koestler witnessed and he was clearly "disturbed." Hughes even speculates, "I guess that was the beginning of *Darkness at Noon*." Hughes himself is surprisingly cavalier: "I did not care much about Atta Kurdov because I didn't like his looks," he writes, adding, "I knew mine was not proper reasoning … and had nothing to do with due process of law. But when I saw that it upset [Koestler], I repeated that night just for fun, 'Well, anyhow Atta Kurdov does look like a rascal'" (135–6).

33 For Freud, the connection between disgust and sex lies at the very foundation of human civilization, when humans "adopted an upright posture," separating "olfactory stimulation" from the genitals. "From that point, the chain of events would have proceeded through the devaluation of olfactory stimuli and the isolation of the menstrual period to the time when visual stimuli were paramount and the genitals became visible, and thence to the continuity of sexual excitation, the founding of the family and so to the threshold of human civilization." Sigmund Freud, *Civilization and Its Discontents*, trans. James Strachey (New York: W.W. Norton, 1961), 54.

34 Central Asian sexuality, Hughes learns, depends on tightly enforced boundaries. Hughes describes a failed sexual encounter with a local

woman that goes awry when he meets violent resistance to his advances. Later he learns that not only was the resistance conventional, his local (male) friends are horrified at the thought of American women *not* resisting. The erotic attraction, it seems, comes from the forced breaching of boundaries (170–8).

35 Koestler's version, on pages 87–8 of *The Invisible Writing*, is signed "Talaal," not Talaat, and is footnoted as "Quoted from Nansen, *Betrogenes Volk, Eine Studienreise durch Georgien und Armenien als Oberkommissar des Völkerbundes*, Brockhaus, 1928."

36 A version of Hitler's "Obersalzberg Speech" (1939) obtained by prosecutors at the Nuremberg trial ends with a promise to "send to death mercilessly and without compassion men, women, and children of Polish derivation and language," and justifies the "physical destruction of the enemy" by invoking the Armenian genocide: "Who, after all, speaks today of the annihilation of the Armenians?" See Margaret Lavinia Anderson, "Who Still Talked about the Extermination of the Armenians?," in Ronald Grigor Suny, Fatma Müge Göçek, and Norman M. Naimark, eds., *A Question of Genocide: Armenians and Turks at the End of the Ottoman Empire* (Oxford: Oxford University Press, 2011), 199. Thank you to Philip Gleissner for pointing out this connection.

37 Menninghaus, *Disgust*, 2.

38 Hughes, *Collected Poems*, 242–3.

39 *The Collected Works of Langston Hughes*, vol. 1: *The Poems: 1921–1940*, 96.

40 *Collected Works*, vol. 1, 247–8. "White Man" concludes by once again connecting anti-racism directly to Marxism: "I hear your name ain't really White Man. / I hear it's something / Marx wrote down / Fifty years ago – / That rich people don't like to read. / Is that true, White Man? // Is your name in a book / Called the *Communist Manifesto*? / Is your name spelled / C-A-P-I-T-A-L-I-S-T? / Are you always a White Man? / Huh?"

7 The Intellectual Migrations of the British Communist Ralph Fox during the 1920s and 1930s

KATERINA CLARK

Many of the contributors to this volume discuss examples of what might be called "red peregrinations" rather than "red migrations" in the sense that their subjects do not move elsewhere with any notion that the shift will be permanent or of long duration.[1] My subject, the English communist Ralph Fox (1900–1937), was one such peregrinator. Although based in London between trips, he spent three extended periods in the Soviet Union during the 1920s, visiting Moscow, the Volga region, and Central Asia, and then made another brief visit in the 1930s. In addition, at the height of the anti-fascist movement in the 1930s Fox yo-yoed back and forth to Paris, headquarters of the literary arm of the campaign, organizing for the cause. He also visited Salazar's Portugal in the summer of 1936 and produced a scathing appraisal of his regime, *Portugal Today* (*Portugaliia segodnia*, published in Moscow in 1937). These peregrinations were cut short in another European country: Fox was killed fighting for the Republicans in the Spanish Civil War in early 1937.

In what follows, I will, however, be looking at Fox less in terms of actual migration, of geographical and national displacement, than in terms of his intellectual migrations. My story will be about how an Oxford graduate specializing in European and Arabic languages and cultures, and whose professors planned for him a career in philological scholarship, "migrated" from the British academic world. Rather than follow the route his professors designated, in 1920 he travelled to the Soviet Union with a group from the Quaker Famine Relief Committee. There, he was dispatched to work in the Central Asian Republics and Mongolia, a journey in space that proved decisive for his intellectual "migration."[2] In the course of his several stays in the Soviet Union, Fox not only became intellectually assimilated but also shifted his own primary geocultural orientation from Western and European culture to the Eastern, somewhat parallel to his shift in ideological orientation.

Intellectual and geographical migrations are not of course distinct phenomena. Journeys to foreign climes are generally reckoned to have a formative influence on the minds of participants – think of the necessity for any would-be English gentleman to undertake the Grand Tour in order to acquire the appropriate degree of cultivation to buttress claims to that status. Fox's peregrinations were no Grand Tours – in the famine-stricken Soviet Union of the early 1920s he lived in often appalling conditions where typhus was rampant. But one must do more than simply travel in geographical space for the experience to trigger a cognitive shift. Xavier de Maistre made this claim with his provocatively titled book, *Voyage around My Room* (*Voyage autour de ma chambre*, 1794), which mischievously parodies Grand Tour narratives; the narrator, confined to his room for six weeks, fastens on the furnishings and other objects there and using a free play of the imagination transforms the familiar setting into scenes from a voyage in a strange land. De Maistre's book was immensely popular in its time and would later influence, among others, Marcel Proust as he wrote *In Search of Lost Time* (*À la recherche du temps perdu*, written between 1906 and 1922 and published between 1913 and 1927). Proust claimed that a crucial factor in his writing of the *Recherche* was his prolonged confinement to his room, which helped evoke for him the memories of that "lost time" of its title.

As Proust well understood, in processing impressions there is always an element of mediation. Past experiences bear on one's perceptions. This is something that Christopher Isherwood, another (then leftist) writer and associate of Fox in the London literary scene of the 1930s, recurrently points to in his travelogue "Travel-Diary," which appeared in *Journey to a War* which he and W.H. Auden produced jointly as a response to their visit to war-torn China in 1938. In "Travel-Diary" Isherwood often describes scenes he witnessed as observed not close at hand but through a ship or train window, a framing that provides a figure for the pair's overall predicament as outsiders to the society and culture they were observing, limited by the gap between their cognitive maps and those of the locals. For example, he remarks during their journey to Shanghai on a riverboat that

> a cabin port-hole is a picture frame. No sooner had we arrived on board than the brass-encircled view became false. The brown river in the rain, the boatmen in their dark bat-wing capes[,] the tree-crowned pagodas on the foreshore, the mountains carved in mist – these were no longer features of the beautiful, prosaic country we had just left behind us; they were the scenery of the traveler's dream; they were the mysterious L'Extrême Orient. Memory in the years to come would prefer this simple theatrical picture to all the subtle and chaotic impressions of the past months. This, I thought – despite all we have seen, heard, experienced – is how I shall finally remember China.[3]

This sense that often one's narratives about experiences are not "realistic" – are "false" – but nevertheless prove more enduring than "actual" experience implicitly challenges those writers who glibly believe that they have gone beyond the colonialist, exoticist clichés to present the "authentic" East.

As we will see, Fox became one of those writers. But at the same time we should note that Isherwood's narrator presents two takes on the scene; one purportedly actual, complex, "subtle and chaotic," the other more streamlined and simple, and that he insists it is the latter "we" shall retain. Here he may have been influenced by any of several theorists from the turn of the last century – with Henri Bergson, Proust's uncle, among them – who investigated the role of past experiences and the memory of them in processing immediate impressions. Images formed are often crystallizations or conflations of discrete memories of experiences from different earlier moments, passages from texts read among them.

Both Isherwood and Auden had earlier been seemingly on the verge of becoming "red." Together they had written two anti-bourgeois, quasi-Marxist plays, some versions of which include worker revolutions.[4] But by the time they reached China their enthusiasm was fading. They, as it were, undertook a reverse "migration." Isherwood's "Travel-Diary" is full of the Bertie Wooster humour and self-deprecating irony that typified the Oxbridge mindset of the pair's undergraduate years there and undercuts any political message.

Fox had meanwhile acquired a different "porthole." In the 1920s he "migrated" to a Marxist-Leninist viewpoint such that he viewed the East through such texts as Lenin's *Imperialism as the Highest Stage of Capitalism* (*Imperializm kak vysshaia stadiia kapitalizma*, 1917). By the late 1930s, after Fox was dead, in a Soviet publishing house an in-house reviewer, A. Krivosheeva, wrote in her appraisal of one of his books (*The Novel and the People*): "Ralph Fox was not our compatriot, but he thought as we do."[5] Fox's intellectual "migration," then, was seen as so complete that he had settled permanently in the new "country" and had acquired the intellectual mindset of the Marxist-Leninist, not to say the Stalinist. Fox himself represented his time in Central Asia as a conversion experience. In his *People of the Steppes* (1925), his account of his first trip to the Soviet Union, he remarks that he had been "brought up to look upon the Latin countries as my spiritual home. I had never regarded them as foreign, but the scene before me now was so utterly different, so new and strange that I could not help feeling like a traveller who had discovered some lost Atlantis."[6] His old "portholes" were inadequate to convey his new experiences. Yet, as I will argue, vestiges of Fox's intellectual and experiential past continued to insinuate themselves into his writings. After all, the metaphor of the porthole is too simplistic and leads to a binaristic account of the process of taking "otherness" on board. Impressions are refracted through a more complex and variegated "frame" (or set of frames) formed from experiences from different time periods, including experiences and readings from *after* the event(s) "remembered."[7] I will nevertheless continue to use the metaphor of the porthole because Fox, rather more than Isherwood, tended to view what he saw in binaristic terms, downplaying the complexity of "actuality."

The framing narratives that guided Fox's accounts of the places he visited in central Eurasia, the informing texts, were often derived from Marxist-Leninist theory and Bolshevik rhetoric, and especially from Marx's and Lenin's writings on colonialism and imperialism. This "porthole" frame was supported by an implicit claim to "scientific objectivity," but at the same time Fox's accounts of the region were inflected by a lingering Romanticism and exoticism. I will establish this point here by looking at the three main texts Fox wrote based on his personal experiences and scholarship about Central Asia: *People of the Steppes*, the novel *Storming Heaven* (1928), and *Genghis Khan* (1936). I will also look, for comparative purposes, at the writings of three Western leftists who also visited Central Asia during the interwar years: Langston Hughes, Arthur Koestler, and Egon Erwin Kisch.

But first, an account of Fox's career.

Fox is largely forgotten today, yet he was in the 1920s and 1930s an important figure of the British communist movement and more broadly in London leftist literary circles of the 1930s. He is all but forgotten today in part because the Cold War has coloured Western accounts of European intellectual life of that decade. Many British writers who in the 1930s had flocked to Comintern-affiliated literary organizations and published in their periodicals (a virtual Who's Who of the literary world of the time) airbrushed out or at least minimized those involvements in their post-war memoirs.

On the British intellectual landscape of the interwar years Fox loomed large and wore a remarkable number of hats. He was a founding member (in 1920) of the Communist Party of Great Britain (CPGB) and became a member of its Executive Committee; he was also associated with the Comintern and helped organize the British Section of the Writers' International, established in 1934 as a branch of the Comintern's International Association of Revolutionary Writers (MORP).[8] He worked tirelessly as a labour organizer and journalist and wrote on current events in the British labour movement for communist periodicals such as *Labour Monthly*, set up by the Comintern in 1921, and later the communist paper *Daily Worker* after it was founded in 1930.[9] And he lectured widely to Party groups and worker audiences. His main source of income was as an editor in the communist publishing house Lawrence and Wishart, and for them he did a number of translations of Marxist publications.[10] Yet he also found time to produce numerous scholarly books and articles of his own on a broad range of subjects, literary, political, and historical.

Fox also had literary aspirations. He wrote poetry and was active in literary circles in London, where he served on the editorial board of both *The Left Review*, which he co-founded, and *New Writing*.[11] Edited by John Lehmann, *New Writing* was self-declaredly unaffiliated politically (although anti-fascist) and attracted some of the leading writers of the time, such as W.H. Auden, Christopher Isherwood, and George Orwell, all of whom published some of their most famous texts of the 1930s there. As Glyn Salton-Cox has observed, the leftist writers in Britain at the time were remarkably parochial; however, the writers who ran *New Writing* were an exception.[12] Proudly cosmopolitan, they travelled all over the continent, often staying for months at a time in one or another locale: Berlin, Vienna, Paris, Belgium, Spain, Denmark, and Portugal. But they were also decidedly Eurocentric – a defining aspect of Isherwood's "porthole" through which he viewed China. Fox, however, had a distinctly Asia-centric perspective, that is, not the perspective of an actual Asian, but rather of the revolutionary movement in Asia. He saw to it that, until his death, *New Writing* published material about Asia; even its literary texts about the Soviet Union were about Asian parts of the country.

This shift by Fox to an anti-colonialist, Asia-centric perspective can be attributed in part to his stints in the Soviet Union in the 1920s. During each of them, although his Soviet affiliation was different, he worked *inter alia* on or in Asia. On his first visit, in 1922–3, Fox was attached to the Friends Relief Mission in Samara but in the course of his duties spent five months living among the nomadic Kyrgyz in Central Asia procuring horses for struggling farmers in European Russia.[13] He drew on these experiences for two of the books I will be discussing, *People of the Steppes* and *Storming Heaven*.

On returning to England in 1923 from his first trip to the Soviet Union, Fox enrolled in 1924 in London's School of Oriental Studies, intending to write a doctoral dissertation on oriental history under its director, Denison Ross.[14] But he did not complete it, probably because the following year, 1925, Fox was sent by the Central Committee of the CPGB to Moscow for his second stint, this time to work in the Comintern's

Colonial Department (as British sources call it, actually the Eastern Department or *Vostochnyi otdel*), concentrating on Indian affairs.[15] Then for his third stay, 1929–32, Fox was based in the English subsection (*Angliiskii kabinet*) of the Marx-Engels Institute (IMEL). While there he researched materials for books he published after his return.[16]

At the time, IMEL's main task was to study and edit the Marx-Engels *Nachlass*, including their statements on literature, which appeared in early volumes of *Literary Heritage* (*Literaturnoe nasledstvo*).[17] One of Fox's colleagues in IMEL was Georg Lukács, who was at the time working on the *Nachlass*. We can assume that they interacted, as can be sensed in Fox's book on literary theory and history, the aforementioned *Novel and the People*. This text provides a contrast with E.M. Forster's *Aspects of the Novel* (1927), which is better known today; Fox's book is now almost forgotten, but in the late 1930s it was an important text for British leftist intellectuals, as Raymond Williams reported.[18] *The Novel and the People* is in most of its positions close to those taken by Lukács in his articles of the 1930s, which together provided a canonical account of the nature and evolution of realism and socialist realism. There were some differences, however, especially in their attitudes towards representations of sex. (Fox was more liberal and called for depicting the "living man.") Tellingly, Lukács in a generally fulsome review criticizes Fox on the few points he made that diverged from Lukács's own.[19]

At the Marx-Engels Institute Fox also wrote educational textbooks for the Lenin School and for the research section of the Soviet Party's Central Committee. Those texts covered the history of the British labour movement and the colonial policy of British imperialism; even his collection of Marxist writings on Ireland was focused on exposing the colonialist nature of British rule there.[20] Additionally, Fox taught at the Communist University for Toilers of the East (KUTV) from 1930, and at the Lenin School from 1931, and from 1930 he served in the bureau of the Party cell at IMEL.[21] In other words, he was integrated into Soviet intellectual life as an expert on both British colonialism and the East.

Fox developed two main areas of Asian expertise, especially during this third Soviet stay, and the two correspond to the main foci of Comintern activity in Asia during the 1920s. The first was China. In the late 1920s, following the Shanghai Debacle of 1927, during which the Nationalist forces of Chiang Kai-shek routed the Communists and dozens of Soviet advisers fled back to the Soviet Union, China policy became a central issue in the power struggle between Stalin and Trotsky that led to Trotsky's expulsion from the Party and then from the Soviet Union. Like Lukács in the literary sphere, Fox, although a foreigner, played a significant role in Soviet controversies of the time, in his case regarding Asia. He published an article titled "Canton Commune" in the journal *Communist* of March 1928 and also participated while at IMEL in a major debate about the theory of the German (then) communist Karl Wittfogel from the Frankfurt School regarding the "Asiatic mode of production." Wittfogel's ideas were debunked by Stalin as part of a rethinking of Asia policies after the 1927 China debacle, even though they had been espoused not only by Karl Wittfogel but also, inconveniently, by Marx.[22]

Of greater interest for Fox during his third Soviet period was the revolutionary situation not in China, but in India. While at IMEL he edited Marx's letters on India that had been published in the *New York Daily Tribune* in the 1850s (and in Russian translation in 1927 in the institute's journal *Chronicles of Marxism* [*Letopisi marksizma*]).[23] Fox drew on these letters in his book *The Colonial Policy of British Imperialism* (1933), written while Fox was at IMEL. Two translated versions appeared in Russian, an indication of Fox's stature among Soviet scholars of imperialism; one came out in 1931, before the British edition of 1933, and an updated, fuller version was published in the Soviet Union in 1934, after he had left.[24] Fox's book proved an important source on India for Soviet scholars, administrators, and politicians, but also for Indians themselves.

On his return to London Fox also functioned as mentor not just to assorted British working-class groups but also to the Indian leftists then based there. In this capacity he served as godfather to the Indian Progressive Writers' Association (IPWA), which was initially founded in London in 1935; all of the founding members recall this in their memoirs.[25] One of the IPWA leaders, Sajjad Zaheer, returned to India to proselytize for the association, and branches were established all over the country. The reach was so great that until the war IPWA was the leading organization of Indian leftist intellectuals.

The member of IPWA whom Fox particularly influenced was Mulk Raj Anand, the most famous Indian writer of the interwar years writing in English. Two of Anand's novels from the mid-1930s, *Untouchable* (1935) and *Coolie* (1936), figure in discussions of world literature to this day. One can only speculate on the extent to which Fox influenced Anand's fiction, although it is known that he walked Anand through *The Novel and the People* as he was writing it. In addition, a marked shift in Anand's writing dates from around 1932, when Fox returned from his third spell in the Soviet Union.[26] And in *Coolie* Anand draws extensively on Fox's *Colonial Policy of British Imperialism* for his account of living conditions for workers in Bombay factories and of how Hindu–Muslim clashes undermined the labour movement.[27]

In 1936 Fox wanted to expand his Asian repertoire and visit Mongolia to collect materials for a future book on that country. He already had British and American publishers lined up, but when he wrote to the Comintern for permission to travel there they refused him on the grounds that there were "infiltrators" in the CPGB and that they, the Comintern, did not trust the intentions of the British government as regards Mongolia.[28] Instead, he was sent to the Spanish Civil War, arriving in late December 1936. There he served as commissar to the British Battalion, and there, soon after he arrived, he was killed on 2 January 1937, while making a quixotic dash through a hail of bullets.

Fox's acquiescing and going to Spain rather than Mongolia suggests that he was a dutiful member of the Comintern and the CPGB. Indeed, many have commented that in the 1930s he seemed overly dogmatic. Yet archival materials indicate that Soviet literary officials and the CPGB accorded him a leading role under sufferance and looked askance at him and several of his publications.[29] Fox comes across as a somewhat idiosyncratic communist functionary, and even problematical; in December 1930 he had to subject himself to self-criticism as overly rightist.[30] Perhaps the British communists tolerated him because he was associated with the Comintern, although they had trouble assimilating Fox because his intellectual purview was broader than that of his Party superiors. Thus, he proves representative of the many prominent intellectuals who were maverick figures yet accommodated themselves to the communist movement of the pre-purge years (such as Wittfogel).

In the mid-1920s Fox published two books based on his experiences in Soviet Russia, *People of the Steppes* and *Storming Heaven*.[31] *People of the Steppes* is a work of non-fiction and *Storming Heaven* a novel. The latter purports to follow the life of a fictional character, John, an American who finds himself in the Soviet Far East and then travels to Central Asia for an extended period before moving on to Moscow. It is a somewhat simplistic novel, in which ideologically freighted pronouncements are scantily clad in an unconvincing plot. Because *People of the Steppes* first appeared in 1925 and *Storming Heaven* in 1928, one might conclude that the former reflects his first Soviet stint and the latter his second, but actually the two books present similar accounts of Soviet Asia. Consequently, I am looking at both as if there were no significant generic distinctions. Both texts include recurrent declarations about the backward and even moribund state of the Asiatic populace, a common judgment among European thinkers of the eighteenth and nineteenth centuries that is also prominent in imperialist writings. One might have expected Marx and Lenin to use a different vocabulary, but the notion of China (or of Asia generally) as in the sleep of centuries typifies their remarks as well. Lenin, however, insisted that there was revolutionary promise in moribund Asia. In one article, "China Renewed," he declared that "four hundred million backward Asians [i.e. the Chinese] have awakened to political life. A fourth of the population of the globe has gone, so to say, from sleeping to the light, to movement, to struggle."[32] In Lenin's scenario the awakening of Asia was not an autochthonous act. Rather, and especially in his statements after the Revolution, the Soviet Union was to function as the prince who would awaken the sleeping princess. In a 1919 speech delivered to the Second All-Russian Congress of Communist Organizations of the Peoples of the East, Lenin declared: "Now it remains for our Soviet republic to gather around itself the peoples of Asia who are awakening, in order to conduct the struggle against international imperialism together with them."[33]

Fox in his account of Soviet Asia identified signs of this awakening, which in a passage from *Storming Heaven* is said to have been sensed by John, who, we are told,

> had ridden across the heart of Asia, over grass steppes and sandy wastes, across swift rivers, through wooded valleys overhung by great mountains, and dimly, obscurely, in the tents of nomads, from wayfaring companions, in the mud-houses of the infrequent towns, he had become aware of a tremendous process. Something was waking after a long sleep, and a stirring was going on over the endless steppe such as the stir that precedes the awakening of spring, when in a night the grass shoots up, tall and green, many-colored tulips flame and dance in the warm breeze, and even on the sandy wastes for a brief day there is a blossom of desert green.

This transformation is no mystery. John's Soviet companion in Central Asia and mentor figure, Yasha, tells him that the area's decline over the centuries is now being reversed because "the Bolsheviks had invented a new weapon called 'electrificatsia' [the Leninist formula for modernization], which was performing miracles in Russia."[34] The "miracles" effected in Russia were coming to Central Asia, too. Yasha continues: "To waken the world. There's a desert to reclaim, all Russia to be covered with railway and air routes, factories to build, new things to be discovered, to make men freer."[35] In the earlier book, *People of the Steppes*, the narrator predicts that in five years' time locals "will be driving tractors across the steppe."[36] For "in every village things were moving, life was stirring again," thanks in part to the restoration of the railways.[37]

The theme of modernization and technological progress is, however, in both books interwoven with a different strand, a romantic vision of exotic otherness that we can sense in the quotation I used earlier about how "the scene before me now was so utterly different, so new and strange that I could not help feeling like a traveller who had discovered some lost Atlantis." In these two books, as the narrator in *People of the Steppes* puts it, "the spirit of great adventure still lingers here." At times that spirit overtakes the narrative of a people brought back to life in scenarios of modernization.[38] To return to Isherwood's comments on his own apprehension of China, "they were the scenery of the traveler's dream; they were the mysterious L'Extrême Orient. Memory in the years to come would prefer this simple theatrical picture to all the subtle and chaotic impressions of the past months."

Fox believed he had broken through the Eurocentric porthole. Arguably, however, he brought to the encounter some of the non-Marxist intellectual baggage of his recent past, and this inflected his accounts, producing a more dramatic and inspiring version of what he observed on the vast steppes of Central Asia. One might speculate that part of this intellectual baggage was the romanticized image of T.E. Lawrence (Lawrence of Arabia). Fox would not have been alone in being drawn in the early 1920s to the image of Lawrence. For example, at about the same time that Fox went to the Soviet Union, in 1923, André Malraux decamped to French Indochina, and commentators on him have suggested that his sudden decision to abandon the Surrealist literary scene in Paris for adventure in the Far East was prompted by a desire to emulate Lawrence.[39]

In the two years immediately before Fox left for his first trip to Russia, 1919–20, an image of Lawrence as a mythic figure was presented to the English public by the American journalist Lowell Thomas, who together with a photographer had dogged Lawrence in the Arabian desert. Thomas presented at Albert Hall in London 200 performances of his show "With Allenby in Palestine and Lawrence in Arabia," in which he screened a film about Lawrence accompanied by an exhibition of photographs and a lecture about Thomas's adventures with Lawrence. With his story of the shy young Oxford archaeologist turned guerilla leader, Thomas was largely responsible for a cult of Lawrence as a genius who, already conversant with the Arab language and culture, single-handedly inspired the Arabs to fight for their own liberation from the Turks. The heroic image of Lawrence that Thomas projected implied that British territorial gains in the Middle East had been the work of a rugged individualist in the desert wilderness rather than that of a highly disciplined British army officer and the strategic deployment of British troops.

We do not know if Fox attended one of the performances. But he had studied Arabic at Oxford and was surely aware of the great excitement over Lawrence while he was there. In his own journalism Fox periodically commented on him. For example, in a 1927 review of *Revolt in the Desert*, the shorter version of Lawrence's *Seven Pillars of Wisdom* (the full text of the *Seven Pillars* was limited to private circulation and available to the general reader only in 1935), Fox expresses his admiration for Lawrence but maintains that he "didn't recognize until later that ... it would be the oil companies, not the Arab nationalists, who would take control and that he had in effect become their tool."[40] Although Lawrence had great potential, Fox suggests, the class and culture that formed him were in decline. The East, on the other hand, was resurgent, a general point he could have drawn from Oswald Spengler's *Decline of the West*, which was widely discussed in Soviet intellectual circles of the early 1920s.

The notion of a resurgent East fired Fox's imagination, but in his presentation of it I sense a possible shaping influence of the Lawrence myth, with the "endless steppe" serving as an analogue to Lawrence's desert; the narrator in the tents of nomads is, like Lawrence, eager to enter into discussions of their cultural heritage.[41] In one passage, for example, from *Storming Heaven*, the narrator enthuses:

> Night after night John learned much history while sitting around the tent fires, and from Ali Hodja's lips [an elderly local] he drained up the life of this great people. He heard for the first time the names of people who had changed the face of the world, Chingiz, Timur, Akbar and the like, and learned with surprise that these great warriors were just such men as Ali Hodja, born in the black tents or mud huts of the Steppe, weaned on the milk of mares – horsemen and wanderers.[42]

Fox, then, glamorizes the process of modernization in Central Asia by identifying its agents with the region's ancient heroes. One sees this in a striking passage from a chapter in *People of the Steppe*, titled "A Dream of Great Conquerors." The narrator describes how he encountered a Kyrgyz, Konat, in a nomad's tent and reports that "as he [Konat] stood there ... I remembered a phrase of Renan's about the hills of Judea. Looking down from them, he said, over the great plains, one feels the immensity of the world and the desire to conquer it."[43] Fox continues: "'Konat,' I ventured, and at the name he turned, and I saw that it was not Konat, but Timur Lenk, Tamerlane the Great, who remade Asia to his own vision." Shortly thereafter the narrator presents a variation on this experience, now with a different local "conqueror": "Turning, I saw Ak Bala [another Kyrgyz], short, strong and sturdy, but as he came up I knew he was not Ak Bala, but Temudjin, Chengiz Khan, Emperor of the World."[44]

In de Maistre's *Voyage autour de ma chambre*, the objects in his room trigger free play of the author's imagination, which conjures up exotic scenes. Here, rather than objects as the trigger, we have humans, and rather than a room as the setting, it is a rude tent of nomads. The narrator's imagination takes him on a journey not in space, but in time, yet the scene he conjures is no less exotic and extravagant. An important "trigger" is Fox's cultural memory as derived from his European education (elsewhere the narrator mentions Herodotus). Throughout these two texts we find an uneasy coupling of imperialist grand visions conveyed in terms of historical precedents and a more democratic vision of an Asia liberated by modernization and drawn into a transnational fraternity.[45] Lawrence may have, in Fox's view, been a liberator of the Arabs manqué, but Fox sees the Russians as the true liberators of this other group of oppressed Asians. There is in these books an isomorphy between the great Asian conquerors of the deep past and the Soviet Russian "liberators" of Central Asia. In *People of the Steppes* the narrator declares: "There is a new Russia today who dominates all Asia, full of life and young vigour. Will it repeat the conquests of the great Mongols and restore the peoples of the steppe to their ancient heritage?"[46]

Fox was not the only traveller from the Western communist orbit to visit Central Asia in the interwar years and write up that experience. The three most prominent among them were the Czech cum Austrian writer Egon Erwin Kisch, who was there in 1931, the Harlem Renaissance writer Langston Hughes, who visited in 1932, and the Hungarian Arthur Koestler, who largely travelled with the same group as Hughes (see chapter 6). Hughes and Koestler each produced two different accounts of their experiences, one published soon after their trip and the other during the Cold War. Hughes's first book on the subject was the Soviet-published booklet *A Negro Looks at Soviet Central Asia* (1934); this was followed more than twenty years later by his memoir *I Wonder as I Wander* (1956), in which he devoted a section to his time in Central Asia. For Koestler the first book was *Von weissen Nächten und roten Tagen*, which he later came to refer to as *Red Days and White Nights*, or, more usually, *Red Days*, although it never managed to appear in English or in the other languages in which editions were planned.[47] Then, again in the mid-1950s, he published a somewhat different account of Central Asia in his memoir *The Invisible Writing* (1954). Both writers had by the 1950s become disillusioned with the Soviet Union so that their Cold War memoirs about Central Asia represent, if not 180 degree turns from their accounts from the early 1930s, views of it seen through a decidedly different "porthole."[48] Kisch, for his part, never abandoned his loyalty to communism, and he died in 1948, so we have no revisionist take on

Soviet Central Asia by him; his main account of the region is his *Changing Asia* (*Asien gründlich verändert*, 1932).

In their texts of the 1930s all three of these writers emphasize, as does Fox in his two books about Central Asia of the 1920s, the tremendous progress that Central Asia has made under the Soviets. They marvel at the great strides made in literacy, education, women's liberation, transportation, agriculture, and the promotion of local culture, and at the impressive efforts at constructing housing, factories, and hydroelectric dams. The enthusiasm is especially marked in Hughes's *A Negro Looks at Central Asia*, which is largely constructed around the stark contrast in the treatment of persons of colour between Central Asia and the United States, where "segregation, peonage, lynching" are rampant and where "negroes" are kept out of leadership positions and given an ersatz education.[49]

Quite striking in all three of the books from the early 1930s – by Kisch, Hughes, and Koestler – and in contrast to Fox's two books from the 1920s (*People of the Steppes* and *Storming Heaven*), is the virtually complete absence of any favourable reference to the Great Conquerors of Asia. This absence is somewhat compensated for with (very occasional) references to the *Arabian Nights*, a text that had for years served as a source for exoticist romance. This absence of reference to the conquerors, actual historical figures, might be explained by the fact that in the Soviet late 1920s and early 1930s any celebration of the ancient past and its heroes was frowned upon officially. As Koestler laments in his Cold War text, *The Invisible Writing*, "it had also been hammered into my head, and into the heads of two hundred million Russians, that to pay undue attention to the relics and monuments of the past was a sign of a morbid, sentimental, romantic and escapist attitude."[50] He describes numerous instances when local authorities have pulled down the ancient monuments and old sections of historic towns, or neglected them so that they are in a sorry state, and how they rebuff all requests that his writers' group be able to see them. Only recent economic achievements are deemed worthy of the group's attention. Accordingly, and somewhat predictably, Kisch in *Asien gründlich verändert* warns against idolizing Tamerlane. He has a "comrade Mustapha" bemoan the fact that visitors from Europe only want to see Tamerlane's tomb and ignore the new institutions and buildings that bear witness to Central Asia's lightning progress (scientific institutes, railways, factories, etc.).[51]

The narrative of Koestler's *Von weissen Nächten und roten Tagen* is shaped by the binary "underdeveloped"/developing. Central Asia is no longer so "backward, fanatical and wild." The same binary shapes his coverage of the economy and of culture. In one section he describes how wandering bards of Central Asia perform their national epics and ballads, the mainstay of the culture of a largely illiterate people. Koestler gives these events a highly negative press, pointing out that the bards' texts were composed under the patronage of the beys (feudal lords) and consequently draw on "mystical religious" material and are irremediably retrograde. He himself is bored by their monotonous renditions and the epics' repetitive plots about medieval "heroes," alternating with love stories, both always ending tragically. Inexplicably, among the locals even the educated, such as schoolteachers, fall into a trance as they listen to these bards' performances; they sometimes even perform themselves. But, he reports, hope is in sight. Some bards, especially the young, have begun to compose "revolutionary Bachschi-songs that have no religious origins" and that sing praise of Lenin and the advent of a new, brighter life under the Soviets. Indeed, this trend is spreading.[52]

Around 1934, however, after Koestler's memoir was composed, the official Soviet policy on ancient history was reversed. Two official pronouncements in particular contributed to this bouleversement. One was Maxim Gorky's first speech to the First Writers' Congress of 1934, where he stipulated that an important role in literature should be played by what he called "the folklore of the toiling people," or more specifically "the ancient folktales, myths and legends."[53] A second shift was reflected in the "Comments on an Outline of a Textbook on the History of the USSR" ("Zamechaniia po povodu konspekta uchebnika po istorii SSSR"), which was co-signed by Stalin, Zhdanov, and Kirov on 8 August 1934, in other words, on the eve of the First Writers' Congress. Their "Comments" called for a positive re-evaluation of the pre-feudal social order, which made more possible glorification of the past.[54]

With such clear indicators of a new official policy, by the mid-1930s the ancient history of Central Asia and its Great Conquerors had become an acceptable topic once again. Much later, in the mid-1950s, when Hughes and Koestler put together new versions of their memoirs (*I Wonder as I Wander* and *Invisible Writing*), although they incorporated some of the same material, presumably derived from their diaries written during their visits to Central Asia, they reshuffled the sections and reframed them, omitting some material and making some critical changes that altered much of the import of their texts (new "portholes"). In particular, they gave greater and more enthusiastic coverage to ancient Central Asia and to the Great Conquerors. Of course, having long abandoned their ties to the communist movement, they were under no constraints in presenting this material; they even indulged periodically in a little romantic exoticism. Hughes in *I Wonder as I Wander*, for example, includes an apostrophe to the glory days of the Great Conquerors (who are not mentioned in the earlier books): "Samarkand! Green-curled Samarkand! City of Tamerlane, the earth shaker; before that the city of Genghis Khan, leader of the Mongols; and before that the sporting ground of Alexander the Great ... lovely song-city of the oriental poets; city of the Turquoise domes – Samarkand! Green-curled Samarkand."[55] Koestler in *The Invisible Writing* also romanticized the wonders of ancient Central Asia, adding that in his childhood he had been very taken by Armin Vambéry's popular *Travels in Asia*, based on his visit of 1863. As it were, Koestler's "porthole" was partly constructed by his take-away from an exotic romance. There were occasional invocations of the exotic romance in Koestler's 1930s text *Von weissen Nächten und roten Tagen*, too, including mentions of Karl May and even Genghis Khan. However, they were largely invoked in chapter headings and not mentioned in the ensuing chapter; in this way, they provided an ironic counterpoint to the factual material offered there.

In their paeans to the Great Conquerors written in the 1950s, neither Hughes nor Koestler was particularly concerned to draw a political message. By contrast, when Fox wrote *Genghis Khan* (1936), he used the khan's biography largely as a vehicle for political allegory.[56] This third Fox text on Central Asia is based heavily on research he did during his third stay in Moscow and is much more scholarly than his previous two books on Central Asian themes; it also features detailed fold-out maps and an extensive bibliography. Fox's account of the Great Khan draws, at times explicitly, on the work of several earlier Russian scholars, two in particular: B.Ia. Vladimirtsov and V.V. Barthold (Bartol'd), who had established careers in the imperial period but continued working in the early Soviet years, updating their findings a little for the new era with a smattering of class analysis. Vladimirtsov was considered a leading scholar of the Mongols and Barthold an expert on Turkestan (roughly Central Asia), but both are also noted for their writings on Genghis Khan. In fact, Barthold's inaugural lecture, delivered at Saint Petersburg University on 8 April 1896, was on "The Formation of the Empire of Genghis Khan" ("Obrazovanie imperii Chingiz-khana"). These two scholars' take on this great conqueror was revisionist and challenged the standard Russian image of the Golden Horde as barbarians who slaughtered and plundered indiscriminately, laying waste to some of the great cities of the time, including their magnificent buildings and irreplaceable libraries.[57] The positive role these scholars accorded to the conquerors bears comparison with the positive account of Genghis Khan and his role in the formation of modern Russia that the Eurasianist Nikolai Trubetskoi presented in his book *The Heritage of Genghis Khan* (*Nasledie Chingiskhana*, 1925).[58]

In his *Genghis Khan*, Fox alluded specifically to Barthold and Vladimirtsov as sources because, as he himself wrote, he wanted to produce a more historically based account of this conqueror than was offered in popular biographies. To this end, he insisted in the initial chapters on referring to Genghis by his real name Temujin (Temudzhin). In crafting a different image of Genghis Khan, he maintained that the military successes of the khan were the result not of a chaotic invasion by his wild hordes but, rather, of fully worked out, strategic plans.[59]

However much it was based on actual historical records, Fox's account of Genghis Khan could not be purely objective and neutral. Since at least the 1920s, intellectuals had been resorting to the Great Conquerors when airing the sensitive topic of whether violence was permissible in the name of historical progress. In their writings about Genghis Khan and Tamerlane, writers and historians produced diametrically opposed evaluations of the conquerors' use of extreme violence. A subject of intense debates among Soviet intellectuals in the early 1920s, the controversy resurfaced in the mid-1930s when the past became an acceptable topic once again. But in both times there were diametrically opposed views. One example from the 1930s of an intellectual giving the conquerors' record a negative appraisal would be Sergei Eisenstein in his conception of the film *The Great Ferghana Canal* (*Bol'shoi Ferganskii kanal*), commissioned to celebrate the construction of the epynomous canal. Although Eisenstein was never able to complete this film, archival records of his plans show that he wanted to organize it as a historical triptych, devoting the first of the story's three parts to how the heinous Tamerlane, in capturing Urgenj, drowned masses of inhabitants by redirecting waters to flood the city.[60] Although he attributes the act to Tamerlane, Eisenstein's proposed representation of the destruction of Urgenj actually conflates the accounts in Barthold of the city's devastation by first Genghis Khan and then Tamerlane.

Fox in his coverage of the Great Khan, by contrast, takes the opposite position and is highly laudatory of the khan's actions. But here the very different historical moment in which he wrote this text as distinct from that of his two Central Asian texts of the 1920s played an important role, opening up, if you will, a different "porthole" through which to project a very different image of the khan. While in the first two texts Fox invokes the cult of the conquerors to suggest a potential and emerging future for the region under Bolshevik guidance, in the third, *Genghis Khan*, feats of the conquerors in the past are used as vehicles for promoting a very different political agenda. A central argument in Fox's *Genghis Khan* is that the tremendous violence of the Mongol conquests effected what Fox recurrently characterizes as a "revolution" that cleared away the many principalities in Eurasia and the Middle East and amalgamated them in the one federation. With their trade barriers and fortified borders gone, the conquered territory, critically, fostered a more open exchange that brought a great leap forward in the development and cultures of both East and West. As Fox puts it:

> It can be said of the Mongols that ... the cavalry of this young feudal power for the first time in history created a real world market ... which gave the impulse to a new civilization in the West ... The Mongol troopers were rough and brutal conquerors. They had little regard for the precious things they stole or destroyed. Yet they made the West and East known to one another for the first time since the death of Alexander the Great. In the wake of the Mongols the knowledge of many things came to Europe from China, printing and navigation, to mention but two.[61]

This positive assessment of Genghis Khan's role in Eurasia is uncannily similar to the account of his impact presented by Viktor Shklovsky in *Marko Polo*, which appeared in the same year as Fox's *Genghis Khan* (1936). Shklovsky's text is (perhaps deliberately) highly ambiguous and engages his recurrent themes of exile (internal and external), alienation, and the lot of the intellectual in an autocratic state, as Fox's does not.[62] But Shklovsky also, here like Fox, emphasizes the advantages that flow from the Great Khan's elimination of borders in terms of the free circulation of languages, cultures, and ideas, although in Fox this point is not given the same degree of emphasis. Both writers admit that this liberation came at the cost of great violence; Fox devotes several pages to a discussion of the wanton massacres and the razing of magnificent cities.[63] Violence is of course endemic to any "revolution," and so inevitable, but Fox's rationalization of it in the case of Genghis Khan could be read as a vindication of the Stalinist purges (in this text Fox uses the epithet "merciless," a code term during the purges).[64] Fox actually wrote *Genghis Khan* before the Great Purge, so he could not comment on it even indirectly, but the issue of violence was always problematical for the Bolsheviks.

Shklovsky in *Marko Polo*, less predictably than Fox in *Genghis Khan*, makes a similar case that violence is necessary to effect political ends. Rather than accuse Shklovsky of having a purge mentality, one could rationalize his adoption of this position by saying that his glorification of the work of the Great Khan in eliminating the borders was implicitly directed against the "iron curtain" that impeded commerce in ideas across the Soviet borders. However, the year after *Marko Polo* appeared, Shklovsky was himself implicated in the great upheavals in Soviet literature that attended the Great Purge. The year 1937 was marked by a rout of Trotskyites and, in literature especially, of former members of VAPP (the All-Union Association of Proletarian Writers), which had enjoyed a prominent presence in Central Asia during the 1920s and early 1930s. In that year Shklovsky joined a literary brigade that went to Soviet Central Asia not actually to purge writers (that was effected by the NKVD), but to recruit reliable replacements for the Writers' Union.[65]

Fox in *Genghis Khan* also idealizes the khan as a great leader. In the service of cold objectivity, as it were, he sometimes accounts for the khan's extraordinary achievements in terms that somewhat echo the Hegelian notion (articulated particularly in Section 5 of his *Philosophy of History*) of a "world-historical figure," that is, someone whose destiny it is to have a major impact on world events because their own propensities happen to coincide with the needs of the time and place in which they operate. In another age, in which different qualities were required, they would not have the same impact. As Fox puts it, "[Temujin's] fate was to be born when the two great feudal states on either side of him [Central Asia and China] were in full decay. It was this combination, which made it the destiny of the Mongol nomad to become the Emperor of the world, the greatest conqueror since Alexander, the godlike prince of Macedon."[66]

"Had China been a strong and united country with a stable economy," Fox remarks later in the text, "no Chingis Khan would ever have conquered it, however 'godlike' his military skill."[67] But Fox does not sustain this line of analysis. Despite such disclaimers, the more clear-headed account of Genghis Khan's role is often crowded out by the narrator's marvelling at precisely the khan's "godlike" "genius";[68] his extraordinary prescience and military skills ensure the emergence of a great empire.[69]

Clearly by the mid-1930s the themes that dominated the coverage of Central Asia in Fox, Kisch, Hughes, and Koestler – modernization, electrification, education, and so on – have been superseded. Now at the forefront is a different theme, to be found in Fox's book and Shklovsky's as well: political amalgamation. Another new policy position presented in both the "Comments on an Outline of a Textbook" and Gorky's addresses to the Writers' Union Congress was the importance of incorporating the culture of Central Asia and its history into the greater Soviet Union (within which Russia would be *primus inter pares*). The 1930s saw a concerted effort to create a *single* Soviet literary tradition that would incorporate all the literatures of this multi-national country. As Gorky put it in his initial speech to the First Congress of the Writers' Union in 1934, Soviet literature for all its variety "must be organized as a unified and collective whole [*edinoe kollektivnoe tseloe*], as a mighty weapon of socialist culture."⁷⁰ This would, in effect, amalgamate the literary traditions of the ethnic minorities with the Euro-Russian tradition that predominated in Soviet Russia. The project of cultural assimilation under Russian leadership and the persecution of the "bourgeois nationalists" among the minority peoples, at its height in 1937, has in recent histories become a standard negative example of Stalinist nefariousness.

It might be assumed that Fox is calling for a "multi-cultured," "multi-national" Soviet Union when in *Genghis Khan* he commends the Khan for eliminating the borders that impede the sort of progress that can be brought about by fruitful exchanges between peoples. He also foregrounds the importance of a strong, centralized government in the national interest – for example, "the absence of a strong central power made it impossible to check the greed of the feudal officials and generals." In consequence, the young feudal society "would welcome the appearance of a strong figure who could impose order on all the turbulence, build a nation out of these quarrelling chiefs," and "the far-sighted ... should turn with a sigh of relief towards the iron discipline of the Mongol army and the organizing genius of Genghis-khan."⁷¹

As we see, in *Genghis Khan* the great progressive force that can transform the East is no longer (Soviet) "Russia," as it was in Fox's two books of the 1920s on Central Asia, but now by implication a leader of genius. In other words, this book can be read as composed in the service of a cult of personality. As Fox puts it at one point, "the greatest commanders ... have always therefore been men ... whose terrible genius possessed something legendary and god-like. Among these few world geniuses, alongside Alexander and Napoleon, Chingis takes his place."⁷²

Genghis Khan has, then, been inscribed into the *European* pantheon of "god-like" military commanders, alongside Alexander and Napoleon. Many leftist intellectuals of this time were also impressed by the way history's great conquerors had melded disparate and even warring principalities to the common good. Lukács, for example, in his second dissertation about Hegel's *Phenomenology of Mind*, on which he worked during his Moscow stay in the 1930s, wrote enthusiastically about Hegel's veneration for Napoleon as a great unifier;⁷³ after Jena, Hegel had celebrated Napoleon's victory over the Prussians as the victory of civilization over feudal barbarism. But important to Hegel's assessment of Napoleon was his own consistent support for the policy of the Confederation of the Rhine.

Some Western readers today might find odious Fox's espousal of territorial amalgamation under an all-powerful leader and his rationalizations of the use of violence. He had, as it were, "migrated" too far from his Oxbridge mindset in the direction of endorsing Stalinist authoritarianism. Unlike Fox, Koestler and Hughes in their memoirs from the Cold War years included apostrophes to the Great Conquerors but more as expressions of a romantic attachment to the exotic than as rationalizations for extreme measures. There was another reason why European leftists of that earlier moment when Shklovsky and Fox's coverage of the Great Khan appeared might want to stress the importance of geopolitical and cultural amalgamation. At the time, Stalin's Soviet Union was the only major country opposing fascism, a fact that drew quite unlikely suspects into the Soviet cultural orbit. Consequently, I would argue, to see Fox as having been guided in writing this book by the new "porthole" of the cult of personality is too glib an assessment. In 1935, as Fox was writing this book, there was a historic meeting of anti-fascist intellectuals from all over the world in Paris called the Congress for the Defence of Culture. Fox attended it as a member of the delegation from the British Section of Writers' International, as did Mulk Raj Anand (classified as British for this purpose) and also John Lehmann, the editor of *New Writing* and so from Fox's literary London set. Auden and Isherwood had been invited to attend and also to go to the 1937 sequel in Spain, but they waivered. However, Auden and several other Western leftists covered in this article – Arthur Koestler, George Orwell, Mulk Raj Anand, Egon Erwin Kisch, and Langston Hughes – went to Spain for another reason, which was to support, in various capacities, the embattled Republican side in the Spanish Civil War. Most of these writers were soon given pause by the intensifying repressiveness of Soviet officialdom, both in Spain and in the Soviet Union. In time, most of them undertook a reverse intellectual "migration," away from the Soviet orbit, but not Fox. One can only speculate about the course his political life might have taken had it not been cut short at the very beginning of that dark year, 1937.

Fox's untimely death was in a sense timely because it meant that he missed most of the Great Purge, the Molotov–Ribbentrop Pact, and the other events in a series that so strongly challenged the faith of European leftists that "Moscow"-oriented internationalist institutions could lead the world in a campaign against fascism and similar political scourges. Unlike those of Isherwood, Auden, Orwell, Koestler, Wittfogel, and many others (but not including Kisch), Fox's intellectual journey Eastward, together with his embrace of Marxism-Leninism, was no peregrination, but a true "red migration."

Notes

1 Admittedly, the amount of time a person has to stay in a new place in order for that to count as a "migration" is subject to dispute.
2 "Pravka v redaktsiiu 'Deili Uorker,'" RGASPI f. 495, op. 198, d. 391, l. 26; A.P. Kiselev, *Ral'f Foks – publitsist kompartii Velikobritanii* (Moscow: Izdatel'stvo moskovskogo universiteta, 1961), 3–5.
3 Christopher Isherwood, "Travel-Diary," in W.H. Auden and Christopher Isherwood, *Journey to a War* (London: Faber and Faber, 1939), 234.
4 Alan Wilde, *Christopher Isherwood* (New York: Twayne, 1971), 80–1.
5 RGALI f. 216, op. 1, d. 430 (Fond Zozulia, E.D.), 1.
6 Ralph Fox, *People of the Steppes* (London: Constable, 1925), 201.
7 Daniel L. Schachter, *The Seven Sins of Memory: How the Mind Forgets* (New York: Houghton Mifflin, 2001).
8 "Avtobiografiia Ral'fa Foksa 3 oktiabria 1929 g.," RGASPI (Komintern) f. 495, op. 198, d. 39, l. 2828; Kiselev, *Ral'f Foks*, 39.
9 Michael Freeman, *Ralph Fox Telling the Times: An English Vista to His Politics of Literature* (2009), unpublished manuscript in the Marx Memorial Library, Clerkenwell Green, London, 77.
10 "Avtobiografiia Ral'fa Foksa," 3. Vii.32, RGASPI (Komintern) f. 495, op. 198, d. 39, l. 28, l. 4.
11 Freeman, *Ralph Fox*, 87; Kiselev, *Ral'f Foks*, 22.
12 Glyn Salton-Cox, "Cobbett and the Comintern: Transnational Provincialism and Revolutionary Desire from the Popular Front to the New Left," PhD diss., Yale University, 2013.
13 Don Hallett, "'The Hand that History Dealt': Ralph Fox (1900–1936)," in *Transactions of the Halifax Antiquarian Society* 17, new series 2009, 113; Freeman, *Ralph Fox*, 27; Ralph Fox, "Catching Tatars," *Daily Worker*, 8 January 1936.
14 Freeman, "Ralph Fox," 54. (I have not been able to ascertain the exact topic of the proposed dissertation.)
15 Listed as a "praktikant referent Vostochnogo otdela," RGASPI Komintern f. 495, op. 198, d. 391 (Angliia), l. 16; Security Service File, NAGB KV 2/1377, 15, 28, 92; Freeman, *Ralph Fox*, 207; Hallett, "'The Hand that History Dealt,'" 114.
16 RGASPI Komintern f. 495, op, 198, d. 391 (Angliia), l. 26; *Seven Writers of the English Left: A Bibliography of Literature and Politics, 1916–1980*, compiled by Alan Munton and Alan Young (New York and London: Garland, 1981), 117–18.
17 Volume 1 of *Literaturnoe nasledstvo* (1931) contains the correspondence of Engels with Paul Ernst; no. 2 of 1932 contains the correspondence between Engels and Margaret Harkness; no. 3 of 1932 contains the correspondence of

Marx and Engels with Lassalle about his play *Franz von Sickingen* (the most complete version of this published to that date); and nos. 7–8 of 1933 contain Engels's letters to Minna Kautsky about her novel *The Old and the New*.
18 Raymond Williams, "Cambridge," in *Politics and Letters: Interviews with New Left Review* (London: NLB, 1979).
19 Ral'f Foks, *Roman i narod*, perevod s angliiskogo i primechaniia V.P. Isakova, vstuplenie R. Miller-Budnitskaia (Leningrad: Goslitizdat, 1939); G. Lukach, "'Roman i narod'," *Literaturnoe obozrenie*, 1939, no. 16, 45.
20 Ralph Fox, *Marx, Engels, and Lenin on Ireland* (New York: International, 1940).
21 "Avtobiografiia Ral'fa Foksa," RGASPI Komintern f. 495 op. 198 d. 391 (Angliia), ll. 34–5.
22 Kiselev, *Ral'f Foks*, 45; *Diskussiia ob aziatskom sposobe proizvodstva po dokladu M. Godesa. Obshchestvo marksistov-vostokovedov pri leningradskom otdelenii Kommunisticheskoi akademii i Leningradskom vostochnom institute im. A. Enukidze* (Leningrad: Gos. sotsial'no-ėkonomicheskoe izdatel'stvo, 1931); R. Foks, "Vzgliady Marksa i Ėngel'sa na aziatskii sposob proizvodstva i ikh istochniki," *Letopisi marksizma* (Institut K. Marksa i F. Ėngel'sa), no. 3 (13) (1930), 3–29.
23 K. Marks, "Pis'ma ob Indii," *Letopisi marksizma*, no. 3 (1927), 36–55; letter of Bill Alexander, 2 May 1978, Marx Memorial Museum and Archive, Ralph Fox files; *Seven Writers of the English Left*, 117–18.
24 Ralph Fox, *The Colonial Policy of British Imperialism* (London: Martin Lawrence, 1933); R. Foks, *Kolonial'naia politika Anglii*, trans. N. Kamionskaia (Moscow and Leningrad: Moskovskii rabochii, 1931); Ral'f Foks, *Angliiskaia kolonial'naia politika (populiarnyi ocherk)* (Moscow and Leningrad: Gos. Sotsial'no-ėkonomicheskoe izdatel'stvo, 1934).
25 Sajjad Zaheer in *Indian Literature*, no. 2 for 1952, cited in *Marxist Cultural Movement in India: Chronicles and Documents (1936–1947)*, vol. 1, compiled and edited by Sudhi Pradhan, 2nd ed. (Calcutta: New Rooplekha Press, 1985), 28; Mulk Raj Anand, "Preface," in Ralph Fox, *The Novel and the People*, 2nd ed. (London: Cobbett, 1944), 9–10.
26 Katerina Clark, "Indian Leftist Writers of the 1930s Maneuver between India, London and Moscow: The Case of Mulk Raj Anand and His Patron Ralph Fox," for a special issue of *Kritika* on South Asia, 18, no. 1 (Winter 2017), 63–87.
27 Foks, *Kolonial'naia politika Anglii*, 17, 38–41; Foks, *Angliiskaia kolonial'naia politika*, 34–7.
28 Letter of Kraevskii of 3.7.1936, RGASPI Komintern f. 495 op. 198 d. 391 (Angliia), ll. 1, 23–5; Hallett, "'The Hand that History Dealt,'" 114. Fox had recently published *The People's Republic of Mongolia* (1935).
29 Note the reproaches of S. Dinamov, President of Anglo American Commission, International Association of Revolutionary Writers,

Moscow, in a letter to Fox of 19 November 1934 (S. Dimanov [sic], NAGB [National Archive of Great Britain] 67a O.F. 42/5 in KV 2/1377, 77; NAGB KV 2/1376, 55.
30 RGASPI (Komintern) F. 495, op. 198, d. 39, l. 35.
31 Fox, *People of the Steppes*; see also Ralph Fox, *Storming Heaven* (London: Constable, 1928).
32 Compare Karl Marx, "Chinese Affairs," *Die Presse*, 7 July 1862; Karl Marx, "Revolution in China and In Europe," in *New York Daily Tribune*, 14 June 1853; and V.I. Lenin, "Obnovlënnyi Kitai," *Polnoe sobranie sochinenii*, vol. 22 (Moscow: Institut marksizma-leninizma pri TsK KPSS, 1958); see also V.I. Lenin, "Probuzhdenie Azii," *Pravda*, 7 May 1913.
33 V.I. Lenin, "Doklad na 2-om vserossiskom s"ezde kommunisticheskikh organizatsii narodov Vostoka," 20 December 1919, reprinted in Lenin, *Polnoe Sobranie sochinenii*, vol. 39 (Moscow: Politizdat, 1970), 330.
34 Fox, *Storming Heaven*, 158.
35 Fox, *Storming Heaven*, 160.
36 Fox, *Storming Heaven*, 114.
37 Fox, *People of the Steppes*, 193.
38 Fox, *People of the Steppes*, 143.
39 Denis Roak, "Malraux and T.E. Lawrence," *Modern Language Review* 61, no. 2 (April 1966): 218–23.
40 The review appeared in *Sunday Daily Worker* for 14 August 1927; see Freeman, *Ralph Fox* (2009).
41 Fox, *Storming Heaven*, 158.
42 Fox, *Storming Heaven*, 113.
43 This passage is in chapter 2, "Departure of the Disciples from Jerusalem. – Second Galilean Life of Jesus," in Ernest Renan's *The Apostles* (1866).
44 Fox, *Storming Heaven*, 170.
45 Fox, *People of the Steppes*, 2.
46 Fox, *People of the Steppes*, 165.
47 This book was originally meant to appear in separate editions in five languages – Russian, German, Ukrainian, Georgian, Armenian – but only the German version was published (in Kharkiv).
48 On Hughes and Koestler's Cold War–era accounts of their travels, see chapter 6 of this book.
49 For example, Langston Hughes, *A Negro Looks at Soviet Central Asia* (Moscow and Leningrad: Co-operative Publishing Society of Foreign Workers in the USSR, 1934), 5, 8, 12–15, 28, 32, 35–7.
50 *The Invisible Writing* being the second volume of *Arrow in the Blue*, an autobiography by Arthur Koestler (New York: Macmillan, 1954), 64.
51 Egon Erwin Kisch, "Rings um das Grab von Tamerlan," *Asien gründlich verändert* (Berlin: Erich Reiss Verlag, 1932), 44.

52 Arthur Koestler, *Von weissen Nächten und roten Tagen* [originally published by Staatsverlag der deutschen Minderheiten der UdSSR, in Kharkiv, 1934] (Vienna: Promedi, 2013), 123–31.
53 M. Gor'kii in *Pervyi vsesoiuznyi s"ezd sovetskikh pisatelei, 1934: Stenograficheskii otchët*, ed. I.K. Luppol (Moscow: Khudozhestvennaia literatura, 1934), 5.
54 *Krasnyi arkhiv* 75 (1936): 6. Publication of this text was delayed, and it appeared in *Pravda* only on 27 January 1936, but it was cited by historians already in 1934, and one might assume that its general drift was widely known in intellectual circles.
55 Langston Hughes, "Farewell to Samarkand," in *I Wonder as I Wander: An Autobiographical Journey* (New York: Reinhart, 1956), 184.
56 Ralph Fox, *Genghis Khan*, with 8 ills. and 2 maps (London: John Lane the Bodley Head, 1936).
57 Among Fox's sources were B.Ia. Vladimirtsov's *Obshchestvennyi stroi mongolov* (Leningrad: Izd-vo Akademii nauk SSSR, 1934); his essay, *The Life of Genghis Khan*, the English translation of which appeared in 1930; and V.V. Bartol'd's *Turkestan* and *Turkestan Down to the Mongol Invasion*.
58 I.R. [i.e., N.S. Trubetzkoi], *Nasledie Chingiskhana. Vzgliad na russkuiu istoriiu ne s Zapada a s Vostoka* (Berlin: Evraziiskoe knigoizdatel'stvo, 1925).
59 Fox, *Genghis Khan*, 21.
60 RGALI, f. 1923, op. 1, d. 520, l. 1; Naum Kleiman, "Ferganskii kanal i bashnia Tamerlana," *Kinovedcheskie zapiski*, nos. 102–3 (2013): 8–9.
61 Fox, *Genghis Khan*, 12.
62 V. Shklovskii, *Marko Polo*, Vvedenie i kommentarii i redaktsiia K. I. Kunina in the series Zhizn' zamechatel'nykh liudei (Moscow: Zhurnal'no-gazetnoe ob"edinenie, 1936); note: an earlier and very different version for children came out in 1931.
63 Fox, *Genghis Khan*, 213–14.
64 For example, Fox, *Genghis Khan*, 96.
65 This information is based on a conversation with Evgeny Dobrenko of 9 May 2021, and on his research for a book on multi-national Soviet literature, which he is now writing; see also *Mezhdu molotom i nakoval'nei. Soiuz sovetskikh pisatelei SSSR. Dokumenty i kommentarii*, vol. 1, 1925-Iun' 1941 (Moscow: Rosspen, 2011), 783.
66 Fox, *Genghis Khan*, 50.
67 Fox, *Genghis Khan*, 249.
68 For example, Fox, *Genghis Khan*, 133.
69 Fox, *Genghis Khan*, 201, 204, 205.
70 *Pervyi vsesoiuznyi s"ezd sovetskikh pisatelei, 1934: Stenograficheskii otchët*, ed. I.K. Luppol (Moscow: Khudozhestvennaia literatura, 1934), 17.

71 Fox, *Genghis Khan*, 136, 67, 188, respectively. Incidentally, Fox's position here also bears comparison with two novels by Heinrich Mann, a leader of the anti-fascist movement (*Die Jugend des Königs Henri Quatre* and *Die Vollendung des Königs Henri Quatre*), which appeared in Russian translation in the 1930s and attracted a great deal of positive critical attention.
72 Fox, *Genghis Khan*, 206.
73 The keynote speech, "Resistance to Theory," given by Galin Tihanov on Zoom on 11 September 2020 for the conference "Red Migrations."

PART III

Identities

8 Revolutionary Violence with Chinese Characteristics: Chinese Migrants in Early Soviet Literature

EDWARD TYERMAN

"We love death! We love it very much!"
(Мы любим смерть! Мы очень ее любим!)
– Chinese soldiers in Andrei Platonov's *Chevengur* (1927–8)

In November 1918, Winston Churchill spoke to his constituents in Dundee, Scotland, about the ongoing civil war in Russia. The Bolsheviks, Churchill declared, were reducing Russia "to an animal form of Barbarism," maintaining their power by "bloody and wholesale butcheries and murders carried out to a large extent by Chinese executions and armoured cars ... Civilization is being completely extinguished."[1] Churchill's identification of "Chinese executions" as a primary agent of civilization's demise evokes the international character of the Russian Civil War, in which his government had intervened on the opposite side. Significant numbers of Chinese soldiers, most of whom had come to the Russian Empire as economic migrants in the late nineteenth century, fought on the side of the Red Army (and, to a much lesser degree, the White). These were not the only international troops to fight in the Red Army, which also contained Romanians, Poles, Czechs, Germans, Hungarians, and Latvians.[2] Nonetheless, the presence of Chinese soldiers in the Red ranks received particular attention. Churchill's account of the Red Army as a barbaric horde spearheaded by Chinese executioners echoed the thrust of much White propaganda. One notorious poster from the period shows a grotesquely Semitic Trotsky leading a band of Chinese soldiers engaged in mass executions (figure 8.1). This image brings together the two dominant racial phobias of late Imperial Russia, both themselves transnational: antisemitism, and the complex of fears around East Asian migration and a modernizing Japan known as the Yellow Peril.[3] Transferred to the context of the Civil War, the

Figure 8.1. "Peace and Freedom in Sovdepia," Kharkov OSVAG (Information-Propaganda Agency of the Armed Forces of Southern Russia), 1919. From the holdings of the Russian State Library.

message of such images was clear. The Red Army constituted a foreign, hostile, invading force driven by ethnic others, whose especial savagery derived from their lack of social connection to the Russian nation.[4]

Soviet historiography of the Civil War would subsequently commemorate these Chinese partisans as heroic internationalists, risking their lives for a revolution of global significance.[5] However, if we turn to the representations of the Civil War that filled early Soviet literature, we find that the Chinese partisan appears there as a constant yet more ambiguous figure. A striking number of major early Soviet writers, including Isaac Babel, Artem Veselyi, Boris Pil'niak, Vsevolod Ivanov, Nikolai Ostrovskii, Andrei Platonov, and Mikhail Bulgakov, foregrounded the figure of the Chinese partisan in their fictional accounts of the Civil War. This chapter contends that the Chinese migrant soldier became a recurring presence in their writing because he concentrated within himself a set of ideological tensions over the social and historical meaning of the Revolution and the Civil War, tensions that revolved around questions of socialist internationalism, national identity, and racial difference. These migrant workers who fought and died for the Russian Revolution offered a vivid symbol of the possibilities of internationalist solidarity. At the same time, even the most pro-Soviet writers in this group shaped their literary images of the Chinese partisan under the influence of biologized conceptions of racial difference that emerged from the transnational discourse of the Yellow Peril, which developed in Europe and its settler colonies as a response to the rise of Japan and the expansion of Chinese and Korean migration in the second half of the nineteenth century.[6] In Russia, the discourse of the Yellow Peril was closely connected to Chinese migration into the Russian Far East. The repeated appearance of the Chinese migrant soldier in these texts thus offers what Frederic Jameson, following the Bakhtin Circle, called an "ideologeme": a literary figure that serves as a point of collision, where contradictory ideological discourses meet, clash, and interpenetrate.[7] The authority of internationalist Marxism to explain the political instability and transnational labour relations of the early twentieth century competes here with a cluster of rival discourses that would frame these same phenomena in terms of civilizational and racial difference.

Around twenty million people migrated out of China between 1840 and 1940, fleeing poverty and the destabilizations of successive rebellions, revolutions, and civil wars.[8] Chinese migration into the Russian Empire was concentrated from the mid-nineteenth century in the Priamur and Primor'e regions, which had been ceded from Chinese control by the treaties of Aigun (1858) and Peking (1860).[9] After the Qing government loosened restrictions on migration into Manchuria, somewhere between 200,000 and 500,000 Chinese migrants entered the Russian Far East between 1878 and 1910.[10] In contrast to Korean migrants, who tended to come as families and settle, Chinese migrants were predominantly single men engaged in seasonal labour.[11] Nonetheless, by 1912 there were around 200,000 Chinese people living in the Amur and Primorsky oblasts.[12] Many of these migrants worked in gold mines: by 1910, 83 per cent of the gold diggers in the Amur region were Chinese.[13] Others worked on the construction of the Trans-Siberian and other railway projects. In both cases, their wages were substantially lower than those of their Russian counterparts.[14] In the context of Russian imperial expansion into East Asia, the presence of these migrants fuelled fears of a demographic invasion from China, fears that from the mid-1890s increasingly spoke an international language of race and Yellow Peril.[15] In 1910 the Russian government implemented labour and land-lease policies that sought to restrict Chinese immigration.[16] Following the outbreak of the First World War, however, Chinese migrant workers began arriving to satisfy an increased demand for cheap labour within Russia, with around 160,000 entering the Russian Empire between January 1915 and April 1917.[17] This marked the first time that Chinese workers migrated in significant numbers into the western part of the Empire. They played a central role in building the Murmansk railway; they also worked in factories and extractive enterprises in the Urals, Donbass, Belorussia, and Karelia and in the cities of Petersburg, Ekaterinburg, Luhansk, and Odessa.[18]

The revolutionary year of 1917 found as many as 300,000 Chinese migrants in Russia.[19] Whether through material need or political commitment, many joined the Red Army: various estimates suggest that between 30,000 and 70,000 Chinese fought on the side of the Reds in the Civil War.[20] After the war ended in Bolshevik victory, many Chinese migrants settled down to run laundries and other enterprises in major Soviet cities. The 1926 census recorded around 100,000 Chinese people in the Soviet Union, concentrated in Vladivostok and the Far East, with 10,000 in European Russia.[21] Walter Benjamin's account of the Soviet capital in "Moscow Diary" (1926) notes the presence of Chinese street traders selling artificial paper flowers and describes the street signs for laundries: "Shirts are usually painted on a board bearing the words *Kitaiskaia prachechnaia* – Chinese laundry."[22] Vladimir Mayakovsky's 1927 poem "Moskovskii Kitai" acknowledges the racial animosity directed at Chinese laundry workers in 1920s Moscow, placing ethnic insults in the mouths of children: "Mal'chishki orut: – U-u-u! Kitaezy! – / Povernetsia, vzgliadom podariv, / ot kotorogo zazhglos' litso osennee ..." (Little boys shout: – Oo-ooh! *Kitayozy*! / He turns, struck by a look / that inflames his autumnal face ...).[23] Nonetheless, the poem ends with the hope that China's imminent revolution – expected to emerge from a Comintern-sponsored United Front between the Chinese Nationalist and Communist Parties – will affirm these migrants as internationalist allies.[24] With the collapse of that alliance and the expulsion of Comintern advisers from China in 1927, Soviet hopes for a fraternal Chinese revolution faded. Instead, the xenophobia of the Stalinist period, fuelled by antagonism with Nationalist China and the growing threat of Japan in East Asia, caused many Soviet Chinese to flee back to China. Others were deported or sent to the Gulag. By the late 1930s, the Soviet Chinese population had disappeared.[25]

The Chinese economic migrants who joined the Red Army also entered Russian literature, where they became symbolic figures burdened with expressing the era's conflicting understandings of the "international": as utopian promise and social threat, as revolutionary triumphalism and migration anxiety. Within the parameters of this volume on Marxism and transnational mobility, then, my chapter takes up this symbolic figure as a site where Marxist-Leninist internationalism and biologized racial discourse vied for the ideological authority to explain the movement of human beings across national borders. At a moment of enormous social upheaval and the collapse of old orders, in a world increasingly globalized by transnational flows of capital, labour, and media, the figure of the Chinese migrant soldier served early Soviet literature as a test case for the limits of the post-revolutionary community. The internationalism of the Bolsheviks and the Comintern described a world unevenly transformed by the forces of a global imperialist capitalism, giving rise in turn to a global anti-imperial alliance of workers and the colonized. (Indeed, these anti-imperial aspects of Bolshevik Marxism played a central role in its appeal among Chinese migrants and within China itself.)[26] But socialist internationalism was just one of the ideological prisms through which the meaning of the Chinese migrant could be processed. Under the Yellow Peril xenophobia that shaped Russian social consciousness in the period immediately before the war, this figure had come to mark precisely the limit of community, the quintessential Other. Fears of invasion from the east, by military force or demographic infiltration, had permeated late imperial society, from official pronouncements to popular journalism.[27] The transnational discourse of Yellow Peril was compounded in Russia with cultural memories of the Mongol conquest to magnify anxieties over Chinese migration and the rise of Japan, anxieties that only grew following Russia's defeat in the Russo-Japanese War of 1905. Indeed, V.I. Diatlov suggests that the collective enemy represented by the "yellow threat" played a central role in the formation of a modern mass political consciousness in Russia in this period.[28] In the sphere of literary culture, the "Panmongolist" prophecies of Vladimir Solov'ev, which interpreted Japan's victory over China in the 1894 Sino-Japanese War as the harbinger of an apocalyptic invasion from the East, exerted a powerful influence over a whole generation of Russian modernists.[29] If socialist internationalism was going to succeed in becoming a mass ideology, it would have to displace and even invert the relationship to East Asia inscribed by the discourse of the Yellow Peril. The figure of the Chinese literary partisan staged the conflict between these ideologies on the pages of early Soviet literature.

My argument will assess the symbolic role of the Chinese literary partisan in two stages. In the first part, fragmented modernist texts by Babel, Veselyi, and Pil'niak deploy the Chinese migrant soldier as a symbol for a world out of joint, where established borders and social distinctions are collapsing. Echoing the impurity anxieties of Yellow Peril ideology, the international appears here as the confusion of nations, a confusion expressed by linguistic distortion and an aesthetic of the grotesque. In the work of Pil'niak, however, this confusion comes to signify a shared experience of revolutionary modernity as disruptive, enabling a sense of civilizational commonality between Russia and China despite the abiding inscription of racial difference. The second part of the chapter considers the Chinese soldiers in the Civil War tales of Ivanov, Ostrovskii, Platonov, and Bulgakov as revolutionary allies, even heroes, who nevertheless remain linguistically and physically other. Undergirding this ambiguous symbolic function, I suggest, was a transnationally circulating, racialized discourse about the Chinese as physiologically different, most importantly in their relationship to pain. This global discourse about the characteristics of Chinese migrant workers – impervious to pain, and thus able to suffer physical deprivation and work harder for less – transmutes into the figure of a Chinese soldier who is fearless and willing to sacrifice himself without hesitation. The qualities of a feared worker become those of an ideal revolutionary soldier, although the anxiety of otherness remains. Thus the figure of the Chinese migrant soldier could celebrate the possibilities of internationalist allegiance while also perpetuating notions of absolute racial difference.

Out of Place: Chinese Migrant Soldiers, Modernist Fragmentation, and Post-Revolutionary Confusion

According to Viktor Shklovsky, Isaac Babel spent the Petrograd winter of 1919 writing "always one and the same story about two Chinese in a brothel ... The Chinese and the women kept changing. They got younger, they got older, they smashed the windows, they beat the woman, they tried it every which way."[30] Although Shklovsky describes Babel leaving Petrograd with the story unfinished, a short text on this theme appeared in 1923 under the title "Khodia" – a colloquial and somewhat derogatory term used in Russian to refer to Chinese migrants in the early twentieth century.[31] Babel was not the first writer to take up the figure of the Chinese migrant. Aleksei Remizov's short story "Kitaets," published in 1916, uses a young Russian boy's fear of a Chinese migrant trader to explore the mechanisms of xenophobia in the context of the First World War.[32] But Babel's dense two-page fragment may be the first time that a Chinese Red soldier appears at the centre of a literary text.

Outside a café on Nevsky Prospect in the dead of a cold winter night stand a prostitute named Glafira and an older man, Aristarkh Terent'ich.

Their speech marks them as members of the former ruling class, and Aristarkh Terent'ich rails against the foreign soldiers propping up the new authorities. "They depend on the Latvians, and the Latvians are Mongols, Glafira," he explains, positioning the Latvian Rifle regiments that supported the Bolsheviks as the latest in a long line of violent foreign invaders. Right on cue, a Chinese man in a leather jacket – the symbolic uniform of the Bolsheviks – emerges from the dark street and propositions Glafira in exchange for a pound of bread. Glafira asks that Aristarkh Terent'ich, who she says is her godfather, be allowed to come with them and sleep by the wall. At the hotel, they drink *khanzha* (i.e. *baijiu*, Chinese grain alcohol); an ellipsis omits the sexual act. As the Chinese man sets off into the night, he wakes Aristarkh Terent'ich and indicates that he, too, should copulate with his god-daughter. "Get away, you dog," she objects, "your Chinese has finished me off" (*ubil*, lit. "killed me").[33] But the Chinese man insists, in heavily accented broken Russian: "– Mi drug, – skazal kitaets. – On – mozhna. E, sterf' …" ("My friend," said the Chinese man. "He can. Eh, slut …")[34] The mangled speech of the migrant here expresses not exclusion but power; the members of the former privileged classes are reduced to obedient supplicants. Babel's story also draws on a wider social perception of Chinese migrants, who were overwhelmingly male, as a sexual threat.[35] Indeed, the story's two sexual encounters are both coded as socially destabilizing: one murderously exogamous, the other excessively endogamous. Babel's short, dark fragment links the collapse of the social order to the enigmatic figure of a Chinese migrant in a leather jacket wandering through post-revolutionary Russia.

Artem Veselyi's short story "Vol'nitsa," published in *LEF* in 1924, likewise places a Chinese migrant at the centre of its account of post-revolutionary confusion. In 1920, Veselyi (the pseudonym of Nikolai Ivanovich Kochkurov) had edited the newspaper of the Red Cossack agit-train as it travelled through the Kuban and Don regions of Ukraine, where some of the earliest Chinese Red brigades had been formed.[36] "Vol'nitsa" presents the chaos of the Civil War through an anarchic, almost plotless stream of linguistic heterogeneity that resists any sense of semantic hierarchy or narrative order. The text jumbles together regional dialecticisms, snippets of Ukrainian, non-standard orthography, and passages of typographical innovation that violate punctuation and even spacing. Into this chaotic linguistic world enters a Chinese worker-soldier, a *khodia* or *kitayoza*:

Стонут качаются дома. Пляшут улицы. Прислонился ходя к России.
По неизвестной причине плачет ходя разливается

Вольгуля мольгуля
Выкатились из России ребятки и навалились на ходю
    Хам
        Гам
            Китаеза
                Черепашьи яйца
                    Что обо-
значают твои слезы?
                Вольгуля мольгуля
Моя лаботала лаботала, все денихи пло-
лаботала – папилоса нету, халепа нету
Ха ха ха
    Гу гу гу[37]

[The houses groan sway. The streets dance. A *khodia* has leaned / against Russia. For an unknown reason the *khodia* weeps and sobs / Vol'gulia mol'gulia / Some boys rolled out of Russia and fell upon the *khodia* / Taunting / Ruckus / *Kitayoza* / Tortoise eggs / What do your / tears mean? / Vol'gulia mol'gulia / Me worked worked, all money worked / through – no cigarette, no bread / Ha ha ha / Gu gu gu]

This migrant's speech suggests Veselyi's passing familiarity with Chinese Pidgin Russian (CPR), a contact language that developed in areas of Sino-Russian economic contact – Kyakhta, Manchuria, and the Russian Far East – from the late seventeenth century.[38] The use of the possessive pronoun "moia" in place of the personal pronoun "ia" is a standard element of CPR, as is the use of the colloquial negative form "netu" at the end of a sentence.[39] The presence of feminine past tense endings ("labotala") may emphasize the linguistic strangeness of a male subject referring to himself with a female pronoun, but it also reflects the tendency in CPR to form past tenses by adding the Chinese suffix *le* 了 – placed after verbs to denote a completed action – to Russian imperative forms (the standard verb form in CPR).[40] Other terms suggest some superficial knowledge of Chinese. The phrase "tortoise egg" (王八蛋 *wangbadan*) is a well-known Chinese insult: Veselyi places it in the mouths of Russian-speaking soldiers, suggesting the spread of such terms together with Chinese migrants. "Gu gu gu" could be the onomatopoeia *gu* 呱, used to denote the crying of a child.

Veselyi is one of several writers from this period whose accounts of Chinese migrants display a generalized awareness of Chinese Pidgin Russian. Unsurprisingly, the most extensive engagements with this pidgin come from writers who spent time in the Russian Far East, such as the prominent LEF member Sergei Tret'iakov and the poet Aleksandr

Alekseevich Bogdanov.[41] However, even writers without direct experience of that region display a vague sense of CPR, reflecting the spread of this contact language alongside Chinese migration. Hence Mayakovsky places the Siberian dialectical term *shibko* ("very," *ochen'*), a common lexical item in CPR, in the mouth of his Chinese laundry worker in "Moskovskii Kitai."[42] A contact language born out of a material history of trade and economic migration, Chinese Pidgin Russian takes on specific artistic valences as it enters the linguistic order of a literary text. In "Vol'nitsa," a text whose linguistic heterogeneity already expresses social chaos, pidgin speech defines a character who is doubly displaced by migration and war and whose misery cannot be understood by those around him ("What do your tears mean?," ask the Russian soldiers). Recruitment into the Red Army amounts to little more than joining a drunken debauch: the remainder of the Chinese character's utterances consist of the pidgin declaration "Moia kalaso" (me good), until the point where he vomits from too much wine.[43] In Veselyi's disordered text, this hybrid contact language expresses a Babelian confusion that cannot resolve itself into a new social relation.

When the figure of the Chinese migrant appears in the Civil War texts of Boris Pil'niak, these themes of distortion and displacement find expression through an aesthetic of the grotesque. Pil'niak's seminal novel *The Naked Year* (*Golyi god*, 1921) plays with the Moscow toponym "Kitai-gorod," which translates as "China-town" yet refers to an old district of the city with no history of Chinese settlement.[44] Pil'niak's "Kitai-gorod" is a bustling commercial district by day, "all bowler-hatted, altogether Europe."[45] At night, however, a grotesque figuration of China emerges into the empty city: "And then, in this desert, out of the courtyards and from under the gates it crawled: China without a bowler hat on, the Celestial Empire, which lies somewhere beyond the steppes to the East, beyond the Great Stone Wall, and looks at the world with slanting eyes, like the buttons of Russian soldiers' greatcoats."[46]

Philip Thomson defines the grotesque as "the unresolved clash of incompatibles in work and response," an aesthetic of unstable ambivalence.[47] Hence, for Thomson, "the grotesque mode in art and literature tends to be prevalent in societies and eras marked by strife, radical change, or disorientation."[48] Pil'niak's China combines incompatible elements to produce a visual description impossible to visualize. While it seems comic to confirm that China is hatless, there is something creepy about an empire that crawls. This empire also has eyes, which Pil'niak both racializes and likens to an object from the realm of the inanimate: the buttons from a soldier's greatcoat. China migrates through Pil'niak's Russia as a repeating motif, showing up again at a market in Nizhny Novgorod. A third appearance at an abandoned factory heightens the grotesque effect by granting those inanimate button-eyes a sinister grin: "China, the soldier's buttons grin (how they can grin!)."[49]

Readers of *The Naked Year* tend to interpret this xenophobic image of China as a symbol for the Asiatic element within Russia's own identity, part of the geographical obsession with Russia's liminal position between East and West that Pil'niak inherited from Solov'ev and his Symbolist epigones.[50] Europe, the West, represents activity, efficiency, and capitalist modernity. China, as East, is linked to inactivity and the desert – an understanding of *kitaishchina* as historical stagnation that entered Russian intellectual discourse of the nineteenth century from Hegel's philosophy of history.[51] Pil'niak's novel, on this reading, seeks to outline an authentic Russian cultural identity that might emerge between these two civilizational poles, a third way to be uncovered by the revolution's transformative violence.[52] Less commented upon is the fact that Pil'niak presents China as a *migrant*. "This is from his, China's, wanderings" (Eto iz ego, Kitaia, brodiazhestv), begins the section of the novel titled "Kitai-gorod."[53] China's spatial location is ambiguous, both proximate and distant. Crawling out into the deserted streets of Moscow, China is simultaneously "somewhere beyond the steppes to the East, beyond the Great Stone Wall." This China emerges at spaces of trade and industry, spaces shaped by the same transnational forces of economic modernization that produced large-scale Chinese labour migration into the Russian Empire. This China, then, is not an immobile East, but an East that is sinister precisely because it *can* move. Just as Pil'niak's visual descriptions combine elements from separate spheres to produce a grotesque effect, so his China has moved from its proper place, beyond the Wall, and now wanders across Russia. The grotesque serves here, then, as an aesthetic of migration. Within the fragmented chaos of *The Naked Year*'s modernist poetics, the wandering of Pil'niak's China expresses the collapse of borders between discrete national and cultural spaces.

By contrast with the abstract, symbolist China of *The Naked Year*, Pil'niak gives a more historically concrete account of the relationship between Chinese migration and the Russian Revolution in the short story "Sankt-Piter-Burkh." Written shortly after *The Naked Year*, and first published in Berlin in 1922, this enigmatic text interweaves Russian and Chinese histories as they oscillate between imperial construction and revolutionary destruction. The weight of historical and cultural detail on China in the story suggests some extensive secondary reading on Pil'niak's part.[54] The opening pages establish a historical parallel between Russia and China by connecting "the First Emperor, Peter Alexeevich" to Shi Huangdi, the First Emperor of China (also known as Qin Shihuang 秦始皇, 259–210 BC), who founded the Qin dynasty, united China into a single empire, and began construction of the Great Wall (figure 8.2).⁵⁵ Peter and Shi Huangdi are linked through construction in stone, although one builds a wall to keep foreigners out and another builds a city-window to let them in: the foreign name Sankt-Piter-Burkh receives a literal translation into Russian in Pil'niak's story, as *Sviatoi-kamen'-gorod* (Sacred Stone City).⁵⁶ The two emperor-builders are also destroyers and revolutionary modernizers: as Peter dismantled the traditional practices and institutions of the Russian elite, so Shi Huangdi, in Pil'niak's summary, "overthrew all ranks and regalia, all princes, thus inflicting 'a mortal blow on feudalism.'"⁵⁷ Their historical trajectories meet again in the present, when both empires fall to revolutions within six years (1911, 1917).

Once these parallel imperial histories are established, the impressionistic outlines of a plot juxtapose Russian and Chinese characters undergoing a common experience of revolutionary disruption. The Chinese peasant Li-yang, born on the Chinese–Mongol border, flees the turmoil of the 1911 Revolution and migrates to Russia, where he becomes the Red Guard Liyanov. In Petersburg, suspected of treason when English coins are found on his person, he is imprisoned by a professor turned Bolshevik revolutionary, Ivan Ivanovich Ivanov, who in turn is compelled to execute a close friend; Liyanov, released from prison, forms one half of the two-man Chinese firing squad. Later he settles down to till the soil on the outskirts of ruined Petersburg, while Ivanov's brother Petr, a White officer in emigration, ends the story begging on the streets of Beijing.

Readings of "Sankt-Piter-Burkh" tend to adopt one of two historically connected ideological frames for understanding the Russia–China relationship in Pil'niak's story: a "Panmongolist" approach that positions the Chinese migrant as threatening, and a "Eurasian" approach that suggests the possibility of Russian–Chinese community.⁵⁸ "Panmongolist" readings, which focus on the second of the story's three chapters, identify "Sankt-Piter-Burkh" as a pastiche of the "Petersburg text," most specifically Bely's *Petersburg*.⁵⁹ Pil'niak's Petersburg, like Bely's, is a nightmarish, delirious, non-Russian city, invaded by both Europe and Asia. The Red Guard Liyanov, a symbol of Asian invasion, inherits the grotesque aesthetic of inscrutable alterity we have seen already in Kitaigorod: "On the Chinese man's face were ... only teeth, strange teeth, the jaw of a horse; he grinned with them: who will understand?"⁶⁰ In Ivanov's nightmares, the map of the world becomes a chessboard across

278   Edward Tyerman

Figure 8.2. Peter the First and Shi Huangdi, the First Emperor (engraving by V.N. Masiutin, Gelikon edition of *Povest' Peterburgskaia ili Sviatoi-kamen'-gorod*, 1922). From the holdings of the Russian State Library.

which Liyanov crawls – the same form of locomotion favoured by Kitai in *The Naked Year*. China crawls across Europe; the sunset above the Neva turns an feverish yellow, and the Great Wall rears up through the fog on the riverbank.[61] No wonder Georges Nivat identifies here the final link in a chain of Russian modernist Yellow Peril anxieties that traces back to Solov'ev's "Panmongolism" and the "sinification" fears of Dmitrii Merezhkovskii.[62] In the 1922 Gelikon edition, this "sinification" is announced on the title page, which translates the name of Sankt-Piter-Burkh into Chinese characters that hover above the Cyrillic title (figure 8.3).[63]

This reading of Liyanov as a symbol of the Yellow Peril, however, takes into account only the second of the story's three chapters, where the shadow of Bely looms largest. By contrast, "Eurasianist" readings of the story note that it begins and ends with images of agricultural, patriarchal tradition that link together premodern Russia and China.[64]

Figure 8.3. Title page for "Sankt-Piter-Burkh," Gelikon 1922. From the holdings of the Russian State Library. The Chinese characters read Bidebao, a phonetic approximation of "Petersburg."

The first chapter describes Li-yang's childhood in northern China as the gradual acquisition of inherited knowledge. Here Pil'niak draws on his readings to bombard the reader with elements of Chinese cultural "tradition": Li-yang learns about yin and yang, studies Daoism through Laozi, and masters the Four Books and Five Classics of Confucian tradition.[65] Li-yang's Chinese world, much like pre-Petrine Russia, is an agricultural civilization that has developed in constant interaction with the nomadic steppe. This world falls into disruption at the hands of forces produced by China's semi-colonial incorporation into the modern world-system: first the anti-foreigner Boxer Rebellion in 1900, and then the 1911 anti-Manchu Republican Revolution, which leads to the death of Li-yang's father. At the story's close, the Chinese migrant reverts to his premodern instincts: in the "wasteland" behind a deserted house, abandoned in a foul state by its previous inhabitants, Li-yang gathers human excrement to fertilize the soil and plant corn, millet, and potatoes. China comes to Russia, on this reading, not as a symbol of sinister stagnation, but rather as a regenerating force that helps Russia recover from its catastrophic experiment with European modernity.

The Chinese migrant thus emerges in Pil'niak's story as a profoundly ambiguous figure, capable of symbolizing both Panmongolist threat and Eurasian affinity. Crucial to note here is that these shifting meanings and aesthetic instantiations depend on perspective and, in particular, place. Pil'niak's protagonist only becomes grotesque and threatening once he appears in Petersburg, a transformation marked by the mutation of his name from Li-yang to Liyanov. In the distorted nightmares of Petersburg's disturbed inhabitants, Liyanov epitomizes the Russian Revolution as chaos, delirium, and murder. Even his speech is grotesquely distorted: the one word we hear him pronounce in Russian is "kius-no," a mangled rendering of "skuchno" (boring).[66] In the agricultural worlds of northern China and ruined Petersburg suburbs, however, Li-yang stands for continuity and the possibility of organic renewal. Thus, I suggest, it is a conscious engagement with the dynamics of migration that represents Pil'niak's crucial addition to his predecessors in the lineage of Silver Age, Slavophile, and proto-Eurasian thought. Li-yang has been driven from home by the violent disruption caused by China's traumatic entry into modernity. As he flees the 1911 Republican Revolution, passing through Mongolia into Russia, "with him went dozens of others, men who had lost, abandoned – fathers, mothers, sons and fatherland."[67] This is hardly the marauding Asiatic army of Solov'ev's apocalyptic nightmares; it is more a trickle of homeless, bereaved individuals, the victims of social upheaval rather than its perpetrators.

The story ends with a diptych of parallel migrations. As Li-yang tills the soil alone in post-revolutionary Petrograd, Ivan Ivanovich's brother, a White officer named Petr, has joined the White migration into China, where he begs on the streets of Beijing. A story that began with the parallel imperial histories of Russia and China ends with a Chinese and a Russian migrant, each alone in the other's land, both refugees from war and revolution. Eurasianist readings of Li-yang's turn to the Russian soil underplay the fact that his presence produces no sense of community with the local Russians. Quite the opposite: just like Mayakovsky's laundry worker, he is taunted and mocked by the local children: "Hey, *khodia*, you slant-eyed devil! Who cut off your pigtail? Watch out, we'll steal your potatoes!"[68] They watch on as he tends his tiny plot of land, trapped in a degrading difference, "alone, foreign to everyone, slant-eyed."[69] Petr is similarly isolated in Beijing, sleeping alone on the city walls amidst "silence and peoplelessness" (*tishina i bezliudie*).[70] Although on opposite sides of the ideological spectrum and the Eurasian continent, these two figures share a common experience of displacement by modern forms of revolution. To be sure, Pil'niak's depiction of Li-yang/Liyanov does not escape from xenophobic stereotype. But his story's close attention to the relationship between strangeness and place allows "Sankt-Piter-Burkh" to outline a new sense of commensurability between Russia and China, as two Eurasian land empires embarked on a belated and disruptive path of modernization. What emerges here is something like a conservative, Eurasianist internationalism, one that laments a common loss of roots and organic community in a world made unevenly whole and unpredictably mobile by a global modernity.

"The Chinese is tough. He fears nothing": Chinese Partisans and Chinese Pain

If Pil'niak's story outlines a transnational migrant condition shorn of any explicit connection to socialism or even class, elsewhere in early Soviet literature the symbolic figure of the Chinese Red partisan serves to explore the possibilities of a specifically socialist internationalism. The *locus classicus* for the Chinese migrant as revolutionary ally is Vsevolod Ivanov's novella *Armoured Train 14–69* (*Bronepoezd No. 14–69*), first published in 1922. This popular Civil War tale, later staged to great success at the Moscow Art Theatre (MKhAT) in 1927, recounts the attempts of a group of Red partisans to stop a White armoured train as it heads towards a town in the Russian Far East. When the original plan to blow up a bridge falls through, the single Chinese member of the partisan brigade, Sin-Bin-U, lies down on the rails and shoots himself. The train stops, the driver is shot, and the partisans capture the train. Ivanov claimed he found the outlines of this plot in a divisional newspaper while serving with the Red Guards in western Siberia: "In order to stop the speeding armoured train even for a moment, a Chinese soldier in the brigade, Sin-Bin-U – one of those coolies whom the Tsarist government hired in large numbers and transported to the front to dig trenches – lay down on the rails and was crushed by the armoured train."[71] Ivanov's story transposed this event from western Siberia to the Russian Far East: a scene of ongoing fighting in the Civil War, but also the focal point of historical anxieties about Chinese migration.[72]

Ivanov's reworking of this raw material allows the Chinese partisan Sin-Bin-U to perform a function that would become pivotal in the ritual narratives of socialist realism: voluntary self-sacrifice for the sake of the Revolution.[73] Whereas Pil'niak's Li-yang joined the Red Army as a confused refugee with no clear ideological commitment, Ivanov gives Sin-Bin-U a distinct political motivation: the Japanese, who at that time were occupying Vladivostok, killed his wife and children. At the same time, Ivanov's Sin-Bin-U, like the Chinese partisans in Veselyi and Pil'niak, remains marked by linguistic hybridity and a certain aesthetic of the grotesque. Take, for example, his first extended set of utterances:

> Син-Бин-У сказал громко:
> – Казаки цхау-жа! Нипонса куна, мадама бери мала-мала. Нехао, казака нехао! Кырасна русска …
> Он, скосив губы, швыркнул слюной сквозь зубы, и лицо его, цвета песка золотых россыпей, с узенькими, как семячки дыни, разрезами глаз, радостно заулыбалось.
> – Шанго!..
> Син-Бин-У в знак одобрения поднял кверху большой палец руки.
> Но не слыша, как всегда, хохота партизан, китаец уныло сказал:
> – Пылыоха-о …
> И тоскливо оглянулся.

[Sin-Bin-U said loudly, "The Cossacks are scoundrels! The Japanese take women … Not good, Cossacks not good! Red Russian …"
Tightening his lips, he flung a gob of spit through his teeth; his face, the colour of the sand of gold mines, with little narrow slits like melon seeds for eyes, broke into a joyful smile, "Good!"
As a sign of approval Sin-Bin-U stuck up his thumb.
But, as usual, he didn't hear the laughter of the partisans and said sadly, "Bad …"
And he looked back wistfully.][74]

Sin-Bin-U's language again displays elements from Chinese Pidgin Russian, including the use of an imperative (*beri*) as an indicative verb and the lexical items *kuna* (girl or young woman, from Chinese *guniang* 姑娘), *mala-mala* (*nemnogo*, "a little"), and *shango* (*khorosho*, "good," possibly from *shanghao* 上好, "first-rate").[75] More inventive are the macaronic utterances "nekhao" (a combination of Russian *ne*, "not," and Chinese *hao* 好, "good") and "pylyokha-o" (a splicing of Russian *plokho* with Chinese *bu hao* 不好, "not good"). These hybrid lexemes, as Roy Chan has observed, ask to be read in the spirit of the time as gesturing towards a utopian linguistic internationalism that might overcome Babelian separation.[76]

Yet the ambivalence at the heart of the Chinese migrant soldier endures in the tension between linguistic form and performative embodiment. Sin-Bin-U's physical appearance shares the grotesque, racialized aesthetic favoured by Pil'niak: his eyes are like like melon seeds, his skin the colour of sand from gold mines (a site where many Chinese migrants worked). Unlike Liyanov, however, Sin-Bin-U's primary affect is not sinister but comic. He speaks loudly, yet incomprehensibly. His simplistic rhetoric and exaggerated body language swing between the absolute poles of "good" and "bad" – now he smiles "joyfully" (*radostno*) with thumb raised in confirmation, then he speaks "sadly" (*unylo*) and looks around "mournfully" (*tosklivo*). Even the scene by the train tracks, wherein Sin-Bin-U shifts from comic performer to self-sacrificing hero, remains shrouded in ambiguity. The partisans decide that someone must lie on the rails, as the driver will have to stop and fill out a report. Red-haired former miner Vas'ka Okorok volunteers. When Vas'ka cries out in fear, Sin-Bin-U rushes up to lie down beside him. Almost immediately Vas'ka abandons him, and the last words any partisan addresses to Sin-Bin-U define him in purely ethnic terms: "Throw the ladle over here, *manza*!.. And you could also leave your livorver [i.e., revolver] here. What do you need it for?"[77] Ivanov's physical descriptions alienate the reader from their sacrificial hero, whose head on the rails appears "flat and emerald-eyed, like a cobra."[78] In response to the request for his gun, he moves to throw it into the bushes, only to shoot himself suddenly in the back of the head. Should we read this as an act of heroic decisiveness or as a rebuke to his erstwhile comrades? At this key moment of self-sacrifice, Ivanov leaves Sin-Bin-U's final actions ambiguous, their psychological motivations unclear.

In Ivanov's original text of 1922, Sin-Bin-U's self-sacrifice combines bravery and comradeship with an unnervingly impenetrable fearlessness in the face of violent death. The Russian partisan loses his nerve, whereas Sin-Bin-U seems to have no nerves at all. Ivanov smoothed out much of this ambiguity for the theatrical production of *Bronepoezd 14–69* that debuted at the MKhAT in November 1927.[79] On the stage of MKhAT, it was Sin-Bin-U himself who proposed that he lie on the rails, framing his self-sacrifice as an explicit affirmation of Comintern internationalism: "If there is no Soviet revolution, there is also no Chinese republic. I lie down here for China."[80] Such ideological motivations remain strikingly unvoiced in the climactic scene of the 1922 text. At the same time, Sin-Bin-U's readiness to sacrifice himself feeds into a common trope in contemporary discussions of the Chinese partisan: his apparent fearlessness in the face of death and suffering. Consider the following assessment by the Soviet military commander I.E. Iakir, whose battalion included Chinese soldiers:

> The Chinese is tough, he fears nothing. His own brother gets killed in battle, and he won't bat an eye: he'll go to him, close his eyes, and that'll be the end of it. Then he'll sit down next to him, with ammunition in his cap, and he'll

calmly fire off round after round. If he understands that he is up against an enemy, that's bad news for the enemy. A Chinese will fight to the last.[81]

Iakir was not alone in his admiration for Chinese soldiers' composure in battle. The newspaper *Ural'skii rabochii* noted in 1918 that Chinese soldiers were distinguished by "resilience and remarkable endurance" (*stoikost'iu i zamechatel'noi vynoslivost'iu*).[82] Another division commander reported that his Chinese soldiers were "fearless, brave and unflappable [*khladnokrovnye*, lit. 'cold-blooded']" in battle.[83]

Literary images of the Chinese partisan frequently emphasize fearlessness in the face of battle and death. Pavel Bliakhin's adventure novel for children *The Red Devils* (*Krasnye d'iavoliata*, 1923) features a Chinese street acrobat who becomes an indomitable Red soldier, "capable, with typically Chinese sang-froid [*khladnokrovie*], of standing or crawling under a hail of bullets, amidst the hellish roar and whine of shells."[84] A similar figure appears in Nikolai Ostrovskii's socialist realist classic *How the Steel Was Tempered* (*Kak zakalialas' stal'*, 1932–34), running at the head of Red Army troops: "A bronzed Chinese with bloodshot eyes, clad in an undershirt and girded with machine-gun belts, runs fully upright, a grenade in each hand."[85] His posture and weaponry suggest a fearless eagerness for battle. Andrei Platonov reduces this image of the Chinese partisan to grotesque simplicity in a brief scene from *Chevengur* (1926–28). Aleksandr Dvanov hops a train home and travels briefly with some "sailors and Chinese" headed for Tsaritsyn (today's Volgograd). On the way, they stop at a meal station so that the sailors can beat up the commandant and take his soup. The participation of the Chinese soldiers in the narrative is confined to two sentences: "The Chinese ate up all the fish soup, which the Russian sailors turned down, then gathered up with bread all the nutritious moisture from the walls of the soup pails and said to the sailors, in response to their question about death: 'We love death! We love it very much!' Then the Chinese, sated, lay down to sleep."[86]

These Chinese soldiers act and speak simplistically and in chorus, displaying a collective interweaving of pleasure and death drives. The communal refrain "We love death!" transforms fearlessness into a child-like enthusiasm for the end of life, followed by a collective mimesis of death in sleep. Platonov's Chinese partisans express the fascination with death that runs through *Chevengur* at its minimalist extreme. Sin-Bin-U's individual act of heroism is replaced by a collective death drive so free of reflection as to become disturbing, and the superhuman elements that Iakir admired take on a subhuman cast.

This image of the fearlessly violent Chinese partisan became sufficiently well established to serve as the object of parody. Mikhail Bulgakov's "Chinese Story" ("Kitaiskaia istoriia," 1923) tells the tale of a Chinese migrant, Sen-Zin-Po, who joins the Red Army and proves highly effective with a machine gun. In a review published in 1925, the critic Leonid Averbakh attacked Bulgakov's piece as a cynical parody of Ivanov.[87] For a start, there is his hero's name, which mimics the double-hyphenated graphic form of Sin-Bin-U and copies two out of three letters in the first two syllables. Then there is his career, which systematically undermines the narrative of internationalist solidarity that Ivanov (ambiguously) endorses. Sen-Zin-Po is given no backstory that might explain his attraction to the Red cause. Instead, Bulgakov has Sen-Zin-Po decide to join the Red Army after Lenin appears to him in an opium dream dressed as a Qing dynasty official, complete with yellow jacket, a black cap with a button on top, and a "huge, shiny, tightly wound queue."[88] Whereas Sin-Bin-U's broken Sino-Russian offers a potential model for the overcoming of Babelian division, Sen-Zin-Po's Russian utterances are limited to a three-word obscenity that draws "a thunderous wave of laughter" from his newfound Red Army comrades.[89]

However, this comic figure turns out to be a highly efficient killing machine. When his commander sees Sen-Zin-Po shoot a Maxim gun, he declares that such "virtuoso" work deserves to be rewarded with bonus payments (*premial'nye*).[90] Several newspaper accounts of Chinese Red Army soldiers emphasized their enthusiasm for the machine gun.[91] Yet when battle comes, Sen-Zin-Po does not consciously sacrifice himself to save his comrades. Instead, he dies because he fails to understand that his side has retreated. Even when his commander shoots himself in front of him, Sen-Zin-Po turns back to his gun and keeps firing – not out of bravery, but in memory of the promised financial rewards for his virtuosity: "Premiali … karasii virtuzi … palata! palati!" (Bonus … red virtuoso … pay! Pay!)[92] Soon after, his voice is silenced when a junker stabs him in the throat. The Chinese partisan realigns here with the image from White propaganda: a threatening stranger who kills for money. If other accounts of Chinese partisans complicate the notion of internationalist solidarity with their grotesque combinations of comedy and violence, Bulgakov's story dismisses the idea of solidarity entirely, reducing Sen-Zin-Po's motivation to confusion and self-interested opportunism.[93]

From Yellow Peril to Red Partisan

In highlighting this repeated literary emphasis on the fearlessness of Chinese partisans, it is not my intention to demean the bravery of those Chinese soldiers who fought for the Red Army in the Civil War.

Nonetheless, the repetition and continuity of this image suggest we are in the presence of an ideologeme: a refraction of lived experience into a codified ideological discourse, which in turn finds itself refracted into a literary text as a character, figure, or trope.[94] If White accounts stressed the brutality and cruelty of Chinese soldiers, the Red side found productive potential in the notion that the Chinese do not fear death or physical pain. The two sides essentially mirror each other and suggest a common origin in pre-revolutionary ideological currents.

Significant images of threatening Chinese violence emerged in the pre-revolutionary period. One important precedent arose from the anti-foreign uprising in China known as the Boxer Rebellion (1900), an event that caused considerable anxiety in the Russian Far East. The Boxers, known in Chinese as the League of Righteousness and Harmony (*Yihetuan* 義和團) or the Righteous and Harmonious Fists (*Yihequan* 義和拳), initiated a mass movement against foreign missionaries and commercial interests in northeastern China that received the tacit support of the Qing government. In July 1900, the administration of Blagoveshchensk on the Russo-Chinese border, fearing an uprising, drove the Chinese population of the city into the Amur River, where several thousand drowned.[95] Russian eyewitness reports of the rebellion, which was eventually suppressed by an international force that included Russian troops, emphasized the Boxers' claims of magical invulnerability to pain.[96] Pil'niak has Li-yang repeatedly sing a song connected with the Boxers, linking the migrant Red soldier to this earlier image of violent Chinese threat.[97] The shadow of the Russo-Japanese War is important here too, not least because several variants of the Yellow Peril discourse, including Solov'ev's "Panmongolism," predicted that a modernizing Japan could mobilize the racial allegiance of China's large population to gather an army and invade the rest of Eurasia.[98] Significant in this regard are the racialized claims of the prominent late-Imperial physical anthropologist Ivan Sikorskii, who declared in a public lecture delivered in 1904 that "in wartime, Yellow races easily became fanatical and gave themselves to feeling and passion rather than to rationality and reason."[99]

But this image of the fearless Chinese soldier also belongs to a wider transnational history. Eric Hayot traces through European modernity a fascinated perception of China as a space of exceptional cruelty, a perception focused in particular on Chinese practices of torture and thus a presumed high tolerance for pain.[100] These ideas circulated with particular intensity in the late nineteenth century, filtered through the biologized language of race, in conjunction with the transnational increase in Chinese labour migration. Perhaps their most famous formulation can be found in the work of Arthur Smith, an American missionary who drew on two decades of residence in China to write the highly influential volume *Chinese Characteristics* (1890).[101] In one of his chapters, titled "The Absence of Nerves," Smith defines "clear-eyed endurance" as "one of the most remarkable phenomena of the [Chinese] race."[102] The Chinese body, according to Smith, can withstand monotony, repetition, and discomfort: "It seems to make no particular difference to a Chinese how long he remains in one position"; the Chinese are "able to sleep anywhere"; and Chinese workers can repeat the same activity "from dewy dawn to dusky eve ... without any variation in the monotony."[103] For Smith, this gives the Chinese a competitive advantage over Europeans, whom he considers excessively afflicted with nervousness in a modern age "of steam and of electricity."[104] Smith's anxieties operated in the context of contemporary medical theories of neurasthenia and the wider discourse of European degeneration, both of which contained a marked racial aspect.[105] Indeed, for Smith, the Chinese absence of nerves becomes a competitive advantage in a Social Darwinist racial struggle to dominate the modern world:

> What the bearing of this pregnant proposition may be on the future impact of this race with our own – an impact likely to become more violent as the years go by – we shall not venture to conjecture. We have come to believe, at least in general, in the survival of the most fit. Which is the best adapted to survive in the struggles of the twentieth century, the "nervous" European or the tireless, all-pervading, and phlegmatic Chinese?[106]

Smith's book had a global impact: it was translated into Chinese and Japanese as well as several European languages.[107] A Russian translation was published in Vladivostok in 1904.[108] This final passage shows, moreover, that Smith's arguments operated within a global perspective that extended beyond the mores of the Chinese in China. Indeed, this preoccupation with Chinese physical resilience cannot be understood apart from a transnational discourse about the threat of Chinese migrant labour.

In North America, responses to heightened Chinese immigration from the mid-nineteenth century coalesced around the perceived threat that the Chinese worker, putatively able to survive on less food and lower wages, posed to native workers. As Hayot notes, this disparity was understood not economically or politically, but physiologically: the physical body of the Chinese migrant worker was "figured as enduring, impervious to physical pain, and mechanical or slavish in its relation to freedom, pleasure, and a volitional relation to history."[109] These dehumanized, mechanical qualities made the Chinese worker better equipped for a dehumanizing, mechanized modernity.[110] Crucially, this biologized discourse actively undermined the possibility of transcultural or transracial solidarity between workers on the basis of common class interests. Many socialists in the US – including Friedrich Sorge, a frequent correspondent with Karl Marx who founded the first North American section of the International Working Men's Association – framed Chinese migrant workers as a threat to the rights and wages of native white workers rather than as common victims of exploitation.[111] In the North American context, this racialized understanding of the Chinese migrant worker's biological difference fundamentally problematized the realization (or even conceptual possibility) of a workers' International. And not only in North America: in 1872, the General Council of the International Working Men's Association voted against expanding its membership to include China and India (Friedrich Engels was among those opposed).[112]

When Russian discussions of threat of the "yellow race" emerged from the 1890s, they did so with an explicit awareness of this global context. The Chinese population in Russia's Far Eastern territories expanded in the 1890s due to growing demand for labour in railway construction and gold mining.[113] Increasingly, the region's economy came to depend on Chinese migrant labour.[114] In turn, Russian discussions of migration in the Far East began to speak an international language of race and migration anxiety. Il'ia Levitov, an engineer on the Chinese Eastern Railway and the author of the pamphlets *The Yellow Race* (*Zheltaia rasa*, 1900) and *Yellow Russia* (*Zheltaia Rossiia*, 1901), framed his analysis of migration in the Russian Far East through a close comparison with the situation in the US.[115] Like his American counterparts, Levitov characterized Chinese workers as inherently possessing "such lesser moral qualities as endurance, [capacity for] mental and physical labour, and persistence at work."[116] V.V. Grave, an official from the Ministry of Foreign Affairs, began his 1912 report on migration in the Priamur region with a comparative gesture towards the "yellow question" as it had played out in North America and the European colonies. Among the "racial characteristics" (*rasovye osobennosti*) of Chinese migrants, Grave included their "complete indifference to death" and consequent ability "to reduce to a minimum their personal needs for clothing, food, housing etc."[117] These characteristics become a direct threat to state security in the writings of Aleksei Kuropatkin, Nicholas II's war minister during the Russo-Japanese War and a famous exponent of Yellow Peril discourse.[118] On the eve of the First World War, Kuropatkin warned of future conflict with China in *The Russia–China Question*, a pamphlet that participated explicitly in a transnational, physiological discourse about "Chinese characteristics":

> With regard to the Chinese tribe, various researchers have expressed highly divergent opinions. But they all concur in defining the main qualities that characterize the Chinese race: a great capacity for labor; endurance; frugality; modest requirements with regard to food, clothing, living quarters and size of wages; persistence in pursuit of established goals; cruelty; strength of the nervous system; and a capacity to greet death calmly.[119]

Kuropatkin here was linking together the absence of nerves and a fearless attitude towards death in order to argue that the Chinese could pose a serious military threat to Russia in the Far East.[120]

Early Soviet policies sought to alter the status of Chinese and other migrant workers: the 1918 constitution of the Russian Soviet Federal Socialist Republic accorded the right of citizenship to all workers on Russian territory, and in 1920 Chinese workers gained representation on the Soviet Council of Nationalities.[121] At the First Congress of the Peoples of the East, held in Baku in September 1920, speakers condemned the role of trade unions in supporting anti-Chinese policies in the US.[122] However, if we look to early Soviet literature as an expression of the social imaginary, we find that the relationship to the Yellow Peril discourse of the past proceeds under an ambiguous blend of inversion and continuity. Some images of the Chinese partisan, seeking to replace a threatening migrant labourer with a class ally, polemicize with earlier stereotypes. Levitov, for example, had claimed that Chinese workers possess an exceptional capacity for physical labour but lack the "loftier moral qualities" of the European worker, including a "sense of duty, public spirit [*obshchestvennyi dukh*], true bravery [*nastoiashchee muzhestvo*]."[123] By contrast, the texts of Ivanov, Bliakhin, and Ostrovskii affirm that the Chinese soldier can be distinguished precisely by bravery and public spirit, the spirit of revolutionary self-sacrifice.

However, this inversion coexists with the lingering presence of the first paradigm, whereby this exceptional bravery and fearlessness can be attained because of an imperviousness to suffering that remains on some level alienating. Bulgakov's Sen-Zin-Po explicitly reduces this fearlessness to ignorance and a pure mechanical aptitude for the most typical tool of modern warfare, the machine gun – a militarized version of the dehumanized, mechanized modern labour that Smith fears the Chinese can better withstand. But the marked absence of psychology in Ivanov, and the automatized death drive in Platonov, make broadly the same claim: Chinese migrants make perfect revolutionary soldiers because their physical difference renders them impervious to pain and thus fearless in the face of death. In the literary figure of the Chinese migrant, the ideals of Soviet internationalism encountered the unaddressed and untheorized traces of modern racial discourse, a system of thought that developed in concord with the expansion of capitalism and imperialism precisely to naturalize divisions and prevent common cause among the workers of the world.[124] The aspiration for a transethnic political affiliation founded in class, grounded in common experiences of exploitation and expressed in heroic deeds, coexists here with the legacies of a racialized discourse of insurmountable otherness and inescapably conflicting interests that served to forestall any possibility of political solidarity.

Notes

1 R.S. Churchill and Martin Gilbert, *Winston S. Churchill*, vol. 4 (London: Heinemann, 1975), 227.
2 David Bullock, *The Russian Civil War 1918–22* (Oxford: Osprey, 2014), 91. Bullock counts "at least 40,000–50,000" international troops in the Red Army by July 1918, not including the Latvian Rifles.
3 A canonical expression of this combination can be found in Andrei Bely's modernist novel *Petersburg* (1916), whose sinister Ukrainian villain, the terrorist revolutionary Lippanchenko, physically resembles "a mix of a Semite and a Mongol." See Henrietta Mondry, "*Petersburg* and Contemporary Racial Thought," in *A Reader's Guide to Andrei Bely's Petersburg*, ed. Leonid Livak (Madison: University of Wisconsin Press, 2018), 124–37.
4 White sources tended to insist that the Chinese partisans were not volunteers but rather hired mercenaries. For a summary and indeed revival of this perspective from the post-Soviet period, see Viktor Suvorov, *Ochishchenie: Zachem Stalin obezglavil svoiu armiiu?* (Moscow: Izd. AST, 1998), 179–89; cf. Vladimir Tikhomirov, "Kak migranty otomstili Rossii," *Istoricheskaia Pravda*, 17 October 2013, http://bratsk.org/2015/09/08/Russia-retaliated-migrants.
5 See, for example, Nikita Popov, *Oni s nami srazhalis' za vlast' sovetov: Kitaiskie dobrovol'tsy na frontakh grazhdanskoi voiny v Rossii, 1918–1922* (Leningrad: Lenizdat, 1959).
6 Heinz Gollwitzer, *Die Gelbe Gefahr* (Göttingen: Vandenhock & Ruprecht, 1962); Richard Austin Thompson, *The Yellow Peril, 1890–1924* (New York: Arno Press, 1978); Colleen Lye, *America's Asia: Racial Form and American Literature, 1893–1945* (Princeton: Princeton University Press, 2005), ch. 1, "A Genealogy of the Yellow Peril," 12–46.

7 Frederic Jameson, *The Political Unconscious: Narrative as a Socially Symbolic Act* (Ithaca: Cornell University Press, 1981), 76, 87–8.
8 Adam McKeown, "Chinese Emigration in Global Context, 1850–1940," *Journal of Global History* 5 (2010): 98.
9 For the history of these negotiations see R.K.I. Quested, *The Expansion of Russia in East Asia, 1857–1860* (Kuala Lumpur: University of Malaya Press, 1968).
10 John Stephan, *The Russian Far East: A History* (Stanford: Stanford University Press, 1994), 71; N.A. Popov, "Kitaiskie proletarii v grazhdanskoi voine v Rossii," in *Kitaiskie dobrovol'tsy v boiakh za sovetskuiu Rossiiu*, ed. Liu Yun-an' [Liu Yong'an] (Moscow: Izdatel'stvo vostochnoi literatury, 1961), 6–7.
11 Susanna Soojung Lim, "Occidental Bullyism? Russia, Yun Ch'iho, and Race in the Early Twentieth-Century Pacific," in *Ideologies of Race: Imperial Russia and the Soviet Union in Global Context*, ed. David Rainbow (Montreal and Kingston: McGill–Queen's University Press, 2019), 267.
12 Popov, "Kitaiskie proletarii v grazhdanskoi voine v Rossii," 6–7.
13 Lewis H. Siegelbaum, "Another 'Yellow Peril': Chinese Migrants in the Russian Far East and the Russian Reaction before 1917," *Modern Asian Studies* 12, no. 2 (1978): 326.
14 In 1897, Chinese workers constituted the largest non-Russian national group of labourers on the Trans-Siberian Railway. Their wages were less than half those of Russian workers. Siegelbaum, "Another 'Yellow Peril,'" 312–13. For lower wages in the Lena gold mines, see Popov, "Kitaiskie proletarii," 8.
15 V.I. Diatlov, "Sindrom 'zheltoi opasnosti' v dorevoliutsionnoi Rossii: ekzotizatsiia kak mekhanizm degumanizatsii i iskliucheniia," in *Pereselencheskoe obshchestvo Aziatskoi Rossii: migratsii, prostranstva, soobshchestva*, ed. Diatlov and K.V. Grigorichev (Irkutskii gosudarstvennyi universitet, 2013), 526–54.
16 Chia Yin Hsu, "A Tale of Two Railroads: 'Yellow Labor,' Agrarian Colonization, and the Making of Russianness at the Far Eastern Frontier, 1890s–1910s," *Ab Imperio* 3 (2006): 239.
17 A.G. Larin, *Kitaitsy v Rossii vchera i segodniia* (Moscow: Muravei, 2003), 68.
18 Popov, "Kitaiskie proletarii," in *Kitaiskie dobrovol'tsy*, ed. Liu, 7; Gregor Benton, *Chinese Migrants and Internationalism* (London: Routledge, 2007), 21.
19 Siegelbaum, "Another 'Yellow Peril,'" 327.
20 Larin, *Kitaitsy v Rossii*, 89. For an argument that foreign recruitment into the Red Army was driven primarily by material need, see Marc Jansen, "International Class Solidarity or Foreign Intervention? Internationalists and Latvian Rifles in the Russian Revolution and the Civil War,"

International Review of Social History 31, no. 1 (1986): 78. For evidence that Chinese recruitment was motivated by political commitment, see the memoirs collected in Liu, *Kitaiskie dobrovol'tsy*, and the discussion in Benton, *Chinese Migrants*, 28–9.
21. Benton, *Chinese Migrants*, 26.
22. Walter Benjamin, "Moscow Diary," *October* 35 (1985), 20, 36.
23. Vladimir Mayakovsky, "Moskovskii Kitai," *Prozhektor* 9 (1927): 28. All translations are my own unless otherwise specified.
24. On the history of the Comintern's engagement with China in the 1920s see Alexander Pantsov, *The Bolsheviks and the Chinese Revolution, 1919–1927* (Honolulu: University of Hawai'i Press, 2000).
25. Terry Martin, *The Affirmative Action Empire: Nations and Nationalism in the Soviet Union, 1923–1939* (Ithaca: Cornell University Press, 2001), 311–43.
26. Liu, *Kitaiskie dobrovol'tsy*; Benton, *Chinese Migrants*, 28–9; John M. Knight, "Savior of the East: Chinese Imaginations of Soviet Russia during the National Revolution, 1925–1927," *Twentieth-Century China* 43, no. 2 (2018): 120–38.
27. Hsu, "A Tale of Two Railroads," passim.
28. Diatlov, "Sindrom 'zheltoi opasnosti'," 535–6.
29. Susanna Soojung Lim, "Between Spiritual Self and Other: Vladimir Solov'ev and the Question of East Asia," *Slavic Review* 67, no. 2 (Summer 2008): 332–9.
30. Viktor Shklovskii, "I. Babel': kriticheskii romans," *LEF* 6 (1924): 153.
31. Isaac Babel', "Khodia," *Siluety* 6–7 (1923). A subtitle described the story as an extract from a longer work, *Peterburg, 1918*, that never appeared. The etymology of *khodia* is disputed. Variants include the Chinese term *huoji* 伙計, meaning a shop assistant; the Russian verb *khodit'*, in the sense of itinerant workers or traders who "come and go"; the Chinese terms *huojia* 貨家 ("trader in goods") or *hejia* 合家 ("the whole family"); or the adverbial expression *kuaidianr* 快點兒, meaning "a little quicker" or "hurry up." See *Slovar' sovremennogo russkogo literaturnogo iazyka*, vol. 17 (Moscow: Nauka, 1965), 302; O.M. Mladenova, "Russkoe khodia," in *Etimologiia, 2006–2008*, ed. Zh.Zh. Varbot et al. (Moscow: Nauka, 2010), 183–91.
32. Aleksei Remizov, "Kitaets," *Birzhevye vedomosti*, 29 May 1916, 2–3. For an analysis, see Jinyi Chu, "Patterns of the World: Chinese Fashion and Cosmopolitan Ideas in Late Imperial Russia," PhD diss., Stanford University, 2019, 229–37.
33. Isaak Babel', *Sobranie sochinenii v chetyrekh tomakh*, vol. 1: *Odesskie rasskazy* (Moscow: Vremia, 2005), 271.
34. Babel', *Sobranie sochinenii*.
35. Chu, "Patterns of the World," 233–4.

36 Yurii V. Luchinskii, "Grazhdanskaia voina na Kubani v rasskaze Artema Veselogo 'Vol'nitsa'," *Nasledie vekov* 2 (2017): 42–4; Benton, *Chinese Migrants and Internationalism*, 23–4; Popov, *Oni s nami srazhalis'*, 68–9.
37 Artem Veselyi, "Vol'nitsa," *LEF* 1 (1924): 42.
38 Dieter Stern, "Myths and Facts about the Kiakhta Trade Pidgin," in *Journal of Pidgin and Creole Languages* 20, no. 1 (2005): 175–87; Olga Bakich, "Did You Speak Harbin Sino-Russian?" *Itinerario* 35, no. 3 (2011): 23–36; Johanna Nichols, "Pidginization and Foreigner Talk," in *Papers from the Fourth International Conference on Historical Linguistics*, ed. Elizabeth Closs Traugott, Rebecca Labrum, and Susan C. Shepherd (Amsterdam: John Benjamins, 1980), 397–408.
39 Bakich, "Did You Speak Harbin Sino-Russian?," 30–2.
40 Bakich, "Do you Speak Harbin Sino-Russian?," 31.
41 Tret'iakov lived in Vladivostok and also visited Harbin while residing in Beijing in 1924–5. His poem "Rychi Kitai" ("Roar China") appeared in the same issue of *LEF* as Veselyi's "Vol'nitsa." For Tret'iakov's use of pidgin, see Mark Gamsa, "Sergei Tret'iakov's *Roar, China!* between Moscow and China," *Itinerario* 36, no. 2 (2012): 95, 106. Bogdanov, who fought in the Russian Far East during the Civil War, included a glossary of pidgin vocabulary and a pidgin rendering of a Russian convict song in *Van Iun-Chan* (1933), a narrative poem about a Chinese migrant's recruitment into the Red Army in Vladivostok. Aleksandr Alekseevich Bogdanov, *Van Iun-Chan: poema* (Moscow: Moskovskoe tovarichestvo pisatelei, 1933).
42 Vladimir Mayakovsky, "Moskovskii Kitai," *Prozhektor* 9 (1927): 28; E. Perekhval'skaia, *Russkie pidzhiny* (St. Petersburg: Aleteia, 2008), 344.
43 Veselyi, "Vol'nitsa," 43, 45.
44 Peter Jensen traces the etymology of "Kitai-gorod" to the word "kita," a kind of rope. Peter Jensen, *Nature as Code: The Achievement of Boris Pilnjak, 1915–1924* (Copenhagen: Rosenkilde and Bagger, 1979), 177. He Fan suggests possible derivations from Turkic ("fortified place") or Mongol ("middle"). Khe Fan, [He Fang], "Evraziistvo i russkaia literatura 1920–1930kh godov XX veka," PhD diss., Moskovskii gosudarstvennyi universitet, 2004, 123–4. At a conference on "Russia in East Asia" at Columbia University in February 2014, Mark Gamsa suggested the "kitai" in "kitai-gorod" could also be a corruption of Italian "città," in reference to Ivan IV's Italian architects (creating a tautology, "city-city"). "Kitai" derives from the Khitan, a Mongolic nomadic people who founded the Liao dynasty and ruled over much of northeast Eurasia in the tenth and eleventh centuries. Susanna Soojung Lim, *China and Japan in the Russian Imagination, 1685–1922: To the Ends of the Orient* (London: Routledge, 2013), 18.
45 Boris Pil'niak, *Golyi god*, in *Sobranie sochinenii v shesti tomakh* (Moscow: Terra-Knizhnyi klub, 2003), vol. 1, 37.

46 Pil'niak, *Golyi god*, 37.
47 Philip Thomson, *The Grotesque* (London: Methuen & Co., 1972), 27.
48 Thomson, *The Grotesque*, 11.
49 Pil'niak, *Golyi god*, 38.
50 Georges Nivat, "Du 'Panmongolisme' au 'Mouvement Eurasien': Histoire d'un thème littéraire," *Cahiers du Monde russe et soviétique*, vol. 7, no. 3 (1966): 460–78.
51 Alexander Lukin, *The Bear Watches the Dragon: Russia's Perceptions of China and the Evolution of Russian–Chinese Relations since the Eighteenth Century* (Armonk: M.E. Sharpe, 2003), 17–20.
52 Jensen, *Nature as Code*, 178; Gary Browning, *Boris Pilniak: Scythian at a Typewriter* (Ann Arbor: Ardis, 1985), 121–2; Tatiana Filimonova, "From Scythia to a Eurasian Empire: The Eastern Trajectory in Russian Literature, 1890–2008," PhD diss., Northwestern University, 2013, 98–104.
53 Pil'niak, *Golyi god*, 37.
54 In September 1921, Pil'niak wrote to M.M. Shkapskaia: "I can lie on the couch for a week and read about China." Cited in Khe Fan, "Evraziistvo i russkaia literatura," 121. The story is dated 20 September 1921. Most of Pil'niak's sources on China are unclear, although one will be considered below.
55 Boris Pil'niak, "Sankt-Piter-Burkh," in *Povest' Peterburgskaia* (Berlin: Gelikon, 1922), 11, 13. Peter took the title "Imperator Vserossiiskii" in 1721. Qin Shihuang was the first Chinese ruler to take the title of *huangdi* 皇帝, "Emperor." See Derk Bodde, "The State and Empire of Ch'in," in *The Cambridge History of China*, vol 1: *The Ch'in and Han Empires, 221 BC– AD 220*, ed. Denis Twitchett, John King Fairbank, and Michael Loewe (Cambridge: Cambridge University Press, 1986), 53.
56 Nirman Moraniak-Bamburach, "B. A. Pil'niak i 'Peterburgskii tekst'," in *B.A. Pil'niak: issledovaniia i materialy* (Kolomna: Kolomenskii pedagogicheskii institut, 1991), 45.
57 Pil'niak, "Sankt-Piter-Burkh," 11. For Qin Shihuang's reforms, including script unification and the mass destruction of books, see Bodde, "The State and Empire of Ch'in," 52–72. For the question of feudalism in China see 22.
58 For a historical genealogy of these terms, see Nivat, "Du 'Panmongolisme.'"
59 V.P. Kriuchkov, *"Povest' Peterburgskaia B. Pil'niaka i "Peterburgskii tekst russkoi literatury"* (Saratov: Nauchnaia kniga, 2005), 45–58; Nivat, "Du 'Panmongolisme,'" 475–6; Nirman Moraniak-Bamburach, "B. A. Pil'niak i 'Peterburgskii tekst'," 40; M.Iu. Liubimova, "O Peterburgskikh povestiiakh B. Pil'niaka," in *Boris Pil'niak: Opyt segodniashchnego prochteniia* (Moscow: Nasledie, 1995), 55–62. Liubimova notes that Pil'niak visited Petersburg for the first time in 1921, the year he wrote the story. Pil'niak's debt to Bely

was open: "I came out of Bely and Bunin," he declared in the foreword to *Machines and Wolves*, written 1923–4. Pil'niak, *Sobranie sochinenii*, vol. 2, 8.
60 Pil'niak, "Sankt-Piter-Burkh," 37.
61 Pil'niak, "Sankt-Piter-Burkh," 40, 47.
62 Nivat, "Du 'Panmongolisme'," 473–7.
63 Pil'niak, "Sankt-Piter-Burkh," 7. The city's name in contemporary Mandarin uses a different character with the sound *bao*, 堡, which gives the meaning of "fortress" to match the German root "Burg."
64 Khe Fan, "Evraziistvo i russkaia literatura," 122–3; Filimonova, "From Scythia to a Eurasian Empire," 104–6.
65 Filimonova, "From Scythia to a Eurasian Empire," 18.
66 Pil'niak, "Sankt-Piter-Burkh," 43. Even here we are reminded of the estrangement produced by a foreign cultural environment when Liyanov introduces himself to a Chinese prison guard in undistorted Chinese: "Vo xin Li Yan" (*wo xing Li Yang*, "my name is Li Yang") (47).
67 Pil'niak, "Sankt-Piter-Burkh," 24.
68 Pil'niak, "Sankt-Piter-Burkh," 53.
69 Pil'niak, "Sankt-Piter-Burkh," 54.
70 Pil'niak, "Sankt-Piter-Burkh," 56.
71 Vsevolod Ivanov, "Kak byl napisan 'Bronepoezd 14–69,'" *Molodaia gvardiia* 1 (1957): 193.
72 Ivanov, "Kak byl napisan 'Bronepoezd 14–69.'"
73 For the classic account see Katerina Clark, *The Soviet Novel: History as Ritual* (Bloomington: Indiana University Press, 2000), 177–9.
74 Vsevolod Ivanov, "Bronepoezd No. 14–69," *Krasnaia nov'* 1 (1922): 81. My translation makes use of Ivanov's own footnotes as well as the English translation by Frank Miller in Evgeny Zamyatin, *The Islanders* / Vsevolod Ivanov, *Armoured Train 14–69* (Ann Arbor: Trilogy, 1978), 55. I make no effort to translate the distortions in Sin-Bin-U's speech.
75 Perekhval'skaia, *Russkie pidzhiny*, 324, 326, 344. For *shango*, see Bakich, "Do you Speak Harbin Sino-Russian?" 32. Wherever Ivanov learned his Chinese and CPR, there seem to be some inconsistencies. His footnotes translate "kuna" as "scoundrel," while "tskhao-zha," which probably originates from *caozhe* 肏者, "fuckers," is rendered as "plokhi" (bad people).
76 Roy Chan, "Broken Tongues: Race, Sacrifice, and Geopolitics in the Far East in Vesvolod Ivanov's *Bronepoezd No. 14–69*," *Sibirica* 10, no. 3 (Winter 2011), 33–4.
77 Ivanov, "Bronepoezd," 110. The peasant's mangling of *revol'ver* as *livorver* illustrates the point that Sin-Bin-U is not the only character in Ivanov's Far East who engages in non-standard speech. See Chan, "Broken Tongues," 35. *Manza* was a term of uncertain origin applied to Chinese inhabitants of Ussuri krai from the time of its acquisition by Russia in 1860. Sergey Glebov,

"Between Foreigners and Subjects: Imperial Subjecthood, Governance, and the Chinese in the Russian Far East, 1860s–1880s," *Ab Imperio* 1 (2017): 95.
78 Ivanov, "Bronepoezd," 110.
79 Staged for the tenth anniversary of the October Revolution, this production appeared in the immediate wake of the collapse of the Comintern's mission in China. For the standard Soviet study, see E.I. Poliakova, *Spektakl' Moskovskogo khudozhestvennogo akademicheskogo teatra "Bronepoezd 14–69"* (Moscow: Nauka, 1965).
80 Vsevolod Ivanov, "Bronepoezd 14–69," *P'esy* (Moscow: Iskusstvo, 1964), 83.
81 Quoted in Larin, *Kitaitsy v Rossii*, 92.
82 Popov, "Kitaiskie proletarii," 22.
83 Popov, "Kitaiskie proletarii," 23.
84 Pavel Bliakhin, *Krasnye d'iavoliata* (Baku: Bakinskii rabochii, 1923), 34.
85 Nikolai Ostrovskii, *Kak zakalialas' stal'* (Moscow: Molodaia gvardiia, 1936), 107. Translation modified from Nikolai Ostrovsky, *How the Steel Was Tempered: A Novel in Two Parts*, trans. R. Prokofieva (Moscow: Progress, 1975), 150.
86 Andrei Platonov, *Chevengur. Kotlovan. Rasskazy* (Moscow: Eksmo, 2011), 95.
87 Leonid Averbakh, "M. Bulgakov. 'Diaboliada,'" *Izvestiia*, 20 September 1925.
88 Mikhail Bulgakov, "Kitaiskaia istoriia," first published in *Illustratsii Petrogradskoi pravdy* 7, 6 May 1923. Reprinted in Mikhail Bulgakov, *Diavolida: rasskazy* (Moscow: Izd-vo Nedra, 1925), 139. Bulgakov's account of Chinese migrants escaping through opium into dreams closely echoes the reportage from 1860s Nevada of Mark Twain, a writer Bulgakov admired. See Jonathan D. Spence, *Chan's Great Continent* (New York: W. W. Norton & Company, 1999), 124; and Ia.S. Lur'e, "Mikhail Bulgakov between Mark Twain and Lev Tolstoy," *Russian Review* 50, no. 2 (April 1991): 203–10. Lenin's hairstyle and clothing were already anachronisms by 1923. For Qing official clothing, see Gary Dickinson and Linda Wrigglesworth, *Imperial Wardrobe* (Berkeley: Ten Speed Press, 2000), 116–17. For the queue (*bianzi* 辮子) or pigtail as a Manchu hairstyle imposed by the Qing and rejected by the Republican Revolution, see Edward J.M. Rhoads, *Manchus and Han: Ethnic Relations and Political Power in Late Qing and Early Republican China, 1861–1928* (Seattle: University of Washington Press, 2000), 60, 252–4.
89 Bulgakov, "Kitaiskaia istoriia," 141.
90 Bulgakov, "Kitaiskaia istoriia," 142.
91 Popov, "Kitaiskie proletarii," 22, 86–7. In July 1919, a local newspaper in Velikie luki reported that a group of Chinese machine gunners, surrounded by the enemy, had continued firing until they ran out of ammunition, whereupon they shot themselves (36).

92 Bulgakov, "Kitaiskaia istoriia," 145.
93 Bulgakov would later rework many of the motifs from "Chinese Story" in his 1926 NEP-era play *Zoika's Apartment* (*Zoikina kvartira*), which features two comic-sinister Chinese laundry workers and drug dealers named Gan-Dza-Lin (aka Gazolin, i.e., Gasoline) and Sen-Zin-Po (aka Kheruvim, i.e., Cherubim). This namesake of the "Chinese Story" machine gunner takes up the themes of violence and sexual threat, murdering the NEP entrepreneur Gus' for his money and eloping to Shanghai with Zoya's maid Maniushka. Mikhail Bulgakov, "Zoikina kvartira," in *Sobranie sochinenii v piati tomakh*, vol. 3: *P'esy* (Moscow: Khudozhestvennaia literatura, 1992), 77–125.
94 Pavel Medvedev, "Formal'nyi metod v literaturovedenii," in M.M. Bakthin (pod maskoi), *Freidizm. Formal'nyi metod v literaturovedenii. Marksizm i filosofiia iazyka. Stat'i* (Moscow: Labirint, 2000), 203–8.
95 Larin, *Kitaitsy v Rossii*, 41–2; Siegelbaum, "Another 'Yellow Peril,'" 318–19. For Russian responses to the Boxer Rebellion, see David Schimmelpennick van der Oye, "Russia's Ambivalent Response to the Boxers," *Cahiers du Monde russe* 41, no. 1 (2000): 57–78; and Alena N. Eskridge-Kosmach, "Russia in the Boxer Rebellion," *Journal of Slavic Military Studies* 21, no. 1 (2008): 47.
96 Dmitrii Grigorevich Ianchevetskii, *U sten nedvizhnovo Kitaia* (St. Petersburg: Izd-vo P. A. Artem'eva, 1903), republished as *1900: Russkie shturmuiut Pekin* (Moscow: Yauza; Eksmo, 2008), 144–5.
97 Pil'niak, "Sankt-Piter-Burkh," 46, 53. Pil'niak probably took the song from Ianchevetskii, *1900*, 145.
98 Lim, "Solov'ev and the East," 321. For similar formulations in the writings of Jack London, see Lye, *America's Asia*, 16.
99 Quoted in Mondry, "*Petersburg* and Contemporary Racial Thought," 134–5.
100 Eric Hayot, *The Hypothetical Mandarin: Sympathy, Modernity, and Chinese Pain* (Oxford: Oxford University Press, 2009), 14–18.
101 Smith's chapters were first published as instalments in Shanghai's *North China Daily News* in 1889, before appearing in book form in 1890. Revised editions appeared in London (1892) and New York (1894). See Lydia Liu, "The Ghost of Arthur H. Smith in the Mirror of Cultural Translation," *Journal of American-East Asian Relations* 20 (2013): 407.
102 Arthur H. Smith, *Chinese Characteristics* (Edinburgh, London: Oliphant, Anderson and Ferrier, 1900), ch. 11, "The Absence of Nerves," 96.
103 Smith, *Chinese Characteristics*, 92–3.
104 Smith, *Chinese Characteristics*, 90.
105 For contemporary theories of neurasthenia and their racialized dimension, see Liu, "The Ghost of Arthur H. Smith," 410–11. On the

connection between theories of European degeneration and the discourse of Yellow Peril, see David Schimmelpenninck van der Oye, *Toward the Rising Sun: Russian Ideologies of Empire and the Path to War with Japan* (DeKalb: Northern Illinois University Press, 2001), 95–6.
106 Smith, *Chinese Characteristics*, 96–7.
107 Liu, "The Ghost of Arthur H. Smith," 407.
108 See A.G. Smith, *Kharakteristiki kitaitsev*, ed. E. Spal'vina (Vladivostok: Dal'nyi Vostok, 1904–7).
109 Hayot, *The Hypothetical Mandarin*, 139.
110 Lye, *America's Asia*, 56–7.
111 Benton, *Chinese Migrants*, 4–6. See also Lye, *America's Asia*, 15–20.
112 Benton, *Chinese Migrants*, 6. In Australia, trade union agitation against Chinese migration played a key role in the formation of the White Australia policy from 1901. See Benton, *Chinese Migrants*, 75–6.
113 Siegelbaum, "Another 'Yellow Peril,'" 310–11.
114 Diatlov, "Sindrom zheltoi opasnosti," 537.
115 See, for example, Il'ia Semenovich Levitov, *Zheltaia rasa* (St Petersburg: tip. inzh. G.A. Bernshtein, 1900), 19–32, 46–9. For a detailed discussion of Levitov and his writings, see Hsu, "A Tale of Two Railroads," 231–4.
116 Quoted in Hsu, "A Tale of Two Railroads," 231.
117 Diatlov, "Sindrom zheltoi opasnosti," 535, 544.
118 Schimmelpenninck, *Toward the Rising Sun*, 82–103.
119 Kuropatkin, *Russko-kitaiskii vopros* (St. Petersburg: A.S. Suvorin, Novoe vremia, 1913), 183.
120 In this regard, Kuropatkin explicitly polemicized with earlier writers such as Nikolai Przheval'skii, who had claimed that Qing China was so weak militarily it could easily be conquered by Russian troops. See Kuropatkin, *Russko-kitaiskii vopros*, 2; Schimmelpenninck, *Toward the Rising Sun*, 33–7.
121 Benton, *Chinese Migrants*, 22.
122 Benton, *Chinese Migrants*, 15.
123 Quoted in Hsu, "A Tale of Two Railroads," 231.
124 For an account of modern racism's historical imbrication with capitalism that draws on the work of Stuart Hall and Cedric Robinson, see Satnam Virdee, "Racialized Capitalism: An Account of its Contested Origins and Consolidation," *The Sociological Review* 67, no. 1 (2019): 3–27.

9 The Feeling and Fragility of Modernity: Red Mobility against the Grand Tour in Nikolai Aseev's *Unmade Beauty* (1928)

MICHAEL KUNICHIKA

La Funicolare Vesuviana, built in 1880, traversed the slopes of Mount Vesuvius, famous for its eruption in AD 79 that destroyed Pompeii. Commonly featured in photography and postcards of the time, the funicular was a feat of modern engineering and an augur of modernization to come. Tourists would gather at the base of the volcano and be shuttled to its heights in eight minutes. From that vantage, they could take in the Neopolitan views and perhaps ponder the millennia-old destruction. Others were said to have wanted to spit into the dormant crater. The funicular, herald of industry, was destroyed by another eruption in 1944.

Among those who visited the site in the 1920s was Nikolai Aseev, who had travelled to Italy in 1927 with his wife Ksenia Aseeva. Funded by the proceeds from his first collected works, Aseev left Moscow with an itinerary that included several other European cities before Italy.[1] Gazing upon the tracery of steel affixed to the mountain, Aseev remarked that "the golden thread of fire on the edge of Vesuvius is, of course, still far from a complete victory over nature."[2] The funicular signalled "the growth of international modernity, the force of whose forms continually breaks through cardboard walls of artificially existing authorities and does not permit itself to be covered by the dust and ash of traditions and ruins."[3] Such signs of modernity acquired heightened legibility in a landscape dominated by ruins as was Italy's, to which tourists – who, in Aseev's view, belonged to a modern-day cult of antiquity – made pilgrimages. Against such worship of the past, Aseev sided with the funicular and all that it represented, espousing a technophilia he shared with other members of his generation, including Aleksei Gastev, Sergei Tret'iakov, and Dziga Vertov.

Aseev's descriptions of the funicular typified his observations during his Italian sojourn, which he would record in two sketches (*ocherki*) published *Novyi LEF*. His celebration of industrial modernity aligned with the overriding concerns of the journal and its editors Nikolai Chuzhak, Vladimir Mayakovsky, Viktor Shklovsky, and Tret'iakov. Aseev later gathered a larger selection of sketches and published them under the title *Razgrimirovannaia krasota* the following year: the adjective "razgrimirovannaia" relates to the theatre, with the verb *grimirovat'* meaning "to make up," so the Russian title can be translated as *Unmade Beauty*.[4] That "beauty" refers to Europe itself and contains a promise that Aseev aims to fulfil. As he explains in the work's concluding remarks, he writes "so the myth about the dazzling Abroad-Beauty [*krasavitsa zagranitsa*] is debunked, her impeccable superiority over us, the powerful force of her cultural tradition is debunked" (225). These lines disclose the polemical edge of the work, which gives force to Aseev's assessment of the progress of industry and culture in both Europe and the Soviet Union.

As a series of travel sketches, the text has other significant concerns beyond industrialization. Throughout *Unmade Beauty*, Aseev remarks on revolutionary culture and its intellectual sources, meditates on figures such as Kropotkin and the Russian literary past, and reflects on European politics and culture, even the nature of shopping in Western European capitals. Aseev envisions various readerships for his dispatches – or at least presents a kind of performance of future readerships. Some of the work's most likely readers are his literary compatriots from *Novyi LEF*; others may need to be convinced that Aseev's new aesthetic values should prevail over those of the past. Indeed, these sketches represent his effort to reformulate travel writing specifically, and writing more generally, as we see advocated by the writers and thinkers Aseev meets and the literary programs they have elaborated for the post-revolutionary period. His itinerary intersects with other mobilities and occasions meetings with particular luminaries, most notably with Maxim Gorky in Sorrento. He also meets Filippo Marinetti, who linked Italian Futurism to the fascist government, and reflects on Benedetto Croce and the dispersal of Italian intellectuals as fascism rises in the country. And throughout, he is guided by the essential text of the Russian cultural estimation of Italy, Pavel Muratov's *Images of Italy* (*Obrazy Italii*, 1911–12), with which Aseev launches an extended polemic in one of the sketches of *Unmade Beauty*, focusing on the debate between antiquity and modernity.[5] It is in this latter vein that he reflects on how he too can contribute to the image of Italy in European and Russian culture by engaging such figures as Nikolai Gogol, Alexander Blok, and Muratov himself, while also thinking about the future of Soviet writing in his encounter with Gorky.

As he travels, he reveals different facets of left cultural movement. The poetics of mobility offered here are neither those of the exile nor those of the émigré, for whom "up-rooting and dislocations" create "such travail [that] there comes an urgency, not to say a precariousness of vision and tentativeness of statement that renders the use of language something much more interesting and provisional than it would otherwise be."[6] It is instead an attempt at a left travel writing that will register the predicaments of writing and culture for modern writers. We shall see this with the three encounters in the work: with Muratov and, by extension, the Russian literary past; with Marinetti, and thus the fate of Futurist aesthetics in the 1920s; and with Gorky, and thus the question of what Soviet writing will be. These encounters in Aseev's work disclose multiple intersecting stories of intellectual life in the 1920s while also occasioning reflections on the purpose of leftist writing and culture as it takes shape in the process of travel and as Aseev aims to establish its legitimacy in the face of antiquity and Western European culture.

An Unsentimental Education: Aseev's Visit to Rome and the Feeling of Modernity

Aseev titled the two instalments of *Unmade Beauty* published in *Novyi LEF* "Abroad (from the Diary of a Journey)" ("Zagranitsa [Iz dnevnika puteshestviia]") and "An Argument with a Travel Guide (from the Diary of a Journey)" ("Spor s putevoditelem [iz dnevnika puteshestviia]"). The latter title signalled immediately to his readers that he would contend with how earlier cultural authorities had codified attitudes and itineraries of Italy in their travel guides.[7] The guide with which Aseev took particular issue was Muratov's *Images of Italy*, the three volumes of which had served as the pre-eminent travelogue for his generation.[8] The work combined Muratov's reflections on his journey with a richly elaborated range of literary references and extensive considerations of Italian Renaissance art. It served as a guide for itineraries throughout the country, as well as to the regimentation of experience and feeling central to the Grand Tour: one could find in it a valorization of the antique and Renaissance past as well as horror at a modernizing Italy. In this way, it supplied Aseev with an ideal counter-model and a source of cultural authority (albeit one that was waning in the post-revolutionary decade) against which he could fashion his own version of the Grand Tour.

What both writers shared was the notion that to go to Italy is to try to understand the nature of experiencing and articulating culture as it underpins the very idea of mobility. Some travel for leisure, others for political, religious, or economic reasons, still others are forced to travel. Here, the motivation for mobility is the pursuit and evaluation of culture and, more specifically, the reassessment of and debate on culture in the aftermath of the Revolution. For Aseev, the trip to Italy, cynosure of Renaissance humanism, was meant not only to gauge the progress of proletarian revolutionary struggle, European industrialization, and socialism (as do so many of the writers and thinkers examined in this volume), but also to newly articulate the relationship between culture and travel. In effect, he was going to Italy to test himself – to test whether he could resist the grandeur of the past celebrated by such figures as Goethe, Stendhal, and others who visited Italy in search of cultivation.[9] That test, however, was not simply the kind of exercise in Futurist bravado that had typified the early movement, as had been announced in the manifesto "A Slap in the Face of Public Taste," with its ostentatious rejection of the past.[10] Aseev was more cautious. Indeed, in the editorial note he affixed to "Argument with a Travel Guide," he disclosed no small anxiety over his tenuous grasp on both modernity and culture itself. In that note, he describes how he is entering into a "polemic about the preservation of all kinds of cultural antiquities" by grappling with Muratov.[11] Where Aseev "rejoices at any manifestation of modernity in Rome," Muratov, he points out, exhibits a "shudder of disgust at any sign of the time, no matter how necessary it may be" (16).

To cultivate both taste and spirit is no less central to Aseev's mission than it had been for Muratov, but the objects of admiration change. One must feel and develop aesthetically, but previous models of experience and their relative objects of veneration no longer suffice. The former Italy weighs upon Aseev; he tries to resist the gravitational force of the past, training his gaze instead upon such signs of modernization as aquariums, funiculars, and tunnels, or searching for signs of labour or the proletariat. His pursuit of modernity reveals another fragility: Aseev is not sure about his own cultural standing. Aseev's "argument" with Muratov hinges on such questions as: What should a Soviet traveller look at? When navigating a landscape in which the signs of the past prevail, how does one remain committed to a feeling for modernity and modern writing? Pondering such questions, Aseev describes travelling through Rome on a tram, from whose mobile vantage point he observes the stultifying landscape of ruins unfolding before him: "Brrrr! Death and ruins amidst the shops and magnolias, the rotting of the spirit like a hash of stones" (3). Indeed, ruins do not just linger in Rome; they seem actually to proliferate, and Aseev notes that Rome aimed toward "producing antiquity" in an effort to satiate the desires of tourists.

What thereby unfurls before Aseev is what he calls a "revolting comedy of human ruins" (3), a place where a millennium, materialized by a monument, looms and threatens to plunge a traveller into antiquity. Confronting a site such as the Colosseum, for example, Aseev revolts against this ever-present antiquity: "Imagine for yourselves," he writes upon seeing the structure, "amidst the large, well-arranged city with its trams, buses, excellent bridges, noisy crows, and entrances to cafes and pubs ... is located an inordinately massive, wind-cracked, dark-brown stony cardboard box" (3). In the face of an antiquity that obdurately persists, Aseev shows here that the Futurist writer must take recourse to rhetorically diminishing it, deflating the status of these markers of antiquity, reducing stone to hardly more than mass-produced wood pulp.

This antagonism towards ruins makes Aseev sound as though he were an Italian Futurist. When Fillipo Marinetti announced the movement's arrival, he alerted the public in his "Founding Manifesto of Futurism" (1909) that he would be taking aim at an Italy freighted by the ballast of ancient ruins and ceaselessly devoted to their celebration: "It is from Italy that we launch through the world this violently upsetting incendiary manifesto of ours. With it, today, we establish *Futurism* because we want to free this land from its smelly gangrene of professors, archaeologists, *ciceroni* and antiquarians. For too long has Italy been a dealer in second-hand clothes. We mean to free her from the numberless museums that cover her like so many graveyards."[12]

Marinetti's Russian counterparts were well acquainted with his views, and his antipathy towards the past served as a powerful forerunner of Aseev's own revolt against ruin and indicated the iconoclastic strain in Futurism internationally that, in the Russian case, extended from the pre-revolutionary into the post-revolutionary period.[13]

Although he echoes Marinetti's vision of Italy, Aseev's iconoclasm has limits. It would be a "pity," he observes, to destroy the Colosseum, suggesting instead that it be made less prominent so as "to hide it from the general urban background" (6). This proposal reveals his conflicted sense of how to treat the past, which inspires "respect" in him but also fear – fear because it "deadens the air, thought, and will" (6). "Ruins," Aseev notes, "which are carried over into modernity, are dangerous because they drive back the present day from us, leading us into melancholy" (6). His encounter with the past in Rome can thus be seen as disclosing a sense of the fragility of modernity and of being modern. Indeed, rather than offering a vision of modernity as either inexorable or unrelenting, Aseev reveals his doubts about modernity's ability to exorcise the past from the present. In effect, he is articulating his awareness of a continual revanchist threat against which many sectors of Soviet cultural production were on guard.

This complex view of the Colosseum also points to some nuances in his assessment of Muratov's *Images of Italy*. The work clearly served him as a guide (or anti-guide): the very chapter on Muratov in *Unmade Beauty*, for example, extensively cites from his predecessor and thereby betrays that he had the book in hand. What Aseev must do is elaborate his own model in order to contradict Muratov's sense that "it frequently occurs to the modern traveller that his predecessors were vastly happier than he in their knowledge of Rome" (15). A statement like this, which accords so much value to the past, could not be more anathema to a Futurist like Aseev. Against such a view, his task is to rewrite Italy for a new generation, overturning the "influence of views and impressions of national travellers at the end of the previous and the start of the present century" (15). The power of past impressions means that "any new sense of a country is treated like a blasphemous perversion of its genuine character" (15). Such passages indicate how the "ideals of behaviour, analytic strategies, ethical postures, cognitive agendas, and ideologies out of which the concept of the logic of culture" arises are all now being contested.[14] In this regard, the value of going to Italy, *locus classicus* for culture, was to carry on a distinctly modernist endeavour (for which Aseev represented one ramified branch of Futurism): How is one to articulate modernity in a country seemingly dominated by antiquity, but also, how is modernity itself to be established as a culture on par with antiquity?

Radical Tourism in the Face of Antiquity

Although staunchly opposed to Muratov's vision, Aseev reveals the challenges facing the modern writer who is bereft of – or, rather, wilfully rejects – a cultural authority based on the past. He notes some hesitation about LEF's own purchase on culture:

> Should I, a modern person, perceive and feel Rome exactly in accordance with [Muratov's] recipe? Should I believe in the reality of the assertion that no rational solicitude could change the course of Rome's history in a more attractive direction? And is it true that against the "feeling of antiquity" [*chuvstvo antichnogo*] I have no right to juxtapose my own "feeling of modernity" [*chuvstvo sovremennosti*] out of a fear of being called an ignoramus or superficial person? (17)

Uncertain about his own cultural status and credentials, Aseev still protests: "No. I decisively should argue with Muratov, behind whose words ... are hidden millennia of the slavish worship of the sacred sites of the ages that continue to deify ruins" (17). Such remarks fill several paragraphs, becoming a kind of LEF catechism, testifying both to Aseev's modernity and, from our perspective, to the possibility that the modern protests too much.

Like his colleagues in *LEF* and later *Novyi LEF*, Aseev faces the multiple challenges that travel writing poses. Their aspiration, as Devin Fore has observed, was "not to veridically reflect reality in [their] work," which could be associated with documentary passivity, but instead "to actively transform reality through" documentary modes.[15] Indeed, both journals endeavoured to render innovative accounts of travel both within the Soviet Union and abroad; a preponderance of these articles highlighted an essential complementarity and attraction between documentary and sites advancing industrialization. Maria Gough, in her account of one such project – Tret'iakov's visit to the commune "The Lighthouse" – labelled this kind of travel "radical tourism."[16] Although what is "radical" about tourism seems often to hinge on the site that is visited, many "radical" itineraries involved travel not only to sites of industrialization but also to places where industrialization seemed quite far off. This is to say that what is "radical" is also the orientation and aesthetic program a given writer brings to a site and not only the site itself.

A typology of what could have constituted radical tourism might be necessary because many of these writers gauged the radical nature of their travel in both geographical and chronological terms: hinterlands and backward territories were places that seemed to test a traveller rather than assuage him that the course of modernization was inexorable.[17] In Tret'iakov, for example, we find a commensurability between his documentary project and socialist constructions, but also a divergence. Other documentary projects, such as those on Georgia, could frequently lament the backwardness of various spaces while also praising modernization efforts. In 1922, Tret'iakov aptly observed how Aseev's "Steel Nightingale" ("Stal'noi solovei") expressed an "industrial worldfeeling" (*industrial'noe mirooshchushchenie*).[18] It is this sensibility, as we saw in his description of the funicular, and thus his own radicality, to which Aseev clings, and which is tested as he enters a space celebrated for its antiquity.

Once there, Aseev faced a local instance of what was a broader predicament for writers of the time: How to conjoin the commitments to formal innovation to the project of documenting societal change? How to narrate one's own experiences of travel, with its attendant impact on fashioning of a self as a Soviet writer? With Aseev, however, Italy poses other challenges: What happens when a writer aspiring to establish his revolutionary credentials visits a site long visited by tourists and essential to various visions of Western or world culture? How does a "radical tourist" prove his own radical commitments in both subject and form in the face of the antique past? Italy, then, was putting to a test Aseev's "feeling of modernity," something he had been cultivating long before his arrival.

In this light, Aseev writes some of his most moving and nuanced accounts of his predecessors. While he frequently polemicizes with Muratov, he benefits from the latter's range of reference, in particular, Muratov's reconstruction of the Italian theme in Russian letters. In an extended series of essays in *Images of Italy*, Muratov discusses how Italy's ruins enchanted Blok and Gogol but made their relationship with Russia impossible. He notes how Blok, whose "Italian Poems" Aseev knew well, faithfully describes the "caressing gloom of Umbria" (34). "In general," he writes, Blok's "Italian verses are entirely precise and subtle in conveying the local colour of Italy." Aseev even gives himself over to describing the landscape his forebears had seen, and he, too, finds the experience revivifying. "After the snow and gloom of the border crossing, the air of Umbria, its land and freshness, how sudden a returning youth" (35). Still, he relies on labour to justify his account of the landscape: "Who says Italians are lazy?," Aseev remarks, as he observes the plethora of gardens and tilled rows throughout the region, everywhere revealing the signs of labour. One of the failures of past writers on Italy is that they either refused to see modernization or lamented it. As a result, in Aseev's analysis, writers attracted to Italy's ruins became ruins themselves. "Both Gogol and Blok," Aseev writes,

> were destroyed by the fragments of ruins, which had been thrown down upon their melted imaginations. The traces of these fragments, like seals, grew cold and remained upon them like impressions of foreign cultures, and, in order to free themselves of them, both tried to rub them off with the dust of their native land. But even this "native" land turned out to be the same convention, the same traditional lie, as was the plaintive exclamations of papal services. (153)

For Aseev, the ruins become an "avalanche of ancient conceptions of culture" (153) that buried both Gogol and Blok. They had been entranced by Italian culture, lured by Roman Catholicism, and neither could recover. The time of antiquity and the attraction to it should be definitively over; Aseev is, at the very least, attempting to bring an end to the mythologization and mythopoetics of Rome, a city that has entranced his predecessors.

What's notable about Aseev's account is his relative candour in conveying how this competition with the past – a Soviet Futurist's version of an ongoing battle of the ancients and moderns – leaves him slightly embarrassed, even anxious about his own cultural status. Aseev, at various moments, discloses not only the bravura of the attempt but also the strain of his position as he shuttles between an antipathy towards the cultural past whose authority he resists and his acknowledgment that such a rejection leaves him bereft of cultural authority himself.

What Aseev admits perhaps more than do others is that iconoclasm represents a crisis facing leftist culture – namely, how to establish one's own cultural credentials and on the basis of which aesthetic values. Italy is thus the premier country in which to test one's resistance to the allure of the past while also trying to prove that LEF can articulate a vision of cultural value: "the protest against this feeling of becoming mute before the archaic is perceived as a LEF tendency, an unwise lack of tact, almost like a bravado against culture" (16). Indeed, as Aseev punctuates his travelogue with verse, the lyric persona he fashions styles himself as a barbarian within the gates:

Римляне!
На чужом языке,
Косноязыкий
варвар
к вашим потомкам
кричу я,
за кем
нет еще
хлама старого?! (241)

[Romans! / In a foreign tongue / A tongue-tied barbarian / to his descendants / Shout I, / behind whom / Is there still not / old junk!?]

Aseev's self-presentation as a barbarian can be approached in various ways. The adjective he chooses for his sense of himself as a barbarian, *kosnoiazykii*, is itself something of a barbarism, since the word *kosnoiazychie*, meaning "confused articulation," has, as its standard adjectival form, *kosnoiazychnyi*.[19] This slight play – a stylistic infelicity about a word signifying confused speech – indicates a kind of linguistic barbarism.

On one level, he announces his own combination of bravado and anxiety that typifies his cultural stance. He knows his views on the past will be viewed as "barbarian" or in bad taste. On another, he taps into two distinct threads of Russian cultural history in which barbarism is polemically adopted as a way to challenge the cultural authority of

Europe.[20] To be sure, this is not only a Russian cultural tendency, but it is one that acquired particular force during the modernist period when, for example, Russian modernists such as Natalia Goncharova and Aleksandr Shevchenko adopted Primitivism as part of their challenge to the cultural tastes of Europe, paralleling European counterparts such as Paul Gauguin and his travels to Tahiti.[21] In this regard, a figure more proximate to Aseev is Blok, whose own shifting visions of culture and poetry may also have served as a positive model for Aseev. One need only recall that Blok had ratified his own transvalued barbarism in his long poem "Skify" ("The Scythians"), which he wrote while he, too, was re-envisioning the poet's role after the Revolution. With his pronouncement "Da, Skify my, Da, Aziaty my" ("Yes, we are Scythians, Yes, we are Asians"), Blok summoned the chauvinisms associated with such fears as the Yellow Peril and adopted them as he threatened Europe, in particular Paestum (a site of Italian ruins).[22] Aseev carries forward that image.[23] In so doing, he inverts what Hayden White has called a "technique of ostensive self-definition by negation" in his reconstruction of the "wild man" *topos* in Western culture, which we see during periods of "sociocultural stress: when the need for positive self-definition appears, it is always possible to say something like: 'I may not know the precise content of my own felt humanity, but I am most certainly *not* like that.'"[24] In this regard, Aseev defines his own position as an inversion of this model – having been licensed by Blok, he styles himself as the wild man within the gates of Rome in order to assert that he certainly does not want "to be like that" – that is, like his predecessors and like the ruin worshippers who venerate the Italian past – as he works towards elaborating a modern, post-revolutionary culture.

Futurism and the Fate of Culture: Aseev's Evening with Marinetti

The challenge Aseev faces in elaborating a vision of Italian modernity and modern culture relates not only its fragility but also to its possible future – in fact, modern Italy was taking a worrisome turn at the time. Shadowing Aseev's experience of Italy is the rise of fascism, whose signs he notes throughout the countryside and whose impact on Italian life he frequently laments. If Muratov represents one kind of past, then so too does Marinetti, who represents for Aseev a past of Futurism itself. Their meeting is a richly textured literary-historical moment, from which Aseev launches a series of reflections on the ultimate failure of the Italian branch of Futurism, the foil to Russia's own branch, whose development in the post-Revolutionary period was a central task of Aseev and his colleagues at *Novyi LEF*. In this regard, he and Marinetti represent the ramifying of Futurism into its two major affiliations in the 1920s, the one with communism, the other fascism.

Aseev recorded a speech Marinetti gave at the Teatro Argentina in 1927. That speech was, in effect, a moment in which a Russian Futurist saw what had become of the Italian Futurist. "I have travelled the whole of Europe," he records Marinetti saying. "I have seen how in France Futurism has degenerated into an artistic-aesthetic tendency, having become stiff in the painterly school of the cubists. I have seen how in Germany it led toward expressionism, degenerating into the epileptic perception of the world by Dadaism" (345). "Only Italian Futurism," Marinetti asserted, "remained an actual, undiluted, unclouded method for the reorganization of the human psyche, which imparts to it all manner and means of the quickest and utilitarian rebirth" (344). Such pronouncements must have appalled Aseev, who could hardly have responded well to the idea that it was in Italy and not in Soviet Russia that Futurism was still capable of elaborating the aesthetic principles for reconstructing society and the human, given that he himself was engaged in precisely that endeavour.

Aseev registers his opposition to Marinetti by observing how, by 1927, the Italian Futurist had become passé (the greatest insult one could level against a Futurist). Marinetti had once been a towering figure in modernist letters; now he had become something of a buffoon: "Marinetti's speech is radical and witty, but I cannot forget that, in the end, his entire pathos was nevertheless theatrical and exaggeratedly exalted. He'd jump from one histrionic [*teatral'shchina*] to another, from the histrionics of antique ruins, remnants, and museums to the props of the caps of gendarmes and the cocky plumage of fascist warmongers."[25]

Assev's commentary links Marinetti's style to the aesthetic and political ideology of the attraction to ruins and what it shares with fascism. For Aseev, both ideologies reflect romantic delusions of restoration. Aseev's criticism of Marinetti hearkens back to his criticism of Muratov's obsession with antiquities, but in this case, he asserts that the worship of the past is central to Marinetti's fascism – in this regard, Marinetti is no longer a Futurist. Indeed, Aseev's views on the erstwhile Futurist's attraction to antiquity recognize a central feature of fascist aesthetics as it was elaborated, for example, by the artist and critic Ardengo Soffici, whose article "Fascist Art" (1928) had asserted that "[it] also must not be the fruit of reaction, or, of subversion, but of discovery, through revolutionary experiences, of characteristics specific to Italianness, that remain from the epoch of Greco-Roman art to the nineteenth century."[26]

The present Marinetti seemed more pathetic than the one Aseev encountered more than a decade earlier, when the Italian visited Moscow in 1914. As recorded by Benedikt Livshits in his own memoir of Futurism, *The One and a Half-Eyed Archer*, Marinetti had caused an uproar among his hosts by insisting on Italian Futurism's pre-eminence, which left Russian Futurism, a movement about the future, both indebted to Italy and belated in comparison with it.[27] Encountering Marinetti again in 1927, Aseev recalls his earlier impression from 1914: "It was strange to look at him – he'd provoked wild ecstasy then and just as much hatred from the audience, but now, 'working' under the protection of the Carabinieri, he finally arrived at our theatrical means of *épater*, no one especially offended or nonplussed by the official exponent of a fascist 'renaissance'" (346).

The confrontation between Aseev and Marinetti was one in which two Futurists, both of whom challenged a previous cultural regime, now found themselves trying to articulate a vision of culture in relation to two prevailing -isms: socialism and fascism. In Vladimir Markov's account of Aseev's attendance at Marinetti's event, "both the play and its author aroused in Aseev nothing but pity – or so he wrote. After 1928, interest in Marinetti seems to have ceased in Russia."[28] The year 1928, in which Aseev published *Unmade Beauty* in full, marked the end of the line for *Russian* engagement with Italian Futurism; in effect, it offered nothing but memories of a past.

The sense of historical lines criss-crossing at this moment is all the more striking when read against Aseev's account of the rise of fascism in Italy. For all the indications of industrial transformation that he valorizes throughout the travelogue, it is the rise of fascism that haunts his account. He records, for example, graffiti scrawled on a wall in Rome, which he incorporates into a poem: "A basso rossa! // Evviva fascisti!" ("Down with the reds! Long live the fascists!," 255). Aseev observes how, lurking behind the seemingly tranquil antiquity of the Italian landscape, the new political regime has transformed ordinary behaviour.

> Local residents told me they don't recognize Italy anymore. Everyone fears one another, fears expressing their opinion, fears telling a joke, for the love of laughter. In inns everyone bites their tongue these days. Conversation about politics – the beloved theme of an Italian at the end of work – is absolutely intolerable. If someone utters the word "fascism" or mentions the last name of you know who, the proprietor of the inn ... asks the unbalanced regular to pay at once and take a walk on the street. The eyes and ears of fascism are on guard everywhere, and so the spontaneity of displaying emotions, which struck me on my first days in Italy, is only a pale shadow of the joie de vivre and temperament of Romans. (248)

Fascism has made Italian life seemingly more pallid, and increasingly threatening. Aseev notes that his own movements are under surveillance.

For example, when the hotel porter in Rome suggests to Aseev that he register at the nearby *questura* (police station), he notices something odd in the relationship of fascism to architecture, which echoes Marinetti's new penchant for antiquities: the new forms of policing under Mussolini have taken up residence in the most ancient of buildings.

All these various interactions remind Aseev that he is a "Soviet." When, for example, he interacts with the police and fascist bureaucrats, they "react with a combination of surprise, wariness, and respect toward a Soviet passport" (255). This mode of constituting his own identity through the experience of travel and in his encounters with other writers is not always conducted through a process of definition by negation – it often positively affirms what being "Soviet" and indeed a "member of LEF" can mean for Aseev. Towards the end, his work builds to an exultant return to the Soviet Union: "We are returning home, full of hale sprits of our proximity to the sole place on earth where there is not such a quantity of human falsity, hypocrisy, where the vast mass of people know their own value, believe in the future, grow, and are filled by the enthusiasm for what will be the tomorrow, and not the yesterday of humanity" (384).

His desentimentalizing Grand Tour ends with this message of anti-travel. One goes to other countries in order to know one's home better. This episode could perhaps have served as a source of inspiration for Mayakovsky's poem "Verses on a Soviet Passport" ("Stikhi o sovetskom pasporte," 1929), which appeared the following year; it likewise concludes with a similar account of how the experience of travel affirms the poet's status as a Soviet citizen. In any case, these lines provide at least one vision of the function and fate of "red mobility": one travels in order to learn that one should have stayed home. While the lesson might seem glib by the end of the work – its ending is not just a return home but an ideology of home – it indicates some of the tension bound up with the term Soviet. As Aseev thinks about Italy, he thinks often of his precursors – Marinetti and Muratov, but also Gogol and Blok. He is attempting to trace what Italy's effect was on those who became too enchanted by it to really come home. In this regard, he is expressing an appeal to national culture, not just Soviet culture. A similar episode, this time with Maxim Gorky, will possess a greater density, while in this case addressing the various possibilities for Soviet letters and Aseev's place within them.

Visiting Gorky in Sorrento: The Crisis of Modern Writing

Aseev devoted four chapters of *Unmade Beauty* to his two-week stay in Sorrento with Gorky, whose "dacha" drew writers and artists in the 1920s. When Aseev and his wife arrive in early November 1927, he encounters various people living at Gorky's, from his son and daughter-in-law, who occupy one small room, to the sickly artist Ivan Nikolaevich, who paints in the style of Henri Rousseau, and Gorky's secretary, civil wife, and translator, Mariia Ignat'evna Budberg. Aseev records his various discussions with Gorky about contemporary literature, along with Gorky's daily life and habits. Indeed, some of the details seem oriented towards providing a journalistic account of a major red émigré's life, for example, how he maintains his literary connections, but also how he has adapted to Italian life.

Gorky has arranged a dinner for some fifteen people to honour Aseev's arrival. The guests include Olga Forsh and an Italian prince from whom Gorky is renting his home. Throughout the experience, Aseev writes character sketches, which are often keyed to an individual's class and thus social-historical significance. Presenting a scene that could have appeared in Giuseppe Tomasi di Lampedusa's *The Leopard* (*Il Gattopardo*, 1958), Aseev remarks on how the prince, for example, is "unconsciously drawn to the next phases of the development of culture, which are foreign and incomprehensible to him, but which bring to him a tempting light continuing in the life of man" (277). In Aseev's view, the collapse of the Italian aristocracy has left that class bereft of a future plot; the prince's Italian daughter and heir seems to be at the end of the historical line: "His daughter, an Italian princess and inheritor of all his villas, contradicts the image of an Italian aristocrat with her appearance and behavior ... She listens to talk of Russia and Soviet life with the hungry attraction of youth to another way of life, to other customs, to unobtainable life" (278).

Many of the figures at Gorky's seem to be losing their place in history and modernity; they are, in their own way, ruins. What occupies both Aseev and Gorky is the nature of writing after the Revolution and thus their place in the historical trajectory of Russian cum Soviet letters. They spend their evenings debating various aspects of the new Soviet writing, with Gorky occasionally taking slight digs at Aseev about his eating habits; all signs, perhaps, that he cannot fully appreciate the newly emerging styles and forms of Soviet poetry. He is generally indifferent to or contemptuous of the poets Aseev reads to him; and his own poetry, in Aseev's view, is "naturalistic" and tends towards "narrative" (*povestvovatel'nyi*). Aseev does not dismiss it out of hand, but Gorky represents an older style and "feels some discomfort from the lowering of that very high style," a lowering that Gorky perceives in Soviet poetry. Reflecting on his stay, Aseev notes:

> I do not know what impression I made on Gorky, but from conversations with him I feel and am convinced that closest of all to him is not only

his literary work, nor his literary production, but the general matters of all Soviet literature, in which there cannot be general tastes and general understandings by virtue of the diversity, various significances, multiple strengths of its constitutive tendencies that justly define the heated development, rapidity, and the freshness of its course. (290)

This pluralistic vision of cultural production, pitted squarely against Gorky's approach to an emerging cultural field, was Aseev's essential statement of his views.

Aseev's travelogue, however, would not be the last word on the matter; Gorky would later have an opportunity to tell the Soviet public his own impressions of Aseev. In his review of Aseev's book, published in *Izvestiia* in 1928, Gorky remarks: "There, in Sorrento, he produced an impression of being rather kind, somewhat cunning, easily able to 'adapt' to people, relatively ignorant, but somewhat capable of hiding this shortcoming, which is shameful for a man of letters. The work unmasks him as surprisingly illiterate, frivolous, and unintelligent."[29]

Gorky concludes: "We are permitted to ask, when will young Soviet men of letters begin to learn to read and write?"[30] The review is all the more stinging because Gorky invokes the discourse of *unmasking* – synonymous during that era with exposing inauthenticity – thus suggesting that Aseev, too, is wearing a mask (*grimirovat'*, to recall the work's title *Razgrimmorovannaia krasota*, means to put on make-up) and has shown himself to be a charlatan.

The blatant quality of Gorky's review generated a sharp debate about Soviet letters, one that drew in various literary camps. Gorky described Aseev's book as "shameful, barely literate" and went so far as to mistitle it *"Razvenchannaia krasavitsa,"* or *The Dethroned Beauty*. And even then, he would not leave the matter alone: a few weeks later, again in the pages of *Izvestiia*, he continued to attack Aseev and, by extension, young Soviet writers in general. In another critical article, this one titled "O nachinaiushchikh pisateliakh" ("On Beginning Writers"), he lambasts the young generation, who betrayed an "aspiration toward knowledge that is poorly developed. They read little. Poets find it superfluous to read prose; prosaists do not read poetry, but one and the other rush to write barely intelligible reviews of each other."[31]

The attacks highlighted the larger problem of literary style as it was being advocated by *Novyi LEF*. When Shklovsky came to Aseev's defence in an article "Gorky as Reviewer" ("Gor'kii kak retsenzent") in *Novyi LEF*, he noted all the errors Gorky had made in his two-column review.[32] Such demonstrations of punctiliousness on both sides amounted to a struggle for various kinds of literary and cultural authority. They are significant here because they indicate how Aseev's work was the subject of a range of literary debates – often heated – that disclose for us today the broader context in which that work was read. In light of this back and forth, Aseev's writing reveals the broader, transnational literary field in which so much of the critical debate of the period took place as it related to the nature of poetry as well as to the relationship of the writer to his or her country. Gorky may have been in Sorrento, but he insisted that his literary authority had not been diminished by distance. But what might have been particularly stinging to him was precisely that distance. He had yet to heed Aseev's conclusion that home was better. Gorky, in 1927, had still not indicated he would return to the Soviet Union. He would repatriate only in 1932.

Perhaps the most interesting defence of Aseev came from Tret'iakov, who defended his work in the article "What's new?" ("Chto novogo?"), which appeared in the same issue of *Novyi LEF* as Shklovsky's rebuttal.[33] He noted that Aseev had undertaken an essential transformation of "his verse into commentary material for prose documentary." Gorky's review, he remarked, revealed its own complete "ignorance of verse that shows to what degree attention takes the side of prose." This was a cutting remark, since Tret'iakov was faulting Gorky precisely with what Gorky had faulted the members of LEF, namely that they failed to read poetry. In this regard, what is notable is another aspect of the travelogue, namely the formal dimensions of the work and how they grapple with particular challenges facing those who write first-hand accounts. It was as though Gorky had faulted Aseev for not resolving the very dilemma of culture he admitted was a challenge to any left traveller to Italy.

Conclusion

This chapter has exposed a multitude of tangles of literary and political history. Its episodes illuminate the movements and dispersals that characterized both international modernism and Soviet letters in the post-revolutionary period. In these, one can sense various historical layers and trajectories and narrative possibilities, but also developments that seem to have been made possible only through mobility. The nature and experience of migration are such that one can track the different developments that modernist aesthetics underwent as various figures encountered one another in different locations. In all this, Italy was the *locus classicus* for the traveller in search of cultivation. For the writers and artists considered in this chapter, the themes and questions concerning red mobility and migration were as much about forging and consolidating cultural networks as they were about elaborating a form of writing in the aftermath of modernism and the Revolution. To migrate – or even to travel – was to grapple with how to represent the transformations a given country or countryside was undergoing in relation to an available repertoire of representational forms. That relationship was either oppositional, insofar as those forms were deemed superannuated or in service of privileged classes; or, it was reformist, reconstituting representational modes that could possess renewed value for the task a writer faced.

Unmade Beauty can thus be seen to be transected by multiple crosscurrents of historical narratives and aesthetic tendencies of the period, which reveal the various facets of the conjuncture of leftist and avantgarde aesthetics with travel and the articulation of cultural value.

In the end, Aseev states: "It is not because I reject this perception of the past that I am a member of LEF, but because I am member of LEF the feeling of the living vanquishes within me the pathos of any ruin" (18). While insisting that he does feel the pull of the past, he also notes that the aesthetic ideology of his modernity intervenes at the moment when someone could slip into a retrograde aesthetic mode. In this regard, one goes to Italy to resist its past, to test one's mettle and commitments as a modern artist, everywhere tempted to fall for the past. One must undergo a desentimentalizing education and journey that is, at the same time, a LEF proclamation for the legitimacy of the modern writer and his subject.

Notes

1 K.M. Aseeva, "Iz vospominanii," in *Vospominaniia o Nikolae Aseeve*, 12–34 (Moskva: Sovetskii pisatel', 1980), 29. No date is given for the recollections.
2 Aseeva, "Iz vospominanii," 82. Unless otherwise indicated, all translations are mine.
3 Aseeva, "Iz vospominanii," 82.
4 *Razgrimirovannaia krasota* was originally published in 1928 by Federatsiia, with a more readily accessible version coming in N.N. Aseev, *Proza: 1916–1963, Sobranie sochinenii v 5 tomakh* (Moskva: Izdatel'stvo khudozhestvennoi literatury, 1964), 205–384. All further citations are to the 1928 edition and will be in parenthetical notes in the text.
5 P.M. Muratov, *Obrazy Italii* (Leipzig: Z.I. Grzhebin, 1924).
6 Edward Said, "Introduction" to *Reflections on Exile and Other Essays* (Cambridge, MA: Harvard University Press, 2000), xv.
7 N. Aseev, "Zagranitsa (*Iz dnevnika puteshestviia*)," *Novyi Lef* 2 (February 1928): 1–7; idem, "Spor s putevoditelem (Iz dnevnika puteshestviia)," *Novyi Lef* 5 (May 1928): 15–23.

8 For a recent study of Muratov's work, see L.M. Lencek, "The Venetian Mirror: Pavel Pavlovich Muratov's 'Obrazy Italii' (1924 and the Literature of Art)," *Znanie, Ponimanie, Umenie* 1 (2015): 344–58.
9 For various accounts of the Grand Tour, see, for example, *Grand Tour: The Lure of Italy in the Eighteenth Century*, ed. Andrew Wilton and Ilaria Bignamini (London: Tate Gallery, 1996).
10 David Burliuk et. al., *Poshchechina obshchestvennomu vkusu* (Moskva: Izd-vo Kuz'mina, 1912). Futurist bravado as a performance of antipathy towards past authority has been long established, and debunked. See, for example, Anna Lawton, "Introduction" to *Russian Futurism through its Manifestoes, 1912–1928* (Ithaca: Cornell University Press, 1988).
11 Aseev, "Spor s putovoditelem," 15.
12 F.T. Marinetti, "The Founding and Manifesto of Futurism," in *Futurist Manifestos*, ed. Marine Umbro Apollonio (London: Thames and Hudson, 1973), 22.
13 See Richard Stites, *Revolutionary Dreams: Utopian Vision and Experimental life in the Russian Revolution* (New York: Oxford University Press, 1989). Notably, Aseev is staking out a different position towards antiquity than other post-Revolutionary iconoclasts, including those affiliated with Futurism and *Novyi LEF*. Consider, for example, a poem from 1927 by Tret'iakov that is cited by Stites: "All for combat. / Force is best. / A bullet in the brain / Of Basil the Blest. / Smash all the icons / And the signs / They have made. / Explode the Iverskaya / With a hand grenade" (Stites, 70). To be sure, Stites advises us to recall that some of this iconoclasm was cast in a jocular pitch. I might add that it recapitulates the general sense that the Russian Futurists had a vastly more complicated relationship to the past than their bravado and statements such as throwing Pushkin and Dostoevsky from the steamship of modernity would otherwise suggest. As we will see below, Aseev, for example, is always thinking about the literary past of figures such as Alexander Blok and Nikolai Gogol. For an account of how categories of "retrospection" and "preservation" form cultural impulses that challenge established accounts of post-Revolutionary culture, see Katerina Clark, "The Avant-Garde and the Retrospectivists as Players in the Evolution of Stalinist Culture," in *Laboratory of Dreams: The Russian Avant-Garde and Cultural Experiment*, ed. John E. Bowlt and Olga Matich (Stanford: Stanford University Press, 1996), 259–76.
14 William Ray, *The Logic of Culture* (New York: Wiley), x.
15 Devin Fore, "Introduction," *October* 118: Special Issue: Soviet Factography, ed. Devin Fore (2006): 8.
16 Maria Gough, "Radical Tourism: Sergei Tret'iakov at the Communist Lighthouse," *October* 118: Special Issue: Soviet Factography (2006): 159–78.
17 To my knowledge, there is no sustained examination of Russian and Soviet modernist reportage. I will note here some preliminary observations of

what I think is a broadly diverse undertaking by a range of writers whose literary production, insofar as it was sponsored by various journalistic publications, had to bend the forms typifying literary modernism to the task of documenting and reporting on reality, in particular after the Revolution. One could pick off the shelf leading journals such as *Krasnaia nov'*, *LEF*, *Novyi LEF*, and *Novyi mir*, in which writers ranging from the Serapion Brothers to the Russian Formalists, Tret'iakov, Boris Pil'niak, Andrei Platonov (none of whom were perceived in their time as friends of mimesis) each had to report on a range of events. To be sure, leading the way in thinking through how modernist concerns would be pressed into service of journalism were likely visual and cinematic artists such as Aleksandr Rodchenko and Dziga Vertov (consider the latter's *Kino-Nedelia* and *Kino-Pravda* series, which are considered by scholars such as John MacKay laboratories for experiments with cinematic form). I have considered some of the challenges reportage poses to these writers in a forthcoming piece on Pil'niak and Platonov's travel writing, in particular, the former's "Rossiia v polete" and the jointly authored "Che-Che-O."

18 O. Smola, *Lirika Aseeva* (Moskva: Khudozhestvennaia literatura, 1980), 67, citing S. Tret'iakov's review of Aseev's poetry collection, "Stal'noi solovei" (*Dal'nevostochnyi put'*, 30 July 1922).

19 The word does not appear in Ushakov; its only entry is in the *Natsional'nyi korpus Russkogo iazyka* (1922).

20 See Harsha Ram, *The Imperial Sublime: A Russian Poetics of Empire* (Madison: University of Wisconsin Press, 2003), 226–33.

21 Hayden White, "The Forms of Wildness: Archaeology of an Idea," in *The Wild Man Within: An Image in Western Thought from the Renaissance to Romanticism*, ed. Edward J. Dudley and Maximillian E. Novak (Pittsburgh: University of Pittsburgh Press, 1973), 151. See also Jane Ashton Sharp, *Russian Modernism between East and West: Natal'ia Goncharova and the Moscow Avant-Garde* (Cambridge: Cambridge University Press, 2006). Other considerations of this dynamic can be found in Irina Shevelenko, *Modernizm kak arkhaizm: Natsionalizm i poiski modernistkoi estitiki v Rossii* (Moskva: Novoe literaturnoe obozrenie, 2017); and my *"Our Native Antiquity": Archaeology and Aesthetics in the Culture of Russian Modernism* (Beacon: Academic Studies Press, 2015).

22 Aleksandr Blok, "Skify" (St. Petersburg: Izd-vo pri tsentral'nom komitete partii levykh sotsialistov-Revoliutsionerov [Internatsionalistov], 1918), 43.

23 The vision of Blok in fact focuses only on his early engagement with Italy in the "Ital'ianskie stikhi," while avoiding his later attempt to think through it in his essay "Cateline." See, for example, Judith Kalb, *Russia's Rome: Imperial Visions, Messianic Dreams 1890–1940* (Madison: University of Wisconsin Press, 2010).

24 White, "The Forms of Wildness," 151.
25 Aseev anticipates here fascism's theatricality; Brecht will give the most robust formulation of this in *Über die Theatralik des Faschismus* (1939), but he does so through the figure of Marinetti as the embodiment of both fascist aesthetics and degraded futurism (345).
26 Ardengo Soffici, "Fascist Art" (1928), in Marla Stone, *The Fascist Revolution in Italy: A Brief History with Documents*, Bedford Series in History and Culture (Boston: Bedford/St. Martin's, 2013), 134.
27 See chapters 1 and 2 of Benedikt Livshits, *Polutoraglazyi strelets* (Leningrad: Izd-vo pisatelei v Leningrade, 1933).
28 Vladimir Markov, *Russian Futurism: A History* (Berkeley: University of California Press, 1968), 163.
29 M. Gorkii, "O dvukh knigakh," *Izvestiia*, 11 September 1928.
30 It's possible that Gorky took a harsher line in his review of Aseev's poetry only after he read the travelogue. K.M. Aseeva recounts that Gorky was brought to tears by Aseev's reading of "Semen Proskakov." Upon learning that the *poéma* had a print run of 3,000, Gorky is alleged to have exclaimed, "Such things should be published in a run of a hundred thousand" (Aseeva, "Iz vospominanii," 30).
31 M. Gorkii, "O nachinaiushchikh pisateliakh," *Izvestiia*, 19 September 1928.
32 V. Shklovskky, "Gorkii kak retsenzent," *Novyi LEF* 9 (1928): 42–4.
33 S. Tret'iakov, "Chto novogo?" *Novyi LEF* 9 (1928): 1–5.

10 Blackness in the Red Land: African Americans and Racial Identity in the "Colourless" Soviet Union

KIMBERLY ST. JULIAN-VARNON

From the moment that this group of Negroes crossed the gang-plank of the steamship "Europa" in Brooklyn on June 14, an aureola of comparative freedom environed them.

– Chatwood Hall[1]

Black journalist Chatwood Hall wrote the above passage in a glowing report on the arrival of twenty-two African Americans in Moscow in late June 1932. The article included grainy photos of typical Moscow tourist attractions, including the Kremlin and the Moscow Radio Station. Nevertheless, what drew the reader – likely a Black reader of the *Baltimore Afro-American*, a leading regional Black newspaper of the time – was the parade-like welcome the Black Americans enjoyed in the land of the Soviets. Hall's description paints an atmosphere of acceptance that was impossible in the US for African Americans. The Black visitors "had just stepped from a train into a small army of assembled, smiling, cheering Russians. A brass band blared a din of welcome into a land where there is no racial prejudice."[2] The twenty-two Black travellers, who included Langston Hughes, had come to the Soviet Union to shoot a film that would indict American racism. The group was part of a broader, unorganized cohort of African Americans who migrated to and worked in the Soviet Union. Their motives were as diverse as the members of this group themselves: some were seeking jobs, others social opportunities, and still others the equality and freedom that racism had denied them in the US.

For all of them, the Soviet Union represented a space where they could live a Black life without the spectre of white supremacy. While enjoying the generally welcoming environment of the Soviet Union, African Americans had experiences that layered international movement, personal and group identities, and the transfer of American racial mores onto a new social and cultural context. Many of their experiences would be shaped by their lives under racial oppression in the US. These Black Americans analysed, reforged, and performed various forms of Black racial identity in ways that in later decades have often been overshadowed in the discussions of their economic motives for relocating to the Soviet Union. Through analysis of first-hand narratives, this chapter traces the experiences of Black Americans in the Soviet Union, including how they interacted with Soviet citizens and white Americans as part of a project of racial identity construction and performance. This chapter also shows how the subjects' previous experiences with racism in the US and engagement with white Americans in the Soviet Union mitigated the impact of transnational migration and travel on racial identity.

Jim Crow America and the "Anti-Racist" Soviet Union

Interwar African American travel to the Soviet Union took place in a unique historical context for both the Soviet Union and the US. The period fundamentally shaped the imaginative possibilities of identity performance for visitors. In the 1920s and 1930s, the Soviet Union set out to build the first socialist country in the world. At the same time, African Americans, particularly those living in the US South, were victims of emotional, psychological, and physical violence because of their skin colour. Race relations and conditions for African Americans worsened as the Great Depression ravaged the US. During the 1920s and 1930s, the Soviet Union became a beacon for those African Americans who hoped to find a better life overseas after suffering the dual catastrophes of economic devastation and racial injustice at home.[3] During the First Five-Year Plan (1928–32), the Soviet people experienced profound changes in their society and culture as they cultivated new identities within the state's Marxist ideology.[4] The Soviet state presented itself as a viable alternative to the failing capitalist economic system as well as to the nation-state (although the Soviet Union itself created and perpetuated regimes of difference). The rapid and sweeping cultural and social changes in the Soviet Union in the 1920s and 1930s provided a unique context for African Americans to explore modes of racial identity that were impossible in the racist and violent climate of Jim Crow America.

In the 1920s, a time when many African Americans were victims of racism in white America, the Soviet Union began promoting itself as an anti-racist regime. The Marxist dialectic posited that racial inequality was a consequence of exploitative capitalism: Black people were placed at the bottom of the racial hierarchy so that their labour could be exploited.[5] Lenin's brief 1913 treatise "Russians and Negroes" compares the plight of post-emancipation African Americans with that of Russian serfs and points to the failures of America and capitalism to provide true freedom and equality to the formerly enslaved.[6] Thus, the specific issues that Black Americans faced as oppressed labourers within a racially organized society did not escape some of the leading Bolsheviks.[7] These writings, and the influence of Black American and Caribbean intellectuals such as Claude McKay and James Ford, shaped the Bolshevik view that African Americans were the most oppressed group of workers.[8] The Party and the Communist International turned their attention to promoting the revolutionary cause in the African American community through the Communist Party of the United States.[9]

In 1928, African Americans were officially categorized by the Soviet Union and the Comintern as an oppressed *nation*, although this categorization was used in Communist Party policy for African Americans in *America*, less so in the Soviet Union.[10] Through propaganda, communist newspapers, and the active recruitment of African American workers and specialists in the US, the Soviet Union promoted the idea that it was free of racial prejudice.[11] From the late 1920s to the mid-1930s, dozens of African Americans went to the Soviet Union, having been promised work as well as freedom from prejudice.[12] Those who made their way there often invited friends and family to join them in the land of equality; most, however, eventually returned home to the US. These travellers' experiences shaped their personal and collective racial identities.

Soviet citizens' limited experience with Black individuals created conditions that provided African Americans a space to examine, redefine, and perform their individual and group identities of Blackness.[13] African Americans' experiences in the Soviet Union speak to the multifaceted nature of identity construction and the internal and external factors that influence identity. They show how subjects responded to changes in their social and cultural environment and to the unique qualities of Soviet culture and society in the 1920s and 1930s. Particularly for the African American men in this study, past struggles with racism were the dominant framework for their racial identity as Black people. Throughout their narratives, Black travellers would compare the anti-racist – race-neutral is the best characterization – society of the Soviets to the racialized society in America. Their comparisons would reveal how daily proximity to racial violence had imprinted itself on the American sense of Blackness. Even in the Soviet Union, the possibility of racial violence was made real by white Americans, who often attempted to apply American racial ideologies and behaviours when encountering Black Americans.[14]

These travellers serve as a case study for how international travel and migration influenced the formation and questioning of racial identity. Soviet ideology emphasized class as the organizing principle of society and did not recognize race as a legitimate means of categorizing people. Thus, the relocation of African Americans to this ideologically unique state often required Black and white Americans to translate or reformulate how race functioned, occasionally through the lens of class as a principle for forging social hierarchies. These travellers also provide a micro-level perspective on transnational migration and globalization that sociologists Luis Eduardo Guarnizo and Michael Peter Smith have emphasized in their work.[15] In contrast to Guarnizo and Smith's research – and many similar studies that focus on the latter decades of the twentieth and early twenty-first centuries – these travellers speak to transnationalism of a different era. A study of the 1930s traces how racial identity and transnational migration functioned together before decolonization, thereby transcending the common periodization of globalization. That white Americans continued to perpetuate American racial hierarchies in the Soviet Union speaks to the transnational function of white supremacy and is an example of this transnational function outside the colonial context.

Historiographical Context and Theoretical Framing

Thanks to works like John Scott's memoir *Behind the Urals: An American Worker in Russia's City of Steel* (1943), American experiences in the Soviet Union have become well-known in academic and public circles.[16] While there has been an increase in studies on the presence of African Americans in the Soviet Union, they tend to focus on the economic motives of Black travel, the Soviet Union's influence on Black artistic production, the history of the Black presence in the region, or the dynamics between the Soviet Union and African Americans regarding the fight for Black civil rights.[17] Furthermore, the Soviet Union's anti-racist ideological stance has gained attention in scholarly literature in the past two decades.[18] This chapter contributes to this literature by adding a nuanced analysis of racial identity as an individual and group construction that tests the experiential horizons of Soviet anti-racism. Finally, there are discussions about the travels of significant African American intellectuals such as Langston Hughes, Paul Robeson, and W.E.B. Du Bois.[19] This chapter broadens the scope of work on African Americans in the Soviet Union by centring the stories of non-elites within the Black community. Their stories help us see how racial equality often superseded economic and ideological concerns for those who travelled or migrated to the Soviet Union.

I argue that African American experiences, the Soviet political context, and racial identity are mutually constitutive elements. The Soviet Union did not have considerable contact with African Americans, nor did many Soviet citizens know of Blacks' experiences with racism in the US under Jim Crow outside of what was depicted in Soviet media. Furthermore, there was no significant physical presence of African Americans in the country before 1928, when the Soviet Union began recruiting African American specialists to work in various capacities.[20] In the 1920s, racism towards Blacks and the exploitation of workers dominated Soviet criticism and narratives about the US.[21] There was no central narrative on African Americans other than that they were oppressed people who experienced violence and discrimination at the hands of white Americans.[22] Nevertheless, the idea of oppressed African Americans often shaped Soviet interactions with and expectations of their Black visitors.[23] Thus, African Americans and Soviet citizens could cultivate various conceptions of racial identity.

This work uses the paradigms of individual and group identity to examine how Black racial identity functioned in the early 1930s.[24] I use political scientist James Fearon's conception of individual identity. This dichotomy distinguishes between social and personal identity to discuss how Black visitors' experiences with racism in the US shaped their expectations of Soviet anti-racism and the fluidity of their performance of Black identity. I then layer Fearon's dichotomy with Rogers Brubaker and Frederick Cooper's conceptualization of collective group identity to demonstrate how racial identity functioned in a group context.[25]

One of the main problems with these theories of identity is that they are static and generally not applied to racial identity. However, Stuart Hall and Judith Butler provide epistemologies that help us understand the links between race, identity, and precarity that African Americans faced in the US, links that shaped how they understood race in the Soviet Union. Stuart Hall argues that race is a discursive, floating signifier. Instead of reifying racial difference as a product of biology, he contends that racial identity is contextual and fluid. Race's meaning and function are products of its social contexts.[26] We can see this in how these Black subjects racialized themselves as Black and their Soviet counterparts as white. Second, Judith Butler's theory of gender as a performance tied to precarity allows us to understand how previous experiences with racism in the US often strongly informed how African Americans performed race in Black-only and mixed-race groups in the Soviet Union.[27] For the Black Americans featured in this chapter, race was intimately tied to the precarity of their economic condition and the spectre of physical and emotional violence. The racial regime in the US influenced how these individuals navigated mixed-race social interactions, which always featured the potential threat of deprivation or violence. These Black travellers read Soviet citizens as white and initially returned to their learned survival behaviours when interacting with their Soviet interlocutors. However, the influences of class and labour occasionally mitigated their expectations of racial discrimination by Soviet people.

Having studied first-person narratives by Black American travellers to the Soviet Union, I argue that a shift from US connotations and prejudices connected with skin colour enabled many African Americans to explore modes of individual racial identity impossible in the US. However, African American identity occasionally clashed with Soviet conceptions of African American group identity. Some African Americans found that the Soviet emphasis on racial equality reinforced their individual and group identity. Together, their experiences and reflections illustrate race's fluid and contested nature and the centrality of the unique Soviet anti-racist social context.

Black and White and Group Identity Performance

For many African Americans, Jim Crow America's oppression and environment of racial hostility felt inescapable. However, the physical and ideological distance between the US and the Soviet Union helped Black travellers see themselves and their surroundings in ways that were impossible in the US. Langston Hughes and twenty-one other African Americans, including writers, performers, and laypeople, made the voyage to the Soviet Union in 1932 to make a movie to be titled *Black and White*.[28] In his memoir *I Wonder as I Wander*, Hughes recalls how the group he travelled with to Moscow came together and decided "to behave themselves" in public.

The group made sure that they did nothing to give Soviet citizens a negative perception of African Americans. "While we were there, the twenty-two coloured folks from Harlem were lionized to no end and at cultural gatherings we were always introduced as 'representatives of the great Negro people.'"[29] Because of this type of introduction, they made a definitive choice for action. "Conscious of being wholeheartedly admired, we solemnly decided ... that we must all do our best to 'uphold the honour of our race' while in Russia."[30] The high expectations of their Soviet hosts influenced the dynamic of groupness, a sense of belonging to a distinctive, bonded group and to a collective identity.[31] Knowing that Soviet citizens' experience with people of their colour was limited, Hughes and his group created a set of acceptable behaviour parameters for African Americans. These strictures included avoiding excessive drinking, always dressing appropriately, and using proper speech. The group even punished members who broke these parameters for "disgracing the race."[32] When a young woman in the group attempted suicide, waking everyone in the hotel, the group got together to discuss the commotion. The women in particular denounced her actions as shameful. When they were alone, the group ostracized her. "A few days later, she was back rehearsing spirituals with us. However, the other girls declared that she, a Negro, had 'disgraced the race,' creating all that excitement in the Grand Hotel."[33] According to Hughes, the group only maintained this standard of behaviour while in the presence of non–African Americans.

This example highlights how they performed a collective identity of Blackness. The twenty-two individuals travelled to and around the Soviet Union in a group setting. They thought that their performance would affect how Soviet people perceived them and, in their minds, the Black race in America. What is notable is that the group developed and projected an identity that was specifically for the consumption of others because their Soviet hosts introduced them as "representatives of the great Negro people." Thus, even the form of group identity was ascribed to them by external actors. Their performance of group identity speaks to Judith Butler's discussion of precarity and identity. Although Butler focuses on the performance of gender, her argument that precarity, which "characterizes that politically induced condition of maximized vulnerability and exposure for populations exposed to arbitrary state violence and other forms of aggression" applies to this group's behaviour as well.[34] Trip organizer and participant Louise Thompson Patterson echoed Hughes's sentiments in a letter to her mother dated 14 August 1932. After the making of the film was postponed (it would eventually be dropped altogether), there was increasing tension within the group regarding the causes of the postponement. Thompson Patterson lamented the behaviour of Ted Poston and Thurston Lewis. "They have been thoroughly irresponsible and Thurston really incorrigible. Their actions have shamed us all for they have acted like two puppies, chained for a while and then let loose. Their attitude toward the Russian women was so obvious as to seem absolute proof of all the things white Americans say about Negro men and white women."[35] Thompson Patterson, an active Black communist, was cognizant of the impact any potential scandal could have on the Soviet attitude towards the group and how Poston and Lewis's behaviour could be interpreted by the US press. By openly pursuing liaisons with white Russian women, the pair broke the group's agreement on appropriate behaviour and placed them all at risk abroad and at home. She was also appalled by

Lewis's constant use of cuss words in mixed company.[36] The precarity of their position as Black Americans who would have to return to the US, dependent upon the goodwill of their Soviet hosts, was an ever-present subtext to how the group behaved and how they interpreted the behaviour of group members in interracial settings. Furthermore, it seems Thompson Patterson was concerned that the skirt-chasing of Poston and Lewis could erode Soviet belief in African Americans' oppression in the US.

The Soviet people they interacted with understood that in the US, Black people were an "oppressed" nation, and treated them with empathy and curiosity, but they also projected their understanding of Blackness onto their foreign visitors. At this juncture, their previous experiences with race-based precarity and violence from racist whites shaped their expectations. The group racialized the Soviets they encountered in Moscow as white people. Thus, there was a possibility that the Soviets would turn their backs on Black Americans. Their fears also demonstrate their insecurity about the Soviet promise of anti-racism, a nuanced result of their reading of Soviet people as white. Essentially, they believed that the Soviets were white and would behave as the whites did in the US. The influence of racism and precarity at home coloured the group's performance of Black identity abroad.

Chatwood Hall's, Hughes's, and Thompson Patterson's accounts reveal that Soviet acceptance of Black Americans was dependent on their behaviour. Furthermore, the group knew they would be returning home to racism and prejudice and that they needed the continued support of the Soviet people in their fight for civil rights and equality in the US. As Chatwood Hall clarified, if any member of the group misbehaved, that behaviour would be communicated to the US as further proof of Black degeneracy and, thus, a justification for the continued brutalization of African Americans. The film's postponement and eventual cancellation weighed heavily in this thought process.[37] Transnational movement and contact offered the group new work opportunities and led them to impose behavioural strictures on themselves that limited their freedom more than in their mostly Black surroundings in the US. The interesting point is that class was not as important a factor in their behaviours or methods of identity performance, as most of the film group were in the Soviet Union for only a short term and were in a self-contained group with a purpose: acting in a Soviet film on race. By contrast, those African Americans who went to the Soviet Union for employment opportunities had more engagement with class as a factor of identity.

Being a Black Soviet Worker: Margaret Glasgoe

The group behaviour Hughes described was unique among Black travellers to the Soviet Union because the *Black and White* group enjoyed incredible privileges during their time in the Soviet Union. While some stayed longer than the few months allotted for filming, most returned to the US.[38] Other Black migrants, such as Margaret Glasgoe, Homer Smith (aka Chatwood Hall), and Robert Robinson, went to the Soviet Union for work. Their lives in the Soviet Union illustrate the dynamism of individual racial identity.

Margaret Glasgoe was a New York City hairdresser who could never get clients because white customers preferred white hairdressers. In her Soviet-published autobiography, Glasgoe mentions that before her move to the Soviet Union, she volunteered with Black and white Communists in the fight for the Scottsboro boys.[39] However, white communists in New York City annoyed her sister-in-law Sarah Patterson, who did not like her having white "comrades" over to her house. "In general, she hated white people, just as I had for many years," Glasgoe remembered.[40] The fear of white people combined with the fear that accusations of communism would be levelled against them. African Americans in urban areas were in a precarious situation in terms of employment and housing. They could be fired or thrown out of their housing on a whim, and to be accused of communism was the last thing Sarah Patterson wanted.

Glasgoe moved to Moscow in June 1934 after her son, Lloyd, a *Black and White* group member, wrote to her from the Soviet Union describing the immense privileges he enjoyed as a Black worker and because he had married and had a child, James Lloydovich Patterson.[41] He wrote to her about the opportunities there that they could never have in the US.[42] In a letter to a Soviet newspaper, Glasgoe quoted her son: "Mammy, life here is boiling like water in a kettle. There's so much work that the workers can't do it all. Here no one even notices my black skin. Only now and then children who meet me cry out – not in spite but only in surprise: 'Oh look, there's a black man!'"[43] What finally enticed her to go was that people of all colours who were oppressed had opportunities there. She could start over and create a new life in a place that did not judge people by their skin colour.

"By the force of habit," she later wrote, "I expected that the white people there, as everywhere else, would treat me with hostility. But to my joy I found just the opposite. 'Comrade' – that was the first word I heard ... I felt at home, among my folks, in my own country."[44] "Comrade" engendered feelings of acceptance for Glasgoe, something she did not expect from Americans who shared the same skin colour as her Russian greeters.

Clearly, Glasgoe had seen an opportunity. But like those in the film group, Glasgoe carried life experiences among American whites and daily engagement with white supremacy that shaped her expectations. She, too, projected a form of racial identity onto the Russians. The new social context of the Soviet Union was still foreign to Glasgoe, so she resorted to a racialized system of understanding that she had experienced in the United States to render her initial contact with Soviet society and race relations legible.

In her short letter to the newspaper, Glasgoe also discusses how she acclimated to her new home and created a new individual identity. In the Soviet Union, she changed her profession and became a factory worker. She even became an *udarnik* (shock worker) and took that identity seriously. She felt that this new identity, which other factory workers recognized and projected onto her, was the identity she wanted to emphasize. She was a top worker in the Stalin Automobile Plant – something that mattered in the new society she was joining. "Now that I am living in one house with Englishmen, Germans, and Letts (in a factory dormitory), I've quite forgotten that I'm black. I simply feel like a human being, that's all. I've been given a special shock-brigader's card for the dining-room."[45] Glasgoe, in the Soviet Union, forged an identity that was not externally defined by her skin colour. She was able to "forget" she was Black because shock workers received privileges that other workers did not, and the state celebrated them. For most of her life in the US, her belonging to the Black group stripped her of her rights and placed her in economic precarity, but Soviet society allowed her to take on a personal identity that included her in a celebrated group.

Moreover, throughout her life, she had been unable to secure enough work to alleviate her and her family's poverty. She witnessed both her deceased husband's and her brother's struggles to find work and was sexually harassed when she laboured as a domestic worker.[46] Thus, the Soviet concept of labour as a form of identity that could be chosen opened doors to new forms of identification and new ways of life for Glasgoe. It is meaningful that of the myriad types of work available, she chose to work in the automobile plant. This was a rare opportunity for a Black woman who had spent most of her working life cleaning up after wealthy and middle-class white and Black families.

Glasgoe was Black, but in her new social environment, her abilities as a worker mattered more, and thus, her primary performance of identity became that of a shock worker. This was still externally defined, but it was an identity she could embody that had social worth. The concept of a worker's identity based on equality is reflected in a 1937 interview she gave during a trip back to the US: "The past three years of her life, she said, has been one [sic] of equality, brotherly attention, a human being among human beings, and not a supposedly 'inferior' among 'superiors.'"[47] By working hard, attending lectures after her shift, and attempting to learn Russian, she was becoming a *Soviet* person. She exhibited the aspects of commonality (sharing a common attribute) and connectedness (relational ties that link people) to Soviet society.[48] She shared a common attribute with her fellow workers: class, a definitive factor in Soviet social relations. Her shock brigader's card, coupled with her work performance, entitled her to and provided her with this new group and individual identity as a Soviet worker. Glasgoe's adoption of the Soviet worker identity was possible because of her international relocation; but even so her previous experience with white supremacy tempered her expectations of equality. Additionally, her engagement with communists in New York, and her ability to choose her work, bolstered her willingness to modify her identity.

The Scribe of Black Russia: Homer Smith

In 1931, at the time of the Scottsboro trial, a Black Mississippian studying journalism in Minnesota turned his attention to the Soviet Union. During that trial, nine Black boys were sentenced to death for the alleged rape of two white girls. Homer Smith – who wrote under the pseudonym Chatwood Hall – decided to leave America the day the sentence was announced.[49] "*The Daily Worker* wrote glowingly that Soviet Russia was the one political state which stood for social justice for all oppressed peoples. Who, I thought, was more oppressed than the Negro? Who else was being lynched with hideous regularity?"[50] Throughout his journalism career in the Soviet Union, Smith reported on Black visitors' experiences, explored the Black community in Abkhazia, and discussed race and fascism with his readers. He used his time there to chronicle the Soviet Union's unique context, becoming what I call "the Scribe of Black Russia." Unlike Glasgoe, Smith was acutely aware of his Blackness in the Soviet Union, and his individual racial identity was reinforced rather than changed.

Smith joined Hughes and his group of Black artists to work on the *Black and White* film project. He travelled with the group on the *Europa* and initially lodged with them, but as it transpired, he did not participate in making the film. Instead, he found work at the Moscow Post Office and became a fourteen-year Soviet resident. Smith thought that those who came over from America were not representative of the

Blacks of the American South and did not correspond to the Soviet conception of Black southerners. "There most certainly were no callous-handed sharecroppers, stevedores or truck drivers – the types the Russians had expected – among them. Furthermore, most of them had never even experienced the ruder and cruder forms of Jim Crow, having lived North of the Mason-Dixon line."[51] Smith's delineation between Blacks from the North and those from the South illustrates his logic of group racial identity. A shared experience of segregation and sharecropping rather than similar skin colour was the attribute he considered when establishing commonality with the Black group. He described how the Soviets crafted a flattened narrative of Black experience that rarely engaged with Blacks' layered and divergent experiences between the North and the South. Even within the US, regional differences influenced the function of race and the shape of racial violence towards African Americans.

The experiences with American racism within the film group were strongly varied. In America, their black skin colour meant *de facto* that they were all second-class citizens. However, once they were in the Soviet Union, Smith separated himself from the group, at least in his writing. Blacks in the North were not subject to Jim Crow laws like Blacks in the South, and Smith's reluctance to identify with the northern artists suggests that his personal and group identity was strongly shaped by his own experience with white supremacy and prejudice. To Smith, skin colour – their shared physical trait – did not lead automatically to feelings of commonality or connectedness to this group. This underscores the salience of Brubaker and Cooper's discussion of collective identity. Although he travelled with and wrote about the group, Smith does not portray a sense of solidarity with its members. This, even though the Soviet people and white Americans read his phenotypic difference as Black group membership. Smith's long stay in the Soviet Union, his employment there, and the mobility he enjoyed in that country make his story unique. So it is plausible that he did not feel affinity with the group because he decided to remain in the Soviet Union to live and work while they were privileged visitors. In this sense, migration allows us to see how a shift in social and cultural context can erase previous affiliations of group racial identity and bolster the importance of experiences in previous countries in the process of forging individual racial identity.

Smith was interested in the race of Russia's great writer, Alexander Pushkin. During his residence in the Soviet Union, Smith met with Pushkin's great-granddaughter, Catherine Pushkin. Catherine apologized to him during their first meeting for not resembling him, although her great-grandfather had Black blood. "Among Catherine's last words were: 'Alexander Sergeevich was dark-complexioned, a few shades lighter than you. I am so sorry that my colour is so light. He would have been fond of you, I'm sure.'"[52] Although these words can be read as a rhetorical flourish rather than accurate reporting, the meeting made Smith contemplate how race worked in Soviet Russia. The apology and a subsequent meeting with Pushkin's grandson Grigorii Pushkin led Smith to wonder whether Pushkin was a Black man. In a seven-page passage in his memoirs, Smith traces Pushkin's African heritage and comes to an interesting conclusion: Pushkin's Blackness depended on where he was and what society he was in. "Indeed, had Pushkin lived in America he would certainly have been classified by the United States Census Bureau as a Negro. There are countless coloured persons living in America who are far lighter in skin than Pushkin was ... Yet, in America they are classified as Negroes."

At the end of his thought exercise, Smith decides that Pushkin was Russian, despite his skin colour, because he felt and lived that way.[53] Smith's conclusion mirrored the conclusions of other Soviets. Even Yuri Lotman denied Pushkin's heritage as African and emphasized that Pushkin's great-grandfather Gannibal was "not a Negro, but a Blackamoor [*arap*]."[54] What is compelling about this thought exercise is that it provides insight into how Smith defined his individual racial identity. In the Soviet Union, no Census Bureau defined him as Black, yet Smith felt and presented that way. Race operates as a language, as Stuart Hall argues, and American Blackness was the language Smith understood and within which he interpreted his life. His previous experiences with whites and American racism shaped his understanding of both his and Pushkin's racial identities.

Additionally, his thought exercise demonstrates a contextual understanding of race. He recognizes that Pushkin lived his life in a country that did not have an office representing state power to define his race. It seems that for Smith, in terms of his individual and group identities, his Blackness was inescapable: US white supremacy had forged his racial identity as a Black man. For him, external factors in America, like segregation, open discrimination, and the threat of lynching – that is, factors of precarity – were definitive.

Moreover, Smith found Soviet anti-racism peculiar. He sought examples of racial equality during the fourteen years he spent there, and he found a situation that was initially hard for him to grasp. "Negroes who were looking only for racial equality found themselves given the full treatment of racial inequality in reverse. Seeing this racial inequality in action, but in reverse order to what I had seen in America, proved intriguing and pleasant."⁵⁵ Because of Soviet citizens' frequent acts of politeness, such as giving up their seats to him on the bus, steering him to the front of shop lines, and even offering their Russian girlfriends for him to dance with – Smith was constantly aware of his Blackness. Smith's placement in the Black racial group was publicly reinforced every time he interacted with Soviet people. The Soviet Union was officially race-blind, but just as in the US, his skin colour defined how he was treated and how people perceived him. This, perhaps, was the point Smith was highlighting when he described what other Black Americans found in the Soviet Union while searching for racial equality. His comment also shows the limits of Soviet claims of anti-racism: the legal denunciation of racism did not prevent Soviet officials and citizens from tokenizing Black Americans. The Soviet people Smith encountered expected, because of his skin colour and what they had been told about America, that he would want to dance with white-presenting Soviet women. This assumption was rooted in racist notions that Black men seek white women and hearkens back to Louise Thompson Patterson's concerns about relations between Black men and Soviet women.

A memorable event during Smith's time in the Soviet Union was an instance of racism on a train from Moscow to Leningrad. He had a ticket for a berth in a sleeper car compartment, which he was to share with a woman, which was not unusual.⁵⁶ However, the woman was a white American, and she became distraught. She demanded repeatedly to be moved to another compartment. The porter, confused by her complaint, told her she was in the right compartment. Finally, she took her things from the compartment and stood in the corridor.⁵⁷ Smith tried to understand why she was so adamant about not sharing a sleeper compartment with him, and wondered whether she thought he would attempt to sexually assault her. (A common trope of American racist propaganda is the threat of uncontrollable African American men raping white women.) While he was considering this, the woman asked him if he was from the United States. He replied, "Madam, whether or not I am from the United States is of no importance. You are not in the United States now."⁵⁸ Smith was satisfied with how he handled the situation, noting that although the woman threw a fit, they were treated equally. The situation, which would have been deadly for him in America, turned out to be embarrassing for the woman who had been prejudiced against him.

The absence of prejudice towards his skin colour in Soviet society did not lead Smith to question or redefine his identity. Rather, the social meaning of his identity was no longer a hindrance to him, although it had been the primary cause of his leaving the United

States in 1931.[59] The incident on the train serves as a reminder of the experiential basis of his individual racialized identity. His experience in the Soviet Union did not change what had happened to him while he was still in the US; therefore, neither did it change his personal or racial identity.

Smith often wrote about his run-ins with white American racism in the Soviet Union. In a June 1933 spread for *Abbott's Monthly*, Smith described his first year as a resident of the Soviet Union. In three separate instances, he encountered white Americans who struggled with the Soviet belief in and enforcement of racial equality. His first encounter occurred on the *Europa*, which was transporting him and the *Black and White* film crew to Europe. A white passenger asked Smith where he was going and was incredulous when he responded that he was going to Russia. He asked Smith, "Don't you realize that America is the greatest country in the world for your people? ... In America there is democracy and freedom; in Russia there is neither."[60] Smith then debated the man's logic and contended that America had no freedom or democracy, especially for Black people.

When the group visited the Black Sea port of Odesa, they had another run-in with white Americans, who expected their understandings of racial hierarchy to be universally applied in the Soviet Union. The Black Sea coast was a popular destination for foreign visitors, even though a state-made famine was ravaging Ukraine at the time. The American tourists "seemed non-plussed to find, especially in such an out-of-the-way place, a Negro lounging about the lobby or eating in the dining-room on full equality with 'white ladies and gentlemen.'"[61] Smith basked in the discomfort of the white Americans, who were unable to use the tools of whiteness available to them in America to remove the Blacks from their presence.

In each of these situations, foreign travel did not initially erase American whites' understanding of their racial supremacy. When their assumptions about white supremacy and, thus, social power were confronted in the Soviet Union, they responded with anger and disbelief. In these examples, Smith saw evidence of the Soviet commitment to racial equality. At the same time, these racist white Americans often reinforced Smith's own individual and group identity. The causes of his experiences with racism and prejudice did not stop at the US border; instead, they followed him to this new land in the shape of the white woman on the train and the white vacationers. These vignettes further demonstrate how white Americans attempted to make their new surroundings culturally legible by applying white supremacist ideas to Black travellers even in the Soviet Union.

The Reluctant Black Soviet: Robert Robinson

Robert Robinson was one of the most remarkable African American visitors to the Soviet Union in the 1930s. He was a member of the Moscow Soviet, was vilified in the American press during the Cold War, was stripped of his US citizenship, gained Soviet citizenship, and returned to the US only in 1986.[62] Among African Americans who worked in the Soviet Union, he was unique in several ways: he was born in Jamaica, grew up in Cuba, then moved to Harlem and eventually Detroit, where he worked in the famous Ford factory.[63] He recounted that he did not experience racism until he arrived in New York: "Cuba at that time was two-thirds Black and one-third white. I never experienced racial prejudice and did not know what it was until I arrived in New York."[64] This background sets him apart from most Black travellers to the Soviet Union. Based on his experiences in the US, he was prepared to expect racial prejudice.

In 1930, Robinson and a number of white workers from his plant were offered employment contracts, free rent, and free passage to Russia to work at the Stalingrad Tractor Plant.[65] In his memoir *Black on Red: My 44 Years Inside the Soviet Union*, he describes how he decided to move to the Soviet Union. The pay and perks would be better, but he also had to consider the negative aspects of the Soviet experiment that were continually in the American news. "I was aware of media accounts criticizing the Soviet system. But to think about the obstacles I was facing, trying to advance within the institutionalized racism in America – and recalling that the cousin of a friend of mine had just been lynched three months earlier – I made up my mind on the spot. I read the contract and signed it."[66] Robinson's logic mirrors that of other Black workers who made the move, including Homer Smith and Margaret Glasgoe. And although the American media did not speak much of this, they knew it was possible that the Soviet Union could offer relief from US racism, and there were jobs for Black people.

Like Smith, Robinson was constantly aware of his racial difference throughout his voyage to Russia and during his first few weeks in the Soviet Union, primarily because of the racial prejudice of the white Americans who were part of his group. Aboard the *Rykov*, sailing from London to Leningrad, two white Americans refused to sit with Robinson at breakfast. When he sat down next to them, the two men walked away, and they did the same the following day.[67] To both Robinson's and their surprise, the ship's captain admonished the men for their racism: "Comrade specialists, you are all invited to work in the Soviet Union … Everyone in Soviet Russia is equal. I am not authorized to segregate anyone on this ship. I am asking that everybody – all of the passengers – obey Soviet law."⁶⁸ Although segregation was the rule in the US, the opposite would be true in the USSR, and Robinson's white counterparts had to accommodate the Soviet enforcement of racial equality.

Notwithstanding Soviet law, Robinson continued to have problems with white Americans. This culminated in a 1930 incident in Stalingrad when he was assaulted by two white American workers, who had been harassing him for two months. Earlier, when warned about the possibility of attack by a group of Americans, he thought, "but this is Russia ... The chances of a black man being murdered in Stalingrad because of the colour of his skin are a lot less than back home."⁶⁹ His assailants attacked him and beat him, and he fought back, biting one until he bled from the throat.⁷⁰ Robinson does not go into significant detail in his memoir about how he felt after the attack, but he does describe his anxiety when facing the police afterward. Like many African American men, he saw the police as a threat to his life. "Their superior officer wanted to hear my version of what had happened with Louis and Brown [the assailants]. Now, I had already learned as a child that the police station was obviously a place to avoid. For a black man especially it could well be the first step to jail, beatings, and oblivion. I was very wary."⁷¹ Fortunately for Robinson, they believed him, and his attackers were convicted and eventually deported.⁷²

Because of the incident, Robinson became a public sensation in Leningrad and eventually throughout the Soviet Union. He was elected as a deputy to the Moscow Soviet, and he was featured in the newspapers the *Moscow Worker* and *Moscow Evening News*.⁷³ However, this notoriety was not something he wanted.⁷⁴ He was uncomfortable with the publicity the trial and his election to the Moscow Soviet brought him, and he does not seem to have interpreted these events the way Homer Smith interpreted his own experiences with Soviet anti-racism. Both Smith and Robinson experienced Soviet citizens emphasizing their racial identity in social interactions. Like Smith, Robinson was invited to dance with Russian women. One Russian woman named Vera "was so sure of herself. But not me. I was the product of my upbringing in a racist society that had beaten into me the need to be leery of white folks, to be always suspicious that when given the chance they would want to destroy a black man like me."⁷⁵ This made Robinson aware of his Black identity, not because of the behaviour of the Soviet people but because of the reaction of the white Americans, who made their displeasure with his behaviour clear.⁷⁶ In this sense, as with Smith, Robinson's racial identity was influenced by external behaviour, yet the nuances were different. The reaction of American white supremacy in a space where that supremacy was actively rejected influenced Robinson's sense and performance of Black identity.

Although the cultural environment had changed, the American-style racism that categorized him as Black and socially inferior limited the freedom Robinson had to develop a social identity as a Soviet worker and resident. Additionally, Robinson, unlike Glasgoe and Smith, laboured in the same industry and in the same class as he had in the US. In the US, Robinson had been a highly skilled automotive worker in a predominantly white industry, and he remained in a mostly white (to him) working environment in the Soviet automotive plant. In this case, transnational migration to the Soviet Union did not create as drastic a change for Robinson as it did for the others.

Robinson's experiences in the first half of the 1930s speak to the dynamic nature of Black identity in the Soviet realm. He accentuated his identity as a worker, one that he had tried to cultivate in the US. After he renewed his contract with the plant, "[I] channeled most of my energy into my work, doing everything I could to become the most productive worker possible. I wanted to be productive, and it was also the best way to avoid getting trapped by social and political problems."[77] In general, Glasgoe was content that she could choose her work and become an exemplary worker in her factory. Robinson was more aware of the ideological underpinnings of the worker identity and the performance of that identity. Focusing on work helped him avoid political conflict in the Soviet Union, much as it had in the US. Robinson was more concerned about attaining the "groupness" characteristic of collective identity construction. The white Americans he worked with still followed American racial hierarchies. The Soviet conception of a collective worker identity was one he could cultivate because he was connected with his Russian co-workers by virtue of being productive. Robinson attempted to subdue the primacy of race by focusing on his belonging to the working class in the Soviet Union. This collective identity was possible for him and Glasgoe because of the unique context of the Soviet Union in the 1930s. The Soviet push to create a new socialist society in the 1930s meant their Soviet co-workers were also in the process of fashioning distinctly Soviet selves that merged class and labour as primary elements of personal and group identity.

Concluding Remarks

The narratives of the film group, Glasgoe, Smith, and Robinson provide a micro-level understanding of the fluidity and instability of racial identity. At the group and individual levels, the shadow of the racial system in the US influenced their performance of Black racial identity in the Soviet Union. To these Black people, their racial and social identity as members of the Black group and their sense of belonging to the Black group were rooted in shared experiences of racial inequality and economic precarity in America. This experience shaped how Hughes, Smith, Glasgoe, and Robinson understood themselves and the function of race within the new Soviet world. On the other hand, the Soviet Union's creation of a distinct, class-based society offered Robinson and Glasgoe space to cultivate personal identities related to a new group identity, the Soviet worker. Class had a complicated relationship with race in their Soviet workplaces. For Glasgoe and Smith, the class-based social organization in the Soviet Union opened doors to engage in types of labour denied to them in the US. They could enter the industrial working class. Robinson was already an industrial labourer in the US, and the assault on him by two white co-workers cemented the connections between his race and his work once he became well known in the Soviet Union.

International travel and migration enabled these individuals to visualize white supremacy's figurative and literal boundaries. As Hughes noted, the all-encompassing nature of racial prejudice in American society was embedded in both Black and white Americans' comprehension of their physical and mental worlds and, thus, their concepts of race. The colour line and the prejudice and discrimination attached to it shaped the experiences of Black Americans' individual and group racial identities. Their lives and narratives highlight a new application of Butler's precarity and identity performance theory within racial identity construction. Equally important, these narratives embody the discursive nature of race even within a society that legally and ideologically rejects it. This cohort's interactions in the Soviet Union with white Americans and their racial prejudice illustrate Guarnizo and Smith's critique that "transnational practices cannot be construed as if they were free from constraints and opportunities that contextuality imposes."[78] The Soviet anti-racist social context thwarted the attempts of white Americans to transpose their ideas of racial hierarchy onto the Soviet space. However, American racism continued to inform African American visitors' identity performance. American racial mores shaped the behaviour of white American migrants to the Soviet Union. Thus, this narrative reveals the tension between racial identity, racial ideologies, and transnationalism. These individuals could not entirely escape the American racial regime if white Americans were in the Soviet Union, if any hint of sexual impropriety with Soviet women could dampen Soviet acceptance of Black men, and if most of these individuals would eventually have to return to the US and its racial hierarchy.

Notes

1 Chatwood Hall, the pseudonym of journalist Homer Smith, "Where Bands of Music Welcomed 22 Black Americans …," *Baltimore Afro-American*, 6 August 1932, 24.
2 Hall [Smith], "Where Bands of Music Welcomed."
3 It is difficult to gauge how many African Americans travelled to and lived in the Soviet Union from the mid-1920s to the end of the 1930s (the lead-up to the Nazi invasion of the Soviet Union). Most sources are memoirs and newspapers that include the stories of travellers.
4 There is a significant body of literature on the nature of Soviet social construction and the role of ideology in that process. Jochen Hellbeck's *Revolution on My Mind: Writing a Diary under Stalin* (Cambridge, MA: Harvard University Press, 2009) and Sheila Fitzpatrick's *Everyday Stalinism: Soviet Russia in the 1930s* (Oxford: Oxford University Press, 2000) offer two competing views on this process.
5 For more thinking on this question, see Leon Trotsky's "On the Negro Question," a letter written to Claude McKay on 13 March 1923 and first printed in *Socialist Appeal* 3, no. 72, 20 September 1939, 1, https://www.marxists.org/archive/trotsky/1923/03/negroq.htm. W.E.B. Du Bois discusses racialized capitalism in the United States and its impact on the Black population in *Black Reconstruction* (1935).
6 V.I. Lenin, "Russians and Negroes," *Collected Works of Lenin*, vol. 18, 543–4, Marxists Internet Archive (2004), https://www.marxists.org/archive/lenin/works/1913/feb/00b.htm.
7 For a detailed analysis of Lenin's comparison between Black slaves and Russian serfs, see Joe Pateman, "V.I. Lenin on the 'Black Question'," *Critique: Journal of Socialist Theory* 48, no. 1 (Feb. 2020): 77–93.
8 Allison Blakely, *Russia and the Negro: Blacks in Russian History and Thought* (Washington, DC: Howard University Press, 1986), 106–9.
9 John L. Gardner, "African Americans in the Soviet Union in the 1920s and 1930s: The Development of Transcontinental Protest," *Western Journal of Black Studies* 23 (Fall 1999): 191.
10 Meredith L. Roman, *Opposing Jim Crow: African Americans and the Soviet Indictment of US Racism, 1928–1937* (Lincoln: University of Nebraska Press, 2012), 6.
11 Kate A. Baldwin, *Beyond the Color Line and the Iron Curtain*, (Durham: Duke University Press, 2002), 9.
12 A small notice in the NAACP monthly *The Crisis* mentions eleven Blacks going to Russia to help with the cotton crop, including chemists from Drake University and Virginia State College. "Along the Color Line, Cotton in Russia," *The Crisis*, January 1933. *The Crisis* online archive, 15.

13 Blackness, in this context, means an individual or group identity based on African-American heritage or membership in the African diaspora.
14 The primary wave of African migration to the Soviet Union occurred in post-Stalinist times, a contextually different period. Furthermore, experiences with racism and colonialism in Africa were different from those of African Americans in the United States and should not be equated.
15 Luis Eduardo Guarnizo and Michael Peter Smith, *Transnationalism from Below: Comparative Urban and Community Research*, 1st ed. (New York: Routledge, 1975), 3–4.
16 John Scott, *Behind the Urals: An American Worker in Russia's City of Steel* [1942] (Bloomington: Indiana University Press, 1989).
17 For examples, see Joy Gleason Carew, *Blacks, Reds, and Russians: Sojourners in Search of the Soviet Promise* (New Brunswick: Rutgers University Press, 2008); Roman, *Opposing Jim Crow*, and Blakely, *Russia and the Negro*.
18 Soviet anti-racism, in this context, is the projection of Soviet society as one in which there was an absence of racism and an absence of racial categorization. Francine Hirsch discusses the intricacies of Soviet views on race in her essay "Race without the Practice of Racial Politics," *Slavic Review* 61, No. 1 (Spring 2002): 30–43.
19 In many American narratives, their experiences and work in the Soviet Union are often treated as a dark period in an otherwise stellar career. Kate A. Baldwin discusses the repercussions of these omissions in work on African-American literature in *Beyond the Color Line*.
20 Roman, *Opposing Jim Crow*, 4.
21 Alan M. Ball, *Imagining America: Influence and Images in Twentieth-Century Russia*, (Lanham: Rowman and Littlefield, 2003), 42. Some Black students from the United States and the French and British colonies participated in Comintern schools from the mid-1920s to the 1930s. See Woodford McClellan, "Africans and Black Americans in the Comintern Schools, 1925–1934," *International Journal of African Historical Studies* 26, no. 2 (1993): 371–90.
22 Roman discusses the constant use of this motif in Soviet propaganda directed towards its population and towards American audiences throughout her work. See Roman, *Opposing Jim Crow*.
23 Christina Kiaer provides an outstanding analysis of the role of the Black as oppressed nation theme in the art of Aleksandr Deineka and in other media of Soviet art. Christina Kiaer, "African Americans in Soviet Socialist Realism: The Case of Aleksandr Deineka," *Russian Review* 75, No. 3 (2016): 402–33.
24 I am drawing from James Fearon's argument that identity has a double sense in the social sciences, one that is personal and one that is social. James Fearon, "What is Identity (As We Now Use the Word)?" Stanford University, unpublished Draft, 1999.

25 Rogers Brubaker and Frederick Cooper, "Beyond Identity," *Theory and Society* 29, no. 1 (2000): 19. The authors define collective identity as an "emotionally laden sense of belonging to a distinctive, bonded group, involving both felt solidarity or oneness with fellow group members and a felt difference from or even antipathy to specified outsiders."

26 See Sut Jhally and Stuart Hall, *Race: The Floating Signifier* (Northampton: Media Education Foundation, 1996), https://www.kanopy.com/product/stuart-hall-race-floating-signifier.

27 See Judith Butler, "Performative Acts and Gender Constitution: An Essay in Phenomenology and Feminist Theory," *Theatre Journal* 40, no. 4 (1988): 519–31. See also Butler, "Performativity, Precarity and Sexual Politics," *Revista de Antropologia Iberoamericana* 4, no. 3 (2009): i–xii.

28 Blakely, *Russia and the Negro*, 93. Their voyage was covered in the Black press. See "21 Movie Players Leave for Moscow: Will Make Film on Negro Life," *New York Amsterdam News*, 15 June 1932, 7. The article includes the list of travellers, among them Dorothy West, Lloyd Patterson, Sylvia Garner, and Wayland Rudd.

29 Langston Hughes, *I Wonder as I Wander* (New York: Thunder's Mouth Press, 1986), 87.

30 Hughes, *I Wonder as I Wander*, 88.

31 Groupness is one of three factors Brubaker and Cooper emphasize in their conception of collective identity. Brubaker and Cooper, "Beyond Identity," 20.

32 Hughes, *I Wonder as I Wander*, 88.

33 Hughes, *I Wonder as I Wander*, 88. In Julia L. Mickenberg's *American Girls in Red Russia* (Chicago: University of Chicago Press, 2017), 257, we discover the name of the woman who caused the scandal, Sylvia Garner. She attempted suicide because of a romantic entanglement.

34 Butler, "Performativity, Precarity and Sexual Politics," ii.

35 Louise Thompson Patterson, "Letter to Mother, August 24, 1932." Louise Thompson Patterson Papers, collection 869, box 1, folder 24, Emory University Archives.

36 Patterson, "Letter to Mother."

37 Steven S. Lee explores the issues of the film's postponement and cancellation in *The Ethnic Avant-Garde: Minority Cultures and World Revolution* (New York: Columbia University Press, 2018), 141–2.

38 Mickenberg, *American Girls in Red Russia*, 270. Mickenberg traces some of the exploits of the women in the group who went to Central Asia, including Dorothy West. The article "Players Denounce Attack on Soviets" includes how the group was treated well and received opportunities above and beyond what was stated in their contracts. *New York Amsterdam News*, 26 October 1932, 16.

39 James Lloydovich Patterson, *Chronicle of the Left Hand: An American Black Family's Story from Slavery to Russia's Hollywood* (Washington, DC: New Academia, 2022), 95.
40 Patterson, *Chronicle of the Left Hand*.
41 Patterson, *Chronicle of the Left Hand*, 97–8. James Lloydovich Patterson is famous for his portrayal of the toddler Jimmy in the 1936 Soviet film *Circus* (see chapter 1 of this volume). The volume includes Glasgoe's autobiography.
42 Margaret Glasgow, "Negro Mother, Now a Shock-Worker," in *60 Letters: Foreign Workers Write of Their Life and Work in the USSR*, ed. NS. Rosenblit and R. Schuller (Moscow: Cooperative Publishing Society of Foreign Workers in the USSR, 1936), 11.
43 Glasgow, "Negro Mother," 12. Glasgoe's letter was written in response to a questionnaire from the workers' newspaper *Za industrializatsiiu*. The purpose of the letters was to show the "new attitude towards labour, which forms the basis of the Stakhanov movement" (xvii–xviii). Note: Glasgoe's name is spelled two ways across publications. I use Glasgoe primarily, but Glasgow when it is spelled as such in the source.
44 Glasgow, "Negro Mother," 12.
45 Patterson, *Chronicle of the Left Hand*, 13.
46 See Patterson, *Chronicle of the Left Hand*, 52, 55, 89–90.
47 Chatwood Hall, "American Woman, formerly of New York and Westfield, is back in U.S. from Russia," *Atlanta Daily World*, 2 November 1937, 5.
48 Brubaker and Cooper's conception of collective identity includes three factors: commonality, connectedness, and groupness. See Brubaker and Cooper, "Beyond Identity," 20.
49 Homer Smith, *Black Man in Red Russia* (Chicago: Johnson, 1964), 2. He also confirms his writing identity on this page.
50 Smith, *Black Man in Red Russia*, 3.
51 Smith, *Black Man in Red Russia*, 26.
52 Smith, *Black Man in Red Russia*, 46. He also details an interview with Catherine in a 1936 article. See "Great-granddaughter of Pushkin not Writer," *Baltimore Afro-American*, 2 May 1936, 2.
53 Smith, *Black Man in Red Russia*, 55. Smith was one of a long line of Black writers to contemplate Pushkin's Blackness. See Anne Lounsberry, "Bound by Blood to the Race: Pushkin in African American Context," in *Under the Sky of My Africa: Alexander Pushkin and Blackness*, ed. Catherine Theimer Nepomnyashchy, Nicole Svobodny, and Ludmilla A. Trigos (Evanston: Northwestern University Press, 2006).
54 Nepomnyaschchy et al., eds., *Under the Sky of My Africa*, 7.
55 Smith, *Black Man in Red Russia*, 57.
56 Smith, *Black Man in Red Russia*.
57 Smith, *Black Man in Red Russia*, 58.

58 Smith, *Black Man in Red Russia*, 58.
59 Writing as Chatwood Hall, Smith gleefully recounts watching white Americans struggle with not having the right to complain about his presence next to them on a beach in Odesa, Ukraine. He notes, "I enjoyed their suffering immensely." "A Black Man in Red Russia," *Abbott's Monthly* 6, no. 6 (1933), 38.
60 Hall, "A Black Man in Red Russia" 8.
61 Hall, "A Black Man in Red Russia" 10.
62 Robert Robinson, *Black on Red: My 44 Years inside the Soviet Union* (Washington, DC: Acropolis, 1988), 19, 417.
63 Robinson, *Black on Red*, 24.
64 Robinson, *Black on Red*, 24.
65 Robinson, *Black on Red*, 29.
66 Robinson, *Black on Red*, 29.
67 Robinson, *Black on Red*, 36. White American workers also refused to room with him in Leningrad, but the hotel staff did not accommodate them. Robinson, *Black on Red*, 42.
68 Robinson, *Black on Red*, 36.
69 Robinson, *Black on Red*, 66.
70 Robinson, *Black on Red*, 67.
71 Robinson, *Black on Red*, 67.
72 Robinson, *Black on Red*, 71. Chatwood Hall loved this result and mentioned it in "A Black Man in Red Russia," 40.
73 Robinson, *Black on Red*, 96, 98, 100.
74 Robinson, *Black on Red*, 70.
75 Robinson, *Black on Red*, 58.
76 Robinson, *Black on Red*, 58.
77 Robinson, *Black on Red*, 75. Robinson was acutely aware of the connection between worker productivity and political behaviour in the Soviet Union. He understood that in the factories, one who was not productive was committing a political slight.
78 Guarnizo and Smith, *Transnationalism from Below*, 11.

PART IV

Communities

11 The "Father of Russian Futurism" in America: David Burliuk and the *Russian Voice*

ANNA ARUSTAMOVA, TRANSLATED FROM THE
RUSSIAN BY ISAAC STACKHOUSE WHEELER

The Russian literary scene in New York in the 1920s both resembled and diverged from that of "Russian Paris." The Parisian branch of the Russian émigré community included a significant number of major poets and writers like Ivan Bunin, Dmitry Merezhkovskii, Vladislav Khodasevich, and Marina Tsvetaeva, who had spent significant portions of their literary careers in Russia and won their fame there. These figures continued their work after they emigrated and played a leading role in the Russian literary scene abroad. The American émigré community, by contrast, hosted markedly fewer writers who had established themselves in pre-revolutionary Russia, such as Grigori Grebenshchikov, Osip Dymov, and, most prominently, David Burliuk. Like Paris, New York was home to a wide range of Russian-language periodicals, including the long-lived *New Russian Word* (*Novoe russkoe slovo*) and the *Russian Voice* (*Russkii golos*). Unlike its Parisian counterpart, the New York émigré community included pro-socialist publications like the *Russian Voice*, which led not only to ideological differences with opponents like the *New Russian Word*, but also to a distinct aesthetic vision and attendant themes and motifs, which were reflected in the circle of authors that formed around them. Furthermore, the *Russian Voice* not only expressed pro-Soviet views but also attempted to establish connections, including literary ones, with Soviet Russia and to integrate itself into the Soviet literary world.

The *Russian Voice* was founded in 1907 by Ivan Okuntsov (who later became the editor of the *New Russian Word*), but closed in 1909 due to financial difficulties.[1] It was resurrected in 1917, once again under Okuntsov, as a cooperative, non-partisan newspaper that was nonetheless sympathetic to the Bolsheviks.[2] By the mid-1920s, the front page proclaimed it the "largest daily cooperative newspaper in the United States and Canada," and by the end of the decade it was calling itself "the largest Russian newspaper in America." In 1920, a new editor took the helm: the writer, poet, and leftist political figure A.Y. Brailovsky, who had left Russia after the revolutionary events of 1905.

Two years later, David Burliuk, the "father of Russian Futurism," as he liked to call himself, arrived in New York, and within a year, he became literary editor at the *Russian Voice*. Burliuk was attracted to the periodical – where he worked for seventeen years, from March 1923 to 1940 with a brief hiatus in 1926 – because of its unapologetic pro-Soviet stance, a point he emphasized often to colleagues and friends.[3] "The *Russian Voice*, where I have been an editor for six years," he wrote in a 1929 letter to Erich Gollerbakh, "is a firmly Soviet newspaper that defends the interests of our Great Motherland in the country of predatory capitalism. I would never work at any other newspaper!"[4] In a 1932 letter to Vasily Kamensky, he wrote that the *Russian Voice* was "the only pro-Soviet Russian newspaper in existence abroad, which has come out every day without fail for fifteen years."[5] Burliuk also emphasized the longevity of his newspaper, which was oriented towards familiarizing the "workers' colony" in the United States with life in the Soviet homeland they had left behind, strengthening ties with the Soviet Union, and, ultimately, setting socialist Russia in opposition to the capitalist world.[6]

Burliuk had founded Hylaea – the first Russian Futurist artistic group – in 1910. It soon attracted Vasily Kamensky, Velimir Khlebnikov, Aleksei Kruchenykh, and Vladimir Mayakovsky. All had become signatories of the Futurist manifesto "A Slap in the Face of Public Taste" (1912) and participants in a scandalous tour through European Russia in 1913–14, during which the poets painted their faces, dressed ridiculously, and heckled their audiences. In 1917, while living in the Urals, Burliuk had welcomed the Revolution, even creating a mixed-media collage called "Revolution" to celebrate the occasion. However, Burliuk's interest in anarchism led him to flee the country in 1918. Travelling east through Siberia, Japan, and Canada, Burliuk eventually found his way to the US, settling in New York. He knew little English but was still avowedly leftist, and he was determined to use his talents and experience in literary organizing in his new homeland.

Over the next two decades, Burliuk worked tirelessly as literary editor at the *Russian Voice*, making the pro-Soviet newspaper into the hub of Russian "proletarian culture" in America. New York might not have had the recognized literary talent of Russian Berlin or Paris, but Burliuk's interests lay elsewhere. He aimed to find and develop untrained talent. On the pages of the newspaper and beyond, Burliuk mobilized his status as the "father of Russian Futurism" to foster a literary community through an active pedagogical strategy that involved many opportunities for first-time publication, creative writing prompts, generous feedback, and constant – and often published – correspondence with aspiring writers. The literary community that formed around the *Russian Voice* thus came to represent not only a creative outlet for those far from home but also a school of leftist proletarian poetry in the US, the land Burliuk called "the country of predatory capitalism."

As such, the *Russian Voice* developed a different kind of émigré literature. If literature of the Russian emigration is often defined by the inaccessibility of home, a sense of alienation in the new host country, and the romantic reconstruction of an irretrievable past, then the poetics of the *Russian Voice* offered something quite different. On the one hand, it set up a sharp opposition between the capitalist world and Soviet Russia, where the workers, who had triumphed in the 1917 Revolution, were building a new and more just society. On the other hand, the cultural interactions and bilateral exchanges of information that the newspaper was attempting to facilitate managed to soften the nostalgia for a lost homeland, the sense of irretrievable loss. To a certain extent, this nostalgia was replaced either by the hope of returning one day or by a belief in the idea of a world revolution, which would lead to the destruction of all the barriers facing the workers of the world.

But the *Russian Voice* did not simply wait for those barriers to fall. The newspaper served as a kind of "bridge" connecting Soviet Russia and the "proletarian" element of the Russian diaspora in the US. It was aimed at disseminating knowledge of contemporary Soviet life, foreign and domestic policy, and cultural life as widely as possible. It included letters from workers in Soviet Russia and travelogues from Russian Americans visiting the country. In the 1920s, the *Russian Voice* had many readers and even subscribers in Russia.[7] The newspaper offered harsh criticisms of the social contradictions of the US and the conditions faced by workers and the lower strata of society; gender and racial problems were also discussed. In this way, the *Russian Voice* – and especially its literary section with Burliuk at the helm – present a less familiar picture of émigrés' cultural life and their connections to the Soviet Union. This chapter explores this previously overlooked mode of émigré cultural production by following Burliuk's creation of a literary community around the *Russian Voice*, then by interrogating the poetics fostered there, and finally by examining the connections made with the Soviet Union before they fell apart in the 1930s.

The *Russian Voice* as Literary Community

Burliuk's work with the newspaper was quite varied; he published satire, sociopolitical essays, sketches of life in New York, and articles about cultural happenings among the Russian diaspora in the US. He also wrote surveys of Soviet life, reviews of Soviet literature, film, and theatre, and reports on performances by touring Soviet theatre troupes. But it is the literary dimension of Burliuk's work that deserves special attention. Each week the paper published a section devoted to literature. Initially called the "Literary Page," it later became "Literary Thursday," and in the second half of the 1920s and the early 1930s, it changed its name twice more, first to the "Literary Corner" and finally to "Colonial Creations." (This chapter uses the longest-lived name, Literary Thursday, throughout.)

The Russian literary situation in the US in the 1920s and 1930s was, to a certain extent, unique. Partly due to the lack of a large circle of great Silver Age writers (most of whom had settled in Berlin and Paris), there was more room for authors who ran the gamut of literary talent and poetic accomplishments in newspapers, magazines, and books. The *Russian Voice* was primarily oriented towards a broad working-class readership and sought to publish, in Burliuk's words, "material that is as modern as possible and is accessible to the reading masses of workers whom we serve."[8]

In addition to "modern" content, the newspaper fostered a lively Russian-language literary scene in New York. The diverse literary community around the *Russian Voice* included professional writers, but it also made room for new writers who were just beginning to become professional, publishable, and readable. Burliuk proved essential to uniting these two currents. He brought together a broad array of literary names new to the Russian diaspora in the US, and many aspiring writers from the "democratic" strata of the Russian émigré community began to gather around the newspaper. Some of them also became members of the Circle of Proletarian Writers and Artists in North America.[9] The Circle published actively in the *Russian Voice* and also produced an almanac, *Toward New Horizons* (*K novym gorizontam*, vol. 1, 1922), a magazine, *Transatlantic Bunting* (*Zaatlanticheskii kumach*, 1924), a collected volume for the Kitovras publishing house, *The Subway's Windpipe* (*Svirel' sobveia*, 1924), and the anthologies *Captives of the Skyscrapers* (*Plenniki neboskrebov*, 1924) and *Hammer and Sickle* (*Serp i molot*, 1932). In each of these publishing ventures, Burliuk, as the leader of the Russian colony's new "proletarian" authors, played a key role.

Burliuk was a capable and experienced organizer who had led Futurism, a new literary movement, to prominence in the 1910s. He had participated in the fierce and complex literary struggles of the pre-revolutionary decade. And when he took the reins of the *Russian Voice*'s literary section, he brought this experience and pedigree with him. He arrived in America as the "father of Russian Futurism" and did his utmost to maintain

Figure 11.1. The front page of the *Russian Voice* on the reactions to Lenin's funeral, 24 February 1924.

Figure 11.2. A typical Literary Thursday with poems from Futurists Aleksei Kruchenykh, Nikolai Aseev, and David Burliuk alongside those of unknown authors, 15 May 1924.

that status. That title appeared in the newspaper often, for instance, in announcements for poetry readings that included, among others, "the father of Russian Futurism, the inimitable David Burliuk."[10] Burliuk's personal archive contains letters that address him with this title, including an invitation to a literary event for "the father of Russian Futurism, the bard of the country of workers and peasants, you, Mr. David Burliuk."[11]

The literature page of the *Russian Voice* immediately began to be associated with his name, which was printed in large letters aside the section title. Correspondence written to Literary Thursday was often addressed to Burliuk himself. And subsequent editions of the page, in turn, published a whole range of readers' letters and verses. For example, a small verse text addressed to the editor of Literary Thursday was published in 1925:

Вы, как орел, изведаете,
И блеск, и тон теней,
И ярко нам поведаете
О красках наших дней.

With talons bright enough to frighten us,
And wings dark with shadowed tones
Our eagle brilliantly enlightens us
To our age's finest prose and poems.

The selection was signed "with greetings from M. Levina" and included a comment on how important Literary Thursday was to Russian proletarians in the US.[12] The author of a poem titled "A Worker's Greeting" used the voice of the workers to indicate what he saw as the essential function of Literary Thursday:

Два года, как пишем и читаем мы,
Два года как «Литературная страница»
Нам место дает.
Призыв верный ее каждый мы слышим,
К прогрессу нас она громко зовет.

For two years, we have written and read,
For two years the Literature page
Has published what we've said
Every one of us heeds its call to progress.[13]

But it wasn't until the celebrations of the "25th Anniversary of David Burliuk's Revolutionary Activities" in early February of 1924 that recognition of his literary mastery, his poetic leadership, and his role as a mentor to young poets fully emerged. On that occasion, a section called "Readers on Our Colleagues" included letters addressed directly to Burliuk, the mentor and organizer of the literary scene around the *Russian Voice*.

This perception of the career and figure of the poet was characteristic not only of participants in the literary scene that had gathered around him and recognized his role in the formation of their poetic identity, but also of the newspaper's audience, that is, other readers who saw themselves as potential writers. Thus, a letter signed simply "Reader" expressed delight at Burliuk's work as an organizer and guide in the world of literature:

Dear Comrade Burliuk,

Do you know who all of us are, we who write and test the strength of our wings before we can soar? All of us are lonely people born in a different land. Do you know who brought us together and gave us the strength of community ... the hope of new pursuits? It was you! Do you know that this literature page is our home, our temple, our rostrum, our only joy?[14]

Burliuk was not only recognized as a prominent poet; he was also the leader of the Futurist literary movement, which gave him the authority of a mentor. The *Russian Voice* published letters from those who regarded Literary Thursday as the newspaper's best section and who expressed the hope that the poet would take on the job of running another section as well. Several contributors stated that they learned from Literary Thursday and expressed gratitude to its editor. Burliuk was perceived as the first among equals in a community of proletarian readers and beginning authors: "Burliuk is a comrade in the truest sense of the word. Burliuk is the soul of our writing colony. Burliuk is the creator of Russian-American literature. Burliuk is a poet and artist in his own right. We, as young writers and poets, entrust our important work to him, not to the stale professors in their ivory bakery."[15]

During the first years of its existence, the function of Literary Thursday was to establish proletarian poets and offer guidance to beginning authors. In the mid-1920s, readers, beginning authors, and those who had become regular contributors were all highly active. Literary Thursday boiled over with poems, stories, and the literary polemics of the Russian proletarian colony. The newspaper printed correspondence between reader-contributors and the editors as well as commentary from those editors elucidating the newspaper's aesthetic and conceptual vision. It was in the pages of the *Russian Voice* that the literary scene of the "proletarian" wing of the Russian émigré community in the US took shape, and one of the most important elements of that scene was literary instruction for those readers of the paper who were beginning authors.

Burliuk wrote that "the goal of the 'Literary and Artistic Thursday' section in the *Russian Voice* newspaper is to gather and unify literature in America and provide a place for beginning and active writers."[16] Various explanations of the role of the literature page were offered in the mid-1920s: "Anyone who joins us will be lonely no more; friendly creative support often proves indispensable. 'Literary Thursday' is the finest beginners' school for journalism and poetry. It is an open rostrum for original, accomplished creators."[17] The *Russian Voice* promoted the idea that it was possible to teach readers to write poetry, to transform a reader into a writer and help that writer mature. The newspaper, like the Circle of Proletarian Writers and Artists in North America, was viewed as a place where pro-Soviet literature could be born, shaped, and strengthened. Burliuk offered the following advice to beginning authors, emphasizing the need for confidence: "Those who write, often send their work in to be published in a newspaper or anthology, and they often send it with modest qualifications: 'I am not a specialist ...' 'I am an amateur.' Modesty is generally a perfectly laudable thing, but not in art ... even just writing a pair of passable poems is impossible unless you consider yourself a great poet at the moment of creation."[18] Later in the same note, he emphasized knowledge and craft, not just talent and inspiration: "If you have talent, you can sometimes write just fine, even if you have no knowledge to speak of, but knowledge is essential for corrections and revisions ... It is essential to study the anatomy of the word, the phrase, the line."[19]

In addition to general recommendations for mastering poetry, he offered personal recommendations. An author who sent in his texts for revision might, for example, receive the following advice: "Your book has been received and accepted with gratitude ... The corrections to your poems were made for a more modern style, which you will notice if you read them both aloud for comparison."[20] By offering this type of commentary in the newspaper, the editor could reach not only New Yorkers but also those in other cities, from New Haven to San Francisco. For those wishing to improve their mastery of poetry who did live in New York, there were Literary Thursday studio classes available on 14th Street, right off Union Square, often announced in the newspaper.

Also, regular opportunities to interact with Burliuk were scheduled for readers who wanted to write, enter the literary world, and eventually become professional writers and poets. "Those who wish to discuss their works personally," ran a note under Burliuk's signature in one issue, "are invited to come by the editorial offices of the *Russian Voice* on Wednesdays and Fridays from 3:00 to 5:00 pm."[21] The paper also frequently printed letters from readers who sought a verdict as to whether or not they had a chance to become a writer or poet. "I am sending you several poems selected from the small number I have ... I have recently arrived from Russia ... I do not know if I am a poet or not, but I would like to know. Who will tell me the truth? I believe in you."[22] This correspondent's poems later appeared in the newspaper. The *Russian Voice* often published authors whom they viewed as promising and often provided complimentary commentary. For example, various responses to Romuald Kornosevich's poems stated that the author was achieving success, gaining poetic mastery from issue to issue, and putting out better and better work.[23] New poets' first (and sometimes only) collections were often published under the auspices of the *Russian Voice*. This was how Kornosevich's debut collection *The Reins of the Stars* found its first publication.[24]

In addition, the *Russian Voice* often published prompts, assignments, and competitions to attract and develop new literary talent.[25] One issue of Literary Thursday presented a contest for the title of "the first poet of the Russian colony." The winner, Alexander Alland, who had arrived in America about a year before from Constantinople, was chosen by a contest committee, chaired by Burliuk. Prizes in this case included a book and a painting by Burliuk.[26] This was a way for the newspaper to build a sense of community; it was also a way to convince people that it was possible to learn to become a writer in the broadest sense of the word, a participant in the literary scene that was taking shape thanks to the editors of the *Russian Voice* and the tight-knit circle of authors that had assembled around it. A typical reader letter illustrates this view of Literary Thursday:

> I am sending you my poems. I am interested in new Russian poetry and literature, and I was tremendously glad to learn that here, in America, oh so far from my beloved homeland, there are people working towards bringing together everything that is warm, beautiful, and Russian. After all, American life is a room I could easily have frozen stiff in otherwise. I have been in America for just four months. I would be overjoyed to become a contributor to your Thursday.[27]

In order to break out of the solitary room of American life, this writer was turning to "new Russian poetry and literature" and "everything that is warm, beautiful, and Russian," both of which were provided in the *Russian Voice*. By melding cutting-edge Russian poetry and literature with the comforts and nostalgia of home, the *Russian Voice* provided the émigré community with a unique way to address the alienation of life abroad while staying politically and culturally engaged.

Poetic innovation was critically important for the *Russian Voice*'s position and for Burliuk as its literary leader. Burliuk, the father of Russian Futurism, as presented in the *Russian Voice* and the publications of the Circle, was closely identified with devotion to the new and rejection of the old art and the old world. "New" came to mean revolutionary, progressive, pro-Soviet proletarian art, the art of the masses. It was precisely in this light that Burliuk constructed certain aspects of his biography; the *Russian Voice* presented him as a key figure in Futurism who wholeheartedly embraced the Revolution.[28] In his own poetry, he constructed a lyric biography that was understandable to his readers and his comrades in America:

Страна Россия … Где рос и я..
Где Горького
Максима прочитав
Среди дворянских арий
И так и сяк
Уверовал: я пролетарий,
Я футурист и сверхбосяк!

The Russian land … where I too was born …
Where I read Maxim
Gorky among the palace arias
And in every way
Proclaimed "I am a proletarian
I am a futurist and a supervagabond!"[29]

In offering his newspaper as a forum for "fosterlings of the red storm" (as one of those fosterlings, Yakov Tarle, phrased it), Burliuk shaped his own biography in the same mould: not just as a Futurist and a supervagabond but as a simple proletarian writer like the others around him.[30] As the preceding fragment indicates, Burliuk emphatically attributed the genesis of his own creative work to reading Gorky; this stance enabled readers and potential authors to see him as one of their own. The combination of this identity with many others – artist and critic, Futurist and supervagabond – is what allowed him to forge the literary community around the *Russian Voice* as a proletarian voice in the US.

A Different Kind of Émigré Literature

This raises the question of how the identity of readers and authors took root and was nurtured by a pro-Soviet émigré newspaper like the *Russian Voice*. On the one hand, the *Russian Voice* was a newspaper for émigrés, and it naturally contained the familiar range of themes, images, and emotions that were characteristic of the first wave of Russian émigrés. On the other hand, it was a pro-Soviet proletarian newspaper that emphasized Soviet ideals, the building of Soviet society, the struggle for the global liberation of working people, and the belief that revolutionary ideas would soon triumph, not just in a single country, but throughout the world.

The parallel existence of these two threads, sometimes within a single text, produced a rather paradoxical effect. For example, the 1927 issue dedicated to the tenth anniversary of the Revolution included the following poem by Yakov Tarle, titled "Oh Country, Be a Mother":

Будь мне матерью, страна!
Мне, с Гудзоном сроднившимся!
В жизни скорбной ты одна
Радуешь мир истомившийся …

… Дай мне к твоим приникнуть порогам,
К розам праздничным венца.

Oh country, be a mother!
To me, a man who has become kin to the Hudson!
In my dolesome life
Only you gladden this weary world …

… Let me touch your thresholds,
And the festival roses of your wreath.[31]

The lyrical subject views Soviet Russia as his motherland, his lodestar. At the same time, he refers to another aspect of his identity, the American side ("kin to the Hudson"). This poem lacks the opposition between foreign and familiar that is so common in émigré literature and proposes instead a synthesis. The lyrical subject does not treat America as foreign – he is "kin" to the country to which he has found himself transplanted. The more relevant opposition here is that between labour and capital, with the "weary world" and "dolesome life" as metonymic references to the world of the exploited and the "thresholds" and "wreath" representing a welcome beyond toil. The implication is that deliverance must come from beyond labour. The broader context – this issue of the newspaper was dedicated to the tenth anniversary of the October Revolution – would prime readers to detect Tarle's symbolism.

Likewise, in his poem "Back in New York," V. Bondarenko describes his warm feelings for the city:

> Мне мил неряшливый беспечный великан
> И бестолочь высот скребущих небо зданий,
> Бродвей и Баури, кино, обжорка-ресторан,
> Все будит в памяти поблекшее воспоминанье.

> This heedless slovenly giant is sweet to me
> And the imbecile heights of its sky-scraping buildings
> Broadway and Bowery, movies and food stalls
> All of it stirs withered recollections in my memories.

This poem unfurls a picture of places that are *already* beloved and familiar and that are linked with the biography of the lyric hero. New York already seems lived in and "sweet," and this motif repeats throughout the poem. This poem is a lyrical formulation of the processes of adapting to the foreign space of emigration, making it one's own:

> И странного в том нет, конечно, ничего,
> Что вместе с остальной разноязычною оравой
> Считаю я, что здесь все – наше, все – мое,
> Что на него я выковал себе неписанное право.

> Of course there is nothing strange about the fact
> That I, along with the rest of the polyglot mob
> Feel that everything here is ours, everything is mine
> That I have forged for myself an unwritten right.

The "foreign" becomes "familiar," and the borders of the "familiar" expand closer to the conclusion of the text:

> И что забыв о местном чудном языке,
> Сквозь шум, я на борту скользящего парома
> На Годсоне, как будто на Москве-реке,
> По-русски звонко говорю и чувствую себя совсем как дома.

> And that, when I have forgotten about the peculiar local language
> Through the noise, I am aboard a ferry gliding
> Over the Hudson, as if down the Moskva River
> I speak in booming Russian and feel utterly at home.³²

Unlike typical émigré poems, whose motifs emphasize the indelible division between foreign and familiar, the sense of alienation in one's country of residence, this poet manifests the sense of belonging to a "we," a polyglot mob of working people, and erases the symbolic borders between the homeland he left behind and the space where he has spent "a quarter century" as an émigré. The nostalgic ruminations and memories of the lost homeland that are characteristic of the first wave of émigrés (and that emphasize the impermeability of borders and the alien culture and society of the host country) give way here to a feeling of belonging to another community, a "polyglot mob" of immigrants and working people.

The Tarle poem cited earlier contains motifs of a hard journey and a hard lot, not just in a foreign land but, first and foremost, in the kingdom of capital and oppression. Those motifs are characteristic of many texts by authors from Burliuk's circle. The opposite pole, obviously, is Soviet Russia, the hope and lodestar not just for proletarian émigrés but for working people the world over. Thus the "I" of these poems becomes a "we." The weary suffering of one's own fate is eased or replaced by hope for revolutionary change on a global scale. In this context, "weary world" alludes to existing in thrall to capital and suffering oppression as one awaits worldwide revolutionary events.

The global scale of these coming changes "above borders and barriers" is affirmed in a significant number of the texts published in the *Russian Voice* around this time. These poems paint a utopian picture of a new world whose foundations have been laid in the homeland, in Soviet Russia. Thus, M. Moskvin writes,

> И старый мир в пожаре
> Растает, как лед от солнца, до конца,
> И на ярко-алом небосводе
> Всех сильней сиять будет красная звезда.
> Народы будут в братстве и свободе,
> Вдохновляясь заветом разумного труда.

> The old world, too, dissolves in flame
> Like ice running in the sun,
> And on the bright scarlet horizon

The red star will shine ever brighter.
The peoples will in brotherhood and freedom
Take inspiration from their vow of reason and labor.³³

As expected, works of this kind, which depict the coming utopia, include motifs of dreams, reveries, and visions, which are also reflected in their titles and subtitles, as in another Moskvin poem, "USSR (Waking Dream)":

Я слышу клич воли народной.
Власть Советов – удел Руси …
И заревом алых зарниц
Окрашается [sic] над миром свобода.
Нет ей предела, нет границ!

I hear the cry of the people's will
Soviet power is the destiny of Rus' …
And in a blaze of scarlet lightning
Freedom shines over the world
Knowing no limits or borders!³⁴

These authors see the Revolution expanding to encompass the entire planet and all who inhabit it.

Burliuk helped set the tone for this trend. In his 1923 poem "May Day Parade," he offered both command and prophecy:

Шагайте, товарищи, смело,
Прошедшему взгляда не кинь!
За правое вечное дело –
РАБОЧИЙ – Земли Господин.

March boldly, comrades
Without a backward glance!
The WORKER, master of the world
Serves his just eternal cause.³⁵

The marching rhythm of this poem can be found among other writers as well, from experienced poets who regularly appeared in the paper to readers who published only one or two texts. For example, R. Kornosevich, a member of Burliuk's circle, published his "March of the Poets" about a month earlier, in which personal identity – "I am an émigré and a working person" – formed a lyrical "we," which simultaneously linked

Russian "working people" in America with the workers in the country of the victorious proletariat, making them part of a single whole that included working people the world over.[36] In August 1924, A. Sanderov, a fixture of Literary Thursday and the Circle's anthologies, outran time itself with his poem "1925," in which he predicted a future in which:

> Бездыханным лежит старый мир!
> Мы справляем по умершим тризну.
> Расцветился размашистый пир
> У ворот в Мировую Отчизну!
>
> The old world lies unbreathing!
> We stage a funeral feast for the departed.
> The spread lies resplendent
> At the gates to the Worldwide Motherland![37]

In this new world, the borders of the speaker's motherland have expanded to encompass the entire planet. Simultaneously, the émigré has become a citizen of the world who now experiences himself as part of a greater "we." The object of exploitation, the worker, has become a revolutionary subject, an active figure able to transform the planet. The palette of emotions and feelings has shifted; there is no place for nostalgia or lonely alienation in a foreign land; instead, there is energy, action, transformation, and cohesion.

The mid-1920s saw a surge of works filled with enthusiasm for the Revolution; these were connected with the optimistic position that the *Russian Voice*, especially its literature page, had taken regarding world revolution. That enthusiasm began to die down somewhat by 1930, and such texts appeared less often. At the same time, the newspaper published more typical émigré reflections on the loss of homeland and the aspiration to return. Such texts frequently featured clichés of the Russian landscape: rye fields, oak trees, birch groves, blue skies, and so on. This lexicon hearkens back to mid-nineteenth-century poetry and specifically the work of Aleksei Koltsov, Nikolai Nekrasov, Aleksei Pleshcheev, and Lev Mei, as well as others who were often included in school primers at the time. The following is highly representative:

> Люблю я землю мою родную
> И влажный шепот зеленых трав.
> Люблю полоску полей ржаную
> И шум лепечущих дубрав.

Всегда готов в свои объятья
Тебя, Россия, заключить.

I love my native land
And the moist murmur of the green grass.
I love the strips of rye in the field
And the rustle of the oaks.
I am always ready to enclose you
In my embrace, Russia.[38]

The same can be said of R. Kornosevich's poem "Foreign Land and Motherland":

Здесь мы на чужбине – наши силы вянут,
А в заводах душных наши жилы тянут.
И в тисках невзгоды крепко нас зажали,
И пришиблен ум наш, груди исхудали.

Here we are on foreign land – we have spent our might
And in the ropeworks of the soul our veins are drawn tight
We are trapped in the vice of woe
And our minds are dejected, our chests sunken.

Russia, in contrast, hosts "native fields" and "groves of aromatic green."[39] In these texts, Russia is often referred to as "Rus." At the same time, these texts depict new realities, imposed by the new socialist order, which is placed directly beside images and innovations from nineteenth-century poetry and early twentieth-century urban romance:

Мечтаю о любви и ласке
Людей мне близких и друзей;
С родного края песни-сказки –
Москвы великий Мавзолей ...
В аккордах песен струн суровых
Есть сила бодрости и жар,
На новых знаменах багровых
Горит жертвенный пожар ...
И с этой вечно юной силой
Я жажду слиться и гореть;
Да будет Русь моей могилой –
Там жить, любить и умереть ...

I dream of love and tenderness
Of friends and dear ones
Songs and tales from my native country
The great Mausoleum of Moscow…
In the chords of harsh-stringed songs
There is the force of vigor and heat
In the new crimson banners
The sacrificial fire burns …
And with that eternally youthful force
I thirst to melt and burn
Yes, Rus' will be my grave
There will I live, love, and die.[40]

In these poems especially, one can sense the conservatism of much of the imagery. Even as these poems express the spirit of the Revolution, in other words, they do so in forms that take little from Burliuk's Futurism.

Other poets, however, were more receptive to formal experimentation. For instance, L. Opalov's poem "Azure Jour-Fix" contains unexpected imagery, describing the poem's addressee as having "lilac babble of rouged braids" ("sitenevyi lepet narumiannykh kos") and "blousy lips" ("usta bluznye"), for example.[41] David Ionkis's poem "In the Metro" follows the Futurists' fascination with urban technology, even incorporating avant-garde rhythms and verbal inventions:

В подземке
Радио-зубки
Чужеземки
И алогубки
Тело – губ.
Но …
Вместо милочки – Сиденье.
И дня – тень.

In the underground
Radio-teeth
Foreigners
And krimsonlips
A body of lips.
But …
Instead of my darling – a seat.
And instead of the day – shadow.[42]

Although some elements of Burliuk's Futurist poetics appeared among the poets of the *Russian Voice*, most often the avant-garde was mixed with the traditional, revolutionary sentiments expressed in older forms.

The key divergence from the literature (and publications) of the broader Russian émigré community apparent in the general stance of the *Russian Voice* and the associated published texts is the possibility of going home to the Soviet Union, and even exhortations to do so. The newspaper regularly published materials on individuals and groups who had returned to the Soviet Union and belittled claims that a tragic fate awaited those who did. The editors printed texts from both readers and poets of the Literary Thursday circle that stated it was possible and even desirable to return to the Soviet Union. They also printed texts by "travellers visiting the motherland," demonstrating the high standard of living in the Soviet Union and the justice of the new social system, as exemplified in the travelogues of Pavel Narodny, serially published in the *Russian Voice* in 1932.[43]

The foreign/familiar dichotomy sometimes persisted in the work of the *Russian Voice*'s authors, but it had ceased to be as urgent and tragic as it had been for representatives of the white émigré community. If the latter's was based on the impossibility of return, then readers of the *Russian Voice* had examples before their very eyes of people who had returned successfully. For instance, the poem "Exhortation" by "Farmer Vas" specifically implored readers to go back:

> Ты здесь как раб!
> Ты здесь чужой.
> Вернись назад туда –
> К стране своей родной! …
> Спеши скорей туда,
> Где льются трели соловья,
> Где так прекрасны рощи, нивы и поля!
> Скорей на родину домой,
> Туда, где жаворонок звонкий
> Еще все реет
> В выси голубой.

> Here you are like a slave
> Here you are a foreigner
> But you can get back there
> To your native country
> Hurry back to the place
> Where the warbles of nightingales resound
> Where the groves, coppices, and fields are so lovely!

Hurry home to your motherland
Where the clear-voiced skylark
Still cries out
In the clear blue sky.[44]

The text is, predictably, built on a system of oppositions: slave labour and free labour, fetters in a foreign land and freedom at home, but it is an inversion of the dichotomy employed by white émigré literature.

The newspaper was constructing a myth of returning, of a "transit" back "there," out of permanent exile, out of movement in the opposite direction, and, indeed, out of movement towards an ideal. On this journey, the *Russian Voice* itself was a guide and mediator. That is precisely how an author writing under the pseudonym "Rossiianin" (or "Russian citizen") describes its role in the poem "To the *Russian Voice*," in which the publication functions as a hero and a speaking subject. At the same time, the text compares the newspaper to a paladin defending the boundaries and liberty of the Russian people:

Из русских лесов и цветистых равнин,
Из гор, и долин, и простора,
В Америку двинулся я, паладин,
Чтоб быть на посту и дозоре.
И голосом русским я здесь загремел:
Я стану на страже свободы,
И буду беречь, чтоб никто не посмел
Обидеть родного народа.

From the Russian woods and flowering ravines
From mountains, valleys, and expanses,
I have made for America like a paladin
To take my post and keep watch
And with my Russian voice I have rumbled
"I will stand on guard for freedom"
I will ensure that no one dares
Harm my kindred people.[45]

But which "people" is the poet referring to? In 1923, this poem offered an interpretation of this phenomenon among the element of the Russian diaspora in the US targeted by the newspaper, explaining the motivations behind their decision to leave their homeland:

Приехал сюда из того далека,
Где жизнь была – мука лихая.

Приехал, чтоб счастье и волю найти,
От зла, беззаконья и рабства уйти.

I came here from that faraway place
Where life was wicked torment.
I came to find happiness and freedom
To depart from evil, anarchy, and slavery.⁴⁶

Here the author is reproducing the classic plot of nineteenth-century Russian literature dealing with American themes – expectation versus reality. America was expected to be a land of freedom and abundance, but in reality it proved to be, in the familiar words of Alexander Herzen, "a corrected reprint of a previous text."⁴⁷

White émigré literature dealing with the experience of departing from Russia generally treated returning as impossible, whereas the *Russian Voice* was a "magical helper" who could lead its "kindred people" into the light:

И я, «Русский голос», ему подсказал:
- Товарищ, тебя не забыли!
Ты, друг, дай мне руку и вместе пойдем
Туда, где нет горя и муки,
Где братство, свободу и счастье найдем ...

And I, the Russian Voice, said to him
Comrade, you are not forgotten
Give me your hand, friend, and we will walk together
To where there is no bitter torment
Where we will find brotherhood, freedom, and happiness ...⁴⁸

The *Russian Voice* was the mediator that could facilitate movement towards the utopian ideals of brotherhood, freedom, and happiness, perhaps even on a global scale.

Connecting to the Soviet Union

Burliuk's best-known Soviet connection developed in 1925, when Vladimir Mayakovsky visited the US.⁴⁹ Burliuk served as his guide in New York, and his trip was covered extensively in the *Russian Voice*. A poem by one of Burliuk's protégés depicting Mayakovsky's arrival was published alongside an excerpt from Mayakovsky's "Vladimir Il'ich Lenin" and a note from Burliuk declaring that "all of us working for the cause of New Russian Literature in America ... unite in sincere friendly greetings to the first poet of New Russia from the bottom of our hearts and awe of his … mighty talent."[50] Frequent updates followed, culminating in an early review of Mayakovsky's cycle *My Discovery of America* (*Moe otkrytie Ameriki*), in which Burliuk hailed the poet as "the first Russian who was able to see America … and give it to us Russians in a way we could understand."[51]

The *Russian Voice* energetically promoted a sense of unity with the motherland that had been left behind, a sense not of distance but of proximity and even participation in the construction of a new way of life there. Issues of the *Russian Voice* were sent to Russia, and the publication regularly printed response letters from readers in the Soviet Union, who offered greetings to the American proletariat and the newspaper, noting its high quality and the interest it was attracting from Soviet readers. Letters arrived from authors in Soviet Russia, who submitted their own texts to the *Russian Voice* (a rarity for Russian-language publications abroad) and who expressed the desire to become correspondents. For example, in 1925, the editors received a letter from Roman Bobach in Moscow titled "Pantomime," offering to expound on the literary scene there. The editors printed his story, offered him greetings "from faraway America," and referred to him as "our newly-minted permanent Moscow correspondent," emphasizing creative connections with the motherland.[52] In January 1924, S. Manenkov, a textile worker, a poet from Burliuk's circle, and a regular author for the *Voice of Textiles*, the newspaper of the Central Committee of the All-Union Union of Textile Workers, published a photograph in the *Russian Voice* accompanied by a call for "friends and colleagues who wish to enter into correspondence with me."[53] There were many such examples of interaction on a personal as well as editorial level in the 1920s. Some Soviet greetings arrived in verse. For example, the paper published a poem by Georgy Shkatullo from Lyuban, with "greetings to you, brothers in a foreign land, sons of Mother Russia!"[54] Such lines helped to construct a sense of unity and kinship and also to shift the emphasis; the *Russian Voice* was not the voice of émigrés who had abandoned Russia, but of "brothers in a foreign land," no less sons of Russia than those who were establishing a new way of life in the Soviet Union.

Throughout the 1920s, the *Russian Voice* was distributed in the Soviet Union. Individual issues of the newspaper were sent to private individuals, often relatives of readers in the US, but there were also actual subscribers, since it was a proletarian newspaper and therefore appropriate from a class perspective. Indeed, it was class, rather than any geographical criterion (its status as a foreign émigré publication) that played the dominant role in how the *Russian Voice* was perceived in the Soviet Union. The newspaper announced that "packages of newspapers are on their way to private individuals and institutions in the USSR ... Lots of private individuals and Soviet institutions are ordering the *Russian Voice*." If subscriptions are any indication, readers and institutions received copies regularly. The *Russian Voice* made the following statement regarding an issue dedicated to the memory of Lenin: "Readers are still coming in to buy copies of our Sunday issue to send back to their comrades and relatives in the Motherland. Many of them are sending five or ten copies at a time to village soviets and other institutions."[55]

The fact that the newspaper was (at least relatively) available in the Soviet Union prompted its more active readers to write letters to the editor. The *Russian Voice* might include, for example, a letter from the Soviet Union in which the author described how the newspaper of the Russian proletarians in America was one of the most interesting and most actively read periodicals in his village's library or workers' club. As communications between the two countries became more difficult by the end of the decade, this bilateral flow of correspondence would dry up, but during the 1920s, readers received regular signs of friendly support from their homeland, which, according to the editors' thinking, could give them the strength they needed to exist in the country of capital and endure the associated suffering and dissatisfaction. It could also promote hope that the situation in the world as a whole would change.

The connection to the Soviet Union was also emphasized on an aesthetic level. The *Russian Voice* frequently pointed to the aesthetic and ideological overlap between the Soviet "art of the masses" and that of the proletarian émigré community in America. Editors rejected any division of Russian literature into two branches (émigré and Soviet) and worked hard to show readers how proletarian writers in America were contributing to the "new" Soviet Russian literature, especially under the auspices of the *Russian Voice*. This idea was even expressed in how the newspaper was formatted; texts from Russia would occasionally be printed on the same page as work from "proletarian poets in America." In one of the May issues of Literary Thursday dedicated to celebrating International Workers' Day, Burliuk's editorial introduction, titled "May Day Spring," highlighted the harmony between US-based "works dedicated to this spring holiday and pieces by representatives of the Moscow Left Front of the Arts, our old compatriots in the first battles against the bourgeois literature of 'yesteryear.'"[56] The promised Soviet poets included Vladimir Mayakovsky, Vasily Kamensky, and Nikolai Aseev. All three were Futurists who had worked alongside Burliuk to shock the bourgeoisie during the pre-revolutionary period. Burliuk's poem in that issue's Literary Thursday appeared directly beside theirs. Thus, on a visual level, this quite literally positioned Burliuk among the ranks of the authors who became Soviet poets after the Revolution, the implicit assertion being that he was co-present in the literary scene in the Soviet Union.

In that same editorial introduction, he repeatedly emphasized the connection between the young Russian proletarian literature of America and Soviet literature:

> Literary Thursday, by uniting young Russian authors in America who have offered their pens in service of the great ideals of the New Russia, by printing the work of our faraway Muscovite brethren in this issue, is reaching across the ocean with comradely greetings and the fervent wish that our old friends on the other side will meet us halfway as we pursue the cause of uniting the primary (Muscovite) proletarian/Left-Front-of-the-Arts literature with the youthful flights of our young Russian-American literature.[57]

Burliuk had created a personal artistic strategy designed to accomplish two goals simultaneously (remaining part of the literature of his homeland and consolidating his position in the American literary space). In a parallel effort, he also directed his efforts as an organizer towards integrating the work of "proletarian" émigrés into Soviet literature.[58] He was also attempting through his polemics against white émigré literature and criticism to assert the emergence of a new "literary movement," or, more accurately, a new segment of Russian literature: the proletarian literature of the Russian émigré community. Burliuk's language at the time frequently invoked concepts like "new," "young," "the people's literature," and "labour literature":

> The young Russian literature in America is an expression of the working people – it is their offspring, growing, getting stronger, and perhaps someday soon, it will burst into a literary movement … we must value, understand, embolden, and love the art of those who have emerged from among the people. The art of the young … the foundation of our strength in the tireless quest for true art – that is something that cannot be seized by our enemies who would like to suffocate and stifle the youthful flights of Russian literature in America … and replace it with the meager rubbish of mechanical reproduction and clippings from dusty places distant in space and time.[59]

Burliuk declared novelty, youth, and the people to be the criteria, which corresponded to the prevailing rhetoric around literature in Soviet Russia in the 1920s, where masses of working people were entering the literary scene and a new literature was being constructed.[60]

In the mid-1920s, the newspaper began including a subsection titled "Our Connection with Russia," where texts by Soviet authors would be printed alongside texts from authors from the *Russian Voice* circle. For example, Literary Thursday might include a "Song of the First Cavalry" by Moscow author B. Cherny (accompanied by a note indicating that the poem had been sent in specifically for this section) alongside a poem titled "Faithlessness" by Lev Levin from Chicago, a regular contributor to the newspaper.[61] An alternative, as an embodiment of the idea of youth and the promise of the future, might be "A Challenge to the Sun," a narrative poem by I. Averbuch, an eighteen-year-old Soviet reader of the *Russian Voice*, that bore a distinct stamp of Mayakovsky's influence. In the accompanying letter, which the editors published, the beginning author indicated that he "accidentally happened upon" the *Russian Voice* on a table in a workers' club and realized that it was precisely in this publication that he could feel "that his poems were entirely at home, surrounded by friends."[62]

It seems that this gesture towards effacing the opposition between here and there, foreign and familiar, was extremely significant to the editors of Literary Thursday. This poem, like other texts submitted from the Soviet Union, was placed directly beside work by local poets and prose writers. It is worth mentioning that the texts under discussion here were submitted from the Soviet Union by readers of the *Russian Voice* specifically for publication in this newspaper. Although, due to political pressures, this practice could not continue long, in the 1920s it reinforced the connection between the young Russian literature of America and the literature of the Soviet Union, to promote a sense of historical optimism among readers of the *Russian Voice* in the US and to serve as yet another way of overcoming the barriers between the here of the émigré world and the there of the country of origin. In the 1920s, this practice coexisted with an abundance of publications of works by representatives of Russian Futurism: Mayakovsky, Kamensky, Aseev, and Lifshitz.

In order to the strengthen the co-presence of young Russian proletarian literature in the literature of the Soviet Union, the editors would, at times, literally copy the initiatives of Soviet publications. If the magazine *Red Field* (*Krasnaia niva*), for instance, announced a poetry contest requiring a specific rhyme scheme, then the *Russian Voice* offered an identical contest, compared the literary mastery of the participants from the Soviet Union and America, and reviewed the results. An introduction by Z. Gisenkin, a regular author and critic for the *Russian Voice* as well as the Circle's anthologies, stated that "we are part of Russia ... it is so good to recognize that we are all walking the same path. We are simply trying not to fall behind."[63]

Across the 1920s and 1930s, the newspaper published work by Soviet authors quite extensively; indeed, Soviet texts were published more frequently as time progressed. The pages of the *Russian Voice* filled up with texts by Aleksei Tolstoy, Mikhail Sholokhov, Alexander Grin, Mikhail Zoshchenko, Boris Pilnyak, Sergei Mikhalkov, and Lev Kassil. There were also frequent surveys of Soviet literature and lesser-known poems by Mayakovsky and Esenin, as well as articles about the Russian classics: Nekrasov, Lermontov, Chekhov, or Tolstoy. This material was either drawn from the Soviet press or produced by a staff writer assigned to the work of a particular author.

In his own criticism, Burliuk often rebuked Soviet authors and poets for losing the spirit of the Revolution, paradoxically declaring that "we are more proletarian here; our art is more proletarian," since it was situated in more difficult social and class conditions, amidst exploitation and oppression.[64] In the same vein, he called on young authors in America to publish regularly, not to lose hope, and not to develop an inferiority complex, so that they could open a way forward for themselves and "straightforwardly announce themselves." Burliuk recommended that "poets put out books, and readers will scurry in from every direction."[65] Burliuk's review was titled "Here and There" emphasizing, again, that the world of émigrés here was equal or superior to that of the home country back there.

In 1930, Burliuk wrote that "for six years in this foreign land, I have used my pen to defend my Soviet motherland, here in this country of predatory capital standing in the ranks of the New Revolutionary Art in the name of creating hitherto unseen aesthetic forms the proletariat is waiting for."[66] These few lines encapsulate the key aspects of Burliuk's literary work following his arrival in the US in 1922. He emphasized his status as the "father of Russian Futurism," a teacher and mentor, and used the *Russian Voice* both as a personal tribune and as a hub of "literary instruction" for beginning poets and authors. His work both cemented his own status and formed a "proletarian literature" in the Russian émigré community.

This proletarian literature aspired to create a new revolutionary art, a poetics of the red emigration that stood against America's predatory capitalism and in contrast to white émigré poetics. The work of the *Russian Voice*'s authors, unlike that of the white émigrés, contained motifs of the world revolution to come, as well as the formation of a lyrical subject that experienced itself as belonging to a broader transnational *we* of working people around the world. Thus, the dichotomy between homeland and host country, foreign and familiar, so characteristic of the first wave of émigrés, was transformed, symbolically surmounting geographical borders, into an dichotomy between labour and capital. The backwards-looking temporality of much émigré literature was flipped to look forward to a future world revolution. On a formal level, the *Russian Voice* encouraged beginning poets to experiment with recent poetic innovations instead of borrowing exclusively from past models, thus encouraging Russian-American working-class poets to forge the poetics of the future.

On a practical level, the *Russian Voice* strengthened connections with Soviet literature, Soviet readers, and Soviet institutions. It published numerous Soviet works, engaged in constant comparisons with new Russian literature, and the drew parallels between the "proletarian literature" of the émigré community and that of the Soviet Union. All of these actions surmounted the barriers of emigration and worked to create a common space of Russian/Soviet literature, a process that gained vibrancy and energy from Burliuk's talent as an organizer. In his work in the *Russian Voice*, he created a new literature, a literature of the red emigration, not only by constructing its reader but also by actively forming its authors, as well as uniting two branches of Russian literature, Soviet and émigré, on the basis of common aesthetics and ideology.

Notes

1 Tat'iana Shugailo, "Osnovnye tendentsii i osobennosti razvitiia russkoiazychnoi pressy v SShA v 1920 – pervoi polovine 1970-kh gg. (na primere riada krupnykh izdanii)," in *Voprosy istorii Kitaisko-vostochnoi zheleznoi dorogi i goroda Kharbina (120-letie stroitel'stva). Sbornik nauchnykh trudov*, ed. Aleksei Buiakov et al. (Vladivostok: Izdatel'stvo VGUES, 2018), 169–79.

2 Mikhail Pavlovets, "Russkii golos," in *Literaturnaia entsiklopediia russkogo zarubezh'ia (1918–1940)*, vol. 2 (Moskva: INION RAN, 1997), 267–8. See also Evgenii Demeniuk, *David Burliuk. Instinkt esteticheskogo samosokhraneniia* (Moskva: Molodaia gvardiia, 2020).

3 Burliuk commented on this in a 1930 letter to Vasily Kamensky: "You[r] book was quite well published indeed ... at the moment, I have been dismissed from work [at] the *Russian Voice* newspaper for six weeks, so I am thoroughly enjoying getting my paints from tubes to canvass. We didn't go anywhere this year, since we have no money and have to live frugally here in the city. Travel, of whatever kind, is just a waste of one's reserves of energy. I want to spend these six weeks concentrating and producing a series of paintings" (RGALI f. 1497, op. 1, ex. 184, l. 28).

4 OR RNB f. 207, ex. 18 l. 1, 15 avg. 1929. Meanwhile, some years later in 1947, Burliuk characterized his service at the *Russian Voice* as follows in a

letter to Kamensky: "I served at the *Russian Voice* from 1923 to 1939. It was exhausting, backbreaking work for miserly pay. I spent every free minute I could snatch painting. The period of fateful change in my life came in 1938, when my paintings started to sell ... In 1940 I left the newspaper racket behind – I would just send in some articles on the side." RGALI f. 1497, op. 1, ex. 184, l. 32–2 ob.

5 Quoted in Nikolai Firtich, ed., *Vasilii Kamenskii. Materialy i issledovaniia* (St. Petersburg: Izd-vo Obshchestva "Apollon," 2019), 310.
6 In the *Russian Voice*, the work of authors from Burliuk's circle, and the poet's own letters, the word "colony" (*koloniia*) is used in the sense of "diaspora."
7 Although the paper circulated to a certain extent in the Soviet Union, Burliuk was always eager for a stronger connection. See, for instance, his 1932 letter to Kamensky, in which he lamented *The Russian Voice*'s low circulation in the USSR: "you write that nobody is interested in the *Russian Voice*. That is very bad." Firthich, *Vasilii Kamenskii*, 310–11.
8 Letter from D. Burliuk to E. Gollerbakh, 21 November 1929. OR RNB f. 207, ex. 18, l. 7.
9 The Circle of Proletarian Writers and Artists in North America deserves a history of its own, but that is outside the bounds of the current study. Among those published on the Literary Thursday page in the 1920s were members of the Circle – Romuald Kornosevich, David Iuzhanin, Aleksandr Sokolovsky, Anna Mark, Robert Magidoff, Leonid Opalov, Alexander Alland, and others.
10 Untitled announcement, *Russkii golos*, 3 February 1923: 5. Hereafter the *Russian Voice* newspaper, *Russkii golos*, is cited as *RG*.
11 Pavel Narodnyi, *Pis'ma k Burliukam D.D.i M.N. 1931–1932*. OR RGB f. 372, k. 13. ex. 54. l.1.
12 Mariia Levina, "Redaktoru Lit. str.," *RG*, 12 April 1925, 9.
13 Levina, "Redaktoru Lit. str."
14 "Chitateli o nashikh sotrudnikakh," *RG*, 31 January 1924, 3.
15 R. Kornosevich, "Prizyv," *RG*, 14 February 1924, 3.
16 D. Burliuk, "Russkii iazyk za granitsei v gody revoliutsii," *RG*, 15 March 1923, 3.
17 Lev Levin, "Pis'mo iz Chikago," *RG*, 21 February 1924, 3.
18 "O professionalakh i liubiteliakh," *RG*, 16 August 1923, 5.
19 "O professionalakh i liubiteliakh," *RG*, 16 August 1923, 5.
20 D. Burliuk, "Otkrytoe pis'mo L. Levinu," *RG*, 18 January 1924, 3.
21 D. Burliuk, "Portfel' 'Literaturnogo chetverga,'" *RG*, 16 August 1923, 4.
22 Zh. Dneprovskii, "Pis'mo iz San-Francisco," *RG*, 6 March 1924, 3.
23 "Pochtovyi iashchik," *RG*, 26 July 1923, 3.
24 Some books by *Russian Voice* authors did remain unpublished. For example, the newspaper printed announcements that a collection of stories

by Nadezhda Odinokaia was being prepared for publication, and an evening was planned to help the author publish her book, but this result was apparently not achieved.

25 Contests were often announced in the *Russian Voice*, and their themes were not always strictly literary. For example, one issue announced a contest with the prompt "Why I Support Soviet Power," and another asked readers to describe why they loved or hated New York. Responses to the contest would be printed for several weeks until a winner was ultimately selected.
26 "Rezul'taty publichnogo konkursa," *RG*, 7 February 1924, 3.
27 Tema Sven, "Pis'mo," *RG*, 7 February 1924, 3.
28 The *Russian Voice* almost never mentioned the European context of Burliuk's previous artistic work (his participation in exhibitions by the Blue Rider group, for instance); yet his magazine *Color and Rhythm*, which was intended for a different audience, strongly emphasized that context.
29 D. Burliuk, "Moia strana," *RG*, 5 April 1925, 9.
30 The phrase "fosterlings of the red storm" or "pitomtsy krasnoi buri" is from Yakov Tarle's poem "Krasnoi burei rozhdennye," *RG*, 8 November 1923, 3.
31 Iakov Tarle, "Bud' mne materiu, strana," *RG*, 13 November 1927, 9.
32 V. Bondarenko, "Opiat' v N'iu-Iorke," *RG*, 7 April 1935, 8.
33 M. Moskvin, "Pamiati Lenina," *RG*, 31 January 1924, 3.
34 Moskvin, "SSSR (Son naiavu)," *RG*, 24 January 1924, 3.
35 Burliuk, "Parad pervomaiskii," *RG*, 1 May 1923, 2.
36 Kornosevich, "Marsh poetov," *RG*, 5 April 1923, 3.
37 Sanderov, "1925 god," *RG*, 9 August 1924, 3.
38 A. Gritsevich, "Chikago," *RG*, 31 January 1924, 3.
39 Kornosevich, "Chuzhbina i Rodina," *RG*, 24 July 1923, 2.
40 Sitkarev, "Toska po rodine," *RG* 18 September 1927, 3.
41 L. Opalov, "Zhurfiks lazurnyi," *RG* 5 April 1925, 9.
42 David Ionkis, "V Metro," *RG* 26 April 1925, 9.
43 Narodnyi, "Moia poezdka v Sovetskii soiuz," *RG* 29 July 1932, 3.
44 Fermer Vas., "Prizyv," *RG*, 13 January 1924, 3.
45 Rossianin, "Russkomu golosu," *RG*, 3 February 1923, 2.
46 Rossianin, "Russkomu golosu," *RG*, 3 February 1923, 2.
47 Aleksandr Gertsen, *S togo berega*, in *Sobranie sochinenii v 30 tomakh*, vol. 6 (Moskva: Izdatel'stvo Akademii nauk SSSR, 1955), 28.
48 Rossianin, "Russkomu golosu."
49 This trip has been treated extensively in secondary literature, so this chapter limits its treatment to a brief discussion of the trip's appearances in the pages of the *Russian Voice*. For an overview of Mayakovsky's visit in English, see Milla Fedorova, *Yankees in Petrograd, Bolsheviks in New York:*

America and Americans in Russian Literary Perception (Dekalb: Northern Illinois University Press, 2013), 52–72.
50 Burliuk, "Pribytie Maiakovskogo," *RG*, 9 August 1925, 9.
51 Burliuk, "Moe otkrytie Ameriki," *RG*, 10 October 1925, 2.
52 Bobach et al. "Nasha sviaz' s Moskvoi," *RG*, 14 June 1925, 2.
53 Manenkov, "'Russkii golos' v Sovetskoi Rossii," *RG*, 13 January 1924, 2.
54 Shkatullo, "Akrostikh," *RG*, 21 June 1925, 9.
55 "'Russkii golos' v Rossiiu," *RG*, 27 January 1924, 1.
56 D. Burliuk, "Vesna nyneshnykh poetov," *RG*, 15 May 1924, 3.
57 D. Burliuk, "Vesna nyneshnykh poetov," *RG*, 15 May 1924, 3
58 Notably, the occasional publications in the USSR by authors from the *Russian Voice* circle were accompanied by effusive reactions in the newspaper.
59 D. Burliuk, "Nasha sila," *RG*, 12 June 1924, 3.
60 For example, compare the poetic strategy of Burliuk's friend and compatriot V. Kamensky, who became a Soviet poet and maintained a reputation as a true believer welcoming the construction of a new form of life. See Zoia Antipina, *Literaturnaia reputatsiia i tvorchestvo V.V. Kamenskogo v istoriko-kul'turnom kontekste 1920–1930-kh godov*, Candidate of Sciences dissertation, Perm State University, 2021.
61 Chernyi, "Pesnia budennovtsev (Kazach'ia)"; Levin, "Izmena," and "Alchno bushuet vokrug menia," in "Nasha sviaz' s Rossiei," *RG*, 26 July 1925, 9.
62 Averbukh, "Solntse – otvod," *RG*, 26 April 1925, 9.
63 Gisenkin, "87 i 5," *RG*, 12 June 1924, 3.
64 Burliuk, "Zdes' i tam," *RG*, 19 June 1924, 3.
65 Burliuk, "Zdes' i tam," *RG*, 19 June 1924, 3.
66 Burliuk, *Entelekhizm* (New York: Izd. Marii Nikiforovny Burliuk, 1930), 5.

12 Exilic Experiments in Education: The Multiple Lives and Journeys of László Radványi, pseud. Johann-Lorenz Schmidt

HELEN FEHERVARY

Refuge

An oar lies over the roof. A moderate wind
Won't carry off the thatch.
In the yard for the children's swings
There are posts knocked in.
The mail comes twice a day
Where letters would be welcome.
Down the sound the ferries sail.
The house has four doors, to flee by.
– Bertolt Brecht, *Svendborg Poems*, 1939[1]

"Unadulterated Marxism"

Like many Marxists of his time from Central and Eastern Europe, László Radványi, born in Hungary, spent a significant portion of his life in political exile: a total of fifty-nine diasporic years in Austria, Weimar Germany, France, Mexico, and the German Democratic Republic. Although he was educated as a philosopher, his most noteworthy contributions were in the field of worker education, an undertaking to which, even when engaged in academic research, he remained devoted throughout his life.

The Marxist Workers School (Marxistische Arbeiterschule) of Greater Berlin, known as the MASCH, which László Radványi directed from 1927 till 1933 under the pseudonym Johann-Lorenz Schmidt, was among the most important educational ventures in the last years of the Weimar Republic, and certainly the most important experiment in worker education. Radványi summarized the school's aims and achievements in a report he submitted in 1931:

> Five years ago, in winter 1926/27, the Marxist Workers School of Berlin opened its doors. Our goal was to create a place of learning available to all, one in which the working population of Berlin could acquire the basic teachings of unadulterated Marxism and their application in all areas of proletarian life ... As a result, in the intervening five years the Berlin Marxist Workers School has developed into a genuine institution of higher learning for the working population in which thousands of blue- and white-collar workers are taught in the spirit of unadulterated Marxism and empowered to think and act in a consistent, class-conscious way.[2]

According to Radványi's report, the school year 1926–7 had offered 19 evening courses to 146 students. By 1930–1 there were roughly 2,000 courses and 4,000 attendees, as well as more than thirty branches of study, from lectures on dialectical materialism, history of the workers' movement, capitalism, imperialism, and fascism to classes on medicine, hygiene, sexuality, mathematics and sciences, history, literary history, art history, stenography, typing, and bookkeeping, in addition to German language classes for foreigners as well as Russian, English, French, and Esperanto. The MASCH was founded at the prompting of the German Communist Party (KPD) but operated independently and was financially self-reliant, its operating costs covered by student fees: 30 Pfennige per two-hour segments for hundreds, later thousands, of students. The school's teachers – communists, socialists, unaffiliated democrats, and progressives – offered their services for free, and members of the Bauhaus teaching at the MASCH donated ample classroom furniture. When Nazi paramilitary gangs disrupted classes in 1931, instruction moved to the backrooms of taverns, where purchase of a glass of beer counted as tuition, and friends of the MASCH like Bertolt Brecht, Hanns Eisler, and Kurt Weill offered their apartments for classroom use. By the time the National Socialists came to power in 1933 and the MASCH was forced to close, it had organized twenty-nine more schools in Germany and was the model for similar schools in Zurich, Vienna, and Amsterdam.[3]

Radványi's reference to "unadulterated Marxism" (*unverfälschter Marxismus*) – not once, but twice in the passage quoted above – deserves attention. This term was not in common use at the time, and it had no official relevance. It appears in this context to have had a triadic polemical edge vis-à-vis the waning Marxism of the German Social Democratic Party (SPD), the KPD's ultra-left campaign against social democracy as social fascism, and the rigid conception of Marxism-Leninism under Stalin. Implying what is unsullied, hence pure, "unadulterated Marxism" has an antecedent in Rosa Luxemburg's call for the return of "true Marxism" (*wahrer Marxismus*) in the newly formed KPD of 1918–19, as opposed to the "official" *ersatz* Marxism of the SPD, which had voted for war credits in 1914.[4] Certainly Radványi's emphasis on "unadulterated Marxism" suggests he had a clear understanding of himself as a Marxist and educator, and of the school he co-founded, then directed for seven years as a teacher and administrator. But this understanding had not progressed directly from his first encounter with Marxism as a youth; rather, it developed in the context of competing approaches to Marxism and his complicated life story.

From Budapest to Berlin: 1918–1933

Born in 1900, László Radványi was still a Gymnasium student in Budapest when he joined the socialist Galileo Circle during the First World War, published a book of Symbolist poetry titled *Black Book (Fekete Könyv)*,[5] and attended the Free School of the Humanities, a self-proclaimed counter-university where learning was based on the Socratic model of question and answer. Radványi and his classmate Tibor Gergely's participation so impressed Béla Balázs, the school's founder, that they were invited into the select Sunday Circle, whose weekly meetings at Balázs's home often lasted into the night. Formed in late 1915, the Sunday Circle and its occasional guests comprised Hungary's intellectual vanguard: poet-dramatist Balázs and artist-writer Anna Lesznai, art historians Lajos Fülep, Frigyes Antal, Károly (Charles) Tolnay, and Arnold Hauser, philosophers Béla Fogarasi and Károly (Karl) Mannheim, composers Béla Bartók and Zoltán Kodály, economist Károly Polányi and scientist Mihály Polányi, psychologist Júlia Láng, and psychoanalyst René Spitz. At the Circle's (and the Free School's) intellectual centre was the philosopher György (Georg) Lukács. In mid-December 1918, having learned that his application for Habilitation at Heidelberg had been rejected because he was a foreigner – his advocate Max Weber suggested it was because he was a Jew – Lukács joined the Hungarian Communist Party.[6] Only a few Sundayers followed his lead, yet all became active in the Hungarian Soviet Republic, the "Commune" as they called it, which lasted from mid-March 1919 till early August, two months longer than its model, the Paris Commune of 1871. As Peoples' Commissar for Education, Lukács opened museums and other cultural sites to the general population, established public education at all levels, and appointed members of the Sunday Circle to key cultural posts. A commission for storytelling, headed by Anna Lesznai, added folk and fairy tales to the school curriculum, while Balázs, director of the division of literature and theatre, recruited Radványi as his assistant. Like his elders Lukács and Balázs, Radványi was likely at the front during the summer of 1919 when Czech and Romanian forces attacked the Republic.[7]

After the Commune's collapse, reactionary forces carried out reprisals against anyone connected to the revolutionary regime. There were arrests by the thousands, pogroms, and torture in police cellars. Internment camps were established that held prisoners for years.[8] Since the majority of communists and half the social democrats among the Republic's commissars were Jewish (as were almost all members of the Sunday Circle), antisemitic propaganda during the White Terror was rife. In the wake of the Republic's defeat, roughly 100,000 Hungarians emigrated, many of them artists and intellectuals, who went on to make major contributions to the cultures of the countries to which they fled – for example, the avant-garde artists Éva Zeisel (a ceramicist and Radványi's cousin), János Mácza (see also Irina Denischenko's chapter in this volume), Lajos Kassák, László Moholy-Nagy, the Korda filmmaker brothers Alexander, Vincent, and Zoltán, and not least the dispersed members of the Budapest Sunday Circle. Radványi was not yet nineteen when the Commune was defeated, and he was forced to flee. The separation from his homeland and its close-knit intellectual and personal community must have devastated him. Thereafter, he lived as a foreigner in foreign lands; in the sixty years remaining to him, he never returned to Hungary. Yet the impact of his youthful experience allowed him to develop a dialectical method that would serve him well on his exilic journey through life, even as this called for an ever more agile dialectical relationship with Marxist theory and praxis.

Radványi attended university in Vienna, where most Hungarians first sought refuge.[9] The Béla Kun faction in the Hungarian Communist Party escaped to the Soviet Union with its "bureaucratic utopias"; Lukács settled instead in Vienna, where he and the social democrat-turned-communist Jenő Landler's moderate policies for the struggling Hungarian underground countered the revolutionary tactics of the Moscow-supported Kun faction.[10] Mannheim, who wanted to escape the shadow of his mentor Lukács, soon left for the University of Heidelberg, as did Radványi in the winter of 1920–1, where he attended lectures by the sociologist Emil Lederer and the philosophers Karl Jaspers and Karl Rickert. Under Jaspers he wrote his doctoral dissertation on chiliasm – the idea of God's kingdom realized on earth, which had its roots in the Books of Daniel, the Maccabees, and the first-century Jewish

Christians, and was later carried forward by John Wycliffe in England, Taborites in Bohemia, and Anabaptists around Thomas Müntzer in Germany.[11] Here, too, Radványi found examples of theory (i.e., theology) combined with political practice.

He completed his dissertation in 1923, the same year that Lukács's revolutionary contribution to Marxist theory, his essay collection *History and Class Consciousness*, appeared. Radványi's enthusiastic marginalia in this book that examined the ethics of revolutionary socialism reveal that his analysis of chiliasm coincided with the messianic currents in those essays contained in *History and Class Consciousness* that were first published in Hungarian during the Commune.[12] The first of these essays clearly affirmed Radványi's intellectual position in 1923: "Orthodox Marxism ... does not imply the uncritical acceptance of the results of Marx's investigations. It is not the 'belief' in this or that thesis, nor the exegesis of a 'sacred' book ... Orthodoxy refers exclusively to *method*."[13] Lukács's approach to Marxism during the Hungarian Commune notably came closer to ideas held by Rosa Luxemburg than to those held by Lenin, who had criticized Lukács for what the venerable Bolshevik called the "infantile disorders" of "left-wing communism."[14] A year later Radványi again revealed his own undoctrinaire approach to Marxism in his substantial review of Karl Korsch's *Marxism and Philosophy* (1923), which like *History and Class Consciousness* is a foundational work of critical Marxism.[15] Korsch subsequently denounced the Stalinization of the Comintern and was expelled from the KPD in 1926. That he, like Lukács, was later invited to teach at the MASCH indicates Radványi's continuing interest in critical Marxism.

The review of Korsch's book was likely written in 1924 in Heidelberg, where Radványi remained unemployed after obtaining his doctorate. Writing to the literary scholar Gyula Földessy, his Gymnasium teacher in Budapest, Radványi lamented that his "Hungarianness and Jewishness" prevented his academic employment in Germany.[16] He was aware that this problem had plagued Lukács in Heidelberg and now also plagued Mannheim. Yet Mannheim eventually was willing to bear the scorn of his Hungarian comrades, severing his ties with Lukács and Marxism in his book *Ideology and Utopia* (1929). To downplay his Hungarian-Jewish heritage, he applied for German citizenship.[17] All this, notwithstanding protests from conservative academics, led to a professorship for Mannheim at Frankfurt. Forced to step down in 1933 by the antisemitic laws governing the civil service, he fled to London, where he taught at its School of Economics.

Although their political and intellectual pursuits were now diverging, Radványi and Mannheim remained on intimate terms in Heidelberg and beyond. Mannheim, never a Marxist, tended ever more towards sociology, while Radványi, a lifelong Marxist, espoused "ethics and metaphysics" and "theology and the history of religion."[18] Radványi's revolutionary commitment, combined with his belief in Christianity's chiliastic communism, hastened his decision to join the KPD in 1924. At this time, he was writing a book on ethics; he was also teaching himself Hebrew to better understand the Book of Daniel, as well as translating into German 150 poems by the Hungarian Symbolist and socialist Endre Ady, whose poetry had become the mantra of the Hungarian avant-garde. Seen as having the moral voice that Bolshevism lacked, Ady was proclaimed the prophet of the Hungarian Revolution.[19]

In January 1925, Radványi found employment with the Soviet Trade Commission in Berlin. This job focused him on economic issues "far removed" from his "true philosophical interests." He complained to Gyula Földessy, "I actually wanted to become a teacher."[20] The reason for Radványi's compromise regarding employment was his forthcoming engagement. His fiancée, Netty Reiling, with whom he had studied in Heidelberg, came from a prominent Jewish family of jewellers with ancestral roots in the Rhineland. Her father, Isidor, who owned a prestigious art and antiquities firm in Mainz, was reluctant to have her wed a penniless East European Jew with few prospects. Yet he finally gave in, and the couple was married in August 1925, then moved to Berlin. There Radványi's wife began writing under the pen name Seghers, then Anna Seghers.

In Berlin, Radványi also assumed a pseudonym. To family and friends in Budapest he was Laci (pronounced Latsi), the Hungarian short form for László. On the title page of his dissertation, he was Ladislaus Radványi. As the youngest member of the Sunday Circle, whose discussions of messianism were inspired by first-century Christianity, he adopted the sobriquet Johann after the youngest disciple John. To this he eventually added "Lorenz," which conveyed his forename, László, less awkwardly than the Latinate Ladislaus; then, in a final effort to Germanize his persona, he chose the common surname Schmidt.[21] Now that he had a German wife – who nicknamed him Rodi in a well-intentioned but erroneous attempt to approximate the first syllable of his last name – and with no prospect of returning to his native land, all this Germanizing was surely an effort to shed the impression of his "Hungarianness and Jewishness" and accommodate his exilic surroundings.

Radványi's chance to develop his talents as a teacher arrived before long, not in academia as he had envisioned, but in the KPD's proposal for a Marxist Workers School of Greater Berlin. The historian, labour movement activist, and Spartacus/KPD co-founder Hermann Duncker, who prior to 1914 taught in SPD workers' schools, co-founded the MASCH in 1925–6 with the young Hungarian expatriate Radványi. The latter's decision to leap from the high ground of academia into the nitty-gritty of worker education was based on his commitment as an idealist to the educational traditions of the Enlightenment, on his commitment as a communist to class justice, and not least on his desire to be part of a meaningful societal venture. He defended his decision to his Gymnasium teacher, Földessy, who had long encouraged him to pursue a university career: "Unfortunately it is still the case today that truly sound and thorough work in the humanistic sciences, especially philosophy, can be conducted only by those who are rich. This is very sad ... also from the standpoint of philosophy. For as the current trend in philosophy makes obvious, it is largely a preoccupation of members of the financially well-situated classes."[22]

Radványi directed the MASCH from 1927 to 1933, and between 1930 and 1933 established twenty-nine more Marxist Workers Schools in major German cities. No records of these schools survived the Nazi era, so we know very little about the their day-to-day activities or the thinking behind Radványi's decisions. He was surely influenced by traditional Marxist approaches to education, by educational reforms during the Hungarian Commune, by Antonio Gramsci's educational theories for Turin's factory councils, and by Anton Makarenko's work at the Gorky Colony in Ukraine. The years of the MASCH coincided with major upheavals in the Soviet Union that saw a shift from Lenin's policies to Stalinism. Thus, Radványi must have tempered some of his early idealism in favour of practicable policies – policies that in fact led to the enormous success of the Berlin MASCH and its affiliates in Germany and abroad. In 1929 he travelled to the Soviet Union to consult with Lenin's widow, Nadezhda Krupskaya – a leading scholar and practitioner in literacy, worker education, and teacher training, as well as Deputy Commissar of Education from 1927 till 1939.[23] Radványi's views at this time probably coincided with those of Krupskaya, who, as Lenin's widow, rejected Stalin in favour of members of the Left Opposition. Yet after this group was defeated, she ended her open opposition to Stalin and devoted herself to her long career in public education.

Under Radványi's direction the MASCH reached across a wide left-internationalist spectrum. Its German and Austrian teachers included the historian Hermann Duncker, economist Alfons Goldschmidt, philosopher Karl Korsch, psychoanalyst Wilhelm Reich, theatre director Erwin Piscator, actress Helene Weigel (her husband, Brecht, attended as a student), composers Hanns Eisler and Kurt Weill, montage artist John Heartfield, and architects Mies van der Rohe, Hannes Meyer, and Walter

Gropius. Among the foreigners Radványi recruited, using pseudonyms to distract the police, were some fellow Hungarians – Lukács, his wife the mathematician Gertrud Bortstieber, Balázs, Andor Gábor, Béla Fogarasi – as well as émigrés from reactionary regimes elsewhere in Europe. A memorable MASCH lecture was given on 28 October 1931, in a North Berlin school auditorium packed with hundreds of workers, by Albert Einstein, who explained to his audience "What a Worker Must Know about the Theory of Relativity."[24]

The Berlin police began patrolling the MASCH's classrooms in 1930, and by 1931 the school was subject to police surveillance, as was Radványi's private residence in Berlin-Zehlendorf. Claiming that they were tracking illegal aliens, the police ransacked the MASCH offices on 25 November 1932, arresting eleven people and confiscating the faculty directory. This action signalled the end of the MASCH, although some classes continued into early 1933.[25] Until then, the MASCH undoubtedly served as a vital crossroads for the red migrations of its time. Many of its teachers and students were revolutionaries fleeing right-wing reactionaries in Eastern Europe and the Balkans, or, in the case of China, they were about to return to their homeland to join the liberation movements there.

Much of what transpired in and around the MASCH during the seven years of Radványi's tenure – notably, eyewitness accounts from the steady stream of migrants among its teachers and students – influenced Anna Seghers's *Die Gefährten* (*The Wayfarers*) of 1932.[26] The novel depicts the experiences of workers and intellectuals who participated in ultimately thwarted uprisings after the First World War and were imprisoned or murdered or fled to the Soviet Union or the West. The home countries and directions of flight describe a cartography reflecting the political-economic geography of that time: on the one hand, countries with agricultural economies and semi-feudal or pre-national traditions – Poland, Italy, Hungary, Bulgaria, and China – where revolutionary movements succeeded for a time but were cut short or overthrown by reactionary or proto-fascist regimes; and on the other, the industrialized nations of Europe – Germany, Belgium, France, England – where émigrés found refuge but remained outsiders living lives largely without purpose or meaning. Beyond this was the Soviet Union, where, after Lenin's death, the Comintern increasingly controlled the international workers' movement. In 1956, Seghers wrote to the Soviet literary scholar Vladimir Steshenskii: "I could show you in this book who related what to me and just when that was. Of course, everything is transformed. This has nothing to do with a *roman à clef*. It's just that the material came to me from the stories I was told."[27] Although identities in *Die Gefährten* have been "transformed," a reader acquainted with the material senses that characters in the novel evoke the Hungarians Lukács, Balázs, Mannheim, Radványi, and other Sundayers; Bulgarian revolutionaries, including Giorgi Dimitroff; and here, as in other works by Seghers, the Chinese revolutionaries Liau Han-sin, Hu Lanqi, Liao Chengzi, and Chen Chi-yin.[28] Beyond this, homage is paid to revolutionaries across the spectrum, whose stories Seghers would have heard at the MASCH but whose identities remain unknown to us.

Marxism and the Popular Front: France, 1933–1941

After the National Socialists came to power in 1933, Radványi and Seghers fled to Paris, where they settled with their children, Peter (b. 1926) and Ruth (b. 1928). Here Seghers wrote some of her best-known works, notably *The Seventh Cross*, a 1942 American bestseller made by Fred Zinnemann into a film starring Spencer Tracy.[29] The Radványis lived in the Paris suburb of Meudon-Bellevue, where on Sundays they held open house for their émigré friends. One of them was the Hungarian cartographer Sándor Radó, who as head of the Swiss branch of the Soviet Union's intelligence network later monitored the German army's Russian campaign and helped speed Allied military successes. For cooperating with British intelligence, he was arrested by the Soviets and imprisoned until 1955.[30] Another Hungarian, Arthur Koestler, remembered Seghers from their Paris writers' group as its only member of international standing, "whom I admired, and still admire, both as a novelist and as an attractive and charming woman, but with whom I never found any personal contact."[31] Karl Mannheim, long in personal contact with the Radványis, visited them in Paris in the mid-1930s, where he and Radványi continued to discuss their political differences, prompting Mannheim's protest: "Can't you understand this, I'm not a communist, I'm a liberal bourgeois thinker; that's how you have to accept and judge me."[32] Radványi later learned that when he and Seghers needed entry visas during the war, Mannheim appealed to Mexico on their behalf.[33]

Radványi wanted to revive in Paris the kind of educational model he had experienced in Budapest and later developed with a working-class focus at the MASCH. The School for Émigrés opened in February 1934 with a lecture by Johann-Lorenz Schmidt on the "Basics of Materialist Dialectics." Within a year it was offering 200 lectures in sixteen disciplines by thirty scholars, writers, and artists, and in November 1935 it was launched as the Free German Academy (Freie Deutsche Hochschule) before an audience of around 700 in the Mutualité. Among its promoters was the German writer and spokesperson for the Popular Front, Heinrich Mann. In the spirit of the Popular Front and what Radványi called a "tradition of German–French scholarly cooperation," lectures in the humanities and natural sciences appealed to émigrés and French citizens.[34] A second educational venture reminiscent of the MASCH, the German Adult Education School (Deutsche Volkshochschule), met in a bookshop in the Latin Quarter. Its courses, consistent with the politics of the Popular Front, included topics about the Soviet Union, fascism, and National Socialism, as well as literature and the arts.[35]

As German territorial expansion in 1938 drove more émigrés into France, resulting in a "brain drain" from Nazi-occupied countries, Radványi founded the *Zeitschrift für deutsche Forschung* (*Journal for German Research*). Its intention, he stated in the first issue, was to give scholars the opportunity to share the results of their research and thus nurture "the best traditions of German scholarship" – as in Albert Einstein's article "Physics and Reality" ("Physik und Realität") in the first issue.[36] Later contributors to the journal and its related projects included the philosopher Ernst Bloch, the critic Walter Benjamin, the rector of the University of Jerusalem Abraham Fraenkel, and the historian Alfred Meusel. The only equivalent émigré journal at this time was the Frankfurt School's *Zeitschrift für Sozialforschung* (*Journal of Social Research*), published in France from 1933 till 1938, when it moved to New York. By presenting what he termed "free, independent research" as a countermodel to the "pseudo-scholarship" practised in Germany, Radványi's journal more or less filled the vacuum left by the Frankfurt School. His own research examined "new forms and methods" by which Nazi ideology exerted influence "over large masses of the German population ... not as a concomitant of the exercise of power, but as an integral part of the structure of the regime."[37] Around this time Radványi was analysing National Socialism in other venues as well, in addition to collaborating with the American Guild for Cultural Freedom, an aid organization for émigré intellectuals founded by the historian and jurist Prince Hubertus of Löwenstein.[38]

In early 1940, Radványi along with other "enemy aliens" was confined by the French police in Paris's Roland Garros Stadium; soon after, he was transported to the concentration camp at Le Vernet in the Pyrenees.[39] After the fall of France in June, living conditions at the camp, which was already holding Republicans from Spain, deteriorated sharply, and the Central Europeans held there feared they would be handed over to the Germans. Amidst this misery and uncertainty, Radványi exercised his gifts as a teacher to great effect. His presentations in

German, French, and Spanish on Marxism and fascism not only served an educational purpose but also established a routine that helped focus the minds and lift the spirits of the incarcerated men.[40] According to the town council of Foix's brochure about Le Vernet, at the camp Radványi wrote for his students an "Histoire de la littérature française."[41] In December 1940, Seghers secured travel papers for her husband's transfer to the transit camp Les Milles. On 24 March 1941 the Radványis and their children departed Marseille on the refugee freighter *Capitaine Paul Lemerle*. Its passengers included André Breton and Victor Serge as well as Claude Lévi-Strauss, who described the treacherous Atlantic crossing in his *Tristes Tropiques* (1955). After being detained on Martinique and on New York's Ellis Island, the family arrived in Veracruz, Mexico, on 30 June; from there, they continued on to the capital, where they settled.[42]

Marxism, Anti-fascism, and Empiricism: Mexico, 1941–1952

Thanks to the liberal asylum policies of President Lázaro Cárdenas of Mexico (1934–40) and his successor, Manuel Ávila Camacho (1940–6), anti-fascists from Europe found safety in Mexico. Still, throughout their stay the Radványis and their comrades in Mexico were monitored not only by the occasional Soviet or German agent but also, more systematically, by the US FBI, which opened and censored their correspondence.[43] Soon after the their arrival, Vicente Lombardo Toledano, leader of the powerful labour union Confederación de Trabajadores de México (CTM), hosted a reception at which Chile's ambassador Pablo Neruda greeted the Radványis with a welcoming speech.[44] In 1936, Lombardo Toledano had founded the Universidad Obrera de México, a working-class educational model for the entire region. Its program was overseen by the Latin America specialist Alfons Goldschmidt, who had served on the MASCH faculty in Berlin. After his death in 1940 his position remained vacant until Lombardo Toledano recognized the recently arrived Radványi as the obvious successor to Goldschmidt and promptly hired him. The thirty-four-page Workers University brochure for 1942 lists twelve individual lectures by Radványi on Marxist philosophy and several more by him on the origins of fascism, twenty-four full-term courses by various anti-fascist émigrés on aspects of National Socialism, and twenty-two individual lectures on the Soviet Union by the Bauhaus architect Hannes Meyer, who in the 1930s developed urban projects in the Soviet Union and in 1939 became director of Mexico's Instituto del Urbanismo y Planificación.[45] Radványi continued teaching at the Workers University until he left

Mexico in 1952. The Confederación de Trabajadores de América Latina regularly sent its members to Mexico so that over the years Radványi's students included a large number of trade union functionaries from Chile, Ecuador, Colombia, and Venezuela.[46]

In 1944, Mexico's National University offered Radványi a professorship. Now that the battle against Hitler was being waged by military rather than political means, Radványi turned to empiricism (as did other Europeans exiled on the American continent, including Paul Lazarsfeld, who took up communication research). Impressed by George Gallup, whose *The Pulse of Democracy: The Public-Opinion Poll and How It Works* (1940) promoted public polling as an antidote to authoritarian policies, Radványi reinvented his educational practice to include the emerging field of opinion research. At the National University he established the Institutes of Mexican Public Opinion and Studies in Social Psychology and Public Opinion, surveying public opinion in the US as well as in Mexico, where very different conditions prevailed. He was editor of the quarterly *International Journal of Opinion and Attitude Research*, to which Harvard, MIT, and Cornell scholars contributed, and the journal *Social Sciences in Mexico and South and Central America*. He was a member of the American Psychological Association, Statistics Association, Association for Adult Education, Association for Public Opinion Research, Academy of Political and Social Science, and National Council on Measurements in Education, as well as the UK's Royal Economics Society. In 1946 he attended the first international conference on public opinion, held in Colorado; in 1947, at a conference held in Massachusetts, with George Gallup and ten others, he was a founding member of the World Association for Public Opinion Research (WAPOR). In 1948, two years into the Cold War, the US denied him entry to attend the next WAPOR conference, held in Pennsylvania.[47] As recently attested by Mexican scholars, during these "'golden years' of vital polling activity," his "contribution to the polling industry in Mexico and at the international level" was "enormous."[48]

Radványi published his research in numerous articles and books, among the latter: *Public Opinion Measurement: A Survey* (1945), *International Directory of Opinion and Attitude Research* (1948), *La Metrópoli No. 1: Lectura de historietas entre la población adulta de la ciudad de México* (1950), *Measurement of the Effectiveness of Basic Education* (1951), *La industrialización de América Latina y el nivel de vida de la población rural* (1952), *Industrialización nacional: como deben industrializarse los paises de América Latina* (1952), and *Ten Years of Sample Surveying in Mexico* (1952). If this last book suggests Radványi's growing scepticism about the value of conventional empirical data, his engagement is obvious in the 1951 volume, whose subtitle reveals his true affinities: *Surveys of the Results of UNESCO's Pilot Project of Basic Education Among the Rural Populations of the Santiago Valley, Nayarit, Mexico*. While Radványi oversaw this project and spent a week in Nayarit evaluating data – wearing his "indispensable gabardine coat" in "Celsius 35-degree temperatures" – most of the native population was interviewed by his graduate students.[49] Some of them later held important positions – for example, Emilio Mújica Montoya was Communication and Transportation Secretary in José López Portillo's government (1976–82), then Mexican ambassador to Costa Rica (1984–7).[50] It was surely Radványi's eleven years of lived experience in Mexico, his affection for its culture and people, and his sympathy with Mexico's indigenous poor that inspired him thereafter to conduct research on socio-economic conditions in Latin America.

Marxism and "Actually Existing Socialism": East Berlin, 1952–1978

Radványi had no interest in returning to Germany, but he did so out of sympathy for his lifelong intellectual partner and wife, Anna Seghers. Internationally acclaimed as Germany's leading anti-fascist author, she longed as a writer to be immersed in her own language and culture, and arrived in Berlin in the spring of 1947. Radványi would delay his return until summer 1952. Fluent in Spanish, he had thrived in Mexico, where he was less a foreigner than a cosmopolitan working within a multicultural society. After fleeing three countries in fear for his life – Hungary in 1919, Germany in 1933, France in 1941 – he relished the liberal atmosphere and lack of overt racism and antisemitism in Mexico. Whereas in Berlin and Paris he had found no employment to suit his education and expertise, in Mexico he was sought after for his intellectual stature; it was there that for the first time in his life he held a professorship. Now in his third exile and in his fifties, he was reluctant to adjust to yet another new and different culture and political regime – and this the East German state calling itself the German Democratic Republic (GDR) would surely be.

Radványi's return to a radically transformed, divided Berlin – his fourth exile, as it were – came one year before Stalin's death and four years before Khrushchev's revelations about Stalin's crimes. Three years earlier, Hungary's Minister of the Interior László Rajk had been subjected to a show trial and executed as a "Titoist." Around this time, the American Quaker Noel Field, who as director of the Unitarian Service Committee had helped the Radványis and other refugees trapped in France, was arrested by the KGB as a US spy and imprisoned in

Budapest. His activities would be used by the prosecution during the Rajk trial. Radványi's Hungarian friend Sándor Radó and others he knew were languishing in Soviet prisons, and in the summer of Radványi's return a show trial was being prepared in Prague at which at least one close comrade and collaborator in Paris and Mexico – Otto Katz, alias André Simone – would be found guilty and executed.[51] Moreover, like other anti-fascists exiled in Western democracies far from Moscow, Radványi was automatically deemed suspicious, as was his place within a tradition of intellectuals who during the upheavals of 1919 had embraced the ideals of the workers' councils. Vulnerable as a "West-émigré" and a foreigner, viz. a Hungarian, in East Germany he was closely monitored. This included an interrogation by the Central Party Control Commission and the Ministry for State Security; the latter subjected him to an "Investigation Process" from mid-1952 to mid-1954.[52]

On the basis of his unwavering KPD membership and his educational work since the 1920s, and with his wife's influence, Radványi was offered a professorial chair in "Problems of Contemporary Imperialism" at Berlin's Humboldt University as well as the directorship of the Institute of Economics at the Academy of Sciences. In Mexico he had used his birth name; in the GDR, he revived his German pseudonym and, once again reinventing his educational practice, analysing socio-economic developments in the Cold War. In 1961 he was appointed president of the German–Latin American Friendship Society, which facilitated scientific and cultural programs and exchanges. Two of its prominent participants were the Mexican immunologist Dr. Mario Salazar Mallén and the sculptor Federico Silva.[53] Radványi's numerous publications in the post-war era focused on the growth of multinational corporations and conditions specific to developing nations. His works included academic series, edited volumes, scholarly articles, and the monographs *Neue Probleme der Krisentheorie* (1956), *Probleme des Neokolonialismus* (1963), *Die Entwicklungsländer: Ursprung, Lage, Perspektive* (2nd rev. ed. 1976), and *Internationale Konzerne* (posth. 1981).

Radványi's international reputation as a scholar with expertise in developing nations drew students from around the world, who wrote their graduate theses with him.[54] His lectures reflected the meticulousness of his publications. Reports by colleagues and students echoed what others had said in earlier years: he was an exceptionally knowledgeable, inspiring teacher; soft-spoken, modest, and polite; punctilious in attire, deportment, and bearing; always punctual and correct; always kind, considerate, and fair. While this conveys the image of a very cautious man, which he undoubtedly was, Radványi retained his quiet sense of humour and rebellion. Just as in 1932 he outwitted the German police seeking to arrest him at the MASCH by seating himself among his students in the classroom, at Humboldt University he disregarded requirements that professors read only from lecture notes approved by the departmental administration. According to his daughter, Dr. Ruth Radvanyi, as he lectured he could be seen glancing now and then at the pages he flipped at the lectern, pages that were in fact empty.[55] Fluent in seven languages and conversant with twelve, he baffled colleagues at international conferences by not wearing headphones and writing notes in, say, Armenian or Georgian.[56] Radványi notably "divided his fellow-beings into two categories: his students and all others," and by the course of a tumultuous life he demanded forbearance at every turn, taking pride above all in his work as a teacher.[57] His greatest influence as an educator within his family was on his grandson Jean Radvanyi, also a polyglot, who as a geographer specializes in the Caucasus. When he began teaching at the Sorbonne in 1975, his grandfather sent him a handwritten letter with nine "Principles" for the teacher in the classroom, of which the first states: "The main thing: winning the trust and respect of the students."[58]

Radványi's reputation as a reserved, reticent man extended far beyond his deportment as a teacher. According to his son, Pierre Radvanyi, a nuclear physicist who worked with Frédéric and Irène Joliot-Curie in Paris-Orsay, his father "never engaged in sectarian arguments; it was his aim in all his affairs to be cautious, yet at the same time conscientious and precise."[59] If this assessment obtains for the methodological rigour of Radványi's scholarship, it applies just as well to his reasoning concerning Party politics. However often he may have disagreed with Communist Party decisions, his objections were never public. According to Pierre Radvanyi, when his parents learned of Khrushchev's secret speech of February 1956 enumerating Stalin's crimes, his mother "was furious and tried, if in vain, to understand and imagine the psychology of Stalin and his entourage," while his father "went into a rage and even later, his anger never let up."[60] Yet neither Radványi nor Seghers revealed their critical views of Stalin at this time or any other, just as they never spoke out against the Soviet show trials and purges, the Soviet invasion of Hungary in 1956, or the Warsaw Pact invasion of Czechoslovakia in 1968. It was evidently their silence in 1968 that prompted their old friend Lukács, who notably opposed the 1968 invasion, to dissociate himself from them when interviewed during his fatal illness in 1971. Accusing Seghers of having "succumbed to Ulbricht's latest literary fashion" in her novel *Trust* (*Das Vertrauen*, 1968), he described Radványi as a not "completely kosher" Hungarian who "slavishly followed the Party line" and thus "had an unfortunate influence" on his wife.[61] The German economist Jürgen Kuczynski, who like Lukács – and Ilya Ehrenburg, Jorge Amado, and other men – had been enamoured of Anna Seghers over the years and perhaps for this reason failed to appreciate her husband, accused Radványi of having been "an informant and slanderous liar regarding other comrades."[62] However, the dissident East German singer-songwriter Wolf Biermann, who in 1960 "enthusiastically" attended lectures at Humboldt University by both Radványi and Kuczynski, described only the latter as a "polymathic Party hack."[63]

Rudolf Bahro, another notable East German dissident, frequented Radványi's lectures while a student of philosophy and economics at Humboldt University from 1954 to 1959. Thereupon Bahro developed his concept of a "non-capitalist road to industrial society" as a "Communist Alternative" to the "actually existing socialism" promoted in the GDR and the Eastern Bloc. An early samizdat version of his book *The Alternative in Eastern Europe* (*Die Alternative: Zur Kritik des real existierenden Sozialismus*, 1978), circulated in 1977, led to him being found guilty of treason and imprisoned, then amnestied after two years and deported to the Federal Republic, where he became active in environmental politics and the Green movement.[64] In the 1960s, Bahro had asked Radványi to critique drafts of his manuscript. According to Bahro, his former professor was extremely receptive and forthcoming. After reading the drafts, he responded with affirmation and great interest, and encouraged Bahro to further develop his analyses. At this same time he also intervened on Bahro's behalf at the Free German Youth magazine *Forum*, where, as deputy editor, Bahro was encountering difficulties. Bahro considered Radványi not simply a Marxist, but a *critical* Marxist.[65]

To be sure, the terms "critical," "orthodox," and "unadulterated Marxism" appear nowhere in Radványi's publications in the GDR. After his exile in France in the 1930s, "unadulterated Marxism," so important to him at the MASCH, became simply "Marxism." Although he still believed in the future of socialism, if not of the East German state, in the 1970s Radványi shared with his son his "serious concerns about the future of the socialist world." Some of the problems he enumerated – consequences of the cult of personality, the impact of bureaucracy, decreasing productivity, absence of open discussion and of first-hand perspectives[66] – coincide with issues raised by Rudolf Bahro. When asked by his son how he thought the Socialist Unity Party (SED) might fare if free elections were held in the GDR, Radványi predicted – correctly, as it turned out in 1990 – that it could not win over more than

20 per cent of the population.[67] And when asked why he didn't write down his thoughts about the "problems of the socialist world" in a comprehensive analysis, he answered with a laugh: "You don't understand, that's impossible" – an answer plainly corroborated by Bahro's arrest and imprisonment in 1977.[68]

All the same, there is no reason to assume that Radványi no longer held what half a century earlier he had described in his doctoral dissertation as a chiliastic worldview. Nor did he, now restricting his scholarship to economics, surrender his early interest in philosophy, religion, and, increasingly, the music of Johann Sebastian Bach. As an aficionado of literature, he still immersed himself in the poetry of the Hungarian Symbolist Endre Ady, and for each novel or story his wife was writing, he was her first and most trusted reader and confidant.[69] Neither Radványi nor Seghers ever revealed publicly how they envisaged the development of communism in the twentieth century, that is, beyond Stalinism and "actually existing socialism." However, a reader attentive to the subtleties of literary allusion and encoding will find in many of Seghers's works alternative suggestions as to the nature of communism, as in *Uprising of the Fishers of St. Barbara* (1928), *The Wayfarers* (1932), *The Trial of Jeanne d'Arc at Rouen, 1431* (1937), "The Finest Tales of Woynok the Brigand" (1938), "Tales of Artemis" (1938), "The Ship of the Argonauts" (1949), "The Light on the Gallows" (1960), and "The Just Judge" (conceived 1956, published posthumously in 1990).[70]

Radványi and Seghers viewed themselves as staunch communists in the tradition of chiliasm reaching back to the first-century Jewish Christians, whom Rosa Luxemburg notably described as Roman proletarians and communists.[71] The history of Christian chiliastic and Jewish messianic movements proved that there were more defeats than victories, more times of waiting and expectation.[72] If the German workers' movement of the 1920s had raised hopes that the politics of "unadulterated Marxism" could bring a communist victory, the German Democratic Republic was experienced by the Radványis as a significant, albeit increasingly failed, attempt to bring about democratic socialism. This was a time of waiting and expectation during which their hopes turned towards anti-colonial liberation movements in developing nations. Radványi's efforts in this regard have been outlined here. After the late 1940s, Seghers was also attentive to social conditions and their history in Latin America, Africa, and Asia – as in her Caribbean tales "High Time in Haiti," "The Reinstatement of Slavery in Guadeloupe" (both 1949), and "The Light on the Gallows" (1960); her Mexican stories "Crisanta" (1950) and "The Genuine Blue" (1968); her novel *Crossing: A Love Story* (1971) about Brazil; and her last collection of tales *Three Women from Haiti* (1980). The Seghers Archive in Berlin has roughly 300 files from the 1940s to 1970s that mostly contain Radványi's responses to his wife's writing and that reveal how Seghers frequently benefited from his advice.[73] "In each case the husband Laszlo Radvanyi's influence on his wife's writing was inspiring, commentative, corrective, in part also censorious," writes Simone Bischoff, who also quotes from a letter Seghers wrote in 1947 when she returned to Berlin without her husband: "I can now feel how spoiled I was by his advice and support for my work, how we tinkered with every sentence and every expression."[74] From their written notes and exchanges we can assume that Radványi was involved in Seghers's creative work, and not only as a consultant or editor; he participated from the very outset in plotting the outline and direction of a story or novel. To this extent he can be viewed as the mastermind behind certain philosophical and political ideas that influenced Seghers's narratives. Thus, it appears that beyond his work as an educator, life had another métier in store for László Radványi, this one more or less anonymous, yet no less inspired by the vision of a better world.

In the fifty-nine years he spent as a transnational exiled from his native land, László Radványi is not known to have complained about his trials and tribulations nor to have bemoaned his fate. What we know about him is summarized by the events of his life and how he responded to them in his actions and writings. From these we can conclude that he was a lifelong Marxist who despite all remained committed to the revolutionary struggle he first joined as a young man of eighteen. I can think of no finer homage to Radványi and his generation than Siegfried Kracauer's review of Seghers's novel *The Wayfarers* in the *Frankfurter Zeitung* in November 1932. Only a few months later the renowned literary critic Kracauer, no revolutionary, would himself be forced to flee his homeland and thereafter live in the diaspora, not unlike the revolutionaries he described in this passage from his review:

> Whoever actively joins the cause of the revolution tends to consider this cause more important than himself. Thus it is easy to understand that the revolutionaries' actions and even more so their sufferings are rarely evident ... The world in which they live can be compared with no other. Whether they become stranded in Berlin or Bologna or Paris, these cities are only provisional, indifferent places to which coincidence has led them. They meet in apartments which could exist in any random city, accustomed to the notion that they must move on the next day. Would they then be nomads without a home? Indeed for them, Russia is at best the hallowed forecourt of their homeland while their homeland itself remains a battlefield. They will find their true home only when they themselves have seized power and their homeland no longer bodes martyrdom for them.[75]

Notes

1 Bertolt Brecht, *The Collected Poems*, trans. and ed. Tom Kuhn and David Constantine with the assistance of Charlotte Ryland (New York: Liveright, 2019), 732.
2 Dr. Johann Schmidt, "Fünf Jahre Marxistische Arbeiterschule," *Der Marxist: Blätter der Marxistischen Arbeiterschule* 1 (1931): 28. Unless otherwise indicated, all translations from German and Hungarian are my own.
3 See Gabriele Gerhard-Sonnenberg, *Marxistische Arbeiterbildung in der Weimarer Zeit (MASCH)* (Cologne: Pahl-Rugenstein Verlag, 1976), 71–9.
4 Wolfgang Fritz Haug, Frigga Haug, Peter Jehle, and Wolfgang Küttler, eds., *Historisch-kritisches Wörterbuch des Marxismus*, INKRIT (Hamburg: Argument-Verlag, 2015), 1865.
5 *Fekete Könyv: Radványi László Versei* (Budapest: Martos Adolf Kiadása), 1916; preface by the popular writer Frigyes Karinthy.
6 Citing Dante's *Inferno* in his 1918 lecture "Science as a Vocation," Weber referenced his advice when asked about Habilitation: "If the young scholar … is a Jew, of course one says 'lasciate ogni speranza' ['abandon all hope']." Quoted in Arpad Kadarkay, *Georg Lukács: Life, Thought, and Politics* (Cambridge, MA: Blackwell, 1991), 193.
7 On the Budapest Sunday Circle, see Éva Karádi and Erzsébet Vezér, eds., *Georg Lukács, Karl Mannheim und der Sonntagskreis* (Frankfurt am Main: Sendler Verlag, 1985). On the influence of Radványi and other Sundayers, see Helen Fehervary, *Anna Seghers: The Mythic Dimension* (Ann Arbor: University of Michigan Press, 2001), 66–147.
8 See Oscar Jászi, *Revolution and Counter-Revolution in Hungary* (London: P.S. King & Son, Ltd., 1924), 153–97.
9 See Lee Congdon, *Exile and Social Thought: Hungarian Intellectuals in Germany and Austria, 1919–1933* (Princeton: Princeton University Press, 1991).
10 See Congdon, *Exile and Social Thought*, 49, 72–3; the reference to "bureaucratic utopias" is by Lukács, in Éva Fekete and Éva Karádi, eds., *György Lukács: His Life in Pictures and Documents*, trans. Péter Balabán and Kenneth McRobbie (Budapest: Corvina Kiadó, 1981), 119.
11 Ladislaus Radványi, *Der Chiliasmus: Ein Versuch zur Erkenntnis der chiliastischen Idee und des chiliastischen Handelns* (1923), ed. Éva Gábor (Budapest: MTA Filozófiai Intézet, 1985).
12 Akademie der Künste, Berlin, Anna-Seghers-Museum, NB 6004. Hereafter ASM.
13 Georg Lukács, *History and Class Consciousness: Studies in Marxist Dialectics*, trans. Rodney Livingstone (Cambridge, MA: MIT Press, 1983), 1.
14 Lenin's *"Left-Wing" Communism: An Infantile Disorder* appeared in 1920. On his subsequent influence on Lukács, see Michel Löwy, *Georg Lukács:*

From Romanticism to Bolshevism, trans. Patrick Camiller (London: New Left Books, 1979), 154–67.
15 *Archiv für Sozialwissenschaft und Sozialpolitik*, ed. Emil Lederer (Tübingen: Mohr/Paul Siebeck, 1925), 528–35.
16 Petöfi Irodalmi Múzeum, Budapest (hereafter PIM), letter to Gyula Földessy, 8 July 1924, 5.
17 For his reference to Radványi on chiliasm, see Karl Mannheim, *Ideology and Utopia: An Introduction to the Sociology of Knowledge* (London: Routledge and Kegan Paul, 1949), 195.
18 PIM, letter to Földessy, 3 October 1924, 4.
19 See Lukács, "Uj magyar líra," in G.L., *Ifjúkori müvek*, 1902–1918, ed. Árpád Timár (Budapest: Magvetö Kiadó, 1977), 249.
20 PIM, letter to Földessy, 17 December 1926, 1, 2–3.
21 The name may have been inspired by the eighteenth-century theologian Johann Lorenz Schmidt (1702–1749), author of the iconoclastic *Wertheim Bible*, with which Radványi would have been familiar.
22 PIM, letter to Földessy, 17 December 1926, 4.
23 See "Johann-Lorenz Schmidt im Gespräch mit Marianne Thoms," Radio DDR II (5/1/1977), ASM.
24 See Anna Seghers, "Einstein in der MASCH," in A.S., *Über Kunstwerk und Wirklichkeit*, ed. Sigrid Bock, vol. 4 (Berlin: Akademie-Verlag, 1979), 112–13.
25 Gerhard-Sonnenberg, *Marxistische Arbeiterbildung in der Weimarer Zeit*, 141–2.
26 In Russian: *Poputchiki*, trans. Izabella Grinberg (Leningrad: Vremia, 1934); in Hungarian: *Út az éjszakából*, trans. Tibor Hollósi (Budapest: Magyar Helikon, 1959). As yet no English version of the novel exists; see, however, Hunter Bivens's translation of its first chapter in *Anna Seghers: The Challenge of History*, ed. Helen Fehervary, Christiane Zehl Romero, and Amy Kepple Strawser (Boston: Brill, 2019), 326–40.
27 Anna Seghers, *Briefe 1953–1983*, ed. Christiane Zehl Romero and Almust Giesecke; Seghers, *Werkausgabe*, vol. 2, ed. Helen Fehervary and Bernhard Spies (Berlin: Aufbau-Verlag, 2010), 43.
28 See Weijia Li, *China und China-Erfahrung in Leben und Werk von Anna Seghers* (Oxford: Peter Lang, 2010), 55–83.
29 See the articles devoted to this novel in *Anna Seghers: The Challenge of History*, 9–118.
30 See Radó's memoir *Codename Dora*, trans. J.A. Underwood (London: Abelard, 1977).
31 Arthur Koestler, *The Invisible Writing: An Autobiography* (Boston: Beacon Press, 1955), 231.
32 Éva Gábor, "Egy 'elfelejtett' vasárnapos emlékeiböl," *Világosság* (23 July 1980), 449.
33 Gábor, "Egy 'elfelejtett' vasárnapos emlékeiböl," 450.

34 Dieter Schiller, *Exil in Frankreich* (Frankfurt am Main: Röderberg-Verlag, 1981), 279.
35 Schiller, *Exil in Frankreich*, 278–9.
36 Schiller, *Exil in Frankreich*, 275.
37 Schiller, *Exil in Frankreich*, 275.
38 See Christiane Zehl Romero, *Anna Seghers: Eine Biographie, 1900–1947* (Berlin: Aufbau-Verlag, 2000), 290–1.
39 Most German nationals were interned at the start of the war.
40 Radványi's sister Lili and her husband, the Hungarian psychoanalyst Léopold Szondi, assumed similar roles when they and their children Vera and Peter were interned in the German concentration camp Bergen-Belsen, June–December 1944. While Lili Szondi-Radványi spent each day teaching children in the camp, Léopold Szondi offered therapy for those in need, and every night in his barracks was the centralizing force for the camp's "Humanistic Circle," which he organized. See Lili Szondi-Radványi, "Ein Tag in Bergen-Belsen," *Szondiana: Zeitschrift für Tiefenpsychologie. Sonderheft: Leopold Szondi zum 100. Geburtstag* (1993): 43–59.
41 Margrid Bircken, "Acht Jahre in zwölf Tagen: Über eine Frankreichreise im April 2000," *Argonautenschiff: Jahrbuch der Anna-Seghers-Gesellschaft* 9 (2000): 136. On Le Vernet, see Lion Feuchtwanger, *The Devil in France*, trans. Elisabeth Abbott (New York: Viking Press, 1941); Bruno Frei, *Die Männer von Le Vernet* (Hildesheim: Gerstenberg Verlag, 1980); and Sibylle Hinze, *Antifaschisten im Camp Le Vernet* (Berlin: Militärverlag der DDR, 1988).
42 On the Atlantic crossing and Mexico, see Olivia Díaz, "Gespräch mit Frau Dr. med. Ruth Radványi," *Argonautenschiff: Jahrbuch der Anna-Seghers-Gesellschaft* 12 (2003): 201–14.
43 See Alexander Stephan, *Communazis: FBI Surveillance of German Émigré Writers*, trans. Jan van Heurck (New Haven: Yale University Press, 2000).
44 On anti-fascists in Mexico, see Marcus C. Patka, *Zu nahe der Sonne: Deutsche Schriftsteller im Exil in Mexico* (Berlin: Aufbau Taschenbuch Verlag, 1999).
45 Wolfgang Kießling, *Brücken nach Mexiko: Traditionen einer Freundschaft* (Berlin: Dietz Verlag, 1989), 343–5.
46 "Lebenslauf von Johann Schmidt (Laszlo Radvanyi)," handwritten, presumably 1952, 9; Akademie der Künste, Berlin, Anna-Seghers-Archiv.
47 Alejandro Moreno and Manuel Sánchez-Castro, "A Lost Decade? László Radványi and the Origins of Public Opinion Research in Mexico, 1941–1952," *International Journal of Public Opinion Research* 21, no. 1 (2009): 14.
48 Moreno and Sánchez-Castro, "A Lost Decade?," 3–4.
49 Kießling, *Brücken nach Mexiko*, 490.
50 Mújica Montoya initially followed Radványi to Berlin's Humboldt University, where he earned a doctorate in economics under his direction. See Kießling, *Brücken nach Mexiko*, 489–90.

51 On the Slánský trial, see Artur London, *The Confession*, trans. Alastair Hamilton (London: MacDonald, 1970).
52 See Christiane Zehl Romero, *Anna Seghers: Eine Biographie, 1947–1983* (Berlin: Aufbau-Verlag, 2003), 111.
53 See Kießling, *Brücken nach Mexiko*, 491.
54 The Humboldt University Archive has fifteen boxes of Radványi's university lectures, student papers, dissertations, correspondence, and other materials, which are as yet inaccessible.
55 Ruth Radvanyi, "Ein Verlust, den ich erst später bemerkte," *Argonautenschiff: Jahrbuch der Anna-Seghers-Gesellschaft* 14 (2005): 292. See also the recollections of Radványi's teaching assistant Dieter Klein, in Moreno and Sánchez-Castro, "A Lost Decade?," 21.
56 Ruth Radvanyi, "Ein Verlust, den ich erst später bemerkte," 292.
57 Pierre Radvanyi, *Jenseits des Stroms: Erinnerungen an meine Mutter Anna Seghers* (Berlin: Aubau-Verlag, 2005), 91.
58 See Jean Radvanyi, "Für mich war Anna Seghers einfach Großmutter Tschibi," *Argonautenschiff* 14 (2005): 300, 306.
59 H.F. telephone conversation with Pierre Radvanyi, Paris-Orsay, February 2021.
60 Pierre Radvanyi, *Jenseits des Stroms*, 128.
61 Georg Lukács, *Record of a Life: An Autobiographical Sketch*, ed. István Eörsi, trans. Rodney Livingstone (London: Verso, 1983), 93.
62 Quoted in Romero, *Anna Seghers … 1947–1983*, 364n63. While these claims cannot be verified, Kuczynski possibly had in mind Radványi's testimony on 4 May 1954 concerning Paul Merker when chief of the KPD group in Mexico. Yet the published text of this testimony reveals nothing "slanderous." See Wolfgang Kießling, *Partner im "Narrenparadies": Der Freundeskreis um Noel Field und Paul Merker* (Berlin: Dietz Verlag, 1994), 185–6.
63 Wolf Biermann, *Warte nicht auf bessre Zeiten: Die Autobiographie* (Berlin: Propyläen, 2016), 73.
64 For an early assessment, see David Bathrick, "The Politics of Culture: Rudolf Bahro and Opposition in the GDR," *New German Critique* 15 (1978): 3–24.
65 H.F. conversation with Rudolf Bahro, Berlin-Pankow, July 1997.
66 Radvanyi, *Jenseits des Stroms*, 136.
67 Telephone conversation with Pierre Radvanyi, Paris-Orsay, April 2020.
68 Radvanyi, *Jenseits des Stroms*, 136.
69 On Radványi and Seghers's frequent written exchanges while she wrote this novel in the 1950s, see Anna Seghers, *Die Entscheidung*, vol. ed. Alexander Stephan, in AS, *Werkausgabe* I/7, ed. Helen Fehervary and Bernhard Spies (Berlin: Aufbau-Verlag, 2003), 683–7.

70 On such encodings and Radványi's influence on her early works, see Fehervary, *Anna Seghers: The Mythic Dimension*, 66–147.
71 Rosa Luxemburg, "Socialism and the Churches," in *Rosa Luxemburg Speaks*, ed. Mary-Alice Waters (New York: Pathfinder Press, 1970), 136–7. First published 1905 in Kraków as "Kościoł a socjalizm" under the pseudonym Jósef Chmura.
72 See Gershom Scholem, *The Messianic Idea in Judaism* (New York: Schocken Books, 1971).
73 List of files sent to H.F. 5 January 2021 by Helga Neumann, the director of the Anna Seghers Archive. Radványi's involvement was surely the same in earlier decades, but police searches in 1931–3 and the exigencies of exile caused such papers to be lost or destroyed.
74 Simone Bischoff, *"Gottes Reich hat begonnen": Der Einfluß chiliastischer Hoffnung auf die DDR-Romane von Anna Seghers* (Frankfurt am Main: Peter Lang, 2009), 17. See Seghers's letter of 9 October 1947 to her Austrian comrade Bruno Frei, in Anna Seghers, *Über Kunstwerk und Wirklichkeit*, vol. 4, 150–1, at 151.
75 Siegfried Kracauer, "Eine Märtyrer-Chronik von heute" (A Martyr Chronicle of Today), *Frankfurter Allgemeine Zeitung* (13 November 1932), in SK, *Werke: Essays, Feuilletons, Rezensionen*, vol. 5.4, 1932–65 (Berlin: Suhrkamp Verlag, 2011), 269–72, at 269–70.

13 Haunting Encounters: Reimagining Hermina Dumont Huiswoud's Trip to the Soviet Union, 1930–1933

TATSIANA SHCHURKO

In her *Caribbean Crusaders and the Harlem Renaissance*, Joyce Moore Turner recollects the despair the Afro-Caribbean radical Hermina Dumont Huiswoud felt about the dissolution of the Soviet Union.[1] Born in Guyana, Huiswoud migrated to the US and later settled in the Netherlands. She had an active political life and travelled widely. While in the Soviet Union, she developed attachments to the region, its peoples, and the socialist ethos that made the dissolution of the Soviet Union more than a geopolitical event; for her, it was personal:

> When the Soviet Union collapsed [Huiswoud] sent for me because she needed to share her grief at the passing of an era in which she and [her husband] Otto had believed that the USSR could be an example of a nation free of exploitation. The apparent demise of socialism, which she had embraced for sixty-five years, seemed to herald her own demise.[2]

Why would a Black woman grieve over the passing of the Soviet Union? This grief may surprise us or look nostalgic or even naive. Many of Huiswoud's Black radical contemporaries, initially enchanted with revolutionary promises, later learned about state atrocities and broke their ties with the Soviet Union. While embracing the reasons for this estrangement and the importance of deconstructing the Soviet project, I am equally concerned about post–Cold War scripts and their memory technologies vis-a-vis the former Soviet region. As a queer feminist scholar from Belarus, I aim in this chapter to read against the conceptual traps of post–Cold War analysis that would catch Husiwoud's grief as merely nostalgic.

By post–Cold War traps, I mean practices that encourage rejecting the past entirely instead of revising it. These practices contribute to the flattening of Soviet-era history and the homogenization of the former

Soviet space. Specifically, rendering the past (and the region) uniform occludes the complexity of mechanisms applied by state power to diverse communities, especially racialized and colonized peoples. Furthermore, compressing the past into one story neglects marginal and alternative practices of cross-border cooperation and resistance, thus depriving non-state actors of agency. Coming myself from this region that has been so overwhelmed and misinterpreted by predominant Western-centric and Russo-centric visions, I expect the archive to reveal subjectivities and relations that do not fit neatly into post–Cold War narratives. Hence, this chapter provides an alternative explanation for what underrpinned Huiswoud's sorrow.

I read Huiswoud's grief as a longing for social justice as a radical lived practice that could span peoples and regions. From 1930 until 1933, Huiswoud worked for and studied at the International Lenin School in Moscow, having accompanied her husband, Otto Huiswoud, a Black communist and a leading Comintern functionary, on his trip to the Soviet Union. The Communist International generated a dense web of contacts and relations during the interwar years. Remarkably, these relations were not limited to formal meetings. Innumerable encounters occurred outside official arrangements. While in the Soviet Union, Huiswoud developed a deep connection to the Soviet project and a unique set of affinities with and attachments to peoples and places. Probably, some connections she forged stuck with her, causing her to grieve their passing even while many celebrated. My interest in Huiswoud's close affinities, daily relations, or solidarities with Soviet subaltern subjects animates this chapter. As I read against the initial impulse to reject this history, I revisit the way Huiswoud potentially connected to another subaltern subject. To learn about her affinities and understand why she had such an attachment to the Soviet Union, I turn to the archive.

Encountering the Archive: Notes on Methodology

I visited the archive in search of traces of past relations and revolutionary subjectivities not accounted for in prevailing historical narratives. But when I explored Huiswoud's papers and photographs at the New York University Special Collections, I found that the available documents about her time in the Soviet Union offered little. They include brief notes about her visit and more than one hundred Soviet postcards from Eastern Europe, the Caucasus, Siberia, and Central Asia dated from 1922 to 1932.[3] Even so, I turn to these to probe the possibilities of reading beyond archival absences. The possibilities suggest not that we look back to recuperate the past but rather that we begin a conversation about how to approach what the archive does provide. What happens when we encounter absences in archival records? What prospects lie at the limits of these records? How can we tell untold stories or engage ethically with stories that escape the archive's gaze? In asking these questions, this chapter intervenes in post–Cold War technologies of memory that rely on traditional historiographies and that, in doing so, determine whose history is worth preserving, what is essential, and what is of minor significance.

Traditional historiographies and positivist methodologies require proof or documentation from archival materials, thus establishing an impermeable border between historical fact and fiction. However, it often happens that evidence does not exist and that absences cannot be filled with more research.[4] Furthermore, the predominant focus on individual historical figures makes it hard to explore archives produced from within social movements, which are marked by dynamic relations and constant border crossings. Also, seemingly factual history focuses too strongly on policy-making and thereby privileges macro-narratives of state actors, parties, institutions, and key leaders over the visions and experiences of marginalized groups and non-state actors and their alternative forms of sociality. In addition, the dominant modes of historical thought cannot fully account for the immense structural violence against racialized and colonized peoples that has kept them out of historical records. Black radicals' lives and activities were severely impacted by anti-Black racism, constant state surveillance, and Cold War rivalries. These factors, among others, explain why archives may be incomplete. Thus, striving to overcome the limits of traditional methodologies, I turn to interdisciplinary humanistic inquiry, relying on Black feminist and queer scholarship that has developed another method of writing history, especially history that has been erased or silenced or that has escaped recording.[5]

Saidiya Hartman presents "critical fabulation" as a method of history writing "with and against the archive."[6] This method of critical and close reading of the archive attempts "to jeopardize the status of the event, to displace the received or authorized account, and to imagine what might have happened or might have been said or might have been done."[7] Specifically, Hartman responds to the limits of the official archive to represent a Black enslaved woman. The archival narratives "yield no picture of the everyday life, no pathway to her thoughts, no glimpse of the vulnerability of her face or of what looking at such a face might demand," she emphasizes.[8] Relying on the worldviews and perspectives of "captors and masters," the official archive produces/conditions absences and fabricates facts, events, and subjects, thus establishing the tropes of their representation.

Hartman's recent book *Wayward Lives, Beautiful Experiments* shows how this historical paradigm continues to influence protocols and modes of research. Against the violent norms, erasures, and fabrications of the official archive, Hartman combines historical research with a fictional narrative to create stories of young Black women at the turn of the twentieth century in New York and Philadelphia. She illuminates and narrates occluded and erased experiences, practices of resistance, and intellectual traditions of Black women. Challenging the authority of the official archive to determine what is worth recalling and how the story should be told, she pushes "the limits of the case file and the document" by imagining "the things whispered in dark bedrooms" and amplifying "moments of withholding, escape and possibility, moments when the vision and dreams of the wayward seemed possible."[9] Against the violence of structural racism that determined the livelihoods of Black women and the possibilities open to them, she foregrounds young Black women as "radical thinkers who tirelessly imagined other ways to live and never failed to consider how the world might be otherwise" and who "struggled to create autonomous and beautiful lives, to escape the new forms of servitude awaiting them, and to live as if they were free."[10]

My reading draws inspiration from Hartman's approach. Huiswoud's scattered archive poses questions about state power and the structural reasons for the scarcity of official records. Anti-Black racism determined the absence of Black women in official narratives and pushed Black women to search for better living conditions and forms of sociality (as Hartman illuminates). For Huiswoud and for many other Black radical women, anti-colonial communism and overseas travel were ways to escape state oppression and to engage in building alternative social models. However, as Turner notes, due to constant state surveillance and suppression of dissent in the US and Europe, she refrained from recording or exposing information about her activities.[11]

Thus, absences in the archive point out for us the vulnerability of histories that counter dominant powers. Hartman's approach helps us think through these multiple erasures and treat the neglected aspects and absences in the archive as more than a historical problem. These absences reflect contextual factors and the conditions of possibility and agency. Through careful analysis of the context and constraints of the time, I map out what and who could have escaped the gaze of the state and the archive, and why, as a means to explore these occluded histories.

At the centre of my exploration in this chapter is a photo depicting a veiled woman* in Central Asia.[12] The image is no different from several others held in Huiswoud's archive that show the life-worlds of Central

Figure 13.1. Undated photographic image of a veiled woman.* Photographer unknown.

Asia.[13] Yet this damaged and seemingly neglected photo postcard, fractured into two pieces, started to haunt me. I do not know why exactly Huiswoud kept this postcard. Might it refer to a relationship between a US Black radical and a Soviet Central Asian woman? In asking this question, I am trying to overcome the void manifested in the absence of any notes on the back and the paucity of the archive pertaining to Huiswoud's trip to the Soviet Union.[14]

This postcard may strike one as not very informative – as marginal, in fact, and lacking any "real story." So why choose it as an object of analysis? I suggest that although it is not strictly amenable to historiographic research, its very ephemerality offers many possibilities for creative speculation and open-ended interpretation. The postcard bears the memory of many travels and encounters and thus may serve as a reference point for Huiswoud's political commitments and experiences of solidarity. It invites us to think about the role and situation of subaltern subjects and their solidarities at the margins, even those beyond any archive. The relationship between Huiswoud and the veiled woman* can be both a historical fact and a fiction. However, I do not aim to prove either. Reading the archive otherwise, I explain why this relationship may be a possibility, whether or not it actually happened. To reveal this possibility, I explore the conditions of the time and the (un)fulfilled aspirations that held out the promise of relations attuned to difference. My research does not claim to be strictly historical; instead, it benefits from an interdisciplinary vision. Drawing on scholarship and available historical evidence, I reflect upon possible relations, reconstructing livelihoods, experiences, and forms of sociality in order to extend them and thereby exceed the available archive. In the following sections, I juxtapose and analyse several dimensions – Huiswoud's impetus for internationalism, the veiled image, the materiality of the postcard, and connections Huiswoud made in the Soviet Union. The context, the artefact, and the conditions of possibility provide windows onto possible solidarity even in the absence of documentary evidence. Furthermore, my exploration discusses Huiswoud's experiences through her relations with others. She did not leave an autobiography but told her story while narrating the stories of others. I follow her lead.

On the Move

Hermina Dumont Huiswoud (1905–98), like many Black radical women, was constantly on the move, crossing physical borders as well as transgressing social boundaries established by the US white supremacist order and Western colonialism. The radicalism of Black women included an overt critique of structural inequity, and not only in the US context. Their activism and visions transcended national borders, connecting local to global and establishing cross-border relations with marginalized communities. Since the 1920s, Huiswoud had been involved in various movements, supported diverse projects, and travelled across multiple spaces. For her, "the struggle was more than words or ideas but life itself," to borrow Cedric Robinson's words.[15] Building on this idea, I suggest, notwithstanding the scant evidence about this period in her life, that Huiswoud's travel to the Soviet Union, which was situated within her political commitments and life-worlds, constituted a radical statement in its own right.

Huiswoud grew up in British Guiana (now Guyana).[16] When her father died, and then her grandmother, and her family lost most of their possessions, Huiswoud and her mother were forced to move.[17] They ended up in Harlem, which by 1919 had established itself as an epicentre of Black radical thought.[18] Huiswoud was fourteen, and her interest in radical politics, which had started through her mother's involvement in Guyanan politics, further developed in her high school years and later under the influence of her husband.[19]

In Harlem, Huiswoud frequented the public library, listened to soapbox orators such as the prominent Black radical internationalist Hubert Harrison, and attended cultural events with Black writers and artists.[20] At that time, the New York City neighbourhood was a complex environment where the legacies of slavery and colonialism informed labour upheavals, diverse struggles for social justice, the creative ferment of the Harlem Renaissance, and the radicalism of Black liberation. Later, Huiswoud met W.A. Domingo, Richard B. Moore, Cyril V. Briggs, Grace P. Campbell, Claudia Jones, and Elizabeth Gurley Flynn, among others.[21]

Importantly, Black radical activists, writers, and artists of that time envisioned Black liberation in the US as a part of struggle against colonialism and capitalism overseas. Gradually, Huiswoud became "convinced that socialism was the answer to the social and economic problems facing the poor."[22] However, following the 1917 Russian Revolution, anti-Black politics intersected with waves of anti-communist persecution that especially targeted Black communists and leftist radicals in an attempt to suppress political dissent.

In those times, Black women were severely affected by economic and social injustices, relegated mostly to domestic servitude, and subjected to surveillance by the police and other state organs.[23] Working against significant restrictions on employment and mobility, left-based activism helped Black women access resources and institutions usually foreclosed in the white supremacist and segregationist US landscape. Huiswoud would remember facing many hardships after finishing high school in 1924 as she studied in college and while working. She had to take different jobs – from real estate office worker to domestic maid – where she experienced racism and unfair treatment.[24] It was during this time that she began working for the National Association for the Advancement of Colored People and the Harlem Tenants League. She joined the American Negro Labour Congress in 1925, the Young Workers League in 1927, and the Communist Party in 1928.[25] She also worked for Cyril Briggs's monthly magazine *The Crusader* and contributed to *The Liberator*.[26]

A central issue for this activist circle was housing.[27] While working for the Harlem Tenants League, Huiswoud, like other Black activists such as Grace Campbell and Williana Burroughs, organized marches, demonstrations, and rent strikes, blocked evictions, demanded that housing regulations be enforced, and agitated on behalf of the community.[28] The league "linked poor housing to broader struggles against global white supremacy, capitalism, and imperialism," as Eric McDuffie has noted.[29] This transnational perspective was a constant presence in Huiswoud's writings and organizing.

For example, while accompanying Otto Huiswoud on his tour of the Caribbean in 1930, she noted how US imperialism and occupation impoverished local communities as it "tr[ied] to establish in Haiti the rule of the South and South Africa." Pointing out the miserable conditions, she also focused on "burning unrest against the American imperialism," emphasizing the active role of women in these struggles: "Demonstrating the keen interest of the Haitian masses in all protest movements, a protest mass meeting called by the Young Women Nationalist Organization brought out over 15,000 people, with house tops and trees crowded with spectators ... A very militant spirit was shown by the entire crowd, demands for Haitian freedom being vigorously applauded. Women were very numerous in the gathering."[30]

This tour prepared the ground for her multiple travels that aligned with her political commitments. Against the backdrop of colonial violence, domestic servitude, and poverty that kept Black women in place, mobility was both a way "to elude capture by never settling" and "an ongoing exploration of what might be," to borrow Hartman's formulation.[31] Travelling allowed Huiswoud to expand her understanding of the global operations of power; all the while, she searched for viable and lived alternatives. Her trip to the Soviet Union was a part of that search. Her interest was sparked in 1927 when she, her mother, and her husband, Otto, heard W.E.B. Du Bois lecture on his own recent visit to the Soviet Union. She recalled: "It was he who convinced me of the value of communism. His final words still ring in my memory. From the pulpit of the fashionable Fifth Avenue Unitarian Church, after summing up all that he'd seen in the USSR, enumerating the results of the 10-year-old Soviet system, Dr. DuBois said: 'If that's Communism, then I'm a Communist.'"[32]

For Du Bois and many other Black radicals, racial logics and anti-Blackness were intrinsic to the emergence and functioning of capitalism and Black labour fuelled and sustained world capitalism. They envisioned Marxist-driven critique as a tool for challenging racial capitalism.[33] In this context, the Soviet Union and the Comintern were an important site for efforts to consolidate the global struggle against racism, imperialism, and capitalism.[34]

Huiswoud left behind Harlem with its complex histories of state violence and radical struggles, arriving in the Soviet Union in search of new visions of the future, free from racial and gender conventions. For Huiswoud, the Soviet Union, with its progressive women and national politics, looked especially attractive as this "imaginary and actual elsewhere furnishe[d] a space to rethink crucial aspects of social and cultural life at home."³⁵ Many radicals, including Comintern functionaries, promoted masculinist and patriarchal visions; Black radical women challenged these erasures, showing how gender and sexuality merged with racial violence and capitalist exploitation.³⁶ Huiswoud complained that Black communist men did not involve "their women kin in their activities, adhering to the theory that the women's place was in the home."³⁷

In the Soviet Union, she was provided with an apartment, employment as a translator in the International Lenin School and a stenographer for the Central Control Commission of the Party, and resources to study.³⁸ Soviet officials also offered her the possibility of improving her health in the sanatorium at Borjomi, in the Caucasus.³⁹ Before discussing Huiswoud's journey in more detail, I want to emphasize that her time in the Soviet Union influenced her further political activities and thus was not an exception but rather an integral part of her growing internationalist commitments.

Returning from the Soviet Union in February 1934, Huiswoud continued to participate in political organizing. After a short period in New York, she joined Otto Huiswoud in Antwerp, Belgium, where she helped edit, publish, and distribute *The Negro Worker*, an official organ of the International Trade Union Committee of Negro Workers.⁴⁰ Under the pseudonym Helen Davis, she published several articles between 1934 and 1937. She was also active in the International Trade Union Committee of Negro Workers until its demise in 1938. In 1939, she moved to New York, where she worked as an assistant to Richard B. Moore, who edited the Pathway Press edition of *Life and Times of Frederick Douglass*. She also worked as a secretary for the Negro Labour Victory Committee and an assistant to Gwendolyn Bennett, director of the George Washington Carver School, where she lectured as well.⁴¹ In 1943, she co-organized a Midwest Black labour conference. In 1949, she moved permanently to Amsterdam to join Otto; there, among many things, they worked for the Association "Ons Suriname," which fought for the independence of Dutch Guiana. This move to the Netherlands helped the Huiswouds escape the Red Scare purges of the early 1950s that many of their friends experienced in the US.⁴²

The Veiled Woman*: Huiswoud and Hughes in the Soviet Landscape of Difference

Huiswoud was passionate about Soviet efforts to free racialized and colonized peoples. Unfortunately, she had few opportunities to engage with diverse Soviet communities. The postcards in her archive are almost the only indications of her desire to interact. Those postcards epitomize a problem that many Black radicals struggled with – how to translate difference across borders and comprehend the heterogeneity of the local context.

While Huiswoud was crossing the Caucasus, Crimea, and Ukraine on her way from Moscow to the spa town of Borjomi and back in 1932, her husband, Otto, accompanied Langston Hughes and a group of Black artists from the film project *Black and White* on their journey to Central Asia. The postcards from Huiswoud's archive bear the memory of these travels. Hughes presented some of them to Huiswoud. Others she received from her husband and some she acquired on her own. How she obtained the photo postcard of the veiled woman* is unclear. Even so, this image has the potential to reveal the complexities of imperial power, difference, and agency that Huiswoud confronted.

The photo offers a quick glimpse into the daily life of a community in Soviet Central Asia. A veiled woman* is at the centre of the image, while in the background, many people are sitting on the ground, apparently waiting. Some are sleeping, some are watching the photographer. The location suggests a transport station or a market before opening or after closing. It is apparent that the photographer has intruded on the space, disrupting the daily routine of a local community, which cannot refuse to be photographed. One may conclude that the photographer was striving to produce the fictional landscape of ethnic difference, focusing on clothing and the district's rural qualities. The picture may call to mind orientalist clichés that recycle images of veiled women to (re)produce homogeneous and stereotypical visions of the East and delineate the racialized gendered boundaries between East and West (on orientalism, see also chapters 6 and 10 in this volume).[43] However, I suggest there are many possible scenarios to explain how and why the photographer created this image. Those scenarios reflect the complicated and often contradictory context in which Huiswoud landed.

After the 1917 Revolution, photographers poured into Central Asia.[44] Among them were Max Penson, Ivan Panov, Arkady Shaikhet, Max Alpert, Mikhail Grachev, and Georgy Zelma, who explored the drastic transformations the region was experiencing since after the Revolution. Many of their photos were printed as postcards and played an instrumental role in the operations of Soviet power.[45] Some images advertised Soviet successes; others conveyed interpretations of indigenous peoples. There were also many amateur photographers. However, as Craig Campbell notes, Soviet photography was a largely Russian- and male-dominated sphere, and this suggested "specific power dynamics in which one group of people had the means to represent another" while the "situated gazes of women and indigenous [peoples], as well as peasants and other people on the margins of power and society, are not present in the framing of the photographs."[46]

This photo, then, reflects a normative Soviet gaze, an attempt to provide a homogeneous image of what state discourse would refer to as "the oppressed woman of the East." In the context of Soviet modernization in Central Asia, ideas about emancipation produced their own racialized gendered hierarchies and pressures.[47] Specifically, through the unveiling campaigns in Central Asia, the Caucasus, and the Volga-Ural region, the Soviet state asserted that women's emancipation depended on their dissociation from traditional environments and supposedly backward cultures.[48] In national anti-colonial narratives, the veil served as a symbol of resistance to Soviet imperial power; for the Soviet state, it unambiguously epitomized seclusion, confinement, and servitude.

So it is easy to propose a reading of the postcard that centres Soviet orientalist practices justifying narratives of progress and modernization. Some scholars argue that Black radical women were enchanted with Soviet emancipation and unveiling campaigns and thus were also guilty of an "Orientalist reading of the status of Soviet Central Asian women."[49] Indeed, Black radical women, including Huiswoud, may have set aside the fact that the Soviet Union achieved much of its progress through violence, exploitation, and the disparagement of indigenous life-worlds. However, while it seems that Black radical women's approaches "resembled those of early twentieth-century European travellers to the region" or embraced the thinking of "Soviet officials, who made unveiling a key part of official Soviet policy of modernizing the region," they also may have offered alternative readings of Soviet practices in an attempt to connect to local communities and their struggles.[50]

For example, Langston Hughes, who may have given this postcard to Huiswoud, was fascinated with Soviet practices of unveiling as he strived to comprehend the possible emancipatory potential that Central Asian women experienced through those practices. Kate Baldwin argues that Hughes attempted to rethink the meaning of unveiling in relation to the context of US racial segregation and Du Bois's notion of the veil as a metaphor for a heterosexual Black male consciousness. Identifying specifically with Uzbek femininity, Hughes envisioned unveiling, in Baldwin's reading, as "the act that best represented transgression, the permeability of so-called natural boundaries, of all previously delimiting delineations as a route to a racialized sexual emancipation."[51] In this way, Baldwin argues, Hughes "complicated any simple decoding of the discourse of the veil," in that his interpretation of unveiling opened up the possibility for "a rewriting of the category of otherness" by linking sexual liberation and racial emancipation.[52]

Perhaps the photo postcard epitomized this desire to connect with local communities of colour – a desire that Hughes may have wanted Huiswoud to share. Hughes's reading connected distant geographies and communities at a time when he was thinking about racial/sexual violence and colonial powers relationally. In centring the experiences of non-European non-Slavic communities, he was challenging the normative Soviet image of a revolutionary. In part through the postcard, Hughes could share his reflections and experiences with Huiswoud as they were "good friends" who had "spent six months together in Moscow."[53] They may well have discussed the potential of revolutionary transformations as well as the barriers limiting their comprehension thereof.

Hughes's opportunities to connect with local communities in Central Asia were significantly restricted by the state, which orchestrated them. In a letter to Matt Crawford on 23 October 1932, for instance, Hughes noted that "the great difficulty here is getting in touch with the native life. The Turkmens sort of step aside, and let the Russians take charge of all the visitors."[54] Similarly, Turner remarks regarding Huiswoud's studies at the Lenin School:

> [Huiswoud] and Peggy Dennis, wife of Eugene Dennis (Frank Waldron), were the two Americans selected by a Comintern commission to attend the regular day program in the fall of 1932. According to Peggy Dennis they studied the writings of Marx, Engels, Lenin, and Stalin, as well as the history of the Russian Revolution and the Russian Party, and also visited factories and villages to glimpse Soviet life; but they never had "direct contact and conversation with ordinary Soviet citizens."[55]

Hughes strived not to approach the Soviet East as a foreign observer, which the limitations imposed by state power made him. Grounded as he was in his embodied experience of violence in the US, he offered a different way of seeing, a methodology of approaching the complexity of the Soviet landscape in which two communities, Black people in the US and indigenous people in Central Asia, were placed in a dynamic relationship to resist colonial racial/sexual logics. It was the desire for this kind of relationship, unfulfilled in practice, that he shared with Huiswoud. Possibly, she preserved the photo postcard as a reminder of her longing for a relationship with Soviet racialized gendered communities of the sort that Hughes forged through his writing.

It is also possible that Hughes's vision, which Huiswoud perhaps shared, was an extention of the orientalist reading of the veil. In his efforts to see agency beyond official Soviet narratives, Hughes – apparently like many Black radical women – viewed unveiling as an uplifting practice, at a time when the veil remained a marker of difference and oppression. For instance, describing her husband's and Hughes's trip to Central Asia, Huiswoud noted: "They visited cities like Tashkent and Samarkand as well as the agricultural regions, where only a decade and a half before women were bartered in marriage and wore veils. Even then, customs were dying hard for many women still adhered to the old customs."[56]

Feminist scholarship has questioned the predominant perception that the veil is inevitably oppressive and has delineated the intricate links between practices of unveiling and the operations of empire.[57] Of course, Hughes and Huiswoud could not have been familiar with this type of critique in the 1930s. Feminist post-colonial readings of the veil do not deny the transformative potential that unveiling may have had for indigenous and Muslim women; nor do they reject transgressive visions like those that Hughes articulated. But they do problematize "unveiling" narratives that reproduce the veil as a symbol of othering, that deny veiled women's agency, and that see women who wear a veil as obedient objects and reduce all agency to state control. So another reading is possible that inverts the agency of the photo.

The photo locates a group of subjects in their social context, thus emphasizing their connections to a larger society and exposing complex and subtle interactions. The camera may indeed be applying its gaze to the veiled woman*, but she responds in an unexpected manner. She and other people in the photo look confidently at the camera as they pose in their familiar environment. Her open posture suggests that she is curious about the process. She does not try to hide, and indeed returns the gaze, refusing to be transparent. The veil allows her to face the camera comfortably without exposing herself. I see the veiled woman* as part of the community to which she belongs but also as a participant in the photo process.

These alternative readings require us not just to challenge the imperial gaze but to unlearn its practices of seeing, thinking, and being. Ariella Aïsha Azoulay suggests that "unlearning imperialism" means unlearning "the stories the [photographic] shutter tells" and foregrounding "a commitment to reversing the shutter's work."[58] Any narrow interpretation of the photo neglects "the possibility of seeing photography as the product and effect of an open-ended encounter among various participants."[59] In this way, she problematizes the negation of "the presence of the persons photographed and the relations of reciprocity that exist between them and the photographer."[60] Just as unveiling may signify simultaneously a multifaceted operation of a transgressive border-crossing and the violent operation of Soviet rule, so the photo may reveal the resilience of indigenous communities and their struggle against the overdetermined Soviet gaze. Non-Slavic non-European communities in the Soviet Union were not mere passive recipients of Soviet orders; they actively challenged and redressed ineffective policies even as their voices were circumscribed by Soviet officials.[61]

Likewise, the function of many Soviet photographers cannot be reduced to the machinery of state rule.[62] The photographer is unnamed; we do not know whether that person was part of the community, so we cannot discard that possibility. The photographer may have creatively adapted some conventions to suit the interests of the community. Specifically, using the medium of the postcard, a photographer could aim to disband the monolithic vision of Soviet spaces or the unified image of the worker by centring multiple communities that navigated these spaces. By angling the camera to capture the woman not from a top-down angle but directly, on equal footing, the photographer seems to engage with the landscape. This photo shows a locally produced order and structure, one that is unavailable for easy understanding.

In this context, Huiswoud could have a more empathic identification with the veiled woman*, privileging the person in the image and female agency rather than operations of state power. Even if she could not fully grasp the drastic difference between official politics and practices, by looking at the image she could inquire about how to engage with local communities, given their differential positionalities and the restrictions imposed by state powers on their bodies and relations. From this perspective, Huiswoud may have kept the photo as a reminder of a Soviet indigenous life-world that had its own agency and with which she could achieve solidarity. This alternative reading of the image illuminates the complexity of the context and also raises questions about the presence of the postcard in the archive and what other layers of Huiswoud's imagined solidarities this presence may reveal.

Postcard in the Archive

While she navigated the complicated Soviet landscape, Huiswoud collected postcards and included them in her archive, in this way participating in an archiving process and revealing histories of a collective search for liberation that she and many others (across the East/West divide) were pursuing at that time. The postcards amount to a material archive of Black–Eurasian interactions. This collection does not contain coherent stories; it does, however, reflect real or desired relations and create new connections. Thus, this section engages with the material presence of a Central Asian postcard (and its afterlives) in the archive of a Black radical woman and what this presence entails.

To deal with the repressed histories that come to the fore in the present as ghosts, Avery Gordon has developed "haunting" as a method that focuses on "feelings, motivations, blind spots, craziness, and desires" that the haunting presence may reveal.[63] Engaging with ghosts and their haunting presences means exploring "what paths have been disavowed, left behind, covered over and remain unseen."[64] Drawing haunting out of the materiality of the postcard, I explore how the veiled woman* emerges as a ghost that calls the viewer to assess the possibility of solidarity. Specifically, the postcard encourages us to revise radical politics for how they can be attuned to the experiences of the veiled women from Central Asia, who have been overshadowed by Eurocentric and Russocentric epistemologies. In this sense, the trouble Huiswoud may have struggled with is still here: how to connect across borders and differences informed by various imperial formations or grasp the nature of an empire so different from Western empires. In other words, the failure to connect or understand the context figuratively manifested in the material presence of the postcard in the archive is an invitation to investigate both the limits of solidarity and why solidarity should have happened.

In archival collections, postcards are often labelled as ephemera – artefacts of nebulous significance, open for creative speculation, since they do not offer an immediately coherent story. Ephemera trouble what is already known or recognized and may reveal forms of subjectivity and sociality that were lost or never fully articulated. In Huiswoud's archive, the postcard is the material evidence of travel and indicates the presence of a Black radical woman in the Soviet Union and the relations she imagined – if we suppose a connection between her and the veiled woman*. In addition, the image encompasses the motion that led to its archiving in the US. Produced in some location in Central Asia, it crossed multiple borders together with Huiswoud and witnessed her life-spaces and communities, finally ending up in the New York archive. Thus, the photo postcard may unlock stories about a Black radical woman's multiple journeys and strivings for solidarity permeated by her commitment to social justice.

The destructions and protrusions of the fractured postcard itself bear witness to its turbulent life and travels. How can we reconstruct the circumstances that led to the crease in the middle of the image and assign meaning to it? As I noted previously, after her time in the Soviet Union, Huiswoud resettled many times, and she could have carried the postcard around, packed and unpacked it, left it in different places, folded it into storage, shifted, handled, or passed it to other people. From this perspective, the fracture may signify those practices and events fuelled by Huiswoud's political commitments, to which the photo bears witness. Thus, the veiled woman* emerges as a ghost calling to mind the violence and resilience of indigenous communities, and the postcard holds the memory of transnational mobility and imagined solidarity, rendering the physical fracture a part of the haunting.

Furthermore, considering the disappointment that Huiswoud expressed over the collapse of the Soviet Union, this postcard could have been a reminder of relationships between struggling peoples around the world that she never managed to forge, although she desired to. Such an engagement could have unlocked the possibility for Black and Soviet indigenous communities to develop their own grammar for transnational solidarity. While looking through her diverse postcards, did Huiswoud pay particular attention to this one? Did she long for a connection with the veiled woman*, recollect the memory of past relationships, or simply pass by indiscriminately? In this case, the fracture may signify Huiswoud's long-held curiosity about the postcard, as well as the way the veiled woman* was attempting to escape or transcend the frozen medium of the photograph to recall solidarities and desires or invite new ones.

The fracture may also signify negligence or violence rather than the work of care and love. One can read the very process of collecting someone's photo as a violent gesture of subjection in which the colonial power's production of Others leads to their objectification in the archive. So, was this act of collecting, owning, and folding someone's photo a violent extension of the practices of colonial power? The fractured postcard of the veiled woman* troubles power hierarchies that could have emerged even from within social justice struggles and practices. This troubling does not deny the possibility of solidarity but rather explores the complex net of power relations that surrounded subjugated communities and mediated their relations of solidarity. This inquiry is addressed not to the past but to the future, as the fracture may unlock conversations about building solidarity against uneven practices of displacement and dispossession across borders.

The fracture may also refer to negligence or violence produced by the archive as an institution. I found the fractured postcard in the archival collection crushed between stacks of other postcards. It appeared to me that for the archive, including all its actors – workers and visitors – this postcard did not seem significant; someone may have placed it inaccurately into the folder, which further led to its destruction, which was aggravated by the brittleness of the paper. This material damage, then, also reflects the gaps and absences in the archive as well as a history of archival disregard for Black women and their potential networks of solidarity with Soviet non-European, non-Slavic women. In the US, the activities of Black radical women are often occluded and their archival collections are scattered and fragmented (if not entirely absent). For the longest time, Western historiography has failed to recognize Black and indigenous women as historical actors, instead privileging normative visions of revolutionary subjects, focusing on leaders, institutions, and organizations. Even less is known about Soviet indigenous women's visions of interactions with US Black radical women. Recognizing these erasures, we are forced to confront the fact that the story is not present in the archive whereas the postcard is. Thus, the veiled woman* haunts us, forcing us to see the absence and to ask how alternative stories or a common realm of belonging can be imagined, where the Black radical woman and Soviet indigenous woman aspire for a connection. It is this void that necessitates the approach of haunting and imagination.

The paucity of the archive may also mark the resistance of subjugated subjects to the expectation that they be "obedient objects" for the conventional gaze, which requires transparency, legibility, consistency, and visibility as its principal paradigms. Just as the veil allowed the woman* from the postcard to gaze back into the camera, so the absence of the archive and the fracture may signify the escape or refusal to be seen by the normative gaze of the archive. The opaqueness and unwholeness that witness the repression also invoke survival when pitted against the violence of colonial power. For instance, Turner recollects that Huiswoud mostly "refused to be interviewed on tape" and "would say, 'Just listen and remember!'"[65] Anti-communist purges and surveillance in the West had contributed to this reserve. Therefore, the fracture may be a way for the ghost to transcend the borders of established interpretations that circumscribe the agency of the subject. Rereading the veil and the fracture alongside each other, I suggest that they mark not only a violent erasure or act of destruction but also escape as a political act against the racial and sexual structures of legibility and illegibility. Furthermore, being present in the archive while veiled and fractured provokes thoughts of escape and refusal and thus opens up creative imagination about what could have been.

This approach foregrounds the value of opaqueness that can speak on its own. Both the veil and the fracture may refer to loss, the abuse of power, or disregard, all of which require critical attention. Such critical inquiry should not be an end point of an exploration; it should invoke alternative readings that situate the veiled woman* and Huiswoud within the diverse web of their relations and communities. The veil and the fracture create the gap or void in the neat operations of power, and the imagination crosses it to point out other ways of seeing agency or relation where no agency or relation is expected to be. This reading reveals the desire for another grammar and methodology to start the conversation between uneven communities and put "life back in where only a vague memory or a bare trace was visible to those who bothered to look."[66] Another reading allows us to see how the material presence of the postcard indicates a desire for solidarity and the barriers facing its development.

"Women I Have Known Personally"

I approach solidarity as a juncture, a coming together, or a connection whereby there is a possibility for change. This definition encompasses both concrete solidarities, where coming together is possible, and imagined ones, where a relationship has all the conditions to emerge but, for some reason, does not. It is these conditions that are important in thinking about imagined solidarities. It is my contention or speculation that Huiswoud and the veiled woman* may have wanted to connect. Linking my imagination to the material conditions surrounding Huiswoud and the veiled woman*, I am convinced that they could have had this desire amidst their experiences with colonial and racial violence, whether or not they had a real possibility to communicate. I also consider this desire as an important point for reflection about the limits for genuine engagement.

In this section, I think about the conditions that could have prepared the ground for Huiswoud's effort to develop a connection of solidarity with Soviet Central Asian women as well as the factors that prevented this solidarity from happening. Against the absence in the archive, I extract Huiswoud's willingness to develop relations from her political commitments and activities and her concrete solidarities. Specifically, I rely on Huiswoud's published articles and her unpublished corpus of writings, titled "Women, Biographical Essays (Women I Have Known Personally)," which consists of a series of portraits of women she knew "either over a long period of time or through an incidental, short encounter."[67] In this series, Huiswoud writes not only about other women but about her life as well, neatly weaving together her own and others' stories. In this series, she presents her experiences in the Soviet Union, describing some of her encounters while clearly keeping others to herself.

The series "Women I Have Known Personally" makes apparent Huiswoud's commitment to transnational solidarity.[68] Her depictions contain some biographical information but also deeply personal and intimate observations about these women in their daily lives. For instance, she developed a close relationship with another Black radical communist, Williana Burroughs, who frequently worked in the Soviet Union and in 1928 moved her children there to be "educated in a society free of the racism prevailing in the United States."[69] Probably they met during her time in the Harlem Tenants League, where they worked together. While in the Soviet Union, Huiswoud cared for Burroughs's two children. And upon returning to the US in 1945, Burroughs lived in Huiswoud's house, having lost all her property and possessions in the US due to her long absence. In contrast to this close relationship, her encounters with other women – for example, Sylvia Chen – were brief, although they do figure in her archive.[70]

Notably, her writings about other radical women create the impression that she cared a great deal about community-building and forging relationships and less about historicizing her own activities. Huiswoud was reserved about her role in explicitly political activities, prioritizing stories about other radical women she knew through communist and artistic networks or women she encountered during her many journeys. In her writings and recollections of the past, Huiswoud describes her interactions with other radical women in the course of daily interactions and fleeting encounters, as well as her reflections along the way, thus also revealing small fragments of her life. She does not focus on prominent events or political meetings, instead privileging those moments of direct quotidian contact that may seem insignificant today. I suggest that however vital her political commitments and activism were for her, she valued small daily interactions that had the potential to weave communities together on a personal level.

Furthermore, Huiswoud was genuinely interested in the worldwide struggles against imperialist powers (the US, Great Britain, Germany, and Italy), capitalism, racism, and warfare. In her published articles, she always emphasized and illuminated the connections between imperialism and capitalism.[71] Huiswoud published several articles about anti-colonial and anti-capitalist protests in Haiti, Cuba, South and East Africa, Palestine, Egypt, and Abyssinia.[72] She stood against "the Imperialist War-makers" who served the interests of "the armament manufacturers, international bankers and trust companies."[73] Her articles describe the multiple injustices imposed on Black communities by capitalism and US imperialism (poverty, labour exploitation, anti-migration laws), focusing on protest movements that emphasize the importance of solidarity. She frequently points out how imperial and capitalist powers attempt to disrupt unity or solidarity among communities.

For example, when describing the Cuban Revolution's beginning, Huiswoud concludes with this call: "Every class conscious worker should rally to the support and defence of the Cuban toilers in their struggle for the establishment of a Workers and Farmers Government."[74] In another article, she writes that "in their efforts to free themselves of the yoke of capitalist exploitation and imperialist rule, the proletariat of all countries seek allies."[75] That same year, in a different article, she declares: "The Fascists say there are differences between nations. Toilers know no national borders."[76] Huiswoud defied nation-states and borders, forging political connections around aspirations for a livable future that would confront transnational entanglements under global capitalism and imperialism. At the same time, she did not demand unification, emphasizing instead the importance of difference and of forging relations across differences:

> [The proletariat of all countries] seek these allies because the world is not composed of only workers and bosses. There is the poor farming population, there are the intellectuals – school teachers, doctors, lawyers, students, writers etc. In short there are many classifications of people in the world beside the rich capitalists and the army of poor workers. These people in one way or another, also feel the effects of capitalist exploitation and from time to time, many of them realise that capitalism must be doomed and a better society established.[77]

Huiswoud published most of her articles after her trip to the Soviet Union, so the visit, "a logical next step in the efforts to emancipate people of colour around the world," may have crystallized her ideas about the need for global solidarity and transnational alliances.[78] At the same time, as I noted earlier, she was interested in more direct connections on the ground. She not only worked and attended classes at the Lenin School but also participated in extracurricular activities.[79] The few existing fragments of her notes from this period show that her interactions with peoples and communities developed within the textures of her daily life as she navigated the Soviet landscape. Her notes indicate that she wanted to build grassroots connections rather than make them through the vanguard party. In the Soviet Union, she participated in often quotidian activities, as Turner reports:

> Frequently Hermie devoted her free day to a voluntary project, or *subbotnik*, such as carting stones and dirt in a wheelbarrow for the bed of a new railway line, cleaning the Park of Culture and Rest in preparation for May Day 1931, helping on the construction of Moscow University, carting away

dirt excavated for construction of the Moscow subway, weeding vegetable patches, threshing wheat, picking tobacco, or unloading a train load of potatoes. She has stated that she appreciated all the work she did because it made her conscious of the tremendous tasks entailed in production.[80]

In Moscow, she met the Spanish communist revolutionary Dolores Ibárruri, Nadezda Krupskaya, and Lenin's sister Maria Ulianova. She presents these women as complex human beings and in this way privileges an intimate or quotidian level of forging relations. For instance, Ibárruri came to Moscow to participate in a Comintern session, but Huiswoud chose to describe an informal gathering where she sang ballads.[81] Although Krupskaya appeared at several meetings of foreign communists, Huiswoud did not describe the content of those meetings or record what Krupskaya said, focusing instead on describing her as a "quiet, self-effacing little woman who, if one did not know it, would never suspect that she had played an important role in helping Lenin to develop and achieve the Russian Revolution." During the meetings, Krupskaya, "diminutive, plain, simply attired, grey-haired," addressed the participants, and then "she would shyly withdraw to the background."[82]

Huiswoud's accounts do not focus solely on key political figures. In her notes, one finds "a most extraordinary woman, who was 60 years old in 1930," working at the Lenin School. She also recounts brief interactions in dining halls and shower rooms.[83] Huiswoud's writings include ruminations about a domestic worker and peasant named Shura who helped her in Moscow and with whom she developed a strong personal connection: "From our first meeting, a bond between Shura and me had been struck for she reminded me of my mother in many ways. As time passed I was to learn her deep affection and devotion to me; someone I could trust and rely on."[84] Turner notes that initially Huiswoud "had difficulty with the idea of having a maid in the egalitarian USSR."[85] However, Shura convinced her that she needed this job: working for families with children was hard on her, and she preferred to take care of the Huiswouds. Huiswoud described how Shura cared about her and the hardships she faced, offering a glimpse into her daily life, in which Shura occupied an important place and served as a maternal figure. However, her archive reveals little about how she made sense of Shura's position and experiences and what conversations they had. Through such interactions, could Huiswoud have developed her sensitivity to the most marginalized and multiply oppressed communities in the Soviet Union and thereby have developed a similar interest in the photo postcard of the veiled woman*?

Given Huiswoud's concrete solidarities, her attentiveness to intimate and quotidian interactions, and her commitment to struggling people of colour, the postcard of the veiled woman* leads us to assume that in the Soviet Union, she may have hoped to connect with racialized communities. However, there were significant restrictions on her doing so. Setting aside language barriers (it is not clear whether she knew Russian well enough to communicate), Huiswoud's interactions were state-managed and surveilled. She could not travel freely to Central Asia to engage with local communities there. It is not clear why she did not join her husband Otto Huiswoud, her friend Langston Hughes, and other Black participants in the film project *Black and White* in Central Asia. Perhaps she was refused official permission, for the region was mostly closed for foreign visitors. Besides, around this time, Huiswoud embarked on a different trip to Borjomi. But even if she had gone to Central Asia, she still would have likely experienced barriers to connecting with local communities. While in Central Asia, could she have spoken to the veiled woman*? Could she even have had direct and unmediated contact? Very likely not, and the postcard may have filled this gap of longing and disappointment.

So, this postcard does more than simply represent the political solidarity that Huiswoud desired; it is also an element and expression of her aspiration to forge quotidian and informal ways of communication. The focus on daily acts and encounters conveyed by the postcard ruptures the monolithic structures of political articulation linked to state institutions of power. One could even suggest that, had she gone to Central Asia within the confines of regulated engagement, she might still have found ways to enjoy moments of genuine reciprocity within the textures of daily life, as she did in Tbilisi, Georgia.

While travelling to Borjomi, Huiswoud missed her train connection and had to spend a night in the open air at a train station. While she was preparing herself to sleep on the ground, a local woman persuaded the station attendant to allow them to spend the night inside the station. They found a vacant bench and "stretched out foot to foot and fell asleep." In the morning, they went together "to the lavatory and refreshed," then "took a strole [sic] on the station heights, while admiring Tiflis that was sleepily awaking." Afterwards they "returned to the station restaurant, took a light breakfast and went to the train platform where our paths diverged, she going to the train that would take her to Armenia and I, the train to Borzhom."[86] Huiswoud's description of this encounter does not explain how these two women communicated, interacted, or came to an agreement. Myriad questions emerge: How did this local woman make sense of Huiswoud's presence at the station in Tbilisi? What did

Huiswoud think about this woman? Did she ask herself: how has this woman navigated this space on her own, to what community does she belong, and what experiences has she had? A great deal is left to our imagination if we dare to pursue this train of thought.

Huiswoud's fleeting descriptions of her encounters demonstrate how she attempted to comprehend Soviet landscapes and also sense the possibilities for solidarity beyond state-sanctioned narratives. Given that conditions made it impossible for her to visit Central Asia and engage with local activists and communities, the postcard of the veiled woman* can easily function as a ghost pushing us to inquire about these missed opportunities. But in addition, her attention to daily interactions allows us to approach the postcard as a haunting reminder of those solidarities Huiswoud valued: coming together and living with others in everyday situations. The postcard depicts a quotidian landscape in which local communities freely occupy their space. Notwithstanding the orientalist gaze of the camera, Huiswoud may have preserved the postcard to help her relate to the quotidian reality of a struggling community about which she cared. Perhaps the postcard reminded Huiswoud of her political aspirations for connection unmediated, unsanctioned, and rooted in the daily realities of a community. This imagined solidarity rooted in the realities of the landscape could have been a way for her to fill a gap she felt within her. Is it possible to add one more story to Huiswoud's series "Women I Have Known Personally"? This inquiry awaits its co-conspirators.

Conclusions

The postcard of the veiled woman* adds something unique to the archive. In this chapter, I have shown how different ways of seeing the postcard produce methodological troubles. But it is also important that this postcard brings to light a community often omitted in explorations of the Comintern and Black radicalism: that of Soviet non-European, non-Slavic indigenous women engaged in transnational political organizing. The photo's archival presence invites the spectator, the veiled woman*, and Huiswoud to meet in a shared space committed to combating capitalist, imperialist, and racist violence. Huiswoud and the veiled woman* probably never met, yet they are unexpectedly brought together in the archival collection, marking a moment of their past geographic proximity. Accounts of the relationship between the Black radical woman and the Soviet indigenous woman are absent from the archive; this chapter has created the conditions of possibility for such a relationship to emerge. It has attempted to rethink the absence of that relationship through the image, the materiality of the postcard, the archive, Huiswoud's political commitments, and imagined solidarities. I approach the postcard as a medium for interconnection through which the veiled woman* escapes the limits of the colonial gaze (and the predominancy of its interpretations) so as to suggest a different set of networks, both local and transnational. The veiled woman* was suppressed and mobilized by state power, but her agency was not defined solely by state narratives. The same is true for Huiswoud. The image haunts us to read beyond the state's "clauses and parentheses" (Hartman) so that we recognize both the limits of and the possibilities for a relationship that privileges the perspectives of subjugated subjects. It becomes a haunting reminder of violent histories and suppressed lifeworlds as well as revolutionary journeys and transformative visions. By offering creative speculation about what could have been, I also aim to challenge the historical genealogies of political dissent (in both the US and the former Soviet spaces) that erase Black and indigenous subjects. This exploration may serve as a departure point for unlocking the conversation about what it may mean to reanimate today these imagined anti-racist solidarities and radical desires to connect in both the US and the post-Soviet context. Huiswoud's disappointment over the collapse of the Soviet Union may thus signify a longing for a vision of global solidarity that we no longer have.

Acknowledgments

This work was made possible by the support of Elizabeth D. Gee Grant for Research in Women's, Gender and Sexuality Studies, an Alumni Grant for Graduate Research and Scholarship, and a Mershon Graduate Student Research Grant. I owe sincere gratitude to the editors of this collection – Bradley Gorski and Philip Gleissner – for their valuable and thorough comments on this manuscript. I am also grateful to Katherine Reischl and participants in the research project Red Migrations: Marxism and Transnational Mobility after 1917, for their support and invaluable feedback on the first version of this chapter.

Notes

1 The term "radical" reflects positionality informed by leftist political ideas and directed towards social justice struggles against diverse systems of oppression, including racism, heterosexism, capitalism, imperialism, and colonialism. See also Barbara Ransby, *Eslanda: The Large and Unconventional Life of Mrs. Paul Robeson* (New Haven: Yale University Press, 2013), 294n8;

and Carole Boyce Davies, *Left of Karl Marx: The Political Life of Black Communist Claudia Jones* (Durham: Duke University Press, 2007), 5.
2 Joyce Moore Turner, *Caribbean Crusaders and the Harlem Renaissance* (Urbana: University of Illinois Press, 2005), ix–x.
3 The archive generally consists of her correspondence with family and other activists, writings that include pieces about Otto Huiswoud and various women she knew, photographs, and Soviet photo postcards. Initially, Huiswoud gave this collection to her biographer and friend Joyce Moore Turner. In 2006, Turner donated it to the New York University Special Collections after publishing her biography of Otto and Hermina Dumont Huiswoud in 2005. This article relies heavily on both Huiswoud's collection and Turner's book. In this chapter, all quotes from the Hermina Dumont Huiswoud Papers and Photographs (hereafter HDHP) are used with permission of the copyright holder.
4 Talbot C. Imlay, "Exploring What Might Have Been: Parallel History, International History, and Post-War Socialist Internationalism," *International History Review* 31, no. 3 (September 2009): 521–57; Jocelyn Fenton Stitt, *Dreams of Archives Unfolded: Absence and Caribbean Life Writing* (New Brunswick: Rutgers University Press, 2021).
5 Specifically, the academic and artistic works of Dionne Brand, Tina M. Campt, Cheryl Dunye, Alexis Pauline Gumbs, M. NourbeSe Phillip, Matt Richardson, and Christina Sharpe centre on Black and Indigenous people and people of color in the archives. They illuminate how encountering gaps and occlusions in the archives (which cannot be filled or recuperated) leads to developing a different approach to history. This approach challenges the stability of historical fact, deconstructs Western historical methodologies and official narratives, and blurs the border between "objective truth" and fiction.
6 Saidiya Hartman, "Venus in Two Acts," *Small Axe* 26, 12, no. 2 (June 2008): 12.
7 Hartman, "Venus in Two Acts," 11.
8 Hartman, "Venus in Two Acts," 2.
9 Saidiya Hartman, *Wayward Lives, Beautiful Experiments: Intimate Histories of Social Upheaval* (New York: W.W. Norton, 2019), xiv–xv.
10 Hartman, *Wayward Lives*, xv, xiii.
11 Turner, *Caribbean Crusaders*, ix.
12 I use an asterisk to trouble my assumption that the person on the photo postcard is a woman. In colonial consciousness, the veil serves as a common trope that enables subject formation through discourse that produces and homogenizes racialized femininity. At the same time, for oppressed communities, the veil may appear as an important site for political resistance against Western racial/sexual logic while not denying

the suppressing role it may play in anti-colonial national narratives. Therefore, in this chapter, an asterisk is used to acknowledge the multiplicity and heterogeneity of bodies, expressions, identities, meanings, and positionalities that may stay behind the loaded image of the veiled figure and go beyond the imposed gender binary.

13 Most of the postcards in this collection are made from photographic prints that depict collective farms, kindergartens, and factories along with urban landscapes, countryside, markets, and portraits of workers. Many of these photo postcards have short handwritten notes in English (such as "Tashkent" or "Baku") or printed descriptions in Russian such as "Soviet cotton farm 'Pakhta Aral'. Mechanical gathering of cotton" or "Everyday life of the peoples of the USSR. Loading grain to Khiva from Charjuy."

14 The postcard is located in Box 1, folder 30 HDHP; TAM 354; Tamiment Library/Robert F. Wagner Labor Archives, Elmer Holmes Bobst Library, New York University Libraries.

15 Cedric J. Robinson, *Black Marxism: The Making of the Black Radical Tradition* (Chapel Hill: University of North Carolina Press, 2000), 184.

16 In Guyana, the imperial powers established a plantation economy based on the labour of Black enslaved peoples and later, after the abolition of slavery, on indentured labour. See Kwame Nimako, Glenn Frank, and Walter Willemsen, *The Dutch Atlantic: Slavery, Abolition, and Emancipation* (New York: Pluto Press, 2011).

17 Turner, *Caribbean Crusaders*, 5.

18 Huiswoud moved to the US at the beginning of the Great Migration. Unjust conditions rooted in anti-Black racism, colonial violence, and capitalist exploitation forced many Black people to migrate from the US South and the Caribbean to the northern parts of the US as well as to Canada in search of better living and working conditions.

19 Turner, *Caribbean Crusaders*, 124.

20 Turner, *Caribbean Crusaders*, 10.

21 Turner, *Caribbean Crusaders*, 25; "Elizabeth Gurley Flynn (1890–1964)" and "Claudia Jones" in folder "Women, Biographical Essays (Women I Have Known Personally)" (hereafter WBE), n.d., box 1, folder 35, HDHP.

22 Turner, *Caribbean Crusaders*, 124.

23 Dayo F. Gore, *Radicalism at the Crossroads: African American Women Activists in the Cold War* (New York: NYU Press, 2011).

24 "Marian Anderson," in folder WBE, n.d., box 1, folder 35, HDHP.

25 Turner, *Caribbean Crusaders*, 7, 136, 154.

26 Turner, *Caribbean Crusaders*, 59.

27 Hartman, *Wayward Lives*, 249–56.

28 Erik S. McDuffie, *Sojourning for Freedom: Black Women, American Communism, and the Making of Black Left Feminism* (Durham: Duke University Press, 2011), 45.

29 McDuffie, *Sojourning for Freedom*, 45.
30 Hermie Dumont, "Notes on the West Indies," *The Liberator* 1, no. 48 (15 March 1930): 3.
31 Hartman, *Wayward Lives*, 227–8.
32 "Shirley Graham (Mrs. W.E.B. Du Bois)," in folder WBE, p. 1, n.d., box 1, folder 35, HDHP.
33 Brent Hayes Edwards, *The Practice of Diaspora: Literature, Translation, and the Rise of Black Internationalism* (Cambridge, MA: Harvard University Press, 2003); Robin D.G. Kelley, "'But a Local Phase of a World Problem': Black History's Global Vision, 1883–1950," *Journal of American History* 86, no. 3 (December 1999): 1045–77; Margaret Stevens, *Red International and Black Caribbean: Communists in New York City, Mexico, and the West Indies, 1919–1939* (London: Pluto Press, 2017).
34 Kate A. Baldwin, *Beyond the Color Line and the Iron Curtain: Reading Encounters between Black and Red, 1922–1963* (Durham: Duke University Press, 2002); Joy Gleason Carew, *Blacks, Reds, and Russians: Sojourners in Search of the Soviet Promise* (New Brunswick: Rutgers University Press, 2008); Meredith L. Roman, *Opposing Jim Crow: African Americans and the Soviet Indictment of US Racism, 1928–1937* (Lincoln: University of Nebraska Press, 2012); Mark Solomon, *The Cry Was Unity: Communists and African Americans*, 1917–1936 (Jackson: University Press of Mississippi, 1998).
35 Baldwin, Beyond the Color Line, 21.
36 Gore, *Radicalism at the Crossroads*, 9. See also Ashley D. Farmer, *Remaking Black Power: How Black Women Transformed an Era* (Chapel Hill: University of North Carolina Press, 2017).
37 Turner, *Caribbean Crusaders*, 78.
38 Turner, *Caribbean Crusaders*, 187.
39 Turner, *Caribbean Crusaders*, 200.
40 Turner, *Caribbean Crusaders*, 59, 215–17. After several months in Antwerp, both Huiswouds were arrested, imprisoned for eight days, and deported to Amsterdam in September 1934. In December 1935, they moved to Paris to re-establish the *Negro Worker*'s headquarters.
41 Turner, *Caribbean Crusaders*, 227. See also "Gwendolyn Bennet" in folder WBE, n.d., box 1, folder 35, HDHP.
42 However, in Amsterdam, the US Consulate issued Hermina Dumont Huiswoud a restricted passport and pushed her to return to the US. In a letter to the American Committee for the Protection of Foreign Born, Huiswoud wrote: "I was told that because I was a communist I could only receive a passport if I agreed to return to the US. From friends in the USA, I had learned that the FBI had shown a lively interest in me." She received a valid passport without restrictions only in 1958. See, letter from Hermina Dumont Huiswoud to American Committee for the Protection of Foreign Born, 5 June 1975, box 1, folder 3, HDHP.

43 See chapters 6 and 10 in the current volume.
44 Boris Golender, "Iz istorii fotoisskustva Tashkenta," *Moi Gorod*, 17 July 2011, http://mg.uz/publish/doc/text56289_iz_istorii_fotoiskusstva _tashkenta.
45 The photo postcard as a genre was invented at the turn of the twentieth century, and, like photography more generally, became a vital tool in the production of ethnographic knowledge and constructions of the "other." Thus, in the 1840s, Sergei Levitsky, a pioneering photographer in the Russian empire, conducted his first experiments with daguerreotype photography, making images of the Caucasus. Russian imperial photography was in line with trends in other Western empires, representing Russia as a modern European power with a civilizing mission directed towards indigenous communities. After 1898, in the Russian Empire, more than 1,000 postcards with images of Central Asia were published. See Ali Behdad and Luke Gartlan, eds., *Photography's Orientalism: New Essays on Colonial Representation* (Los Angeles: Getty Research Institute, 2013); Inessa Koutienikova, "The Colonial Photography of Central Asia (1865–1923)," in *Dal Paleolitico al Genocidio Armeno Ricerche su Caucaso e Asia Centralea* cura di Aldo Ferrari, Erica Ianiro (Venice: Edizioni Ca' Foscari, 2015), 85–108; and David Prochaska and Jordana Mendelson, eds., *Postcards: Ephemeral Histories of Modernity* (University Park: Pennsylvania State University Press, 2010).
46 Craig Campbell, *Agitating Images: Photography against History in Indigenous Siberia* (Minneapolis: University of Minnesota Press, 2014), 184.
47 For similar critique, see Alastair Bonnett, "Communists Like Us: Ethnicized Modernity and the Idea of 'the West' in the Soviet Union," *Ethnicities* 2, no. 4 (December 2002): 435–67; Adeeb Khalid, "Backwardness and the Quest for Civilization: Early Soviet Central Asia in Comparative Perspective," *Slavic Review* 65, no. 2 (Summer 2006): 231–51; and Madina Tlostanova, "Why the Postsocialist Cannot Speak: on Caucasian Blacks, Imperial Difference, and Decolonial Horizons," in *Postcoloniality–Decoloniality–Black Critique: Joints and Fissures*, ed. Sabine Broeck and Carsten Junker (Frankfurt am Main: Campus Verlag, 2015), 159–74.
48 Stephanie Cronin, *Anti-Veiling Campaigns in the Muslim World: Gender, Modernism, and the Politics of Dress* (London: Routledge, 2014); Adrienne Edgar, "Emancipation of the Unveiled: Turkmen Women under Soviet Rule, 1924–29," *Russian Review* 62, no. 1 (2003): 132–49; Marianne Kamp, *The New Woman in Uzbekistan: Islam, Modernity, and Unveiling under Communism* (Seattle: University of Washington Press, 2006); Douglas Northrop, *Veiled Empire* (Ithaca: Cornell University Press, 2004); Mohira Suyarkulova, "Fashioning the Nation: Gender and Politics of Dress in Contemporary Kyrgyzstan," *Nationalities Papers* 44, no. 2 (2016): 247–65.
49 McDuffie, *Sojourning for Freedom*, 72.

50 McDuffie, *Sojourning for Freedom*, 73.
51 Baldwin, *Beyond the Color Line*, 90.
52 Baldwin, *Beyond the Color Lin*, 108, 115–16. See also Jennifer Wilson, "Queer Harlem, Queer Tashkent: Langston Hughes's 'Boy Dancers of Uzbekistan,'" *Slavic Review* 76, no. 3 (2017). Reading Hughes's "Boy Dancers of Uzbekistan" along with his writings on the 1920s Harlem queer scene within communities of colour, Wilson states that Hughes "gesture[s] not only towards an ethnic transnational awakened by Soviet internationalism, but to a translocal queer collective whose revolt was its own revolution." In his reading of Soviet practices, Hughes focuses on such figures as Tamara Khanum as well as "boy dancers" who challenge the normative Soviet image of a revolutionary as a heterosexual, cisgender Russian/Slavic male.
53 Turner, *Caribbean Crusaders*, 2.
54 Evelyn Louise Crawford and Mary Louise Patterson, eds., *Letters from Langston: From the Harlem Renaissance to the Red Scare and Beyond* (Berkeley: University of California Press, 2016), 97–8.
55 Turner, *Caribbean Crusaders*, 191.
56 "Louise Thompson" in folder WBE, n.d., page 2, box 1, folder 35, HDHP.
57 Lila Abu-Lughod, *Veiled Sentiments: Honor and Poetry in a Bedouin Society* (Berkeley: University of California Press, 1986); Saba Mahmood, *Politics of Piety: The Islamic Revival and the Feminist Subject* (Princeton: Princeton University Press, 2005); Fatima Mernissi, *Beyond the Veil: Male–Female Dynamics in Modern Muslim Society*, rev. ed. (Bloomington: Indiana University Press, 1987).
58 Ariella Aïsha Azoulay, *Potential History: Unlearning Imperialism* (New York: Verso, 2019), 6–7.
59 Ariella Aïsha Azoulay, *Civil Imagination: A Political Ontology of Photography*, trans. Louise Bethlehem (New York: Verso, 2015), 80.
60 Azoulay, *Civil Imagination*, 53.
61 Ali Iğmen, *Speaking Soviet with an Accent: Culture and Power in Kyrgyzstan* (Pittsburgh: University of Pittsburgh Press, 2012); Anara Moldosheva, "'Naberites' khrabrosti i prochtite vse!' Perepiska rabotnits Zhenotdelov Kyrgyzstana 1920-kh godov," in *Poniatiia o sovetskom v Tsentral'noi Azii: Al'manakh Shtaba*, no. 2, ed. Georgiia Mamedova and Oksany Shatalovoi (Bishkek: SHTAB Press, 2016), 210–69.
62 Some scholars underscore how early Soviet photo postcards served as a medium to disrupt the orientalist gaze. Photographers invented alternative techniques that strove to overcome unequal power dynamics between the photographer and the photographed. See Alexander D. Borovsky, "Max Penson in Uzbekistan," *History of Photography* 22, no. 1 (1998): 80–4; Anja Burghardt, "Picturing Non-Russian Ethnicities in

the Journals *Sovetskoe Foto* and *SSSR na Stroike* (1920s–1930s)," *Russian Literature* 103–5 (2019): 209–33; Helena Holzberger, "National in Front of the Camera, Soviet Behind It: Central Asia in Press Photography, 1925–1937," *Journal of Modern European History* 16, no. 4 (2018): 487–508; Timothy A. Nunan, "Soviet Nationalities Policy, *USSR in Construction*, and Soviet Documentary Photography in Comparative Context, 1931–1937," *Ab Imperio* 2 (2010): 47–92; Nunan, "A Union Reframed: Sovinformbiuro, Postwar Soviet Photography, and Visual Orders in Soviet Central Asia," *Kritika: Explorations in Russian and Eurasian History* 17, no. 3 (Summer 2016): 553–83; Alison Rowley, *Open Letters: Russian Popular Culture and the Picture Postcard, 1880–1922* (Toronto: University of Toronto Press, 2013); and Olga V. Shaburova, *Sovetskii mir v otkrytke* (Moskva: Kabinetnyi uchenyi, 2017).

63 Avery F. Gordon, *Ghostly Matters: Haunting and the Sociological Imagination* (Minneapolis: University of Minnesota Press. 1997), 98.
64 Gordon, *Ghostly Matters*, 41.
65 Turner, *Caribbean Crusaders*, ix.
66 Gordon, *Ghostly Matters*, 22.
67 WBE, n.d., box 1, folder 35, HDHP.
68 WBE. The 85-page corpus contains her notes about many radical and communist women she met in the US and around the world, such as Dolores Ibárruri, Ella Reeve Bloor, Sylvia Chen, Williana Burroughs, Grace Campbell, Thyra Edwards, Elizabeth Gurley Flynn, Shirley Graham Du Bois, Claudia Jones, Louise Thompson Patterson, Maria Ulianova, and Nadezhda Krupskaya. See also Anne Donlon, "Hermina Huiswoud, 'Thyra Edwards,' Women I Have Known Personally," *Palimpsest: A Journal on Women, Gender, and the Black International* 9, no. 1 (2020): 28–34.
69 Turner, *Caribbean Crusaders*, 191; "Williana Burroughs (1882–1945)" in WBE.
70 "Mme Benes" in WBE.
71 Helen Davis, "Who Really Rules Britania," *The Negro Worker* 7, no. 1 (January 1937): 5–7.
72 She published these articles under her pseudonym Helen Davis. Helen Davis, "Supporters of Colonial Rule," *The Negro Worker* 5, nos. 2–3 (February–March 1935): 13–15; Davis, "Egypt Awakes," *The Negro Worker* 5, no. 11 (December 1935): 18–19, 24; Davis, "Hitler Germany Demands Colonies," *The Negro Worker* 6, no. 2 (April 1936): 12–15, 22; Davis, "Palestine Arabs Revolt," *The Negro Worker* 6, no. 5 (July 1936): 8–11; Davis, "Abyssinia – A Year after Great Roman Holiday," *The Negro Worker* 7, no. 6 (June 1937): 6.
73 Helen Davis, "The Approaching War of 'Defence,'" *The Negro Worker* 4, no. 8 (December 1934): 5.
74 Helen Davis, "The Negro Workers and the Cuban Revolution," *The Negro Worker* 4, no. 1 (May 1934): 29.

75 Helen Davis, "The Rise and Fall of George Padmore as a Revolutionary Fighter," *The Negro Worker* 4, no.4 (August 1934): 15.
76 Helen Davis, "Stop the Disruptive Tactics of the Negro 'Leaders,'" *The Negro Worker* 4, no. 2 (June 1934): 22.
77 Davis, "The Rise and Fall of George Padmore," 15.
78 Turner, *Caribbean Crusaders*, 186.
79 Turner, *Caribbean Crusaders*, 191.
80 Turner, *Caribbean Crusaders*, 191.
81 "'La Pasionaria' (Dolores Ibárruri)" in folder WBE, undated, box 1, folder 35, HDHP.
82 "Krupskaya" in folder WBE, n.d., box 1, folder 35, HDHP.
83 "Polskaya (Translator)" in folder WBE, n.d., box 1, folder 35, HDHP.
84 "Shura," in folder WBE, p. 2, n.d., box 1, folder 35, *Hermina* HDHP.
85 Turner, Caribbean Crusaders, 190.
86 "Shura," in folder WBE, p. 5, n.d., box 1, folder 35, HDHP.

14 Desiring the USSR: Writers from Two Germanys in the Soviet Contact Zone

PHILIP GLEISSNER

In November 1965, the writer Hans Magnus Enzensberger (1929–2022), at the time a rising star among the West German leftist intelligentsia, wrote a letter to Ilya Ehrenburg in the Soviet Union. A future issue of his literary journal *Kursbuch* (*Railway Guide*), he explained, was going to feature an article titled "Our Catechism" ("Unser Katechismus"), which had developed a plan for peaceful coexistence and collaboration between the two German states.[1] Ehrenburg, Enzensberger suggested, could send a short comment that would be printed alongside the article. Nothing came of this request, which the seasoned Soviet writer declined politely, pleading his lack of knowledge on the matter.[2] This encounter is paradigmatic of the red migrations of German postwar intellectuals. I subsume under this term various kinds of global mobility that include but are not limited to long-term relocation as well as short-term displacement because of their similar patterns of cultural engagement. These eastward mobilities and transnational networks involving the Soviet Union relied on a unique constellation of institutional frameworks, literary practices, and personal relations, which are the three thematic foci of this chapter.

First, the networks rested on the foundations of official institutions that facilitated literary and cultural exchange: conferences and official visits arranged by the Union of Soviet Writers, as well as periodicals and publishing houses dedicated to literature in translation. Enzensberger initially met Ehrenburg at a reception that the latter hosted at his Moscow apartment following a 1963 writers' conference. Second, events such as this conference initiated or further shaped the contact zones for transnational literary exchanges in which political agendas, like Enzensberger's intervention into German postwar politics, could be realized via literary practice and projects like the *Kursbuch*. Third, these networks assumed a deeply personal dimension. Enzensberger recounts in his memoir how he connected with Ehrenburg on an intimate level in French – talking about the latter's Paris years, Picasso, Apollinaire, and the Café Rotonde.³ But it is the archival location of the correspondence that bears witness to another level of transnational intimacy: Enzensberger's letter is held in the archive of the Soviet poet Margarita Aliger at the Russian State Archive of Literature and Art (RGALI).⁴ Between 1967 and 1979, the West German author was married to the daughter of Aliger and Aleksandr Fadeev, Maria.

Through these three dimensions – institutional, literary, and personal – this chapter develops a model of the processes and structures that facilitated the emergence of transnational networks involving East and West Germans in the 1960s and 1970s. What this model cannot explain on its own, however, is the underlying mode of attraction that drew these actors towards the Soviet Union. Born in 1929, Enzensberger did not belong to the generation of socialists who were attracted to the project of a communist utopia, as was the case for the intellectuals of the 1920s and 1930s who figure in other chapters of this volume. The same applies to the West German literary organizer Hans Werner Richter (1908–93) and the East German writers Erwin (1912–94) and Eva Strittmatter (1930–2011, married 1956). Each of them struggled to realize their respective leftist agendas within the political realities that defined post-war Germany and the world during the Cold War at large.⁵ At the same time, the connections that these actors developed to the Soviet Union are very different from the West German left's later ties with the Soviet dissident movement, epitomized by Heinrich Böll's involvement in paving the path towards exile for Lev Kopelev and Alexander Solzhenitsyn.⁶

Determined by the pragmatism of post-Stalinist renegotiations of socialist ideals, the eastward mobilities of the 1960s cannot be explained solely in terms of oppositional solidarities or in terms of the revolutionary endeavour and enthusiasm for the Soviet project that had shaped the pre-war years. To explore alternative drivers of mobility, I follow scholarship in migration studies that eschews the schematic representations of migration in terms of push and pull factors, either as an escape from oppression or an attraction to economic improvement – a model that traditionally "relies on an idea of the migrant as a utility-maximizing individual."⁷ In pursuit of alternative ways to theorize migration, recent scholarship has instead positioned desire as a central element in the production of global mobility. Employing this conceptual framework, Francis Collins proposes, in the tradition of Gilles Deleuze and Félix Guattari, an understanding of "desire as the energies that draw different entities – human, non-human, symbolic – into relation with each other and [which] in the process generates social forms and affects."[8] In this chapter, I show that it is this kind of desire that generated a multiplicity of political and ideological meanings countering common twentieth-century narratives both of global mobility as movements of utility maximization and of Cold War East–West encounters as binary confrontation. It first found expression in the institutionally determined transnational contact zones of the 1960s and intensified through literary engagement and personal relationships. The desire for the post-Stalinist Soviet Union discussed in this chapter, I argue, occupies a unique position in that it does not incorporate the socialist state as an explicit ideal. In light of the experience of state terror and the continuous acts of encroachment by the Moscow political regime – from the suppression of the East German uprising of 17 June 1953 and the Hungarian Revolution of 1956 by the Soviet army to the campaign against Pasternak in 1958 – such idealism would have been naive. Instead, the Soviet Union figures as a screen for projecting alternative modes of cultural and social life in rejection of Western capitalist models.

"May Russian Writers Transcend the Borders of Socialist Realism": Institutions of the Contact Zone

In early August 1963, while representatives of the US, British, and Soviet governments convened in Moscow to sign the Partial Nuclear Test Ban Treaty, a very different kind of international meeting was held in Leningrad. It had been initiated by the Italian-based Association of European Writers (Comunità europea degli scrittori, or COMES). Founded by Giovanni Battista Angioletti and managed by Giancarlo Vigorelli and Giuseppe Ungaretti, COMES aimed to foster literary exchange across national borders in post-war Europe. The choice of Leningrad as the site of their conference gestured towards efforts to support dialogue between East and West.[9] Since COMES did not have a governing body or affiliated institutions aside from the literary journal *L'Europa letteraria* (*Literary Europe*, 1960–5), the logistics for the Leningrad meeting were managed by the Union of Soviet Writers.

Reports from the conference give the impression of a carefully orchestrated event that also offered opportunities for spontaneous exchange and unscripted encounters. In her work on colonial writing and travel, Mary Louise Pratt describes environments like this as contact zones, "social spaces where disparate cultures meet, clash, and grapple with each other, often in highly asymmetrical relations of domination and subordination."[10] These zones generate their own kinds of discourses and cultures, often hybrid assemblages from elements of the two systems clashing. That this approach lends itself well to the Soviet context has been demonstrated by Rossen Djagalov and Masha Salazkina, who apply it to the annual Tashkent Festival of African and Asian Cinema (started 1968). They argue that as a space of cultural exchange, the festival did not partake in Cold War binaries of East and West or North and South; rather, it had its own modes of operation with a noteworthy "variety and instability of hegemonies at play."[11] Indeed, the 1950s and 1960s contact zones of literary conferences and film and youth festivals generated new power dynamics and tactics that were rooted in the emergence of new transnational modes of organizing, which replaced the earlier internationalist model of the pre-war era.[12]

Literary conferences reflect a long history of Soviet ambitions in cultural internationalism and the project of shaping socialist world literature, beginning in the 1930s. In early iterations of these conferences, participants seem to have been able to align their political and ideological commitments somewhat consistently with the program of the Soviet state.[13] This political commitment became, in subsequent years, closely entangled with socialist realism as an "institution of control, normalization, and terror [that] was served by a doctrine whose main feature was maximum vagueness and main function was to conceal its real political functions," as Evgeny Dobrenko proposes.[14] The vast majority of German representatives among the forty foreign participants at the First Congress of the Union of Soviet Writers in 1934, for instance, had been either members of the German Communist Party or closely affiliated with Marxist groups or proletarian cultural organizations.[15] For them, the conferences were not merely a venue to develop socialist literature but also occasions for anti-fascist organizing.[16]

Between the pre-war conferences and the events of the 1960s lies the transition from the Soviet-dominated Comintern internationalism in culture to a more loosely defined transnational mode of collaboration that still relied on the Soviet space as the contact zone but that shifted power dynamics and, at least for a brief period, allowed for relative openness in terms of aesthetic doctrine. Moreover, the very cast of the literary networks had undergone a generational shift, although luminaries of the pre-war global literary left, such as Ilya Ehrenburg and Anna Seghers, continued to provide symbolic capital – as the letter from Enzensberger to Ehrenburg illustrates.

The political affiliations of the participants in 1963 were diverse. COMES's selection criteria seem to have been rather broad; the conference was open to writers with varying degrees of political attachment to the Soviet Union, but not to fascists and pronounced anti-communists, because, as the organizer Vigorelli explained, by announcing oneself as anti-communist, "one automatically falls into the fascist camp."[17] Among the attendees, representatives from France and Italy were in the majority. The French delegation included Jean-Paul Sartre and Simone de Beauvoir. Angus Wilson and William Golding came from the United Kingdom. Most East European nations were represented as well: Tibor Déry from Hungary, Dušan Matić from Yugoslavia, Ryszard Matuszewski from Poland, Jiří Hájek from Czechoslovakia, and Pantaley Zarev from Bulgaria, among others. Besides Erwin Strittmatter, the East German delegation featured three additional participants: the literary functionary Hans Koch, Buchenwald survivor and author of the concentration camp novel *Naked among Wolves* (*Nackt unter Wölfen*) Bruno Apitz, and the poet Paul Wiens.[18] West Germany was represented only by Richter and Enzensberger.

The choice of representatives was undoubtedly subject to pragmatic considerations that were particularly challenging with regard to the two German delegations. Authors from the GDR had to be in good standing with their own government, while their Western colleagues had to fulfil the minimal requirements in terms of ideological vetting. Both sides, however, had to contend with an issue that concerned most of the German post-war political and cultural elite: the requirement to not have been entangled with the Nazi regime. Richter checked this box easily, as did the thirty-four-year-old Enzensberger. Strittmatter's past was at the time largely unknown, and he had accumulated political capital in his leading position in the East German literary system.[19]

All three belonged to a new generation of writers who emerged in their respective German states after the war. Erwin Strittmatter's career as a prose author began in the early 1950s while he was working with Bertolt Brecht in East Berlin.[20] Although not always fully in line with the cultural bureaucracy of the GDR, he was awarded five National Prizes. Similarly, Hans Werner Richter emerged on the literary stage in the late 1940s as the initiator of the group of writers known as Gruppe 47. As organizer of this network, he had a foundational influence on the formation of West German literature and especially its branch that became closely affiliated with German social democracy under Willy Brandt in the 1960s. Starting with the 1955 meeting of Gruppe 47, Enzensberger became one of its recurring participants. Born in 1929, Enzensberger belonged to a different generation, one that did not have to account for its engagement with the Nazi regime and the war years, and his politics were rather noncommittal, aligning in fluctuating and, at times, rather radical ways with the German student movement of the late 1960s.

This group of relatively young German writers was met at the 1963 conference by the elite of the Soviet literary establishment: Mikhail Sholokhov, Konstantin Fedin, Konstantin Simonov, Ilya Ehrenburg, Leonid Leonov, and Boris Riurikov, who had just started his tenure as editor of the journal *Inostrannaia literatura* (*Foreign Literature*). The acclaimed Soviet writers' speeches at the congress were immediately published in *Literaturnaia gazeta* (*The Literary Newspaper*) and *Pravda*, and they focused, rather predictably, on the achievements of the Soviet novel as the key genre of the twentieth century. Across the board, their addresses turned the congress of the Association of European Writers into a domesticated Soviet event, a showcase of the achievements of socialist literature that did little to engage with the current literary moment outside the country.

After a lengthy discussion of the Soviet tradition of the novel, Fedin sought to pre-empt the objection of provincialism: "Those who conclude from this that Soviet literature proclaims artistic isolationism are mistaken."[21] He rightly emphasized that the Soviet Union was a world leader in literary translation. At the same time, he singled out the works of Proust, Joyce, and especially Kafka, acclaimed in the West, as particularly worthy of critique: "We do not believe that one should turn to this variety of decadence in the pursuit of innovation."[22] Proust and Joyce were accessible in Russian translation, Kafka less so. The significance of his work was fiercely disputed in Eastern Europe at the time.[23] In the discussions that unfolded at the 1963 conference, Kafka, Proust, and Joyce were recurring names, coming to serve as shorthand for deviations from the realist novel that the Soviet hosts consistently reprimanded.

Konstantin Simonov's address to the congress further alienated some of the West European visitors. Dedicated to the theme of the writer's responsibility to society, it attacked artistic individualism; some of the guests later objected to this in their own contributions.[24] Here, the contact zone was provided its raison d'être by the symbolic re-enactment of socialist realist discourse. At the same time, however, the dominant role played by Moscow in literary organizing was no longer enough to bring together a closed front of socialist realism among its partners abroad. As Dobrenko observes with regard to the post-Stalinist Soviet Union, the aesthetic doctrine's "institutional existence was pretty much guaranteed but [was], at the same time, deprived of its instrumental status"; it "had only symbolic value and belonged to a category of an almost epic past."[25] The foreign guests were thus allowed to operate outside the regime of socialist realism. While the presentations from the Soviet side seem to have been consistently conservative, the fact that the dissenting positions of some of the conference guests from abroad found their way into the Soviet press attests to an atmosphere of openness.

Inostrannaia literatura printed excerpts from the Western authors' responses. They showed that within the space of the contact zone, ideological and aesthetic positions that might not have been possible in domestic Soviet discourse were permissible for foreign authors. Pratt calls this process transculturation, which describes "how subordinated or marginal groups select and invent from materials transmitted to them by a dominant or metropolitan culture."[26] As Pratt explains, while the repertoire of ideas and forms is predetermined, there is a degree of freedom when it comes to choosing and appropriating from that repertoire. Richter was probably furthest away from such a hybrid approach, dismissing the debate about Kafka and Joyce as dated, and he concluded his speech with the rather daring expression of his hope "that Russian writers may soon transcend the boundaries of socialist realism."[27] Richter's own reminiscences corroborate this: irritated by a severe hangover and a disengaged audience, he "declared Soviet literature of the last years backwards" and claimed it yielded incomprehension among readers – comments that, as he found out later, made him an instant favourite among the convention's interpreters.[28]

Enzensberger made a somewhat half-hearted attempt at transcending the distinction between realism and experimental prose by suggesting an alternative focus on the novel as a genre committed to history and proposing that a multiplicity of aesthetics were available and necessary to aptly describe it. As he explained, Kafka, Proust, and Joyce modelled a mode of exploring history that could be appropriate for specific topics. Realism, he continued, was not always sufficient for the exploration of history; there had been times when he experienced his own life as Kafkaesque – especially his encounters with fascism, which he defined as a phenomenon that cannot be fully explained, a mystery.[29] This laconic statement made him the focus of his older East German colleagues' attention and scorn.

The most productive and contentious element in the German visitors' tactics of transculturation was thus not the question of socialist realism but history. While the colleagues from the GDR also sought a more nuanced and affirmative take on the realist novel and the writer's responsibility, they quite aggressively fixated on Enzensberger and his reference to fascism as a mystery. In his diary, Strittmatter found harsh words for his West German colleague: "How powerful Simonov appeared yesterday compared to the West German windbag and know-it-all Enzensberger. As village youths, we met visitors from the city like this: For a while we watched as they'd intrude upon our sacred games and things. By the third day at the latest, we would beat them up."[30] Other members of the East German delegation directly targeted Enzensberger in their addresses. Paul Wiens described in detail the sadism he had witnessed in the concentration camp, polemically adding that Enzensberger declaring this kind of violence mysterious was the only thing that was truly Kafkaesque. Hans Koch expanded the discussion by listing literary texts that had successfully dealt with fascism beyond the established binary.[31]

In his recent book, *From Internationalism to Postcolonialism*, Djagalov revisits Pratt's theory, highlighting that Soviet contact zones, which often included representatives from the Global South, "lacked the obvious violence" that Pratt had identified in the colonial era.[32] The same cannot be said of the 1963 conference as a contact zone because it involved actors from the two German states at a time when both the recent past of German aggression and the contemporary threats of the Cold War loomed large. On top of that, the conference brought them to an urban space traumatized by the genocidal ambitions of Nazi warfare during the Siege of Leningrad less than twenty years prior.

On an excursion to the Leningrad Siege Memorial at the Piskarevskoe Cemetery, Strittmatter took a leading role in representing Germany. Overwhelmed by what he called "collective shame," he reports that he wrote the following in the guestbook: "Whatever lies within our power to do we will do to make sure that war will never again be brought to Leningrad *from the German side* [italics in the original]."[33] Enzensberger signed Strittmatter's statement, but the latter remained mistrustful of his colleague's sincerity. Facing German guilt did not unify representatives from East and West. One does not need to dig deep into the participants' reminiscences of the events to detect an atmosphere of mutual disregard, suspicion, and even contempt between the two small German delegations; their incompatibility inhibited any exchange on matters of politics, ideology, or even literary aesthetics, which was, after all, the primary subject of the meeting.

The disconnect between East and West German authors can be seen as a failure of the COMES project of East–West dialogue. This is surprising in light of the aspirations of détente that Richter and Enzensberger pursued elsewhere. Here, they withdrew from dialogue with writers respected by the socialist state. Ultimately, the Soviet contact zone, even with its relative freedom, did not allow for the intertwining of the two German camps. The rejection of the writer Uwe Johnson exemplifies this. Originally slotted to travel as part of the West German delegation, he was denied participation by the Soviet side, the concrete circumstances of which remain unclear. Johnson had left the GDR in

1959 and settled in West Germany; his ambitions to travel east would have blurred borders, creating a kind of ambiguity that was politically impermissible. After the conference, Johnson's efforts to visit the Soviet Union, supported by Enzensberger, continued for several years.[34]

The longing Johnson had for the Soviet space is noteworthy. His "move" (*Umzug*), as he called it, to the Federal Republic was a result of the publication of his second novel, *Mutmassungen über Jakob* (*Speculations about Jakob*), with the West German publisher Suhrkamp after his work was rejected in East Germany.[35] Although he maintained connections to the GDR, Johnson was thus well aware of the oppressive conditions of the country's cultural and political system, which mirrored the Soviet one. This is the paradox of German desires for eastward mobility: the simultaneous possibility to envision a productive space for the realization of cultural and political agendas and the acknowledgment of its politically insufficient realities. For East Germans, especially during the Thaw, the Soviet Union may have appeared to be a more liberal space.[36] But, as should be clear from the transcripts of conference discussions in Leningrad, for the West German writers, the Soviet Union was ideologically unattractive, which sets the 1960s contact zone apart from the contact zone of early 1930s internationalism. But as Johnson's correspondence reveals, a different kind of desire for the Soviet space persisted. As Collins suggests in his theory of desire as a driver of migration, desire is not about the pursuit of a clearly defined object; rather, it "manifests in terms of becoming otherwise, being drawn into another world that is expressed by these possibilities, becoming migrant."[37] Of course, Richter, Enzensberger, and Strittmatter were not migrants – an issue I will address in the following section – but their transnational involvements nonetheless opened trajectories towards becoming, towards "dynamic social and material assemblages" that constitute the desirable element also of global mobility.[38] The contact zone of 1963 provided a stage for this kind of realization of desire.

The Writers' Intourist: Mobile Desires and Their Literary Assemblage

After conference sessions and the accompanying sightseeing program had ended, the German participants enjoyed their time off in Moscow. Strittmatter noted in his diary: "Shopping stroll. On my own. Gorky Street, GUM. Nice. Many observations. On your own you see more."[39] While Strittmatter took advantage of the Soviet capital, Enzensberger joined a small delegation of authors who had been invited to meet Nikita Khrushchev in Gagra, an event that he recalls in his 2015 memoir

Tumult. The stiff, ceremonious nature of the meeting was relieved only by a brief swim in the Black Sea together with Khrushchev, for which Enzensberger claims to have borrowed one of the Soviet leader's bathing suits.[40]

It is not surprising that the visits facilitated by the Union of Soviet Writers were as much welcome occasions for leisure travel, inspiring literary productivity, as they were opportunities for official business. Writers were not the only ones keen to travel to the Soviet Union. Tourists had been visiting the country since the late 1950s, and about one million of them were coming to the Soviet Union annually by 1965.[41] What they shared with some of the authors was a curiosity about how Soviet socialist modernity blended with local colour in an orientalist key. This section focuses on the writers' touristic proclivities in addition to their deeper intellectual involvement. I demonstrate how the Soviet space beyond the literary contact zone of the conference became a destination for leftist intellectuals and an object of desire, which ultimately found expression in literary productivity. I argue that if "social production is purely and simply desiring-production itself under determinate conditions," as Deleuze and Guattari suggest, we can consider literary works, travelogues, memoirs, and even literary correspondence as actualizations of the desire for Soviet assemblages by the writers.[42]

Of course, these short-term encounters with the Soviet Union were different from the long-term displacements of migrants. As Caren Kaplan observes, "all displacements are not the same," but there is still a significant overlap between travel and other kinds of global displacement.[43] The figure of the migrant permeates imaginaries of mobility as a trope, and travel and migration are often propelled by the same kinds of attraction: consumerism, adventure, ideological proclivities. Reading the accounts of the German writers, one may get the impression that they treated the Union of Soviet Writers as an alternative to the state travel agency Intourist, effectively creating their own boutique writers' Intourist.

The point person for travel arrangements at the Union of Soviet Writers was Aleksei Surkov, who had been its secretary until 1959 and who organized the visits of Western writers, such as Enzensberger's attendance at his second, politically engaged congress, a 1966 writers' conference on behalf of the Vietnamese people in Baku, Azerbaijan. As Enzensberger laid out in his response to the initial invitation, he had doubts as to whether he could contribute to the goals of the congress and whether a literary meeting could make any difference with regard to the Vietnam War. Nonetheless, he was pleased "to take advantage of the opportunity to get to know the Soviet Union better," and wrote that he would like to also "see the Asian parts of [the] country, especially Tashkent, Alma Ata, and Siberia," talk to Soviet scientists in Akademgorodok, and realize his "long-held dream" of travelling on the Trans-Siberian Railway.[44] A shift from the conferences of the 1930s is tangible here. Participation was no longer imagined as a politically meaningful engagement but was simply an opportunity to travel, which appears to have been acceptable to the Union of Soviet Writers.

The same place names can be found in the writings of other authors who attended Soviet literary conferences. Eva Strittmatter's correspondence with her family's closest Soviet friends, Lev Kopelev and Raisa Orlova, demonstrates her enchantment with Soviet localities. In 1965, Samarkand had captivated her attention, but then she moved on to Kirghizia: "I remember something about Issikul (?) and a lake, mountains and warmth, healthy mountain air and especially horses ... Erwin is ignited by the thought of THIS journey."[45] Next, the "famous name" of the Russian city Vladimir attracted her. Like the city of Tula, it "has a beautiful sound to [her] ear."[46] For another visit, Erwin and Eva considered a cruise on the Volga and trips to the Caucasus.[47] Georgia and Armenia and sanatoriums in Yalta, Yerevan, and Kislovodsk were recurring items on her list. Then, a trip to the Russian North seemed appealing – as long as it was not with a large group of tourists.[48] Over a period of nearly ten years, barely a letter went by without a passionate discussion of these possible destinations, only a fraction of which bore fruit.

Richter petitioned the Union of Soviet Writers for an extensive tour of the Tajik, Turkmen, and Uzbek Republics, in service of a specific literary goal. His interest in the region had likely been aroused by a voluminous body of travel literature on the Soviet Union. There is a long German tradition of writing about Russia – both pre-revolutionary and early Soviet.[49] Politically engaged themselves, the earlier authors of such works transcended the gaze of the travel writer, demonstrating in their contribution to the internationalist project the "multiplicity of involvements" that is characteristic of transnational social networks.[50]

Among the most noteworthy products of these early Soviet encounters were Egon Erwin Kisch's two books of reportage, which were instant successes in Germany but were later banned by the Nazis (see also Katerina Clark's account of Kisch in chapter 7). Contemporary Soviet commentators such as Anatoly Lunacharsky viewed Kisch favourably.[51] In Russia, Kisch's success endured. In a 1958 essay, critic Aleksandr Dymshits refers to him as "a proletarian internationalist," "a devoted friend of the Soviet people," and "a writer dedicated with his whole heart to the workers' struggle for socialism."[52] The Slavist Harold

Segel, on the other hand, has raised doubts about Kisch's commitment to communism.[53] Thus, evaluating the Revolution and the nascent socialist utopia as a genuine pull factor motivating leftist mobilities may be an insufficient approach even in this earlier context. This is further illustrated by a scene from Kisch's 1932 work *Asien gründlich verändert* (*Changing Asia*, 1932). In response to Kisch's fascination with the cultural heritage of Uzbekistan, one of his local informants exclaims: "To hell with all of you! ... You come to Samarkand, you Europeans – workmen, economists, Marxists, scholars, writers – and not one of you cares to look at our technical plants, our experimental institutes, our factories, our housing schemes, our waterworks in Revat-Khodsha, our clubs, our Farmers' Home, our hospitals and maternity wards. All you come here for is to see something romantic."[54] Thus, instead of interest in the achievements of the First Five-Year Plan in Central Asia, the visitor has displayed a romanticism that his interlocutor finds abominable: an essentialization of local culture of the past has obstructed the guest's view of the modernization project of the present.

Kisch's ironic retelling of this incident shows some distance, however. After all, the goal of his trip was not to produce an exoticizing account of this East – at least not exclusively. His reportage makes it clear that what most engaged him was the contrasts he observed. Already in his 1927 book *Tsars, Priests, Bolsheviks* (*Zaren, Popen, Bolschewiken*), he combines national tradition and socialist innovation: he describes factories, reformed prisons, lectures about sexually transmitted infections, and an enthusiastic visit to the Marx-Engels Institute; May Day celebrations figure alongside Easter processions and ethnographic reports from the Caucasus republics about the "curious demeanour of a Turkish bath attendant" in Tbilisi and about a traditional theatre performance in Azerbaijan, attended "by the whole Bible – Lea, Rahel, Rebekka, and Hagar – and the rest of the Orient – Scheherazade, Fatmé, Salome, and their comrades."[55] Kisch's reportage satisfies the German readers' demand for exotic imagery, which he weaves into the spectacle of a new social order.

Kisch applies the same approach in *Changing Asia*, but the observations he makes at the end of the First Five-Year Plan are even more enthusiastic with regard to Soviet social progress. About thirty years later, Richter would continue this approach in *Karl Marx in Samarkand: A Journey to the Border of China* (*Karl Marx in Samarkand. Eine Reise an die Grenzen Chinas*, 1966). In fact, that book would not have been feasible without Kisch's text as a forerunner. It prominently features a photo of Kisch on the first pages, retraces his steps, and often makes references to his writing. And it was not just Richter who armed himself with Kisch;

the representative of the Union of Soviet Writers who was in charge of the West German guest had also "read the book carefully." As Richter recalls, "In places, he knows it by memory. Kisch quotes are a matter of course."[56]

As John Zilcosky has observed, "we inevitably experience foreign lands in terms of the books we read, and these lands eventually *become* [italics in the original] the texts we write about them."[57] Similarly, Richter's *Karl Marx in Samarkand* triangulates earlier texts, Soviet realities, and the writer's own political and aesthetic program. The book's investment in intertextual topographies materializes in the form of maps that were included with the first edition as individual postcard inserts: "Central Asia in the Times of Kisch" and "Central Asia Today." The former is a reproduction of the map included in earlier editions of *Changing Asia* (figure 14.1). Relying on numerous pictographs – of tiny mosques, hydroelectric power stations, cotton plants, trains, and airplanes – this map expresses Richter's fascination with local culture, Soviet modernity, and exotic adventure, which were so central also to the 1932 book. A large-scale rendering of Europe and the Soviet Union inserted in the bottom left corner reminds the reader of the distance between Berlin and Central Asia. The second map, "Central Asia Today," merely depicts cities, rivers, and borders, which, of course, remain largely unchanged from Kisch's day. The most notable change, unrelated to these authors' travels, is the emergence of independent nation-states south of the Soviet border after the independence of British India. Topographically, however, Richter is visiting the same Central Asia, and the publisher of his book could easily have done without the second map altogether. The biggest difference between the maps has to do with the level of representation of society, culture, and economy, now absent, conveying a loss of adventure, exoticism, and the notion of a nascent Soviet utopia, which the author now needs to re-create through intertextual reference. Desire for this social space is not a longing for a concrete locality but a "force involved in the production and arrangements of social forms."[58] The traces of Kisch's past engagement with Central Asia are among those social forms available to Richter.

This act of desiring precedes the political, even for Richter, who worked closely with the Social Democratic Party under Willy Brandt in Germany.[59] In *Karl Marx in Samarkand*, his engagement with ideology and politics is slippery, often limited to observations about the rhetoric of Soviet communism. Again and again, Richter notices statues and portraits of Karl Marx. From a mural at the Tashkent airport, Marx "smiles at [Richter], as if he wanted to say, 'Well, my friend, theoretically, Tashkent is only one step removed from Trier [Marx's German birthplace] –

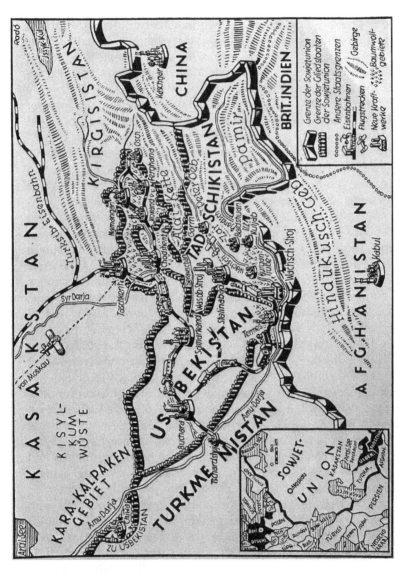

Figure 14.1. Intertextual geographies: "Central Asia in the Times of Kisch," an insert from Richter's book. The key of the map explains the different pictographs. Aside from borders (of the Soviet Union, between Soviet republics, and other states), it features: railways, aviation routes, new power plants, mountain ranges, and cotton-farming areas.

dialectically speaking.'"⁶⁰ Richter proposes that it is in Central Asia, "where there has never been a proletariat," that Marx did more for the people than in Europe.⁶¹ Yet the author appears entirely uninterested in Marx's actual ideas – something that surprised his Soviet interlocutors. "[In Central Asia], Karl Marx is a god of German descent, and no one can understand how a German could not admire him."⁶² It is on this point that Richter and Kisch part ways, revealing a change in the perception of revolutionary geographies. Kisch expresses greater admiration for Marxist research and teaching in the early Soviet Union; Richter engages with Marxism in Central Asia rather superficially if not light-heartedly, making it more digestible for his West German readers, most of whom had, by the 1960s, lost their taste for Soviet-style communism.

Kisch's presence in the text allows Richter to rely largely on a comparative mode of description to take inventory of social and industrial progress. The small airplanes of Kisch's time, limited in reach and comfort, have been replaced by one of the achievements of late Soviet aviation, the Ilyushin Il-18. New irrigation projects and large-scale agriculture make Richter optimistic about the future. Silk factories and automated weaving mills have replaced the small textile workshops, and it appears that the industrial modernization of Central Asia has gone hand in hand with new roles for women in society. Richter, like his predecessor in the 1930s, focuses almost obsessively on the declining presence of veils as an indicator of women's liberation (see also Bradley Gorski's discussion of the interest of Western visitors in Soviet deveiling in chapter 6). He repeatedly states, not without satisfaction, that the past has been left further behind, although he is still startled by the invisibility of women in public. All of these observations speak to modernization in relative rather than absolute terms. References to Kisch enable Richter to make a compelling case about social and technological progress.

The desire that generated *Karl Marx in Samarkand* seems to have been short-lived. Looking through the page proofs in 1966, Richter himself concedes in his diary that the book "now appears somewhat clumsy."⁶³ Like the map of "Central Asia Today," Richter's experience of actually existing socialism has become depleted. Moreover, the assemblages that emerged for Richter were not meaningful for his Soviet counterparts – much like how Kisch's host had no interest in his seemingly romantic attachment to ancient Central Asian history. In *Karl Marx in Samarkand*, Richter repeatedly asks his hosts about their recollections of the visit of his venerated Kisch but finds most of them uninterested. His personal translator, Kostja, is "irritated by the constant 'Kisch-ing'" and considers Kisch a "banal travel writer."⁶⁴ Richter further reports how the Uzbek poet Nassyrulla Akhundi remembers an evening with Kisch and André Gide, who, as is later confirmed, had never been to Tashkent. Confronted with this historical inaccuracy, Akhundi shrugs his shoulders and says, "Then it must have been someone else."[65] It appears that by the 1960s, Western European intellectuals visiting Central Asia have become indistinguishable and that they have little lasting impact locally. The desire involved in the eastward mobility of German intellectuals remains unintelligible to local interlocutors, who do not recognize their own current reality in the literary assemblages of the visitors.

Kostja, Lowa, Mascha: The Personal

While the individual itineraries of German visitors to the Soviet Union in the 1960s varied, their paths through the country intersected in the person who served as their interpreter, fondly referred to as Kostja.[66] The Soviet Germanist and translator Konstantin Bogatyrev is one node of the friendship networks that initially emerged around official institutional frameworks and literary travel. These networks involved an increasing level of intimacy and brought to the fore transnational desires as a social force.

Bogatyrev was a Germanist by training and a survivor of the Gulag, where he spent six years (1951–6). Upon his return, he became an avid translator of Rainer Maria Rilke and Erich Kästner and cultivated connections with writers and Slavists in the West.[67] As their translator at the 1963 conference, Bogatyrev approached Richter and Enzensberger with such openness and familiarity that they initially suspected him of being a provocateur – a thought that was quickly abandoned.[68] In a humorous tone, Richter's reminiscences present Bogatyrev as a thoughtful guide who explained to him the workings of Soviet culture, helped with bureaucratic transactions, accompanied him on fur shopping sprees, warned him about the advances of sex workers, and even helped him retrieve his lost dentures.[69] After Bogatyrev was brutally murdered in 1976, presumably by the KGB, Richter wrote a moving essay about his friend, remembering their last farewell at the Moscow airport about ten years prior, after Bogatyrev had accompanied him on his trip to Central Asia to work on *Karl Marx in Samarkand*: "Tears were falling from your eyes, and you kept repeating again and again: 'Take me with you, take me with you.' But I couldn't take you with me, and had I been able to, everything would have been very different: our travel and our conversations. And maybe you would not even have wanted to leave with me."[70]

It is in personal relationships that the multidirectional nature of transnational desire becomes visible. Bogatyrev's longing was, of course, not for Richter as a person, nor did he truly seem to long for relocation to the West. Even in the late 1960s, when he was increasingly at odds with the state, Bogatyrev refused to consider leaving the country, not wanting to sacrifice "the close relationship to the Russian language" that a departure would have meant.[71] What is therefore desired is a constellation, an unattainable realm, similar to what Aleksey Yurchak calls the Imaginary West, which "signif[ies] an imaginary place that was simultaneously knowable and unattainable, tangible and abstract, mundane and exotic. This concept was disconnected from any 'real' abroad and located in some unspecified place."[72] But for Bogatyrev, Germany was certainly more concrete, involving a wide network of contacts with Western intellectuals. A 1982 volume compiled in his honour by the German Slavist Wolfgang Kasack bears witness to the friendship networks he built: the book includes contributions by Heinrich Böll, Gleb Struve, and Roman Jakobson, as well as by Soviet dissidents and émigrés such as Lev Kopelev and Vasily Aksenov.

Much like the literary work discussed earlier, these personal relationships operated within spaces that were shaped neither by complete imagination and absolute projection nor by unmediated access. The German visitors' desires for transnational networks and literary production involving the Soviet Union are remarkable for their concurrent capacity to perceive Soviet reality and project onto it. The simultaneous involvement of German writers and their Soviet counterparts in these red migrations created situations of ideological ambivalence, constellations that Caren Kaplan and Inderpal Grewal have described through the concept of scattered hegemonies, challenging "the master narrative of cultural imperialism through specific articulations of transnational identities and relationships."[73] The relationships cannot be understood in terms of Cold War dichotomies of socialist and pro-Soviet versus dissident and anti-Soviet. Yet for Richter, witnessing his friend's longing for mobility generated the desire to help. He repeatedly tried to invite Bogatyrev to Germany, including to one of his Gruppe 47 conferences. At a meeting in East Berlin in early 1964, he approached Lev Kopelev in the hope that he could mediate with the Union of Soviet Writers to arrange a visit.[74] The mobility of the German actors was thus closely intertwined with the *im*mobility of the Soviet one, at times generating enough energy for the Soviet counterpart to join in the migrations – as was the case for Richter's friend Enzensberger.

Although Enzensberger, too, met Bogatyrev, the translator plays only a minor role in his reminiscences. The major relationship that he developed in the Soviet Union created transnational social assemblages that were more disruptive – politically and aesthetically as well as socially – ultimately displacing a Soviet citizen to the West. This mobility came about as a result of a relationship that unfolded after Enzensberger's participation in the above-mentioned 1966 meeting of the Soviet Committee for Relations with Writers from Africa and Asia in Baku, dedicated to the Vietnam War.[75] Enzensberger may have been viewed as a desirable presence in this thematic context, since he had emerged as a prominent voice in the West German movement against the war. A note in *Literaturnaia gazeta* explains that "his poems evoke great interest among readers, especially in progressive circles among the youth."[76] It is around this time that Enzensberger's attitude vis-à-vis the society and politics of the Federal Republic became increasingly unforgiving; he radically rejected the country's political system as unsalvageable, a position that may have contributed significantly to how he approached transnational relationships. German commentators have labelled his stance a performance of anti-bourgeois *épatage* that still relied on the society it was trying to provoke.[77]

This oppositional stance may have paved Enzensberger's way to Baku and his contact with the Soviet literary elite. At an official dinner, he was seated next to poet Margarita Aliger and twenty-three-year-old Mascha – Maria Makarova, the daughter of Aliger and the acclaimed Soviet writer Aleksandr Fadeev. Enzensberger seems to have been intrigued by the literary gossip around the family and their connections to the upper echelons of Soviet literature.[78] The romantic affair that unfolded with Makarova shifted the focus of his Soviet desire. Enzensberger quickly lost interest in the trip around the Soviet Union that had been arranged at his request by the Union of Soviet Writers; he now felt compelled to embark on it.[79] Upon his return to Moscow, the liaison with Makarova took its course. Their 1967 wedding, following Enzensberger's divorce from his first wife, Dagrun, finally allowed the couple to relocate to Berlin.

International statistics of contemporary migration indicate that family ties are the most common motivating (and legitimizing) factor in global mobility.[80] The case of Enzensberger, as documented in his memoir, which covers both his personal turmoil and his politically most radical years, exemplifies how a political dimension can figure in transnational family networks. His relationship seems embedded in his performance of the role of a public intellectual, and his "amour fou," he claims, can explain where he ended up "geographically and politically."[81] And while marriage to a Soviet citizen inevitably reinforced his various efforts to sever his ties with the conservative society of the Federal Republic, it did not bring him closer to the Soviet Union, geographically or politically, for neither did he seem particularly interested in relocating eastward, nor did he succeed in getting continuously involved in that country's literary process.

Already at the meeting of poets that Enzensberger attended in Tbilisi after his journey around the Soviet Union in 1966, he defended the instability of poetic identities, in defiance of the dominant understanding of the social significance of literature.[82] Responding to the preceding speaker, his Soviet benefactor Aleksei Surkov, he rejected the tendency to ascribe specific roles or responsibilities to poets, a practice that he identified as a specifically Soviet problem.[83] It appears that whenever Enzensberger took public positions on Soviet culture, they were antagonistic. In 1967, he published the essay "Kronstadt 1921 or the Third Revolution," a piece that examined the failure of the revolutionary project.[84] As a consequence of these repeated statements, Enzensberger's goodwill in the Soviet Union finally ran out, and he was no longer invited as an official representative of German literature.[85]

Enzensberger's red migrations – although born of commitments to the political left or possibly the desire to disrupt what he found to be a stagnant German society – manifested themselves not as an affirmative search for ideological alternatives but rather as mobilities of negation, with the Soviet Union serving merely as the locus for antagonistic positioning.[86] The country figures in his political imagination along destructive lines. In February 1968 he wrote to his wife, "Have you heard about the big fascist demonstration in Berlin? It's going to be more and more of a dangerous place to live in. I wish the Soviets would put their foot down. A few days of blockade would be a good thing."[87] While it is doubtful that Enzensberger truly desired an escalation of the Cold War on German territory, the statement points to his general experience of disconnect from the Federal Republic and its politics, mirrored in his constant geographic relocations.

Enzensberger's relationship with Maria motivated his travels and his search for a new home for the two. Berlin quickly proved to be an unlivable place for the couple. His attempt to take a fellowship year at Wesleyan University in Connecticut failed. Protesting the war in Vietnam and US foreign policy at large, Enzensberger withdrew from the position after a few months, not missing the opportunity to publicly perform his outrage by printing his letter of resignation in the *New York Review of Books* in January 1968.[88] Correspondence between the couple, archived with the Margarita Aliger papers, documents how constant relocation, political torment, and difficult personal relations aligned. In letters to his wife from California, Tahiti, Australia, and Singapore, the tone he takes about political events is increasingly aggressive and the quest for a place to settle consistently challenging. The only constant seems to have been Enzensberger's lack of interest in living in the Soviet Union. Ultimately, Cuba presented itself as an option for the couple, but it was a rather short-lived one.[89]

The end of Enzensberger's marriage to Maria also marks an end point of the German author's engagement with the Soviet Union. When the couple's discontent, documented in archival sources, is placed alongside Enzensberger's sensationalist treatment of the turmoil of the 1960s in his memoir, an unfortunate image of a marriage appears – one that appears like part of a political and artistic performance.[90] This is where transnational desire exhausts itself, where the social assemblages that it generates deteriorate. As Deleuze and Guattari suggest, "desiring-machines," which could be understood here as the mechanisms that generate transnational social assemblages, "continually break down as they run, and in fact run only when they are not functioning properly: the product is always an offshoot of production, implanting itself like a graft, and at the same time the parts of the machine are the fuel that makes it run."[91]

The development of intense attachment and its breakdown can also be seen in the correspondence between Eva and Erwin Strittmatter and a Soviet couple, the Germanist Lev Kopelev and the translator Raisa Orlova. The two families were connected by their literary work. Kopelev had published reviews of Erwin's work and helped make it popular in the Soviet Union.[92] Erwin Strittmatter, for his part, had valuable information for Kopelev's project, a biography of Bertolt Brecht, since he had worked as Brecht's assistant in the 1950s.[93]

The Kopelev Archive holds more than sixty letters from the Strittmatters, most of them written by Eva. Often many pages long, they suggest significant intimacy between the families.[94] But like Bogatyrev's officially sanctioned work with foreign guests, this relationship featured elements of both the official and the subversive. The couples were intertwined in ways that became challenging to navigate by the late 1960s, by which time Kopelev's involvement with the dissident movement can be felt in the letters. Increasingly, the two parties could only be held together by personal affection, which slowly dissipated as well. This attachment is evident in letters from Eva Strittmatter to Kopelev, whom she fondly addresses as Lowa: "I am full of longing for you, for Moscow, your country, for our friends, for a bit of freedom and levity, ideas and poems."[95] In the assemblage of the desire for eastward mobility, friendship is woven in with literary passion and with attraction to the country as a destination and, for the East Germans, as a space of intellectual freedom.

Aside from the continuous travel planning, correspondence between the two families included conversations about everyday events and arrangements for exchanging goods (gifts, consumer products, medications, and even spare parts for a samovar that had stopped functioning, much to Eva's disappointment).[96] The most important topic, however, remained literature. Kopelev shared with Eva Strittmatter – who continued to study Russian – poems by Alexander Pushkin and Anna Akhmatova in interlinear translation.[97] While some of these works were available in the GDR, the exchange with Kopelev seems to have given the Strittmatters a different kind of access to Russian literature, as Eva expressed regarding a current volume of German translations of another poet: "of the Pasternak that I have encountered through the two of you, nothing remains."[98] Eva shared with Kopelev her own poetry and her thoughts on recently published translations; she also provided updates about her progress in learning Russian and reports from increasingly frequent trips to literary conferences in the Soviet Union and Yugoslavia. Her decade's worth of letters, which are imbued with longing to connect to the rest of the socialist world, reveal that transnational "desire as a social force is necessarily affirmative in that it emphasizes the processes of becoming that migration entails."[99]

By the late 1960s, it was clear that the Strittmatters' investment in the Soviet space did not align with the increasingly oppositional position that Kopelev had assumed. In the case of the German–Soviet transnational desires, the continuous breakdown of the desiring-machines – to again use Deleuze and Guattari's term – was accelerated as those machines were worn out by the grit of the political turn at the end of the Thaw – by the crackdown in Czechoslovakia and the intensification of dissident resistance to the Soviet regime, which had already set in after the Sinyavsky–Daniel trial of 1965–6. A letter from Eva Strittmatter to Kopelev from early 1968 expresses disappointment over their failure to meet during a recent trip, alluding to restrictions that were the result of his political statements: "We are not sure if the price that you are paying for certain things isn't too high? And it should be clear that this is the price for certain things."[100] Gaps between letters grow, and sadness over a dissolving friendship begins to dominate, interrupted only occasionally by the hope for renewed closeness. In a letter from December 1968, Eva writes: "The old differences between us remain, dear Raja and dear Lowa (although in recent years it appeared to us as if Raja stood a little closer to our opinions).

As a result, we'll have to do without you, now that we cannot visit. It has been hard to get used to this thought. In our life, you were something unique and irreplaceable."[101]

The archive holds several more years of letters, which oscillate between celebration of friendship and sadness over its dissipation, before it cuts off in 1974.[102] The enthusiasm and affection with which the East German intellectuals arranged their transnational assemblages made the disappointment over their inevitable breakdown all the more potent. Neither the desire that led to these assemblages nor its exhaustion can be explained in terms of political motivations alone: the Strittmatters made continuous efforts to maintain their friendship with Kopelev and Orlova in spite of "certain things," while Enzensberger and Richter withdrew from their Soviet networks earlier and without specific reference to changes in the political climate in Moscow. And while the disintegration processes of East and West German relations to the Soviet Union were parallel, the "grit" that accelerated the deterioration of the desiring-machines was somewhat different, although originating from the same political source. For the West Germans it was their disillusionment with the again increasingly oppressive Soviet regime, whereas for the East Germans it was the impossibility of maintaining relations with dissidents.

Breaks were clearer at the institutional level. In the late 1960s, the Union of Soviet Writers cut ties with COMES over the organization's defence of the dissidents Andrei Sinyavsky and Alexander Solzhenitsyn, among others, thus scattering the constellation that had initiated the eastward mobilities of Richter and Enzensberger.[103] But as I have shown in this chapter, the authors had at that point no need for COMES, as they had found and finally moved on from their own strategies for realizing intellectual and political becoming through mobility to the Soviet Union. If desire is a force aimed at this becoming, it will necessarily have to change once a new stage in this process is reached. In the Soviet literary contact zone, it was a powerful force that inspired both East and West German writers of the post-war generation to pursue their projects of transnational intellectual and social assemblage: events of cultural exchange, literary production, and personal relationships. This desire's unique feature was its capacity to exist in parallel with or even detached from clear and stable political commitments, to be realized in an ideologically eclectic manner. But as the cases discussed in this chapter show, the downside of the desire-driven red migrations in the 1960s and early 1970s was the tendency for this desire to ultimately exhaust itself.

Acknowledgments

I would like to thank Bradley Gorski for his thoughtful feedback on multiple drafts of this chapter, and Roman Utkin for his discussant comments to my presentation of this project at the Red Migrations symposium. Helen Fehervary's discerning remarks regarding the politics of East and West German literature have been particularly helpful. Deeply saddened by her passing in April 2023, I am grateful to have had the chance to get to know her as a brilliant scholar of East German literature and as a kind and caring person.

Notes

1 The text appeared as "Katechismus zur deutschen Frage" ("Catechism on the German Question") in *Kursbuch* 4 (1966): 1–55.
2 Hans Magnus Enzensberger, "Letter to Il'ia Erenburg" (Moscow, 20 November 1965), 2219/2/601, RGALI.
3 Hans Magnus Enzensberger, *Tumult* (Frankfurt am Main: Suhrkamp Verlag, 2015), 17.
4 The archive holds some letters that reveal intimate details about the relationship between Maria Makarova and Hans Magnus Enzensberger. As the author himself had already chosen to make much of this relationship public in his 2015 memoir *Tumult*, twenty-three years after his second wife's death, I believe it is justifiable to selectively cite from this correspondence.
5 The most obvious case here is Erwin Strittmatter, who found himself at the will of the East German literary bureaucracy and also served as the secretary of the East German Writers' Union between 1959 and 1961. In West Germany, Richter and Enzensberger developed their alliances with the Social Democratic Party under Willy Brandt and the West German student movement respectively.
6 For a detailed discussion of this involvement, see Peter Bruhn and Henry Glade, Heinrich Böll in der Sowjetunion, 1952–1979: Einführung in die sowjetische Böll-Rezeption und Bibliographie der in der UdSSR in russischer Sprache erschienenen Schriften von und über Heinrich Böll (Berlin: E. Schmidt Verlag, 1980).
7 Francis L. Collins, "Desire as a Theory for Migration Studies: Temporality, Assemblage, and Becoming in the Narratives of Migrants," *Journal of Ethnic and Migration Studies* 44, no. 6 (2018): 965.
8 Collins, "Desire as a Theory," 967. It is worth adding here that flows of population themselves also figure prominently in the work of Deleuze

and Guattari, such as Deleuze's *Difference and Repetition* and, later, in Deleuze and Guattari's *A Thousand Plateaus*.
9. Dzhankarlo Vigorelli, "Sposobstvovat' delu mira," *Literaturnaia gazeta*, 6 August 1963.
10. Mary Louise Pratt, *Imperial Eyes: Travel Writing and Transculturation* (London: Routledge, 1992), 4.
11. Rossen Djagalov and Masha Salazkina, "Tashkent '68: A Cinematic Contact Zone," *Slavic Review* 75, no. 2 (2016): 281.
12. A detailed discussion of multilayered cultural activities of and around the Comintern's internationalism can be found in Amelia Glaser and Steven S. Lee, eds., *Comintern Aesthetics* (Toronto: University of Toronto Press, 2019).
13. Katerina Clark, *Moscow, the Fourth Rome: Stalinism, Cosmopolitanism, and the Evolution of Soviet Culture, 1931–1941* (Cambridge, MA: Harvard University Press, 2011), 44.
14. Evgeny Dobrenko, "When Comintern and Cominform Aesthetics Meet: Socialist Realism in Eastern Europe, 1956 and Beyond," in Glaser and Lee, *Comintern Aesthetics*, 422.
15. Among them were Willi Bredel, Franz Weiskopf, Wieland Herzfelde, Balder Olden, and Adam Scharrer. The only participant in the conference who remained somewhat outside the politically active circles was Klaus Mann.
16. Of the participants at the pre-war congresses, several returned to the second and third congresses in 1954 and 1959. At the second one, East Germany was represented by Seghers and Bredel, as well as Stefan Heym and Erwin Strittmatter; at the third, by Bredel, Otto Gotsche, Seghers, and Strittmatter. The Federal Republic of Germany was represented for the first time in 1959 by the relatively secondary Karl Ludwig Opitz. See M. Bazhan et al., eds., *Vtoroi vsesoiuznyi s″ezd sovetskikh pisatelei. Stenograficheskii otchet* (Moskva: Sovetskii pisatel', 1956), 604; and P. Brovka et al., eds., *Tretii s″ezd pisatelei SSSR. Stenograficheskii otchet* (Moskva: Sovetskii pisatel', 1959), 268.
17. "Forum pisatelei Evropy," *Literaturnaia gazeta*, 6 August 1963.
18. In the 1960s, Wiens was already serving as an informant for the Ministry of State Security (more commonly known as the Stasi). An incident in 1978 showed that writers' travel to the Soviet Union could also be sanctioned by this organization. Wiens, who had won the trust of Lev Kopelev, visited Moscow as an unofficial collaborator (IM) of the Stasi to gather more information on Soviet dissidents. As a disguise, the Union of Soviet Writers approved the visit as a vacation trip. Joachim Walther, *Sicherungsbereich Literatur: Schriftsteller und Staatssicherheit in der Deutschen Demokratischen Republik* (Berlin: Ch. Links, 1996), 604.
19. In the early war years, he became a member of a reserve police unit that was later integrated into the SS. He spent most of the war in Slovenia,

Poland, Finland, and Greece – much of this was not public knowledge in the 1960s. More recent discoveries about Strittmatter's war years suggest involvement in SS units responsible for the Kraków ghetto and the deportation of the Jewish population of Athens. "Erwin Strittmatter: Das unbefragte Schweigen," https://www.tagesspiegel.de/kultur/ns-debatte-erwin-strittmatter-das-unbefragte-schweigen/1450528.html.

20 Annette Leo, *Erwin Strittmatter: Die Biographie* (Berlin: Aufbau-Verlag, 2012), 230ff.
21 Konstantin Fedin, "Sud'ba romana," *Literaturnaia gazeta*, 6 August 1963.
22 Fedin, "Sud'ba romana."
23 A selection of Kafka's prose, including "The Metamorphosis" and "In the Penal Colony" was published in *Inostrannaia literatura* in 1964. The Kafka conference in Liblice, Bohemia, in 1963, became a landmark political event of the Prague Spring. The emerging reception of Kafka's work in 1960s Czechoslovakia catalysed the German literary scene's investment in exchange with their colleagues in Prague, where Richter had even planned to hold a Gruppe 47 meeting, which was cancelled due to the 1968 Soviet invasion. Hans Werner Richter et al., *Mittendrin: Die Tagebücher 1966–1972* (München: C.H. Beck, 2012), 105ff.
24 Konstantin Simonov, "Otvetstvennost'," *Literaturnaia gazeta*, 8 August 1963.
25 Dobrenko, "When Comintern and Cominform Aesthetics Meet," 444.
26 Pratt, *Imperial Eyes*, 6.
27 "Roman, chelovek, obshchestvo. Na vstreche pisatelei Evropy v Leningrade," *Inostrannaia literatura*, no. 11 (1963): 242.
28 Hans Werner Richter, *Im Etablissement der Schmetterlinge: Einundzwanzig Portraits aus der Gruppe 47* (München: Hanser, 1986), 108.
29 "Roman, chelovek, obshchestvo," 218.
30 Erwin Strittmatter, *Nachrichten aus meinem Leben: Aus den Tagebüchern 1954–1973* (Berlin: Aufbau, 2012), 211.
31 "Roman, chelovek, obshchestvo," 223.
32 Rossen Djagalov, *From Internationalism to Postcolonialism: Literature and Cinema between the Second and the Third Worlds* (Montreal and Kingston: McGill–Queen's University Press, 2020), 17.
33 Strittmatter, *Nachrichten aus meinem Leben*, 212.
34 Hans Magnus Enzensberger and Uwe Johnson, *"Für Zwecke der brutalen Verständigung": Hans Magnus Enzensberger, Uwe Johnson: Der Briefwechsel*, ed. Henning Marmulla and Claus Kröger (Frankfurt am Main: Suhrkamp, 2009), 78ff.
35 Michael Hofmann, *Uwe Johnson*, Nr. 17625 (Stuttgart: Reclam, 2001), 24–6.
36 An example of the East German interest in the Soviet Union as an at times politically more progressive alternative can be found in the history of the

East German publishing house for literature in translation, Volk und Welt. Here, Lektorat I, the department for Soviet literature, was considered to be the politically most interesting and "dangerous." Fritz Mierau, "Angewandte Literaturgeschichtsschreibung," in *Fenster Zur Welt. Eine Geschichte Des DDR-Verlages Volk & Welt*, ed. Simone Barck and Siegfried Lokatis (Berlin: Ch. Links Verlag, 2003), 44.
37 Collins, "Desire as a Theory for Migration Studies," 971.
38 Collins, "Desire as a Theory for Migration Studies," 968.
39 Strittmatter, *Nachrichten aus meinem Leben*, 212.
40 Enzensberger, *Tumult*, 23. This episode is also recounted in Richter's reminiscences of his travels with Enzensberger; his book features additional colourful and at times cliché-ridden descriptions of their escapades. Richter, *Im Etablissement der Schmetterlinge*, 110.
41 Shawn Salmon, "Marketing Socialism: Inturist in the Late 1950s and Early 1960s," in *Turizm: The Russian and East European Tourist under Capitalism and Socialism*, ed. Anne E. Gorsuch and Diane P. Koenker (Ithaca: Cornell University Press, 2006), 190.
42 Gilles Deleuze and Félix Guattari, *Anti-Oedipus: Capitalism and Schizophrenia* (Minneapolis: University of Minnesota Press, 1983), 29.
43 Caren Kaplan, *Questions of Travel: Postmodern Discourses of Displacement* (Durham: Duke University Press, 1996), 4.
44 Hans Magnus Enzensberger, letter to Aleksei Surkov (19 July 1966), 1899/1/610, RGALI. As he remembers in *Tumult*, the request was fulfilled as a rushed "grand tour" of the Soviet East after the conference, since his attraction had by then moved to a different object. In only two weeks, Enzensberger travelled to Tashkent, Bukhara, Samarkand, Irkutsk, Bratsk, Novosibirsk, and Akademgorodok, followed by another conference in Tbilisi. Enzensberger, *Tumult*, 25.
45 Eva Strittmatter, letter to Lev Kopelev and Raisa Orlova (26 December 1965), 2549/1/463, RGALI.
46 Eva Strittmatter, letter to Lev Kopelev and Raisa Orlova (31 January 1966), 2549/1/463, RGALI.
47 Eva Strittmatter, letter to Lev Kopelev and Raisa Orlova (2 June 1970), 2549/1/463, RGALI.
48 Eva Strittmatter, letter to Lev Kopelev (12 March 1970), 2549/1/463, RGALI.
49 In the 1920s and early 1930s, intellectuals from various segments of the leftist spectrum visited and published in German about their encounters, among them Arthur Hollitscher, Klara Zetkin, and Otto Friedländer, to name just a few. For further discussion, see Harold Segel, *Egon Erwin Kisch, the Raging Reporter: A Bio-Anthology* (West Lafayette: Purdue University Press, 1997), 31–2.
50 Nina Glick Schiller, Cristina Szanton Blanc, and Linda G. Basch, *Nations Unbound: Transnational Projects, Postcolonial Predicaments, and Deterritorialized Nation-States* (Langhorne: Gordon and Breach, 1994), 7.

51 Anatolii Lunacharskii, "Egon Ervin Kish," *Literaturnaia gazeta*, 8 July 1929, 1.
52 Aleksandr Dymshits, "Egon Ervin Kish i iskusstvo reportazha," *Zvezda*, no. 2 (1958): 233.
53 Segel, Egon Erwin Kisch, 32.
54 Egon Erwin Kisch, *Changing Asia*, trans. Rita Reil (New York: Alfred A. Knopf, 1935), 41. Kisch's German original, "Alle kommt ihr nach Samarkand, um Romantik anzuglotzen," is even more effective. The phrasing evokes Bertolt Brecht's famous distancing effect of installing a banner on stage that reads "Glotzt nicht so romantisch" (roughly: "Stop that romantic gawking."). Egon Erwin Kisch, *Gesammelte Werke in Einzelausgaben*, 3rd ed., vol. 3: *Zaren, Popen, Bolschewiken. Asien gründliche verändert. China geheim* (Berlin: Aufbau, 1980), 248.
55 Kisch, Gesammelte Werke in Einzelausgaben, 3, 147, 169, 104.
56 Hans Werner Richter, *Karl Marx in Samarkand: Eine Reise an die Grenzen Chinas* (Neuwied: Luchterhand, 1966), 6. In 1990, the German publisher Luchterhand released a second edition of Richter's book. Its new title, *Durchs rote Turkestan: Eine Reise von Taschkent bis Samarkand* (*Crossing Red Turkestan: A Journey from Tashkent to Samarkand*), alludes unmistakably to the popular orientalist adventure novel *Durchs wilde Kurdistan* (*Wild Kurdistan*) by the German nineteenth-century author Karl May. The ongoing dissolution of the Soviet Union seemed to rekindle German readers' interest in Central Asia and its socialist realities in an orientalizing key.
57 John Zilcosky, *Writing Travel: The Poetics and Politics of the Modern Journey* (Toronto: University of Toronto Press, 2008), 6.
58 Collins, "Desire as a Theory for Migration Studies," 967.
59 Richter, *Mittendrin*, 260.
60 Hans Werner Richter, *Durchs Rote Turkestan. Eine Reise von Taschkent bis Samarkand* (Frankfurt am Main: Luchterhand, 1992), 11.
61 Richter, *Durchs Rote Turkestan*, 110.
62 Richter, *Durchs Rote Turkestan*, 110.
63 Richter et al., *Mittendrin*, 83.
64 Richter, *Durchs Rote Turkestan*, 37.
65 Richter, *Durchs Rote Turkestan*, 17.
66 It appears that Enzensberger and especially Richter spent significant amounts of time with Bogatyrev. Strittmatter only mentions him once, noting in his diary that "Kostja takes us to the airport." Strittmatter, *Nachrichten aus meinem Leben*, 212.
67 Wolfgang Kasack et al., *Ein Leben nach dem Todesurteil: Mit Pasternak, Rilke und Kästner: Freundesgabe für Konstantin Bogatyrjow* (Bornheim: Lamuv, 1982).
68 Hans Werner Richter, "Verspäteter Brief an einen Freund," in *Ein Leben nach dem Todesurteil*, 127.
69 Richter, *Im Etablissement der Schmetterlinge*, 106; Richter, "Verspäteter Brief an einen Freund," 127.

70 Richter, "Verspäteter Brief an einen Freund," 132.
71 August R. Lindt, "Zwei Begnungen mit Konstantin Bogatyrjow," in *Ein Leben nach dem Todesurteil*, 136.
72 Alexei Yurchak, *Everything Was Forever, Until It Was No More: The Last Soviet Generation* (Princeton: Princeton University Press, 2006), 159.
73 Kaplan, *Questions of Travel*, 18.
74 R.D. Orlova and Lev Kopelev, *My zhili v Moskve: 1956–1980* (Moskva: Kniga, 1990), 95.
75 Enzensberger's presence at the event was an exception, since most of the participants were from the Global South. As conference reports indicate, the agenda of the meeting also featured administrative issues that would have been of very little interest to him. Mulud Mammeri, "Solidarnost'," *Literaturnaia gazeta*, 27 August 1966.
76 "Bakinskii dnevnik," *Literaturnaia gazeta*, 1 September 1966.
77 Hans Dieter Zimmermann, *Der Wahnsinn des Jahrhunderts: Die Verantwortung der Schriftsteller in der Politik: Überlegungen zu Johannes R. Becher ... und anderen* (Stuttgart: Kohlhammer, 1992), 31.
78 Enzensberger, *Tumult*, 51.
79 Enzensberger, "Letter to Aleksei Surkov."
80 For instance, recent immigration statistics for the US indicate that more than 70 per cent of all individuals granted permanent resident status received it based on family ties. "Persons Obtaining Lawful Permanent Resident Status by Type and Major Class of Admission: Fiscal Years 2017 to 2019," Department of Homeland Security, 20 September 2020, https://www.dhs.gov/immigration-statistics/yearbook/2019/table6.
81 Enzensberger, *Tumult*, 110.
82 "Spory o poezii nashego vremeni (Mezhdunarodnaia vstrecha poetov v Gruzii)," *Inostrannaia literatura*, no. 2 (1967): 201 f.
83 In this regard, Enzensberger differs from Evgenii Evtushenko, to whom he was sometimes compared due to their generational proximity (Evtushenko was born in 1931, three years after Enzensberger) and their broad popularity. Evtushenko had, however, famously proclaimed the role of the poet as a social institution and authority in the opening verse of his 1965 *poema* "Bratskaia GES" (The Bratsk Hydroelectric Station): "A poet in Russia is more than a poet."
84 Hans Magnus Enzensberger, "Kronstadt 1921 oder die dritte Revolution," *Kursbuch*, no. 9 (1967).
85 Enzensberger, *Tumult*, 102.
86 This phase in Enzensberger's work has been labelled anarchist in the sense of an all-encompassing rejection of authority, if not an attraction to political statements geared towards the creation of chaotic conditions.

See, for example, Reinhold Grimm, "Poetic Anarchism? The Case of Hans Magnus Enzensberger," *MLN* 97, no. 3 (1982): 745–58.
87 Hans Magnus Enzensberger, "Letter to Maria Enzensberger" (27 February 1968), 2219/2/600, RGALI.
88 Hans Magnus Enzensberger, "On Leaving America," *New York Review of Books*, 29 February 1968.
89 In a way, Enzensberger's engagement with Cuba parallels his Soviet experience, transitioning from an initially more enthusiastic embrace of its politics to a more critical stance after his actual visit to the country in 1968–9. Charlotte Melin and Cecile Cazort Zorach, "Cuba as Paradise, Paradigm, and Paradox in German Literature," *Monatshefte* 78, no. 4 (1986): 487–91.
90 Maria Enzensberger's obituary, on the other hand, speaks of the hardship she experienced after settling in London, where she traded in her Soviet nomenclature origins for the relative invisibility of émigré existence. Rosalind Delmar, "Masha Enzensberger 1943–1992," *History Workshop Journal* 33, no. 1 (March 1, 1992): 298–302.
91 Deleuze and Guattari, *Anti-Oedipus*, 31.
92 Orlova and Kopelev, *My zhili v Moskve*, 92.
93 The book appeared in 1966 in the *Zhizn' zamechatel'nykh liudei* series.
94 As in the case of the Makarova–Enzensberger correspondence, my discussion of these archival holdings follows the publishing of Erwin Strittmatter's diaries and correspondence (between 2012 and 2019), which has already brought much of the family's life to public attention.
95 Eva Strittmatter, letter to Lev Kopelev, 16 August 1966, 2549/1/463, RGALI.
96 Eva Strittmatter, letter to Lev Kopelev and Raisa Orlova, 10 January 1968, 2549/1/463, RGALI.
97 Strittmatter, letter to Lev Kopelev and Raisa Orlova," 31 January 1966, 2549/1/463, RGALI.
98 Eva Strittmatter, letter to Lev Kopelev, 26 March 1966, 2549/1/463, RGALI.
99 Collins, "Desire as a Theory for Migration Studies," 968.
100 Eva Strittmatter, letter to Lev Kopelev, 9 February 1968, 2549/1/463, RGALI.
101 Eva Strittmatter, letter to Lev Kopelev and Raisa Orlova, 6 December 1968, 2549/1/463, RGALI.
102 Kopelev and Orlova's emigration in 1980 put a definitive stop to their exchange. In January 1981, Strittmatter notes in his diary: "Emigrating means becoming weak, giving up. One can live and do creative work in any country." But he also concedes: "Of course I do not know if I would see it the same way and say this if I had spent years unlawfully in Soviet prison camps." Erwin Strittmatter, *Der Zustand meiner Welt: Aus den Tagebüchern 1974–1994* (Berlin: Aufbau, 2014), 161f.

103 Evgeniia Litvin, "'Evropeiskoe soobshchestvo pisatelei': K voprosu o sovetskoi kul'ture ottepeli," *Novye rossiiskie gumanitarnye issledovaniia*, no. 14 (2019): 108.

Contributors

Anna Arustamova is a doctor of Philology and professor in the Department of Russian Literature at Perm State University. She is a specialist on nineteenth- and twentieth-century Russian literature and the literature of the first wave of Russian emigration. She is author of *Russian-American Dialogue in the Nineteenth Century* (in Russian, 2007).

Katerina Clark (1941–2024) was a B.E. Bensinger Professor of Comparative Literature and of Slavic Languages and Literatures at Yale University. Her books include the seminal *The Soviet Novel: History as Ritual*; *Eurasia without Borders*; *Moscow, the Fourth Rome*; *Petersburg: Crucible of Cultural Revolution*; and, with Michael Holquist, *Mikhail Bakhtin*.

Irina Denischenko is an assistant professor in the Department of Slavic Languages and the Women's and Gender Studies Program at Georgetown University. She is co-editor of *Cannibalizing the Canon: Dada Techniques in East-Central Europe* and is currently finishing her book manuscript, *Lyrical Nomadism: Vladimir Mayakovsky and Democratic Representation in Art*.

Helen Fehervary (1942–2023) was a professor of German Studies at the Ohio State University. She published extensively on twentieth-century German literature, theatre, and intellectual history, and the works of Anna Seghers, Bertolt Brecht, Heiner Müller, and Christa Wolf. She co-translated plays by Müller and stories by Seghers and was general editor, with Carsten Jakobi of the Universität Mainz, of the multi-volume text-critical and annotated *Anna Seghers Werkausgabe* (Berlin: Aufbau Verlag).

Philip Gleissner is an assistant professor in the Department of Slavic and East European Languages and Cultures at Ohio State, specializing in migration, periodical studies, and queer studies in the Soviet Union and socialist East Central Europe. His *Subscribing to Sovietdom: The Lives of the Socialist Literary Journal* is forthcoming with University of Toronto Press.

Bradley A. Gorski is an assistant professor of post-Soviet literature and culture at Georgetown University. He is the author of *Cultural Capitalism: Literature and the Market after Socialism* (2025). His writing has appeared in *World Literature Today*, *Public Books*, the *Times Literary Supplement*, and elsewhere.

Michael Kunichika teaches at Amherst College, where he is professor and chair of Russian. He also directs the College's Amherst Center for Humanistic Inquiry. His first book, *"Our Native Antiquity": Archaeology and Aesthetics in the Aesthetics of Russian Modernism*, appeared in 2015 and received honourable mention for the Wayne S. Vucinich Prize. Along with publications on modern Russian literature, he has also written on both cinema studies and the history of art.

Serguei Alex. Oushakine is professor of Anthropology and Slavic Languages and Literatures at Princeton University. Recently, he published a two-volume Russian-language edition of foundational texts of Soviet practitioners of the Formal method (*The Formal Method: An Anthology of Russian Modernism*. Vol. 4. Functions. Ekaterinburg-Moscow: Kabinetnyi uchenyi, 2023). In 2022, together with Marina Balina, he co-edited the volume *The Pedagogy of Images: Depicting Communism for Children*. University of Toronto Press, 2022), which received the best edited volume award from the American Association of Teachers of Slavic and Eastern European Languages in 2024.

Tatsiana Shchurko, PhD, a postdoctoral ACLS Fellow at Ohio State University, is a Belarusian researcher and queer feminist activist specializing in transnational feminist theorizing. Her work focuses on anticolonial feminist theory, exploring multiple imperialisms. Her book project investigates the relationship between US Black women's transnational activism and Eurasian knowledge production.

Elizabeth H. Stern is an independent scholar, editor, and translator currently based in Heidelberg, Germany. She holds a PhD from Princeton University, an MPhil from the University of Oxford, and a BA from Brown University.

Kimberly St. Julian-Varnon is a PhD candidate in History at the University of Pennsylvania. Her research focuses on Soviet and East German ideas on race and Blackness by examining the experiences of Africans and African Americans, popular media, and state archives. She holds a MA in Russian, Eastern European, and Central Asian Studies from Harvard University and a MA in History from the University of Pennsylvania.

Edward Tyerman is an associate professor in the Department of Slavic Languages and Literatures at the University of California, Berkeley. His research focuses on cultural connections and exchanges between Russia and China from the early 20th century to the present, within the broader historical contexts of socialist internationalism and postsocialism. He is the author of *Internationalist Aesthetics: China and Early Soviet Culture* (Columbia University Press, 2021).

Roman Utkin is an associate professor of Russian, East European and Eurasian Studies at Wesleyan University. He is the author of *Charlottengrad: Russian Culture in Weimar Berlin* (University of Wisconsin Press, 2023).

Trevor Wilson is an assistant professor at Virginia Tech. His research focuses on the history of Russo-Soviet philosophy and cultural theory. His forthcoming book, *Alexandre Kojève and the Specters of Russian Philosophy* (Northwestern University Press, 2025) examines the work of Kojève through the lens of Russian philosophy abroad.

Index

Page locators in *italics* indicate illustrations.

abjection, 216–18, 234. *See also* disgust
abstraction: cosmopolitan, 29–30, 66–7, 71, 73; in Marxist thought, 160, 162–6, 172–7; in modern art, 88–90, *89*, 137, 192, 194
Academy of Sciences of the Soviet Union, 165, 167, 169–70
Activism (artistic movement): agitation/work of, 94–6, 101, 116; Mácza on origins of, 109, *111*, 112–14, 124n61; in Mácza's "new art" diagrams, *92, 106, 108, 110–11*
"actually existing socialism," 390–1, 443
Ady, Endre, 380, 391
aestheticism, 64–5, 68–70, 73
affect. *See* desire; disgust; grief/disappointment
African Americans. *See* Black Americans; US race relations
African peoples, 213n75, 330–1, 339n14, 405, 416, 432, 446
agitation: art as tool for, 94–7, 100, 113–14; in Bely's writing, 199–200; by Black radical women, 404–5; Communist Party's department of, 63, 70, 76; Dadaism and, 98–101, *99*; Proletkult and, 96–7, 100–1
aid organizations, 5, 219–20, 239, 243, 384, 387
Akademie der Künste (AdK), 131, 135, 145–7
Akhmatova, Anna, 449
Akhundi, Nassyrulla, 444
Aksenov, Vasily, 445
Aleksandrov, Grigorii: films of, 31, *34*, 35, 40–2, 44; international travels of, 10, 17, 33–9, *34, 36–7, 39*, 40; on Soviet/US filmmaking, 31–2, 36, 39–40, 76. *See also* Circus
Alexander the Great, 253, 255–7
alienation. *See* exile
Aliger, Margarita, 430, 446
Alland, Alexander, 354, 372n9
Alpert, Max, 407
Althusser, Louis, 161, 176
Amado, Jorge, 390
Amerikanizm, 38, 46, 60–2, 73–6, *74*
Anand, Mulk Raj, 245, 258
anarchism, 7, 95, *110*, 112, 119n13, 346, 456n86
Anderson, Perry, 174–5
Angioletti, Giovanni Battista, 431

Antal, Frigyes, 377
anthroposophy, 189, 196–7, 200
anti-colonialism, 10, 14, 243, 387, 391, 401, 408, 416
anti-fascist movement: in GDR, 132, 388; leftist writers and, 243, 257–8, 387, 417, 432; in Mexico, 385–6; Paris headquarters of, 5, 239, 258; Popular Front, 263n71, 383–5
antiquity: fascism's attraction to, 309–11; modernist writers' engagement with, 304–8; vs. modernity, 299–305, 314–15, 440
antisemitism, 60–1, 98, 267, *268*, 377–8, 387
Antsiferov, Nikolai, 212n70
Any, Carol, 208n17
Apitz, Bruno, 433
Apollinaire, Guillaume, 430
Appiah, Kwame Anthony, 14
Arabian Nights, 251
arbitrage. *See* cultural arbitrage
architecture, *106*, *108*, 113–14, 193, 293n44, 311, 381
Archive of the Russian Revolution, 191
archives: absences in, 399–403, 414–15, 420–1; colonizing work of, 413–14; fractured objects in, 402, *402*, 412–15; "haunting" in, 412–15, 420–1; Huiswoud's, 406–7, 411, 422n3, 423n13; transnational intimacy evidenced in, 430, 447–50
Armenia, 231–2, 419, 439
Art of Contemporary Europe, The (Mácza): compositional history of, 96–8, 105, 124n61, 127n91; vs. hegemonic art histories, 109–14; Marxist method in, 91–3, *92*, 105, 112–14; "social psychic" in, 91, *92*, 105, 109, *110*; theory of "new" art in, 105–9, *106*, *108*, *110–11*, 113–16
Arvatov, Boris, 38, 62

Aseev, Nikolai: in Italy, 10, 18, 299–304, 309–15; poetry by, 305, 307, 310, 318n30; in *Russian Voice*, *350*, 367, 369. *See also Unmade Beauty*
Aseeva, Ksenia, 299, 311, 318n30
Association of European Writers (COMES), 431–7, 444, 450
Astaire, Fred, 51
Auden, W.H., 240–1, 243, 258
Auerbach, Erich, 115
Ausdruckstanz (modern/expressionist dance), 130, 132–4, 137–8, 145
Australia, 298n112, 447
Austria: Hungarian émigrés in, 95–7, 102, 124n61, 128n94, 378; leftist British writers in, 243; Radványi/MASCH in, 375–6, 378–9, 381–2
autobiography, 44, 94, 96, 186, 190, 200
automobile industry, 32, 38, *39*, 328–9, 334, 336
avant-garde: comparative approaches to, 110–13, 115; diagrammatic imagination of, 88, *89–90*, 90–3, 105, 108–9, 126n69; embeddedness and, 208n17; formalist approach to, 91–3, 109; genealogical models of, 71, 88–91, *90*, 105–7, 109–10, 115; "little magazines" of, 97–8; Mácza's transnational theory of, *92*, 105–9, *106*, *108*, *110–11*, 113–16; manifestos of, 97, 100, 118n10, 302–3, 346; political leftism of, 94–7, 100–2, 113–14, 193–4; Proletkult/proletariat and, 96–7, 100–2, 112–14; revolution and, 95–6, 101–2, 104–5, 112, 114, 116, 192
Averbakh, Leonid, 285
Averbuch, I., 369
Ávila Camacho, Manuel, 385
Azerbaijan, 438, 440, 446
Azoulay, Ariella Aïsha, 410

Babel, Isaak, 42, 268, 271–3
Bach, Johann Sebastian, 133, 391
Bacon, Lloyd, 33, 51
Bahro, Rudolf, 390–1
Bakhtin, Mikhail, 43–4, 51, 57, 269
Balázs, Béla: on Aleksandrov's *Circus*, 25–8, 46, 51, 71, 76; Hungarian avant-garde/émigré community and, 94, 116, 377–8, 382–3
Baldwin, Kate A., 221–2, 339n19, 408
Banfi, Antonio, 169
barbarism, 253, 257, 267–8, *268*, 307–8
Barr, Alfred H., Jr., 88, *89*, 91–2, 105
Barta, Sándor, 100, 102–4, *103*, 113, 115
Barthold, V.V., 253–4
Bartók, Béla, 377
Basch, Linda G., 132
Bauhaus, *89*, 193, 376, 385
Bazin, Jérôme, 136
Beauvoir, Simone de, 433
Belfrage, Cedric, 30
Belgium, 243, 382, 406
Belinskii, Vissarion, 66–7
Belodubrovskaya, Maria, 62
Bely, Andrei: Berlin poems of, 213n74; migrations of, 10, 189, 196–8; *Petersburg*, 191, 198–9, 201, 277–8, 290n3. *See also One of the Mansions of the Kingdom of Shades*
Benjamin, Walter, 270, 384
Bennett, Gwendolyn, 406
Berberova, Nina, 8
Berg, Hubert van den, 117n5
Bergson, Henri, 241
Berkeley, Busby, 51, *52*
Berlin: authors/artists in, 100, 228, 243, 346, 348, 433, 446–7; as centre of modernity, 192–4, 206; class divides in, 187–8, 193–5, 201–3, 205–6; vs. countryside, 193–4, 203–4; dance in, 129, 134, 145, 149; as decaying mythopoetic space, 188, 197–200, 206; film industry in, 5, 33–5; Hungarian émigrés in, 95, 102, 387; police in, 382, 389, 397n73. *See also* Marxist Workers School of Greater Berlin; Russian Berlin
Bethea, David, 199
Bezymenskii, Aleksandr, 42
Bible, 378–9, 394n21, 440
Biermann, Wolf, 390
Bischoff, Simone, 392
Black Americans: 1932 Soviet contingent of, 220, 319, 324–7, 329–30, 333, 407, 419; in American South, 220, 225, 232–3; double consciousness of, 221; encounters with white Americans in the Soviet Union, 320–2, 332–3; Great Migration of, 423n18; motifs of dirt/racism, 232–4; as oppressed nation, 6, 321, 324, 326, 400–1, 404–5; racial identity constructed/performed by, 319–26, 335–7; recruited to Soviet Union, 321, 323, 334, 399, 405–6; as Soviet workers, 327–9, 334–7, 338n12; tokenizing of, 331–2. *See also* Hughes, Langston; Soviet race relations; US race relations
Black and White (planned Soviet film), 220, 319, 324–7, 329–30, 333, 407, 419
Black liberation: envisioned as global struggle, 404–6, 416–17; material evidence of search for, 411–13; mobility as enabling, 221–2, 225, 401, 405–6, 412–13, 416; unveiling and, 408–10
Blackness: glossed, 339n13; performed/constructed, 319–26; Pushkin's, 330–1; reinforced by Soviet experience, 329–33
Black radicalism: absented in archive, 400–3, 414–15, 420–1;

Black radicalism (*continued*)
desired connections, 19, 406–11;
fractures/absences/missed
connections, 411–15, 419–21; Harlem
as site of, 250, 403–5, 416, 426n52;
imagined vs. concrete solidarities
and, 415–21; internationalism of,
401, 403–6; leftist positionality of,
421n1. *See also* Huiswoud, Hermina
Dumont
Blanc, Cristina Szanton, 132
Bliakhin, Pavel, 284, 289
Bloch, Ernst, 384
Blok, Alexander, 122n36, 197, 300,
306, 308, 311, 316n13
Bobach, Roman, 366
Bogatyrev, Konstantin, 443–5, 448
Bogdanov, Aleksandr Alekseevich,
274–5
Böhme, Fritz, 152n12
Böll, Heinrich, 430, 445
Bol'shakov, Ivan, 72–3
Bolshevik Revolution. *See* October
Revolution
Bolshoi Theatre, 43, 147, 150–1
Boltanski, Christian, 27
Bondarenko, V., 357–8
Bornyik, Sándor, 100
Borshchagovskii, Aleksandr, 60, 74
Bortnyik, Sándor, 101–2, 119n13
Bortstieber, Gertrud, 382
Botar, Oliver, 121n32
Botka, Ferenc, 121n26
bourgeois art: FAKC campaign and,
30, 68, 71–3; vs. proletarian, 94–5,
100–1, 112, 367; Soviet views on,
25–8, 51, 62
bourgeois intellectuals, 229, 383
bourgeois nationalism, 75–6, 257
bourgeois psyche/culture, 107,
198–203, 205, 227
Braidotti, Rosi, 116, 117n8

Brailovsky, A.Y., 346
Brandt, Willy, 433, 441, 451n5
Brecht, Bertolt, 135, 318n25, 375–6,
381, 433, 448, 455n54
Bredel, Willi, 452nn15–16
Breton, André, 385
Briggs, Cyril V., 404
Brubaker, Rogers, 323, 330, 341n48
Budberg, Mariia Ignat'evna, 312
Bulgakov, Mikhail, 268, 272, 285, 289
Bulgaria, 17, 161, 164–7, 171, 205,
382–3, 433
Bullock, David, 290n2
Bunin, Ivan, 7–8, 294n59, 345
Buñuel, Luis, 39
Bürger, Peter, 91
Burghardt, Max, 137, 145
Burliuk, David: in émigré
community, 7, 345; as father of
Russian Futurism, 346, 348, 351–2,
355, 362–3, 367, 370; as literary
editor of *Russian Voice*, 5, 19,
346–7, 350, 351–5, 358–9, 365–71;
as painter, 346, 354, 371nn3–4; as
poet, 350, 355, 359, 367–8. *See also*
Russian Futurism; *Russian Voice*
Burroughs, Williana, 404, 416, 427n68
Butler, Judith, 323, 325, 337

Campanella, Tommaso, 104
Campbell, Craig, 407–8
Campbell, Grace P., 404, 427n68
capitalism: Dadaist attacks on,
100–1; disgust induced by, 227,
235n15; global impoverishment
due to, 403–6, 416–17; Great
Depression and, 320; late stage of,
15, 105, 107–9, *108*, *110*, 112–14,
203, 271; Marx's reception under,
180n56; modernity and, 276; racial
inequality and, 238n40, 320–4,
403–6, 420; self-estrangement

under, 166; as synonymous for
United States, 7, 133, 346–7, 358,
363–5, 370; value-form under, 160,
172–3, 175

Cárdenas, Lázaro, 385

Caribbean, 321, 334, 398, 403, 405–6,
416–17, 448. *See also* Huiswoud,
Hermina Dumont

censorship: in cinema, 38, 60, 62,
64; in dance/music, 139, 150,
158n97, 169; Glavlit and, 196–7; in
philosophy, 165, 169–71; in print
cultures, 94, 195–7, 249, 392

Central Asia: awakening/
modernization of, 246–52, 256,
407–8, 440–4; exoticizing of,
241–2, 247–53, 258, 407–8, 440–1;
Great Conquerors of, 249, 251–8;
imaginings of, 18, 57, *58*, 214,
215, 220–2, 249–50, 258; living
conditions in, 216, 223–4, 232,
240; mappings of, 441–3, *442*;
racialized population of, 19,
220–2, 234, 251; sexuality in, 229,
237n34; Soviet photography in,
407–8, 410–11; veiling/unveiling
in, 221–2, 230, 401–3, *402*, 407–15,
418–21, 443. *See also* Fox, Ralph;
Hughes, Langston; Koestler,
Arthur

Certeau, Michel de, 212n73

Chagall, Marc, 185

Chan, Roy, 282

Chaplin, Charlie, 10, 31, 33, 36, *36*,
48, 73; *The Circus*, 44–6, *45*

Chekhov, Anton, 64, 370

Chen, Sylvia, 416, 427n68

Chen Chi-yin, 383

Cherny, B., 369

Chiang Kai-shek, 244

Chicherin, Georgii, 119n13

chiliasm, 378–80, 391

China: commensurability with
Russia, 5–6, 276–81; figured as
migrant, 275–6, 278; Genghis Khan
and, 256; Isherwood on, 240–1, 243,
248; MASCH and, 382–3; religions
of, 279; revolution/rebellion/wars
in, 244–5, 269–71, 277, 279–80, 286;
Russians in, 5, 280, 293n41

Chinese migrants: grotesque
figurations of, 272, 275–8, 280,
282–4; as impervious to pain, 272,
281, 283–90; *khodia/kitayoza/manza*
(colloquialisms), 272–3, 280, 283;
linguistic distortions and, 272–5,
279, 280, 282–3, 285; mining/
railroad work by, 269–70, 282–3,
288; Moscow laundry workers,
270, 275, 280, 297n93; statistics for,
269–70, 287–8; in United States,
287–9, 296n88

Chinese migrant soldiers: as barbarian
horde, 267–8, *268*, 280, 285–6; as
doubly displaced, 273–5, 280–1; as
early Soviet "ideologeme," 11, 18,
268–72, 286, 289–90; as Eurasian/
revolutionary ally, 269, 277–81, 283,
289; as fearless, 272, 281, 283–6,
288–90; as Panmongolist threat, 271,
273, 277–80, *279*

Chinese Pidgin Russian (CPR),
274–5, 282

Christianity, 21n23, 33, 306,
378–80, 391

Churchill, Winston, 267

Chuzhak, Nikolai, 300

Circle of Proletarian Writers and
Artists in North America, 348, 353,
360, 369

Circus (Aleksandrov): *Amerikanizm*
in, 46, 60–2; Balázs's review of, 25–
8, 46, 51, 71, 76; cultural arbitrage
in, 29, 46–7, 51, 56–7, 61–2, 76–7;

Circus (Aleksandrov) [*continued*]
  formal borrowings in, 25–7, *26*, 48, *50*, 51, *52*; Soviet talents in, 42–3, 57, 341n41; spherical cosmopolitanism in, 43–4, *45*, *47*, 51, 53–7, *54–6*, *58*, 61; storyline/parallels in, 46–8, *48–50*
city writing: city guides and, 186–9; literary/topographical mapping in, 200–6; mythologizing of Rome, 302–4, 306, 308; "Petersburg text," 277–8, 280; Pil'niak's grotesque approach to, 275–8, 280, 282–3. *See also* Russian Berlin
Clair, René, 42, 81n66
Clark, Katerina, 9, 11, 140, 209n36
classical ballet, 130, 133–4, 137, 139–40, 142–3, 145, 148–9. *See also drambalet*
Cold War: anti-*Amerikanizm*, 73–6, *74*; anti-Soviet sentiment, 219–20, 242, 250, 334; binary/reductivist thinking of, 4, 8–9, 398–400, 430–2, 445; cultural, 133, 434–7; Iron Curtain, 130, 231, 255, 386; pan-Soviet culture and, 130–1, 144–5; Red Scare, 219–20, 225–6, 231–4, 406; Warsaw Pact, 389, 453n23
Colletti, Lucio, 166, 174–5
Collins, Francis, 430–1, 437
Comintern (Communist International): congresses of, 4, 102; international reach of, 226, 242–5, 270, 296n79, 382; mediation of contact with local citizens, 246, 409, 418–21; political internationalism of, 4, 9–14, 271, 283, 432, 437; recruitment of Black Americans by, 321, 323, 334, 399, 405–6; Stalinization of, 379; studies of, 6
Communist Party: China, 270; Czechoslovakia (KSČ), 96; Germany (KPD), 132, 226–8, 376–7, 379–81, 388–90, 432; Great Britain, 16, 242–4, 246; Hungary (KMP), 96–7, 100, 102, 377–8; Italy (PCI), 17, 164, 168–9, 172, 174, 177; United States, 5, 321, 327, 404
Communist Party of the Soviet Union (CPSU): ballet/cinema and, 73, 141; Ilienkov's censure by, 160–2, 164–5, 167, 170–1; loosening grip of, 171–2, 176–7; propaganda/agitation by, 63, 70, 76, 216, 219; red star, 202–3, 359
Constitutional Democratic Party (Kadets, imperial Russia), 185, 191, 197
Constructivism: in Mácza's theory of "new art," 92, 105, *106*, 108, *108*, *110*; other theorists on, 90, 97, 100, 126n66, 185, 194, 208n17
contact zone. *See* Soviet contact zone
Conway, Jack, 42
Cooper, Frederick, 323, 330, 341n48
cosmopolitanism: conceptualized, 13–14; cultural arbitrage and, 29–30; denounced, 133–4, 137; geographic knowledge and, 29, 53, 72–6; vs. internationalism, 12–14, 58, 66–7; Mexico as site of, 387; vs. patriotism, 68–9, 71–3, 193; as pejorative, 13, 17, 58, 60, 65–71, 73, 115; spherical vision of, 43–4, *45*, *47*, 51, 53–7, *54–6*, 61, 74; Stalin's typology of, 68. *See also* FAKC campaign
Crawford, Matt, 409
critical fabulation, 400–3, 420–1
Croce, Benedetto, 174, 300
Cuba, 334, 416–17, 448
Cubism: in diagrams of avant-garde, 88, *89–90*; in Mácza's theory of "new art," 92, *106*, *108*, *110*, 125n65, 126n69, 309; societal decline and, 309

cult of personality, 256–8, 390
cultural arbitrage: Aleksandrov's playful/grounded model, 29, 46–7, 51, 56–7, 61–2, 76–7; conceptualized, 17, 28–30; particular/universal in, 29–30, 42, 53, 72–3. *See also Circus*; FAKC campaign
Czechoslovakia: art/literature of, 91, 112, 433; Communist Party (KSČ), 96; international conflicts and, 267, 378, 389, 449, 453n23; Mácza in, 95–102; Marxism in, 161, 171; Prague Spring, 453n23. *See also* Kisch, Egon Erwin

Dadaism: in diagrams of avant-garde, 88, *89–90*; Mácza's creative/agitational work and, 97–101, *99*; in Mácza's theory of "new art," 105, *106*, 108, *108*, *110*, 114; societal decline and, 200, 309. *See also* Mácza, János
dance: "boy dancers," 426n52; folk, 134, 137, 139, 143, 145, 149; foxtrot, 198, 203; in GDR, 129; mass performances, 139–40, 142; modern, 131, 136–8, 143, 148–50; Nazism and, 130, 132, 134, 136–8; revolutionary, 135–6, 139–45, 147, 151; Soviet dancers, 143, 147–8, 152n8. *See also Ausdruckstanz*; *drambalet*; theatre
D'Angelo, Sergio, 168–70
Daniel, Yuli, 449
Dante Alighieri, 393n6
Deborin, Abram, 177n2, 179n29
Decadence, 107, 143
Decembrist Uprising, 144
Deineka, Aleksandr, 339n23
Deleuze, Gilles, 430, 438, 448–9
Della Volpe, Galvano, 174–7
Del Ruth, Roy, 51

Dennis, Eugene, 409
Dennis, Peggy, 409
Derrida, Jacques, 27
Déry, Tibor, 433
desire: for boundaries, 214–15, 224–6; breakdown of, 446–8; for connection, 409, 413, 415–16, 419–21, 449–50; as driver of global mobility, 19, 430–1, 437, 441, 445; multidirectionality of, 444–5; processes of becoming and, 437, 441, 449–50; for purges, 218; sex and, 227–9; shared food/drink and, 223–4; for Soviet space, 436–9, 441–4, 448
de-Stalinization, 150, 160, 162
D'iakova, Olga, 191
dialectical materialism: coining of, 162; Ilienkov on, 17, 160–5, 167, 172–4; on racial inequality/capitalism, 238n40, 320–4, 405–6; "revisionist" strands of, 160, 165–7, 170–1, 174–7; Russian/Soviet diamat, 162–7, 170, 174, 177; in worker education curriculum, 383; Zhdanov on, 63, 66. *See also* Marxist philosophy
Diatlov, V.I., 271
Dietrich, Marlene, 33–5, 82n85
Dimitroff, Giorgi, 383
Diogenes the Cynic, 13
disgust: affective desire for boundaries and, 18, 214–15, 224–6, 230–1, 234; conceptualized, 215–18, 231; ethical/political nausea, 227–33; food/drink/sex and, 216–17, 223–5, 227–30; grime/dirt and, 216, 219–20, 223–4, 227, 230, 232–4, 279; infection/disease and, 219, 223–7; revolution and, 214, 218–20, 230; ruins/modernity and, 302–3; at suffering/poverty, 235n15

Disney, Walt, 10, 37, 42, 81n66
displacement, 16, 115, 186, 190, 275, 281, 392, 413, 438
dissident movement, 390, 430, 445, 448–50, 452n18
Djagalov, Rossen, 432, 436
Dobrenko, Evgeny, 21n22, 178n8, 262n65, 432, 434
documentary films/modes, 33, 39, 56, *56*, 57, 305, 316n17
Dolinin, Alexander, 199
Domingo, W.A., 404
Dostoevsky, Fyodor, 64, 316n13
Douglas, Mary, 216
Douglass, Frederick, 406
Dovzhenko, Aleksandr, 41
drambalet: GDR transplantation of, 11, 17, 137–8, 142, 144–6, 150; key features of, 139–41; motivation behind, 129–34; post-Stalin, 146–51; Tanzkonferenz and, 134–8, 143, 146–9; usage of term, 147, 149–50, 151n4, 152nn5–6. *See also Flames of Paris, The*
Dreiser, Theodore, 33, 219, 227
Du Bois, W.E.B., 221–2, 322, 338n5, 405, 408
Duchamp, Marcel, 27
Dunaevskii, Isaak, 42–3, 57
Duncker, Hermann, 380–1
Durov circus dynasty, 43
Dvořák, Antonín, 158n83
Dymov, Osip, 345
Dymshits, Aleksandr, 439

East Germany (German Democratic Republic, GDR): heritage appropriation in, 133, 137, 140; literary conferences and, 433–7, 449, 452n16; Ministry of State Security (Stasi), 452n18; oppressive conditions in, 431, 437; pan-German cooperation/culture, 146–7, 149; Radványi in, 375, 387–92; reshaping of national culture in, 17, 129–34, 142, 146–50; socialist realism in, 130, 133–8, 143–9; Socialist Unity Party (SED), 130, 132–4, 390–1; transnational networks and, 19, 430; view of Soviet Union as progressive, 437, 449–50. *See also drambalet*; Strittmatter, Erwin
education: Comintern schools, 339n21; foreign experts and, 32, 35–6, 38, 79n21; Hungarian curriculum, 377–8; periodicals as space of, 97–8, 346–7, 352–4, 370; primers/textbooks, 68–9, *69*, 244, 252, 360; theatre/dance, 62–4, 94, 130, 138; worker, 19, 375–6, 381, 383–5. *See also* Marxist Workers School of Greater Berlin
Efros, Abram, 71
Ehrenburg, Ilya: as émigré/literary personality, 7, 390, 434; Enzensberger and, 429–30, 432; migrations of, 10, 189, 200, 206, 430; publications by, 12–13, 191–4. *See also Letters from Cafés*
Eichberg, Richard, 38
Eikhenbaum, Boris, 189–91
Einstein, Albert, 33, 382, 384
Eisenstein, Sergei: films of, 31, 33, *34*, 35, 254; film technology and, 25, 31–2, 86n142; international travels of, 10, 33–6, *34*, 36–7, 40; at Soviet film festival, 81n66
Eisler, Hanns, 376, 381
Eliseev, Konstantin, *67*
El'sberg, Iakov, 66
émigré poetics: vs. *Russian voice*, 347, 356–8, 363–5, 370–1; vs. travel writing, 301, 311

Index   471

émigré studies, 4, 19, 188–9. *See also* migration; white émigrés
empiricism, 160, 174, 217, 386–7
Engels, Friedrich, 162–3, 177, 244, 288
Enzensberger, Hans Magnus: attraction towards Soviet Union, 430, 437–9, 446, 450; Ehrenburg and, 429–30, 432; literary conferences and, 433–6, 438, 444, 446–7; Makarova and, 430, 445–8; *Tumult*, 437–8, 451n4, 454n44
Erich-Weinert Ensemble, 137
Erlich, Victor, 208n17
Esenin, Sergei, 192, 370
Eurasianism, 212n62, 253–5, 277–81
Evtushenko, Evgenii, 456n83
exile: alienation of, 161, 166, 187, 255, 280, 347, 354–5, 358, 360; as moral choice, 7–9; vs. nomadic subjectivity, 114–16, 392; paradigm of, 93, 95, 115–16; vs. poetics of travel writing, 301, 311; pseudonym usage and, 380
exoticism, 140, 241–2, 247–53, 258, 286, 407–8, 440–1
Expressionism: in diagrams of avant-garde, *89–90*; leftist orientation of, 94, 97, 113–14, 119n13; in Mácza's theory of "new art," *92*, *106*, *107*, *108*, *110*, 125n65, 126n69; societal decline and, 200, 309
Ezrahi, Christina, 140

Fadeev, Aleksandr, 65–6, 68, 76, 430, 446
Fairbanks, Douglas, 31, *32*
FAKC campaign: anti-*Amerikanizm* of, 73–6, *74*; cultural adoption critiqued by, 70–3, 75; cultural arbitrage in, 30, 57, 61–2, 65–6, 67, 69–74, 76–7; "kinless"/"passportless"/ "rootless" and, 13, 58, 60, 66–72, 67, 84n99; theatre/theatre criticism as target of, 62–4, 68–71, *69*; trials of honour and, 58–60, *59*, 70
Fan, He, 293n44
fascism: antiquity and, 309–11; art and, 73, 108, 113–14, 309; black colour and, 212n60, 213n75; Futurism and, 108, 114, 300, 308–11; leftist opposition to, 9–10, 227, 385, 432–3, 435–6, 447. *See also* anti-fascist movement; Nazism
Fearon, James, 323
Federal Republic of Germany. *See* West Germany
Fedin, Konstantin, 207n10, 434
Fedoseev, Petr, 170, 172, 174
Feltrinelli, Giangiacomo, 161, 168–70, 176
Field, Noel, 387
First Congress for the Defence of Culture, 5, 258
First World War: capitalism and, 105, 108, 112; Chinese migrant workers and, 270, 272, 288; destruction/displacement of, 6, 218–19, 382; modernity and, 193, 202; Second International, 12–13; Treaty of Versailles, 98, 100–1, 203
Five-Year Plans, 38–9, 320, 440
Flames of Paris, The (Vainonen/Gruber): GDR premiere of, 131, 134, 138, 141; re-evaluations/restagings of, 146–51; as socialist realist exemplar, 135, 138–44, 146; staging/reception in GDR, 142–6
Fleishman, Lazar, 211n59
Flynn, Elizabeth Gurley, 404, 427n68
Fogarasi, Béla, 377, 382
Földessy, Gyula, 379–81
Ford, James, 321
Ford automotive factory, 38, *39*, 334
Fore, Devin, 305

Forgács, Éva, 118n11, 122n43
form: vs. function, 26–9, 46, 53, 57, 141, 144–5, 150–1; Futurism's destruction of, 107; literary everyday and, 189–91, 205–6; "national," 130, 136–7; proletarian, 100–1, 114, 370–1
Formalism: denounced, 133–4, 137; disciplinary divides of, 128n92; literary everyday theorized, 189–91; vs. Marxist method, 91–3, 109, 205; as pejorative, 64–5, 68–70, 73, 134; periodical culture and, 316n17; relaxed campaign against, 146. *See also* Shklovsky, Viktor
Forsh, Olga, 312
Forster, E.M., 244
Fox, Ralph: in Central Asia, 18, 239, 241–3, 246–50, 253, 256; death of, 239, 246, 258; *Genghis Khan*, 242, 253–8; intellectual/geographical migration of, 239–42, 248, 257–8; in London literary scene, 240, 242–3, 245, 258; in Moscow, 11, 239, 243–5, 253; *The Novel and the People*, 241, 244–5; *People of the Steppes*, 241–3, 246–51, 254, 256–7; *Storming Heaven*, 242–3, 246–51, 254, 256–7
Fraenkel, Abraham, 384
France: anti-fascist movement in, 5, 239, 258, 263n71, 383–5; arts/culture of, 5, 10, 91, 110, 248, 309; émigré community in, 189, 197, 345–6, 348, 382–4, 430; leftist British writers in, 243; literary conferences and, 433; Radványi in, 375, 383–5, 387, 390; Soviet ballet avoided in, 141, 145, 147–8
Frankfurt School, 245, 384
Frantzev, Georgii, 76
French Revolution, 139–42, 144–5; Paris Commune, 377

Freud, Sigmund, 33, 237n33
Friche, Vladimir, 109, 125n64, 127n80
Fülep, Lajos, 377
Futurism. *See* Italian Futurism; Russian Futurism

Gábor, Andor, 382
Gaevskii, Vadim, 139
Galich, Aleksandr, 64
Gallup, George, 386
Gal'perin, Aleksandr, 84n98
Galushkin, Aleksandr, 210n40
Gamsa, Mark, 293n44
Ganf, Iulii, 74
Gannibal, Abram Petrovich, 331
Garner, Sylvia, 340n28, 340n33
Gastev, Alexei, 38, 299
Gauguin, Paul, 308
Genghis Khan, 18, 242, 249, 253–8
Georgia (Soviet state), 228, 305, 419–20, 437, 439–40, 447, 454n44
Gerasimov, Aleksandr, 71
Gergely, Tibor, 377
German Democratic Republic. *See* East Germany
German idealism. *See* idealism
Germany (pre-1945): avant-garde of, 91, 110, 112, 118n11, 309, 373n28; classical heritage of, 133, 137, 140; Communist Party (KPD), 132, 226–8, 376–7, 379–81, 388–90, 432; film studios, 5, 72–3; First World War and, 98, 100–1, 186, 203; interwar transition of, 193, 202–3, 432; Radványi in, 375, 379–84, 387–9; in Russian Civil War, 267; sanitation in, 224–5; Second World War and, 231, 258, 436; Social Democratic Party (SPD), 132, 188, 376–7, 381; SS, 452n19; Third Reich, 129, 132, 134, 142, 154n30; travel writing in, 439–44, 442; worker education

in, 19, 375–6. *See also* Berlin; East Germany; Nazism; Russian Berlin; West Germany
Gessen, Iosef Vladimirovich, 197
Gide, André, 236n20, 444
Giersdorf, Jens, 150, 152n9
Gippius, Zinaida, 7–8
Gisenkin, Z., 369
Glaser, Amelia, 12
Glasgoe, Margaret, 11, 327–9, 334, 336–7
Gluck, Mary, 128n94
Goethe, Johann Wolfgang von, 133, 302
Gogol, Nikolai, 161, 300, 306, 311, 316n13
Golding, William, 433
Goldschmidt, Alfons, 381, 385
Goleizovskii, Kasian, 43, *50*
Gollerbakh, Erich, 346
Goncharova, Natalia, 117n4, 308
Gordon, Avery, 412
Gorky, Maxim: Aseev and, 10, 300–1, 311–14; as émigré personality, 7, 194; filmmaking and, 40; on jazz, 41; on Lenin, 235n15; proletariat readers and, 355; publishing houses and, 4, 196, 209n28; on Soviet literary traditions, 252, 256–7, 312–13
Gough, Maria, 305
Gouzenko, Igor, 87n143
Grachev, Mikhail, 407
Gramsci, Antonio, 11, 174, 381
Grand Tour, 240, 301–2, 311, 454n44
Grave, V.V., 288
Great Britain: Communist Party, 16, 242–4, 246; émigrés in, 6, 379, 382, 457n90; imperialism of, 416; labour movement in, 242–5; Lawrence of Arabia romanticized in, 248–9; literary conferences and, 433; London literary scene, 239–40, 242–3, 245, 258; in Russian Civil War, 267. *See also* Fox, Ralph
Great Soviet Encyclopaedia, 7
Grebenshchikov, Grigori, 345
Grewal, Inderpal, 445
grief/disappointment, 398–9, 413, 421, 449–50
Griffith, D.W., 73
Grin, Alexander, 370
Grinberg, Iosif, 71
Grivtsov, Georgii, 42
Gropius, Walter, 381–2
grotesque aesthetic, 272, 275–8, 280, 282–4
Gruber, Lilo, 129–30, 139, 141–2, 145, 147, 149–50. *See also Flames of Paris, The*
Gruppe 47 (literary network), 433, 445, 453n23
Grzhebin, Zinovy, 191, 197
Gsovsky, Tatjana, 143
Guarnizo, Luis Eduardo, 322, 337
Guattari, Félix, 430, 438, 448–9
Gul', Roman, 211n55
Gulag, 270, 444, 457n102
Guyana, 398, 403–4

Haiti, 405, 416
Hájek, Jiří, 433
Hall, Chatwood. *See* Smith, Homer
Hall, Stuart, 323, 331
Harlem Tenants League, 404–5, 416
Hartman, Saidiya, 400–1, 405, 421
Harvey, David, 29
"haunting," 412–15, 419–21
Hauser, Arnold, 377
Hawks, Howard, 42
Hayot, Eric, 286–7
Haywood, Harry, 6
Heartfield, John, 381

Hegel, Georg Wilhelm Friedrich: on China/stagnation, 276; on great leaders, 256–7; Ilienkov's engagement with, 161, 167, 172; Lenin on, 165–6; Marx's debt to, 160–2, 164, 172, 174–7
Herodotus, 250
Herzen, Alexander, 365
Hevesy, Iván, 125n65
Hirsch, Francine, 339n18
historiography: alternatives to imperialist readings, 408–11; archival absences and, 399–403, 414–15; critical fabulation as, 400–3, 420–1; hegemonic art histories, 109–14; Soviet, 71–3, 251–5, 268
Hitler, Adolf, 51, 228, 231, 386
Ho Chi Minh, 6
Hoersch, Werner, 149
Hollywood: revues/musicals, 25–8, 41–2, 51, *52*; "Soviet," 43; Soviet filmmakers' visit to, 10, 35–6, *36*–7, 82n77; as training ground for Soviets, 17, 31–2, *32*, 40, 51, 72–3. *See also* Circus
Holocaust, 224, 238n36, 384–5, 433, 436, 452n19
Homer, 149
hospitality, 43, 46, 51, 53, *54–6*, 77, 223
Hubert, Harrison, 404
Hughes, Langston: in 1932 contingent of Black artists, 220, 319, 324, 329, 337, 407, 419; in Cold War, 219–20, 226, 231–4, 258; on "honour of our race," 324–7; Huiswoud and, 322, 407–10, 419; and imaginings of Central Asia, 214, *215*, 221–2, 242, 258; Koestler and, 11, 18, 214, *215*, 222–6, 232, 234, 237n32; *A Negro Looks at Soviet Central Asia*, 236n28, 250–1, 256;

poetry of, 222, 232–4. *See also I Wonder as I Wander*
Hughes, Robert, 211n59
Huiswoud, Hermina Dumont (pseud. Helen Davis): focus on the quotidian, 416–20; fractured photo postcard of veiled woman, 401–3, *402*, 407–10, 412–15, 418–21; grief at Soviet Union's collapse, 398–9, 413, 421; Hughes and, 407–10, 419; internationalism/radicalism of, 19, 398–9, 401, 403–6; scattered archive of, 399–403, 411–12, 414–15; travel to Moscow/Soviet Union, 399, 402–3, 405–7, 411, 417–20; "Women I Have Known Personally," 415–20
Huiswoud, Otto, 398–9, 404–7, 410, 419, 422n3
Hu Lanqi, 383
Humboldt University, 388–90, 395n50
Hungarian Commune/Soviet Republic, 17, 94–5, 112, 115, 377–9, 381
Hungarian Uprising/Revolution, 167, 172, 380, 382, 431
Hungary: avant-garde of, 91, 93–7, 100–5, 110, 112–14, 128n94, 377–8, 380; Communist Party (KMP), 96–7, 100, 102, 377–8; émigrés from, 93, 95–7, 100–4, 112–16, 128n94, 378; literary conferences and, 433; Radványi in, 375, 377–8, 387; revolution/conflicts in, 112, 267, 378, 389; show trials and, 387–8; Social Democratic Party (SPD), 120n24, 378. *See also* Koestler, Arthur; Mácza, János; Radványi, László
hygiene campaigns, 216, 219, 223–4, 376
Hylaea, 346

Iakir, I.E., 283–4
Ibárruri, Dolores, 418, 427n68
idealism, 102, 107, 160, 163, 165–6, 175–6, 212n62
identity: group/collective, 321, 323–6, 329–31, 333, 336–7; individual/personal, 322–4, 327–37; performance/construction of, 319–23; precarity and, 323–6, 331, 337; racial, 319–26, 330–1; Soviet worker's, 327–9, 336–7; theorized, 323–4. *See also* Blackness; whiteness
ideologeme, 269, 286, 289–90
Il'f, Ilya, 42
Ilienkov, Eval'd: censure of, 160–2, 164–5, 167, 170–1; international connections of, 17, 167–8, 170–2, 174–7; on Marx's concretized abstraction, 160–1, 172–7; philosophical "Theses" of, 162–5, 171–2; review of Lukács, 167, 170–2; translations of, 161, 168–71, 174, 179n24
Ilienkov, Vasilii, 169–70
Illesh, Elena, 165, 169, 180n33
Imaginary West, 445
imperialism: global impoverishment due to, 403–6, 416–17; Lenin on, 241–2, 246–7, 321; Radványi's professorship on, 388; "unlearning" of, 410–11; warmongering and, 133, 416
Impressionism, 71, 107
India, 5, 243, 245, 288, 441
infection/disease, 219, 223–7, 240, 303
intellectual migration, 239–42, 248, 257–8. *See also* Fox, Ralph
International Association of Revolutionary Writers (MORP), 5, 242, 258, 260n29
International Bureau of Revolutionary Literature (MBRL), 4–5

internationalism: academic cooperation and, 381–2, 384, 388; avant-garde and, 96–7, 119nn12–13; Black radicalism and, 401, 403–6, 426n52; conflicting understandings of, 269–71; vs. cosmopolitanism, 12–14, 58, 66–7; as counternarrative, 9–11; disgust's rejection of, 214; linguistic diversity/confusion and, 53, *54*, 60, 272–5, 282; of Marxist thought, 161–2, 164–5; vs. nationalism, 12–13, 66, 202; solidarity in, 269–70, 277–81, 285; Soviet/socialist, 4–5, 9–11, 269, 271, 281, 283, 290
International Lenin School, 244, 399, 406, 409, 417–18
International Workers' Day, 96, 359, 367
Invisible Writing, The (Koestler): agenda of, 219–20, 231–3, 250; disgust in, 214–17, 226; ethical/political nausea in, 227–33; Hughes in, 222–3, 226; romantic exoticism in, 251–3, 258
Ionkis, David, 362
Isaev, Konstantin, 64
Isherwood, Christopher, 240–1, 243, 248, 258
Italian Futurism: in diagrams of avant-garde, 88, *89–90*, *92*, *106*; fascist links of, 108, 114, 300, 308–11; Mácza on, *92*, 105–8, *106*, *108*, *110*, 114, 127n80; manifesto of, 303. *See also* Marinetti, Filippo; Russian Futurism
Italy: art of, 91, 110, 301; Aseev's travels in, 299–304, 309–15; *città*, 293n44; COMES (writers association), 431–7, 444, 450; Communist Party (PCI), 17, 164,

Italy (*continued*)
168–9, 172, 174, 177; fascism in, 300, 308–11, 382; in Gogol/Blok, 306; Gorky in, 10, 300–1, 311–14; Ilienkov's publication in, 167–71; imperialism of, 416; Marxism in, 161, 164–5, 167–8, 170, 172, 174–7, 179n24, 381; Muratov's guide to, 300–2, 304–6; Pasternak's publication in, 161, 169–70; ruins vs. modernization in, 299, 302–4, 306–9
Iutkevich, Sergei, 86n142
Iuzovskii, Iosif, 70–1, 74
Ivan IV, 293n44
Ivanov, Viacheslav, 7
Ivanov, Vsevolod, 268, 272, 281–5, 289
I Wonder as I Wander (Hughes): agenda of, 231–4, 250; boundaries surpassed in, 224–6, 234, 408–9; disgust in, 214–17, 219–20, 222–6, 228, 230, 234; Koestler in, 222–6, 232, 234, 237n32; readers of, 224–5, 231–2, 234; romantic exoticism in, 252–3, 258; Soviet experiment encountered in, 220–1

Jakobson, Roman, 445
James, C.L.R., 6
Jameson, Frederic, 269
Jannings, Emil, 34
Japan, 267, 269–71, 282, 286–8, 346
Jaspers, Karl, 378
Jensen, Peter, 293n44
Jewish Antifascist Committee (JAC), 60, 66
Jewish Christians, 378–9, 391
Jews: denied university admission/employment, 377, 379–80, 387; targeted as "cosmopolitan," 13, 61, 115. *See also* antisemitism
Johnson, Uwe, 436–7

Joliot-Curie, Frédéric and Irène, 389
Jolson, Al, 33
Jones, Claudia, 404, 427n68
journals. *See* periodicals
Joyce, James, 434–5

Kadets. *See* Constitutional Democratic Party
Kafka, Franz, 434–5
Kalinin, Il'ia, 210n40
Kalinin, Mikhail, 41
Kamensky, Vasily, 346, 367, 369, 371nn3–4, 372n7, 374n60
Kandinsky, Vasily, 117n4
Kant, Immanuel, 43, 77, 161
Kant, Marion, 132, 152n9, 154n26
Kaplan, Caren, 16, 438, 445
Kasack, Wolfgang, 445
Kassák, Lajos, 93–5, 97–8, 101, 104, 119n13, 122n43, 378
Kassil, Lev, 370
Kästner, Erich, 444
Kataev, Valentin, 42
Katz, Otto (André Simone), 388
Käutner, Helmut, 158n83
Kavelin, Konstantin, 66
Keller, Gottfried, 158n83
Kelly, Daniel, 217
Kéri, Pál, 94
Khanum, Tamara, 426n52
Khazanovskii, Mikhail, 59
Khlebnikov, Velimir, 346
Khodasevich, Vladislav, 7, 185, 196, 345
Khrushchev, Nikita, 160, 387, 389, 437–8
Kiaer, Christina, 339n23
kinless cosmopolites. *See* FAKC campaign
Kirchner, Otto, 191
Kirov, Sergei, 252
Kirsanov, Semen, 42

Index   477

Kisch, Egon Erwin: *Changing Asia*, 251, 440–1; life/travels of, 242, 250–1, 256, 258; Richter and, 439–44, *442*
kitsch, 25, 28, 133, 151
Kliueva, Nina, 59
Koch, Hans, 433, 436
Kodály, Zoltán, 377
Koestler, Arthur: Cold War–era agenda of, 231–3; *Darkness at Noon*, 219, 237n32; early Marxism/communism of, 219, 226–9; Hughes and, 11, 18, 214, *215*, 222–6, 232, 234, 237n32; and imaginings of Central Asia, 214, *215*, 242, 258; *Of White Nights and Red Days*, 226, 229, 250–3, 256; on Seghers, 383; in Spain, 258. See also *Invisible Writing, The*
Kollontai, Aleksandra, 218
Koltsov, Aleksei, 360
Komját, Aldár, 113, 123n48
Kondakov, Nikolai, 68–9, *69*
Kopelev, Lev, 430, 439, 445, 448–50, 452n18
Korda brothers, 378
Korean migration, 269
Kornosevich, Romuald, 354, 359–61, 372n9
Korovikov, Valentin, 162–5, 171–2
Korsch, Karl, 379, 381
Kracauer, Siegfried, 392
Kristeva, Julia, 43, 216–18
Krivosheeva, A., 241
Kropotkin, Peter, 300
Kruchenykh, Aleksei, 346, *350*
Krupskaya, Nadezhda, 381, 418, 427n68
Kuczynski, Jürgen, 390
Kuleshov, Lev, 38, 86n142
Kun, Béla, 95, 120n24, 121n31, 378
Kurdov, Atta, 237n32

Kuropatkin, Aleksei, 288–9
Kyrgyz people, 243, 249–50, 439

Laban, Rudolf, 138, 151n3
Labriola, Antonio, 174
Laemmle, Carl, 35
Lamanova, Nadezhda, 43
Landler, Jenő, 120n24, 121n31, 378
Láng, Júlia, 377
Laozi, 279
Larionov, Mikhail, 117n4
Latour, Bruno, 14
Latvian Rifles, 267, 273
Lawrence, T.E. (Lawrence of Arabia), 248–50
Lazarsfeld, Paul, 386
Lebedev-Kumach, Vasilii, 43
Lederer, Emil, 378
Lee, Steven, 12, 221
LEF (group), 274–5, 304–5, 307, 311, 314–15; *LEF* (journal), 124n61, 273, 293n41, 305, 316n17; *Novyi LEF* (journal), 300–1, 305, 308, 313–14, 316n13, 316n17
leftism (cultural/political): antifascism and, 257–8, 387, 417, 432; avant-garde and, 94–7, 100–2, 113–14, 193–4; of Black radicals, 404–6, 421n1; fascist oppression of, 9–10; iconoclasm/oppositionalism, 302–4, 307, 446–7; internationalism and, 5–6, 96, 119nn12–13, 381–2; poetics of mobility and, 301–2, 305–6, 311, 314–15; of Russian émigrés, 5, 185–6, 346–7; Soviet leanings of, 430, 432, 438–9
Lehmann, John, 243, 258
Leipziger Ballett. See *Flames of Paris, The*
Lektorskii, Vladislav, 160–1, 178n14
Lenin, Vladimir: on abstraction, 163, 165–7; death of, *349*, 381–2; on

Lenin, Vladimir (*continued*)
imperialism/capitalism, 241–2, 246–7, 321; memorialized/praised, 235n15, 252, 285, 365, 367; Soviet divides and, 6, 218, 379; widow of, 381, 418, 427n68
Leningrad, 72, 139, 198, 332, 334–5, 431, 436
Leonov, Leonid, 434
Lermontov, Mikhail, 370
LeRoy, Mervyn, 51
Leslie, Lew, 37
Lesznai, Anna, 377–8
Letters from Cafés (Ehrenburg): Berlin mapped in, 201–6; on Soviet/émigré life, 187–9, 192–4, 200
Levin, Lev, 369
Lévi-Strauss, Claude, 385
Levitov, Il'ia, 288–9
Levitsky, Sergei, 425n45
Lewis, Thurston, 325–6
Liao Chengzi, 383
Liau Han-sin, 383
Lidin, Vladimir, 211n57
Lifshitz, Mikhail, 167, 369
linguistic distortion: Chinese migrants and, 272–5, *279*, 280, 282–3, 285; Dadaism/Futurism and, 98–101, *99*, 307
Lissitzky, El, 105, 192
literary conferences: in 1920s, 4–5; in 1930s, 432, 437, 439; in 1960s, 429, 431–9, 444, 446–7, 449, 453n23
literary everyday, 189–91, 197, 205–6
Liubimova, M.Iu., 294n59
Livshits, Benedikt, 309–10
Lombardo Toledano, Vicente, 385
López Portillo, José, 387
Lotman, Yuri, 331
Löwenstein, Hubertus, Prince of, 384
Lozovskii, Solomon, 58, 60
Luchishkin, Sergei, 42–3

Lukács, Georg (György): dissociation from Radványi, 389–90; Hungarian avant-garde and, 94–6, 113–15, 123n50, 377–8; Ilienkov's review of, 167, 170–2; Marxism of, 11, 166–7, 176–7, 244, 257, 379, 382–3
Lunacharsky, Anatoly, 4–5, 33, 439
Luxemburg, Rosa, 377, 379, 391
Lysenkoism, 171

Machine Aesthetics, *89*, *92*, *106*, *108*, *110*
MacKay, John, 316n17
Mácza, János: Budapest archive of, 124nn60–61; in Czechoslovakia, 95–102; life of, 17, 91, 93–4, 124n60, 378; in Moscow, 11, 102–5, 114, 121n31; nomadic subjectivity of, 93, 114–16; periodical culture and, 93–5, 97–8, *99*, 101–2, 105, 113, 125n65; plays by, 94, 96, 98–101, *99*, 124n60; Proletkult work of, 96–7, 100–2; on Russian literature, 104, 128n92. *See also Art of Contemporary Europe, The*
Magri, Lucio, 179n18
Maistre, Xavier de, 240, 250
Makarenko, Anton, 381
Makarova, Maria (Mascha), 430, 446–8
Maliugin, Leonid, 74
Malraux, André, 248
Mandelshtam, Osip, 6
Manenkov, S., 366
Mann, Heinrich, 263n71, 383–4
Mannheim, Károly (Karl), 377–80, 383
Mao Zedong, 5–6
Mariinsky Theatre, 139–40, 158n97
Marinetti, Filippo, 33, 127n80; Aseev and, 300–1, 303, 308–11; tree of Futurism, 88, *90*, 105. *See also* Italian Futurism

Markizova, Gelia, *58*
Markov, Vladimir, 310
Marx, Karl: on colonialism/
  imperialism, 242, 244–6; on
  commodity and value-form,
  160, 172–3, 175; concretized
  abstraction in, 172–7; debt to
  Hegel, 160–2, 164, 172, 174–7;
  on form/function, 26; German
  vs. Soviet takes on, 441–3; US
  socialists and, 288
Marx-Engels Institute (IMEL), 11,
  161, 179n31, 244–5, 440
Marxism-Leninism: anti-imperialism
  of, 241–2, 246–7, 321, 403–6, 416–
  17; vs. biologized racial discourse,
  269, 271, 288–90; intellectuals'
  turn away from, 164, 219, 241,
  252, 258, 443; on racial inequality/
  capitalism, 238n40, 320–4, 405–6;
  vs. "unadulterated Marxism,"
  376–7, 390–1
Marxist method: vs. Formalism,
  91–3, 109, 205; vs. hegemonic
  art histories, 109–14; nomadic
  subjectivity and, 114–16; as
  orthodox Marxism, 379, 390; vs.
  Russian/Soviet diamat, 177; on
  unity of -isms, 91–2, *92*, 105–9, *106*
Marxist philosophy: vs.
  anthroposophy, 197; vs.
  cosmopolitanism, 71–2; pseudo-,
  205–6; race and, 238n40;
  Radványi's espousal of, 376–81,
  385, 390–2; Russian/Soviet diamat
  vs. "revisionist" thought, 160–7,
  170–1, 174–7; Western, 17, 161, 167,
  174–7. *See also* Ilienkov, Eval'd;
  Mácza, János; Radványi, László
Marxist Workers School of Greater
  Berlin (MASCH): aims/offerings
  of, 375–6, 385; founding of, 380–1;

French/Mexican offshoots of,
  383–6; Radványi's direction of, 5,
  376–7, 381–3, 389; "unadulterated
  Marxism" at, 376–7, 390–1
masculinity, 229–30
Masiutin, V.N., *278*
Matić, Dušan, 433
Matuszewski, Ryszard, 433
May, Karl, 253, 455n56
Mayakovsky, Vladimir: Burliuk and,
  346, 365–7, 369–70; *LEF* and, 300,
  311; "Moskovskii Kitai," 270, 275,
  280; propaganda campaigns and,
  235n16
May Day celebrations, 96, 359, 367,
  417, 440
McDuffie, Eric, 404
McKay, Claude, 321
Mechanism, 177n2
Mei, Lev, 360
melodramas, 25–6, 28, 53, 94
memory: borne in objects, 401–3,
  402, 407, 412–15; crystallization/
  refraction of, 240–2, 248;
  memoirs/revisionism and, 219,
  222–4, 226, 250, 252; post–Cold
  War technologies of, 399–401; war
  memorials, 436
Menninghaus, Winfried, 216–17,
  223, 232
Mensheviks, 7, 160, 185, 197,
  210n40
Merezhkovskii, Dmitry, 7–8, 278, 345
Merker, Paul, 396n62
Messerer, Mikhail, 150–1
messianism, 379–80, 391
Meusel, Alfred, 384
Mexico, 5, 19, 40, 42, 375, 383, 385–8,
  396n62
Meyer, Hannes, 381, 385
Mezhrabpom (International
  Workers' Aid Organization), 5, 220

Mickenberg, Julia L., 340n33, 340n38
Mies van der Rohe, Ludwig, 381
migration: disciplinary studies of, 11, 15–16, 430–1, 437, 441; first wave of Russian emigration, 6–9, 14, 356, 358, 370; trope of migrant, 438. *See also* red migrations
Mikhalkov, Sergei, 370
Mikhoels, Solomon, 54, 60
Miliukov, Pavel, 207n1
Miller, Tyrus, 118n11
Miller, William Ian, 217, 225, 227–8
Mirsky, D.S., 189–90
modernity: vs. antiquity, 299–305, 314–15, 440; Berlin as centre of, 192–4, 206; European, 276, 280, 286–8, 299–300, 302, 308; First World War and, 193, 202; forced, 216, 279–81, 407–8; mechanized/industrial, 287–8, 299–300; Soviet/socialist, 18–19, 216, 220–1, 272, 407–8, 438–44
Moholy-Nagy, László, 105, 378
MoMA, 88, *89*, 91–2, 117n4, 117n5
Mongolia, 239, 246, 253–7, 277, 280
Moore, Richard B., 404, 406
Morson, Gary Saul, 204
Moscow: arts in, 41–2, 135, 193, 309–10; vs. Berlin, 193–4, 197–8; Black Americans in, 319, 324–7, 329, 332, 334–5; as centre of Marxist thought, 161, 164–5, 170–2; Chinese laundry workers in, 270, 275, 280, 297n93; as city of sun/promise, 102–4, *103*, 115, 198; as fourth Rome, 9, 11; Fox in, 11, 239, 243–5, 253; German writers in, 437, 446; Huiswoud in, 399, 406, 409, 417–18; Hungarian émigrés in, 102–4, *103*, 121n31, 378; Italian presence in, 168–70; Kitai-gorod in, 275–7; *Russian Voice* readers in, 366, 369. *See also* Marx-Engels Institute
Moscow Art Theatre (MKhAT), 281, 283
Moscow Soviet, 334–5
Moscow State University, 161–5, 417
Moskvin, M., 358–9
Mossalskii, Pavel, 46, *49*, 54
Mújica Montoya, Emilio, 387
Müntzer, Thomas, 379
Muratov, Pavel, 300–2, 304–6, 308–9, 311
music: censorship of, 169; folk/mass songs, 42–3, 145, 193; jazz, 25, 37, 41; in studies of avant-garde, 113
musical comedies, 40–2, 64
Mussolini, Benito, 311
mysticism, *110*, 137

Nabokov, Vladimir (author), 8, 187–9, 191–2, 201, 206, 210n41
Nabokov, Vladimir D. (statesman), 185
Nagy, Imre, 167
Naiman, Eric, 235n14
Napoleon Bonaparte, 257
narodnost', 134–5, 137
Narodny, Pavel, 363
National Association for the Advancement of Colored People (NAACP), 338n12, 404
nationalism: affirmed through travel, 311, 313–15; bourgeois, 75–6, 257; of form, 130, 136–7; GDR project of, 129–30, 146–7, 149; vs. internationalism, 12–13, 66, 202; negotiated in exile, 188–9, 192; vs. nomadic subjectivity, 93, 392; Slavophilism, 198–9
NATO, 12, 75–6
Nazism (National Socialism): arts and, 17, 130, 132, 134, 136–8, 169, 433; nationalism of, 75, 136–7,

154n30, 439; Radványi/MASCH and, 376, 382–5, 389; swastika of, 202, 228. *See also* Germany; Holocaust
Nekhotin, Vladimir, 210n40
Nekrasov, Nikolai, 360, 370
Neo-Primitivism, *106*, 107, 126n69, 308
Neruda, Pablo, 385
Netherlands, 376, 398, 406
New Economic Policy (NEP), 297n93
newspapers. *See* periodicals
New York: Frankfurt School in, 384; Harlem/Black radicalism in, 250, 399, 403–5, 416, 426n52; Russian émigrés in, 345–6, 353, 356–8, 365–6, 373n25. *See also Russian Voice*
Nicholas II, 288
Nikitin, Nikolai, 208n15
Nikolaevich, Ivan, 312
Nil'sen, Vladimir, 42
Nivat, Georges, 278
nomadic subjectivity, 93, 114–16, 392
nostalgia, 151, 188, 347, 354–5, 358, 360, 363, 398–400
novel form, 166, 244, 434–5
Nusinov, Isaak, 66
Nussbaum, Martha, 14, 43

October Revolution, 7, 35, 94, 104, 141, 144–5, 185–6, 192, 197; anniversary celebrations of, 141, 145, 296n79, 356–7. *See also* Russian Revolution (1917)
Odinokaia, Nadezhda, 372n24
Odoevskii, A.I., 157n72
Okuntsov, Ivan, 345
One of the Mansions of the Kingdom of Shades (Bely): Berlin mapped in, 197–8, 201–6; on Soviet/émigré life, 187–9, 191, 197–200, *199*
Opalov, Leonid, 362–3, 372n9

orientalism, 243, 253, 407–9, 420, 426n62, 438–41
Orlova, Liubov, *45*, 46, *48–50*, *55–6*, *58*
Orlova, Raisa, 439, 448–50
orthography, 192, 273
Orwell, George, 243, 258
Ostrovskii, Nikolai, 268, 272, 284, 289
Ottoman Empire, 231–2
Oushakine, Serguei, 190

Palucca, Gret, 143, 151n3, 152n12
Panmongolism, 271, 273, 277–80, *279*, 286
Panov, Ivan, 407
Papernyi, Zinovii, 66–7
parody, 27, 98–100, *99*, 200, 240, 285
Partial Nuclear Test Ban Treaty, 431
Pasternak, Boris, 161, 169–70, 192, 431, 449
patriotism, 57, 64–9, *69*, 71–3, 193, 202. *See also* FAKC campaign
Patterson, James Lloydovich, *54–5*, *58*, 327
Patterson, Lloyd, 340n28
Patterson, Sarah, 327
Pavlov, Evgeny, 163
Pavlov, Todor, 164–7, 171
Payette, Jessica, 154n26
Penson, Max, 407
periodical culture: in Berlin, 196–7; expansion of, 190; in Hungary, 93–5, 97–8, *99*, 101–2, 105, 113, 125n65; in New York, 345–7; as space of education, 97–8, 346–7, 352–4, 370, 406; travel writing and, 305, 316n17; in Western Europe, 242–3, 384
periodicals: *Abbott's Monthly*, 333; *Akasztott Ember*, 100–2; *A Tett*, 93–4; *Baltimore Afro-American*, 319; *Beseda*, 196–7; *Chronicles of Marxism*, 245; *Color and Rhythm*,

periodicals (*continued*)
373n28; *Communist*, 245; *Crisis*, 338n12; *Crusader*, 404; *Daily Worker*, 243, 329; *Die Aktion*, 118n11; *Dni*, 197; *Egység*, 123n48; *Ék*, 102–4, 103, 113; *Epopeia*, 197; *Forum*, 390; *Frankfurter Zeitung*, 392; *Hollywood Reporter*, 57; *Inostrannaia literatura*, 434–5, 453n23; *International Journal of Opinion and Attitude Research*, 386; *Iskra*, 157n72; *Iskusstvo kino*, 25; *Izvestiia*, 187, 192, 313; *Kassai Munkás*, 96–7; *Kino*, 41–2; *Krasnaia niva*, 369; *Krasnaia zvezda*, 187; *Krokodil*, 67, 74; *Kul'tura i zhizn'*, 65; *Kursbuch*, 429; *Labour Monthly*, 243; *Left Review*, 243; *L'Europa letteraria*, 431; *Liberator*, 404; *Literatura mirovoi revoliutsii*, 5; *Literaturnaia gazeta*, 42, 66, 69–70, 434, 446; *Literaturnoe nasledstvo*, 244; *Ma*, 94–5, 97–101, 99, 124n54, 125n65; *Moscow Evening News*, 335; *Moscow Worker*, 335; *Musik und Gesellschaft*, 134; *Napkelet*, 97; *Negro Worker*, 406; *New Russian Word*, 345; *New Writing*, 243, 258; *New York Daily Tribune*, 245; *New York Review of Books*, 447; *Novyi mir*, 73–5, 316n17; *Pravda*, 31, 41, 67–72, 76, 81n73, 218, 262n54, 434; *Social Sciences in Mexico and South and Central America*, 386; *Sonntag*, 134; *Sovetskii ekran*, 31, 32, 79n22; *Sovetskoe iskusstvo*, 64, 68, 70; *Teatr*, 64, 68; *Transatlantic Bunting*, 348; *Ural'skii rabochii*, 284; *Vecherniaia Moskva*, 36; *Veshch'/Gegenstand/Object*, 192, 194; *Vestnik inostrannoi literatury*, 5; *Voice of Textiles*, 366; *Voprosy filosofii*, 164, 167–8; *Voprosy istorii*, 71–2; *Weltbühne*, 134, 143; *Za industrializatsiiu*, 341n43; *Zeitschrift für deutsche Forschung*, 384; *Zeitschrift für Sozialforschung*, 384. *See also* LEF; *Russian Voice*
Peter I, 277, *278*
Petersburg, vs. Berlin, 198–9, 201
"Petersburg text," 277–8, 280
petite bourgeoisie, *92*, 107–8, *108*, *110*, 112, 188, 218, 235n14
Petrov, Evgenii, 42
Petrov, Petre, 136
Pfemfert, Franz, 118n11
philosophy. *See* dialectical materialism; Marxist philosophy
photo postcards: divergent readings of, 408–11; history of, 425n45, 426n62; in Huiswoud's archive, 406–7, 411–15, 422n3, 423n13; Huiswoud's veiled woman postcard, 401–3, *402*, 407–10, 412–15, 418–21; normative Soviet gaze and, 407–8, 414, 420–1; subject's agency in, 410–11, 413–15
Picabia, Francis, 88
Picasso, Pablo, 33, 226, 430
Pickford, Mary, 31, *32*
Pil'niak, Boris, 268, 271–2, 316n17, 370; *The Naked Year*, 275–8; "Sankt-Piter-Burkh," 276–83, *278–9*, 286
Piscator, Erwin, 381
Platonov, Andrei, 267–8, 272, 284, 289, 316n17
Platt, Kevin, 30
Plekhanov, Georgii, 162–3
Pleshcheev, Aleksei, 360
Poggioli, Renato, 91
Poland/Poles, 4, 172, 238n36, 267, 382, 433, 452n19
Polányi, Károly, 377
Polányi, Mihály, 377
Politburo, 79n21
polyglotism: cosmopolitan hospitality and, 53, *54*, 60;

Mácza's, 96, 116, 117n8; Radványi's, 376, 384–5, 389; of space of emigration, 357–8
Portugal, 239, 243
positivism, 160, 177n2, 400
Poston, Ted, 325–6
Pouncy, Carolyn, 155n50
Prague Spring, 453n23
Pratt, Mary Louise, 431, 435–6
Primitivism. *See* Neo-Primitivism
proletarian literature: anthologies of, 348; associations of, 4–5, 252, 256–7, 348, 353, 360, 369, 432; *Russian Voice* and, 346–8, 352–6, 358–60, 366–71. *See also* writers/artists organizations
proletariat: as absent from Central Asia, 443; audiences of, 94–7, 100–1; Black Americans in, 327–9, 338n12; disgust experienced by, 218, 229; education of, 133, 375–6, 381, 383–5; global struggle of, 416–17, 439; as reading masses, 348, 351–5, 366–9; US "workers' colony," 346–8, 351–5, 366–8; worldwide kinship/unity of, 366–71
Proletkult, 96–7, 100–2
Proust, Marcel, 240–1, 434–5
Przheval'skii, Nikolai, 298n120
public polling, 386–7
publishing houses: Berne Convention and, 209n27; D'iakova, 191; Epokha, 191, 197; Gelikon, 191, 194–5, 197, 278, 278–9; Gosizdat, 197; Grzhebin, 191, 197; Kirchner, 191; Kitovras, 348; Ladyzhnikov, 191; Lawrence and Wishart, 243; Luchterhand, 455n56; Mednyi Vsadnik, 191; Obelisk, 191; Petropolis, 191; Politizdat, 160; Slovo, 191, 197;

Suhrkamp, 437; Volk und Welt, 453n36; World Literature, 4
Pudovkin, Vsevolod, 31
purges, 58, 60, 115, 218, 246, 255–6, 258
Purist Aesthetics/Purism, *89–90, 92, 106, 108, 110*
Pushkin, Alexander, 66, 161, 316n13, 330–1, 449
Pushkin, Catherine, 330–1
Pushkin, Grigorii, 331
Putin, Vladimir, 3, 151
Pyr'ev, Ivan, 64

queerness/queer methodologies, 221–2, 398, 400–3, 426n52

Rabinow, Paul, 14
race: biologized conceptions of, 269, 271–2, 286–90, 323; as discursive signifier, 323–4, 331, 337; Imperial Russian racial phobias, 267, *268*; intersectional precarities, 327–9, 404; modernist fascination with, 213n75, 286–7; normative Soviet gaze and, 407–8, 414, 420–1; queerness and, 221–2; racialized "Chinese" features, 275–7, 282–3, 285; structural racism, 400–1, 403–6. *See also* Black Americans; Soviet race relations; US race relations
radio, 62, 168–9, 319
Radó, Sándor, 383, 388
Radvanyi, Jean, 389
Radványi, László (pseud. Johann-Lorenz Schmidt): in France/Mexico, 375, 383–8, 390, 396n62; in GDR, 375, 387–92; in Hungary/Germany pre-MASCH, 375, 377–80, 387, 391; international reputation of, 19, 386, 388–90; as MASCH director, 376–7, 381–3, 389; pseudonym usage by, 380, 388

484   Index

Radvanyi, Pierre (Peter), 383, 389
Radvanyi, Ruth, 383, 389
Raeff, Marc, 6, 8
Raevsky-Hughes, Olga, 211n59
Rajk, László, 387–8
Ratmansky, Alexei, 150–1
Rebling, Eberhard, 134–8
red migrations: cultural exchanges of, 105, 115, 367–71, 429; intellectual, 239–42, 248, 257–8; vs. peregrinations, 239; transnational lens of, 4, 17–18; vs. white émigré narrative, 9, 11–12, 19, 189. *See also* Soviet contact zone
reflection, theory of, 164–6, 174
Reich, Wilhelm, 381
Reiling, Isidor, 380
Reisner, Larisa, 187–8
Remizov, Aleksei, 272
Révai, József, 120n22
revues, 25–8, *26*, 41, 48, *50*, 51, *52*. *See also Circus*
Riazanov, David, 178n6
Ricardo, David, 173
Richter, Hans Werner: attraction towards Soviet Union, 430, 437, 439, 454n40; Bogatyrev and, 443–5; career of, 433, 450; *Karl Marx in Samarkand*, 440–4, *442*; literary conferences and, 433–5, 444, 453n23
Rickert, Karl, 378
Rilke, Rainer Maria, 444
ritual, 140, 145, 217–18, 281–3
Riurikov, Boris, 434
Robeson, Paul, 322
Robinson, Cedric, 403
Robinson, Robert, 11, 327, 334–7
Rogers, Ginger, 51
Roman, Meredith L., 339n22
Romania, 267, 378
Romberg, Kristin, 208n17

Ronen, Omry, 210n41
Room, Abram, 59–60, *59*, 76
Roskin, Grigorii, 59
Ross, Denison, 243
Rousseau, Henri, 312
Rubenshtein, Nikolai, 72
Rubenstein, Joshua, 192
Rudd, Wayland, *54*, 340n28
ruins. *See* antiquity
Russia: commensurability with China, 276–81; Constitutional Democratic Party (Kadets), 185, 191, 197; contemporary era, 3, 13, 20n12, 151; liminal position of, 275–7; Socialist Revolutionary Party, 185, 189, 194, 197. *See also* Moscow; Soviet Union
Russia Abroad, 6–9, 19
Russian Association of Proletarian Writers (RAPP), 4–5
Russian Berlin: Bely's view of, 187–9, 191, 196–206; "city guides" to, 186–9, 200; cultural/political diversity of, 185–7, 191, 197; Ehrenburg's view of, 187–9, 192–4, 201–6; literary everyday of, 189–91, 197, 205–6; literary/topographical mapping of, 18, 201–6; Nabokov's guide to, 187–9, 201, 206, 210n41; publishing houses of, 190–2, 196–7, 200, 276, *278*; Shklovsky's view of, 186–9, 191, 194–6, 201–2, 204–6. *See also* Berlin
Russian Civil War: displacement/destruction due to, 6, 185, 194, 218–19, 280–1; prose after, 189–90; Red vs. White in, 7, 21n23, 267–8, *268*, 270, 275, 277, 280–1, 284–6, 293n41. *See also* Chinese migrant soldiers
Russian Futurism: bravado/iconoclasm of, 302–4, 307, 355,

367; Italian Futurism and, 309–10; literary struggles over, 196, 348; poems of, *350*, 362–3, 369; "A Slap in the Face of Public Taste," 302, 346. *See also* Aseev, Nikolai; Burliuk, David
Russian modernism, 18, 271–2, 276, 304–8
Russian Revolution (1905), 185
Russian Revolution (1917): competing cosmoses after, 14; destruction/destabilization of, 218–19, 227, 276–7, 279–80; displacement due to, 6, 194–5, 280–1; expansive geography of, 214–15, 219–22, 225–6, 230–1, 234, 407–8, 441–3, *442*; Krupskaya's role in, 418; new Soviet writing after, 312–15, 355–8, 365–71; as rupture, 4, 6–8, 192, 302, 307–8; self-sacrifice for, 281–3, 289; as spiritual rejuvenation, 197, 279–80, 355, 362; US leftist activism after, 404; as world revolution, 4–5, 10, 70, 130–1, 144–5, 199, 221–2, 247, 250, 347, 358–60
Russian/Soviet Far East, 246, 269–70, 274–5, 281–3, 286, 288–9
Russian Voice: as bridge/guide, 347, 363–8, 370–1; circulation/readership of, 347, 351–3, 356, 363, 366–7, 369; conservative/pastoral threads in, 360–4; founding/growth of, 345–7; literary instruction/community and, 5, 346–8, 351–5, 370; Literary Thursday column, 348, *350*, 351–4, 360, 363, 367–9; poetic innovation in, 353–5, 362–3, 365–6, 371; pro-Soviet position of, 7, 345–6, *349*, 353, 355–6, 363–4, 370–1, 373n25; synthesis of émigré/Soviet threads in, 19, 356–60. *See also* Burliuk, David
Russo-Japanese War, 271, 286, 288

Said, Edward, 115
Salazar, António de Oliveira, 239
Salazar Mallén, Mario, 388
Salazkina, Masha, 432
Salton-Cox, Glyn, 243
Salys, Rimgaila, 41
samizdat, 162, 177, 390
Sanderov, A., 360
Saraeva-Bondar', Avgusta, 84n100
Sartre, Jean-Paul, 433
Schenk, Joseph, 31
Schiller, Friedrich, 133
Schiller, Nina Glick, 132
Schilling, Tom, 149–50
Schlögel, Karl, 186, 201
Schmidt, Johann-Lorenz (Marxist). *See* Radványi, László
Schmidt, Johann Lorenz (theologian), 394n21
School for Émigrés (Paris), 383–4
Schrire, David, 25
Scott, John, 322
Scottsboro boys, 327, 329
Second International, 12–13. *See also* Comintern
Second World War: cultural transfer during, 28; displacements of, 115, 384–5; German aggression during, 231, 383, 436; German reconstruction after, 129–32, 149; Molotov–Ribbentrop Pact, 258; Slavic studies after, 8–9; Soviet film industry after, 62, 72–3. *See also* Holocaust
Segel, Harold, 439–40
Seghers, Anna (Netty Reiling), 380, 385, 387, 389–92, 432, 452n16; *The Wayfarers*, 382–3, 391–2

Serge, Victor, 385
Sergeev, Konstantin, 150, 152n8
sex/sexuality, 216–17, 224–5, 227–30, 244, 273, 444
sexually transmitted diseases, 25, 216, 224–5, 440
Shaikhet, Arkady, 407
Shakespeare, William, 70–1
Shakhty Affair, 35
Shchupak, Nadezhda, 211n59
Shevchenko, Aleksandr, 308
Shi Huangdi (Qin Shihuang), 277, *278*
Shkapskaia, M.M., 294n54
Shkatullo, Georgy, 366
Shklovsky, Viktor: on Central Asia, 255–6, 258; as émigré personality, 7, 191; on literature/writers, 224, 272, 313–14; migrations of, 10, 189, 195–6, 200, 205–6; periodical culture and, 42, 196, 300, 313–14; purges and, 255–6; "social indifference" of, 65. *See also Zoo, or Letters Not about Love*
Sholokhov, Mikhail, 370, 434
show trials/executions, 82n77; early (1920s/30s), 35, 61, 64, 214, 227, 232; later (1940s/50s/60s), 58–60, *59*, 60–1, 64–5, 70, 387–9, 449. *See also* FAKC campaign
Shtein, Aleksandr, 59–60, 76
Shub, Esther, 41
Shumiatskii, Boris, 40–2, 82n77
Shuvalov, Nikolai, 141
Siege of Leningrad, 436
Sikorskii, Ivan, 286
Silva, Federico, 388
Simonov, Konstantin, 64, 73–6, 434–5
Simultanism, *92*, 95, *106*, 107, *110*, 126n69
Sinclair, Upton, 40
Sino-Japanese War, 271

Sinyavsky, Andrei, 449–50
Slavic and East European studies, 4, 6–9, 11, 19, 398–400, 430–1
Slavophilism, 198–9, 280
Slobin, Greta, 7, 21n20
Smith, Adam, 173
Smith, Arthur, 287, 289
Smith, Homer (pseud. Chatwood Hall), 319, 326–7, 329–37
Smith, Michael Peter, 322, 337
Social Darwinism, 287
Social Democratic Party (SPD) (Germany, Hungary): in first wave of émigrés, 7; Germany, 132, 188, 376–7, 381; Hungary, 120n24, 378; West Germany, 433, 441, 451n5
"socialism in one country," 5, 9
socialist realism: aesthetic doctrine of, 130, 133, 244; debated in GDR, 134–8, 143–9; distancing from, 5, 147–9, 434–5; exemplars of, 135, 138–44, 146; political work of, 21n22, 73, 133, 432; in twenty-first century, 150–1; voluntary self-sacrifice in, 281–4. *See also drambalet*
Socialist Revolutionary Party (imperial Russia), 185, 189, 194, 197
Socialist Unity Party (SED), 130, 132–4, 390–1
Soffici, Ardengo, 309
solidarity: biologized discourse as hindrance to, 287–90; Chinese migrant soldiers as symbol of, 269, 277–80, 285; group identity and, 330, 340n25; imagined vs. concrete, 3, 19, 415–20; limits of, 412–13, 415, 419; at the margins, 399, 402–3, 409–15, 418, 420–1
Sollertinskii, Ivan, 156n54
Solov'ev, Vladimir, 271, 276, 278, 280, 286

Solzhenitsyn, Alexander, 430, 450
Sorge, Friedrich, 288
Soviet cinema: censorship's effect on, 60, 62, 64; film festival, 41–2; Hollywood as training ground for, 17, 31–2, *32*, 40, 51, 72–3; ideological/propagandistic, 43, 57, *58*, 72–3, 220, 254; musical comedies in, 40–2, 64; revues in, 25–8, *26*, 41, 48, *50*, 51, *52*. *See also* Aleksandrov, Grigorii; *Black and White*; *Circus*; documentary films/modes; Eisenstein, Sergei
Soviet contact zone: conceptualized, 431–2, 436; institutional frameworks of, 429–37; literary practices of, 429–31, 437–44; personal networks of, 429–31, 444–50
Soviet historiography, 71–3, 251–5, 268
Soviet literature, 244, 434, 447; criticism/self-criticism and, 63–5, 74–5, 102, 146–7, 246, 313. *See also* socialist realism; *individual authors*
Soviet race relations: African migration and, 339n14; anti-racist rhetoric and, 18–19, 51, 320–4, 326, 331–2, 335, 337; Black American workers and, 327–9, 334–7, 338n12; compulsory unveiling and, 221–2, 230, 408–11, 443; Hughes's observations of, 18, 220–2, 225, 234, 251; idealistic/propagandistic portrayals of, 53, *54*–5, 57, *58*, 251; imagined as liberatory, 11, 221–2, 225, 319–21, 327–9, 405–6, 416; white Americans and, 320–2, 332–7. *See also* Black Americans; *Black and White*; Central Asia; US race relations
Soviet Union: Asian policy of, 243–5, 247; as beacon of hope, 10–11, 320; Chinese migrant population in, 270, 288–9; collapse of, 398–9, 455n56; Commissariat of State Security, 64; as cultural model for GDR, 129–32, 134–8, 142; early living conditions in, 216, 219, 223–4, 232, 240; in First and Second World Wars, 186, 193, 258; Great Appropriation and, 133, 140; international relief efforts in, 219, 239, 243; KGB, 387–8, 444; Ministry of Foreign Affairs, 76, 288; trade commission of, 380; unity-building strategies of, 130–1, 142, 256–8. *See also* Central Asia; Communist Party of the Soviet Union; Moscow; Russia
Spain, 39, 258
Spanish Civil War, 227, 239, 246, 258, 384, 418
Spassova, Kamelia, 179n26
Spengler, Oswald, 200, 249
Spitz, René, 377
Spivak, Monika, 198, 200
Sporck, Martin, 134–8, 143
Stabel, Ralf, 152n9
Stakhanov movement, 341n43
Stakuko, 131, 134, 146
Stalin, Joseph: China policy of, 244–5; on cosmopolitanism, 68; cult of personality of, 256–8, 390; death of, 129, 131, 134, 146, 160–1, 164, 387; Germany and, 129, 132, 134; on history teaching, 252, 256; Koestler on, 229; Marxist thought under, 160–1, 163, 377; opposition to, 6, 381; on silencing/criticism, 70–1; on socialism/Marxism, 5, 9, 14, 163; Soviet arts and, 31, 40–1, 43, 57, *58*, 62–3, 138, 192; violence under, 9, 13, 255–6, 258, 387, 389, 409

Stalin Prize, 84n98, 138
State Academic Theatre of Opera and Ballet (GATOB), 139, 141
Steiner, Rudolf, 200
Stendhal (Marie-Henri Beyle), 302
Stengers, Isabelle, 14
Sternberg, Josef von, 34–5
Steshenskii, Vladimir, 382
Stites, Richard, 316n13
Stoics, 43
Stoliarov, Sergei, 46, *49–50, 55*
Stoll-Peterka, Anni, 147–8
Strada, Vittorio, 169–70
Strittmatter, Erwin: attraction towards Soviet Union, 430, 437, 439; literary conferences attended by, 433, 435–6, 452n16; personal networks and, 448–50, 455n66
Strittmatter, Eva, 430, 439, 448–50
Strong, Anna Louise, 219
Struchkova, Raisa, 143, 152n8
Struve, Gleb, 7, 445
Studer, Brigitte, 12
Subotskii, Lev, 67, *74*
Sullivan, Noël, 236n28
Summers, Walter, 38
Sunday Circle (Hungarian group), 377–8, 380, 383
Surkov, Aleksei, 438, 447
Surrealism, 39, *89–90*, 117n5, 248
Switzerland, 33, 100, 376
syllogisms, 68–9, *69*, 71
Symbolism, 107, 189, 276, 377, 380, 391
Szondi, Léopold, 395n40
Szondi-Radványi, Lili, 395n40

Talaat Pasha, 231
Tamerlane, 18, 249, 251, 253–4
Tanzkonferenz, 134–8, 143, 146–9
Tanztheater, 131
Tapp, Alyson, 190
Tarle, Yakov, 355–8

Tashkent. *See* Uzbek people
Tatlin, Vladimir, 12, 104, 126n66
Taut, Bruno, 193
temporalities, 193, 197–8, 201, 249–50
textile industry, 366, 443
Thaw, 130, 149, 168–9, 171–2, 174, 177, 437, 449
theatre: Brechtian, 381, 455n54; Chinese migrants portrayed in, 281, 283; criticism, 62–4, 68–9, *69*, 71, 94, 348; fascism's theatricality, 309–10; Mácza's playwriting, 94, 96, 98–101, *99*; proletarian audiences and, 94–7, 100–1; "razgrimirovannaia" and, 300; traditional/folk, 440. *See also* dance; FAKC campaign
theology, 378–80, 391
theory and praxis, 96, 135–7, 147, 163, 167, 170
Third International. *See* Comintern
Thomas, Lowell, 248
Thompson, Philip, 275
Thompson Patterson, Louise, 220, 324–6, 332, 427n68
Tisse, Eduard, 10, 33–6, *34, 37,* 40
Titoism, 227, 387
Titunik, I.R., 208n17
Toepfer, Karl, 133, 154n26
Togliatti, Palmiro, 164–5, 167, 170, 172, 174
Tokin, Boško, 97
Tolnay, Károly (Charles), 377
Tolstoy, Aleksei, 370
Tolstoy, Leo, 370
Tomasi di Lampedusa, Giuseppe, 312
Torre, Guillermo de, 110, 113
tourism, 38, 187, 189, 299, 302–3, 319, 333, 437–40; radical, 305–6, 311
Tracy, Spencer, 383
transculturation, 435

translation: cultural, 141; of Ilienkov/Pasternak, 161, 168–71, 174, 179n24, 449; Mácza and, 96, 117n8; personal networks and, 443–5, 448; Soviet Union as leader in, 434
transmigrants, 15–16
transnationalism: conceptualized, 4, 14–17, 132; institutional frameworks of, 429–37, 444, 450; of interwar Berlin, 186; literary engagements of, 429–31, 437–44; personal networks of, 429–30, 443–50; philosophical exchange and, 161, 165, 170–1, 174, 176–7; of Russian revolutionary era, 270–1; solidarities of, 416–17, 419–21. See also Soviet contact zone
Trans-Siberian Railway, 269, 439
Trauberg, Leonid, 41, 72–3, 81n66
travel agencies, 429, 431, 437–41, 438, 452n18
travelogues: Aseev's reformulation of, 300–2, 311, 314–15; disgust/desire in, 219, 438; by Kisch/Richter, 439–44, 442; mediated nature of, 240–1; radical tourism and, 305–6, 311; in *Russian Voice*, 347, 363, 366. See also *Invisible Writing, The*; *I Wonder as I Wander*; Russian Berlin; *Unmade Beauty*
Tret'iakov, Sergei, 274–5, 299–300, 305, 314, 316n13, 316n17
Trotsky, Leon, 5, 35, 65, 205, 227, 244, 267, *268*
Trubetskoi, Nikolai, 253
Tsvetaeva, Marina, 192, 345
Turkestan/Turkmenistan, 215, 216, 220, 223, 225–6, 230, 253, 409, 439
Turner, Joyce Moore, 398, 401, 409, 414, 417–18, 422n3
Twain, Mark, 296n88

Tyerman, Edward, 12
Tynianov, Yuri, 27

Uitz, Béla, 102, 104, 113, 123n48
Újvári, Erzsébet, 104
Ukraine, 93, 273, 290n3, 333, 342n59, 381, 407; Russian invasion of, 3, 20n12, 158n97
Ulanova, Galina, 147–8
Ulbricht, Walter, 389
Ulianova, Maria, 418, 427n68
Ungaretti, Giuseppe, 431
Union of Soviet Writers: congresses of, 252, 256–7, 432, 452n16; nativism of, 20n2, 65–6; travel arrangements by, 16, 429, 431, 437–41, 445–6, 450, 452n18
United Nations, 12, 16
United States: *Amerikanizm*, 38, 46, 60–2, 73–6, *74*; Communist Party, 5, 321, 327, 404; FBI, 385, 424n42; Great Depression, 320; Huiswoud in, 398, 403–4, 406; imperialism/capitalism of, 7, 133, 346–7, 358, 363–5, 370, 416; migration/mobility patterns and, 15, 456n80; Red Scare, 219–20, 225–6, 231–4, 406; Vietnam War, 438, 446–7; "workers' colony" in, 346–8, 351–5, 366–8. See also New York; US race relations
University of Heidelberg, 377–80
Unmade Beauty (Aseev): author's mission in, 301–4; Gorky in, 300–1, 311–14; Marinetti's Futurism in, 300–1, 303, 308–11; on modernists' engagements with antiquity, 304–8; Muratov's *Images of Italy* and, 300–2, 304–6, 308–9, 311; poetics of mobility in, 301–2, 305–6, 311, 314–15; title of, 300–1, 313

US race relations: Black precarity and, 324–8, 331, 337, 409; Chinese migrants and, 288–9, 296n88; colour line and, 221–2, 233–4, 337; economic factors in, 320–1, 323, 328, 337; Great Migration and, 423n18; Jim Crow, 222, 225, 320, 323–4, 330; lynchings, 44, 222, 232–3, 251, 329, 331, 334; miscegenation fears, 38, 51, 325, 332, 335; in North, 329–30, 334; segregation, 251, 330–1, 334–5, 404, 408; in South, 214, 220, 225, 232–3, 320, 330; Soviet awareness/ understandings of, 37–8, 323–6, 330, 332; white supremacy and, 73, 319–24, 332–7, 404, 416. *See also* Black Americans; *Black and White*; Soviet race relations
Utesov, Leonid, 41
utopianism, 102, 222, 227, 271, 282, 358–60, 430, 439–41
Uzbek people, 214, 225, 237n29, 408, 432, 439–41, 444

Vaganova technique, 130
Vainonen, Vasilii, 143
Vambéry, Armin, 253
Vasiliev brothers, 81n66
Vertov, Dziga, 41, 57, *58*, 299, 316n17
Veselyi, Artem (Nikolai Ivanovich Kochkurov), 268, 271, 273–5, 282
Vietnam, 6, 248, 438, 446–7
Vigorelli, Giancarlo, 431–2
Vkhutemas, 193
Vladimirtsov, B.Ia., 253–4
Vogelsang, Marianne, 129–30
Volga region, 239, 243, 334–5, 408, 439
Voltaire, 204–5

Wagner, Richard, 169
Weber, Max, 377
Wechsler, Lazar, 33, *34*

Weidt, Jean, 135–6
Weigel, Helene, 381
Weill, Kurt, 376, 381
Wellek, René, 115
Wellman, William, 42, 73
West, Dorothy, 340n28, 340n38
Western cultural hegemony, 88, 90–1, 109–10, 199–200, 445
Westernizers, 198–9
Western Marxism, 17, 161, 167, 174–7
West Germany (Federal Republic of Germany): division with GDR, 129–30, 133, 143, 434–6; GDR transplants in, 143, 390; literary conferences and, 433–7, 446–7, 452n16; pan-German cooperation/ culture, 146–7, 149, 429; Social Democratic Party (SPD), 433, 441, 451n5; travel writing in, 440–4, 442; writers/cultural exchange and, 19, 429–30, 445, 450. *See also* Enzensberger, Hans Magnus; Richter, Hans Werner
Wetter, Gustav, 170
White, Hayden, 308
White, James D., 178n10
white émigrés: "Changing Landmarks" movement and, 211n59; common narratives of, 6–9, 185, 363–5, 370–1; cosmopolitanism of, 14
whiteness, 8–9, 221, 238n40, 333
Wiens, Paul, 433, 436
Wigman, Mary, 138, 151n3, 152n12
"wild man" *topos*, 308
Williams, Raymond, 244
Wilson, Angus, 433
Wilson, Jennifer, 221–2, 426n52
Wittfogel, Karl, 245–6, 258
Wölfflin, Heinrich, 127n80
women/gender issues: abortion, 33, *34*; Berlin sexuality, 228; Butler's

translation: cultural, 141; of Ilienkov/Pasternak, 161, 168–71, 174, 179n24, 449; Mácza and, 96, 117n8; personal networks and, 443–5, 448; Soviet Union as leader in, 434
transmigrants, 15–16
transnationalism: conceptualized, 4, 14–17, 132; institutional frameworks of, 429–37, 444, 450; of interwar Berlin, 186; literary engagements of, 429–31, 437–44; personal networks of, 429–30, 443–50; philosophical exchange and, 161, 165, 170–1, 174, 176–7; of Russian revolutionary era, 270–1; solidarities of, 416–17, 419–21. *See also* Soviet contact zone
Trans-Siberian Railway, 269, 439
Trauberg, Leonid, 41, 72–3, 81n66
travel agencies, 429, 431, 437–41, 438, 452n18
travelogues: Aseev's reformulation of, 300–2, 311, 314–15; disgust/desire in, 219, 438; by Kisch/Richter, 439–44, *442*; mediated nature of, 240–1; radical tourism and, 305–6, 311; in *Russian Voice*, 347, 363, 366. *See also Invisible Writing, The*; *I Wonder as I Wander*; Russian Berlin; *Unmade Beauty*
Tret'iakov, Sergei, 274–5, 299–300, 305, 314, 316n13, 316n17
Trotsky, Leon, 5, 35, 65, 205, 227, 244, 267, *268*
Trubetskoi, Nikolai, 253
Tsvetaeva, Marina, 192, 345
Turkestan/Turkmenistan, *215*, 216, 220, 223, 225–6, 230, 253, 409, 439
Turner, Joyce Moore, 398, 401, 409, 414, 417–18, 422n3
Twain, Mark, 296n88

Tyerman, Edward, 12
Tynianov, Yuri, 27

Uitz, Béla, 102, 104, 113, 123n48
Újvári, Erzsébet, 104
Ukraine, 93, 273, 290n3, 333, 342n59, 381, 407; Russian invasion of, 3, 20n12, 158n97
Ulanova, Galina, 147–8
Ulbricht, Walter, 389
Ulianova, Maria, 418, 427n68
Ungaretti, Giuseppe, 431
Union of Soviet Writers: congresses of, 252, 256–7, 432, 452n16; nativism of, 20n2, 65–6; travel arrangements by, 16, 429, 431, 437–41, 445–6, 450, 452n18
United Nations, 12, 16
United States: *Amerikanizm*, 38, 46, 60–2, 73–6, *74*; Communist Party, 5, 321, 327, 404; FBI, 385, 424n42; Great Depression, 320; Huiswoud in, 398, 403–4, 406; imperialism/capitalism of, 7, 133, 346–7, 358, 363–5, 370, 416; migration/mobility patterns and, 15, 456n80; Red Scare, 219–20, 225–6, 231–4, 406; Vietnam War, 438, 446–7; "workers' colony" in, 346–8, 351–5, 366–8. *See also* New York; US race relations
University of Heidelberg, 377–80
Unmade Beauty (Aseev): author's mission in, 301–4; Gorky in, 300–1, 311–14; Marinetti's Futurism in, 300–1, 303, 308–11; on modernists' engagements with antiquity, 304–8; Muratov's *Images of Italy* and, 300–2, 304–6, 308–9, 311; poetics of mobility in, 301–2, 305–6, 311, 314–15; title of, 300–1, 313

US race relations: Black precarity and, 324–8, 331, 337, 409; Chinese migrants and, 288–9, 296n88; colour line and, 221–2, 233–4, 337; economic factors in, 320–1, 323, 328, 337; Great Migration and, 423n18; Jim Crow, 222, 225, 320, 323–4, 330; lynchings, 44, 222, 232–3, 251, 329, 331, 334; miscegenation fears, 38, 51, 325, 332, 335; in North, 329–30, 334; segregation, 251, 330–1, 334–5, 404, 408; in South, 214, 220, 225, 232–3, 320, 330; Soviet awareness/understandings of, 37–8, 323–6, 330, 332; white supremacy and, 73, 319–24, 332–7, 404, 416. *See also* Black Americans; *Black and White*; Soviet race relations

Utesov, Leonid, 41

utopianism, 102, 222, 227, 271, 282, 358–60, 430, 439–41

Uzbek people, 214, 225, 237n29, 408, 432, 439–41, 444

Vaganova technique, 130

Vainonen, Vasilii, 143

Vambéry, Armin, 253

Vasiliev brothers, 81n66

Vertov, Dziga, 41, 57, *58*, 299, 316n17

Veselyi, Artem (Nikolai Ivanovich Kochkurov), 268, 271, 273–5, 282

Vietnam, 6, 248, 438, 446–7

Vigorelli, Giancarlo, 431–2

Vkhutemas, 193

Vladimirtsov, B.Ia., 253–4

Vogelsang, Marianne, 129–30

Volga region, 239, 243, 334–5, 408, 439

Voltaire, 204–5

Wagner, Richard, 169

Weber, Max, 377

Wechsler, Lazar, 33, *34*

Weidt, Jean, 135–6

Weigel, Helene, 381

Weill, Kurt, 376, 381

Wellek, René, 115

Wellman, William, 42, 73

West, Dorothy, 340n28, 340n38

Western cultural hegemony, 88, 90–1, 109–10, 199–200, 445

Westernizers, 198–9

Western Marxism, 17, 161, 167, 174–7

West Germany (Federal Republic of Germany): division with GDR, 129–30, 133, 143, 434–6; GDR transplants in, 143, 390; literary conferences and, 433–7, 446–7, 452n16; pan-German cooperation/culture, 146–7, 149, 429; Social Democratic Party (SPD), 433, 441, 451n5; travel writing in, 440–4, 442; writers/cultural exchange and, 19, 429–30, 445, 450. *See also* Enzensberger, Hans Magnus; Richter, Hans Werner

Wetter, Gustav, 170

White, Hayden, 308

White, James D., 178n10

white émigrés: "Changing Landmarks" movement and, 211n59; common narratives of, 6–9, 185, 363–5, 370–1; cosmopolitanism of, 14

whiteness, 8–9, 221, 238n40, 333

Wiens, Paul, 433, 436

Wigman, Mary, 138, 151n3, 152n12

"wild man" *topos*, 308

Williams, Raymond, 244

Wilson, Angus, 433

Wilson, Jennifer, 221–2, 426n52

Wittfogel, Karl, 245–6, 258

Wölfflin, Heinrich, 127n80

women/gender issues: abortion, 33, *34*; Berlin sexuality, 228; Butler's

theory of gender, 323; Central Asian childbirth practices, 223–4; Central Asian sexuality, 229, 237n34; feminist methodologies and, 400–3, 413–15, 422n12; intersectional precarities, 327–9, 404; normative Soviet gaze and, 407–8, 414, 420–1; poverty and, 188, 418; publishing and, 191, 383; US miscegenation fears, 38, 51, 325, 332, 335; veiling/unveiling in Central Asia, 221–2, 230, 401–3, *402*, 407–15, 418–21, 443. *See also* Huiswoud, Hermina Dumont; sex/sexuality; solidarity
Wong, Anna May, 38
workers/labour organizations, 247, 288–9, 366, 385–6, 404, 406
Workers University (Mexico), 385–6
World Association for Public Opinion Research (WAPOR), 386
world wars. *See* First World War; Second World War
writers/artists organizations, 197, 245, 438, 446; COMES, 431–7, 444, 450; MBRL/MORP, 4–5, 242, 258, 260n29. *See also* proletarian literature; Union of Soviet Writers
Wycliff, John, 379

Yellow Peril, 267–72, 277–8, 286–9, 308
Yugoslavia, 91, 97, 112, 433, 449
Yurchak, Aleksey, 445

Zaheer, Sajjad, 245
Zarev, Pantaley, 433
Zaslavskii, David, 68
Zeisel, Éva, 378
Zelenskii, Boris, *26*, 44
Zelma, Georgy, 407
Zemlinsky, Alexander, 158n83
Zenitism, *92*, 97–8, *106*, *108*, 109, *110–11*
Zhdanov, Andrei, 63–4, 66–7, 74–6, 134–6, 153n17, 252
Zilcosky, John, 441
Zinnemann, Fred, 383
Zoo, or Letters Not about Love (Shklovsky): Berlin mapped in, 201–2, 204–6; on Soviet/émigré life in Berlin, 186–9, 191, 194–6, 200
Zoshchenko, Mikhail, 370